The Church Triumphant
A History of Christianity up to 1300

□□□

□□□

To

Donna K. Hopkins

*friend
and minister of Christ.*

□□□

□□□

*The publication of this volume is made possible by a generous grant
from the John and Mary Franklin Foundation, Atlanta, Georgia.*

□□□

The Church Triumphant

A History of Christianity up to 1300

□□□

E. Glenn Hinson

□□□

MERCER
1995

ISBN 0-86554-436-0   MUP/H347

The Church Triumphant. A History of Christianity up to 1300.
Copyright © 1995
Mercer University Press, Macon, Georgia 31210-3960 USA
All rights reserved
Printed in the United States of America
First printing, June 1995

□□□

The paper used in this publication meets the minimum requirements
of American National Standard for Information Sciences—
Permanence of Paper for Printed Library Materials, ANSI Z39.48-1984.

□□□

Mercer University Press
6316 Peake Road
Macon, Georgia 31210-3960 USA
Telephone 912-752-2880   FAX 912-752-2264

Cover photograph (Prague, 1993)
by Jon Parrish Peede for Mercer University Press.

□□□

Library of Congress Cataloging-in-Publication Data

The church triumphant :
a history of Christianity up to 1300 / by E. Glenn Hinson.
xxii+494 pages. 7x10" (17.8x25.4 cm.).
Includes bibliographical references and index.
ISBN 0-86554-436-0 (alk. paper)
1. Church history—Primitive and early church, ca. 30–600.
2. Church history—Middle Ages, 600–1500. I. Title.
BR162.2.H56   1995
270—dc20   95-17517

CIP

Contents

Lists, Maps

Lists

Maps

Preface

This history of Christianity up to 1300 represents the fruit of more than thirty years of research and teaching, first at the Southern Baptist Theological Seminary in Louisville, Kentucky, then at Oxford University and other institutions, and finally at Baptist Theological Seminary at Richmond. It began as a joint endeavor projected by the Sunday School Board of the Southern Baptist Convention. By the time I had completed this lengthy volume, however, the takeover of the Convention by a fundamentalist faction precluded publication by Broadman Press. I am very grateful, therefore, that Mercer University Press promptly agreed to undertake such a demanding enterprise. Authors do not relish seeing ten years' labor lay on a shelf unseen by anybody except themselves.

In this history I have attempted to do some things not found in most earlier textbooks, especially Protestant textbooks. One of these is to take into account the whole Christian story, insofar as possible, rather than focusing more or less exclusively on the West. Most earlier histories have neglected Eastern Christendom from the time of the Germanic invasions on, despite the fact that Christianity remained very vital there throughout Christian history.

A second feature of this history is that it lays to rest the notion so widely entertained in the Free Church tradition of a "Fall" of the church, either with Constantine or before. There is no question that Constantine's conversion markedly affected the situation of the churches in the Roman Empire and posed new challenges for them. At the time, however, most Christians must have rejoiced in what happened in the same way Westerners have celebrated the collapse of Communism in Eastern Europe.

Closely related to this, a third concern involved an effort to look more objectively at groups traditionally labeled heretical in Christian histories. Some groups, such as the Gnostic Basilideans, the Manichaeans, or the Albigensian Cathari, undoubtedly existed on the margin of Christianity, but many of those often labeled "heretics"—the Valentinians, Montanists, Novationists, Donatists, Waldensians, and numerous others—stood much closer to the center and should not be dismissed too readily as non-Christian. Accordingly, I have tried to avoid pejorative terms which lead to dismissal of groups that, in their own way, helped to clarify what early Christianity was.

Another strong emphasis in this history is inclusiveness, especially regarding women. One can safely guess that as many, if not more, women as men chose to belong to early and medieval Christian churches. Although women obviously were not welcomed into the Christian hierarchy, they may have fulfilled certain official duties. More importantly, they held prominent places among the martyrs and played major roles in the shaping of Christian spirituality. In monasticism they had freedom the culture did not grant married women. Women in the Middle Ages left a valuable literary legacy in their accounts of intimate spiritual experiences and did some creative theological thinking.

As a way of facilitating inclusiveness, I have tried to present a balanced picture. Older histories have focused on theological development, official actions, and institutional growth, happenings fairly easy to trace. I employ what I call a socio-institutional approach wherein I try to look at what was taking place through the eyes of ordinary saints. Accordingly, in each major period I have set Christianity within its social and cultural context, explained how it went about evangelizing or Christianizing the society, looked at its struggle to attain or retain Christian identity as it incorporated streams of converts, examined important developments in spirituality, and sketched the growth of corporate life and thought. Christian asceticism and monasticism, usually receiving short and essentially negative shrift, receive more favorable treatment here as efforts of some to sustain a high level of Christian commitment to God. Doctrinal developments, on the other hand, are given less prominence than usual because of attention directed to other facets of the story. In my opinion, Christian identity does not depend on doctrine alone but on a complex array of factors.

One other accent of this book arises out of my personal shaping in the Baptist and Free Church tradition with its appreciation for the voluntary principle in religion. I have devoted special attention to Christian coercion of others, especially of the Jewish people. Insofar as I have observed, not many Christian historians have highlighted this sad facet of the Christian story. Most general histories have glossed over it altogether. This side of Hitler's holocaust, however, we can no longer continue this selective inattention to what happened. Consequently I have put in bold relief those fateful steps taken first as Constantine threw his support to Christianity and continued in the Inquisition, the crusades against marginal Christian groups and then Muslims, and the Northern Crusades designed to vanquish the unconverted of Europe by force of arms.

I express special appreciation to those who have studied the history of Christianity under my direction. Many have helped me to frame questions that illuminate the Christian story. They have taught me even as I have tried to teach them to embrace all of church history as the history of us all. I pray that this book will heighten the affection and appreciation many have for the church universal, its faults and foibles notwithstanding.

Richmond, Virginia *E. Glenn Hinson*
February 1995

Emperors, Popes, and Patriarchs

□ Roman Emperors □

I. The Principate—27 B.C.E. to 285 C.E.

27 B.C.E.–14 C.E. . . . . . . Octavian (Augustus)	193–211 . . . . Septimius Severus
14–37 . . . . Tiberius	211–217 . . . . . . Caracalla (briefly with Geta)
37–41 . . . . Gaius Caligula	217–222 . Elagabalus (briefly with Macrinus)
41–54 . . . . Claudius	222–235 . . . . Severus Alexander
54–68 . . . . Nero	235–238 . . . . Maximinus Thrax
68–69 . . . . Galba, Otho, Vitellius	238–244 . . . . Gordian III
	244–249 . . . . Philip the Arabian
Flavians	249–251 . . . . Decius
69–79 . . . . Vespasian	251–253 . . . . Gallus
79–81 . . . . Titus	253 . . . . Aemilian
81–96 . . . . Domitian	253–260 Valerian (East) and Gallienus (West)
96–98 . . . . Nerva	260–268 . . . . Gallienus
98–117 . . . . Trajan	268–270 . . . . Claudius
117–138 . . . . Hadrian	270 . . . . Quintillus
	270–275 . . . . Aurelian
Antonines	275–276 . . . . Tacitus
138–161 . . . . Antoninus Pius	276 . . . . Florian
161–180 . . . . Marcus Aurelius	276–282 . . . . Probus
180–192 . . . . Commodus	282–285 . . . . Carus and sons
193 . . . . Pertinax	

II. The Dominate (emperor given title of Dominus)

285–304 . . . . First Tetrarchy	305–311 . . . . Second Tetrarchy
Diocletian (East) and Maximian (West),	Galerius (East) and Constantius (West),
Augusti	Augusti
Galerius (East) and Constantius Chlorus (West),	Maxentius (East) and Constantine (West),
Caesares	Caesares
304–305 . . . . Diocletian and Galerius	312–324 Licinius (East) and Constantine (West)

324–337 .... Constantine
337–340   Constans and Constantine II (West),
                          Constantius II (East)
340–351 ...... Constans and Constantius II
351–361 .... Constantius II
361–363 .... Julian
363–375 .... Valentinian (West)
                          and Valens (East)

375–379 .... Gratian and Valentian II (West)
                          and Valens (East)
379–383 .... Gratian and Valentian II (West)
                          and Theodosius I (East)
383–392 .... Valentinian II (West)
                          and Theodosius I (East)
392–395 .... Theodosius I

III. After the Permanent Divison of the Empire
Italicized = not recognized in the Eastern Empire.

A. In the East

395–408 .... Arcadius
408–450 .... Theodosius II

450–457 .... Marcian

457–474 .... Leo I

473–474 .... Leo II
474–491 .... Zeno
475–476 .... *Basiliscus*

B. In the West

393–423 .... Honorius
407–411 .... *Constantine III*
421 .... Constantius III
423–425 .... *John*
425–455 .... Valentinian III [Galla Placidia]
455 .... *Maximus*
455–456 .... Avitus
457–461 .... Majorian
461–465 .... *Severus*
467–472 .... Anthemius
472 .... *Olybrius*
473 .... *Glycerius*
473–480 .... Julius Nepos

475–476 .... *Romulus*

IV. Byzantine Emperors after the Fall of the West

474–491 .... Zeno
491–518 .... Anastasius I
518–527 .... Justin I
527–565 .... Justinian I
565–578 .... Justin II
578–582 .... Tiberius II
582–602 .... Maurice
602–610 .... Phocas
610–641 .... Heraclius
641 .... Constantine III
641 .... Heraclonas (Heracleon)

641–668 .... Constans II
668–685 .... Constantine IV
685–695 .... Justinian II Rhinotmetus
695–698 .... Leontius
698–705 ...... Tiberius III (Apsimar)
705–711 .... Justinian II (for a second time)
711–713 .... Philippicus Bardanes
713–715 .... Anastasius II (Artemius)
715–717 .... Theodosius III
717–741 .... Leo III
[Line continues next page, left column]

741–775 . . . . Constantine V Copronymus
775–780 . . . . . . Leo IV the Khazar (Chazar)
780–797 . . . . Constantine VI
797–802 . . . . Irene
802–811 . . . . Nicephorus I
811 . . . . Stauricius
811–813 . . . . Michael I Rangabe
813–820 . . . . Leo V the Armenian
820–829 . . . . Michael II the Stammerer
829–842 . . . . Theophilus
842–867 . . . . Michael III
867–886 . . . . Basil I
886–912 . . Leo VI the Philosopher (the Wise)

912–913 . . . . Alexander
913–959 . . . Constantine VII Porphyrogenitus

919–944 . Romanus I Lecapenus (coemperor)
944–945 . . . . Stephen and Constantine,
Romanus Lecapenus's sons
959–963 . . . . Romanus II
963–969 . . . . Nicephorus II Phocas
969–976 . . . . John I Tzimisces
976–1025 . . . . Basil II Bulgaroctonus

1025–1028 . . . . Constantine VIII
1028–1034 . . . . Romanus III Argyrus
1034–1041 . . . Michael IV the Paphlagonian
1041–1042 . . . . Michael V Calaphates
1042 . . . . Theodora and Zoe
1042–1055 . . . . Constantine IX Monomachus
1055–1056 . . . . Theodora
1056–1057 . . . . Michael VI Stratioticus
1057–1059 . . . . Isaac I Comnenus
1059–1067 . . . . Constantine X Ducas
1068–1071 . . . . Romanus IV Diogenes
1071–1078 . . Michael VII Ducas Parapinakes

The Frankish Kingdom

741–768 . . . . Pippin III
768–814 . . . . Charlemagne

814–840 . . . . Louis the Pious

840–855 . . . . Lothaire
855–875 . . . . Louis II (in Italy)
875–877 . . . . Charles II the Bald
881–887 . . . . Charles III the Fat
888–891 . . . . interregnum
891–894 . . . . Guido (in Italy)
894–898 . . . . Lambert (in Italy)
896–899 . . . . Arnulf (E. Frankish)
899–911 . . . . Louis the Child
901 . . . . Louis III (in Italy)
911–918 . . . . Conrad I

915 . . . . Berengar (in Italy)

Rulers of the Holy Roman Empire

919–936 . . . . Henry I of Saxony
936–973 . . . . Otto I (crowned 962)

973–983 . . . . Otto II
983–1002 . . . . Otto III
1002–1024 . . . . Henry II
1024–1039 . . Conrad II (House of Franconia)

1039–1056 . . . . Henry III

1056–1106 . . . . Henry IV

1077–1081 . . . . . . Rudolph of Swabia (rival)

1078–1081 . . . . . . Nicephorus III Botaniates	
1081–1118 . . . . Alexius I Comnenus	1081–1093 . . . Herman of Luxemburg (rival)
	1093–1101 . . . . . Conrad of Franconia (rival)
1118–1143 . . . . John II	1106–1125 . . . . Henry V
	1125–1137 . . . . Lothaire II of Saxony
1143–1180 . . . . Manuel I	1138–1152 . . . . Conrad III
	. . . . (House of Hohenstauffen)
1180–1183 . . . . Alexius II	1152–1190 . . . . Frederick I Barbarossa
1183–1185 . . . . Andronicus I	
1185–1195 . . . . Isaac II Angelus	
1195–1203 . . . . Alexius III	1190–1197 . . . . Henry VI
1203–1204 . . . . Isaac (second time)	1197–1208 . . . . Philip of Swabia
. . . . and Alexius IV	. . . . and Otto IV
1204 . . . . . . Alexius V Ducas Mourtzouphlos	
1206–1222 . . . . Theodore I Lascaris	
	1208–1212 . . Otto IV (House of Brunswick)
1222–1254 . . . . John III Ducas Vatatzes	
	1212–1250 . . . . Frederick II
	1250–1254 . . . . Conrad IV
	1254–1257 . . . . (interregnum)
	1257–1273 . . . . . Richard of Cornwall (rival)
1258–1261 . . . . John IV	1257–1272 . . . . Alfonso X of Castile (rival)
1261–1282 . . . . . . Michael VIII Palaeologus	
1282–1328 . . . . Andronicus II	1273–1292 . . . . Rudolph I of Habsburg
1295–1320 . . . . Michael IX	1292–1298 . . . . Adolph of Nassau
	1298–1308 . . . . Albert I of Habsburg
	1308–1314 . . . . . . Henry VII of Luxemburg
1328–1341 . . . . Andronicus III	1314–1347 . . . . Ludwig IV of Bavaria
1341–1391 . . . . John V	1314–1322 . . . . . Frederick of Austria (rival)
1347–1354 . . . . John VI Contacuzene	1347–1378 . . . . . . Charles IV of Luxemburg
	1347–1349 . Guenther of Schwarzburg (rival)
1376–1379 . . . . Andronicus IV	1378–1400 . . . . Wenzel of Luxemburg
1390 . . . . John VII	
1391–1425 . . . . Manuel II	
	1400–1410 . . . . Rupert of Palatinate
	1410–1437 . . . . . Sigismund of Luxemburg
1425–1448 . . . . John VIII	1410–1411 . . . . . . Jobst of Moravia (rival)
	1438–1439 . . . . Albert II of Habsburg
	1440–1493 . . . . Frederick III
1448–1453 . . . . Constantine XI Dragases	

□ *Bishops of Rome (Popes)* □

The Roman Catholic Church names Peter as founder of the church in Rome, the first bishop of the church at Rome, and thus the first "pope." (Bishops were called *papa*, literally "papa," whence "pope.") The pope's temporal title is Sovereign of the State of Vatican City; the pope's ecclesiastical titles are Bishop of Rome, Vicar of Jesus Christ, Successor of St. Peter, Prince of the Apostles, Supreme Pontiff of the Universal Church, Patriarch of the West, Primate of Italy, and/or Archbishop and Metropolitan of the Roman Province.

[ ] = not counted in papal lineage; or antipopes, illegitimate claimants of or pretenders to the papacy.

67?–78?	Linus	337–352	Julius I
78?–90?	Anacletus	352–356	Liberius
90?–99?	Clement I	355–358	[Felix II]
99?–105	Evaristus	366–384	Damasus I
105?–115?	Alexander I	366–367	[Ursinus]
115?–125?	Sixtus I	384–399	Siricius
125?–136?	Telesphorus	399–401	Anastasius I
136?–140?	Hyginus	401–417	Innocent I
140?–155?	Pius I	417–418	Zosimus
155?–166?	Anicetus	418–422	Boniface I
166?–175	Soter	422–432	Celestine I
175?–189	Eleutherus	432–440	Sixtus III
189–199	Victor I	440–461	Leo I
199–217	Zephyrinus	461–468	Hilary
217–222	Callistus I	468–483	Simplicius
217–235	[Hippolytus]	483–492	Felix III
222–230	Urban I	492–496	Gelasius I
230–235	Pontianus	496–498	Anastasius
235–236	Anterus	498–514	Symmachus
236–250	Fabian	498–501	Laurentius
251–253	Cornelius	514–523	Hormisdas
251–258	[Novatian]	523–526	John I
253–254	Lucius I	526–530	Felix IV
254–257	Stephen I	530–532	Boniface II
257–268	Dionysius	530	Dioscurus
269–274	Felix I	533–535	John II
275–283	Eutychianus	535–536	Agapitus I
283–296	Cajus	536–537	Silverius
296–304	Marcellinus	537–555	Vigilius
308–309	Marcellus I	556–561	Pelagius I
309	Eusebius	561–574	John III
311–314	Melchiades	575–579	Benedict I
314–335	Silvester I	579–590	Pelagius II
336	Marcus	590–604	Gregory I

604–606	Sabinianus	847–855	Leo IV
607	Boniface III	855–858	Benedict III
608–615	Boniface IV	855	[Anastasius]
615–618	Adeodatus I	858–867	Nicholas I
619–625	Boniface V	867–872	Adrian II
625–638	Honorius I	872–882	John VIII
640	Severinus	882–884	Marinus I
640–642	John IV	884–885	Adrian III
642–649	Theodore I	885–891	Stephen VI
649–653	Martin I	891–896	Formosus
654–657	Eugenius I	896	Boniface VI
657–672	Vitalian	896–897	Stephen VII
672–676	Adeodatus II	897	Romanus
676–678	Donus	897	Theodore II
678–681	Agatho	898–900	John IX
682–683	Leo II	900–903	Benedict IV
684–685	Benedict II	903	Leo V
685–686	John V	903–904	[Christophorus]
686–687	Conon	904–911	Sergius III
687	[Theodore]	911–913	Anastasius III
687	[Pashcal]	913–914	Lando
687–701	Sergius I	914–928	John X
701–705	John VI	928	Leo VI
705–707	John VII	928–931	Stephen VIII
708	Sisinnius	931–935	John XI
708–715	Constantine I	936–939	Leo VII
715–731	Gregory II	939–942	Stephen IX
731–741	Gregory III	942–946	Marinus II
741–752	Zachary	946–955	Agapitus II
752	Stephen II	955–964	John XII
752–757	Stephen III	963–964	Leo VIII
757–767	Paul I	964	Benedict V
767–769	[Constantine II]	965–972	John XIII
768	Philip	973–974	Benedict VI
768–772	Stephen IV	974	[Boniface VII]
772–795	Adrian I	974–983	Benedict VII
795–816	Leo III	983–984	John XIV
816–817	Stephen V	985–996	John XV
817–824	Pashcal I	996–999	Gregory V
824–827	Eugenius II	997–998	[John XVI]
827	Valentine	999–1003	Silvester II
827–844	Gregory IV	1003	John XVII
844–847	Sergius II	1004–1009	John XVIII
844	[John]	1009–1012	Sergius IV

1012–1024	Benedict VIII
1012	[Gregor]
1024–1032	John XIX
1032–1044	Benedict IX
1045	Silvester III
1045	Gregory VI
1046–1047	Clement II
1048	Damasus II
1049–1054	Leo IX
1055–1057	Victor II
1057–1058	Stephen X
1058–1059	[Benedict X]
1059–1061	Nicholas II
1061–1073	Alexander II
1072	[Honorius II]
1073–1085	Gregory VII
1080–1100	[Clement III]
1086–1087	Victor III
1088–1099	Urban II
1099–1118	Paschal II
1100	[Theodoric]
1102	[Albert]
1105–1111	[Silvester IV]
1118–1119	Gelasius II
1118–1121	[Gregory VIII]
1119–1124	Callistus II
1124–1130	Honorius II
1124	[Celestine]
1130–1143	Innocent II
1130–1138	[Anacletus II]
1138	[Victor IV]
1143–1144	Celestine II
1144–1145	Lucius II
1145–1153	Eugenius III
1153–1154	Anastasius IV
1154–1159	Adrian IV
1159–1181	Alexander III

1159–1164	[Victor IV]
1164–1168	[Paschal III]
1168–1178	[Callistus III]
1179–1180	[Innocent III]
1181–1185	Lucius III
1185–1187	Urban III
1187	Gregory VIII
1187–1191	Clement III
1191–1198	Celestine III
1198–1216	Innocent III
1216–1227	Honorius III
1227–1241	Gregory IX
1241	Celestine IV
1243–1254	Innocent IV
1254–1261	Alexander IV
1261–1264	Urban IV
1265–1268	Clement IV
1271–1276	Gregory X
1276	Innocent V
1276	Adrian V
1276–1277	John XXI
1277–1280	Nicholas III
1281–1285	Martin IV
1285–1287	Honorius IV
1288–1292	Nicholas IV
1294	Celestine V
1294–1303	Boniface VIII
1303–1304	Benedict XI
1305–1314	Clement V
1316–1334	John XXII
1328–1330	[Nicholas V]
1334–1342	Benedict XII
1342–1352	Clement VI
1352–1362	Innocent VI
1362–1370	Urban V
1370–1378	Gregory XI

[Line continues below, left column.]

Popes of the Papal Schism

1378–1389	Urban VI
1389–1404	Boniface IX
1404–1406	Innocent VII

[Line concludes below, next page.]

	Avignon Popes	Pisan Popes
1378–1394	[Clement VII]	
1394–1417	[Benedict XIII]	
1409–1410		[Alexander V]

1406–1415	. . . . Gregory XII	1410–1415	. . . . [John XXIII]
1417–1431	. . . . Martin V	1458–1464	. . . . Pius II
1431–1447	. . . . Eugenius IV	1464–1471	. . . . Paul II
1439–1449	. . . . Felix V	1471–1484	. . . . Sixtus IV
1447–1455	. . . . Nicholas V	1484–1492	. . . . Innocent VIII
1455–1458	. . . . Callistus III	1492–1503	. . . . Alexander VI

□ *Patriarchs of Constantinople* □

381–397	. . . . Nectarius	674–676	. . . . Constantine I
398–404	. . . . John I (Chrysostom)	676–678	. . . . Theodore I
404–405	. . . . Arsacius	678–683	. . . . George I
406–425	. . . . Atticus	683–686	. . . . Theodore I
426–427	. . . . Sisinius I	686–693	. . . . Paul III
428–431	. . . . Nestorius	693–705	. . . . Callinicus I
431–434	. . . . Maximian	705–711	. . . . Cyrus
434–447	. . . . Proclus	711–715	. . . . John VI
447–449	. . . . Flavian	715–730	. . . . Germanus I
449–458	. . . . Anatolius	730–754	. . . . Anastasius
458–471	. . . . Gennadius	754–766	. . . . Constantine II
471–489	. . . . Acacius	766–780	. . . . Nicetas I
489	. . . . Fravitta	780–784	. . . . Paul IV
489–495	. . . . Euphemius	784–806	. . . . Tarasius
496–511	. . . . Macedonius II	806–815	. . . . Nicephorus I
511–518	. . . . Timothy	815–821	. . . . Theodotus I
518–520	. . . . John II	821–832	. . . . Antony I
520–535	. . . . Epiphanius	832–842	. . . . John VII
535–536	. . . . Anthimus I	842–846	. . . . Methodius I
536–552	. . . . Menas	846–858	. . . . Ignatius
552–565	. . . . Eutychius	858–867	. . . . Photius
566–577	. . . . John III	867–878	. . . . Ignatius
577–582	. . . . Eutychius	878–886	. . . . Photius
582–595	. . . . John IV	886–893	. . . . Stephen I
595–606	. . . . Cyriacus I	893–895	. . . . Antony II
607–610	. . . . Thomas I	895–906	. . . . Nicholas I, Mysticus
610–638	. . . . Sergius I	906–911	. . . . Euthymius I
638–641	. . . . Pyrrhus	911–925	. . . . Nicholas I
641–652	. . . . Paul II	925–928	. . . . Stephen II
651–652	. . . . Pyrrhus	928–931	. . . . Tryphon
652–664	. . . . Peter	933–956	. . . . Theophylactus
665–668	. . . . Thomas II	956–970	. . . . Polyeuctus
668–674	. . . . John V	970–974	. . . . Basil I

974–980	Antony III
984–995	Nicholas II
995–998	Sisinius II
999–1019	Sergius II
1019–1025	Eustathius
1025–1043	Alexius
1043–1058	Michael Cerularius
1059–1063	Constantine III, Leuchudes
1064–1075	John VIII, Xiphilinus
1075–1081	Cosmas I, Hierosolymites
1081–1084	Eustratius Garidus
1084–1111	Nicholas III
1111–1134	John IX, Agapetus
1134–1142	Leo Styppes
1143–1146	Michael II, Kurkuas (Oxzeites)
1146–1147	Cosmas II, Atticus
1147–1151	Nicholas IV, Muzalon
1151–1153	Theodotus II
1153	Neophytus I
1154–1156	Constantine IV, Chliarenus
1156–1169	Lucas Chrysoberges
1169–1177	Michael III
1177–1178	Chariton, Eugeniotes
1178–1183	Theodosius I
1183–1187	Basil II, Camaterus
1187–1190	Nicetas II, Muntanes
1190–1191	Leontius, Theotocites
1191–1192	Dositheus
1192–1199	George II, Xiphilinus
1199–1206	John X, Camaterus
1206–1212	Michael IV (Autorianus)
1212–1215	Theodore II (Irenicus; Copas)
1215	Maximus II
1215–1222	Manuel I
1222–1240	Germanus II
1240	Methodius
1244–1255	Manuel II
1255–1260	Arsenius
1260–1261	Nicephorus II
1261–1267	Arsenius
1267	Germanus III
1268–1275	Joseph I
1275–1282	John XI (Beccus)
1282–1283	Joseph I
1283–1289	Gregory II
1289–1293	Athanasius I
1294–1303	John XII
1303–1311	Athanasius I
1331–1315	Nephon I
1316–1320	John XIII
1320–1321	Gerasimus I
1323–1334	Jesias
1334–1347	John XIV
1347–1349	Isidore I
1350–1354	Callistus I
1354–1355	Philotheus
1355–1363	Callistus I
1364–1376	Philotheus
1376–1379	Macarius
1380–1388	Nilus
1389–1390	Antony IV
1390–1391	Macarius
1391–1397	Antony IV
1397–1410	Matthias
1410–1416	Euthymius II
1416–1439	Joseph II
1440–1442	Metrophanes II
1443–1450	Gregory III
1450	Athanasius II
1453–1459	Gennadius II

Part 1

The Beginnings to 70 C.E.

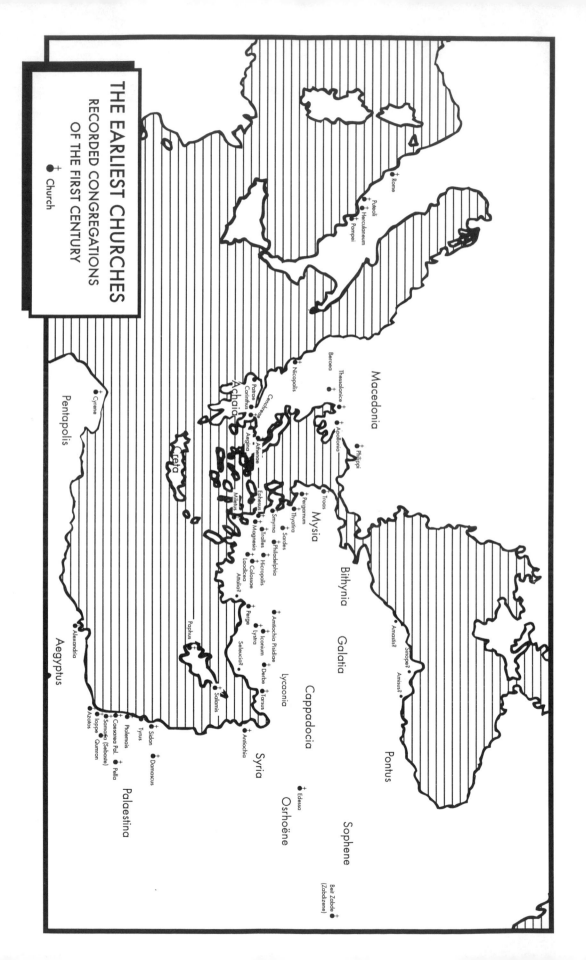

THE EARLIEST CHURCHES
RECORDED CONGREGATIONS
OF THE FIRST CENTURY

+ ● Church

Rome
Puteoli
Herculaneum
Pompei

Cyrene
Pentapolis

Creta

Aegyptus
Alexandria

Beroea
Nicopolis
Thessalonice
Apollonia
Philippi
Macedonia

Achaia
Patrae
Corinthus
Cenchreae
Aegina
Athenae

Troas
Pergamum
Ephesus
Thyatira
Smyrna
Sardes
Magnesia
Tralles
Philadelphia
Hierapolis
Laodicea
Colossae
Attalia?
Mysia

Miletus

Bithynia

Galatia

Paphus

Perge
Antiochia Pisidiae
Iconium
Lystra
Derbe
Tarsus
Seleucia?
Salamis
Lycaonia

Cappadocia

Amastis?
Sinope?
Amisus?
Pontus

Sophene

Edessa
Osrhoëne

Syria
Antiochia
Damascus
Sidon
Tyrus
Ptolemais
Caesarea Pal.
Pella
Samaria (Sebaste)
Ioppe
Qumran
Azotus
Palaestina

Beit Zabde
(Zabdizene)

Chapter 1

An Ancient New People

Christianity began with a history. The first Christians did not consider themselves a new people but an ancient people, Israel, under a new covenant. Stated another way, they thought of themselves as the true Israel having experienced the fulfillment of Jewish messianic hopes through Jesus of Nazareth.

Jesus was a Jew, an heir of centuries of Hebrew history extending from Abraham to his own day. He limited his ministry to the Jewish people and forbade his disciples to witness to any except Jews. He did not intend to begin a new religion. He wanted, rather, to awaken his own people to the dawning of an age of fulfillment of long-nourished hopes in and through him. He failed; yet in failing, he succeeded, for his death and the experience of resurrection which followed it inaugurated a movement which, within a few centuries, spread from Judea and Samaria throughout the civilized world.

Judaism furnished Christianity both with its most salient and central concepts and with a well-tilled field in which to plant them. From Judaism came the concept of one God who had sought a people and entered into covenant with them for the purpose of bringing all peoples and nations into relationship with God and with one another. From it came the hopes for a messiah who would redeem a people, a strong ethical sensitivity, a habit of regular worship, and a sense of duty to broadcast the message of one God who offers salvation to all.

The Covenant People

At the heart of Hebrew self-understanding was the conviction that Yahweh had chosen them out of merciful love to be the People of the Covenant. Beyond the more general covenant made with Noah (Gen. 6:8ff.) Yahweh entered into a special covenant first with Abram (Gen. 16:18) and then through Moses (Exod. 19:4-6). The latter, based on God's deliverance of the people from bondage in Egypt, emphasized both favor and demand.

> You yourselves have seen what I did with the Egyptians, how I carried you on eagle's wings and brought you to myself. From this you know that now, if you obey my voice and hold fast to my covenant, you of all the nations shall be my very own, for all the earth is mine. I will count you a kingdom of priests, a consecrated nation.   (JB)

Much of the story related in the Old Testament concerns Israel's success or failure as the Covenant People, a theme Christians picked up on to establish the validity of Christianity against Jewish claims. When Moses delayed on Mount Sinai, the People demanded a golden calf (Exod.

32:1), symbolic of their subsequent apostasies. During the conquest of the promised land, they regularly went "whoring after other gods," that is, the Canaanite deities Baal and Astarte. In the period of the Kingdom the prophets repeatedly thundered warnings against violation of the covenant. Israel's and Judah's collapse, the prophets concluded, resulted from failure to abide by the demands of the covenant for faithfulness and justice and mercy. The eighth century prophets still held out hopes that a repentant people might avert disaster, but their successors in later centuries saw these dashed on the rock of reality. Jeremiah, rebuffed in his efforts to get his bitter pill swallowed, pointed to the future and to the effecting of a new covenant unlike the one the people broke.

> Deep within them I will plant my Law, writing it on their hearts. Then I will be their God and they shall be my people. There will be no further need for neighbor to try to teach neighbor, or brother to say to brother, "Learn to know Yahweh!" No, they will all know me, the least no less than the greatest—it is Yahweh who speaks—since I will forgive their iniquity and never call their sin to mind.   (Jer. 31:33-34, JB)

Jeremiah and prophets in the exile such as Ezekiel and Deutero-Isaiah (Isa. 40-55) entertained hopes of a Remnant of the People which would return. Indeed, Deutero-Isaiah narrowed the Remnant to one, the Servant of Yahweh (Isa. 42:1-4; 49:1-6; 50:4-9; 52:13–53:12).

Surprisingly the earliest Christian writers seldom cited the new covenant in their arguments for Christianity. The author of Hebrews excepted, New Testament writers based their case on the older covenant references. The Apostle Paul, who deserves more credit than any other for extension of the covenant to include Gentiles, cited the covenant with Abraham as a covenant predicated on faith rather than works (Gal. 3:6-14). The author of 1 Peter applied Exodus 19:5-6 directly to Christians with added allusions to Isaiah 43:20-21 and Hosea 1:6-9 and 2:3, 25.

> But you are a chosen race, a royal priesthood, a consecrated nation, a people set apart to sing the praises of God who called you out of darkness into his wonderful light. Once you were not a people at all and now you are the People of God; once you were outside the mercy and now you have been given mercy.   (1 Pet. 2:9-10)

Christianity, led by the Apostle Paul, departed from its parent religion in its incorporation of Gentiles without requiring them first to become Jews by circumcision and the offering of a sacrifice. It continued, however, to insist on baptism as a symbol of entrance into the Covenant People. Letting down certain of these barriers opened the way for this messianic sect to expand in a way its parent religion could not, but it also generated bitter feelings which lead to an eventual rupture. In Jerusalem Christians met opposition to their continuance in the Temple; outside Jerusalem, to their participation in the synagogues. Differing sharply over messianic views, Christianity gradually emerged as a separate religion which, within three centuries, would become the dominant religion of the Roman Empire and in other nations beyond the borders of the Empire. As Christianity accommodated itself to Hellenistic culture in the process, the exclusiveness of the Covenant was put to the test again and again when masses knocked on church doors seeking admission.

Jewish Corporate Life

In the first century, Jewish corporate life revolved chiefly around two institutions—the Temple and the Law. The Temple had a long history which endeared it to Jews living in Palestine, but its destruction in 589 B.C.E. and the scattering of the Jewish people undercut its importance even before Jesus' day. To make matters worse, Herod the Great's reconstruction of the Second Temple, begun in 19 B.C.E. was politically unpopular. Nevertheless, the Temple retained a central place in Jewish life until its destruction by the Roman armies in 70 C.E.

In theory Temple worship entailed the offering of sacrifices symbolic of covenant renewal. The calendar dramatized the "great moments" in the history of the Covenant People when God had acted on their behalf. The Sabbath, Passover, New Year's, the Day of Atonement, Pentecost, Purim—all said something about Yahweh mighty to save. Sacrifices offered within the context of liturgical recitals allowed the individual symbolically to renew commitments as the People gathered to renew the Covenant. In practice, criticisms from ancient times indicate Temple worship often became perfunctory, making little impact on the worshipers. Weightier matters— justice, mercy, peace, etc.—had to get attention elsewhere.

As the Temple's importance decreased, the Law's increased. During the exile in Babylon (589–520/519 B.C.E.), for obvious reasons, study of the Law took the place of Temple worship. Such study contributed to the development of synagogues as gathering places for Jewish communities in the Dispersion.

Synagogue worship consisted chiefly of reading and exposition of the scriptures. In Jesus' day readings from the Torah, the Pentateuch, were prescribed; those from other writings, however, were optional (cf. Luke 4:17). The Old Testament canon did not achieve its present form in Judaism until 99 or 119 C.E., when rabbis at the Jewish school of Jamnia settled the matter.

One other institution played an important role in a society in which religion intersected with everything. In Jerusalem the Sanhedrin resolved matters of dispute in interpretation of the Torah which synagogues could not settle. Composed of seventy elders presided over by the high priest, it served as a kind of Supreme Court.

The Sects of Judaism

Judaism was by no means monolithic in the first century. It consisted, rather, of numerous parties or sects as well as the "professional" interpreters of the Law called Scribes.

The Sadducees represented the priestly aristocracy, claiming descent from Zadok. As the ruling party, they favored accommodation to Roman hegemony. Religiously, however, they were skeptical of views which came to prominence during the interbiblical period, for instance, resurrection of the dead, judgment, eternal life, and angels or demons. They acknowledged the authority only of the Pentateuch.

The Pharisees were the party most zealous for keeping of the Law. Originating during the Maccabean era, they sought "separation" from Gentile customs and the process of hellenization which Judaism experienced in the third to second centuries B.C.E. In pursuit of this goal, they espoused strict adherence to the oral tradition being developed at the time. They are not to be equated with the Scribes, professional interpreters of the Law, but many Scribes would have belonged to the party of Pharisees. Unlike the Sadducees, the Pharisees believed in a resurrection of the dead, final judgment, and life in the age-to-come, and accepted other writings besides the Pentateuch.

The Essenes or Covenanters entertained the most pronounced messianic hopes of all parties in Judaism. Withdrawing during the Maccabean era in protest of corruption of the Temple and the priesthood in Jerusalem, they established a monastery near the Dead Sea. Like the Pharisees, they were zealous in study and application of the Law and developed an interpretive method which related scriptures in a particular way to their own experience. They were more strongly influenced, however, by Jewish apocalyptic thought. They conceived of themselves as "the Sons of Light" preparing for the final cataclysmic battle against "the Sons of Darkness," whom they eventually identified as the Romans. In 68 C.E., thinking the end had come, they joined battle. Most were killed or taken captive.

Essene influence on early Christianity was significant but difficult to establish with precision. The Essenes shared with early Christians strong expectations of the coming of a Messiah. They practiced some kind of ritual ablutions related to purification as the Covenant People and observed a messianic meal similar to the Christian Lord's Supper. In addition, they organized in hierarchical fashion similar to the Jerusalem community depicted in Acts. At the top was a Council of Twelve, including or plus Three Priests; next came Presbyters or Priests; at the bottom were "the Many." A "Superintendent" (*Mebaqqer*) also played some kind of executive role. The fact that Essenes are never mentioned in New Testament writings has been attributed to familiarity; so many Essenes joined the early Church, no one needed to mention them.

Zealots were extreme Jewish nationalists. Impatient to free their homeland and people from Roman domination, they carried on guerrilla warfare. Jesus' ties with Zealots are uncertain, but at least one of his followers, Simon, was called "the Zealot," and Judas may have belonged to the still more radical Sicarii, for the name Iscariot can be construed in that way. Yet efforts to turn Jesus into a Zealot require such a vast amount of rewriting of early Christian history as to remain unconvincing.

Herodians supported the royal family whose Idumean ancestry aroused bitter feelings among the Jews. Herod the Great widened the rift by catering to the Romans and by his brutal rule in the last years of his reign (37–4 B.C.E.). His sons did not fare much better.

Besides these parties or sects, first century Judaism had guilds of priests, temple singers, and Levites who attended to Temple functions and a guild of scribes who, from the time of Jesus Ben Sirach (ca. 180 B.C.E.), concentrated on the Law. At the time of Jesus scribes were divided into two schools—a strict, Shammaite, and a liberal, Hillelite. Whereas Shammaites emphasized rigorous adherence to the Law, Hillelites stressed love and conciliation.

A New Sect among the Old

Christianity came to birth in this complex setting. How did it differ from the others? For one thing, in eschatological expectations. Whereas the other sects looked *forward* to the coming of Messiah, Christianity looked *backward* from the vantagepoint of the death and resurrection of Jesus of Nazareth. The age-to-come had dawned. The promises had begun to be fulfilled.

This central conviction, however, contained other implications which would push Christianity away from the others. John the Baptist, possibly reared by the Essenes as an orphan, had become impatient with waiting in the desert and gone forth to announce the "coming one." Expectations fulfilled, Christians pressed forth still further. The monotheistic motive which prompted the Jewish mission was not heightened to fever pitch. The time within which the message could be proclaimed was short; soon the risen Lord would return to consummate the plan of God for human history.

The urgency with which the mission was pursued, however, soon evoked a third distinction. Zealous to share the "good news" of the inbreaking of the Kingdom of God in and through Jesus, Israel's Messiah, Christians soon invited the "godfearers" and marginal people connected with Jewish communities to full membership in the Covenant People without insisting on their receiving the marks of Jews or observing Jewish ritual law. This radical action precipitated a massive debate.

In the words and works of Jesus Christians found the precedent they needed. Jesus, to be sure, had not extended his ministry beyond the bounds of Judaism. However, he had ministered to the outcasts—the tax collectors and sinners—and earned the reputation of a "friend of tax collectors and sinners." Not the well but the sick need a doctor, he had said in defense. The parables of the lost sheep, the lost coin, and the prodigal son demonstrated God's love for the sinner. God's mercy is wide enough to receive even these.

Like the prophets of old, Jesus also placed human need above observance of the Law. "The sabbath was made for man, not man for the sabbath" (Mk. 2:27), he argued against rigid interpreters. Those who make a fetish of observance can end up missing the whole purpose of the Law. Tithing mint, dill, and cummin, they neglect the things that really matter (Matt. 23:23-24). Preoccupation with observance may also lead to self-righteousness which inhibits true justification. Not the self-righteous Pharisee who boasted about his scrupulous observance of the *Halakah* but the lowly tax collector who refused to lift his eyes heavenward and beat his breast in abasement "went home justified" (Lk. 18:14).

However much Jesus had done to prepare for the separation of Christianity from other sects of Judaism, it was the Apostle Paul who merits the most credit or blame for the break. Membership in the Covenant People, the Apostle contended, depends on God's grace and the believers' faith, not on doing the Law. Salvation depends purely on God's unmerited favor, for all, Jews and Gentiles alike, have "sinned and forfeited God's glory" (Rom. 3:23). In Christ God has opened a way to do what we could not do for ourselves, that is, obey God. By his death on the cross Christ has taken on himself our condemnation, so that there is now no more condemnation for us (Rom. 8:1). How do we appropriate the benefits of his death? By simple faith. Neither circumcision nor observance of the ritual law will do any good. What is required is simply to trust God. As for Greek, so too for Jew.

Here the apostle undercut the very essence of Jewish piety. Tolerant as Judaism was at many points, on this issue a rift was unavoidable.

Chapter 2

The World of Early Christianity

Judaism gave birth to Christianity, but it did not provide a spawning ground for long. The world of early Christianity was the Roman Empire and its environs—from the British Isles to the Tigris-Euphrates and from central Europe to northern Africa. By the end of the first century Christian communities dotted this entire area, in some places rather heavily, in others thinly.

The Roman Colossus

When Jesus was born, Rome dominated the world around the Mediterranean. Still expanding, it reached its greatest extent under Hadrian around 115 C.E. Continuous expansion, however, came at a price. It required increasing concentration of power in the hands of the Emperor, constant attention to the strengthening of external boundaries, and the reforming of provincial administration during the succession of emperors from Octavian to Nero (27 B.C.E. to 68 C.E.). In addition, as a means for enhancing imperial authority, the Roman Senate fostered Caesar worship, beginning with Julius. Although Octavian forbade such honors in Rome, he permitted it in the provinces. His successors in the Julio-Claudian line held back few claims, thus setting up a headon clash with Christianity, which demanded absolute allegiance to Jesus as Lord. Caligula (37–41) was the first to demand universal homage to his statue. Though Domitian (91–96) was

the first to use real force, the first clash with Christians came under Nero (60–68).

Roman society in the first century exhibited many features similar to American society today. It was cosmopolitan, a vast melting pot composed of many ancient peoples. The Romans were themselves a composite people. By virtue of their conquests they absorbed dozens more, everywhere taking captives who would toss their cultures into the pot. The Romans also admired hellenistic culture, itself cosmopolitan, and spread it wherever they went.

The population of the Empire, approximately 70,000,000, was concentrated chiefly in cities. Rome's population numbered about 700,000. Alexandria and Antioch on the Orantes were only slightly smaller. Ephesus, Corinth, Athens, and several other cities vied for third place behind these. Such cities offered both the opportunities and the disadvantages of modern ones. Rome especially drew hundreds because of its "bread and circuses." Alexandria boasted the world's greatest library and immense cultural resources. Nevertheless, all of the cities suffered from cramped living quarters, poor sanitation, inadequate water supplies, vermin infestation, and a host of similar problems. Poorly constructed apartments six stories high frequently crumpled to the ground with a roar, snuffing out the lives of occupants. The half-mad Emperor Nero probably had urban renewal on his mind when he set fire to the city of Rome in 64 C.E. and then blamed the arson on Christians.

The Empire was characterized also by enormous disparities in wealth. Although there was a middle class, most of the populace clustered at opposite poles. The wealthy lived in grand villas on the outskirts of the city. They enjoyed comforts and conveniences put at their disposal by slaves. The poor squeaked by with bare subsistence of food, clothing, and the necessities. Unable to maintain their families, they frequently exposed newborn children, especially girls. A letter dated June 17, 1 B.C.E. tells the poignant story from a personal standpoint: "If you have a baby," a husband unsympathetically instructed his wife, "if it is a male, let it live; if it is a female, cast it out." Christians were to adopt many of these unfortunates in the next several centuries, as the custom continued until the sixth century.

An increasing number of persons depended on state maintenance. Rome's conquests, of course, enabled emperors to draw supplies from elsewhere to curry favor with the masses. The dole became so burdensome, however, that Octavian was compelled to limit it to 150,000 and later to 100,000 persons.

Side by side with greater brutality were signs of growing sensitivity to human beings. The Roman army, challenged to conquer more and more new territories, conscripted all and sundry. Thoughtful persons such as the Stoic Seneca, however, composed treatises *On Clemency* in criticism of careless regard for human life.

Roman society was divided into several layers. At the lowest level, where Christianity made its first inroads, people waged a daily struggle for survival and worried about losing their property, heavy taxation, the draft, and other matters familiar today. Moral standards varied widely, ranging from the admirable thought of the Stoics—Seneca, Epictetus, Cicero—to the deplorable outlook of masses. Illiteracy was common. The uneducated hired professional scribes to write letters for them and then signed

them with an X. Families strained to survive. Children manipulated parents for money.

> When my father came to me [a young soldier complained to his mother] he did not give me an *obolus* or a cloak or anything. All will laugh at me. His father is a soldier, they will say, and yet he gives him nothing. My father said, when I get home, I will send you everything, but he has sent me nothing. Why? The mother of Valerius sent him a pair of girdles, and a jar of oil, and a basket of dainties, and two hundred drachmae. Wherefore I beg you mother, send me something. Do not leave me in this condition.

People despaired in the face of sickness and death. "I was as sorry and wept over the departed on as I wept for Didymas," a second-century letter said. "And all things, whatsoever fitting, I, and all mine, did. . . . But, nevertheless, against such things one can do nothing. Therefore comfort one another."

The Religions of Rome

Paul's compliment to the Athenians about their being "in all respects very religious" (Acts 17:22) would have suited the people of the Roman Empire quite well, for the word he used, *deisdaimonia*, meant both "religious" and "superstitious." The religions of the Roman Empire fell into three categories: the state cultus revived by Octavian, the oriental religions which attracted the masses, and the philosophies which functioned increasingly as the religion of the better educated. The state cultus still retained much vitality among the masses. An amalgam of many sources, particularly the Greek pantheon, it suffered from impersonalism and formalism. What had made Rome great, the Romans believed, was not merely the gods but their devotion to the gods manifested in precise rituals and observances. When Rome conquered other nations, they tried to incorporate the defeated countries' deities into the pantheon so that none might be neglected. The addition of the cult of the emperor with the goddess Roma helped momentarily, but state religion proved too perfunctory to satisfy all. It lacked the warmth of personal appeal found in oriental cults.

Numerous oriental religions thrived in the West when Christianity put in its appearance. The Mysteries of Eleusis, originating several centuries before the Christian era, were patronized by emperors from Octavian on. They used the planting of seed as a symbol of the promise of life which lies beyond death. Mysteries of Dionysus, found also under the name of Orpheus, extended throughout the Graeco-Roman world. They were noted for enthusiasm and ecstatic prophesying. The three stoutest competitors in the first several centuries, however, were Cybele or the Great Mother, Isis and Osiris, and Mithra.

The cult of the Great Mother, a fertility goddess connected with agricultural rites, enjoyed wide currency in the ancient world as far West as the British Isles. Acknowledged in Rome as a legitimate foreign cult in 205 B.C.E., by the time of Augustus it had gained immense popularity. Originally a wild and enthusiastic cult, involving even human sacrifices, it was modified by combination with the cult of Attis. The mythology of a dying and rising god replaced earlier orgiastic rites. A colorful pageantry combined with the promise of immortality to attract many. In time Cybele adopted the *taurobolium*, a bath in bull's blood, popularized by Mithra. Symbolically "buried" in a pit covered by a latticework of boards, the devotee was said to be purified of sins and raised to new life.

Isis an Osiris, an ancient Egyptian cult, was introduced in the West by the Ptolemies. Soldiers, sailors, slaves, and popular writings disseminated it all over the Empire. Its most attractive features were the myth of a dying and rising god and an appealing liturgy. The myth told how the young god Osiris, civilizer of Egypt, was hacked to pieces by the jealous Typhon and the remains scattered along the Nile River. Osiris's faithful wife Isis, however, searched diligently until she found all parts save the male sexual organ and restored her husband to life. Periodically Osiris would return to visit his wife and son. Daily rituals and two impressive annual ceremonies dramatized this myth. On March 5 a magnificent processional to the river celebrated the reopening of the seas at the end of winter. From October 26 to November 3 the cult dramatized the "Finding of Osiris." Here worshipers simulated funeral lamentations for the fallen god Osiris, then rejoiced as Horus, son of Osiris, overcame Typhon. An impressive initiation rite added to the appeal of this religion. "About midnight," Lucius reported in Apuleius's *Metamorphoses*, "I saw the sun brightly shine, I saw likewise the gods celestial and the gods infernal, before whom I presented myself and worshiped them."

Mithra, a Persian sect growing out of Zoroastrianism, advanced westward by way of the Roman army during the Flavian era (68–96). Remarkably similar to Christianity in many respects, it turned out to be the strongest competitor, though limited by the fact that the cult excluded women. Like Judaism and Christianity, Mithraism emphasized morality. It viewed life as a perpetual struggle between good and evil, light and darkness, the gods and demons. Mithra, one of the lesser deities in the Zoroastrian hierarchy, identified with human beings in their struggle. Mithraic altars depicted Mithra astride the back of a powerful bull hurling his dagger into its side as a serpent twines around one leg to lap up the blood spurting from the wound. To underline the importance of morality, Mithraism emphasized judgment. At death anyone stained with evil would be dragged by the emissaries of Ahriman to the depths of hell to suffer indescribable tortures, whereas the pure would ascend to the celestial realm where the supreme God Ormuzd ruled. Enroute, Mithra himself would serve as the guide past the seven planetary spheres guarded over by angels. After a general resurrection

Mithra would judge all humanity once for all and cause fire to consume all wicked spirits. Mithraism developed rites and organization similar to Christianity's but, since they were of late origin, most were probably borrowed. The most important rite was the *taurobolium*, which promised immortality.

There has been much debate about the similarities between the mystery cults and Christianity. At one time the German history of religions school theorized that Christianity was an oriental mystery cult which Paul had given historical credence by attaching to the person of Jesus. Some scholars doubted whether Jesus ever existed. Much subsequent research, in Jewish and Greek or Roman as well as Christian sources, however, has demolished this view. There remains, nevertheless, considerable question as to the extent of borrowing. The very nature of Christianity as an offspring of Judaism favors, at most, a cautious accommodation, but there is evidence of increasing borrowing of language and ideas as time passed.

The Philosophies

At the beginning Christianity competed chiefly with the oriental religions in enlisting converts among non-Jews. From the first, however, persons of education and culture manifested an interest in this offspring of Judaism, just as they had in Judaism itself. By the mid-second century apologists were presenting Christianity as "the true philosophy," a competitor of the philosophies which responded to the religious needs of the better educated and more sophisticated upper classes.

A multiplicity of philosophies vied with one another, but the one which attracted the largest following in this period and left the deepest mark on Christian thought was Stoicism. Originating about 300 B.C.E. with Zeno of Citium, this school entered its third major phase in the New Testament era with such representatives as Seneca, Epictetus, and, in the second century, Marcus Aurelius. Stoicism was based on the assumption that only matter is real. Yet, unlike Democritus, who ascribed the operation of the universe more or less to chance movement of the atom, the Stoics believed all things hold together in a coherent, indeed monistic, system. Zeus, destiny, providence, universal law, nature, or God penetrated and gave order to all things. The world operated according to divine law, which even God must obey. To live a happy life, human beings had to know and obey this law, which is equivalent to God's will. To discover the law of nature, they had to use their reason. Living according to nature was the same thing as living according to reason. The key lay in constant self-examination, probing of conscience. Conscience and duty were the cornerstones of Stoic ethics. Acting out of enlightened self-interest necessitated concern for all persons. The ideal, however, was to become self-sufficient, controlling actions by reason rather than by passion or desire.

By the second century, Platonism began to edge out Stoicism. Christianity encountered Platonism first in its middle phase chiefly in the popular form known as Gnosticism. There is considerable debate about the origins of Gnosticism. The older theory was that it represented the radical hellenization of Christianity. Discovery of a Gnostic library at Chenoboskion in Egypt in 1947, however, has forced scholars to abandon this theory. Some have interpreted Gnosticism as a pre-Christian religion, others as the result of a failure of apocalyptic thought in Judaism and Christianity. The Nag Hammadi (Chenoboskion) documents indicate that Gnosticism took a variety of forms—some non-Christian, some Jewish, some Christian. Since Christian Gnosticism will receive specific attention later, it suffices here to mention general tenets which may have impressed themselves on early Christian thinking in the first century.

Gnosticism was characterized in its more extreme forms by a metaphysical dualism. Matter is evil; the spirit alone good. Between these there should be no contact. Since matter is evil, the visible, physical world cannot have been created by God, who was by definition pure spirit. God entrusted this work to a Demiurge, a secondary deity. To keep the material from intermingling with the spiritual, a series of concentric spheres, aeons, separated the world from God. Demons kept watch over these spheres, allowing no one to ascend without a password. As in Platonism, human beings were bipartite, consisting of body and soul. Since the body is material, it could not be saved. The soul, however, if enlightened by *Gnosis*, could be. Indeed, souls fell into three categories: the spiritual, who would ascend like helium-filled balloons; the material, who had no prospect of salvation; and the psychic, who could be saved through *gnosis* or knowledge. *Gnosis*, though, meant mystical rather than cognitive apprehension. Where did one obtain *gnosis*? From the Redeemer who descended from the realm of the One, God, taught secret knowledge, and reascended. Not all Gnostic systems, as indicated above, were Christian, but those which attached themselves to Christianity identified Jesus as the Redeemer, a phantom rather than a human being.

The extent to which Gnostic thought shaped that of New Testament writers is debatable. Rudolf Bultmann believed Paul drew the basic framework for his theology from Gnosticism, but many other scholars have demonstrated its essentially Jewish structure. Some New Testament writings, particularly the Johannine, explicitly repudiated Gnostic dualism, docetism (belief that Jesus was a phantom), and moral indifferentism.

Other philosophical schools attracted fewer adherents and exerted more limited influence on early Christianity. Cynics, claiming origins in the fifth century B.C.E., still traveled around preaching that salvation lies in a return to nature. Their diatribes may have affected the form of some early Christian literature. Cynicism later merged with Stoicism. Neo-Pythagoreanism, a Greco-Alexandrian school, thrived during the first century. Its most famous representative was Apollonius of Tyana (c. 1–98 C.E.), whom Philostratus celebrated in the third century as the miracle-working pagan answer to Jesus. Neo-Pythagoreanism combined Platonism and Pythagoreanism (sixth century B.C.E.), thus introducing a religious element into pagan philosophy. Dualistic like Gnosticism, the Neo-Pythagoreans encouraged asceticism as a path to liberation from the body. They shared many ideas with the oriental mystery cults.

The Common Person's Outlook

What has not been covered in connection with religions and philosophies can be adequately summed up under two headings: fate and demons. A profound fatalism gripped the minds of most persons in the ancient world. The Romans took over the Greek deity *Tyche*, Chance or Fortune.

The philosophers commented often and at length on chance and necessity. The Stoics obviated the problem of chance with their doctrine of Providence, but it, too, amounted to a virtual determinism of nature's law. The average person had little sense of control over life. "Assuredly, if Fortune is against it," Apuleius said on behalf of many, "nothing good can come to mortal man."

Belief in occult powers resulted in a similar sense of the futility of life. The average person lived in a world teeming with demons, sprites, spirits of departed ancestors, "ghosties, and things that go bump in the night." Both good and bad, such beings controlled one's fate. If one drank a glass of water, he or she might swallow a demon and become deathly ill, go insane, or drop dead. Another person might invoke a curse through the agency of a demon. Having none of the testing instruments of modern science and technology, only the very skeptical denied and questioned this worldview. The average person searched frantically for ways to get the good demons and powers on their side and to placate the evil. They consulted soothsayers. They employed magicians to compose formulas to ward off evil. They probed the entrails of animals and birds. They carried amulets and magic charms. They entreated the gods with votive offerings. They erected temples and public buildings. Anything to bring a proper balance to the fearful unknown.

We can see here the challenge to early Christianity if it was to attract and enlist converts in a world so unlike the one in which it began. Like the oriental cults flowing westward at the time, it had to respond to the cry for infallible revelation, for assurance as to the meaning of life, for victory over the malign forces which threatened to engulf human beings, for hope. Yet, like those same cults, it could have lost its own identity as it incorporated the diverse and syncretistic peoples of the Empire and beyond. It needed a historical anchorage in its parent religion and, more specifically, its founder.

Chapter 3

The Founder of Christianity

Since the late nineteenth century scholars have debated whether Jesus should be regarded as the founder of Christianity or only as the "presupposition" for it. Was Christianity rooted in his life and thought and ministry? Or did it arise only out of the conviction of the first believers that Jesus, though crucified and buried, has been raised by God? Or, phrased in the words of the noted French Catholic Alfred Loisy, was the church, Christianity, not the *result* of Jesus' preaching of the Kingdom of God rather than something he himself founded?

Such questions cannot be answered easily. Few scholars today would defend the view held since primitive times that Jesus founded the church essentially as it now exists save for growth and development. Nevertheless, it does seem important to insist that Christianity has some connections not merely with the resurrection experience but with what antedated it. Paul, to be sure, accentuated the resurrection as the *sine qua non* for Christianity (1 Cor. 15:17-19), and he seemed to devalue the historical when he declared that "Even if we did once know Christ in the flesh, that is not how we know him now" (2 Cor. 5:16). Yet he could make a word of Jesus about divorce assume the force of command contrasted with his own word of advice (I Cor. 7:10, 12), and he counted traditions about Jesus essential to the very existence of Christianity (cf. 1 Cor. 14:3ff.). Paul himself certainly, important as

he was to early Christian self-understanding, cannot be regarded as the founder of Christianity as some scholars once contended.

The Life and Ministry of Jesus

If critical studies of the century and a half since David Friedrich Strauss published his *Life of Jesus* (1835) have reached any firm conclusion, it is that the sources at our disposal will not allow us to write a biography of Jesus. Jesus' existence, of course, is no longer open to question, as it was for a time, but some scholars do doubt the possibility of reconstructing a framework for Jesus' life and ministry. The first witnesses were not writing biography but giving testimony about the "good news" which they had heard and taken part in.

Some high points in Jesus' life and ministry, however, are evident. Since Herod the Great was still alive when he was born, his birth must have occurred before 4 B.C.E., when Herod died, perhaps about 6 B.C.E. Though December 25 has been celebrated as his birth date since about 335 C.E., there is no evidence to indicate even the time of the year. Prior to 335, Christians in the East celebrated January 6 as the day of birth.

Because Joseph and Mary were devout Jews, Jesus doubtless received an upbringing similar to that of other Jewish youth. Accordingly, he was circumcised on the eighth day and presented in the Temple, as prescribed by Numbers 6:10 (Luke 2:22). "Presentation" had to do with dedication of a "firstborn" son (1 Kgs. 1:24f.). Although Catholic tradition has held that Mary had no more children, the Gospels named four brothers—James, Joses, Jude, and Simon (Mark 6:3; cf. Matt. 27:56). Joseph may have died early in Jesus' life, leaving him with responsibility for support of the family, for he is not mentioned anywhere during Jesus' ministry.

Jesus' ministry began in connection with John the Baptist. At first he may have contemplated following or actually have followed John. Eventually, however, he gathered a following of his own. Subsequently a John the Baptist sect competed with early Christianity (cf. Acts 19:1ff.). This sect claimed that, because John baptized Jesus, he was the superior one. Christians replied by noting that John himself claimed only to be a forerunner.

John's mission and message reflect close enough similarities to those of the Qumran or Essene sect that many scholars have theorized a direct connection, for instance, his adoption as an orphan on the death of his parents. Like the Essenes, John denounced Jewish society, especially priests; insisted on a baptism of repentance for all, Jews as well as Gentiles; and proclaimed a judgment of fire soon to come. Unlike them, however, he administered baptism rather than let people baptize themselves, and he carried his message to the main arteries of traffic rather than waiting for something to happen. If he was once an Essene, he broke with them, perhaps over the timing of the age of fulfillment.

Luke dated the beginning of John's ministry "in the fifteenth year of the reign of Tiberius as Caesar" (Luke 3:1), which could mean either 28/29 or possibly 25/26, depending on whether it is dated from the death of Augustus (August 19, 14 C.E.) or from Tiberius's coreign with him. John did not minister long, however, for his criticisms of Herod Antipas soon led to imprisonment (Luke 3:19-20) and beheading (Mark 6:17-29).

There can be no question that Jesus was baptized by John, for his baptism supplied support for the argument of the John the Baptist sect, and since John's baptism had to do with repentance for sins, posed a serious problem for Christian theology. Why was Jesus baptized? According to the Synoptic accounts, his baptism had something to do with his self-understanding and mission. Through this acted parable, as it were, Jesus proclaimed his identification with his people as the Messiah of the Remnant conceived in terms of the Servant of the Lord in Deutero-Isaiah. At the same time God confirmed his perception. The voice from heaven conflated two passages of scriptures: Psalm 2:7 and Isaiah 42:1, the first a messianic text, the other a servant text. The "temptation" experiences which followed depicted an interior struggle concerning these options. Would Jesus be a messiah like David, gather an army and drive out the Romans? Or would he take the servant route, submitting his cause to God?

Jesus' ministry may have begun in Judaea and continued in Galilee. Not only is this made evident in John 1–3; it is also implied by Mark's report that "after John was arrested, Jesus came into Galilee . . . " (Mark 1:14). However that may be, the most extensive part of Jesus' ministry took place in his homeland, centering on the little town of Capernaum nestling in a cove alongside the Sea of Galilee. It was a natural site for his ministry, for all Galilee converged on Capernaum, from which Jesus drew his most ardent supporters.

The sequence of events cannot be accurately reconstructed. Combining proclamation of the advent of the Kingdom of God with a ministry of healing, Jesus impressed people in different ways. Some thought of him as a rabbi; others as John the Baptist restored to life; others as Elijah, popularly anticipated as the forerunner of the Messiah; others as Jeremiah or one of the prophets; and some, evidently very few, as the Messiah (cf. Matt. 16:14-16). Even his closest disciples, however, had difficulty comprehending the Servant/Messiah concept which the phrase "Son of Man" encompassed. Nationalistic concepts of Messiah precluded the idea of suffering and death of the coming ideal king.

With whom did the concept originate? Jesus or the "early church"? Some scholars have argued the latter. According to some, Jesus may actually have led a revolt which the Romans ruthlessly put down (the cleansing of the Temple). Thence he was tried and sentenced to death as a revolutionary. Subsequently some early Christian or Christians rewrote the story from the point of view of his crucifixion, superimposing the Servant motif.

One cannot speak dogmatically here, but this interpretation ascribes a level of sophistication to the early disciples which the sources would seem to deny. It assumes a massive rewriting such as neither a committee nor an individual could pull off within the brief time span in which it would have had to occur. The Apostle Paul, for instance, converted no more than two to five years after the death of Jesus, had no suspicions of this; he simply assumed the Servant motif derived from Jesus himself, and he passed on early baptismal traditions which incorporated this motif (cf. Rom. 6:8-11). The evidence certainly favors Jesus as the originator of the idea.

Jesus gained enough of a following to generate considerable concern among authorities. In a land bubbling with resistance to authority it is not hard to see why his purpose would be misunderstood.

Somewhere in the Galilean period Jesus selected a band of Twelve from the larger following. Although some scholars have ascribed this symbolic group to the early community rather than to Jesus himself, Paul's acquaintance with it as part of early tradition makes that unlikely (1 Cor. 15:5). It is more likely Jesus, facing the prospect of death before God consummated his purpose in history, wanted to leave this remnant to continue his ministry. Whereas the twelve

tribes and the twelve patriarchs provided the foundation of Israel under the old covenant, this Twelve would supply the foundation for Israel under the new. The Last Supper, one of many fellowship meals Jesus shared with his followers, confirms this interpretation. The "cup" of his death was to be the "new covenant" in which they would share (Mark 14:24).

Although Jesus had the reputation of a rabbi, his calling of disciples differed from that of other rabbis. In the latter case, the disciples sought the teacher; in Jesus' case, the teacher sought the disciple and issued an authoritative call not just to repentance and faith but to follow Jesus himself. His call left no room for equivocation. "Here! Behind me" he exclaimed. Following meant renunciation of family (Matt. 19:29; Mark 10:29-30; Luke 18:19b-30), participation in Jesus' suffering and even in his death (Mark 8:34).

According to Matthew's account, Jesus withdrew from Galilee after sending the Twelve on a mission like his own. This trip to Syria, beyond the bounds of Israel, appears to have been a kind of watershed in his career, for thereafter he set out directly for Jerusalem, the heart of Israel but also the stoner of the prophets. Neither Jesus nor the disciples had gotten a kind reception in Galilee (Matt. 13:56; Mark 6:4; Luke 4:24; cf. John 1:11). Rejected in his home town of Nazareth (Luke 4:28-30), he went to Capernaum. The Twelve extended his ministry. But neither Jesus' nor their efforts produced the repentance among the people which Jesus expected to usher in the kingdom (Matt. 10:23). The Galileans went on playing like children in the market place. Jesus had to pull back and dig deeper into himself to sort things out. The Servant image loomed larger and larger.

Jesus probably took the "pilgrim way" to Jerusalem, via Capernaum, Samaria, and Jericho. On the way he continued to proclaim the message of the kingdom and to try to explain his mission to the disciples, preparing them for his death. By this time the opposition of religious authorities was reaching a high pitch. The cleansing of the Temple came as the last straw in his criticisms of the twin pillars of Judaism—the Law and the Temple.

The Message of Jesus

What in Jesus' self-understanding led to this event? By what authority, religious leaders demanded, did he act? Was he a prophet? Or, as his actions indicated, was he more than a prophet?

In some respects Jesus did act like a prophet, and it is not difficult to understand why some identified him as one. The Temple cleansing fit the prophetic category. He acted too like a rabbi. Nevertheless, he went beyond both prophet and rabbi in claiming to act in God's stead. He taught "as one who had authority, and not as the scribes" (Mark 1:22; Matt. 7:29; cf. Luke 4:32). Though he employed the rabbinic formula, "You have heard that it was said . . . ," he diverged from them with the authoritative, "But I say. . . . " He not only interpreted; he also corrected Moses (Matt. 19:8). If this were not enough to bring an indictment for blasphemy, he had the audacity to offer forgiveness of sins, a prerogative which religious leaders reserved for God alone (Mark 2:7).

Behind both the rabbinic and the prophetic consciousness of Jesus must be seen a "filial" consciousness. He was "Son of God" in a unique sense, one which transcended or swerved from even Jewish expectations of a Messiah. Nothing is so revealing of Jesus' self-understanding as his address of God as *Abba*, an intimate Aramaic term. This was not merely *a* way Jesus addressed God; as Joachim Jeremias has demonstrated, it was *the* way, unique in itself. By contrast, God was seldom referred to as Father either in the Old Testament or in Judaism prior to the first century, and then usually in the corporate sense.

Jesus taught his followers to approach God as a loving parent. They did not need to badger God with their demands, piling up words and phrases, for "your father knows what you need before you ask him" (Matt. 6:8). If earthly parents supply their children's needs, how much more should one expect that of a heavenly parent (Matt. 7:9-11).

A major inference from this understanding of God precipitated a vigorous debate. Jesus' embracing of sinners and outcasts. Is it fair, his critics wanted to know, that God accepts those who have scorned his demands and gone their own way? Maybe not, Jesus responded, but it belongs to his paternal nature. If a poor woman lost a coin, wouldn't she put other coins down and find the lost one? If a shepherd found one sheep had strayed, wouldn't he leave the other ninety-nine to find that one? If a son took his inheritance and squandered it in a foreign country, wouldn't his father keep watching and welcome him home when he repented and returned (Luke 15)? God acts not on the basis of human merit but out of grace, like the owner of a vineyard who paid those who worked one hour the same wage he agreed to pay those who labored twelve. The latter had no complaint. They got what they agreed to work for (Matt. 20:1-16).

The heart of Jesus' message had to do with the kingdom of God. According to Mark, Jesus proclaimed, "The time has come and the kingdom of God is close at hand. Repent, and believe the good news" (Mark 1:14). In what way was the kingdom "close at hand"? Scholars have disputed this question at length. Albert Schweitzer, in his famous *Quest of the Historical Jesus*, contended that Jesus expected the kingdom to come within his own lifetime, and, disappointed that it did not, tried to force God's hand. Thus he, as it were, "hurled himself on the wheel of the world," which turned and crushed him, "the one immeasurably great man." C. H. Dodd, contrariwise, interpreted Mark 1:14 in terms of a present realization. In Jesus himself, in his life and work, the kingdom was already present. Accordingly, Jesus' response to critics of his healing ministry, which they attributed to Satan, was: "If I by the finger of God cast out demons, then the kingdom of God has come upon you" (Matt. 12:28; cf. Luke 11:20). Other scholars have spoken of an "inaugurated eschatology." The Kingdom in its full expression is still future, but it has been inaugurated in and through Jesus' ministry.

A look at Jesus' understanding of the kingdom may help to resolve the problem. The kingdom or rule of God had to do, first of all, with a relationship which God and not human beings would establish, a rebuke evidently to Jewish nationalists. Like seed or like leaven, the kingdom grows by itself in a mysterious way (Mark 4:26-30; Matt. 13:33; Luke 13:20-21), a point which makes the question of present or future virtually irrelevant. In his deeds and words Jesus announced the day of salvation. The kingdom was present in restoration of sight to the blind, in recovery of physical faculties by the lame, in cleansing of lepers, in the deaf hearing again, and in the poor receiving relief (Luke 7:22; Matt. 11:5).

The imminence of the kingdom in Jesus altered the situation of Jesus' disciples vis-à-vis Jewish observances. They did not have to fast, as the Pharisees or John's followers did, for wedding guests do not fast so long as the bridegroom is still with them (Mark 2:19).

Its imminence also sounded a warning about an imminent catastrophe, God's judgment, and called for repentance. The day of the Son of Man coming as judge would occur suddenly, unexpectedly, and without warning, like the flood in Noah's day (Matt. 24:37-41; Luke 17:28ff.). People ought to act with dispatch, like the debtor who sought to settle accounts before being taken to court (Matt. 5:25-26; Luke 12:57-59). They should also act wisely and not like the foolish maidens who did not bring extra oil for their lamps (Matt. 25:1-13).

What did the kingdom signify morally and ethically to Jesus? How did its demands differ from those of the scribes and Pharisees? How did a life based on grace differ from one based on adherence to the Jewish *halakah*?

In the Sermon on the Mount, which contains the essence of Jesus' teaching, those who enter the kingdom are instructed to exceed the scribes and Pharisees in their righteousness. Given the commendable ethic of the scribes and Pharisees, how could that be?

Jesus gave several examples. Whereas they said, "Don't kill," Jesus said, "Don't be angry or insult your brother. Instead, seek reconciliation" (Matt. 5:21-26). Whereas they said, "Don't commit adultery," Jesus said, "Remove the source of infidelity, the inner desire which leads astray" (5:27-30). Whereas they would protect the wife's interest by giving a legal document, Jesus forbade divorce altogether on the grounds that it forced the wife into adultery (5:31-32). Whereas the Old Testament condoned oathtaking, Jesus urged the disciples to make their word their bond (5:33-37). Whereas they encouraged exact retaliation, he promoted nonresistance, reconciliation, and giving without expectation of return (5:33-42).

How could anyone meet such high expectations? Some have insisted Jesus did not mean for them to be met. They have spiritualized, relegated them to the future ideal kingdom, or accommodated them to present exigencies in some way. Such explanations, however, seem to miss the point, that is, that grace alone suffices. Human beings have to be changed from within, become pure in heart, single of mind, downright good. Is this not the point of the parable of the Judgment of the Nations in Matthew 25:31-46? Those whom the "king" invited to enter his kingdom did good out of the goodness of their hearts without even knowing it. They had to ask, "Lord, when did we see you hungry and feed you; or thirsty and give you drink? etc." Good trees bear edible fruit, bad trees inedible (Matt. 5:18; cf. Luke 6:43). Persons made righteous by God would not invoke the Corban rule to escape an obligation to parents. They would not play-act at religion. They would not let sabbath observance or rules and regulations concerning food and fasting get in the way of "weightier matters."

That is how kingdom righteousness exceeds that of scribes and Pharisees.

One additional question should be asked about Jesus' teaching: Did he intend the church? Was his expectation of the consummation so intense, as Albert Schweitzer thought, that he left no room for the remnant of Israel? Hardly anyone would contend that Jesus envisioned the church as an institution, but several bits of evidence point to the direction of the remnant concept. First, some direct sayings—parables about fasting, passages in which Jesus called for allegiance to himself, and the term "Son of Man" with its corporate implications—point to Jesus' expectation that the disciples might carry on after his death. Second, challenges to faith, calling for allegiance not only to himself but to the Father, imply a continuation of the people of God. Third, his calling of the Twelve offers direct evidence of the continuance of his ministry. Fourth, the meals he shared with the disciples suggest a continuing fellowship. Fifth, his ethical teaching would have no meaning unless he envisioned a time in which it would apply. As a prophet, he doubtless foreshortened the time of the consummation, but he did not presume to determine the schedule and forewarned his followers against that.

Jesus' Death

The least debated and debatable aspect of the Jesus story is his death. No Christian, surely, would have invented the crucifixion story. Resurrection maybe, crucifixion no!

The sequence and details of the passion narrative, however, are open to question. Among the many disputed points, the most important is: Why was Jesus put to death? According to all early accounts, the Romans did so because they feared Jesus was a revolutionary. Confronted by Rome's demand that he keep the peace no matter how volatile and explosive the situation, a weak governor like Pontius Pilate could have been expected to take decisive action. His one question of Jesus was: "Are you the king of the Jews?"

(Mark 15:2; Matt. 27:11; Luke 23:3). The fact that Jesus had Zealots in his entourage and replied somewhat evasively (Mark 15:3; John 18:34) did not help his case. If he had been a Zealot and the Temple cleansing an abortive coup, Pilate would not have equivocated at all. But this theory, as we noted earlier, poses massive problems.

Behind the Roman action, according to the evangelists, lay a conspiracy among Jewish officials. Many contemporary scholars have questioned the "conspiracy" idea, particularly in light of the flames of anti-Semitism which it has sometimes fanned. How should the evidence be evaluated? Admittedly, the gospel writers may have sometimes overblown the case. John, for instance, virtually isolated Jesus from his heritage when he lumped Jesus' opponents together under one label, "the Jews." Such general opposition to Jesus can hardly have existed among the Jewish people, for he was popular with the masses. Thus we must handle the reports with care.

Strong opposition to Jesus originated chiefly with religious leaders: Herod Antipas, son of Herod the Great and Tetrarch of Galilea and Perea; the scribes and Pharisees; the Sadducees; and the Zealots. According to Mark, the Pharisees counseled with "Herodians" regarding Jesus' death (Mark 3:6; Matt. 12:4; cf. Mark 12:13). Herodian antipathy may have stemmed from Jesus' association with John the Baptist (Mark 6:14ff.). Jesus himself had warned his followers against "the leaven of the Pharisees and the leaven of Herod" (Mark 8:15). Herod, too, was zealous about the observance of the Law.

The scribes and Pharisees smarted over the cavalier attitude of Jesus and his disciples toward the Law. Though Jesus never disputed the seriousness of their intention, he did question the effect of their call for punctilious observance. They generated "sons of the Gehenna" (Matt. 23:15) rather than children of God. In contrast, he sought to discover in the Law God's intentions for humankind, sometimes correcting the Law itself. To the scribes and Pharisees this was insufferable, for it could do nothing but undermine the whole Jewish legal system, and, in claiming to speak for God, Jesus asserted authority in a blasphemous way.

More directly responsible for the "plot" against Jesus were the Sadducees. Anxious to guard the Temple and to preserve the civil peace under Roman occupation, the Sanhedrin indicted Jesus for blasphemy on two charges: his statement regarding the destruction of the temple and his claims to messiahship. Although some scholars hold that the charge of blasphemy was restricted in the first century to saying the divine name, YHWH, it may have been construed more broadly on many occasions, thus bringing these two charges under a broader umbrella. Whatever else it may have signified, Jesus' cleansing of the Temple represented a flagrant violation of the authority of the priestly aristocracy. The accusation laid against him was the boast: "I will destroy this temple that is made with hands" (Mark 14:58; Matt. 26:61; cf. John 2:19). Further, his citation of the Son of Man saying from Daniel 7:13 came dangerously near to a direct claim of divinity. He was not claiming messiahship merely of the Davidic type but of the heavenly Son of Man type. All religious leaders needed to confirm their suspicions of blasphemy was this quotation from Daniel.

The Zealots may have attached considerable hopes to Jesus at one time, but, as it dawned on them that he was not the Messiah like David, their crushed hopes turned to opposition. Disappointment of this kind possibly figured prominently in Judas's betrayal of Jesus. Although other motives may have entered the picture (money, for example; cf. Matt. 26:15; John 12:13), Judas may have acted from a nobler concern. He might have been the first of the disciples to grasp what Jesus was trying to say and decided he would no longer be a party to a suicidal mission.

Numerous problems arise concerning the Last Supper; date, type of meal, words spoken, and meaning. From the first century on, there were two traditions concerning date, Nisan 14 (John) or Nisan 15 (the other three Gospels), which led to a second century controversy over the celebration of Easter, to which we will return later. Although early tradition considered the Supper a Passover meal, several things conflict with what we know of Passover observances in the first century. Scholars have speculated that the meal may have been of another type: a *Haburah*, a fellowship meal celebrated on many occasions; a sabbath-*kiddush*, at which the head of a household said a prayer of sanctification over a cup of wine and drank it along with other members of a household; and a Qumran-type messianic banquet. Two major traditions (Mark/Matthew versus Luke/Paul) exist concerning the words of Jesus. Interpretation of the words has, of course, divided Christians for centuries. Views range from the more literalist interpretation of the words "This is my body. . . . This is my blood. . . . " by Roman Catholics or Orthodox to the more metaphorical interpretation of many Protestants.

Certainty is no longer possible on the *place* of crucifixion and burial of Jesus. Since 336 C.E., when Constantine's mother Helena had a church erected there, the traditional site of crucifixion and burial has been the Church of the Holy Sepulchre. Another is the "Garden Tomb" located near a cliff weathermarked or quarried to resemble a human skull. Scourging, a horrible form of beating meant to weaken the prisoner and hasten death, preceded the impalement at 9:00 a.m. In this cruel method of execution, reserved for runaway salves and criminals of the worst sort, the victim was either tied or nailed to a crossbeam attached to an upright post. The whole apparatus was then hoisted and dropped into a deep hole. Wine mixed with myrrh was often given to deaden the pain (Mark 15:23). Jesus died at 3:00 p.m., strangled perhaps, like most others, as the body sagged further and further.

The Resurrection

Though some would pronounce "The End" here, to stop with the death of Jesus will in no way explain the origins of Christianity. Neither a noble life nor, surely, an ignominious death can account for the movement which soon spread from Jerusalem throughout the ancient world. The only thing which can account for that is the conviction of some of his earlier followers that God had raised Jesus from the dead.

Now historians, *qua* historians, cannot "prove" Christian claims about resurrection for two reasons. One is that the resurrection is a singular event, one of a kind. Although there have been resuscitations, temporary restorations of life processes, there have been no other resurrections such as Christians ascribe to Jesus. The other is that resurrection, as attested in early Christian writings, is suprahistorical as well as historical. By its very nature it goes beyond the powers of the historian to examine by the empirical methods historians employ.

Does this leave the historian, then, with nothing to say about the resurrection of Jesus? Not at all. Historians can examine the *impact* of this belief (and Christians have always made this an article of belief) on the Christian movement and the ways in which Christians understood it.

Two kinds of evidence substantiate the conviction of the first disciples that Jesus had been raised from the dead. One is the empty tomb accounts. Since the earliest written reports about the resurrection, the Apostle Paul's (1 Cor. 15:3ff.), make no mention of an empty tomb, many scholars regard these as later and less reliable than evidence from experience. From the time of Cerinthus (about 90 C.E.) attempts have been made to explain this evidence away. Cerinthus, a Jewish Gnostic of Asia Minor, thought the "Christ" descended on "Jesus" at the baptism and forsook him at the Cross. The body laid in the tomb, therefore, was Jesus' and not the Christ's.

The other kind of evidence is appearances of the risen Christ to his followers. Although reports of these may have underwent editing in response to Gnostic threat, belief in these alone will explain the church and particularly the vigorous mission of early Christianity. For any other historical event, the witnesses listed by Paul in the tradition he had received would offer overwhelming confirmation: Peter; the Twelve; "more than five hundred brethren at one time, most of whom are still alive, though some have died;" James; "all the apostles;" and finally Peter himself. The fact that the resurrection was "suprahistorical," however, takes it beyond the historian's realm of competence and puts it into the realm of faith.

Chapter 4

Jerusalem and Beyond

The chief task in writing the history of early Christianity is to explain its remarkable success in thrusting beyond its Jewish homeland to the boundaries of the Roman Empire and beyond. Little in its origins would have assured success. It began in a "corner" of the Empire among a people not at all popular with those who ruled them. Its founder suffered an ignominious death as a revolutionary. Its first adherents belonged chiefly to the lower levels of Jewish society, possessing limited education for the task of propagandizing for their faith. Indeed, the death of their leader left them shattered and disillusioned. How, then, can one account not merely for the survival of this sect of Judaism but its phenomenal spread, outstripping not only numerous competitors but its own parent?

The complex answer is best brought forth by unfolding the story of Christianity step by step. A major factor was the bursting of the bonds which tied Christianity to Judaism. The key figure in that was the Apostle Paul, self-designated "Apostle to the Gentiles." But Paul did not singlehandedly precipitate this break. He simply gave further momentum to an impulse which this new/old religion had within which was already impelling it away from its parent and its homeland.

The earliest part of the story is most accurately related in connection with certain centers of this messianic movement, for Christianity assumed a variety of forms in different places. In Palestine alone, the subject of this chapter, for instance, Christian missionaries fanned out from Jerusalem to Samaria (Acts 8:4-25), the coastal strip stretching from Gaza to Caesarea (8:26-40), Damascus (9:25; Gal. 1:17), Galilee (Mark 16:7), and Antioch in Syria (Acts 11:18–13:3). Studies of Christianity in both Galilee and Samaria have further confirmed the thesis of Walter Bauer that, in its origins, Christianity exhibited great variety. Though it has been popular throughout Christian history to hang heterodox labels on Christianity in places like Samaria, therefore, today scholars proceed with greater caution.

In this chapter Jerusalem and Antioch will receive the most attention chiefly because we possess the most detailed information about them and because both played exceptional roles in the spread of early Christianity. Neither Damascus nor Caesarea should be glossed over entirely, however, for both served as centers of Christianity from which the gospel would radiate outward to the surrounding region.

Jerusalem

Jerusalem is where Christianity began. There Jesus died. There his disillusioned and disheartened disciples came to the conviction that God had raised him from the dead. There, according to Luke, they organized for the mission which would carry them to the "ends of the earth."

The Jerusalem community exhibited already the diversity which would characterize Christianity everywhere for at least two centuries. At Pentecost Jews and Jewish proselytes from Parthia, Medea, Elam, Mesopotamia, Judaea, Cappadocia, Pontus, Asia, Phrygia, Pamphylia, Egypt, Libya, Cyrene, Rome, Crete, and Arabia were present in Jerusalem. If, as Luke recorded, any substantial number of these adopted Christianity, they would have multiplied the diversity Palestinian Judaism already assured. Not surprisingly, tension arose quickly between "Hellenists," Greek-speaking Jews, and "Hebrews," Aramaic-speaking natives of Palestine (Acts 6:1). Since Judaism was highly diversified both inside and outside of Palestine, its offspring could have been expected to take on the same characteristic. Variety is visible in theology, worship and organization.

Although the beliefs of individual members of the community cannot be reconstructed with precision, it is possible to note points of difference. James, the brother of Jesus, was, according to early tradition, highly respected by the Pharisees. In Galatians 2:12 Paul indicates that James headed a conservative group zealous about continued observance of the Law (cf. Acts 15:13-21). Stephen, on the other hand, represented a position which challenged the place both of the Law and of the Temple. Hailed before the Sanhedrin, he was accused of "always making speeches against this Holy Place and the Law." His accusers charged, "We have heard him say that Jesus the Nazarene is going to destroy this Place and alter the traditions that Moses handed down to us" (Acts 6:13-14). His reply, as William Manson noted, corresponds in many ways with the argument of the so-called Epistle to the Hebrews.

> You stubborn people, with your pagan hearts and pagan ears. You are always resisting the Holy Spirit, just as your ancestors used to do. Can you name a single prophet your ancestors never persecuted? In the past they killed those who foretold the coming of the

Just One, and now you have become his betrayers, his murderers. You who had the Law brought to you by angels are the very ones who have not kept it.   (Acts 7:51-53)

This radical position vis-à-vis Temple and Law has been associated with the Hellenists, but it should be noted that Jews from Cyrene, Alexandria, Cilicia, and Asia were Stephen's accusers (Acts 6:9).

Some scholars have noted parallels between Stephen's thought, especially his criticisms of the Temple, and that of the Essenes. Peter evidently tried to straddle the fence on this highly controverted issue of Christianity's relationship to Jewish institutions. The Apostle Paul, at any rate, accused him of vacillating at Antioch. "His custom had been to eat with the pagans, but after certain friends of James arrived he stopped doing this and kept away from them altogether for fear of the group that insisted on circumcision" (Gal. 2:11-12). This led other Jewish Christians, including Barnabas, astray on the same point. Peter's speech in Acts 2:14-36, if indicative of this thought, exhibits a much more moderate tone than Stephen's. From this speech C. H. Dodd drew his outline of the "apostolic preaching," but it represents only one type of message. The age of fulfillment has dawned through the death and resurrection of Jesus Christ. This is signified by the outpouring of the Holy Spirit upon all persons. Jesus is going to return to consummate what he has initiated. Repent, and become a member of the community of the new covenant.

The Jerusalem disciples participated in at least two types of worship. As would be expected where the lines separating Christianity from Judaism had not yet formed, they continued to worship in the Temple and in the synagogues. According to Acts 2:46, "they went as a body to the Temple every day" (JB), obviously thinking themselves observant Jews. Until the persecution scattered them, the leaders evidently made the Temple area their base of operations, resisting warnings from the Sanhedrin to stop (Acts 4:20). There were no synagogues in Jerusalem where they would have gathered, but outside of the holy city Christians participated in them as they had before. The Apostle Paul chose the synagogue as his point of entry for spreading the gospel in cities throughout the ancient world.

The distinctive beliefs of Christians about Jesus also necessitated special gatherings. From the very first these beliefs generated a sense of community distinct from the larger Jewish community or any of the other sects or parties. When persecuted or threatened, the community became still more closeknit and well defined. According to the somewhat idealized picture presented in Acts, it was sufficiently close to allow sharing of goods (Acts 4:32). It also provided the context for a more distinctively Christian type of worship. "They persisted," Luke reported, "in the teaching of the apostles, in fellowship, and in the breaking of bread and prayers" (Acts 2:42). The heart of this worship was doubtless some kind of fellowship meal which believers participated in daily in various homes (Acts 2:46). From Luke's terminology it is not possible to determine the degree to which this approximated the Lord's supper described by Paul in I Corinthians 11:17-34, which consisted both of an actual and of a symbolic meal. There can be little doubt, however, that "the breaking of bread" reminded them of the crucified and risen Christ who had called their community into existence. Where Essene converts were present, it may have taken on features of the Qumran meal.

The organization of household meetings cannot be determined. Presumably the apostles, a much larger group than the Twelve, would have presided and taught. For the total community, however, the structure seems to have paralleled closely that at Qumran. James, by virtue of his relationship to Jesus, played a distinctive role like the Essene *Mebaqqer* (Superintendent or Overseer). Peter and others evidently deferred to him on important matters such as the admission of Gentiles, and James issued the so-called apostolic decree (acts 15:19-21) on this matter. Peter, James (the son of Zebedee), and John were what Paul called "the three pillars" (2:9), meaning perhaps they held a position of esteem by virtue of their association with Jesus. The Twelve had symbolic importance, for the community elected Matthias to replace Judas (Acts 1:15-26), but they seem not to have had a special function. The Twelve plus the three pillars sound remarkably like the Council of Twelve laymen plus or including three priests at Qumran. The larger group of apostles and elders apparently carried the burden of decision making just as the priests did at Qumran. They were the ones who, with concurrence of the whole church, chose delegates to go to Antioch with Paul and Barnabas (Acts 15:22), and it was they whose names headed the official letter about the decision reached at Jerusalem regarding admission of Gentiles (Acts 15:23). Finally, "the many" participated in administration of discipline (Acts 15:22) just as they did at Qumran. Although the Essenes are never mentioned in Acts, the number of correspondences is too great to ascribe to coincidence. The Essenes, ardent apocalytists that they were, would have made the likeliest prospects for the Christian message. They could have dominated the Jerusalem community's outlook at a number of points, including community of goods.

A number of factors encouraged adoption of this custom: anticipation of Christ's return, the poverty of many especially of the Essenes, the interknittedness of the persecuted believers, strongly reliant on faith alone, and a famine which struck during the early phase of Christian history. Although Luke had a special predilection for communitarianism, he did paint a realistic picture. Alongside Barnabases (Acts 4:36-37), there were Ananiases and Sapphiras (5:1-11) who did not fully embody the ideal—from each according to ability, to each according to need (Acts 2:44-45; 4:32). The enterprise also broke down with reference to the Greek-speaking converts living in Jerusalem, requiring a new distribution of responsibility.

The appointment of the "seven" has traditionally been regarded as the beginning of the diaconate in early Christianity. According to the account in Acts, these were to wait on tables" (Acts 6:4), which probably means take charge of the charities. It should be noted, however, that none of the seven, all of whom had Greek names, functioned solely in this way. The two mentioned subsequently in Acts, Stephen and Philip, had much to do with the inauguration of the mission to the Gentiles which the Apostle Paul continued with such elan. In Lucan thought the number seven probably symbolized the Gentile mission.

Dispersion and Expansion

Christianity might have sundered its bonds with Judaism more slowly had persecution not scattered the Jerusalem community far and wide (Acts 8:1). Leader of the onslaught was the Pharisee Saul of Tarsus (Acts 8:3; 9:1-2; 1 Cor. 15:9; Gal. 1:13; Phil. 3:6; 1 Tim. 1:13), zealous to conserve his ancestral faith now threatened by the growth of Christianity. There can be little doubt that the faith was taking hold rapidly in Jerusalem and beyond.

Indicative of the spread of Christianity in Palestine prior even to this persecution is its vitality in Damascus, capital of Syria. According to Luke, Paul sought authorization of the high priest to arrest and take to Jerusalem "any followers of the Way" he could find, whether men or women (Acts 9:2). The Damascus community subsequently furnished the converted persecutor a context within which to sort out his faith (Gal. 1:17; Acts 9:23-30). There perhaps he began to glimpse the missionary dream which absorbed the remaining years of his life. In future years Damascus was destined to play an important role in the planting of Christianity in the East, for it was the logical route for the faith to have spread to Edessa, a major center for eastern Christianity.

Why did the faith catch on in Damascus so early and so vigorously? Like other cities of Syria, Damascus boasted a strong Jewish population including Essenes. One Essene document which laid down prescriptions for Essene "camp communities" was entitled *The Damascus Document*. Messianic ideas could have gotten a foothold long before Christian missionaries came with their message.

Following the persecution, the scattered community transported the gospel to numerous cities throughout Palestine. Samaria was evangelized by one of the Hellenists, Phillip (Acts 8:4ff.). This was fortuitous, for, as Raymond E. Brown has pointed out, the Samaritans accepted neither Jewish messianic beliefs nor the Temple, so that the more critical Hellenist theology would accord more readily with their desire to worship God "in spirit and truth" (John 4:23). The "beloved disciple" who wrote the Gospel was acquainted with a community consisting at one time of a considerable number of converts of Samaritan background, whose conversion the evangelist ascribed to Jesus' meeting with the Samaritan woman (John 4:39). This community later broke up, with a substantial part of it becoming heterodox. Luke recounted how Simon Magus tried to obtain the disciples' secret for conferring the Holy Spirit (Acts 8:9-24), presumably to supplement his magical act. The early church fathers, however, regarded Simon as the first of the heretics. Another to come from this locale was the Gnostic teacher Basilides.

Among towns dotting the coastline to which missionaries carried the gospel the port city of Caesarea would eventually play a stellar role in the history of Christianity in Palestine. The old Phoenician city called Strato's Tower, the Romans, on capturing it from the Maccabees in 63 B.C.E., gave it to Herod the Great. Herod lavishly rebuilt it and renamed it in honor of Caesar Augustus (Octavian). It became the official seat of the procurators and the capital of Palestine. Though predominantly pagan, it had a strong

Jewish minority. Interestingly, a Roman, the centurion Cornelius, opened the door to Christianity. A "godfearer," that is, a devout monotheist not yet received into the Jewish community, and a generous contributor to Jewish causes (Acts 10:1-2), he may have been fairly typical of converts to Christianity in this city. The notable feature of the conversion story was the extreme reluctance of "middle-of-the-road" Peter to let Cornelius become a Christian until he first became a Jew. Yet Peter had to defend his actions in Jerusalem (Acts 11:1-18).

Caesarea subsequently figured prominently in the Apostle Paul's missionary journeys and career. He passed through this port going to and returning from Cilicia (Acts 9:30; 18:22). On his fateful journey to Jerusalem bearing the relief offering he hoped would gain Jewish Christian sanction for the Gentile mission, some of the disciples from Caesarea accompanied him and his party and took them to lodge in the house of a Cypriote named Mnason, "one of the earliest disciples" (Acts 21:16). A Caesarea cohort spirited him away from Jerusalem. During his two-year imprisonment and trial in Caesarea before Felix, Festus, and Herod Agrippa, he doubtless experienced the solicitude of the community many times. After the destruction of Jerusalem in 70 C.E. and again in 135, Caesarea became the seat of Palestinian bishops and a center of learning under Origen (who came in 232), Pamphilius (240–309), and Eusebius (260–340).

Antioch

Next to Jerusalem, Antioch played the most crucial role in the expansion of Christianity beyond the bounds of Judaism. Where in other places cultural diversity was stretching the cords which still held Christianity fast, in Antioch, Luke observed, "the disciples were first called 'Christians' " (Acts 11:26), a term indicating separate identity. If previously people could not tell the difference, now they could.

Located at the head of navigation on the Orontes River, Antioch was an important trading center connecting the Mediterranean world with the Syrian hinterlands and eastern countries. Founded in 300 B.C.E. by Seleucus, it attained a political and cultural importance in the east rivaled only by Alexandria. When Roman armies occupied it in 64 B.C.E., they made it the capital and military headquarters of the new province of Syria. A large and ancient Jewish colony attracted numerous Gentiles, perhaps including Nicolaus of Antioch chosen as one of the "seven" (Acts 6:5). More tolerant than Jews in Jerusalem as a consequence of their pluralistic surroundings, Antiochene Jews would have received Christianity with sympathetic interest.

According to Luke, Christianity came to Antioch by way of persons scattered by persecution (Acts 11:19). Although the latter usually confined their preaching to Jews, Hellenists from Cyprus and Cyrene started preaching to Gentiles, "and a great number believed and were converted to the Lord" (Acts 11:21). Hearing about this, the church in Jerusalem sent the Cypriote Barnabas to check on the report (Acts 11:21-23). Impressed with the success of the mission, Barnabas went to Tarsus and brought Paul back with him to Antioch, where the two spent a year instructing the converts (Acts 11:25-26).

When a famine struck Jerusalem in 46 C.E., the community at Antioch sent Paul and Barnabas with a relief offering (Acts 11:17-30). There they had to defend the incorporation of Gentiles without requiring circumcision and observance of the law. Some understanding was evidently reached, allowing Gentiles to become Christians without observing the law strictly (Acts 15:19-35; Gal. 2:1-10). Yet the issue remained in dispute. Peter visited Antioch and ate with Gentile Christians (Gal. 2:11-12), but, when James sent Judas Barsabbas and Silas as emissaries to win over the Jewish Christians to the view that Gentiles had to observe the law strictly (Acts 15:22-29; Gal.

2:12), Peter and Barnabas broke with Paul, pulling others away with them.

Antioch sponsored the missionary journeys of Barnabas and Paul, presumably supplying financial aid as they could (Acts 13:3-4). These two parted company, however, when Paul refused to let John Mark accompany them on a second tour; Paul took Silas instead (Acts 15:36-40). After his third journey, Paul returned not to Antioch but to Jerusalem (Acts 18:22–31:18), thus ending his connections with that community.

The letters of Ignatius, bishop of Antioch, composed between 108 and 117, reveal a continuing division in Antioch over the question of Christian affiliation with Judaism. Ignatius himself, as will be shown later, tried to steer between two extremes—those who endangered Christianity by surrendering faith in the incarnation, on the one hand, and those who wanted Christianity to return to observance of the Jewish law, on the other. Virginia Corwin has suggested that the latter were Essene converts to Christianity. To unite the fractured church, Ignatius emphasized adherence to the bishop, oneness of doctrine, and commonness of worship. Obviously, none of these prevailed in his day.

Antioch, however, did not stand alone in diversity and division. With strong Gentile influence it may have represented the extremes more than other churches. But Judaea, Samaria, and Galilee as well as Syria knew more variety than unity as Christianity tried to define its identity in relationship to its parent within the context of the multifaceted and variegated cultures of the ancient world. Some wanted to loosen all ties with the parent. Others wanted to surrender none of them. Others strove for a middle ground.

Chapter 5

The Pauline Mission

The Christian story cannot be told without special attention to Paul, "the Apostle to the Gentiles" (Rom. 11:13) or "the minister of Christ to the Gentiles" (Rom. 15:16). Though he did not originate the idea of incorporating Gentiles into the church without circumcision or fulfillment of other requirements of the Jewish law, he supplied a rationale for this, developed a strategy for the mission to the Gentiles, and gave momentum to the mission such as it had received from no other. Had there been no Paul, erudite rabbi who once persecuted but then became a zealous convert, the Christian story would have turned out far differently than it did. While he cannot be credited with the founding of Christianity, he deserves at least the title of "refounder."

Paul's own story is difficult to reconstruct. References to his life and activities are fragmentary in the letters which bear his name. Additional evidence found in the Book of Acts sometimes provides a different framework for his life than the letters suggest. Fortunately his thought, though never presented systematically, is more readily ascertainable from the eight letters now usually considered his without question (Romans, 1 and 2 Corinthians, Galatians, Philippians, 1 and 2 Thessalonians, and Philemon) with additional help from those which some scholars label post-Pauline (Colossians, Ephesians, 1 and 2 Timothy and Titus). Hebrews, once ascribed to Paul and in-

cluded in the canon on that basis, reflects a wholly different mindset and outlook and cannot be used to frame his thought.

For the historian of Christianity, however, Paul is of interest not only for his own life and thought but also for the kind of Christianity which emerged from his labors. Born and reared in a hellenistic setting, once converted he held a very different perspective on his new faith than did James and Peter and many other Palestinian converts and even many hellenistic converts. His outlook probably had its roots in the thought of Hellenists such as Stephen and those from Cyprus, Cyrene, and Antioch who did not let cultural differences pose major barriers to the admission of Gentiles. He, however, was better equipped than any of these to sort out and define this position, and the churches which he planted throughout Asia Minor and the Greek peninsula took on a character of their own.

The boldness of Paul in detaching Christianity from its parent, nevertheless, opened the door to massive problems on two sides. Externally Judaists dogged his steps, mounting a campaign to stop him which led eventually to his imprisonment, trial, and death. Internally communities he founded misconstrued his conviction that "Christ is the end of the law" (Rom. 10:4), some taking it as a license to do whatever they pleased, others reverting to the safer havens promised by Judaists. In the end, however, Paul's decision was to be "all things to all persons" that he might win as many as possible (1 Cor. 9:22).

Paul

Born of Jewish parents and reared in Tarsus in the Roman province of Cilicia (Acts 9:11; 21:39), Paul was educated at the feet of Gamaliel II, one of the leading rabbis in Jerusalem in the first century (Acts 22:3). Self-depicted as being "of the race of Israel and of the tribe of Benjamin, a Hebrew born of Hebrew parents," he belonged to the party of Pharisees (Phil. 3:5). Zealous for the Law, like most Pharisees, he carried his commitment to it to the extreme, and it is not difficult to see how this induced him to become a persecutor of the sect which threatened the institution he revered (Phil. 3:6; Acts 23:6; 26:5).

Somewhere in his savage effort to destroy the church (1 Cor. 15:9; Gal. 1:13; Phil. 3:6), whether, as Luke depicted it, on the road to Damascus (Acts 9:1-19; 22:6; 26:12) or elsewhere (Paul himself speaks only of Arabia in Gal. 1:17 as the place where he recuperated before returning to Damascus), Paul experienced a radical conversion. Conversion entailed a mystical encounter with the risen Christ which Paul counted the equivalent of experiences which other apostles had had, despite the fact that it occurred two or more years later, "as though I was born when no one expected it" (1 Cor. 15:8; JB). According to the third person account of 2 Corinthians 12:1-4, he was caught up "right into the third heaven" or "into paradise," where he heard things human beings cannot put in words; he could not say whether this happened "in the body or out of the body."

The confrontation with the Christ whom he had persecuted changed things completely. On the one side, it smashed his loyalty to the law. Whatever advantages he had possessed by right of birth as a Jew now became disadvantageous. All that was refuse (Phil. 3:7-8). On the other

side, it generated a different loyalty, zealous as the old one, but now directed to Jesus Christ.

> For him I have accepted the loss of everything, and I look on everything as so much rubbish if only I can have Christ and be given a place in him. . . . All I want is to know Christ and the power of his resurrection and to share his sufferings by reproducing the pattern of his death.
>
> (Phil. 3:8, 10, JB)

This new fealty carried with it a commission to be the Apostle to the Gentiles.

Paul's claims to apostleship provoked heated debate even in communities which he started. Others had credentials he lacked: they had been eyewitnesses and participants in Jesus' life. So Paul, suspect for a time because of his activities as a persecutor, had to base his case on his encounter with the risen Lord he now served. Though not deserving of the name of apostle because he had persecuted the church (1 Cor. 15:19), he insisted, he was, by God's grace, no less an apostle than the others (1 Cor. 9:1-3), especially so to those congregations he had founded. The Corinthians were "the seal" of his apostleship (1 Cor. 9:2). Yet Christ himself had given the certification he needed (Rom. 1:1; 1 Cor. 1:1; 2 Cor. 1:1; Gal. 1:1; also Col. 1:1; Eph. 1:1; 1 Tim. 1:1; Tit. 1:1), not merely as an apostle but as his "minister to the Gentiles" (Rom. 15:16). Unable or unwilling to defend himself on grounds of competency, Paul rested his case on God's grace in Christ. "He is the one who has given us the qualifications to be the administrators of this new covenant, which is not a covenant of written letters but of the Spirit" (2 Cor. 3:6; JB). Paul was only a clay pot into which God had placed the treasure of the gospel, "to make it clear that such an overwhelming power comes from God and not from us" (2 Cor. 4:7).

Subsequent to his conversion, Paul stayed for a brief time in Damascus (Acts 9:20-25) and then sequestered himself in Arabia, probably meaning the region near Damascus, for three years. He went to Jerusalem for the first time three years after his conversion (Gal. 1:18), where he spent fifteen days conferring with Peter and James, Jesus' brother (Gal. 1:19-20). From thence he proceeded via Caesarea to Tarsus (Acts 9:26-30). In his homeland he evidently carried on mission work until Barnabas came from Antioch to bring him there to work with new converts (Acts 11:25-26), a period of at least eleven and perhaps as much as fourteen years (Gal. 2:1), when Paul participated in the so-called Jerusalem Conference (Acts 15). Calculating backwards from the latter, which took place in 49 C.E., Paul would have been converted about 32 C.E., perhaps two years after the crucifixion, returned to Damascus after three years in Arabia in 35 C.E. and gone to Antioch in 48 C.E., working a year before going with Barnabas to Jerusalem with the relief offering (Acts 11:27-30).

Scholars have usually divided Paul's missionary journeys into three phases, although the divisions are quite artificial. On the first, Barnabas and Paul, commissioned by the church of Antioch (Acts 13:3) and accompanied by John Mark, evangelized first Barnabas's (Cyprus) and then Paul's (Pamphilia, Pisidia, Lycaonia, and Cilicia) home territories. On the mission to Cyprus Barnabas led (Acts 13:3), on that to Asia Minor Paul led (Acts 13:13). If accurately depicted by Luke, the strategy differed at this early stage from that which Paul was later to employ. Here the missionaries sought to win over Jewish synagogues, as they did later, but they seem not to have intended lengthy residency, as Paul did later, thus allowing them to nurse the churches along until they became well established. The entire journey lasted only a few months. Although Luke mentions the appointment of elders church by church, this would appear to view what happened in retrospect many years later (Acts 14:23).

By the *second* journey, on which Paul and Barnabas parted company, now taking Silas with

him while Barnabas took John Mark again (Acts 15:39-40), Paul had worked out his strategy more fully. He would plant churches in major centers in each of the Roman provinces from which the gospel could radiate outward like spokes on a wheel, staying long enough, unless prohibited, to see the seed sprout and become strong. On this particular journey he evidently hoped to reach Ephesus, largest of all the cities of Asia Minor and a center of culture. This plan, however, was deferred. From the provinces they had worked in during the first journey, they proceeded through Mysia to Troas and from there crossed over into Europe. They labored with considerable success in Philippi, a leading city of the province of Macedonia (Acts 16:11-40). After three weeks in Thessalonica, however, they came near being mobbed (Acts 17:1-9). Trouble followed them from there to Beroea, where they were having some success also (Acts 17:10-15). After a brief encounter with sophisticated Athens, where they made few converts (Acts 17:34), they put down roots for a long stay of a year and a half in one of the most important cities on the Greek peninsula, Corinth (Acts 18:11). Although Luke has telescoped this important ministry into a brief paragraph, we can gain much insight into the struggle of Pauline churches from Paul's correspondence with them.

Following his work at Corinth, which ended in controversy with Judaists as that in other cities had, Paul finally achieved his diverted goals of establishing a base of operations in Ephesus. Interrupting this with a brief visit to Caesarea, Antioch, and the cities of Asia Minor he had worked in earlier, he remained in Ephesus possibly three years and wrote 1 Corinthians there.

A curious aspect of the planting of Christianity in Ephesus was its anticipation by a sect knowing only the baptism of John the Baptist, one of whom was the Alexandrian Jew named Apollos (Acts 18:1–19:7). Prisca and Aquila, the refugees from Rome who had just come to Corinth (Acts 18:2), evidently converted Apollos

(Acts 18:26) when he came there from Ephesus, but Paul converted twelve others when he arrived in Ephesus (Acts 19:1-6). Very likely, this John the Baptist sect drew recruits from the Essenes whose "camp communities" dotted the Empire. The eloquent Apollos became the focus for at least a part of the Corinthians criticism and opposition to Paul (1 Cor. 1:12; 3:4-6; 4:6). Apart from this, Paul's work in Ephesus followed the now well-established pattern. For three months he presented his case in the synagogue until the congregation polarized over his teaching. Then he withdrew with converts to hold daily discussions in the lecture room of Tyrannus for two years. Both Jews and Gentiles thus had a chance to hear the message (Acts 19:8-10). Inevitably, however, a public disturbance broke out as Christianity began to have economic effects, notably on the manufacture and sale of idols. The confrontation between Christ and Artemis, goddess of the Ephesians, triggered Paul's plan to go to Jerusalem in hopes of gaining acceptance for the Gentile mission among conservative Christians there.

Meantime, Paul's relations with the Corinthian church had simmered. He wrote an early letter which some scholars think may survive at least in part in 2 Corinthians 6:14–7:1 urging them to shun persons living immorally (1 Cor. 5:9). The Corinthians responded by sending a delegation to report on the Corinthian situation and writing a letter in which they raised several questions. To these Paul replied in 1 Corinthians. Some at Corinth, however, remained recalcitrant. When they received 1 Corinthians borne by Timothy, they reacted in anger at Paul's interference and attacked his claims to speak as an apostle. A quick visit to Corinth only exacerbated the problem, and Paul returned to Ephesus to write a "harsh" letter (2 Cor. 2:1-4) which many scholars think is to be found in 2 Corinthians 10–13, sending it by Titus. Worried about the state of the situation as Titus delayed in returning to Ephesus he then set out for Corinth via Troas. Meeting Titus bearing

good news, he dashed off the much happier and more optimistic 2 Corinthians 1–10.

From this point on, Paul fixed his attention on the Gentile mission. He sought zealously to collect relief funds for the church in Jerusalem in the hope that it would gain their approval for the inclusion of the Gentiles (2 Cor. 8–9). He did not dare to entrust either the collection or its delivery into anyone else's hands. He had to deliver them himself (Rom. 15:25-27). From Philippi (Acts 20:6) Paul and his entourage headed for Jerusalem via Troas (Acts 20:7-12) and Miletus (Acts 13:13-16), where Paul addressed the Ephesian elders (17:38). Dire warnings of prophets along the way were no deterrent to the determined apostle (Acts 21:10-14).

Jerusalem dashed the Apostle's dream. Charged with bringing uncircumcised Gentiles into the restricted area of the Temple, he was barely able to escape with his life. A Roman cohort, fearful of a riot, rescued him from a mob about to stone him (Acts 21:30-31). When the tribune ordered him flogged to find out why he had caused such a tumult, he appealed to his Roman citizenship (Acts 22:25). After a contentious encounter with the Sanhedrin, threatened with assassination, Paul was removed to Caesarea, spending two years in prison before finally being sent to Rome for trial.

Paul had wanted to go to Rome and be sent by the Romans still further to the West, to Spain (Rom. 15:24). He would have arrived in Rome about 62 C.E. and spent considerable time there awaiting trial. Whether he ever went to Spain is debated, but early Christian tradition reported that he was released after one trial, went to Spain as well as visiting other areas he had worked in earlier, and then returned to Rome. There he went through a second trial which ended in condemnation and beheading, probably about 66 C.E. By this time the Neronian persecution was in full swing.

Corinth

Thanks to the difficulties Paul encountered there, Corinth opens a window on the embodiment of Christianity in a predominantly Gentile setting. It reveals once more the immense diversity of early Christianity and the struggle Christians went through when detaching themselves from either Greek or Jewish moorings to establish their identity as Christians.

An ancient Greek city, Corinth was destroyed by the Roman consul L. Mummius in 146 B.C.E. Refounded as a Roman colony by decree of Julius Caesar in 44 B.C.E., it became a thriving center of East/West trade. In 66 or 67 C.E. Nero attempted to cut a canal across the three and a half mile isthmus over which goods and ships were hauled, but the project was abandoned. By the second century C.E. Corinth surpassed all other Greek cities.

A large and diverse Jewish community existed there when the Apostle Paul arrived about 50 C.E. A partial inscription reading "Synagogue of the Hebrews" found on a lintel in recent excavation may represent the successor of the synagogue in which Paul preached (Acts 8:4). The community would have been comprised of Jews from Rome, Naples, Alexandria, or Antioch. Some proselytes and "godfearers" also belonged. Aquila and Prisca brought the Christian message when an edict of Claudius expelled them from Rome in 49 C.E. (Acts 18:27), where riots had resulted from debate over a certain "Chrestos," according to Suetonius. Paul arrived in 50 C.E.

The Corinthian Christian community soon came to consist predominantly of Gentiles, for, according to Paul, not many were well educated, influential, or of noble background (1 Cor. 1:26). They also knew "gods many and lords many" (1 Cor. 8:5), a comment hardly applicable to Jews. And some had been "people of immoral lives, idolaters, adulterers, catamites, sodomites, thieves, usurers, drunkards, slanderers and swindlers" (1 Cor. 6:9-11), indicative surely of lower socioeconomic status among Gentiles. Jewish converts would likely have belonged to the middle or upper middle classes.

Typically of early Christian communities the faithful may have congregated in several different homes, doubtless of the more wealthy, and here they may have split into parties: one for Paul, another for Peter (Cephas), another for Apollos, and even another for Christ (1 Cor. 1:12). The differences in views cannot be established, but, given the variegated background of this church, one would expect much confusion. Questions which the Corinthians themselves raised with Paul had to do with marriage and virginity (1 Cor. 7), eating food which had come from pagan temples (1 Cor. 8–10), conduct of public worship, including spiritual gifts (1 Cor. 11–14), and the resurrection (1 Cor. 15). The larger agenda, however, was: How should the Corinthians relate to their natural cultural backgrounds now that they were Christians?

Paul's stance had created a lot of difficulty on this issue. "Christ has set you free," he proclaimed. "He has brought an end to legalism. Believe and do what you will." For Paul this translated into Jews going on as Jews, Gentiles as Gentiles vis-à-vis their customs, save where these were blatantly immoral or kept others from knowing Christ (1 Cor. 9:19-23). Whatever one does, Paul insisted, it should redound to the praise of God (Col. 3:17). To some persons at Corinth, however, this message translated into. "Anything goes!" Or, worse still, into ridicule of those they regarded as "weak" because they could not live freely in the same way the "strong" could. With these the Apostle could agree that "there are no forbidden things," but he had to add, "If my exercise of freedom causes others to stumble, then I should limit my freedom" (1 Cor. 10:23-33). Otherwise God will not be glorified and the church will not be built up.

Some scholars have classified the Corinthian opponents of Paul as Gnostics, but this is too simple a solution to a complex problem. Although the Corinthian community doubtless had some persons in it who entertained views similar to those held by Gnostics in the second century and after, the evidence of the letters does not suggest well defined and consistent views. On the resurrection, for instance, some persons denied the resurrection altogether (1 Cor. 15:12ff.) while others expected resurrection of a crassly literal sort (15:35ff.). Some may have combined Jewish and Gentile ideas in hodge podge fashion as they tried to sort out their new faith.

In response to this challenge Paul struggled to define faith more precisely by citing tradition and patterned instruction. In his letters he left specimens of confessions of faith, catalogues of virtues and vices, household codes for new converts, and assorted instructional materials used to instruct the uninstructed. Contrary to what many have said in the past, Paul did not operate independently of tradition. Indeed, he commended the Corinthians for "maintaining the traditions just as I passed them on to you" (1 Cor. 11:2).

To believers in "gods and lords a plenty" he reminded that

> for us there is one God, the Father, from whom all things come and for whom we exist; and there is one Lord, Jesus Christ, through whom all things come and through whom we exist. (1 Cor. 8:6)

To persons sketical of resurrection, he reiterated what he had received:

> Namely that Christ died for our sins, in accordance with the scriptures; that he was buried; and that he was raised to life on the third day, in accordance with the scriptures; that he appeared first to Cephas and secondly to the Twelve. Next he appeared to more than five hundred of the brothers at the same time, most of whom are still alive, though some have died; then he appeared to James, and then to all the apostles; . . .
> (1 Cor. 15:3-7)

Innovative as the Apostle was, he anchored Christianity to the actual events out of which the Christian perception of God springs, that is, the life, death, and resurrection of Jesus of Nazareth.

Worship at Corinth differed substantially from that at Jerusalem. Although Christians began in the synagogue, they did not remain there long (Acts 18:16-17), and the Corinthian letters do not show much evidence of synagogue influence on worship. Two types of gatherings, rather, stand out. One was the "Lord's supper" described in 1 Corinthians 11, the other a more charismatic type worship. The former combined an actual meal concluded by the symbolic observance now called the Lord's supper. The purpose of the meal seems to have been charitable. The "haves" were to supply food for the "have nots." In this community, however, good intentions went awry, for the "haves" ate what they brought before the poor arrived (1 Cor. 11:22-23). This, Paul remonstrated, contradicted the very essence of the symbolic meal. Whoever eats and drinks without paying heed to the Body, the Church, stands self-condemned (v. 39).

The charismatic gathering included some elements similar to synagogue worship, but it evidently majored on prophetic preaching rather than interpretation of scriptures. Here is where speaking in tongues entered in and went out of control. Alongside these, however, the service also included chanting of psalms, singing of hymns, and some other items (1 Cor. 14:26ff.).

The Corinthian community seems to have had much difficulty settling on a suitable structure. Paul himself may not have commended a particular structure to them, emphasizing instead openness to the Spirit of Christ. Although some communities which he founded, for example, that at Philippi, eventually adopted the twofold pattern of bishops or presbyters and deacons, the Corinthians resisted that as late as the end of the first century when Clement of Rome pleaded with them to restore the presbyters and deacons they had kicked out. Instead of drawing models from Judaism, they may have looked to their predominately Gentile context represented by competing religions, funerary societies, or guilds of craftsmen. Their main concern, however, was control by the Spirit, and, in response, the Apostle had to underline boldly the importance of order within the Body. Not only did he not think of the church as a "purely spiritual entity," as the Roman jurist Rudolph Sohm held, but he enumerated at least three roles so as to single them out from what he counted "gifts" of lesser importance.

> In the Church [he wrote] God has given the first place to apostles, the second to prophets, the third to teachers; after them, miracles, and after them the gift of healing; helpers, good leaders, those who speak in tongues. (1 Cor. 12:28)

From the sequel to 1 Corinthians we can see that the Corinthians were not prepared to accord the Apostle Paul special status as he claimed here.

Other Churches Founded by Paul

Other churches founded by Paul seem not to have caused him the grief the Corinthian community did. That impression, of course, may be due to the scantiness of the information available on these churches, to the briefer time he spent in these by comparison, or to the disappearance of many of them. Obviously none was without problems. The churches of Galatia experienced terrible turmoil vis-à-vis the reception of Gentiles without circumcision, but, so far as Paul's letters tell, not over worship or organization. The Philippian community was also disturbed by Judaists (Phil. 3:2-16), whom Paul called "the circumcision" party, but, otherwise, they pleased the Apostle immensely by their good sense and personal support. A stronger Jewish constituency may have assisted in this, as their structure suggests. The church at Thessalonica engaged in much debate over Paul's eschatological teachings, some idly waiting for the Second Coming (2 Thess. 3:6-15), and they misunderstood Paul's instructions about the resurrection and other matters (2 Thess. 2). Unless Romans 16 is a letter to the Ephesians, as personal references suggest, we do not have much information from Paul on this community. By the second century this church assumed a place of great prominence in the development of Christianity in Asia Minor. If it was the site of the Johannine community as tradition has assumed, it led the way in the formation of Logos christology. If Paul wrote Colossians, we can see again the powerful struggle of communities he founded to determine the relationship of Christians to Jewish culture on the one hand and Gentile culture on the other, for some of the Colossians found themselves pulled toward a hodge podge of both. At the same time Paul's letter to Philemon opens up a more personal scenario concerning the runaway slave Onesimus, whom Paul sent back with instructions to obey his master as he did the Lord Jesus.

By the end of his career Paul had scattered quite a few seeds through Asia Minor and the Greek peninsula. Most of the communities he founded would have been small, struggling congregations barely able to survive. Most, however, possessed a powerful sense of responsibility for extending the message beyond themselves. The Apostle had also invested them with a strategy for mission. From these would come powerful competition for the other religions moving westward at the same time, now largely without the structures of Judaism.

Part 2

Into All the World,
70–180 C.E.

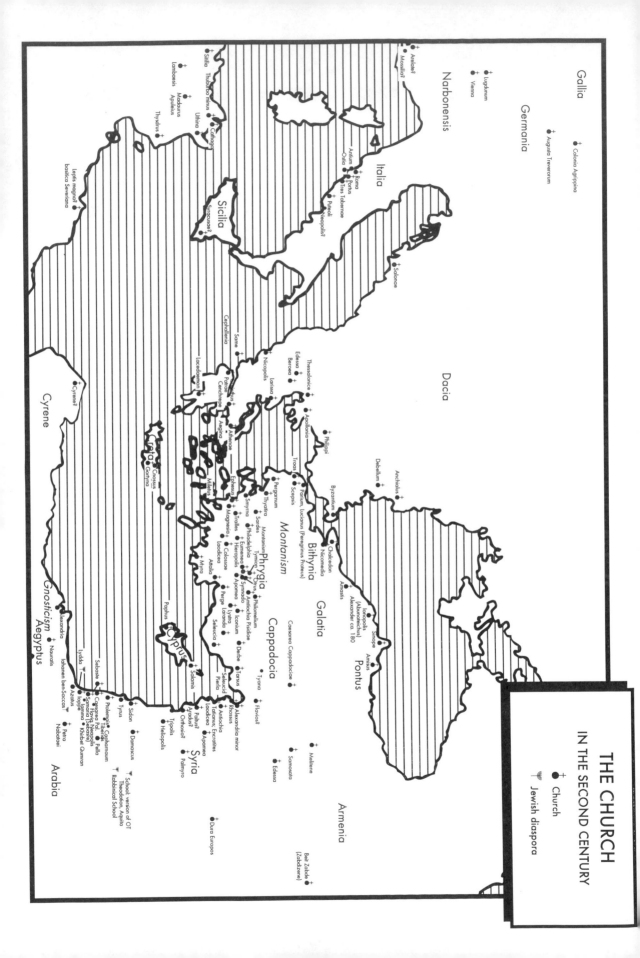

THE CHURCH
IN THE SECOND CENTURY

✝ Church
🕎 Jewish diaspora

Gallia

✝ Arelate?
✝ Massilia?

Germania

✝ Lugdunum
✝ Vienna

✝ Colonia Agrippina
✝ Augusta Treverorum

Narbonensis

✝ Sicilia
✝ Lambaesis
✝ Madaurus Apuleius
✝ Thysdrus
✝ Uthina
✝ Carthago
✝ Thabraba minus

✝ Leptis magna? basilica Severiana

✝ Antium
✝ Roma
Ostia — Portus
Tres Tabernae
✝ Puteoli
Nicopolis?

Italia

Sicilia
✝ Syracusae?

✝ Salonae

Dacia

Cyrene
✝ Cyrene?

Cephalenia
Same
Nicopolis
Lacedaemon
Patrae Cenchreae
Aegina
Athenae
Crete Cnossus
Gortyna
Miletus
Tralles
Magnesia
Ephesus

Thessalonice
Beroea
Edessa
Larissa
Apollonia
✝ Philippi
Byzantium

Troas
Scepsis
Parium, Lucianus (Peregrinus Proteus)
Pergamum
Thyatira
Sardes
Montanism
Smyrna
Tymion
Philadelphia
Eumeneia
Hierapolis
Colossae
Laodicea
Attalia
Myra

Phrygia
Montanism
Otrus, Philomelium
Synnoda
Apamea
Perge
Laranda
Iconium
Lystra
Derbe
Seleucia

Chalcedon
Nicomedia

Bithynia

Galatia

Caesarea Cappadocica

Cappadocia

Pontus
✝ Amastris
✝ Archelais
✝ Debeltum
Sinope
Amisus
✝ Ioopolis (Abanoteichus) Alexander ca. 180

✝ Tyana
✝ Flavias?
✝ Melitene
✝ Samosata
✝ Edessa

Tarsus
Seleucia Pieria
Rhossus
Alexandria minor
Antiochia, Encratites
Tarsus?
Laodicea
Apamea
Orthosia?
Arados?
Paltus?

Syria
✝ Tripolis
✝ Heliopolis
✝ Damascus
Palmyra

✝ Sidon
✝ Tyrus

Armenia
✝ Bei Zabde [Zabdizene]

✝ Dura Europos

Cyprus
Paphos
Salamis

Aegyptus
Gnosticism
Alexandria
Naucratis

Iahanen ben-Soccai
Lydda
Azotus
Ioppama • Khirbet Qumran
Samaria (Sebaste)
Caesarea Pal.
Tiberias
Pella
Ptolemais Capharnaum

Arabia
Petra
Nabataei

School: version of OT Theodotion, Aquila
🔺 Rabbinical School

Chapter 6

Broadcasting the Seed

Although the first Christians spoke of the world as their field, they were acquainted with only a fraction of the vast planet which subsequent generations would evangelize. In the main this world consisted of the Roman Empire and its immediate environs, but here and there it reached some distance beyond, particularly to the east to what is now Iran and possibly to India. Riding the crest of a wave with the oriental religions sweeping westward, Christians struggled during this period to retain their identity as a monotheistic missionary people as they incorporated the syncretistic peoples of the Roman Empire who sought infallible revelation and assurance of salvation. By 180 C.E. they had succeeded in scattering the seed of their religion all over the Mediterranean world and were beginning to attract an educated and cultured constituency which had once despised this "alien" cult, convincing them that Christianity was "the true philosophy."

The Geographical Spread

The ancients' lack of concern for statistics prohibits one from tallying precisely the number of Christians or the many places in which they planted churches. It is possible, however, to discern some areas in which Christianity showed enough strength to evoke the attention of the upper echelons of Roman society and sometimes popular resentment and persecution. The fact that persecution remained local, spasmodic, and

unofficial until the third century shows that Christianity impacted more heavily on some areas than on others but had a limited effect on the Empire as a whole. Occasionally more specific reports of Christian activity come from reports such as the letter of Pliny, the governor of Bithynia, to the Emperor Trajan (112).

Christianity made little impact on Jesus' homeland and people after the first wave of conversions. During the Jewish revolt, 66–70 C.E., Palestinian Christians probably identified largely with the Jewish people and grieved with them in 70 C.E. over the destruction of the Temple. A succession of conservative leaders assured they would not depart far from their native faith. After the Bar Kochba Rebellion, 132–135 C.E., however, the Romans turned Jerusalem into a pagan city, Aelia Capitolina, expelling the Jewish population. Jewish Christians fled to Pella in Transjordan, where they continued under the name of Ebionites ("the Poor"?). Caesarea, the Roman capital of Palestine, replaced Jerusalem as the center of Palestinian Christianity, whose constituency consisted largely of Gentiles by this time. When Origen migrated to Caesarea in 232, the Palestinian star began to rise again. Apart from these cities there is little specific information on the state of Christianity in the holy land.

Churches existed in Tyre, Sidon, and other cities of Phoenicia during this period, but Antioch in Syria replaced Jerusalem as the chief Christian center along the Palestinian littoral. Composed predominantly of Gentile converts almost from the start, it continued the vigorous mission effort begun in apostolic times. Ignatius, the second bishop, who gained fame by virtue of his martyrdom in Rome, called himself "the bishop of Antioch and Syria," implying some sense of responsibility for the evangelization of the entire province. Antioch probably played a part in the planting of churches in Edessa, itself a center of eastern Christianity, and Mesopotamia as well as throughout Syria. Antioch's prestige in the East is manifest in the synods over which the bishops of Antioch presided from the mid-third century on. Besides Ignatius, the church boasted one other noted author among its early bishops; Theophilus composed an apology addressed to an official named Autolycus shortly after 180 as well as several other works now lost.

As both direct evidence and persecutions indicate, Asia Minor provided the most fertile field for Christian witness. Like some of the great cities of the Empire, this region was dotted with Jewish communities which had accommodated themselves already to hellenistic thought and life. Cults such as Zeus Sabazios, an amalgam of Jewish and pagan ideas, show the extremes to which this process was at work. It is not surprising that the person who bridged the gulf between Jewish and Gentile worlds, the apostle Paul, came from Tarsus in Cilicia, one of the provinces of Asia Minor.

Christianity evidently grew slowly and steadily in Paul's home state and in others which he evangelized during his travels through Asia Minor, notably Galatia and Asia. During the second century, Ephesus in the Roman province of Asia vied with Antioch and Rome as one of the most prominent Christian centers in the Empire. The Revelation and the letters of Ignatius of Antioch, however, highlight other churches in Asia at Smyrna, Pergamum, Sardes, Philadelphia, Thyatira, Troas, Magnesia on the Maeander, and Tralles. The letter of Polycrates, bishop of Ephesus, to Victor, bishop of Rome, during the controversy over the date of observing Easter (about 190), points up the self-consciousness of the churches of Asia in the late second century. Speaking for the bishops of Asia, Polycrates reminded Victor that

> in Asia also great lights have fallen asleep. . . . Among these are Philip, one of the twelve apostles, who fell asleep in Hierapolis; and his two aged virgin daughters, and another daughter, who lived in the Holy Spirit and now rests at Ephesus; and, moreover, John, who was both a witness and a teacher, . . . fell asleep at Ephesus. And Polycarp in Smyrna, who was a bishop and martyr; and Thraseas, bishop and martyr from Eumenia, who fell asleep in Smyrna. Why need I mention the bishop and martyr Sagaris who fell asleep in Laodicea, or the blessed Papias, or Melito, the Eunuch who lived altogether in the Holy Spirit, who lives in Sardis, awaiting the episcopate from heaven, when he shall rise from the dead.
>
> (Eusebius, H.E. 5.24)

First Peter and Pliny's letter to Trajan in 112 furnish testimony of the wide diffusion of Christianity in Bithynia and Pontus during the late first and early second centuries. The governor spoke of "a great variety of cases" brought before him and "an anonymous pamphlet . . . containing many names." Using torture he "found nothing but a depraved and extravagant superstition," but he consulted the emperor "on account of the number of those imperiled; for many persons of all ages and classes and of both sexes are being put in peril by accusation." He feared the "contagion" had "spread not only in the cities, but in the villages and rural districts as well" but was confident it could be checked. The temples had been "almost deserted" but were again being frequented and sale of sacrificial victims increasing.

Lucian confirmed the vitality of Christianity in Pontus around 170 when he wrote that "the whole country is full of atheists and Christians" (*Alex. Abon.* 25.38). Dionysius of Corinth addressed letters to churches there also during the reigns of Marcus Aurelius and Commodus. Amastris was the chief city.

Phrygia had a thriving Christian populace when the Montanist sect emerged about 156 or 172. Montanus gained a considerable following in Galatia and Ancyra as well as Phyrgia. Cappadocia probably did not become a strongly Christian area until the third century when Gregory of NeoCaesarea, "the Miracle Worker," evangelized it, but 1 Peter 1:1 implies that there were already Christians there in the first century. Tertullian reported persecution in Cappadocia between 180 and 196 perpetrated by Claudius Lucius Herminianus, who became enraged when his wife converted to Christianity (*Ad Scap.* 3).

Christianity established an early hold on the islands in the Mediterranean. There is not much evidence in this period concerning the growth of the churches planted by Barnabas and Paul, but the Gnostic leader Valentinus is reputed to have spent his last years on Cyprus. Churches founded during the Pauline era by Titus thrived in the second century. Dionysius of Corinth wrote a letter about 170 "to the church of Gortyna and to the other churches of Crete" and a second to the church at Gnossus, whose bishop, Pinytus, replied (Eusebius, H.E. 4.23). The smaller islands around Crete were probably evangelized, too, in this period, but we have limited evidence for them.

In the Balkans and the Greek peninsula there were vigorous churches in cities evangelized by Paul. Polycarp's letter to the Philippians, which served as a cover letter for the letters of Ignatius about 115 (perhaps a later section about 135), demonstrates the continuation of the church started in Philippi by Paul. For Thessalonica and Athens the Emperor Antoninus Pius left evidence of a noticeable Christian constituency when he forbade a pagan uprising against them (Melito in Eusebius, H.E. 4.26). Dionysius of Corinth accused them "almost of apostasy from the faith

since the death of their martyred bishop Publius" but mentioned a revival under Quadratus (Eusebius, H.E. 4.23). Athens was the home of the apologist Aristides and perhaps of Clement of Alexandria. The church at Corinth which troubled Paul so much was the most thriving of the churches in the Greek peninsula. Clement of Rome intervened in the expulsion of presbyters by the congregation in 96 C.E. Dionysius played a notable role in the affairs of churches in the region during the second half of the second century. Dionysius' letter to Lacedaemon urging peace and unity would attest that the Corinthians had done mission work throughout the Peloponnese.

Christian communities dotted other cities and provinces in Europe. Antoninus Pius forbade an uprising against Christians in Larissa in Thessaly (Melito in Eusebius H.E. 4.20). There was a bishop at Debeltum and Anchialus in Thrace near the end of the second century (Eusebius, H.E. 5.19).

In the West Christianity took hold significantly in Italy, Gaul, and Spain. In Rome it spread first among the Greek-speaking population, Victor (189–199), an African, being the first Roman bishop to write letters in Latin. Antedating Paul's advent there, the Roman church acquired a reputation for faith (Rom. 1:8) and charity early on. Clement's letter to the Corinthians evinces a consciousness that the Roman church held a unique place among all the churches. Ignatius's letter to the Romans reveals that others shared the feeling as he extolled it as "the leading church in the region of the Romans" and "the leader of love." That the Roman church had extensive means at its disposal in the second century is evidenced in the letter of Dionysius of Corinth to Soter praising the Romans for sending contributions to "many churches in every city" to relieve the wants of the needy and to make provision for Christian prisoners (Eusebius, H.E. 4.23). The church, as the Shepherd of Hermas substantiates, had not only large numbers but some quite wealthy ones who could give liberally to "charity's chest." On joining a Roman congregation about 140 C.E. Marcion, a wealthy shipbuilder of Pontus who made shipwreck of his own faith, made a huge contribution of 200,000 sesterces. Apologists such as Justin (martyred in 165) founded evangelistic-apologetic schools for the purpose of enlisting the cultured and better educated who knocked on church doors from about the mid-second century on. Meantime virtually all sects and heresies—Marcionites, Valentinians, Montanists—gravitated toward Rome, creating an immense problem for Christian unity and resulting in a heavy handed effort by Victor to enforce uniformity of faith and practice.

Some evidence can be cited for Christian communities in the south of Italy, little in the north. In Gaul, however, the emergence of churches at Lyons and Vienne resulted in a violent outburst of persecution in 177. Although the number of victims was not large (no more than 49), the severity of the pogrom would indicate that pagans viewed Christianity as a major threat. Victims included the aged Pothinus, whose successor Irenaeus escaped by virtue of being sent to Rome beforehand. He returned to lead the church at Lyons in a vigorous mission effort not only in Gaul but also in Germania. About 185 Irenaeus claimed that the beliefs and traditions of the German churches did not differ from those in Gaul or elsewhere (*Adv. haer.* 1.10), but he did not name specific locations.

Critical scholarship raises serious doubt about Christianity in the British Isles before about 300, but churches emerged early in Spain. In addition to the early tradition that the Apostle Paul visited Spain, both Irenaeus and Tertullian (*Adv. Jud.* 7) reported churches there. A letter of Cyprian (about 250) listed Christian communities at Leon, Astorga, Merida, and Saragossa.

The Roman province of Africa competed with Asia Minor for rapidity of church growth during the late second and third centuries, aided again by Jewish antecedents. The extensive writings of Tertullian, converted to Christianity in 195, presupposes a large church at Carthage and a scattering of churches throughout the province. Contemporary evidence of Christianity in the neighboring province of Numidia may be found in the martyrdom of several persons from Madaura and Scilium. Africans began translating the Bible into Latin during the second century and, in Tertullian, produced the first great Latin theologian.

Historians draw almost a complete blank when searching for information about Christianity in Egypt before 180, when the Alexandrian church first appeared in daylight under Demetrius. The church which emerged, however, was a powerful one. Attached to it was the famous school founded by Pantaenus, the "Sicilian bee," which attracted Clement and later the brilliant Origen. Egypt drew Gnostic scholars, too, like Basilides and Valentinus. A Gnostic library was discovered at Chenoboskion or Nag Hammadi in 1947; many of its writings date from the second century.

The Method of the Mission

In this period as in the one before it, Christianity spread chiefly through the sustained effort of organized Christian communities, vying with Judaism and the mystery cults to win adherents. The typical convert probably heard about Christianity by chance—a word dropped by a friend or neighbor, witnessing a martyrdom, overhearing a conversation—for, in time of persecution, direct and open efforts to solicit members would have evoked popular or governmental reaction and endangered the lives of many persons.

Numerous features exerted an attraction to Christianity. Charity offered without expectation of return or consideration of merit; fellowship opened to all social levels—masters and slaves, men and women, young and old, rich and poor; Christian steadfastness in the face of persecution; high moral standards; Christian assurance of victory over demons; the Christian rejection of fate and belief in providence; sacraments conveying tangible assurances of salvation; and numerous other things.

Christians astounded the ancients with their charity. Although Romans were noted for their largesse, they gave expecting return in kind, at least in honor and friendship. Stoic sages regularly cautioned them to single out the deserving. Social aid, therefore, as A. R. Hands has shown, seldom reached the most needy, those belonging to the very dregs of society. And it was precisely these whom Christians sought to help, regularly exhorting their constituency to openhanded and openhearted giving. The *Didache* and the *Epistle of Barnabas*, for instance, urged complete community of "corruptible things" on analogy to the complete community of "incorruptible" (*Did.* 1; Barn. 19.8). The pagan Lucian knew that Christians "despise all things equally and count them common property." (*Pereg.* 13). Although most Christians did not divest themselves of all possessions, the rich heard plenty of pleas to liberal giving. In an elaborate appeal for stewardship Hermas counseled the rich to "circumcise" their riches.

> For just as the round stone cannot be square unless some of it is cut and pared away, so also those now rich cannot be useful to the Lord unless their wealth be cut. (*Vis.* 3.6.6)

Riches, he said elsewhere, distract one from devotion. Yet in assisting a poor person, the rich person may become rich by attracting the poor one's intercession. The two thus become partners in righteousness.

The chief means of charity was alms collected in connection with the main worship service on "the Lord's day." As in Judaism, Christians ascribed immense religious potency to almsgiving. For many, charity supplied the ultimate test of true worship and faith. Matthew could speak of doing "righteousness," the ideal of religious service in Jewish thought, and almsgiving almost synonymously (Matt. 6:1-2). A virtual slogan of early writings is "equipped for every good deed"

(1 Tim. 2:10; 5:10; 2 Tim. 2:21; 3:17; Tit. 2:14; 3:1; Heb. 10:24; 13:21; 1 Cl. 2:7; 33:1, 7).

Besides money, the faithful also brought "oblations" or offerings consisting of all kinds of foodstuffs—oil, grain, eggs, meat, cheese, olives, bread and wine. According to Justin, when the needs of the liturgy were met, the remaining portions were distributed to the poor, prisoners, and other needy. Most of the alms and other gifts doubtless went to the Christian poor, for the resources were too limited to expect more. Nevertheless, the advice of the *Didache* to "let your alms sweat in your hands" is exceptional, obviously sensitive to abuses (*Did.* 1:5). Actually, he contradicted his own reserve in quoting the words of Jesus, "Give to everyone who asks" (Luke 6:30; Matt. 5:42). It was more characteristic to give without attaching strings. Hermas, for example, insisted,

> Give to all who are in want unreservedly, not distinguishing between those to whom you give or those to whom you do not give. Give to all, for God wishes that all be given some of their own free gifts. (*Mand.* 2.4.6; cf. James 1:5; Barn. 19:11; 2 Cl. 16:4)

The range of charity was broad: care of widows and orphans; care of the sick, poor and disabled; ransom and care of prisoners and captives; burial of the poor and other dead; redemption of slaves; furnishing work for the unemployed; and aid to victims of calamities. By the end of the first century, if not from the first, the churches had a formal roll of widows (1 Tim. 5:9). For the most part widows were recipients of charity—food, shelter, clothing, but they also rendered extensive diaconal service. Along with widows, orphans imposed an awesome charitable challenge on the churches. The custom of child exposure still prevailed in the Empire. There are no statistics, but hundreds, even thousands of foundlings must have been rescued from the waste heaps and reared by Christian families, widows, or in special homes.

Christianity competed with other cults such as that of Asclepios, god of healing, for care of the sick and disabled. Besides miraculous cures still attested frequently during the second century, the churches provided sustained care for the sick and incurable. Although it has been argued that Asclepios gave free medical assistance, there is little evidence to show the existence of such a program before the second century C.E. Christianity stepped in to supply the need among the lower classes, once again assuring itself of their commitment. It was here that Christian charities had their most telling impact.

Prisoners and captives, mostly Christian, posed another challenge for Christian charity. Prisoners became the object of special concern early in Christian history, and notable examples of sacrificial care abound. Ignatius left generous evidence of the solicitude of Christians in Asia Minor as he made the arduous journey to Rome (cf. *Smyrn.* 10.2). Justin named visitation of prisoners among the regular duties of deacons (1 *Apol.* 66). The apocryphal second century *Acts of Paul and Thecla* (3.19-20) hinted at the risks some took in their care of prisoners when it reported the care of various communities for Paul and Thecla. Lucian's story about Christian care of the charlatan Peregrinus illustrates how far some went in their zeal. Dionysius of Corinth commended the Romans for their special provisions "for the brethren in the mines" (in Eusebius, H.E. 4.23.10).

The otherworldly outlook of early Christianity produced an understandably pronounced concern for the dead which capitalized on similar sentiments held by Romans generally. But it was among the poor that Christianity made its initial impact. For where the deceased among the wealthy received adequate and even excessive care, the poor had to fend for themselves by forming burial *collegia*. The legal provisions for collegia supplied an umbrella under which otherwise prohibited congregations could function without close scrutiny. Christianity's empire-wide network of "burial clubs" exercised a potent attraction to the masses. In the manner of burial *collegia*, the churches purchased cemetery plots to be given at minimal charge to the poor. Gradually they made provision for the burial of all members.

That early Christianity undertook no campaign to eliminate slavery goes without saying. Nevertheless, within the Christian fellowship itself class distinctions ceased to have meaning. Slaves, like other members of Christ's body, were accorded the name "brothers" (Tatian, *Or.* 11) and possessed full rights to be appointed to the clergy. Thus, according to ancient tradition, Onesimus became a bishop of Ephesus (Papias in Eusebius H.E. 3.36.5); Pius, possibly the brother of Hermas, the tenth bishop of Rome (139–154 C.E.); and Callistus (217–222) a bishop of Rome. Within the churches slaves were esteemed as free persons. A number of slaves obtained the crown of martyrdom, for example, Blandina, one of the martyrs of the Lyons-Vienne massacre. Eventually Christianity sowed the seeds for the decay of the institution of slavery. The inherent implications of Christian faith as a religion of redemption gave substantial encouragement to the freeing of slaves. Clement of Rome boasted that "many" Christians had voluntarily "placed themselves in bondage so that they might ransom others" (1 Cl. 55.2). Hermas listed redemption of "the slaves of God" from their distress among key Christian duties (*Mand.* 8.10). Ignatius' injunction that slaves not ask to be set free from the common fund, "lest they be found slaves of lusts," would appear to be a response to excessive urgency of some slaves to benefit from the practice (*Pol.* 4.3).

Early Christianity also strengthened its appeal by providing employment help for the working classes to whom it appealed most in the first two centuries. Christians held work in high esteem. The author of the *Didache*, for instance, wanted travelling teachers to settle in a Christian community only if they possessed skill (12.3).

Barnabas prescribed working in the conversion and care of others or manual labor "for the redemption of your sins" (19.10). More important still from the charitable side, the early churches provided work for traveling apostles and the unemployed. The demands made of converts probably created many of the instances in which provisions had to be made, for some occupations were not countenanced in the churches. The latter, therefore, served as informal employment agencies.

Finally, early Christianity distinguished itself by its ministry to persons or groups struck down by disasters of one kind or another. The author of Hebrews commended his readers for their participation in aiding sufferers of unnamed afflictions (Heb. 10:32-33). The Roman church gained an exalted reputation for the extent of its assistance to victims everywhere.

Like charity, the fellowship which communities of believers shared openly with all comers would have proved powerfully attractive to the masses. The oriental cults offered some of the same appeal in their intimate gatherings for communal meals, but, where they used only local organizations, Christianity developed an empire-wide network of churches open to travelers. Besides liturgical services stressing community, the churches also continued *agape* meals chiefly for charitable purposes. At first connected with the Lord's Supper or eucharist, these gradually became separated. The *Letter of Pliny to Trajan*, usually dated around 112, reported a eucharist before dawn and "the taking of food" at a later assembly. In the East, however, Alexandria may have continued the joint services until the time of Clement (*Paed.* 2.10.96).

Christian steadfastness in the face of persecution evoked both criticism and admiration from pagans. The latter sometimes censured Christians for "obstinacy," but, more often than not they expressed begrudging praise that common folk died "like philosophers." Epictetus (died ca. 135), for instance, paid a backhanded compliment when he

argued that, if the "Galileans" could face death with such courage when "conditioned by madness and custom," surely the intelligent person could "learn by reason and demonstration" God is the universal Creator and arranger of all things (*Diatr.* 4.7.6). The Emperor Marcus Aurelius (161–180) lauded the person ready for death "not out of sheer obstinacy like the Christians, but rationally and reverently and without theatrics, so as to persuade others" (*Medit.* 11.3). Lucian of Samosata (died after 180) was amazed both at the gullibility of Christians and at the courage, arising, he thought, out of their belief in immortality, which would allow them to despise death or even to put themselves voluntarily into the hands of the authorities (*Peregr.* 13). Justin, a martyr himself, attributed to his viewing of a martyrdom a complete change of heart regarding Christianity.

> For I myself, too [he said] when I was delighting in the doctrines of Plato, and heard the Christians slandered, and saw them fearless of death, and of all other things which are counted fearful, perceived that it was impossible that they could be living in wickedness and pleasure. (2 *Apol.* 12)

In the last analysis, Christianity had to back up its claims in its product, above all, in the lives of its members. Pagans scrutinized Christian moral behavior closely. In his letter to Trajan, Pliny reported a morally favorable impression based on direct investigation. Though he faulted Christians' "inflexible obstinacy," he found nothing socially harmful in their meetings. Likewise, the physician Galen (129–199), like many other intellectuals of his day, criticized Christianity for philosophical naivete, but expressed appreciation for Christian courage in the face of death and self-restraint in regard to their passion. Demonstrated high moral standards doubtless had a major effect in the conversions of both Justin and Clement of Alexandria, for the writings of both clearly indicates the centrality of Christian ethical behavior.

Those who sought Christian conventicles for the same reason they turned to the mystery cults demanded tangible psychological assurances also. Living in abject fear of the demonic and of fate, they responded gladly to promises that believers could participate in the victory of Christ over demons and in his rule over the universe. Where cults such as Mithra or Cybele attached their assurances of eternal rebirth and life to expensive rites such as the taurobolium, however, Christianity used baptism and eucharist to do so. Through the action of the Holy Spirit or the risen and living Christ, Christians promised, the believer could experience the power of resurrection in sacramental rites.

> It is to the font, to salvation, to enlightenment that He invites us [cried Clement of Alexandria], almost crying out and saying: Earth and sea I give thee, my child; heaven too, and all things living in earth and heaven are freely thine. Only, my child, do thou thirst for the Father; without cost shall God be revealed to thee.
>
> (*Protr.* 10)

Or:

> Come, O madman, not leaning on the thyrsus, not crowned with ivy, be exhorted [he pleaded, alluding to the eucharist]. Throw away the mitre, throw away the fawnskin. Come to your senses! I will show you the Word and the mysteries of the Word, explaining them in your own manner.
>
> (*Protr.* 12.119.1)

The actual incorporation of converts occurred through a process which centered around a catechumenate and baptism. At the beginning the process was relatively simple, but by the end of this period Christians tightened it up out of concern for lapses from faith and betrayals. *The Apostolic Tradition* of Hippolytus composed in

217 outlined a four or possibly five stage process employed in the Roman church during the late second and early third centuries.

Although organized communities deserve the most credit for the spread of Christianity, contributions of individual Christians should not be forgotten. Soldiers, sailors, merchants, artisans, and travelers of all kinds scattered the word all over the ancient world. Wherever Christians traveled, they could expect hospitality from others. They preferred to have charlatans take advantage of them, as often happened, than deny "angels unawares" (Heb. 13:2) or Christ himself in the guise of a stranger. In time the churches did feel compelled to search for safeguards. Second John 10-11 forbade entertaining and even greeting anyone who did not bear orthodox teaching. The *Didache* limited hospitality for traveling "prophets" to two days and a single day's bread supply and forbade giving money or allowing the prophet to eat during an ecstatic trance (11.5ff.). Christians preferred, however, to err on charity's side. Third John, for instance, commended Gaius for his hospitality to "the brothers and strangers at that" and condemned the usurper Diotrephes not only for a lack of hospitality but for prohibiting those who wished to give it to do so. And Lucian chided them for caring for the charlatan Alexander of Abonoteichos, for whom they risked life and limb by going to feed and tend him in prison.

As Christianity spiraled upward socially during this period, traveling philosopher-evangelists and schools also played an important role in winning adherents. Although some schools originated in the catechumenate, many others were at least begun by individual initiative. Christian "philosophers" such as Valentinus, Justin, or Pantaenus attracted a following much as Stoic or Platonist philosophers did. Little is known of the activities of Pantaenus in founding the Alexandrian school, but he blazed a trail for Clement and Origen. In Rome Justin assisted the transition of Christianity from Jewish to Gentile cultures and from competition with the religions alone to competition with both religions and philosophies.

Born in Flavia Neapolis (modern Nablus), Justin studied in succession with a Stoic, an Aristotelian (Peripatetic), a Neo-Pythagorean, and finally with a Platonist. The Stoic taught him little about God. The Aristotelian only wanted money. The Neo-Pythagorean rejected him on account of his "ignorance." The Platonist pleased him, but served chiefly as a guide toward Christianity. Witnessing martyrdoms and encounter with an aged Christian who directed him to the "prophets" resulted in his conversion. After a period in Ephesus, where he may have come in contact with the saintly Polycarp, bishop of Smyrna, Justin made his way to Rome, where he founded an apologetic school. Here he attracted persons of education and culture who had formerly spurned Christianity. His pupils included Tatian, founder of the Encratite sect, and Irenaeus, bishop of Lyons and antiheretical writer of some distinction.

The schools may have made few converts, but they rendered an incalculable service in helping Christianity to reach a constituency whose needs it might otherwise have neglected. Even the heretical schools aided the cause, for they pushed Christianity toward the outer limits of accommodation and forced the churches to define their faith with greater precision. Though their intense evangelistic fervor pushed them too far, they tried to make an essentially "alien" Jewish idiom intelligible to persons of Platonist mindset. In pursuit of this goal they fashioned the first commentaries on scriptures and applied radical methods to solve problems of interpretation and application to different contexts. They also posed many of the great theological questions which later generations would have to answer.

A New Day Dawning

At the beginning of this period Christian communities were shifting from a predominantly Jewish to a Gentile constituency. Though Irenaeus could still say in his day (about 185–189) that Jews were easier to reach than Gentiles because they knew the Old Testament promises, most churches would have consisted of persons of non-Jewish culture and outlook. Among Gentiles Christianity at first attracted predominantly persons of lower socioeconomic status, but that had changed noticeably by the last quarter of the second century. Early on, even, Christian communities claimed some persons of wealth and culture among its constituency. By 175 the number of such persons multiplied as the churches ascended the social ladder and presented their appeals in more sophisticated ways. A new day was dawning.

Chapter 7

Like Master, So Disciples

Christianity's success within the Roman Empire proved threatening enough in some regions to evoke violent responses not only from officials but also from the Roman public. In some respects this is strange, for the Romans were tolerant in religious matters. In their Pantheon they made room for the gods of all nations they conquered and would gladly have done so for the God of Jews and Christians had either of them permitted that. The Romans could comprehend even Jewish tenacity in adhering to their ancestral divinity and did not feel threatened by the few who trickled into the Jewish synagogues. What boggled their minds in the case of Christianity was the fact that great numbers of *Romans* abandoned their ancestral gods to worship the God of Jews and Christians, separating themselves not only from the worship but also from the public life of Rome. Such a religion, demanding allegiance to a law and throne other than the Roman, had to have sinister and subversive implications.

Christ and Caesar

In this period Christians were by no means uniform in their attitudes toward Roman society. At one end of the spectrum stood those who clung tightly to Christianity's Jewish roots and repudiated all things Greek and Roman. Tatian, for example, founder of an ascetic sect called the Encratites after the martyrdom of his teacher Jus-tin around 165, attributed any fragment of truth found among Gentiles to borrowing from the Jews. He derided the philosophers, including Plato and Aristotle, for errors and vices and particularly for their varied opinions, which are nothing "but the crude fancies of the moment." Still worse, Greek mythology and the doctrine of Fate have been perpetrated by demons. Philosophy is "the art of getting money," its teaching "a labyrinth."

On the opposite end of the spectrum were some who usually wear the label of "Gnostics" who undertook to detach Christianity completely from its Jewish moorings and radically to "hellenize" it. Marcion, somewhere on the periphery of these, for instance, pointed up a row of "antitheses" between Christianity and Judaism, especially between the God of the Old Testament, which he interpreted literally to emphasize its crudity, and God the Father of Jesus Christ. Evidently smarting over his excommunication for "defiling a virgin" in his father's church in Pontus, he rejected totally the idea of judgment. The supreme God for whom Jesus Christ spoke is a God of love and forgiveness. As an explanation for Old Testament evidences about God which conflicted with those found in the letters of Paul (exclusive of 1 and 2 Timothy and Titus) and in the Gospel according to Luke, both of course edited to suit his theology, Marcion seized on the Gnostic theory of two gods—the supreme God who is purely spiritual and not contaminated by contact with matter and the Demiurge who created the universe. Like the supreme God, Christ too could not have anything to do with matter and thus only "appeared" to be human. Unlike Gnostics in the true sense of the word, Marcion founded a church which functioned very much like other churches in his day. His delineation of a New Testament canon in opposition to the Old probably accelerated the decision of other churches to list writings which would complement the Old Testament canon and which formed the core of the present western New Testament.

"Gnostics" in the proper sense of the term varied quite widely in their views, but most inclined toward some kind of syncretism, mixing a hodge podge of ingredients from religions and philosophies of the day. The Carpocratians, according to Irenaeus, practiced magic, used incantations and spells, consulted spirits of the departed, and sought in other ways to control the nether world. They painted pictures of Jesus and philosophers such as Pythagoras, Plato, and Aristotle; put crowns on them; and venerated their images. Introduced to Rome during the era of Anicetus (155–166) by a woman named Marcellina, they encouraged promiscuous sexual indulgence as a way to avoid reincarnation. Epiphanes, son of Carpocrates, combined an attack on private property with his father's argument for uncontrolled liberty in sexual matters.

Not all Gnostics inclined toward libertinism, however. Valentinus, who labored first in Alexandria and later in Rome, advocated pure behavior and asceticism as the way to free oneself from the grip of matter. According to Valentinus, Jesus practiced continence to the extent that he did not evacuate his food (Clement of Alexandria, *Strom.* 3.59.3). In the *Gospel of Truth*, his chief writing, Valentinus depicted Jesus as a Platonist teacher whom people hated because they were ignorant. Jesus disclosed the "Gospel of truth," that is, the elaborate Gnostic scheme of salvation by escape from matter and reunion with the One. Many

turned to the light, but the "materialistic" could not comprehend it and thus rejected him.

Valentinus's successor in Alexandria, Ptolemaeus, elaborated the cosmological scheme of Valentinus and applied allergorical method not only to the Old but even to the New Testament writings to sustain it. He, for instance, sustained his "mystery" of thirty aeons by adding up the hours at which the laborers in Jesus' parable entered the vineyard (1+3+6+9+11 = 30). To solve the problem of the Old Testament, he divided scriptures into three classes corresponding to three classes of human beings: (1) the material, "which necessarily perishes since it cannot possibly receive the breath of imperishability"; (2) the psychic, "which lies between the spiritual and the material and extends to either one as it has the inclination"; and (3) the spiritual, "which was sent forth to be shaped in union with the psychic and to be instructed with it in its conduct" (Irenaeus, *Adv. Haer.* 1.6.1-2). In his famous *Letter to Flora* Ptolemaeus ascribed some parts of the "Law" to God himself, some to Moses, and some to the elders. He subdivided the first part into three further parts—"the pure legislation not mixed with evil," that "which is interwoven with inferiority and injustice," and that "which is exemplary and symbolic."

Somewhere between these extremes, others saw good in both Jewish and Graeco-Roman antecedents, insisting on adherence to central tenets of Judaism such as monotheism, high moral standards, historical teleology, but recognizing the importance of accommodating Christian faith to the Roman context. The *Epistle to Diognetus*, an anonymous apology of uncertain date but probably second century, for instance, offered a critique of both pagan and Jewish worship. Then, the author proceeded to spell out the true distinction Christians could claim. They differed, he said, "neither in country nor language nor customs" but in respect to the citizenship they held. For "while living in Greek and barbarian [Jewish] cities. . . . and following local customs, both in clothing and food and in the rest of life, they show forth the wonderful and confessedly strange character of the constitution of their own citizenship. . . . They pass their time upon earth, but they have their citizenship in heaven" (5.3-10). After commenting on the behavior and modesty which characterized Christians, he added, "to put it briefly what the soul is in the body, that the Christians are in the world" (6.1).

Justin, guarding against both extremes, took a mediating position which both preserved Christianity's Jewish connections and freed Gentiles to appropriate the best of their own culture. Reminded by Trypho, a Jewish apologist, that Christians were not "separated in any particular" from Gentiles and did not distinguish themselves from Gentiles in mode of living by such observances as the sabbath or the rite of circumcision, Justin replied that, though Christians worshipped the same God as the Jews, they trusted him through Christ rather than through Moses and the law. Scriptures pointed to him as the one through whom God would effect a new covenant for "the true spiritual Israel" (*Dial.* 10-11). Responding to pagan attacks, on the other side, Justin accentuated the correspondences between Christian teaching and behavior and the best in Gentile as well as Jewish teaching. He explained the affinities in two different and conflicting ways—by pagans borrowing from Moses and by inspiration of the divine Logos. The Logos instructed both the prophets of Israel and the Greek greats such as Heraclitus, Socrates, Plato, and others. Both of these, therefore, prepared for the advent of Christ, and all who "lived reasonably" in previous centuries—Socrates, Heraclitus, and persons like them—are "Christians" (1 *Apol.* 46). In Jesus the Logos became incarnate and taught explicitly the complete truth which previous generations had grasped in a partial and fragmented way.

At the level of everyday life Christians had to struggle hard to maintain their identity over against the absorptive culture of Rome. Conservative Christians sought security in a clan approach.

They refused to attend parties in the homes of neighbors, thus earning scorn for being too aloof; send their children to public school where they would be exposed to pagan myths; witness athletic contests in the arenas; serve in the army; hold public offices, most of which had some connection with pagan religion; or do other things which might result in compromises of faith. The first evidence for Christians serving in the army, for example, comes from the end of this era in connection with the famous "thundering legion," reputed to have consisted chiefly of Christians. Most opposed military service for two reasons: dominance of the military by the state religion and biblical injunctions against killing. Soldiers in the ranks could often avoid the obligation to offer sacrifices, though officers could not. None, however, could avoid killing. If soldiers decided to join a church, therefore, they would likely be asked to surrender their commissions in the army.

Persecution and Martyrdom

Roman absorptionism and Christian exclusivism made a clash between Christ and Caesar inevitable. Pagans, relying usually on hearsay often about heretical sects for their understanding, found a variety of Christian ideas and customs offensive. Christianity sundered families and discouraged marriage. Some Christians espoused voluntary poverty and community of goods and sowed seeds for the decay of slavery. They held "secret" meetings at nighttime and spoke of "eating the body" and "drinking the blood" of Christ or exchanging "the kiss of peace," customs which invited pagan charges of cannibalism and incest. The very best of Christian intention turned against them in the dark imagination of pagan minds. Some supposed that Christians took unwanted infants deposited along with human excrement to die, chopped them into pieces, and ate their bodies and drank their blood. Or in their nocturnal assemblies gorged themselves with food, turned dogs loose to scramble across the tables and turn over the lamps, and then engaged in sexual orgies (Tertullian, *Apol.* 7). Christian martyrdom was construed as a perverse "obstinacy"; their refusal to hold public office, serve in the army, or attend public games acts of disloyalty; their breaking away from customs of Jews or Romans impiety; and their abandonment of altars, images, and temples "a sure token of an obscure and secret society" (so Celsus).

Roman officials were intensely circumspect of new religions on two counts—immorality such as occurred in the Baccanalian rites of the second century B.C.E. and danger to the state. For the period at hand persecution arose much less from officials than from mobs, but some charges were set forth for trial and punishment of Christians. Scholars have offered three theories about the specific nature of the charges. (1) Christians were punished under no specific charge but only by virtue of the power of coercion. (2) They were accused and tried for violation of Roman criminal law, particularly for the crime of treason and also for sacrilege, immorality, magic, incest, murder, and the like. (3) They were dealt with under a special law issued by Nero which proscribed Christianity as such, that is, made it illegal to be a Christian. Whether the third was in effect as early as Nero, however, is unlikely. The first definite evidence for punishment simply for "the name" appeared in the time of Trajan (98–117). It is more likely Christians were punished for the general charges of "hatred of the human race, cannibalism, and incest" until, in the second century, Christianity itself became illegal.

There is only the scantiest evidence of Jewish harassment and persecution for the period under discussion, although synagogue and church continued their debate. "Dialogues" such as Justin's with "Trypho" may have occurred publicly on occasion, but pagan use of Jewish arguments against Christianity necessitated written replies. As the Christian mission to the Gentiles waxed strong, however, the Jewish mission relented and drew back, thus undercutting the debate. When Christianity chose the route of accommodation to Gentile culture, as Marcel Simon pointed out, it left Judaism with the option either of accommodating still more radically or else withdrawing and emphasizing Jewishness. When Jewish leaders opted for the latter, they virtually took the synagogue out of the competition altogether.

For a study of persecution in this era, therefore, it suffices to focus on persecution which arose from popular resentment and misunderstanding or from official action. After some respite from the brief pogrom during the late years of Nero's reign (64–68 C.E.), intermittent persecution broke out in 91 C.E. under Domitian (d. 96 C.E.). Fiercest in Asia Minor, where Christianity was growing rapidly, it claimed the lives, among others, of Flavius Clemens, cousin of the emperor, his wife Domitilla, and Achilius Glabrio, an ex-consul.

Under Trajan (98–117 C.E.) hostility to Christianity threatened to run out of control. At the request of Pliny, the governor of Bithynia, where the number of believers had reached significant proportions, the emperor laid down the following guidelines: (1) Christians were not to be sought out, and anonymous accusations were to be ignored. (2) Those regularly accused and who admitted they were Christians were to be punished. (3) But those who denied they had ever been Christians or declared that they had ceased to be such and proved it by offering a sacrifice were to be pardoned. This rescript remained in force until Septimius Severus (195–211). The most celebrated martyr in this persecution was Ignatius, bishop of Antioch, who pleaded in a letter that Roman Christians do nothing to prevent him from imitating "the example of the death of my God." He longed to be "crushed like wheat between the teeth of wild beasts" that he might "attain to Jesus Christ."

During Hadrian's reign (117–138) Christians enjoyed comparative peace. In a directive to Minucius Fundanus, governor of the province of

Asia, Hadrian repeated the first two provisions of Trajan's rescript.

Antonius Pius (138–161) reiterated the same provisions in rescripts to cities of Macedonia, Thessaly, and Achaia. The most celebrated martyr of the persecution was Polycarp, eighty-six year old bishop of Smyrna. The twelfth martyr in Smyrna, his "birthdate into the eternal realm" on February 23, 155 was celebrated annually and became the subject of the first martyrology. The careful gathering up of his bones as as "to have fellowship with his holy flesh" (*Mar. Pol.*) initiated the cult of relics which became so important in subsequent centuries.

Marcus Aurelius (161–180), a Stoic philosopher of considerable distinction, intensified the persecution by reissuing the third provision of Trajan's rescript. Numerous martyrdoms occurred in the province of Africa and in Gaul as well as in Rome and Asia Minor. Popular suspicion of the now thriving sect fanned the flames of official action. In Rome, Crescens, a philosopher whom Justin had bested in an argument, vented his anger on his opponent by having him brought to trial and put to death. In Scilli, a city in Africa whose location is unknown, numerous persons, both men and women, suffered martyrdom on July 17, 180. Their boldness in the face of death was extolled in *The Acts of the Scillitan Martyrs*. In Lyons and Vienne in Gaul Christians were first excluded from homes, public baths, and markets and then attacked with vehemence—being beaten, dragged through the streets, robbed, stoned, imprisoned, tortured in the most inhumane ways, and then killed. The martyrs included several persons of upper class status, especially women, willing to expose themselves in defense of Christian friends.

Persecution had both positive and negative effects on early Christianity. On the positive side, it helped separate wheat from chaff and offered an opportunity for some to demonstrate what Christian faith meant. Even Stoic philosophers, the Emperor Marcus Aurelius included, could

express begrudging admiration that simple and uneducated persons "died like philosophers." On the negative side, persecution obviously diminished the ranks and discouraged public witness and conversions. Reverence for the martyrs and their remains led also to certain distortions of faith, wherein some viewed martyrdom as the true certification of commitment and relics of martyrs as objects of veneration. In the third and fourth centuries, moreover, debate over persons who abandoned their pledges under torture or threat of torture produced two major schisms, and letters of indulgence which martyrs supplied the lapsed who sought readmission to the churches opened the way for a system of indulgences.

The steadfastness of large numbers of Christians in persecution is in itself an interesting phenomenon which has received several explanations. Some scholars have pointed to analogous accounts of Greek and Roman heroes, but the analogies break down when motives are closely examined. Donald W. Riddle emphasized instead the conditioning process which converts went through in the catechumenate that prepared them for such opposition. Although this would offer a partial explanation, it too overlooks the deeper theological perspective out of which the martyrs themselves acted. As W. H. C. Frend has established, the martyrs belonged to the lineage of Jewish martyrs and inherited from Judaism the idea of martyrdom as personal witness to the truth of their faith over against heathendom, the hope of personal resurrection and vengeance on apostates and persecutors in the hereafter, and the view that the true oppressors were not earthly powers but cosmic and demonic ones. It was not by chance that pictures of Daniel among the lions and three "children" in the fiery furnace turned up frequently in the catacombs, for the stories of the Maccabean era fed the Christian faithful just as it had fed the Jewish. The impact of the Jewish tradition is confirmed by the fact that Gnostics such as Basilides, a Platonizer, openly attacked the idea that martyrdom had spiritual value. Salvation, according to Basilides, meant the abolition of death and not acceptance of it through martyrdom.

The Christian Apologia

Christian defense against attacks, whether Jewish or Gentile, did not reach the sophisticated level it would achieve in the subsequent phase of Christian history, but it gradually improved as Christianity attracted an increasing number of cultured constituents. The earliest apology, the so-called *Preaching of Peter*, appearing between 100 and 110 C.E. probably in Egypt, is known only from quotations in Clement and Origen. An Athenian named Quadratus addressed a formal appeal to the emperor Hadrian on his visit to Athens in 125 or 129, but this work too exists only in citations by Eusebius. The *Apology of Aristides* addressed to Antoninus Pius (138–147), recovered in an almost complete text in Syriac in 1889, argued the superiority of Christian to Chaldean, Greek, Egyptian and Jewish worship. About 140 Aristo of Pella established a model for apologies addressed to Jews or replies to Jewish arguments with *The Christian Dialogue*, but his composition is known only from quotations in Origen's treatise *Against Celsus* (246). Justin defended Christianity on two fronts with his *Dialogue with Trypho* and two apologies (ca. 150). His pupil Tatian wrote his bitter invective against Greek arts and letters, *Address to the Greeks*, about 152–155. Only small fragments survive of Melito of Sardis's *Apology* written about 169 to 176. Athenagoras, evidently writing from Rome to Marcus Aurelius and Commodus, joint emperors between 177 and 180, tried an upbeat approach with some success. Repelling stock charges of atheism, cannibalism, and incest, he argued that Christian worship and doctrine were more reasonable and moral than those of the accusers, appealing to Greek philosophers and poets in support. Finally, about 180, Theophilus of Antioch addressed an influential treatise *To Autolycus* in favor of Christian doctrine and against pagan.

Many scholars dispute whether the "dialogues" represent actual encounter of synagogue and church after the first century, but a growing number seem to think that they do. Even if designed, as some think, to reply to Jewish arguments raised by pagans such as Celsus in his *True Discourse*, they played an important role in Christian apologetics as a whole. According to Justin's *Dialogue with Trypho*, the Jewish people objected to the Christian use of the Greek Old Testament known as the Septuagint (LXX); the claim that Jesus was the messiah; the claim that Jesus was God; Christian contempt for the Law, that is, the ritual Law (fasting, sabbath observance, feast days); the concept of a crucified messiah; and the resurrection, both the idea and the conviction that Jesus had been raised.

In response to objections to the Septuagint both Jews and Christians produced more literal versions. About 140 Aquila, a native of Sinope in Pontus who converted to Judaism, reproduced individual Hebrew words and phrases exactly. Later in the second century Symmachus and Theodotion responded with freer and more readable translations, but Origen judged Symmachus's version more faithful to the Hebrew than the LXX. In answer to the further charge of quoting only passages supportive of the Christian argument, Justin contended that other passages were given on account of the nature of Israel. He met the other five objections by citing scriptures, sometimes literally and sometimes as types. Although his handling of scriptures would not have convinced many Jews, modern scholarship has shown that he was familiar with rabbinic methods of interpretation. As a clinching argument, he cited the facts of history to prove that not the Jews but Christians were the chosen people: the dispersal of the Jews, the destruction of the Temple, the cessation of sacrifices, the disappearance of the princes of the house of Judah, and the reception of the good news by the Gentiles.

Pagan charges varied from time to time and place to place, but some of the main themes appeared consistently. As noted earlier, polemicists accused Christians of cannibalism and incest, treason, social aloofness, atheism, theological absurdity, and responsibility for the calamities befalling Rome and the decline of the state.

Christians responded to moral charges with outright denials. Then they turned them by pointing out that their own philosophers and poets had condemned pagans for the unspeakable things of which they accused Christians.

The charge of treason was trickier. Christians had to admit they did not and could not worship the emperor and fulfill perfunctory obligations in the state cultus. Yet, they went on to say, this did not mean disloyalty or bad citizenship. They prayed for the emperor. They paid taxes and discharged other duties. Justin cited the emperors themselves writing about Christian innocence, clinching with a spurious account of the "thundering legion" supposedly by Marcus Aurelius who had saved him and the rest of the Roman army at Carnuntum by prayer.

The apologists accepted the charge of social aloofness and turned it to their advantage. Christians differed in commendable ways from both Jews and Gentiles, they said, and thus deserved to be called "a third race," as pagans chidingly suggested.

Some apologists rejected the charge of atheism arbitrarily, but those better equipped in philosophy cited the arguments of Socrates, Plato, and others in favor of monotheism and against polytheism and idolatry (so Aristides and Theolphilus). They made much of the immorality of Homeric gods and heroes.

Charges that Christian teachings were absurd could not be easily refuted because of vastly different ways in which Jews and Gentiles sometimes approached reality. Occasionally an apologist responded by citing parallels to beliefs such as resurrection (Theophilus), but at other times they emphasized the uniqueness of Christianity (Tatian) and its antiquity (Justin). To these arguments they added "proofs" from miracles, prophecy, the correspondence of the gospel to the moral nature of humankind, Christian life, and the spread of the gospel (Justin).

Christians rebutted the remaining charge, that they were responsible for the calamities and the decline of Rome, by framing a doctrine of providence based on the Old Testament and Christian belief. Not Fate but God controls history, they argued. Those faithful to God, therefore, the Christians, are responsible for saving the world from more horrible events than were happening. They are in the world, the author of the *Epistle to Diognetus* observed, what the soul is in the body.

As numbers increased and influence spread, Christian apologies attacked their highly vulnerable competitors more and spent less time in defense. They lambasted polytheism and immorality. They argued for Christianity as "the true philosophy" (Justin) superior to all others and noted the positive contributions of Christianity to the peace and security not only of individuals but of the Empire. A new day had indeed begun to dawn.

Chapter 8

Life Together

The period under discussion is often referred to as a "tunnel Period" from which Christianity emerged with its institutional life more or less fully elaborated but during which the process of formation remained hidden. Although this characterization holds some truth, it is somewhat misleading, for writings dated in this era do give glimpses of development and allow one to make some judgments about the reasons for it.

In the past Protestants have often viewed development in a negative way, as a kind of "fall" of the church analogous to the "fall" of humankind. According to the German jurist Rudolph Sohm, the church began as a "purely spiritual entity" and became, during the second century, a church of law far removed from the intention of Jesus. Sohm's opponents, from Adolph Harnack on, have correctly pointed out that Sohm imposed a modern (i.e. nineteenth century) concept of law on the early church which created a false conflict between spirit and institution. Harnack himself, however, also defined "catholicism" as "the church of apostolic tradition fixed as law" and ascribed this development, evident first around 200 C.E., to "hellenization." The weakness of Harnack's analysis was that it focused one-sidedly on doctrine and neglected the church in its total corporate life. If one views the issue in that broad scope, one comes away with a more positive view of development and is more impressed with early Christianity's understanding of itself as a covenant missionary people as the major motive for the changes which occurred. Institutional development would not represent some kind of sinister power play by opportunistic bishops, although occasional instances of that can be cited, but a natural consequence of Christian effort to discharge what they perceived to be Christ's commission.

In its total corporate life early Christianity confronted during this period the awesome challenge of conserving its identity as a covenant missionary people while attracting and incorporating the syncretistic peoples of the Roman Empire and beyond. The churches' institutional forms—catechumenate and baptism, the eucharist as the central act of worship, discipline, scriptures and creed, and apostolic ministry—helped in two ways. On the one hand, they drilled into converts an exclusive identity as the People of God under a new covenant. The one God whom Christians came to know in Jesus Christ demanded complete and final commitment. One could not serve Christ and other gods at the same time. On the other hand, accommodated to the Graeco-Roman setting, they served as a basis of appeal for conversion. Accommodation, far from a lapse from genuine Christianity, dispelled the "alien" character and enabled the average Roman to feel at home in a subgroup that began as a sect of Judaism. Because of its security in its own identity, Christianity proved more capable of genuine assimilation to Roman culture than its syncretistic competitors, the oriental mystery religions.

The ideology under which Christians interpreted themselves and their mission in this period was that of the army of Christ doing battle with Satan and his hosts. Borrowed originally from the Essenes, in the Roman context it was elaborated with terminology and imagery taken from Roman military parlance. In some ways this is ironic, for Christians held strong reservations about military service, but it was a case of an inherited ideology fitting into the frame of a dominant cultural motif; the Romans employed a military structure even in administration of the provinces.

Baptism: The Soldier's Oath

The use of the catechumenate and baptism in the enlistment of converts was discussed in an earlier chapter and need not receive further attention here. It will be worthwhile, however, to spell out some developments in baptismal theology and practice during this crucial phase of early Christian history. The debate between those who practice infant- and those who practice believer-baptism, unfortunately, has often diverted attention from broader considerations. For this particular period it suffices to point out that there is no explicit evidence for baptism of infants. The chief support for the view that the early churches baptized infants derives from references to baptism of "households" (1 Cor. 1:16; Acts 16:15, 33; 18:8; 11:14; Ignatius, *Smyrn*. 13.1) and the assumption that Christian baptism followed on the track of Jewish proselyte baptism and circumcision. Apart from this, until Tertullian supplied the first explicit evidence about 206, all evidence is indirect, for example, Polycarp's boast to the Proconsul of Asia that he has served Christ eighty-six years (surely meaning from birth) and Irenaeus's statement that Christ had come to save all, "all these, I say, who through him are reborn into God, infants, young children, boys, the mature and older people" (*Against Heresies* 2.22.4).

The major themes under which the Christians of this era interpreted baptism reflect their concern to reassure the masses groveling in fear of demons and ridden with anxiety about fate, sin and guilt, and death that there was hope. The chief theme was that of participation through the Spirit in Christ's victory over demons. Exorcism during the catechumenate, of course, gave palpable expression to this theme. Baptism supplied the Christian's armament against the powers of evil (Ignatius). "Though the devil is ever at hand to resist us, . . . " Justin would say, "yet the angel of God, i.e., the Power of God sent to us through Jesus Christ, rebukes him, and he departs from us" (*Dial*. 116).

A second theme centered on forgiveness of sin. Derived from John the Baptist's urging of baptism on the basis of repentance for forgiveness of sin," this concept was elaborated more by western than by eastern writers, but it had universal application in a culture where people sought remedies for their guilt. A major debate arose in Rome as to whether one should be allowed to repent a serious sin (murder, apostasy, adultery) after baptism. *The Shepherd of Hermas* permitted one such formal repentance, a view which gained wide currency for a century or more.

Closely connected with the application of baptism to the problem of sin and guilt was the theme of renewal or regeneration. Christianity's main competitors also promised rebirth through rites such as the taurobolium, in which devotees were proclaimed to be *renatus in aeternum* ("reborn forever"). The idea of rebirth received strong emphasis in the Johannine writings and 1 Peter in the New Testament, so it is not surprising to find it often in later writings such as the Epistle of Barnabas and Justin. Irenaeus molded his recapitulation theory around the idea of regeneration; he liked to speak of baptism as "the laver of regeneration."

Finally, the theme of illumination appears often, particularly in eastern writings. The Epistle to the Hebrews almost certainly alluded to baptism when speaking of "those once enlightened" (6:4). Justin Martyr, however, was the first to call baptism *photismos* ("illumination"). This understanding appealed to those who, like Justin or Clement of Alexandria, sought "the true Philosophy," for it suggested a recovery of faculties by which one could grasp truth intuitively in the Platonist sense. Gnostics who did not reject baptism altogether also majored on the theme of illumination.

Already in this period baptism clearly distinguished passage from the old to the new, the kingdom Satan to the kingdom of Christ. The *Didache*, an early church manual, restricted the eucharist to the baptized, indicating that instruction in "the two ways" preceded baptism. Whether instruction in "the mysteries" (baptism and eucharist) was withheld until after baptism is unlikely, for Hippolytus seems to suggest that candidates for baptism received such information *before* baptism. There can be little question, however, that those who took the *sacramentum* ("oath") were expected to dispense with all other ties. The fashioning of an increasingly elaborate process for incorporation of new converts in the army of Christ was obviously designed to help effect exactly that.

The Eucharist and Worship: Covenant Renewal

Where baptism was a kind of acted parable of a convert's initial owning of the covenant, the eucharist or Lord's supper represented a repeating of this first pledge. As a special Christian rite par excellence, it was restricted to the baptized and, perhaps as early as 112 (*Pliny's Letter to Trajan*), the unbaptized or excommunicates were dismissed during observance.

Two themes, sacrifice and real presence, dominated eucharistic theology. Although New Testament writings did not construe the Lord's supper as a sacrifice, the very nature of it made the connection natural as Christians developed an apology both to Judaism and to the Graeco-Roman world, in which the concept played a signal role in both theory and practice. Clement of Rome, for instance, related Christian to Old Testament sacrificial concepts easily and naturally when he spoke of "those who offer their oblations at the appointed seasons" (40.4). The medieval concept of the eucharist as sacrifice was not in evidence, but the apologists did no hesitate to claim that this observance supplanted both Jewish and pagan sacrifices. It represented "the true sacrifice" or "oblation," of course, "Christ's death."

The concept of real presence was deeply rooted in the earliest Christian tradition of the Lord's supper. Before Paul already, Christians gathered on "the Lord's day" at "the Lord's table" to eat "the Lord's supper," a combined charitable (*agape*) and fellowship meal. Against docetists, those who denied Jesus' real humanity, John and Ignatius cited the eucharist as significative of genuine incarnation. Ignatius charged that docetists abstained from the eucharist "because they do not confess that the Eucharist is the flesh of our Savior Jesus Christ who suffered for our sins" (*Smyrn.* 7). For him the bread and wine were "the medicine of immortality, the antidote that we should not die, but live forever in Jesus Christ" (*Eph.* 20.2). Justin explained how the bread and wine were "changed." As the words "This is my body" and "This is my blood" are spoken, the divine Logos "transmutes" them and thus the blood and flesh of the risen Christ "nourish" the recipient (1 *Apol.* 66). Later church Fathers would advance this thinking further as they explained how the eucharist fortified believers against demonic poisons and assaults.

Although information in this period is fragmented and difficult to find, Justin supplies the first outline of a Lord's day or Sunday liturgy (1 *Apol.* 68) used in Rome. It consisted of the following:

- Readings from the "memoirs" of the apostles and writings of the prophets "as long as time permits"

- Verbal instruction by the "president" (that is, presiding presbyter or bishop)
- Prayer standing
- Presentation of "oblations" (offerings of food for the clergy and the poor as well as bread and wine)
- Prayers and thanksgivings offered by the "president" according to his ability
- "Amen!" by the congregation
- Distribution of bread and wine mixed with water by deacons
- Delivery of remaining portions to those who were absent
- Collection of money deposited with the "president" for distribution to widows and orphans, the sick, the imprisoned, and strangers

Some interesting changes took place in Christian worship during the eighty years since the primitive era.

First, Christians were now observing a Roman rather than a Jewish calendar, meeting on Sunday morning rather than Saturday evening after 6:00 p.m. when the Jewish sabbath ended, a change already reported in *Pliny's Letter to Trajan.* Obviously the constituencies of the congregations in Rome, and probably elsewhere, were no longer predominantly Jewish but Gentile.

Second, the eucharist was no longer attached to an actual meal, the agape. Abuses attested at Corinth in Paul's day and after (cf. 2 Peter 2:13) undoubtedly exerted pressure toward the separation. According to Pliny's letter to Trajan, Christians "departed and reassembled to take food," perhaps in the evening (Goguel).

Instead of this conjunction, third, the eucharist had been attached to a preaching service, modeled either after synagogue worship or after the charismatic type service described by Paul in 1 Corinthians 14. Justin does not allude to a dismissal of catechumens following the "service of the Word," but the "Amen!" hints at the distinction between the "Mass of the catechumens" and the "Mass of the faithful" which was characteristic by the late second century.

Aids to a Common Life

A number of other developments accompanied those related to baptism and eucharist which assisted Christians in their private and corporate lives. One of these was a schedule of prayer and fasting for individuals and families. According to the *Didache,* which still reflects strongly the interaction of church and synagogue, the devout said the Lord's prayer three times daily—at the third, sixth and ninth hours (9:00 a.m., noon, 3:00 p.m.)—and prayed extemporary prayers on arising and going to bed. They fasted twice a week—Wednesdays and Fridays (rather than Tuesdays and Thursdays, as in Jewish custom). Sects such as the Montanists who believed the return of Christ was imminent increased the number of prayer hours and fasts.

In early Christian as in Jewish thinking fasting and prayer were closely connected. Fasting prepared one for a deeper level of communion with God. It may also have served a second purpose as well. Food not consumed was brought on Sunday to the communion table as "oblations" which the poor or the clergy could eat.

A second aid to the common life was a calendar, partly taken over and adapted from either the Jewish or the Gentile worlds but partly framed with distinctively Christian concerns in mind. One of the earliest and most significant of calendar observances was the "Lord's day" or, as it was sometimes called, "the eighth day," the day of resurrection. Observed first in line with the Jewish week, by the mid-second century Christians had shifted to Roman reckoning and were reluctantly using the Roman nomenclature, "day of the sun." Hesitancy in using the term stemmed from the fact that the day honored the *Sol Invictus,* the supreme deity of the solar monotheism of cults such as Mithra. By the time Christianity had triumphed in the fourth century, Christians, led by the Emperor Constantine, had overcome enough of their qualms to depict Christ as the *Sol Invictus* in old St. Peter's as well as in the catacombs.

A second observance was Easter. How soon Christians began to set aside one day annually in commemoration of the resurrection cannot be established, but in the controversy over the correct date during the mid-second century both sides claimed ancient precedents. Christians of Asia Minor ended their fast, thus marking the resurrection, on the fourteenth of Nisan, that is, according to the Jewish passover. Christians in Rome, however, celebrated Easter on the first Sunday after the first full moon after the spring equinox. The difference posed no problem until Anicetus (155–166) tried to pressure a congregation of Asian Christians living in Rome to observe the Roman custom. Direct intercession of the saintly Polycarp, however, caused him to relent and the controversy died down. It heated up again in the time of Victor (189–199) and nearly, if not actually, resulted in excommunication of Christians of the province of Asia. This time, Irenaeus, a native of Asia who by then was a towering figure in the West, interceded with Victor to avert a more serious rupture. The issue surfaced again at the council of Nicaea in 325, which decided in favor of the Roman custom.

A third was Pentecost. "Pentecost" is a Greek word meaning "fiftieth"; it designated the fiftieth day after Passover in the Jewish calendar. Originally an agricultural festival, it took on a different nuance for Christians, a celebration of the gift of the Spirit and the beginning of the Church. In the early third century Tertullian noted that converts could receive baptism on Pentecost as well as Easter Sunday.

"Birthdays" of martyrs began to enter the calendars of some churches during the second century with the martyrdom of Polycarp (155). Gathering up the bones of the martyr, the faithful of Smyrna put them where they could "come together according to our power in gladness and joy, and celebrate the birthday of his martyrdom,

both in memory of those who have already contested, and for the practice and training of those whose fate it shall be" (*Martyrdom of Polycarp,* 18). After persecution ceased it took only a short step to include "saints" in the calendar.

There is no reliable evidence concerning observances in honor of Christ's birth prior to the fourth century. Clement of Alexandria, however, speculated privately that Jesus was born on April 18 or 19 or even as late as May 29. In the East January 6 became the preferred date during the fourth century. In the West December 25, a festival in honor of the "Unconquered Sun," was adopted by 335, evidently under urging of Constantine, who had been torn before conversion between solar monotheism and Christianity. It was he who made Sunday a legal holiday in 321 and fostered depictions of Christ as the *Sol Invictus.*

A third aid to worship was hymnody. Already prominent in churches founded by Paul (cf. Col. 3:16; Eph. 5:19), what are usually called prose hymns can be found in many other early Christian writings (cf. 1 Tim. 3:16; 1 Pet. 3:18-22). The Revelation of John contains numerous "songs" similar to the Palms of the Old Testament and Qumran. Pliny's Letter to Trajan (112) reported that Christians were singing hymns antiphonally to Christ. Metrical Greek hymnody developed gradually toward the end of the second century. Some Gnostics wrote hymns. Clement of Alexandria composed hymns still sung today. The churches of Syria distinguished themselves early by composition of psalms or hymns in the vernacular. The *Odes of Solomon* is a collection of forty-two hymns now dated as early as the first or second centuries. Although scholars debate whether they were composed originally in Greek or in Syriac, they reflect distinctive emphasis upon Christ as the Wisdom of God. Hymns in Latin, Coptic, and other languages appeared gradually but not as early as Syriac hymns.

A fourth aid to the common life of Christians was art. From Judaism Christians inherited some ambivalence toward art. Though the second commandment forbade "graven images," Jewish burial places and synagogues both in Palestine and elsewhere were adorned with carvings and paintings of a symbolic character. When Christians took over Jewish catacombs, they also took over art traditions which they expanded along Christian lines. The catacombs of Rome contain numerous paintings from the second century and after which depict God's saving ways from Adam and Eve to the age of the apostles and martyrs. No one can determine the extent to which such art may have adorned Christian homes and then churches, but it is likely that wealthy converts retained artwork in their homes and perhaps christianized it after conversion. Houses remodeled to serve as church buildings would have carried this process further.

No building specially designed to accommodate Christian worship have survived from the second century, but it is quite possible that many houses were refurbished like the house church at Dura Europos, a Roman frontier fortress on the Euphrates. The first floor of this building, which dates from about 232, consisted of three rooms—the largest evidently used for worship, a medium-sized one for an agape meal, and the smallest for baptism. The walls of the baptistry were adorned with biblical themes emphasizing assurance of salvation. On the back wall of the baptistry proper a good shepherd motif stood above one depicting Adam and Eve tempted by a serpent. The point was: Christ has overturned the "Fall" of humankind; in baptism one participates in his victory. Around the sides of the room were depictions of the healing of the paralytic, the ten maidens, and other scenes stressing Christ's power to deliver the helpless.

Rescuing the Fallen

Protestants have usually held the view that Christian discipline deteriorated in the postapostolic age, progressing from "strict" to "lax" treatment of offenders. It is more accurate to say that early Christian churches differed from one another from the start and continued to do so, torn between concern for the purity of the church and for restoration of offenders. Now one and now the other attitude dominated in different churches.

Some favored severe treatment of persons who committed serious sins such as apostasy, adultery, or murder. Hermas, for instance, cited a group in Rome who refused to allow for any repentance save that which preceded baptism. They based their argument chiefly on the Letter to the Hebrews, which carried great weight in the Roman congregations. Around 171 C.E. Pinytus, bishop of Cnossus on the island of Crete, remonstrated with Dionysius of Corinth, who had advocated milder treatment of the people found guilty of adultery. The Montanist sect, which originated in Phrygia about his time, was characterized by a rigorous exclusion of a whole range of offenders including persons who married a second time. Their rigorism evidently was the main attraction for Tertullian, who became a member about 206.

A more lenient approach based on the parable of the wheat and tares in Matthew's Gospel, however, existed alongside this rigorous one. Against the rigorists of Rome Hermas proposed one repentance for serious offenses committed after baptism, a view which gained wide acceptance in other places. Second Clement, composed around 140 C.E. perhaps in Rome, urged almsgiving as a form of repentance which "covers a multitude of sins." The handbook called the *Didache*, representing Syrian practice, counseled public confession before prayer and worship with the implication that the guilty could be absolved. The clearest proof of the prevalence of this outlook, however, is Tertullian's change of attitude after he became a Montanist. In a treatise *On Repentance* composed before he converted to Montanism in 206 he urged one repentance after baptism as proposed by Hermas and excluded no sins from the churches' absolution. In a later work *On Purity* he denounced Hermas as "the shepherd of adulterers" and distinguished between forgivable and unforgivable sins. The latter included several offenses besides apostasy, adultery, and murder.

Known instances of excommunication during this period show that all of the churches took discipline seriously, but some more seriously than others. Tertullian's treatise *On Repentance* describes the formal confession (*Exhomologesis*) required in his day in the church at Carthage. A contemporary account concerning the repentance of a Roman Christian named Natalius, who had become a bishop in a heretical sect, confirms that the Roman churches used a similar procedure (Eusebius H.E. 5.28.12). Persons excommunicated for serious offenses were required to put on sackcloth and ashes, fast (taking "simple things for meat and drink") and pray, lament their sins with groaning and weeping, prostrate themselves before the elders of the church, and kneel before the congregation, entreating them to intercede with the elders for their restoration to communion. Exactly when or how this procedure was fashioned cannot be determined, but Justin hinted at it in asking, "How can the impure and utterly abandoned if they weep not, and mourn not, and repent not, entertain the hope that the Lord will not impute to them sin?" (*Dialogue with Trypho* 141). Still earlier writings urged public confession (James 5:16; *Didache* 4.14, 14.1ff.; Barnabas 6.2), but these did not outline a process for it.

The reason for a more exacting and formal approach was given by Tertullian himself. "Since this second and last repentance is so serious a matter," he said, "it must be tested in a way which is proportionately laborious" (*On Repentance* 9). All too many had probably done as Marcion's teacher in Rome, Cerdo, had done when excommunicated for heretical teaching; they repented frequently, thus embarrassing the churches (Irenaeus, *Against Heresies* 3.4.3).

Structuring for Mission

During the period 70–180 C.E., churches of both east and west moved from a predominantly twofold to a predominantly threefold pattern of ministry. Several motives can be seen in this. One was the struggle of the churches to discover or maintain their identity as they incorporated people who had a radically different cultural background (a hellenistic one) than the one with which Christianity began (a Jewish one). A single authoritative figure, the bishop, assured greater consistency of interpretation and instruction. This factor, however, has often received too much emphasis to the neglect of one which played a far more significant role, that is, the demands of the Christian mission itself. As the churches reached outward and drew converts inward, they revised old structures and fashioned additional ones which worked best. In a context where the military motif was the prevailing social model, it was natural for them to construe what they were doing in terms of that motif.

According to Acts 11:30 and 14:23 and Titus 1:5, the apostles "appointed" presbyters "church by church." Whether this happened universally or not, as J.B. Lightfoot demonstrated a century ago, at the beginning of this period the twofold pattern of presbyter-bishops and deacons alluded to in Philippians 1:1 prevailed in most churches. The terms "presbyter" and "bishop" or, in Greek, *episkopos* were used interchangeably. *Episkopos* was a functional term meaning "overseer" or "superintendent" which described the work of the presbyter, a term inherited from the Jewish synagogue but which signified no more than an older person in the Gentile world. "Church" (*ekklesia*) normally delineated all Christians living within a *polis* (city), however many house churches or congregations that may have involved. Each polis-church would have had a number of presbyter-bishops or deacons who cooperated in meeting the varied needs of the area.

Like the presbyters of Jewish synagogues, presbyter-bishops exercised general oversight, administered finances, presided over public worship, taught, and supervised the charitable ministries (cf. 1 Tim. 3:2-7). In the Palestinian context the shepherd motif supplied an image for the manner in which they would go about their tasks (Acts 20:17 ff.; 1 Pet. 5:1-4). Deacons discharged most of the same functions under supervision of the presbyter-bishops (cf. Acts 6:1-6; 1 Tim. 3:8-13). Unlike the latter office, however, the Christian diaconate probably had no direct antecedent in Judaism but arose directly from the interpretation of Jesus' role in terms of the Servant of Isaiah. In the early churches, women as well as men functioned as deacons from the time of Paul on (Rom. 16:1; 1 Tim. 3:11). The Greek word *diakonos* designated the single office until the late second or early third century when women deacons came to be called "deaconesses."

The threefold office (bishop, presbyters, deacons) emerged gradually from the twofold office during the late first and early second centuries. Some scholars discern a threefold office in the Pastoral Epistles, but it seems fairly clear from Titus 1:5, 7 that the terms presbyter and bishop were still used interchangeably as they continued to be until the late second century in some places. Ignatius of Antioch (110–117) urged the churches of Asia Minor to "do nothing without the bishop," but the frequency with which he repeated that refrain proves they had not yet adopted the threefold pattern. Indeed, many scholars have observed that Ignatius's obsession with the idea, as well as some direct statements in his letters, indicates that this form was not yet secure in Antioch either. The Roman church definitely had not opted for it, for Ignatius addressed his letter to the Roman church rather than its bishop. Although lists of bishops subsequently cited names of bishops of Rome, those listed first functioned as chairpersons of a college of presbyter-bishops and not as monarchical bishops.

How did the transition from the twofold to the threefold pattern take place? Some scholars have cited the crisis of leadership which arose as a result of the fall of Jerusalem in 70 C.E. When the star fell there, it rose in Antioch, putting pressure on the church to elevate its leader to the position of monarchical bishop. It was this concept which Ignatius carried through Asia Minor on his way to martyrdom in Rome.

The difficulty with this theory is obvious in the light of Ignatius's nervous effort to make a case for a monarchical episcopate and the varied rates at which different churches adopted it. A more likely explanation is J.B. Lightfoot's hypothesis that one presbyter-bishop emerged naturally from the position of chairperson of the board of presbyter-bishops to become a monarchical bishop. When this happened, it was natural that the term *episkopos* would be reserved little by little for the persons whose powers were elevated. Threats to the welfare of the churches such as schism or heresy supplied some of the motive, but the normal processes of a vital corporate life of the churches required a level of coordination which the twofold pattern did not supply. Threats to identity added to the need for further coordination.

Still to be explained is how the churches, sprawled all over the vast Roman Empire, opted gradually for the monarchical episcopate. Rudolf Sohm and Walter Bauer attributed this to a gigantic power play by the Roman church which eventuated in Roman dominance and the office of the papacy. The evidence outlined earlier makes their theories highly unlikely. Powerful organizations could hardly have imposed their will on others, and the Roman church was by no means powerful. Far from a single church imposing on others, the churches throughout the Empire, especially those in giant metropolis, impacted mutually on one another.

In this period, as Jerusalem faded, the at least symbolic importance of cities such as Antioch, Ephesus, Corinth, and Alexandria as well as Rome increased. Due to the Pauline strategy of planting churches in major centers which could serve as channels to surrounding regions, these cities had already established themselves as parental figures for other churches in their own provinces and beyond. If Rome had an advantage, it was as the capital of the Empire to which all roads led. Thus Clement felt free to send a fraternal letter to the Corinthians to exhort them to restore their leaders whom they had expelled. Ignatius flattered the Romans, too, by speaking of their preeminence in the country of the Romans. Early lists of bishops enhanced Rome's position still more. Other churches, however, moved ahead of Rome in adoption of the threefold pattern of organization, leaving little room to think about the imposing of a Roman pattern on other churches. Far more crucial was the intimate interaction of the churches everywhere which led eventually to a common organization.

Accompanying the structural changes described previously was a tendency to distinguish more sharply between clergy and laity. In the primitive period such a distinction was not evident. The whole church was referred to as *laos*, the people. First Clement introduced the first sharp distinction. Alluding to the Old Testament priesthood, he distinguished an order of clergy and an order of the laity. "The layperson," he proceeded to argue against the rebels of Corinth, "is bound by the ordinances of the laity" (1 Clement 40). He undergirded this with the germ of a doctrine of apostolic succession. The apostles appointed presbyters "and afterwards added the provision that if they should die, other approved men should succeed to their ministry" (44.2). Ignatius's emphasis upon the exalted place of the bishop sharpened the distinction further. The bishop, he contended, stands in the place of Christ and even of God. Thence whatever happens in the church must have the bishop's supervision—the eucharist, marriages, baptisms, everything. A list of bishops compiled near the end of this period by Hegesippus laid the foundation for the fullblown theory of apostolic succession found in Irenaeus.

Chapter 9

Struggle for Identity and Unity

The unity of Christianity has been viewed in different ways. The early church Fathers saw it as a given which heretics and schismatics threatened to destroy. According to Tertullian's classical formulation in *Prescriptions against Heretics*, Christ laid down "one definite system of truth" for his disciples. The disciples preached the same doctrine everywhere and established churches which would transmit this to others. "These churches, then, numerous as they are, are identical with that one primitive apostolic church from which they all come." Heresy thus represents a departure from the apostolic tradition, an intrusion of an alien culture. Heretics have no real concern for differences in theology "as long as they are all agreed in attacking the truth." They lack discipline of any kind. They are far from unity.

Modern scholarship allows nothing so simple. In his classic treatise on *Orthodoxy and Heresy in Earliest Christianity* Walter Bauer reversed the traditional formulation. Whereas the Fathers would say first orthodoxy and then heresy, Bauer argued first "heresy" (that is diverse expressions of Christianity) and then orthodoxy, the latter imposed as a result of a power struggle. In this struggle, Bauer thought, the church of Rome carried out a major coup. In Clement's intervention in the Corinthian squabble in 96 C.E. "Rome succeeded in imposing its will on Corinth" and "casting its spell" over that church from then on. Subsequently she intervened also in Antioch at

the time of Ignatius and then, "in a more limited manner more than one hundred years later," in Alexandria, using various tactics but especially grants of money in time of desperate need to do so. After overpowering diverse groups in Rome itself, the church turned elsewhere.

> Essentially unanimous in the faith and in the standards of Christian living, tightly organized and methodically governed by the monarchical bishop, the Roman church toward the close of the second century feels inclined and able to extend further the boundaries of her influence. (*Orthodoxy and Heresy*, 129)

Few scholars now would agree with Bauer's theory of a sinister Roman campaign to impose orthodoxy, but most would acknowledge the idea of the initial diversity of early Christianity which generated problems for Christian unity. In reply to Bauer, H. E. W. Turner suggested an interlacing of "fixed" and "flexible" elements in Christian doctrine which eventually helped to establish a *Pattern of Christian Truth*. Along similar lines, most contemporary explanations make room for some kind of unity in diversity, whether or not the common elements were known and articulated. The center around which Christian identity and unity revolved was, of course, Christ himself, but it was not long before Christians realized that they depended on tangible means such as baptismal confessions, scriptures, and authoritative teachers to guide them safely to Christ. By the end of the period discussed here, they were laying down more definite formulas which could assure them that they were on the right track.

The Roman Situation

Early Christianity's problems can be placed in relief by considering the situation of one church, the Roman, on which information is fairly extensive. In the period under study here the congregations were highly diverse in background and character. Judging by writings reliably ascribed to Rome (Mark, Hebrews, 1 Peter, 1 Clement, Hermas, Justin), many of them had a substantial constituency of Jewish background and outlook. The Jewish constituency, too, was diverse, some from a synagogue, others from an Essene background. Both Hebrews and the Shepherd of Hermas reflect vivid Essene ideas. Hermas, a former slave, may well have been, as one scholar has hypothesized, a son of Essene parents brought to Rome as captives after the Jewish revolt of 66–70 C.E. At any rate he reveals deep and explicit influence of Essene ideas. First Clement, moreover, argued for maintenance of proper church order in Corinth on analogy to the hierarchy found only in Essene camp communities—the high priest, priests, Levites, and lay persons (1 Clement 40.5) and alluded to "captains of fifties," a designation found only in Exodus 18:15, 1 Maccabees 3.55, and in Essene writings.

A whole row of Gnostic teachers turned up in Rome during the late first and second centuries: Simon Magus and his consort Helena; Menander, Simon's successor; Marcellina, a disciple of Carpocrates, who came during the time of Anicetus (155–165); Cerdo, teacher of Marcion; Valentinus, who migrated from Alexandria about 140; Ptolemaeus, Valentinus's successor; Marcus, a Valentinian who seduced gullible women; and others. Justin opened his school in Rome about the middle of the second century, educating such notables as Irenaeus and Tatian. Marcion, excluded from his father's church in Pontus, moved to Rome about 139. When excommunicated from the Roman church, he began his own, which proved strongly competitive. Montanism appeared in Rome by 177 C.E.

Besides these groups, Rome attracted Christians from all over the Empire. Christians from the province of Asia were numerous enough to form their own congregation. When Anicetus (155–165) and Victor (189–199) sought to effect greater unity in Rome by pressing for conformity, they created a crisis for the Asians, who observed Asia customs concerning Easter. Polycarp interceded with Anicetus and persuaded him to relent in his insistence that the Asians observe the Roman Easter, that is, the first Sunday after the first full moon after the spring equinox, rather than the Asian custom of breaking their fast on Nisan 14, the Jewish Passover. Victor, however, exerted far greater pressure and may actually have excommunicated Christians in the Roman province of Asia despite the intercession of Irenaeus.

This depiction of their multifarious character should not mislead one into thinking that the Roman churches had no centrifugal forces pulling them toward one another. They were using confessions of some type in catechumenate and baptism. They relied on the Old Testament and certain Christian writings for public worship and instruction. They followed the lead of presbyters and deacons appointed by established procedures. What dissonant voices such as Marcion's did was to speed up a process of definition—a more precise confession, a canon or list of New Testament writings to supplement the Old (which Marcion and most Gnostics rejected), and a more centralized organization. What is known as the Old Roman Symbol dates from the middle of the second century and may respond to Marcion at one or two points. The so-called Muratorian canon, which lists New Testament writings, was composed about 175. Victor was the first highly authoritarian bishop of Rome. Pressures he exerted toward uniformity, however, were unwise; they certainly had a mixed effect on the unity of the churches as a whole.

Jewish Christianity

The struggle for Christian identity proceeded in two directions at the same time. One involved the continuing relationship of Jewish Christians to their parent religion, the other the accommodation of Christianity to its increasingly hellenistic constituency and milieu. Christians of Jewish ancestry were anxious, understandably, about the severing of ties with Judaism and radical adaptation to another cultural setting. Some chose to throw in their lot with Gentile Christianity, others to return to Judaism, still others to go their own way, retaining something from both faiths.

Any depiction of Jewish Christianity will be sketchy by virtue of fragmentary information about it. It continued alongside Gentile Christianity, however, in a variety of forms. In Palestine a group known as Ebionites (from the Hebrew *ebyon*, "the poor") fled to Pella in Transjordan after the fall of Jerusalem in 70 C.E., where they survived until the fifth century. Successors of "believers who belonged to the party of the Pharisees" mentioned in Acts 15:5 and possibly the "false brethren secretly brought in" cited in Gal. 2:4 (see H. J. Schoeps), they espoused views surprisingly close to Essene as well as Christian teachings. They observed ritual baths daily. They believed God has established two beings—Christ and the Devil—one to rule the world to come, the other this world. They rejected the virgin birth, but they believed the Spirit descended on Jesus at baptism in the form of a dove. Jesus came to teach righteousness and to destroy sacrifices. They observed the Law faithfully.

A second Jewish Christian sect known as the Elkesaites appeared in Alexandria and Rome. Originating during the third year of Trajan's reign (101 C.E.), they had several points of similarity with the Ebionites. Both remained faithful to Jewish customs, rejected certain portions of scriptures (the Apostle Paul), and looked on Christ as a human being inspired to discharge the role of a prophet. The Elkesaites, however, claimed special revelations concerning forgiveness of sins after baptism, a view reminiscent of the *Shepherd of Hermas*.

In Ephesus Cerinthus combined Jewish practices with Christian millenarianism. He believed in creation of the world by angels, an establishment of the kingdom of Christ on earth, and restoration of the Temple of Jerusalem and of sacrifices. He also practiced circumcision and kept the sabbath. At the same time he rejected the resurrection of Christ and baptized for the dead.

Several Jewish-Christian sects leaned in the direction of Gnosticism: Simon Magus, Satornilus, Sethians, Ophites, and Naasenes. Gnostic influences on Jewish sects prior to the advent of Christianity are quite evident. It was natural that these would draw elements of Christianity into their hodge podge of doctrine.

Marcion

No early Christian thinker, heterodox or orthodox, did more than Marcion to bring to a head the question of Christianity's relation to Judaism. Although often classified as a Gnostic, he is more accurately viewed as an ardent opponent of legalism and thus of Christianity's ties with Judaism. Behind this opposition lay a personal story.

Marcion was excommunicated for "defiling a virgin" by his own father. Although this statement has often been construed as a reference to his heresy, it fits better Marcion's views if taken literally. On joining the Roman Church he gave a gift of 200,000 sestercii, but he soon got into trouble regarding his theology and was excommunicated a second time. He founded a church about 144 C.E. It thrived during Anicetus's reign. Although it declined during the third century in the West, it remained strong in the East.

Marcion entitled his major work *Antitheses*. Although this work has not survived, its chief tenets can be reconstructed from Tertullian's detailed reply. Marcion established a series of antitheses between the God of the Old Testament, whom he viewed as the Demiurge who created the world and humankind, and the Supreme God who has revealed himself in Jesus. (1) The God of the Old Testament caused fire to come down from heaven; Jesus forbade this. (2) Stealing was encouraged in the Old Testament, forbidden in the New. (3) The God of creation is neither omnipotent nor omniscient; the Supreme God knows all and is all powerful. (4) The Old Testament with its ceremonial law and low standard of morality is fit only for that God, not for the God of Jesus. To emphasize the crudity of the Old Testament, Marcion rejected allegorical or spiritual interpretation and insisted on a literal approach. Having thrown out the Old Testament, he elected for his canon ten letters of Paul (exclusive of the Pastorals) and the Gospel according to Luke, both edited. His emphasis upon Paul as the only true apostle led Adolf Harnack and John Knox to characterize him as a Paulinist rather than a Gnostic. For although he adopted the Gnostic idea of Demiurge and thought Christ only "appeared" to be human, his primary emphasis lay on the gospel of the free grace of God. Christ revealed the God of Love and forgiveness. There will be no resurrection of the flesh, second coming or judgment by Christ. Marcion vehemently repudiated the idea of judgment. The God of the Old Testament was going to send a messiah to collect the chosen people into his kingdom to rule over the whole earth and then to exercise judgment over sinners. But at this point the good God appeared, showing mercy on sinners and freeing all from the bonds of the God of the Jews. Curiously, Marcion also preached strict asceticism, denied the right of marriage, and formulated stern regulations concerning fasting.

The Gnostics

Until 1945, when Egyptian peasants found an entire library consisting of thirteen codices, nine complete with leather covers, containing fifty-two treatises, Gnosticism was known almost exclu-

sively from the writings of opponents, notably Irenaeus, Tertullian, Hippolytus, and other Fathers. This cache of writings, all written in Coptic but dependent on Greek originals and dating from the mid-third to the first half of the fourth century, confirms the church Fathers' impression that Gnosticism was highly diverse. Some of the texts, such as *The Gospel of Thomas*, a collection of sayings of Jesus, and Valentinus's *Gospel of Truth*, claim to be explicitly Christian, although gnosticized. Others, such as *The Apocalypse of Adam*, reflect a Jewish type of gnosis based on allegorical interpretation of the Old Testament. Others, such as *Zostianos and Allogenes* or *Trimorphic Protennoia*, are more philosophical and Neoplatonic than Christian or Jewish.

The variegated character of this library has added weight to the view that Gnosticism was not merely an "acute hellenization" of Christianity, as Adolf Harnack and F. C. Burkitt conjectured. Yet it would not seem to establish the theory of Richard Reitzenstein, Wilhelm Bousset, Hans Jonas, and Rudolf Bultmann that Gnosticism was a pre-Christian religion. It is more accurately characterized, as James M. Robinson (*The Nag Hammadi Library*) has said, as

> a radical trend of release from the dominion of evil or of inner transcendence that swept through antiquity and emerged within Christianity, Judaism, Neoplatonism, the mystery religions, and the like and subsequently became a religion in its own right.

Gnostic sects appeared in various parts of the Christian world. Associated with *Egypt* were Nassenes, Sethians, Cainites, Ophites, Basilidians, and Valentinians; with *Syria* Simonians (after Simon Magus), Dositheans, Menanderians, Basilidians, and Saturnilians; with *Asia Minor* Cerinthians, Nicolaitans, and the Jewish syncretistic cults of Zeus Hypsistos and Zeus Sabazios; and with *Rome* most of the above. It is impossible to catalogue all of these, but the main tenets can be summarized.

All of the Gnostic sects were concerned about redemption by liberation from the material world and reintegration with the spiritual, the One. A profound metaphysical dualism formed the base for their systems of thought. Matter is evil, the spirit alone is good. Consequently, these two must have no contact. Dualism necessitated a theory of creation by some being other than the Supreme God, who is pure spirit. The Valentinians, who leaned strongly toward Platonism, explained creation by way of a series of emanations from the One. Others ascribed creation to a lesser deity usually called the *Demiurgos*. Gnostic cosmology pictured a three-storied universe with a series of concentric spheres or aeons rising above and around the earth to serve as filters between the spiritual and the material worlds. Some projected thirty and others as many as 365 (for the days of the year) spheres. Ruling over these spheres were lesser deities called *archai*, *daimones*, *exousiai*, etc. (cf. Col. 1–2).

Redemption requires first a release of the soul from the body, which since it is material is a "tomb." The soul is a "divine spark" flicked off of the One and trapped in a body. Gnostic groups differed sharply on the way a soul could obtain its freedom. Death, of course, would release it, but one could prepare for liberation before death. Many Gnostics encouraged ascetic practices and self-mortification, rites of purification, and regulation of life according to the dictates of the higher elements within. The Carpocratians, however, urged indulgence, seeking every human experience for the soul so that they would not be forced into another body, which they believed would happen if they did not exercise wanton freedom.

Release from the body is only the first stage in redemption. The second is a return through the heavenly spheres ruled over by demonic forces. Here the later Gnostics usually divided people into three categories: the *pneumatikoi* or "spiritual" who would reascend like helium-filled balloons; the *hylic* or "material" who had no pros-

pect of salvation; and the *psychikoi* or "semispiritual" who could be saved if they followed the right prescription. The key lay, they thought, in *gnosis*, a special knowledge of the names of the ruling powers and "passwords" to obtain their permission to ascend through the aeons. The goal of most Gnostics was a mystical vision and enlightenment which would bring deification.

Where would one obtain *gnosis*? From the Redeemer sent from above to lead the soul on its journey. Here Gnostics could make use of Christ, although most viewed him as a kind of loose addendum to their systems. In some systems he could be seen as the Redeemer whose purpose was to reveal the secret *gnosis* to selected teachers. Accordingly, the Gnostics produced Gospels and apostolic writings of their own. *The Gospel of Truth* is a treatise on the Valentinian system with scant reference to Jesus, but *The Gospel of Thomas* combines sayings parallel to those in the canonical gospels with otherwise unknown sayings of Jesus, some of which have a gnostic flavor. When challenged to authenticate their teachings, Gnostics either allegorized canonical writings or rejected them on the grounds that they had received Jesus' secret teachings by way of apostles other than those who composed canonical writings.

Valentinians made a significant contribution to interpretation of the Bible. Those who did not reject the Old Testament out of hand faced seriously the problems it posed for Christian use. In his famous *Letter to Flora* Ptolemaeus, Valentinus's successor, pointed to subtle distinctions which should be made between various parts of the Old Testament. One part must be attributed to God himself, a second part to Moses, and a third to the elders of the people. Even the first part must be subdivided further. It contains "the pure legislation not mixed with evil," that "interwoven with inferiority and injustice," and that "which is exemplary and symbolic." As examples of the first class, Ptolemaeus cited the decalogue; of the second, the eye for eye, tooth for tooth legislation; of the third, such things as offerings, circumcision, sabbath, fasting, passover, unleavened bread, and the like. His examples of what could be "spiritualized" are not unlike those given by orthodox writers such as Irenaeus and Tertullian.

Montanism

Montanism does not belong in the same category as Gnosticism and Marcionism, but it too mottled the early Christian picture and heightened the struggle for unity. This charismatic sect originated in Phyrgia in Asia Minor either in 156 or 172, the conflicting dates given by different sources, when a converted priest of Cybele named Montanus began to prophesy and speak in tongues. Montanus's first disciples included two women, Priscilla and Maximilla, who also claimed prophetic inspiration. The movement spread quickly throughout Asia Minor and to Rome and Carthage. In Carthage it attracted a number of martyrs and, in 206, the brilliant apologist and theologian Tertullian. Tertullian, however, separated from the Montanists about 222 and formed a sect of his own. As its first prophets disappeared from the scene, the influence of the movement waned, but it continued as late as the sixth century.

Unlike the Gnostics or Marcion, the Montanists espoused no views which would have been judged heretical by contemporary or even later standards. Later orthodox writers, it is true, accused Montanus of claiming to be Christ or the Holy Spirit, but Tertullian, whose orthodoxy was never questioned, could hardly have joined a sect whose theology would have deviated so far from the center.

Montanists designated their sect "the prophecy" or "the new prophecy." They divided history into three stages: that of Old Testament prophecy, that of the "instruction of the Lord," and that of the Paraclete. The last, promised by Jesus (John 14), opened the way for new revelations. Montanus was quoted as saying: "Lo, man is as a lyre and I play on it as a plectron. Man sleeps and I

awaken (him). Lo, it is the Lord who sets human hearts in ecstasy and who in it gives men hearts" (Ephiphanius, *Heresies*, 84.4D). Glossolalia was a form of prophecy.

In accordance with their view of history, the Montanists expected Christ to return soon and set up the millenial kingdom with headquarters at Pepuza, Montanus's home town. Living on the eve of the Parousia, they demanded a higher level of discipline than other churches. Accordingly, they extended the churches' fasts. According to Jerome, they kept three lents a year (*Comm. on Matthew* 9.15; *Ep. to Marcella* 41), and they observed two weeks of what Tertullian called *Xerophagia* or *Raphanophagia* during which they abstained from meats, wine-flavored drinks, and baths (*On Fasting* 1). Moreover, where other churches encouraged voluntary fasting, they required it. Montanists also forbade second marriages even in instances where a spouse died. Tertullian denounced remarriage as "nothing but a type of fornication" (*Exhortation to Chastity* 9). Along similar lines, Montanists elevated virginity. Tertullian listed three levels of purity: virginity from birth, virginity from the new birth, and faithfulness in marriage. He did, however, defend marriage against Gnostic teaching that it is evil.

On line with their eschatology Montanists held rigorous views about exclusion and restoration of offenders. Nothing makes this clearer than Tertullian's hardening of his views after conversion. In his treatise *On Chastity* he repudiated his own earlier statements that grace is free and unlimited, divided offenses into remissible and irremissible, and refused readmission of persons in the latter category only. Montanists gloried in martyrdom and forbade flight to avoid persecution. Opponents charged that they provoked and counseled others to provoke persecution and preferred apostasy under torture to flight.

Montanists emphasized the Spirit in their concept of the church. They liked to label themselves "pneumatics" and other Christians as "psychics," though they did not deny that the latter were Christian. Pneumatics have the advantage of possessing the Spirit, and it is the Spirit which guarantees discipline and order and whatever else the church requires. The Spirit, not ordination, determines leadership; thus women, such as the prophetesses Priscilla and Maximilla, could assume dominant roles. If there were grades or degrees, they would depend on prophetic inspiration and not official classifications. "Are not even we lay persons priests?" asked Tertullian.

Chapter 10

Confessing Faith

Adolf Harnack viewed canon, creed, and episcopate as the three bulwarks which early Christianity erected against heresy. Although each of these did serve this purpose in some way, recognition of the diversity of early Christian life and thought necessitate a more complex depiction of Christian efforts to discern and retain their identity as the churches incorporated the peoples of the Roman Empire and beyond. Side by side with the process of defining a New Testament canon, the framing of confessional statements for baptism which could serve as summaries of faith and guides to interpretation, and location of the teaching function increasingly in the hands of bishops went a process of theological reflection in response to questions posed both within and outside of the churches. The apologists in particular sought to meet this challenge and merit recognition as the early church's first theologians.

Presenting Christ

For early Christians theology was christology. The major question was always: Why do we ascribe to Jesus the honor which belongs to God, whom we believe to be One?

Early Christians stood between two worlds as they wrestled with this question. One was the monotheistic world of Judaism, the other was the polytheistic world of Greece and Rome. Early on, Jewish perspectives dominated, but as the Jewish constituency of the churches diminished, they faded into the background and hellenistic perspectives overshadowed them. The transition was risky and led in many instances to theological shipwrecks. Some, however, managed to steer the ship safely between reefs on either side, relying heavily on baptismal confessions as their pilots in interpreting scriptures.

Two christologies vied with one another during this period. One, known as pneumatic christology, reflected continuing Jewish influences; the other, known as logos christology, addressed itself more sharply to the Gentile setting.

Pneumatic christology probably originated in Jewish Christianity, but it continued to have strong play in Rome and other centers where there was a basic Jewish constituency. It tended toward adoptionism but differed from it in emphasizing Christ's preexistence. Clement of Rome accentuated the monotheism of the Old Testament. He conceived of Christ as the preexistent Servant of Isaiah 53. He expected the Second Coming and bodily resurrection. Similarly, Hermas was strongly monotheistic. He viewed the incarnation as a union of "the holy, preexistent Spirit that created every creature" with human flesh (*Similitudes* 5.6; 9.1). Some scholars have charged him with adoptionism, but he differed from adoptionists in his theory of preexistence.

Near the end of the second century, a divergent form of pneumatic Christianity known as monarchianism developed in Rome and elsewhere. Monarchianism emphasized the single rule (*monarche*) of God. One form of it was known as dynamistic or adoptionistic monarchianism. According to this view, Christ was a man endowed at birth or baptism with divine power (*dynamis*) and thus able to perform miracles. Because he fulfilled the divine will perfectly, he was raised from the dead, given divine authority, and appointed judge and savior of humankind. In this sense he can be recognized as Lord and worshipped as such. The first exponent of this view was Theodotus the Tanner, who migrated to Rome from Smyrna about 190. He was succeeded by his student, Theodotus the Money Changer, Asclepiodotus, and Artemas. The most influential representative, however, was Paul of Samosata, bishop of Antioch and a civil official under Zenobia, Queen of Palmyra, who was condemned at the Synod of Antioch in 268.

The other form of monarchianism was known as Modalism or Sabellianism (after its leading exponent) or Patripassianism. Beginning with the basic premise that there is only one God, the Father, Modalists proceeded to equate Father and Son. If Christ is God, he is surely the Father. If he suffered, then the Father suffered (thus Patripassianism). To avoid charges of Patripassianism, some Modalists distinguished between the flesh (the Son) and the spirit (the Father). But the cardinal tenet of Modalists was that Father, Son and Spirit are identical. These are merely names or modes (thus Modalism). God is at one time in the mode or role (*prosopon*) of Father, at another time in the mode or role of Son, at another time in the mode or role of the Spirit. The chief representatives of this view were Praxeas, who flourished under Victor (189–199); Sabellius, who flourished under Zephyrinum and Callistus (198–222); and Noetus (d. ca. 250). Modalism also gained adherents in Asia Minor and Africa.

The christology which eventually triumphed was logos christology. The early Christian proclamation had posed the question: *Who* was with God—became human—and reascended? Jewish thought supplied several possible answers. Torah, the revealed will of God, was thought of by the rabbis in near-anthropomorphic terms. Wisdom was feted in a highly personal way in Proverbs 8, Ben Sirach, and the Wisdom of Solomon. The Word of God (*dabhar*) figured prominently in Old Testament understanding of creation (Gen. 1:1), revelation, and redemption. Translated *Logos* in Greek, the concept of the Word had some affinities in the Stoic and Platonic ideas of the universal Reason which gives order and illumines understanding. Philo of Alexandria, moreover, had already blended elements of both traditions in his apology for Judaism.

Logos christology caught on in Asia Minor. The prologue to the Gospel according to John, which tradition associates with Ephesus, combined both Old Testament and Greek motifs concerning the Logos, but it added also the profound assertion: "And the Logos became flesh and dwelt among us" (1:14). Not long afterwards, Ignatius of Antioch spoke in like manner of Christ as the Logos, contesting some of the same errors of doctrine John argued against. The Logos is the revealer of God, "the mind," "the unerring mouth of the Father" who "proceeds from silence" (*Magnesians* 9). He was not a phantom, merely appearing to be human, but rather he "was truly born, . . . truly persecuted under Pontius Pilate, . . . truly crucified and died, . . . truly raised from the dead" (*Trallians* 9). Ignatius subordinated the Son or Logos to the Father, but he ascribed divine attributes to him (*Ephesians* 1.7; *Romans* 1). Christianity thus supercedes Judaism. "It is monstrous to talk of Jesus Christ and to practice Judaism," he asserted, standing history on its head. "For Christianity did not base its faith on Judaism, but Judaism on Christianity" (*Magnesians* 10).

In the mid-second century Justin brought the Logos concept to Rome, where he fashioned an apologetic based on it. The Logos was for him the key to morality. Human beings have free will which sets them apart from all other creatures.

However, they do not exercise this because they have been misled by demons and custom or example. To be saved, they must become convinced that God demands virtue and will reward and punish them according to their deserts. Yet they will not repent unless they have knowledge of what is demanded, that is, God's purpose of rewarding the good and punishing the wicked. This knowledge is to be found in Christianity, in its high moral standards and in Christ, the divine messenger sent to reveal God's will and truth. He is the Logos, who became human so as to teach truth and thus to reveal God. Justin viewed the Logos more as the universal Reason of Stoic-Platonic thought than as the Word of the Old Testament. But he could refer to him as the "second God" of the Old Testament theophanies. This Logos inspired the prophets and illuminated the minds of great philosophers such as Heraclitus and Socrates. In Christ, however, he became incarnate. Thus although he spoke to and through the others, in Christ humankind came to possess complete truth.

Tatian (ca. 175), Athenagoras (ca. 177), Theophilus of Antioch (ca. 180), and other apologists echoed Justin's basic thought. Theophilus, however, advanced the logos concept further than any of his predecessors by distinguishing the "internal Logos" (*logos endiathetos*) and the "uttered Logos" (*logos prophorikos*) through whom creation occurred (*To Autolycus* 2.10, 22). "For before anything came into being He had Him as a counsellor, being His own mind and thought. But when God wished to make all that He determined on, He begot this Word, uttered (*prophorikos*), the firstborn of all creation, not Himself being emptied of the Word, but having begotten Reason, and always conversing with His Reason" (2.22). Theophilus was also the first to apply the word *Trias* ("threefold") to the Godhead.

The Charters of the Church

As a sect of Judaism, early Christianity inherited at least one means for conserving its identity, namely the Old Testament law and prophets. Christian attitudes toward the ritual law, however, made these writings highly problematic. If some instructions were to be disregarded, why not all?

Early Christian thinkers were eventually to frame a response to that question, but one (Jewish) Christian touched instinctively on the right answer when he said, "If I don't find it in the charters, I do not believe in the gospel" (in Ignatius, *Philadelphians* 8.2). However many elements Christians choose to ignore, they nevertheless rooted their faith in the Old Testament. Thus when Marcion decided to scrap the Old Testament and emphasize the newness of Christianity, he precipitated a massive identity crisis. That he himself recognized the problem is evident in the fact that he created a canon to replace the one he discarded. The arbitrary way in which he went about this forced the churches to delineate a canon or list of writings which they used in public worship alongside the Old Testament. In actual usage a canon of some kind already existed, but it was Marcion who narrowed the list and forced a process of reflection upon the churches.

Apart from Marcion's the earliest known canon of scriptures is one discovered by L.A. Muratori in an eighth century manuscript. Most scholars date it between 170 and 200 C.E. on the basis of the author's allusions to Pius I, Hermas, Marcion, Basilides, and Montanus as his contemporaries. Although the first part of the manuscript is missing, the list included the four Gospels and all other writings now found in the western New Testament except Hebrews, James and 1 and 2 Peter. It mentioned also the Revelation of Peter and the Wisdom of Solomon and rejected some other writings, including the Shepherd of Hermas. It is quite clear that the core of a New Testament canon was solidly formed by this time. Did such a core precede Marcion?

Probably. Barnabas, the *Didache*, Ignatius, Papias, and Marcion himself all noted one or more of the Gospels. About 170 Tatian produced his *Diatessaron*, a harmony of the four Gospels. The letters which bear Paul's name were circulating as a collection when 2 Peter was written (ca. 130). They may have been gathered in small collections by exchange of letters between churches Paul visited or, as E. J. Goodspeed theorized, been collected suddenly after the appearance of Luke-Acts about 90 C.E. The Apostolic Fathers cited most of Paul's letters. Writing to the Ephesians, Ignatius cited Paul, "who in every letter mentions you in Christ Jesus" (*Ephesians* 12:2). Marcion himself used a ten-letter collection, but later Marcionites used all thirteen letters. Acts probably circulated with the Gospel according to Luke. First John and I Peter were also widely used.

What authority did New Testament writings have? At first, for obvious reasons, not as much as the ancient scriptures of Judaism. Clement of Rome (96 C.E.) quoted only the Old Testament or words of Jesus as scripture; otherwise, he invoked Peter and Paul as examples. Ignatius, however, seldom cited the Old Testament. For him, on the contrary, "the charters are Jesus Christ, the inviolable charter is his cross, and death, and resurrection, and the faith which is through him" (*Philadelphians* 8.2). This would mean not Christ as known through New Testament writings but through the bishop as the sure and safe guide to the gospel. Like Ignatius, Polycarp put apostolic writings a rung higher than the Old Testament. He echoed the thoughts and sometimes quoted many New Testament writings, especially Paul's. Justin based his argument for Christianity principally on the Old Testament viewed in its entirety as prophetic, whether he debated Jews or Gentiles. The divine Logos spoke through the prophets about Christ. Justin asked:

> For with what reason should we believe of a crucified man that He is the firstborn of the Unbegotten God, and Himself will pass judgment on the whole human race, unless we had found testimonies concerning Him published before He came and was born as man, . . . ? (1 *Apology* 53)

The *Dialogue with Trypho* is essentially a collection of proof texts from the Old Testament. For Trypho and his companions would not "have tolerated your conversation," they declared, "had you not referred everything to the scriptures" (*Dialogue* 56).

Not all theories of inspiration of scriptures were as subtle as Justin's. Other apologists, such as Athenagoras, employed a theory of mantic inspiration, according to which the Spirit was believed to move the lips of the prophets "as if they were musical instruments" (Athenagoras, *Embassy* 7), "their own reasoning falling into abeyance and the Spirit making use of them as a flutist might play upon his flute" (9). This near-mechanical theory opened the way for an immensely difficult problem of interpretation, for it necessitated the spiritualizing or allegorizing of obscure or difficult passages and the discovery of meaning in every jot and tittle.

The Gnostics led the way here, but they were not alone in spiritualizing. The *Epistle of Barnabas*, composed in the early second century perhaps in Alexandria, was written as a dissuasive against Jewish literalistic interpretation of the ritual law and an application of the same to morality. Justin tried to steer a course between Jewish literalism and Gnostic allegorism. In some instances he came close enough to the latter to evoke warnings from his opponent Trypho. In the main, however, he ventured no further than typology. Unlike allegorism, which discards the historical, typology was predicated on the assumption that there are real historical correspondences between Israel under the Old Covenant and Israel under the New. Nevertheless, it was only a short step from typology to allegory. And both could be defended on the basis of claims of special gifts for interpretation. As Christianity distanced itself further and further from Judaism, Christians felt less and less pressure to adhere to the historical sense with ominous consequences for their reading of the Bible and application to life.

The Living Voice

The most significant locus for the handing on of Christian tradition and thus for the safeguarding of the faith would have been the catechumenate. Here inquirers and converts got their first taste of Christian doctrine and guidance in interpreting the scriptures. Some New Testament writings such as Matthew's Gospel were assembled in such a context for instruction of new converts. So also early manuals such as the *Didache* and apologies such as Justin's and confessions of faith. Confessions drew together the whole instructional process and served as beacons for their Christian lives from then on. When the churches disciplined errant members, they alluded back to the catechumenate and baptism, particularly to the confessions learned there. Christians had made their pledge in that process, and they had to answer for it.

Although confessions took shape in the catechumenate and baptismal process, they were invoked in numerous contexts: exorcism of demons, reply to persecutors, worship, and doctrinal disputes. Exorcists made the sign of the cross and invoked the name of Christ or the Trinity, symbolizing a believer's participation in Christ's victory. In persecution situations Christian martyrs responded to their persecutors with simple confessions. Because they were often punished simply for being Christians, they replied as Polycarp did in Smyrna, "I am a Christian." Sometimes, however, they took advantage of the occasion to deliver a full confession in God the Father and in Jesus Christ, the Son of God, as Justin did when brought before the prefect Rusticus in 165. Confessions did not become a regular part of the Christian liturgy until the fifth or sixth centuries, but they were used on occasion. The *Letter of Pliny to Trajan* reported the recitation of hymns to Christ and the taking of oaths in services which authorities investigated.

Scholars debate the extent to which theological controversy shaped confessions of faith. There can be little doubt that confessions antedated controversy, for some type of confession existed from the beginning. The earliest New Testament writings contain both one and two-part and also formulas which paved the way for three-part confessions. It is not necessary to assume from this, as Oscar Cullmann did, that confessions were first christological, then bipartite, and then trinitarian. The experience of God to which early Christians bore witness demanded trinitarian expression. What doctrinal debate did was to spur forward a process of refinement and elaboration.

The so-called Old Roman Symbol, a catechetical-baptismal statement employed in the Roman church in the mid-second century that eventually evolved into what came to be called "the Apostles' Creed," reflects the predominantly traditional or biblical character of such confessions. Only three or four clauses can be construed as addressing Gnostic or Marcionite challenges to faith.

> I believe in God, the Father Almighty.
> And in Jesus Christ, his only Son, our Lord,
>   who was born of the Holy Spirit
>   and the virgin Mary;
> crucified under Pontius Pilate, and buried;
> the third day he rose from the dead;
> he ascended into heaven,
>   and sits on the right of the Father;
> from thence he shall come
>   to judge the living and the dead.
> And in the Holy Spirit;
>   the holy Church;
>   the forgiveness of sins;
>   the resurrection of the flesh;
>   eternal life.

This confession contains no word or phrase which is not found also in scriptures, but some of its phrases could be viewed as darts thrown at Marcion or the Gnostics, and possibly even the Montanists. "Father Almighty" could be a repudiation of the idea that a lesser deity, the Demiurge, created the world. Emphasis on judgment could respond to Marcion's obstinate hostility to any idea of judgment. "Forgiveness of sins" could oppose the Montanist unwillingness to restore communion to persons excommunicated for serious offenses. "Resurrection of the *flesh*" could throw up a bulwark against Gnostic docetism. Except for the last statement, however, none of these phrases was specific enough to require opposition to heresy as an explanation. They certainly lacked the precision of later creeds such as the Nicene, and it is wise to conclude that the normal process of instructing converts supplied the chief motive for the framing of the Old Roman Symbol. Catechists would have interacted with contemporary currents as they taught the uninstructed, but that would not have forced a constant revision of the confession itself.

Who Teaches?

The crucial issue in the definition of identity by early Christians lay, as Ignatius perceived, not in what was taught whom but in who taught what. Both scriptures and tradition, even confessions of faith, required interpretation. The question was: *Who* should teach authoritatively?

One group who lay claim to that role was the teachers both in catechetical schools and in schools founded on private initiative such as Justin's in Rome or Pantaenus's in Alexandria or Valentinus's in both Alexandria and Rome. Jesus was a teacher, and a teaching office existed in early Christianity at least as early as the Apostle Paul. "Now God has appointed in the church," he said, "first apostles, second prophets, third teachers, . . . " (1 Cor. 12:28). Teachers such as John Mark traveled with apostles and continued the instruction of converts. A teaching tradition developed out of a strongly felt sense of responsibility for Christianity's evangelistic and missionary enterprise.

For a time the separateness of the teaching office posed no serious threat to Christian identity, but that was no longer true by the late first or early second century. The incorporation of more and more peoples of highly diversified backgrounds complicated matters immensely. Gradually bishops emerged as successors of the apostles and thus the authoritative teachers and interpreters of Christian identity.

Acts, the Pastoral Epistles, and first Clement delineated the basic scheme: Jesus taught the apostles. The apostles preached city by city and appointed selected converts to be their successors as presbyter-bishops and deacons (Acts 14:23; Titus 1:5; 1 Clement 42ff.). According to Clement, they did so because they knew "there would be strife for the title of bishop" (1 Clement 44.1). Ignatius of Antioch did not develop the succession idea, claiming for himself direct inspiration of the Spirit, but rather seems to have thought of the apostles as in some way subordinate to the bishop. The bishop presided in God's place, the presbyters in that of the apostles (*Magnesians* 6.1). Nothing was to be done without the bishop. Contrariwise, Ignatius disparaged the role of teachers. "It is better to be silent and be," he remarked, "than to talk and not be." Christ is the only Teacher (*Ephesians* 15:1f.).

A fullblown theory of episcopal succession appeared about 180 C.E. in Hegesippus's *Memoirs*. According to Eusebius, on a journey to Rome Hegesippus, a converted Jew, received the same doctrine from all the bishops he met and concluded that "In every succession, and in every city that is held which is preached by the law and the prophets of the Lord" (Eusebius, H.E. 4.22.1, 3). He proceeded to draw up a succession list of the church of Rome. His succession list and theory were elaborated by Irenaeus a few years later in his treatise *Against Heresies*.

Teachers continued to have an important function in early Christianity until the time of Origen (185–254/255). By the end of this period, however, bishops were gradually supplanting them as the chief interpreters of Christian doctrine.

Part 3

New Status,
175–313 C.E.

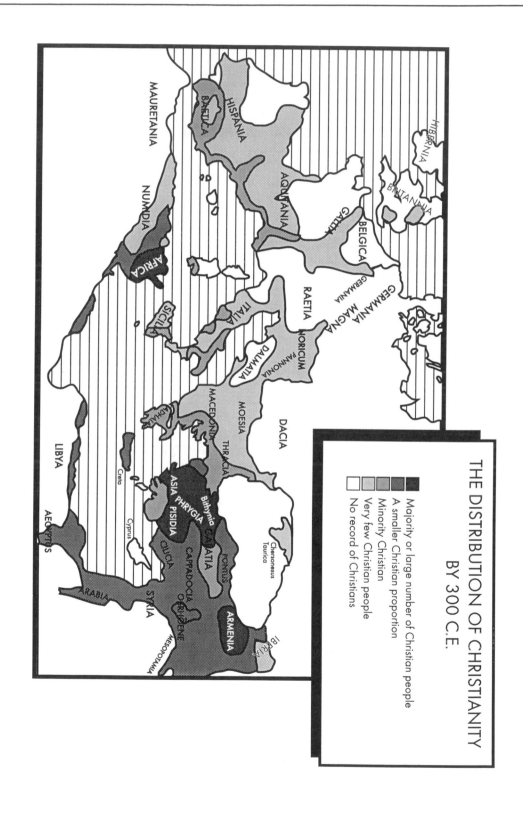

THE DISTRIBUTION OF CHRISTIANITY
BY 300 C.E.

Majority or large number of Christian people
A smaller Christian proportion
Minority Christian
Very few Christian people
No record of Christians

Chapter 11

Victorious Victims

Christianity experienced a dramatic change of status within the Roman Empire after about 175–180. Largely unnoticed or ignored by people of wealth and status up to that point, it began to attract sufficient numbers from the middle to upper echelons to invite comment and attack from pagans. Celsus, Autolycus, Marcus Aurelius, and the satirist Lucian have been mentioned. Before 217 Philostratus put forth a first century pagan miracle worker named Apollonius of Tyana as the pagan answer to Jesus. The distinguished Neoplatonist Porphyry (ca. 232–ca. 303) composed a bitter invective *Against the Christians* for their lack of patriotism and unwillingness to support the religious revivals fostered by the Emperors Decius (248–253) and Aurelian (253–260). Persecution, once local and spasmodic and unofficial, became universal, systematic, and official as Decius perceived Christianity as "an empire within the Empire" and a serious threat to his control. When persecution abated, as it did from 203 until 250 and again from 260 until 303, the churches mushroomed. Slowly gaining confidence of toleration, they witnessed with growing boldness and even built buildings specially designed for their assemblies. A new era was dawning.

Why Christianity Succeeded

What accounts for this substantive change in pagan perceptions and fears of Christianity? One factor was the deterioration in the situation of the Empire itself. The prosperous years of the Antonines (96–180 C.E.) were followed by a period of continuous internal struggle and threats from new enemies on the frontier—the Alamanni, the Franks (236), the Goths (247–251), and the Sassanids or Neo-Persians (260–268). As in other perilous periods, the fear-ridden responded with suspicion. Emperors increased their control, Diocletian finally consolidating complete power in 284 as he took the title of Dominus. They, like Augustus, sought to undergird centralization by reviving the state cultus. Yet the masses looked for reassurance not to the formalized and ritualized cult of Rome but to oriental cults such as Mithra, Isis and Osiris, Cybele, Judaism, and Christianity—all of which addressed their anxiety and fear.

The anxiety of the masses already visible in earlier centuries heightened. A cursory survey of magical papyri from the period reveals an increase in resort to the occult to control fate, overcome the demonic, ward off illnesses, gain power over enemies, escape death, and otherwise cope with the fearful unknown. Men and women consulted prophetesses and prophets, augurs, entrails of birds and animals, pebbles, horoscopes, sages, and spirits of the departed to gain insight into reality. They sought healing through cults such as that of Aesclepius, which came to new prominence with the publication of *The Life of Apollonius* by Philostratus, or Isis and Osiris, which Lucian propagated in his *Metamorphoses* or *Golden Ass*. Philostratus claimed healings of all kinds—demoniacs, the blind, paralytics, the lame—power to predict plagues and earthquakes or other natural disasters, and even resuscitations of the dead by his hero.

Christianity benefited also from a shift of consciousness which occurred during this era. Platonism eclipsed Stoicism as the dominant philosophy in the latter half of the second century, blended into the mystery cults to pull off a coup for solar monotheism. Neoplatonism, created during the mid-third century by Plotinus (ca. 205–270) and, some scholars argue, Origen, both of whom had studied under Ammonius Saccas (ca. 175–242), emphasized return of the rational soul to unity with the One as the path of salvation. Philosopher preachers itinerated everywhere urging repentance and moral reform with a view to purging the soul for its reascent to unity. The *Corpus Hermeticum*, popular Platonist writings dating from the second to the fourth centuries, pled with the masses to be "born again" in order to overcome "destiny" (*heimarmene*) or "fate." Some Platonists repeated Plutarch's hierarchical scheme: the sun god—planetary gods—demons or Olympian gods—spirits, hobgoblins, ghosties, and "things that go bump in the night."

Nearly every popular religion aligned itself in some way with solar monotheism. The sun-cult of Mithraism, attuned in so many ways with this trend, however, captured the interest of the emperors. The initiation of the Emperor Commodus (182–192), spurred on by his wife Julia Domna, inaugurated the first great period of growth for the sun cult. Septimius Severus (193–211) had erected an elaborate three-story facade called the Septizodium or Septizonium which had zodiacal implications. On coins he portrayed the sun god wearing the emperor's beard and carrying the imperial title "Invictus" (unconquerable). Caracalla (211–218) boasted that when driving his chariot he was imitating the sun. Elagabalus (218–222), whose name was a variant of Heliogabalus (devotee of the sun), adopted it when he entered the hereditary priesthood of the sun god at Emesa and made an elaborate point of installing this deity in Rome when he ascended the imperial throne. Although he failed to convince the Roman populace of the supremacy of his cult, he did not destroy it by his excesses. His successor Severus Alexander (222–235) featured the sun god on his coins. It remained, however, for Aurelian (270–275) to establish the sun as the supreme god of Rome. Emperors from Aurelian to Constantine pledged their allegiance to the Unconquered Sun, and Constantine himself had to choose between this faith and the monotheism of Christianity when he was "converted." After he opted for the latter, he worked diligently to translate images of the sun into Christian symbols.

Why Christianity and not Mithraism? The two obviously had much in common: some form of monotheism, strong moral teachings, promise of life after death, rites of initiation and passage which brought tangible assurance. Christianity differed from Mithraism both in inclusiveness and in exclusiveness. Mithra evidently restricted its membership to men, although it may have sponsored some affiliate societies for women; Christianity included all persons. Contrariwise, Mithra tolerated crossing lines to join other cults; Christianity did not. Yet what may have attracted an emperor looking for a religion to hold a shattering Empire together was the structural cohesiveness of Christianity. Mithra could not match Christianity's empire-wide network of churches, charities, mission effort, etc. Nor could it point to a personality and teaching like Jesus' which accounted for the uniqueness of Christianity. Renan was far from accurate when he remarked that if Christianity had not triumphed, Mithra would have. None of the other religions possessed the intense motive for mission which was inspired by the Christian conviction that in Jesus of Nazareth the "last days" had begun.

The Expansion of Christianity

Christianity continued its geographical expansion in most parts of the Empire and beyond its fringes during this era. After the establishment of Aelia Capitolina on the site of ancient Jerusalem the focus shifted to other cities, particularly Caesarea, which became the metropolitanate of Palestine when that system came into existence about 190. A list of bishops can be traced from 190 on: Theophilus, Theoktistus, Domnus, Theoteknus, Agapius, and Eusebius. Eusebius, the first church historian, became bishop about 315 and spent much of his career (d. ca. 340) trumpeting the advent of the "millennium" with Constantine. Caesarea's star rose, however, when Origen took up permanent residence there in 232 and established it as "a second Alexandria" in terms of learning and influence. Pamphilus (ca. 240–309), Origen's pupil and successor, collected a great library which survived until the Arab invasions of the seventh century.

In Palestine at large Christianity survived chiefly in cities and towns with predominantly Gentile populations. The Council of Nicaea in 325 was attended by bishops of Jerusalem, Neapolis (ancient Shechem), Sebaste (Samaria), Caesarea, Gadara, Ascalon, Nicopolis, Jamnia, Eleutheropolis, Maximianopolis, Jericho, Sebulon, Lydda, Azotus, Scythopolis, Aila, and Capitolinas. Evidence of Christian presence in other cities exists, but information is skimpy. Jewish Christians continued, too, in Pella, but Christianity did not survive in Jewish centers such as Tiberias, Diocaesarea, Nazareth, or Capernaum, where rabbinic influence prevailed.

Although Jerusalem, as Aelia Capitolina, lost most of its Christian as well as Jewish populace, it recouped much of its significance during the third and later centuries by virtue of Christian pilgrimages there. Alexander, bishop of Jerusalem, established a library in Aelia in the early third century. By the time Constantine was converted Jerusalem was drawing pilgrims from everywhere. By erecting churches on holy sites Constantine and his mother Helena encouraged a revival whose outcome was the restoration of Jerusalem to a select status alongside Rome, Constantinople, Antioch, and Alexandria at the Council of Constantinople in 381.

Christianity gained a stronger hold in Phoenicia, particularly in coastal cities with largely Greek populaces. Eleven bishops from Phoenicia—Tyre, Plotemais, Damascus, Sidon, Tripolis, Paneas, Berytus (Beirut), Palmyra, Alassus, Emesa, and Antaradus—attended the Council of Nicaea. The center was, of course, Tyre, the leading manufacturing and trading city in the East. The bishop of Tyre played a major role in a Palestinian synod convened to deal with the date of observing Easter. During the persecution under Diocletian, Tyre suffered numerous martyrdoms. Tyre was to Phoenicia what Caesarea was to Palestine.

In Coele-Syria Antioch remained the chief Christian city. Most bishops had Greek names—Euodius, Ignatius, Heron, Cornelius, Eros, Theophilus, Maximinus, Serapion, Asclepiades, Philetus, Zebinus, Babylas, Fabius, Demetrianus, Paul, Domnus, Timaeus, Cyrillus, and Tyrannus—indicating a predominantly Gentile constituency in the church. Antioch rivaled Alexandria as a center of Christian learning under the presbyters Malchion, Dorotheus, and Lucian. Lucian was the teacher of Arius. Antioch took part in numerous theological controversies—Montanist, Origenist, Novatianist, as well as Arian. When Rome could not decide between Cornelius and Novatian, they sought the counsel of Fabius of Antioch, Dionysius of Alexandria, and Cyprian of Carthage. Antioch also mediated between the Greek and Latin West and Syriac East. And it hosted numerous synods during the late-third and fourth centuries. The synod which tried Paul of Samosata, bishop of Antioch, in 268 drew no less than seventy or eighty bishops from all provinces stretching from Pontus to Egypt. According to the unflattering description of Paul supplied by Eusebius, the bishop of Antioch had by this time taken on the customs and manners of a high public official. Paul had close ties with the royal family of Palmyra. In the late fourth century Chrysostom estimated that half of the 200,000 citizens (excluding slaves and children) belonged to the chief church. It would be safe to guess that by 313 anywhere between one-fourth and one-half of the populace had become Christian.

Little is known of Christianity in Syria outside of Antioch. By 313 numerous other cities had churches of some size. Bishops came to Nicaea from twenty-one of these—Antioch, Seleucia, Laodicea, Apamea, Raphanaae, Hierapolis, Germanicia, Samosata, Doliche, Balaneae, Gabula, Zeugma, Larisa, Epiphania, Arethusa, Neocaesarea, Cyrrhus, Gindaron, Arethusa, Arbokadama, and Gabbala. Two country bishops (*chorepiskopoi*) also attended, attesting that the spread covered most of the province.

To the East Edessa was the center of Syriac-speaking Christianity. Although the legendary correspondence between King Abgar of Edessa and Jesus and the *Doctrine of Addai* (Thaddaeus) conjectured apostolic foundations of the church in Edessa, solid evidence for Christianity is lacking until the third century. One of the first widely known figures was Bardaisan or Bardesanes, a native of Edessa who fled to Armenia around 216. Converted about 179 C.E., he and his followers composed a large number of hymns in Syriac as a means of disseminating an astrological fatalism. Although not properly classified as a Gnostic, Bardaisan shared the Gnostic belief that Christ was not truly human and rejected the idea of bodily resurrection. By 300 Christianity had established itself strongly in Edessa. A reliable martyrology records the deaths of simple village folk in the great persecution under Diocletian. Bishop Qona began to construct the cathedral of Edessa, probably in 313, and initiated a line of bishops extending into the middle ages. Edessa was represented at Nicaea and at all important councils thereafter. One interesting peculiarity of the church in Edessa was the use of Tatian's *Diatessaron* until the time of Rabbula (ca. 420).

Outside of Edessa Christianity did not have strong representation in Mesopotamia and the East. Bishops of Nisibis, Resaina, Macedonopolis, and Persa, all in the vicinity of Edessa, attended the Council of Nicaea. The *Chronicle of Arbela*, a sixth century work, recorded the founding of churches in numerous cities in Mesopotamia and Persia during the third century, a fact confirmed by the martyrdoms during the Persian persecution of the fourth century. Constantine's conversion aroused suspicion among the Sassanids that Christians were subversives. According to Origen, the Apostle Thomas evangelized Parthia and Andrew Scythia. The third century *Acts of Thomas* ascribed the evangelization of northwest India to Thomas. Although these traditions have little credibility, they would indicate there were Christians in all three areas in the third century.

Christian churches also existed in Arabia, the region south of the Dead Sea, during this period. Hippolytus alluded to a Christian heretic whom he called "the Arabian Monoimus." Origen referred to bishoprics grouped together in a single synod. According to Eusebius, "a large number of bishops" disputed with Beryllus of Bostra about 240 when he questioned the concept of Christ's preexistence. Origen participated in two synods at Bostra, one of which was attended by fourteen bishops. In the latter bishops debated whether the soul expired and was resurrected with the body. These disputes indicate a continuing semitic influence on the theology of the area which countered hellenistic perspectives. About the mid-third century Arabian Christians, according to Dionysius of Alexandria, sought assistance from Rome. Bishops from Philadelphia, Esbus, Sodom, Bostra, and Beritana (whose location is unknown) participated in the Council of Nicaea.

As in the preceding era, so too in this one Asia Minor supplied Christianity with its most fertile field. Maximinus Daza's edicts against

Christians declared that "almost all persons" had gone over to Christianity in Asia Minor (Eusebius, H.E. 9.9). Lucian of Antioch cited "whole cities" which had become Christian by the time of this persecution, a statement which can be corroborated from other sources.

Paul's home province of Cilicia sent three bishops to the synod of Ancyra in 314 and nine, along with one "country bishop," to the Council of Nicaea in 325. Many Christians from other areas were deported to the mines of Cilicia during the persecution under Diocletian.

Cappadocia was deeply permeated by Christianity in the third century. Tertullian reported a persecution in the province between 180 and 196. In 258 Gothic invaders dragged off many Christian captives, including some clergy and the parents of Ulfilas, the apostle to the Goths. Caesarea, the metropolis of Cappadocia, gained esteem through Alexander, a bishop who later became bishop of Jerusalem, and Firmilian, bishop from ca. 230 until ca. 268. Alexander hosted Clement after he fled Alexandria during the persecution of Septimius Severus. Both he and Firmilian were admirers and supporters of Origen and transmitted Origen's influence to their native province. Cappadocia sent seven bishops and five "country bishops" to Nicaea, testimony surely of its vitality. Through Ulfilas, moreover, Cappadocia was home base for evangelization of the Goths.

In Armenia Christianity existed at least as early as Marcus Aurelius (161–180), for the Thundering Legion, which was composed largely of Christians, quartered in Armenia Minor. Dionysius of Alexandria (died ca. 264) wrote to "the brethren in Armenia, whose bishop is Meruzanes" (Eusebius, H.E. 6.46). The persecution of Licinius claimed the lives of forty martyrs in Sebaste, confirmation of the wide dissemination of the gospel throughout Armenia Minor. Bishop Eulalius of Sebaste and Euethius of Satala attended the Council of Nicaea. In 300 C.E. Armenia Major became the first country officially to adopt Christianity. Curiously the evangelization came from two sources—the Greek Christianity of Caesarea in Cappadocia and the Syriac Christianity of Edessa. The "apostle to Armenia" par excellence was Gregory the Illuminator, who fled to Caesarea due to a Persian persecution and returned to win over King Tiridates (261–317), who evidently adopted Christianity as a bulwark against the Persians. After the conversion of the king Gregory proceeded systematically to overthrow the Zoroastrian priesthood and to install Christian bishops.

In Pontus Christianity had a firm grip by 170. Lucian of Samosata charged that "the whole country is full of atheists and Christians" (*Alexander Abonuteichos* 25.38). Hippolytus reported that a millenarian caused numerous farmers to desert their fields and sell their property in expectation of the return of Jesus a year hence (*Commentary on Daniel*). Bishops from Pompeiopolis, Ionopolis, and Amastris in Pontus and from Amasia, Comana and Zela in Diospontus attended the Council of Nicaea. Amasia was recognized as an episcopal see and metropolis as early as Greogry Thaumaturgus.

In Bithynia Christianity existed from apostolic times with Nicomedia as the capital. Origen spent time there about 240 C.E. When Diocletian's persecution began, the imperial court itself was full of Christians. The rescript of Maximinus Daza attests the large number of Christians in Nicomedia and throughout the province. Both Hierocles and the other unnamed attacker of Christians lived in Bithynia. Bishops from Nicaea, Chalcedon, Kius, Prusa, Apollonia, Prusias, Adriani, Caesarea, and Nicomedia and two "country bishops" from Bithynia attended the Council of Nicaea. Novatianists had numerous churches both in Pontus and in Bithynia.

Christianity was also strong in Phrygia when "the New Prophecy" broke out in the late second century, for it met stern resistance. This movement quickly spilled over into Galatia and Asia. Large synods attended by bishops from Phrygia,

Galatia, Cilicia, and Cappadocia were held at Iconium and Synnada between 230 and 235 to discuss the validity of heretical baptisms.

The province of Asia continued to be the focal point of Christianity in Asia Minor. Polycrates, bishop of Ephesus, took the lead against Victor of Rome during the Easter controversy. He invoked an origin and heritage equal to Rome's: Philip and John and Polycarp and other martyrs. Then, he added, "I, too, Polycrates, hold by the tradition of my relatives, some of whom I have closely followed; for seven of my relatives were bishops, and I am the eighth" (Eusebius, H.E. 5.24). Though this controversy resulted in a decline of Asian influence, the number of Christians there remained large. Lucian reported that people came "from several towns of Asia" to tend to Christian prisoners. Irenaeus, himself a native of Smyrna, gives evidence of the close ties between Christians of this province and of Rome and Lyons. When the terrible pogrom claimed many lives in Lyons and Vienne in 177, they communicated with the churches of Asia. Asia and Caria sent no less than sixteen bishops to Nicaea.

Little specific information is available on Christianity in the three southernmost provinces of Asia Minor (Lycia, Pamphylia, and Isauria), but they sent no less than twenty-five bishops to Nicaea. One notable figure in Lycia was Methodius, bishop of Olympus, martyred during the persecution under Diocletian. He assailed Origen's teaching about resurrection but upheld his emphasis on free will against the Gnostics.

There is no information about the state of Christianity on the island of Crete after the second century, and no Cretan bishop attended Nicaea. Bishops from Rhodes, Cos, Lemnos, and Corcyra, however, the other islands, attended. Three bishops of Cyprus (Salamis, Paphos, and Trimithus) came to the Council.

The Greek peninsula, unlike Asia Minor, did not provide a uniformly good field for Christianity. The hold was strong in Thrace and in cities such as Athens, Corinth, and Thessalonica, but most of the peninsula had a thin Christian population before Constantine's conversion. Thracian Christianity was tied closely to Bithynia. Origen mentioned the Athenian church in his treatise *Against Celsus* (248) as "a peaceable and orderly body" not deserving comparison with the refractory civic assembly. He spoke of Corinth in a similar vein. Several bishops from the peninsula were present at Nicaea. These included Pistus, bishop of Athens, and Alexander, Metropolitan of Thessalonica.

Christianity was beginning to gain a strong foothold in the Balkans in the provinces of Moesia, Dacia, Pannonia, and Dalmatia by the end of this period, for the acts of martyrs recorded numerous martyrdoms during the persecution under Diocletian. Few bishops from Moesia and Pannonia attended the Council of Nicaea, signifying probably there were few to attend. Pannonia could claim at least one notable writer in Victorinus of Pettau.

Christianity was thriving in Rome, middle and lower Italy, Sicily and Sardinia by 325. Even though only four western bishops (Hosius of Cordova, Marcus of Calabria, Caecilian of Carthage, and Nicasius of Duja in Gaul) attended the Council of Nicaea, the evidence of western synods at Carthage, Elvira in Spain, Rome, and Arles in Gaul leave little doubt of the strength of Rome. By the time of Fabian (236–250) the Roman church had increased sufficiently to necessitate two major organizational changes: creation of a lower clergy with five ranks and division of the Roman church into seven districts corresponding to the ancient quarters, each under a deacon. Cornelius (251–253) reported that the Roman rolls included forty-six presbyters, seven deacons, seven subdeacons, forty-two acolytes, fifty-two exorcists, readers and doorkeepers, and 1,500 widows or otherwise indigent persons. Forty-six presbyters may indicate the number of congregations in the city, and the total Christian constituency must have been over 30,000. A synod convened in connection with the Novatianist schism was attended by sixty bishops and a still greater number of presbyters and deacons. Dionysius of Rome (259–268) established a system of dioceses under the bishop of Rome and possibly began the division of Rome into something like parishes. Even before Constantine, emperors began to show some deference to the church because of its obvious influence. Gallienus (260–268) inaugurated a long reign of peace, perhaps yielding to pleas from his own household. Even the usurper Maxentius feigned friendliness to Christianity "in order to cajole the people of Rome" (Eusebius, H.E. 8.14), though he soon took off the mask and became a persecutor.

Under Roman influence middle and lower Italy had at least a hundred bishoprics by about 250. Upper Italy, however, was less hospitable to the Christian faith. By about 300 C.E. the only known bishoprics were located in Milan, Aquileia, Brescia, Verona, Bologna, and Imola. During the last half of the fourth century, Ambrose of Milan still looked on the province of Aemilia and Liguria as pioneer mission fields.

Missionary efforts of bishops like Irenaeus of Lyons were effective in Gaul and provinces bordering on it. From lists of bishops at synods in Rome (313) and Arles (314) and martyrologies it is possible to determine that there were bishops at Vienne, Arles, Marseilles, Vaison, Nizza, Orange, Apta Julia, Toulouse, Lyons, Autun, Rouen, Die, Paris, Sens, Bordeaux, Eauze, Mende, Bourges, Treves, and Rheims. Nevertheless, like northern Italy, much of Gaul remained unevangelized until the late fourth century when Martin of Tours (ca. 375–ca. 397) carried out his remarkable work.

Christian communities existed in Germany as early as 185 C.E. when Irenaeus remarked that the churches planted there adhered to the same kind of tradition as those in Gaul (*Against Heresies* 1.10). A bishop of Cologne attended the synod of Rome in 313, a deacon the synod of Arles in 314; yet the Roman historian Ammianus Marcellinus called the church in Cologne a "little gathering" still in 355. Evidence for other churches is post-Constantinian. There is, however, evidence for congregations in Augsburg and Regensburg in what was then the Roman province of Rhaetia, which separated Germany and Italy.

It is impossible to determine when Christianity first penetrated the British Isles. Pious legend ascribed the conversion of the first Britons to Joseph of Arimathea and another to missionaries sent in 167 by Pope Eleutherus at the request of Lucius, King of the Britons, but such accounts cannot be given credence. The first of the Church Fathers to include Britons among peoples who had accepted Christ was Tertullian, about 200 C.E. Fifty years later, Origen referred numerous times to Christians in Britain. By the time of Constantine there were numerous churches. Three British bishops (of London, York, and Lincoln) attended the Synod of Arles in 314, but none seems to have been present at Nicaea.

Christianity was thriving in Spain by the time Constantine issued the Edict of Milan in 313. Both Irenaeus (185) and Tertullian (ca. 210) mentioned the existence of churches in Spain. By the mid-third century Cyprian's reply to a letter from Spanish bishops alluded to Christian communities in Leon, Astorga, Merida, and Sargossa—all cities having large Latin communities. No fewer than thirty-seven Spanish bishops signed the canons of the Synod of Elvira (modern Granada) in 305. The range of issues touched on by the canons suggests rapidly expanding membership in the churches which was generating huge problems in sorting out the demands of Christian faith. A canon disallowing martyrdom for those who attacked images would point to a buildup of a violent campaign against paganism, only possible if Christians constituted the majority of the populace in some areas.

Christianity blossomed in North Africa during this period. While Proconsular Africa was reaching its peak of prosperity during the third century, the churches there rivaled those in Asia Minor for growth. Tertullian's writings presupposed a large and strong Christian populace in Carthage, the capital city, and its environs. The deaths of several Christians in Scilli, a town probably located in Numidia, indicate a strong Christian presence there by 180. Tertullian also mentions persecution of Christians in Mauretania. As one might expect, Christianity made its greatest gains among the Latin population at first, but it also won converts among the Punic (Phoenician) settlers who preceded the Roman colonists and even among the Berbers, for the Donatist schism represented in part a native protest against the Latins.

Carthage, of course, remained the center of African Christianity. Between the time of Tertullian and the time of Cyprian (converted in 248) the church grew rapidly in the capital city of Africa. Seventy African and Numidian bishops attended a synod convened by Agrippinus (no later than 218) to discuss the issue of heretical baptisms, ninety a synod convened by Cyprian's predecessor Donatus (no later than 240), eighty-seven a synod convened by Cyprian himself in 256 or 257. Cyprian's treatise concerning *The Lapsed* shows that Christianity had penetrated all classes of society and obtained a kind of legal status. The Church included enough persons of wealth to contribute 100,000 sesterces toward the ransoming of Numidian Christians captured by brigands. The Decian persecution understandably took a heavy toll in the number of persons who apostatized during persecution.

The African churches enjoyed a second period of rapid growth between 260 and 303. Once again, the persecution of Diocletian, although lasting only a couple of years, took a heavy toll in both casualties and apostates, for, by this time, Christianity stood on the verge of converting most of the populace. The number of bishoprics nearly doubled between the death of Cyprian in 258 and the outbreak of persecution. No less than 270 Donatist bishops assembled in Carthage in 330. Like Asia Minor, North Africa had a profusion of bishops, while Italy and Egypt had few.

In Egypt Christianity evidently had an earlier start, but the church there did not emerge into the clear light of day until 180 (Demetrius). The famous school of Alexandria began to thrive about the time Clement arrived. During the persecution under Septimius Severus in 202, Christians were rounded up not only in Alexandria but also dragged there "from Egypt and all of Thebes" (Eusebius, H.E. 6.1). When Origen wrote his reply to Celsus in 248, however, he still had to admit that the number of Christians was "extremely scanty" by comparison with the total population; yet he was witnessing sufficient success to contemplate the triumph of Christianity even among the affluent. Although Christianity began among Greek-speaking Christians, it soon spread among those who spoke Coptic, necessitating translation of scriptures into that language, probably as early as the third century. Significant of the growth in the late third and early fourth century, Alexander reported the assembling of almost a hundred bishops for a synod around 320, despite the fact that the Egyptian churches opted for fewer bishops.

Missionaries and Their Methods

Missionary methods did not undergo any significant alteration during this period. Church planting and churches assembling and worshipping and pursuing the many facets of corporate life remained the lynchpin for the mission. Two long periods when persecution virtually ceased (203–250 and 260–303) permitted the churches to operate more openly and to engage in evangelization with increased effect. The sudden flurry of persecution which burst forth under Diocletian resulted in the destruction of numerous buildings erected during the preceding peaceful interlude.

Itinerants still spread the word. Origen, for instance, knew of persons "who make it their business to itinerate not only through cities, but even villages and country houses that they might make converts to God" (*Against Celsus* 3.9). Soldiers, sailors, merchants, and travelers of all kinds carried the word wherever they went.

Evangelistic schools also continued their efforts. In Alexandria Clement adapted his appeals and instruction to the wealthy and well educated who increasingly inquired concerning Christianity. In *Protrepticus* or *Exhortation to the Greeks* he urged pagan hearers to forsake their worship of vain and lifeless idols and to worship the Truth, the Logos, who became human for the salvation of humankind. He derided pagan religions for immorality and unreasonableness in worshipping idols. Idol statues, he insisted, are only blocks of wood and stone. Even philosophers failed to adhere to the Truth, though some moved in the right direction. Plato, for instance, argued for one God. More reliable were the Old Testament prophets. Ultimately, however, it is to the Word that one must come because the Word has brought all truth. He is the one human beings must imitate. In *Paedagogos* or *The Instructor* Clement offered converts guidance for Christian living. Above all, he enjoined, Christians must follow the Word, who is *the* Instructor, as the unerring Guide. They must come as little children to the Paedagogue, the model of the true life, both human and divine. Looking at specific items, he argued like a good Stoic for the golden mean—in the use of foods, drink, household furnishings, conduct at parties, speech, adornments, sleep, sexual indulgence, clothing, jewelry, and everything else. Christianity in Alexandria had obviously moved up the social ladder, enough so that Clement addressed himself also to an explanation as to how a rich person could be saved even though Jesus' words (Mark 10:17-31) seemed to leave little hope. Jesus' words, spiritually or allegorically interpreted, urged good works rather than literal dispensing of wealth. In *Stromateis* Clement carried his hearers beyond the level of "faith" to the realm of "gnosis," mystical knowledge, perfection in love. The "gnostic" alone is truly pious.

When Clement fled Alexandria during the persecution under Septimius Severus, Origen, then only seventeen, continued his educational, evangelistic, and apologetic efforts. In 232, however, he moved permanently to Caesarea, where he carried on a dialogue with both Jews and Gentiles and trained a cadre of missionary personnel. A major feature of his apology to Judaism was the *Hexapla*, a six-column Old Testament indicating points at which the Greek versions differed from the Hebrew. After supplying the Hebrew and a Greek transliteration in columns 1 and 2, Origen published current Greek versions proceeding from the most literal ones by the Jew Aquila and the Jewish Christian Symmachus to the less literal ones of the Septuagint and Theodotion. At the request of a wealthy sponsor named Ambrose he replied point by point to the attack on Christianity made by Celsus. Although seventy years old by Origen's day, Celsus's *True Discourse* continued to unsettle conscientious Christians enough that Ambrose thought it should have a reply. More important still from the point of view of the Christian mission, Origen won over and inspired persons like Gregory of Neocaesarea and his brother Athenodorus to return to their native lands as missionaries. Gregory turned out to be one of early Christianity's most innovative missionaries.

Born of pagan parents in Neocaesarea in Pontus around 213, he was trained in law. Brought (as Gregory thought) "providentially" in 233 to Berytus (Beirut) as companions for their sister, whose husband had already been employed there as a lawyer by the governor of Palestine, to engage in further legal studies, Athenodorus and Gregory proceeded on to Caesarea where they fell into Origen's net. Although they intended to extract themselves and return either to Berytus or Pontus, they could not escape Origen's personal attentions and persuasive arguments from Greek philosophy. "And thus," Gregory wrote in his *Panegyric*, "like some spark lighting upon our inmost soul, love was kindled and burst into flame within us—a love at once for the Holy Word, the most lovely object of all, who attracts all irresistibly toward Himself by His unutterable beauty, and to this man, His friend and advocate." Like a skillful farmer, Origen cultivated his students for philosophy, insisting over and over that they probe more deeply into the nature of things. Through physics and geometry and astronomy he led them toward the study of morality and the love of virtue. Diverting their attention from useless and harmful writings, he guided them through the labyrinth of Greek philosophies to the prophets and thence to God.

After five years under Origen's tutelage Gregory returned to his native city where he was reluctantly appointed bishop of the church. According to popular legends, he overwhelmed the pagan population by performing miracles (thus the surname Thaumaturgus, "Miracle Worker") such as the moving of a mountain and the drying up of a swamp. In reality he performed his evangelistic feats in much more ordinary ways. When Christian discipline disintegrated during the invasion of Pontus by the Goths in 253–254, he established grades or degrees of repentance which could restore order. An early biographer claimed that whereas there were but seventeen Christians in Pontus when he returned, when he died about 270 there were but seventeen pagans.

At the end of this period new approaches to evangelization emerged with the conversion of nations or peoples to the Christian faith through the conversion of their rulers. The first example was Armenia, supposedly won over through the work of Gregory the Illuminator (ca. 240–332). Reared as a Christian in Cappadocia, he returned to Armenia around 280 and succeeded in converting the King, Tiridates (ca. 238–314), to the Christian faith. The king proceeded to establish Christianity as the official religion of the country. Gregory's son Aristakes, who succeeded him as bishop, attended the Council of Nicaea.

Emphasis upon the miraculous in accounts of Christian missionary endeavors was not uncommon from apostolic times on and seems to have increased as Christians came more and more into contact with the barbarians. Claims of healing, prophecy, and other phenomena associated with the effort to win the heathen probably inspired anti-Christian treatises such as Philostratus's *Life of Apollonius of Tyana*, composed about 220. Hierocles, governor of Bithynia, wrote a second life about 303, which evoked a refutation by Eusebius of Caesarea. Pagans, too, could play the power game.

Chapter 12

The Seed of the Church

The success of Christianity in attracting not only persons of lower socioeconomic status but also those of the upper classes brought it increasingly into public view and precipitated a more serious danger. Whereas prior to this period harassment and persecution arose largely from popular hostility, now they came increasingly from official sources and took on a more systematic and organized form. The more Christianity succeeded, the more it threatened a deteriorating and unstable government. The emperors, however, were by no means consistent, and the churches took advantage of every respite to enlist converts and to solidify their own constituency. Four severe spates of persecution came as heavy blows, but they did not destroy the growing movement. The blood of martyrs only served, as Tertullian insisted, as "seed."

Septimius Severus's Severity

Christianity survived four major imperial efforts to suppress it and nullify its influence within the Empire. The first occurred under Septimius Severus (193–211). At the beginning of his reign, judging from Tertullian's writings, Christians stood in danger still of punishment for the name alone. They could be summarily condemned if they admitted to being Christians. If they did not admit their faith, they could be tortured or even executed. No punishment was too cruel—beheading, piercing with a red hot tong, crucifixion, feeding to wild beasts (Tertullian, *Apol.* 12). Some judges loved to dishonor Christian women rather than put them to death (*Apol.* 50). Although Septimius Severus, like his predecessor Commodus, showed some sympathy for Christianity early in his reign, he issued a severe edict against it in 202 during a sojourn in Palestine, prohibiting conversions either to Judaism or Christianity under threat of severe penalties (Spartian, *Severus*, 17). For the first time an emperor, evidently alarmed by rapid expansion, sought to put a stop to the growth of the Church by punishing converts and their converters.

Severus's edict struck hard at centers of Christian growth. It was implemented first in Alexandria, which Severus entered via Arabia in 202, where the famous school begun by Pantaenus flourished under the leadership of Clement. Clement, citing Jesus' instruction to flee from one city to another, took flight. Many other devout Christians, including Leonides, father of Origen, lost their lives. Origen would have followed his father in martyrdom save for the quick thinking of his mother in hiding his clothes. At age eighteen he succeeded Clement as head of the school. Many of his students, evidently adhering to his strictures against flight to avoid persecution, went bravely to their deaths (Eusebius, H.E. 6.1-3).

Severus's persecution also dealt a blow to Christianity in the Roman province of Africa, especially Carthage, a thriving center of growth. According to Tertullian, not only individuals but also congregations paid to escape persecution and martyrdom (*On Flight in Persecution*, 13). Tertullian, soon to join the Montanists, took a dim view of flight to avoid persecution. The names of many African martyrs are known. Most were ordinary saints like the catechumens Perpetua and Felicitas, whose unflinching faithfulness in the face of torture and death bears witness to the excellence of Christian formation in this period. The account of the *Passion of Saints Perpetua and Felicitas*, its Montanist flavor aside, sheds much light on the rigors of the persecution and the aid and support Christians provided the confessors. Two deacons, Tertius and Pomponius, tended the needs of Perpetua and her companions, giving their jailers money.

In the province of Asia the edict of Severus also claimed numerous victims. Although not as well documented as the African persecution, it coincided with the Montanist heyday and claimed many in that sect. Less is known of Severus's persecution in Rome and Gaul, but we do have evidence of martyrdom among the disciples of Irenaeus of Lyons if not of Irenaeus himself (Gregory of Tours, *History of the Franks* 1.27).

Thirty-Seven Years of Peace

Severus's son and successor Caracalla continued his father's effort at suppression of Christianity for only a few years. Persecution was especially bitter in Africa under Scapula Tertullus, the proconsul to whom Tertullian addressed his brief but strong letter. After 212 the churches enjoyed thirty-seven years of relative peace. Neither Elagabalus nor Alexander Severus wished to disturb Christians. Elagabalus viewed anything oriental, including Judaism and Christianity, useful in fostering his solar monotheism. Alexander Severus (222–235) not only tolerated but proved a benefactor of Christianity. His mother Mamme had studied Christianity and, during a stay at Antioch, received Origen with great

honors (Eusebius, H.E. 6.21). From her or Christians who filled his palace Alexander gained respect for Christian discipline and the maxims of the gospel, inscribing the Golden Rule on the facade of his palace and ordering it heralded during execution of criminals (Lampridius, *Alexander Severus* 51). He himself practiced syncretism, including in his pantheon statues of Alexander the Great, the more noble caesars, Apollonius of Tyana, Orpheus, Abraham, and Jesus (Lampridius 29)! According to his biographer Lampridius (43), he wanted to build a temple to Christ and elevate him to the rank of the gods. More important for the churches, Alexander permitted churches to hold title to property. Unfortunately the emperor's relative impotence as a ruler permitted still much popular violence against Christians.

A brief flurry of localized persecution under Alexander's successor Maximin (235–238) interrupted the calm. Maximin, alarmed by the number of Christians in the imperial household, directed his repression at church leaders as those responsible for teaching. In Rome authorities exiled Pontianus, bishop of Rome, and Hippolytus, a presbyter who separated from the Roman Church in 217, to Sardinia. Pontianus died as a result of tortures a year later. His successor Anteros may also have suffered martyrdom, dying after just over a month in office. In Caesarea Maximin summoned Ambrose, Origen's benefactor who had followed him from Alexandria, a scholarly priest named Prototectus and several others to Germany to appear before him. It was in these circumstances that Origen composed his *Exhortation to Martyrdom*, addressed to Ambrose. Ambrose, however, if he answered the summons at all, lived to tell about it, for he was still living in 247 or 249 during the reign of Philip (242–249), according to Jerome (*On Illustrious Men*, 54), "the first Christian emperor."

Philip, a native of Trachonitis in Transjordan, may have been born into a Christian family. His ruthless seizure of power from Gordian, however, caused Christians to look askance at him. When he sought to participate in the paschal vigil at Antioch, the bishop required him to do penance "on account of many charges made concerning him" (Eusebius, H.E. 6.34). Although Philip sought to improve public morality, he continued traditional religious observances, and we can see little of the effects of Christianity, save perhaps in the omission of gladiatorial combats. He, however, did issue a rescript declaring "a general amnesty which permits the return of exiles and deportees" (*Codex Just.* IX 51.7). Even more than Alexander Severus, Philip allowed Christians to be Christians. The Empress Otacilia Severa made no mystery of her faith. She corresponded with Origen, and according to Eusebius (H.E. 6.36), Origen wrote to both emperor and empress. Fabian, bishop of Rome, was permitted to retrieve the body of Pontianus and return it for burial in the cemetery of Callistus in Rome, an act dependent entirely on imperial permission. Origen's wide travels during the period bear witness to the favorable situation for Christianity's expansion. Success, however, resulted in a dampening of discipline that left the churches poorly prepared for the reversal of imperial favor under Decius (249–253) and Valerian (253–260).

Decius's Devastation

Partiality shown by Philip to Christianity evidently enraged pagans throughout the empire and precipitated a savage rebellion that led to his overthrow and death and replacement by Decius, a Pannonian serving as a commander of legions in Mysia and Pannonia. Dionysius, bishop of Alexandria, described how, a year before Philip's defeat at the hands of Decius, pagan mobs unleashed their fury against hapless Christians. Christians could not pass through any street or alley without risking life and limb. Only the intervention of imperial troops restored order during the remainder of Philip's reign (Eusebius, H.E. 6.41.1-11). Such outbursts doubtless took place throughout the Empire and prepared the

way for Decius's vicious edict against Christianity.

Like ancient predecessors, Decius could not distinguish loyalty to the ancestral gods from loyalty to the state. Reacting, Christians thought, against Philip (Eusebius, H.E. 6.39; Jerome, *Chron.* for the year 253; Rufinus, H.E. 6.29; Orosius, 7.21), he saw in this fast-growing religion a little empire within the Empire. Faced with severe threats from barbarians on the frontier, he sought to consolidate his control within, viewing Christianity as the major obstacle to that goal. There were a great number of Christian soldiers in the army, as even Tertullian conceded despite objections to Christians serving there (*Apol.* 37, 42; *On the Crown of the Soldier*). Yet Christians did act circumspectly regarding those aspects of military or public service which bore so heavily the imprint of the state cultus. Some groups such as Montanists took a still stronger and often belligerent stand against either, as Tertullian shows in his late Montanist treatise *On Idolatry*.

For the first time persecution arose not from religious fanaticism or popular hatred but from cold and calculated administrative logic designed to destroy Christianity as a fearful threat to the Empire. To kill all of them was impossible, given their numbers. The aim was to terrify by examples and thus frighten away any who would join them—using long prison terms, torture, temptations, seizure of children to be raised as pagans. Where Septimius Severus concentrated on converts and converters and Maximin on bishops and teachers, Decius ordered all citizens, not just Christians, to obtain a *libellus* stating they had poured a libation, offered a sacrifice, and eaten meat offered in sacrifice. Three types of punishments were prescribed—banishment, confiscation of property, and capital punishment. Judging by actual cases, local authorities could exercise considerable discretion in how they applied each. The number of deaths was relatively small since Decius sought to induce conformity and commitment and destroy Christianity's infrastructure rather than kill.

The Decian persecution had a far more devastating effect than earlier ones, partly because of its systematic, organized, and universal character, but more particularly because Christians converted during the long era of peace were unprepared for it. Having gotten accustomed to tolerance and, in some places, even favor, they would not have understood fully what constituted Christian commitment. Throughout the Empire, therefore, a considerable portion of the flock stepped forward voluntarily to offer sacrifices. Others obtained the required certificates by secret means to avoid outright apostasy. Leading bishops such as Cyprian in Carthage, himself a recent convert, and Dionysius of Alexandria went into hiding at the urging of fellow clergy and people, a decision that caused serious problems later on. Some other bishops and clergy shamelessly hastened to deny their faith, thus giving the authorities exactly what they sought—apostasy rather than martyrdom. At Saturnum Bishop Repostus led a group of his people to offer the sacrifice. Fortunatus, Jovinus and Maximus, three other bishops also gave in. According to Cyprian, Spanish bishops Basilides of Sargossa and Martial of Merida complied with some eagerness. Subsequently Basilides repented, sought restoration as a layman, and then tried to regain his office by appealing to Stephen, bishop of Rome, without telling him of his apostasy (Cyprian, *Ep.* 67.6).

Not all acted unfaithfully. There were notable martyrs. Although the Decian persecution did not single out bishops and other leaders, it turned in that direction as a way to force them to set an example of unfaithfulness. Since Decius left considerable leeway for local enforcement, however, persecution varied from place to place and so too did steadfastness. At Rome Fabian was martyred on January 20, 250, scarcely three months after Decius ascended the throne. Other Roman clergy and some lay persons received lengthy prison sentences designed to break their spirits. In

Africa, about which we have the most extensive information thanks to Cyprian's letters, persecution was particularly severe. Although Cyprian escaped for a time by taking advantage of connections in the upper echelons of society, others did not. Alongside a huge number of apostates were many others among both clergy and laity who offered faithful witness in prison as "confessors." Presbyters, deacons and lay persons alike risked imprisonment themselves to tend the physical and spiritual needs of the confessors. Despite such solicitude, a number perished of hunger or of other causes.

At Alexandria, where the revolt took place against Philip, Christians also suffered harsh treatment, especially at the hands of irate mobs anxious to see the edict of Decius enforced. Although Decius's edict achieved its aim here, too, among large numbers, it met resistance. Dionysius related the story of an old man named Julian who, enfeebled by gout, had to be carried by two others before the authorities. One of his helpers immediately capitulated, but the aged Julian and the other man, Eunus Cronion, refused to yield despite being carried on camels throughout the city and beaten. The mob finally burned them in quicklime. A soldier named Besas standing by as they were led away opposed their attackers and, after a vain battle, was beheaded (Eusebius, H.E. 6.41,14-16). On another occasion when an old man named Theophilus started to renounce his faith before the court, four soldiers ground their teeth, glared at him, made gestures, and ran to the prisoner's dock to say they were Christians. They so frightened the governor and judges, all of them marched out of the court with impunity (ibid., 22-23).

Many Egyptian Christians fled, like Dionysius, to regions almost as dangerous as Alexandria, wandering in deserts and mountains, and dying of hunger, thirst, cold, disease, robbers, or wild beasts (ibid., 6.42). Dionysius survived in a wild section of Libya until the persecution ended. In his absence four presbyters—Maximus, Dioscurus, Demetrius, and Lucius—and three dea-cons—Faustinus, Eusebius, and Chaeremon—carried on in Alexandria.

Martyrdoms also occurred in other places—Italy, Gaul, Greece, Asia Minor—but evidence is scanty and unreliable. In Antioch Babylas, who had refused the Emperor Philip permission to celebrate Easter before doing penance, died in prison (Eusebius, H.E. 6.39.4) or, as Chrysostom reported (*Saint Babylas* 11), was beheaded. At Caesarea in Palestine Alexander, an intimate friend of Origen, also died in prison (Eusebius, H.E. 6.39.2). Origen, then in his sixties, survived severe treatment. Obviously hoping so eminent a figure would renounce the faith, the authorities stretched his feet four notches apart in the stocks "for many days," threatened him with fire, and inflicted numerous other cruelties. The great Adamantius (Flint) did not flinch, but such tortures hastened his death in 254 or 255.

Fortunately Decius's devastation did not last long. By mid-251 most prisoners had been freed and persecution had ceased. Decius had evidently concluded by this time that the Empire had worse enemies than Christians. Although he did not revoke his edict, he ceased to incite magistrates and governors to enforce it. Meantime, his attention turned again to the Gothic threat on the Danube. The Goths had already sacked Thrace and were threatening Macedonia. Departing from Rome in the spring of 251, Decius perished soon afterwards along with his sons in a battle against the Goths.

Although Decius's successor, Gallus, revived the persecution, Christians proved better equipped to face it. Besides experience of persecution, an Empire-wide plague, during which Christians distinguished themselves by caring for the dying, toughened them. In Alexandria, according to Dionysius (in Eusebius, H.E. 7.22), while pagans fled abandoning even their dearest, Christians tended not only to their own but to their neigh-bors as well. In Carthage Cyprian rallied his decimated "troops" to imitate the example of

Christ in pouring out their lives for others (Pon-tius, *Life of Cyprian* 9-10). In Cappadocia terri-fied pagans appealed to Gregory Thaumaturgus for prayers and "a great number gave themselves to Christ" (Gregory of Nyssa, *Life of S. Gregory Th.*). Unfortunately most pagans blamed Chris-tians for this calamity as they did for others. In Carthage the cry went up, "Cyprian to the lion!"

Gallus, frightened by the progress of the epidemic, wanted to revitalize worship of the gods and thus commanded celebration of solemn sacrifices in all cities. Like his mentor Decius, he attacked first the bishop of Rome, Cornelius, shipping him off into exile in Centumcelles, where he died in June, 253. He also dispatched Cornelius's successor, Lucius, elected in July. Contrary to their behavior under Decius, Roman Christians surprised pagans by imitating their leader in seeking exile, prison, or martyrdom. Some of the lapsed of the Decian persecution proved boldest, many shedding their blood as martyrs. Cyprian repudiated Demetrian's charge that Christians provoked the gods and thence caused all kinds of maladies to befall people. Dionysius of Alexandria, likewise, reproved the emperor for persecuting those who sustained the Empire by their prayers. Gallus did not have long to pursue his policy of persecution. He and his son Volusian were killed by the legate of Pan-nonia, Emilian, who had halted a Gothic inva-sion. When Volusian's own forces revolted and killed him, Valerian, dispatched earlier by Gallus to stop Volusian, was acclaimed emperor by his troops. Wanting widespread popular support, he immediately halted the persecution of Christians.

Valerian's Vindictiveness

After four years of peace Christians did not anticipate the severe persecution initiated by Valerian in 257. Dionysius of Alexandria re-marked that the emperor's household "was full of devout believers and a church of God" (in Euse-bius, H.E. 7.10.3). A ruler who tended to rely on advice of intimates, early on he not only tolerated but showed partiality toward Christianity. What, therefore, changed his mind? Several controversies rocked the churches—the Novatianist schism; efforts of Spanish bishops of Leon and Merida labeled *libellatici* to dethrone Stephen, the bishop of Rome, and retain their sees; the rebaptismal controversy—and could have caused a shift of opinion. More likely, however, the key issue was financial. In documents relative to his persecution Christianity was denounced for its powerful hierarchy, extensive properties, and wealth. At the time of Cornelius the Roman Church cared for 1500 indigents. In Carthage Cyprian raised 100,000 sesterces to redeem captives taken by nomadic tribes in Numidia. Such charities astounded pagans and aroused suspicions of sinister hoards of money that weakened the already flagging economy. The question of money figured heavily in Valerian's attack on the churches. Before Valerian's edict he interrogated and put to death a wealthy family of Christians noted for their charities. His counselors apparently convinced him that the material prosperity of the churches, if tolerated too long, posed a real danger to the Empire.

Valerian's edict, unlike Decius', did not demand a denial of faith but sought rather to secure a recommitment to the national religion by sacrificing to the gods of the Empire. Christians could continue to worship Christ so long as they also took part in official ceremonies and burned incense at the feet of the gods—kind of a pledge of allegiance. In addition, the edict sought to dissolve Christian control over cemeteries, the legal base for Christian assemblies. Instead of making general application, it named only bishops, presbyters, and deacons for submission. Valerian sought to make neither numerous victims nor apostates. He wanted, rather, to obtain an official adherence to the gods of the state by way of the submission of the chief leaders in the churches. The laity would run into trouble only if they tried to frequent the cemeteries or hold assemblies. Refusal to swear allegiance to the

gods was punishable by exile, visiting cemeteries or holding assemblies punishable by death. In the latter Valerian surpassed the intolerance of Decius and Gallus.

Valerian's first edict resulted in the exile of some of Christianity's most cultured and well educated leaders. Cyprian, the transcript of whose hearing before the Proconsul Paternus has been preserved, was exiled for a time and then put to death. When the proconsul asked why he hadn't followed the emperor's directive, he replied, "I am a Christian and a bishop. I don't know any gods except the one true God who has made heaven and earth, the sea and all that they contain. It is this God that we Christians serve. It is to him that we pray day and night, for ourselves and for all persons, and for the safety of the emperors (Valerian and Gallienus) themselves." When he refused to budge from this decision, Paternus sentenced him to be exiled to Curubis. Cyprian, trained in law, readily accepted this order, but he refused to divulge the names of his presbyters on the grounds that Roman law forbade *delatio*. The proconsul declared that he would find them and noted that the rest of the edict prohibited holding assemblies and entering cemeteries on penalty of death (*Acts of Saint Cyprian*). The exile, according to Cyprian's biographer Pontius, was not harsh. The authorities, however, arrested other bishops, presbyters, and deacons as well as lay persons and sentenced most to the mines, evidently because they continued to meet or use cemeteries in contravention of the edict, some to death. Cyprian corresponded with confessors from exile, encouraging and counseling them in their frightful situation. Judging by letters exchanged, the prisoners were whipped, branded on the forehead, chained to avoid escape, and forced to labor long hours extracting gold and silver without adequate food or bodily care.

Dionysius of Alexandria received a more lenient treatment at the hands of Aemelian, the prefect of Egypt. Accompanied by a presbyter named Maximus, three deacons (Faustus, Eusebius, and Chaermon), and a visiting "brother" from Rome, he rejected the prefect's demand that they hold no more assemblies, saying, "We must obey God rather than human beings" (Acts 5:29). Aemilian sentenced him to exile in a little village named Cephro in Libya, threatening due punishment either for assembling or frequenting cemeteries. When Dionysius gathered a flock in Cephro, Aemelian transferred him to "rougher and more Libyan-like places," but these turned out to be still more favorable for gathering with other Christians. In his letter (in Eusebius, H.E. 7.12) Dionysius proceeded to list a whole row of indignities heaped on the faithful—imprisonment, confiscation, proscription, plundering of goods, loss of dignities, etc. Those brought to trial for violation of the edict usually were tortured and put to death.

Valerian toughened his edict in 258. In a rescript sent the Roman senate he ordered that "bishops and priests and deacons should be put to death immediately; senators and outstanding men and Roman knights should lose their rank and also be deprived of their goods and, if, after this, they still persevered as Christians, they should be decapitated; matrons should have their goods confiscated and be sent into exile; members of the imperial household who had confessed either before or now, should have their goods confiscated and be sent as prisoners to the emperor's estates" (Cyprian, Ep. 80). The emperor aimed to bring Christianity down from the top.

The new edict resulted almost immediately in the death of Sixtus, bishop of Rome for one year, on August 6, 258, and four deacons. According to early legend, when the Roman prefect ordered one of the surviving deacons, Lawrence, to gather all of the treasures of the Church and have them ready to be collected at a certain time, Lawrence filled the church with the poor. "These," he said, "are the treasures of the Church." The prefect ordered him roasted alive on a grill (Ambrose, *Duties*, 2.28). The schismatic bishop Hippolytus,

a confessor during the persecution of Maximin, also suffered martyrdom. In Africa, Galerius Maximus, succeeding Paternus as proconsul, recalled Cyprian from exile in Curubus and confined him to a residence in Carthage. On August 24, 258 the proconsul surprised a great number of believers of every age at worship and summarily had them decapitated or, according to Prudentius, buried alive in a lime pit (*On the Crown* 3.76-87). A short time afterwards he summoned Cyprian and, when the bishop refused to repudiate his faith, sentenced him to be beheaded.

In this persecution, unlike the Decian, the faithful did not apostatize *en masse*. To the contrary in this instance, as Cyprian thanked God for the sentence, a multitude cried out, "We, too, we want to be beheaded with him." Because the execution took place in a level area, many climbed trees to witness. Others placed handkerchiefs on the ground under his bowed head in order the catch drops of blood.

Cyprian's martyrdom flashed the signal for persecution throughout Africa. This time, most remained firm in their commitment. Indeed, in Africa hysteria may have impelled some deliberately to seek martyrdom in imitation of Cyprian's example. The persecution was more violent still in the neighboring province of Numidia, where nomadic tribes threatened and heightened Roman fears of Christianity. The authorities enforced the letter of the second edict, recalling many exiles to put them to death. In Caesarea, according to Eusebius (H.E. 7.12), three persons presented themselves to the imperial legate and were fed to wild beasts. Here and there, some did lapse, but we find few references of this type in the Valerian era. In Antioch a presbyter named Sapricius, for instance, boldly refusing to honor the edict and proclaiming faith in Christ, was sentenced to be decapitated. An old Christian named Nicephorus begged him to reconsider and, when Sapricius remained silent, asked the authorities to impose the death sentence on him.

In the summer of 258 Valerian headed east to head the campaign against the Neo-Persian or Sassanid armies threatening to overrun Asia Minor, leaving Gallienus in charge of the West. A disorganized and weakened army left the northern frontier exposed to barbarians. In north Africa Berbers continued to create havoc. While both emperors were engaged in wars on different fronts, the Boradi and then the Goths invaded Asia Minor. Valerian succeeded in preventing a union of Gothic and Persian forces but could do little more. Leading an army half-decimated by famine and disease, he suffered a humiliating defeat at the hands of Shapur and was taken captive to spend the rest of his years in chains as a personal slave of the Persian king. Christians looked on this as a just retribution for the vicious persecution he had inflicted on them.

Forty Years of Peace

Very soon after receiving news of his father's capture, Gallienus rescinded his edicts against the churches and, according to Eusebius, "directed the bishops to perform in freedom their customary duties" (H.E., 7.13). For the first time since Nero Christianity became a *religio licita*, permitted to reclaim churches and cemeteries, the former having been sold and the latter merely closed by authorities. The Edict of Milan in 313 granted no more than this. What Gallienus's motives were cannot be definitely established. Some point to his Neoplatonism, others to the influence of his wife, Salonina, believed to have been a Christian; but evidence is scanty.

Christianity fared well under the so-called Thirty Tyrants who shared Gallienus's rule in different parts of the Empire. Where persecution occurred, it was due to local hostility or confusion about Christian legal status. One incident occurred while Macrian, a usurper, still ruled in the East. A soldier named Marinus stationed at Caesarea in Palestine stood next in line for appointment as a centurion. Another soldier who coveted the position stepped forward and denounced him as unworthy because he was a Christian. The tribune Achaeus gave Marinus three hours to decide whether he would sacrifice to the gods as required of officers in the army. Theotecnus, bishop of Caesarea, took him to the church and, placing a copy of the Gospels before him, told him to choose between the sword at his side and the scriptures. Without hesitation he chose the latter. When he returned to the tribunal and declared his faith, he was beheaded (Eusebius, H.E. 7.15). In Alexandria Emilian, the prefect who had sent Dionysius into exile, delayed the application of Gallienus's edict during a brief coup attempt, but his revolt was quickly squelched. Christians once again gained popular support through heroic deeds during a plague that struck the city at the time.

For more than forty years (260–304) Christians enjoyed only relative and not unqualified peace. Under Claudius (268–270), a Dalmatian, Gallienus's edict remained in effect, but the Senate may have expressed its hatred of Gallienus by making Christians expiatory victims for a war against the Goths (in 269), for Rome and Italy were the only areas from which came reports of martyrdom. Aurelian (270–275), however, intending to restore both religious and imperial unity by way of Mithraic solar monotheism, found Christianity standing in his path. In the late fourth century Mithraism, a cult in which Aurelian's mother was a priestess at Sirmium in Pannonia, was the most widespread form of solar monotheism, especially in the camps along the Danube. Valerian erected a temple of the sun on the Quirinal in 274 that surpassed all others in magnificence and proclaimed the Sol Invictus "lord and master of the Empire." Despite Christian unwillingness to be merged into his syncretistic religion, Aurelian did not begin persecution until his later years. In 272, as a matter of fact, he forced Paul of Samosata, renounced for heresy by a council of bishops in 268, to relinquish church properties to "those in communion with the bishops of Italy and the bishop of Rome"

(Eusebius, H.E. 7.30.19), an indication of Christianity's standing at the time. Aurelian evidently initiated some persecution during a foray through Gaul, threatened by several barbarian tribes, on his return from the East in 274, but accounts are not reliable. If he issued a general edict, it has not survived and Aurelian was assassinated in March, 275 before his edict could have had widespread effect. In the seven month interregnum following his death, however, the still predominantly pagan senate continued persecuting Christians in Rome and its environs on the charge that they abandoned and led others to abandon Rome's ancestral gods. A delayed effect of Valerian's order may also have caused some deaths in other provinces after his demise.

Assumption of imperial office by Tacitus, an old senator descended from the famous historian, on September 25, 275, signaled a new period of peace, but Tacitus died after holding office only six months. His successor, Probus, a highly competent army captain leading in victories over barbarians, showed little interest in religion. Here and there, however, popular fear and hostility resulted in the martyring of Christians, especially in instances where Christians let their zeal get out of hand. Two martyrs of Antioch in Pisidia, Trophimus and Sabbazius, for instance, interrupted a celebration in honor of Apollo by crying out, "O Christ, deliver them from error!" Hauled before the city magistrate, they were ordered to sacrifice to the gods. When they refused, guards brutally gouged them with spears and pummeled them. Sabbazius died on the spot. Trophimus was imprisoned, tortured still more, and finally beheaded at Synnada along with a senator named Dorymedon who visited him in prison and, when he failed to attend a religious function, was stripped of his rank and sentenced to death.

The Great Persecution

Nothing definite can be said about persecution of Christians during the brief joint reigns of Carus and his two sons, Carinus, who ruled the West, and Numerian, who ruled the East. Christianity's worst hour, however, occurred under Carinus's competitor for rule of the West, Diocletian, who ruled longer than any other emperor (284–304). Scattered instance of persecution occurred during the joint reign of Diocletian and Maximian (286–292), a bitter opponent of Christianity. Early on, however, Diocletian himself seemed to favor Christianity. His wife Prisca and daughter Valeria were either Christians or catechumens (Lactantius, *On the Deaths of Persecutors*, 15). Many Christians held positions in the imperial household and, according to Eusebius, Diocletian "treated them like his own children" (H.E. 8.6.1). He also extended favors to Christians who wanted to hold public office, dispensing them from the duty of offering sacrifices as he did his wife and daughter. One small town in Phrygia had only Christian officials (Eusebius, H.E. 8.11). Many cities extended Christians, who represented a sizeable part of the populace of Asia Minor, considerable freedom vis-à-vis public religious observances. Governors and magistrates accorded bishops of churches genuine respect (Eusebius, H.E. 8.1). The churches built houses of worship comparable to public buildings. Canons of the Synod of Elvira in Spain (ca. 305) illustrate how Christians struggled to sort out their proper relationship with prevailing customs, for example, whether to adorn churches and homes with paintings (Canon 36). In Rome Christians enlarged and adorned the catacombs and erected new buildings in the very center of the city. Many churches, believing themselves secure, forgot the still present dangers.

At Milan in 292 Diocletian and Maximian, who both held the title of Augusti, decided further to partition imperial administration by appointing Galerius and Constantius Chlorus as caesars to serve under them. Diocletian, as chief Emperor, retained the East with Egypt, Libya, the islands, and Thrace. Galerius, his caesar, took charge of the Danubian provinces, Illyria, Macedonia, Greece and Crete. Maximian kept Italy,

Africa, and Spain. Constantinus Chlorus ruled in Gaul and Britain. Galerius hated Christianity passionately; Constantius Chlorus, though a pagan, was at least tolerant.

During the period of the tetrarchy (292–302), Diocletian issued a rigorous edict against the Manichaeans as a Persian sect dangerous to the Empire (*Gregorian Code* 14.4.4). Among Christians, however, he seems first to have undertaken to purge them from the army, where they served under all four rulers in substantial numbers. Only in Africa did Christians still manifest much reserve about military service, perhaps under influence of Tertullian, and it may have been an incident there in 295 that touched the rulers' alarm button. Maximilian, the son of a soldier, twenty-one years of age, refused conscription on the grounds that a Christian could not serve in the army. Repeated pleas of Dion Cassius, proconsul of Africa, citing Christian service in all the rulers' armies, failed to change his mind. He was beheaded. According to Eusebius, the persecution was first initiated by Galerius, who now gave vent to a long restrained hatred of Christianity (H.E. 8.1.7-8). Galerius proceeded cautiously at first, stripping officers of their titles and mustering out the rank and file, but he gradually ordered more and more put to death (Eusebius, H.E. 8.4.4-5). Many Christians hastened to leave the army, but numerous others remained and died as martyrs. Diocletian and Constantius Chlorus evidently were not directly involved in this military purge, though it occurred in the East under Galerius and in the West under Maximian. Diocletian apparently changed his mind in 302 during a visit to Antioch when a Christian disrupted a sacrifice by making the sign of the cross. The offender was not put to death but expelled from the palace guard (Lactantius, *On the Deaths of Persecutors* 10).

Diocletian issued his first general edict in February 303, commanding that churches be leveled to the ground, scriptures burned, persons holding places of honor degraded, and household servants (perhaps commoners) who refused to submit deprived of freedom (Eusebius, H.E. 8.2.4). Galerius wanted the emperor to require all Christians to sacrifice, but he resisted in the first edict. The edict went into immediate effect in Nicomedia where city authorities tore down the doors of the main church, burned scriptures, and took whatever booty they could lay hands on (Lactantius, *Deaths of Persecutors* 12). Watching from a window of the palace, Diocletian vetoed Galerius's suggestion that they burn the building for fear of a city wide conflagration. According to Lactantius, no friend of Galerius, however, the caesar, not content with the destruction of the building, had secret agents set fire to the palace and blamed Christians for it. Diocletian had his domestics tortured to discover the truth. When he failed to obtain confessions, Galerius set fire to the palace again and fled. The whole affair threw Diocletian into a mad rage of persecution, compelling all in the city of Nicomedia to offer sacrifices and sending an order to Maximian and Constantius Chlorus to require the same (ibid., 14-15). Magistrates in Nicomedia and in surrounding cities proceeded to do the same. The edict, however, made its way slowly to other parts of the Empire, requiring at least two or three months, for instance, to reach Palestine. In the West Maximian enforced the edict vigorously in Italy, Africa, and Spain. Constantius Chlorus, however, seems to have enforced only the provision calling for destruction of churches. During this phase of persecution, authorities forced many to surrender copies of scripture, precipitating a bitter debate concerning apostasy in 311 that resulted in the Donatist schism.

Some kind of an uprising in Cappadocia and Syria became the pretext for two new edicts against Christianity. The second edict ordered all ecclesiastical leaders arrested and imprisoned. A third arranged for all prisoners to be set free on the condition that they offer sacrifices to the gods but stipulated that those who refused be punished (Eusebius, H.E. 8.6.8-10). The issuance of these new edicts may have had something to do with Christian refusal to accept military conscription in some areas. From 303 on Diocletian sought to build up his army in order to fortify the frontiers. When he levied in Cappadocia, some Christians refused. Troops stationed there proceeded either to demolish or set fire to churches.

Illness struck the emperor late in the year 303. At first he resisted Galerius's demand that he step aside, along with Maximian, but they finally relinquished their titles to Galerius and Constantius Chlorus, appointing Severus as caesar in the West and Maximin Daia, Galerius's nephew, as caesar in the East. Galerius intensified the persecution. This tetrarchy did not last long, however, for Constantius Chlorus, in ill health, recalled his son Constantine, whom Galerius reluctantly appointed caesar, elevating Severus to Augustus. On the death of Constantius in 306, Maximin's nephew Maxentius sought to usurp the title Maximian had abdicated, but Constantine's soldiers proclaimed Constantine emperor instead and Galerius declared Severus Augustus. Maximian, however, defeated Severus and had him imprisoned and executed. In his place Galerius appointed Licinius. From 308 to 310, therefore, Galerius and Maximin Daia ruled the East, Licinius, Constantine, and Maxentius the West after removal of Maximian. On the death of Galerius in 311, Maximin Daia seized control of the East. In 312 combined forces of Licinius and Constantine defeated and killed Maxentius at the Milvian Bridge in Rome. The next year Licinius defeated Maximin and seized control of the East. Constantine continued to rule the West. In 324 Constantine became sole emperor after defeating Licinius.

Following Diocletian's retirement, from 304 to 311, Christians suffered severely in the eastern and in part of the western portion of the Empire. Many, unaccustomed after years of relative security to such severity, defected. Some authorities, squeamish about applying the edict, encouraged confessors to fulfill the requirement in minimal ways, perhaps creating confusion in the process. Yet many remained steadfast and unyielding when confronted with the order to sacrifice to the gods. They continued to gather for worship, sometimes secretly but often openly, until authorities seized them and dragged them away. Some believers of Abitena and Carthage, for example, founded a new congregation after authorities closed their churches. One Sunday authorities apprehended them during celebration of the eucharist. The whole assembly—composed of the presbyter Saturninus, his four children, twenty-six men, and sixteen women—openly admitted their activities and defended it on the grounds that the law of Christ commanded it. All, even the children, were sent to prison, most after being tortured.

In 304, Diocletian sick and discouraged, Galerius issued a fourth edict requiring "that all citizens in every country in each city offer sacrifices publicly and libations to the idols" (Eusebius, *Martyrs of Palestine* 3). Here was a declaration of war not only on churches, scriptures, and members of the clergy but on all the faithful without regard to status, age, or sex. Galerius probably applied the edict first in areas he ruled, Macedonia and Pannonia. From there persecution spread elsewhere—Cilicia, Thrace, Galatia, Cappadocia, Syria, Phoenicia, Palestine, Egypt, Rome, Italy, Sicily, Africa, and Spain. Everywhere authorities did their best to force apostasies. Acts of martyrs recount the process repeated with dull regularity. "Why didn't you sacrifice to the gods as the emperors ordered?" . . . "Because I am a Christian." . . . "Don't you realize the penalties for disobedience?" . . . "Yes, but I am happy to suffer for Christ." . . . Beatings, torture, other indignities. . . . Sentencing to prison or death. What is remarkable is that so many remained faithful in the face of such sufferings, witnessing perhaps to the effectiveness of preparation and support they received.

By the end of 305 the persecution appears to have diminished somewhat even in the East, becoming less frequent and less widespread. Maximin Daia, Caesar at the time in the East, recorded later that when he first came to the East he learned of persons banished for refusal to worship the gods "who were able to serve the public good" and thus ordered magistrates not to "deal harshly with the provincials, but rather by persuasive words and exhortations to recall them to the worship of the gods" (Eusebius, H.E. 9.9.13). Eusebius, however, questioned the truthfulness of this claim; Christians could not trust the superstitious Maximin (9.10.1). In the first half of 306 a "second war" of extermination renewed the old fervency in all provinces governed by Maximin (Eusebius, *Martyrs of Palestine* 4.8) and Galerius. This edict did not change the situation of Christians in the areas ruled by Constantius and then by Constantine, Licinius, and to some extent under the pretender Maxentius.

In 310 Galerius contracted a cancer that claimed his life within a year. Finding no remedy in doctors or pagan cults of Apollo and Asclepius, according to Eusebius and Lactantius, he turned in desperation to Christians, halting the persecution and permitting them to exist and to reestablish their assemblies with the proviso that they pray for his healing, for the welfare of the state, and for their own (Lactantius, *Deaths of Persecutors* 34; Eusebius, H.E. 8.17). Although probably written in 310, the edict was not promulgated until April 30, 311. The names of Constantine and Licinius also headed it. Since Maximin Daia's name was not attached, it did not apply in Cilicia, Syria, and Egypt, but it had some effect there anyway. Sabinus, prefect of the Praetorium, circulated an order to provincial governors that, in effect, recognized the rescript of Galerius without preserving his apology for earlier policies and recognizing the Christian right to exist.

Maximin Daia continued insidious attacks on Christianity during the following year. Licinius challenged his rule in the East, however, and took control of the European part of Galerius's territory. As soon as Constantine and Licinius consolidated power in the West by defeating Maxentius, they put pressure on Maximin. In 313 they jointly issued the Edict of Milan that firmly established freedom of religion in the Roman Empire, specifically addressing the situation of Christians.

In the edict the emperors

> resolved to make such decrees as should secure respect and reverence for the Deity, namely, to grant both to Christians and to all the free choice of following whatever form of worship they pleased, to the intent that all the divine and heavenly powers that be might be favorable to us and all those living under our authority. (Eusebius, H.E. 10.5.4)

The document went on to direct care that Christians have "free and unrestricted authority to observe their own form of worship" and that places of worship destroyed earlier be restored along with other properties (Eusebius, H.E. 10.5.2-17). Not surprisingly, some Christians viewed this as the beginning of the millennium.

Chapter 13

Aliens in Their Own Homeland

Advancement not only numerically but also socially and culturally brought Christianity to the attention of literate Romans such as the emperor Marcus Aurelius, the physician Galen, and the Platonist philosopher Celsus and generated commentary. The larger Christianity loomed in the consciousness of educated Romans the more seriously they tried to respond to its claims and the harder Christians had to work to frame an adequate case for their religion. On the whole the Roman elite treated the Christian religion somewhat more graciously than Christians treated Roman religions. So long as Christians remained a clear minority, of course, pagans could speak diffidently and confidently; as Christians grew strong enough to pose a threat to an empire in which devotion to the gods and not just the gods was viewed as the source of health and prosperity, pagan polemicists took the offenders more seriously.

Christians in Roman Eyes

Cultured Romans grudgingly admired Christians for living and dying like philosophers but faulted them for their "inflexible obstinacy" and mystifying motives. The Stoic philosopher-emperor Marcus Aurelius (161–180) lauded readiness for the soul to leave the body "not from mere obstinacy, as with the Christians, but considerately and with dignity and in a way to persuade another without tragic show" (*Meditations* 11.3). The famous Roman physician Galen (129–199) evidently considered adoption of the Christian "philosophy" at one point, but decided against it on account of Christian gullibility. "For one might more easily teach novelties to the followers of Moses and Christ than to the physicians and philosophers who cling fast to their schools" (*Differences of Pulses* 3.3). Both Jews and Christians accepted the irrational and illogical "on faith." Yet Galen had to admit, even if reluctantly, that Christians sometimes did as philosophers should on the basis not of reason but of "parables" promising future rewards and punishments. What especially evoked his admiration and interest was the fact that

> their contempt of death and of its sequel is patent to us everyday, and likewise their constraint in cohabitation. For they include not only men but also women who refrain from cohabiting all through their lives; and they also number individuals who in self-discipline and self-control in matters of food and drink and in their keen pursuit of justice have attained a pitch not inferior to that of genuine philosophers.   (Walzer, 65)

Galen's point stirred sufficient interest among Theodotus the Tanner and his followers in Rome to inspire them to develop a theology based on reason rather than authority (Eusebius, H.E.

5.28.13-14), applying Greek philological methods to scriptures.

Not all of those who took an interest in Christianity were as objectively curious and appreciative as Galen. Celsus, about 175–178, and Porphyry, at the beginning of persecution under Diocletian, put together much harsher and more thoroughgoing critiques. In his *True Discourse*, about seventy percent of which can be reconstructed from Origen's reply, Celsus sought not only to point up the weaknesses of Christianity but to make a case for Roman ancestral religion. A Platonist, he knew Christianity intimately and could highlight its weak points. Like Galen, Celsus criticized Christians for lack of concern for reason and reliance on faith alone. He depicted Christians as "wool workers, cobblers, laundry workers, and the most illiterate and bucolic yokels, who could not dare to say anything at all in front of their elders and more intelligent masters" (Origen, *Against Celsus* 3.55). He was the first to label Jesus a magician and to charge Christians with practicing magic. By magic Jesus performed miracles; by magic his followers do some of the feats they do using spells and incantations (1.6). Claims that Jesus is the Son of God were based on his sorcery and not due to divine endowment (1.68). Replying perhaps to Justin's arguments for Christianity as "the true philosophy" (Andresen), he insisted that Christianity taught little that was new, actually deriving most of its doctrines from the ancient Greeks. What it teaches, he went on to say, it distorts. Celsus criticized especially the Christian doctrines of incarnation, resurrection, and the divinity of Jesus. Incarnation would require a change of God's nature, which is impossible if God is omnipotent and omniscient (4.14). Resurrection, Celsus maintained, is contrary to reason; God would never desire to preserve the flesh (5.14). If there is only one God, Christians err in worshipping a man who had ended on a cross. Better to worship Jonah with his gourd or Daniel delivered from lions (7.53). Jesus was no more than a low-

grade magician. By making Jesus equal with the Father, moreover, Christians violate their monotheism, thus robbing the highest God of his due.

Celsus went to a lot of trouble to discredit Jesus. He was not born of a virgin, a fabricated story (1.28), but of a peasant who earned her living by spinning and a Roman soldier named Panthera (1.32). Growing up in Egypt, he learned sorcery from the Egyptians (1.28). Stories recorded in the gospels about him, for example, his baptism or his resurrection, have no basis in fact. They are concoctions of his followers designed to make him a hero. The resurrection tale is a fabrication of a "hysterical woman" deluded by sorcery or perhaps given to hallucinations (2.55). Christianity, Celsus went on to argue, abandoned its parent, Judaism, and thus disqualified itself by no longer adhering to Jewish teachings set forth in scriptures—circumcision, Sabbath observance, festivals, food laws.

Christians also showed poor citizenship. If they were good citizens, they would serve in the army and fight for the emperor (8.73), accept public office (8.75), and worship the gods (8.2). Worshipping the hierarchy of gods does not offend but rather honors the Supreme God, whose intermediaries they are (8.63). If Christians became too numerous, they would disrupt the stability of the Empire because they would undermine the Law that assures order to it.

Christianity encountered numerous critics during the third century. The most learned was Porphyry, biographer of Plotinus, founder of Neoplatonism and editor of the *Enneads*. Whereas the *True Discourse* of Celsus drew a reply only from Origen, and that seventy years or more after he wrote it, Porphyry's polemic merited responses from Eusebius, Methodius, Apollinarius, Jerome, and Augustine. Unfortunately his treatise *Against the Christians* has not survived, and ideas it contains must be reconstructed from replies, always a tricky business. Writing as Diocletian inaugurated a new persecution, Porphyry may have undertaken the task at the emperor's request. From extant fragments scholars have established that much of Porphyry's argument centered on the Old Testament, refuting, among other things, Christian interpretation of Daniel as future prophecy and arguing that it was a writing of the Maccabean era. Eusebius, Methodius, Apollinarius, and Jerome all replied at length to this contention. The issue was crucial, for Porphyry struck at the very foundations of Christian claims, namely proof from prophecy. Porphyry also refuted Christian arguments about the antiquity of Moses and made fun of the story of Jonah being swallowed by a whale and God's command that Hosea marry a whore and have children by her.

Porphyry evidently did a critique of the New Testament as well. In doing so he must have raised some of the same objections Celsus voiced about Christian worship of Christ as God, thus dishonoring the Supreme God. If Augustine alluded to Porphyry when he spoke of pagan critics in his *Harmony of the Gospels* (1.11), the distinguished Neoplatonist thought Christians should honor Christ "as the wisest of men" but not worship him as God. The substantive part of his argument, however, was not philosophical but biblical. He proceeded through the Gospels chapter by chapter, pointing out their differences, inconsistencies, and contradictions. He may have done the same for the rest of the New Testament.

In a second work, *Philosophy from Oracles*, Porphyry assembled a defense of the traditional religions of the Graeco-Roman world and sought to locate Christianity within his scheme. Unlike other writings where he used philosophical arguments, in this one he argued from authoritative texts for a hierarchical system of deities: one high God, the Olympian deities, stars and heavenly beings, demons, heroes and divine human beings. He placed Jesus among the heroes. He conceded "that the gods have pronounced Christ to have been extremely devout, and have said that he has become immortal, and that they mention him in terms of commendation" (Augus-

tine, *City of God* 19.22-23) because he taught people to worship the high God. Christians, on the contrary, have led people into error by worshipping him rather than the gods. The number of responses Christians penned indicates the danger they saw here. Eusebius, citing Porphyry almost a hundred times, wrote his *Preparation for the Gospel* chiefly to prove that Christianity was not unreasonable to depart from Roman traditional religion. Christianity faced a graver threat to its identity from absorption into the Roman sponge than it did from persecution.

Romans in Christian Eyes

In this era as in the preceding one, Christians varied widely in their attitudes toward their fellow Romans, their culture, and their religious competitors. As Christianity incorporated more and more persons of wealth and culture, however, they moderated extreme views and increased their efforts to give more adequate replies to polemicists like Celsus and Porphyry as well as the illiterate masses. In the East Clement of Alexandria, Theophilus of Antioch, and Athenagoras of Athens, all writing in the last quarter of the second century, represented the "new breed" of apologists. In the West Tertullian and Minucius Felix marked the transition in the early third century. Subsequently Christianity could list among its supporters such distinguished advocates as Origen of Alexandria and Caesarea, Arnobius of Sicca, Lactantius, and Eusebius of Caesarea, foreshadowing a day when Christianity would dominate the Roman religious scene and play a major part in shaping its outlook.

On one end of the spectrum stood Tertullian, especially Tertullian the Montanist, insisting that though Christians had to live with pagans, they didn't have to "sin" with them. Behind this rejection of culture lay a strong sense of a "Fall" from its original purpose. Since God created the universe and the soul, they are good, but "there is a vast difference between the corrupted state and that of primal purity" (*Spectacles* 2). Within the society he lived in Tertullian judged the religions more corrupted than anything else, but Christians should deliberately set themselves over against their society and shun other activities as well because religion pervades them all. They ought to avoid attendance at games, public service, military service, and teaching in pagan schools. "What has Athens to do with Jerusalem?" Tertullian wanted to know. "What in common have the disciples of Greece and the disciples of heaven?" Idolatry has crept into even the best of pagan culture (*Idolatry* 10). Where challenged on the unreasonableness of some Christian doctrine, he would reply, "I believe because it is absurd" (*Resurrection of the Flesh* 18).

To assume that Tertullian was consistent in his "Christ against culture" stance would be to ignore his own learning and culture, but he did represent an extreme which Montanism only intensified. Toward the opposite end of the spectrum stood Christian Gnostics such as Clement of Alexandria, who earnestly yearned to win the flocks of affluent and better educated Romans who inquired of the churches and schools how they might attain salvation. Like Tertullian and virtually all other apologists, he spoke harshly about other religions. He ridiculed fables about the gods, sacrifices, worship of images, and immoral behavior connected with them. He cited the philosophers' criticism of them. In reply to persons like Celsus who insisted that Romans should not have abandoned the customs of their fathers, he argued that the divine gift of truth in Jesus Christ made this the only sensible alternative. Quite different, however, was his attitude toward philosophy. He rejected some elements of Greek thought and blamed some philosophers for leading Christian sects astray. He had no patience, however, for those who said "faith alone" or who considered all philosophy a product of a malign influence. For him it was "in a sense a work of Divine Providence" (*Stromateis* 1.19), discerning no real conflict between Greek philosophy in its best expressions and the Judeo-Christian tradition. Both are pedagogues leading to Christ, in whom the divine Logos became incarnate. In *The Instructor* Clement fashioned a Christian Stoicism, a kind of "liberal Puritanism" (so Henry Chadwick), wherein the rule of moderation would guide Christians as it had Stoics. Although he undergirded his counsels with words of Jesus, *the* Teacher, where he could, Clement was not keenly aware of highly visible differences between Christian and genteel pagan behavior. The distinction would be an interior and invisible one, for the Word, Christ, would instruct and guide them just as he had illumined sages for centuries, whether Jewish or Gentile.

Clement's student and successor Origen took a much more critical stand vis-à-vis even philosophy, despite the fact that Platonism influenced him far more deeply than it did Clement. In a letter to his disciple Gregory (Thaumaturgus) of Neocaesarea, Origen advised the missionary-to-be to focus his efforts on what benefited Christianity and "to extract from the philosophy of the Greeks what may serve as a course of study or a preparation for Christianity, and from geometry and astronomy what will serve to explain the sacred scriptures." (1) Christians should imitate the Jews departing from Egypt in the Exodus. They should "steal" only the valuable items and reject the rest (2). In theory he operated along these lines, but in practice he could not avoid crossing over them. Above everything else, of course, he aspired to explain the truth found in scriptures, every jot and tittle of which is inspired. Finding three senses—literal, moral, and spiritual or symbolic—in them opened a wide avenue for engaging his culture. The prevailing Platonism of his day consequently impacted what he said and wrote far more heavily than it did what Clement said and wrote. Yet, as Henry Chadwick has shown, Origen could differentiate Christian thought from philosophy with much greater precision than Clement. By temperament, moreover, he would never have felt comfortable in the polite circles Clement frequented. On issues such as flight to avoid persecution or public service he took positions nearer Tertullian's than Clement's.

Lactantius, invited by Diocletian to be a teacher of Latin rhetoric in his new capital of Nicomedia, was forced to resign his office when persecution broke out in 304 and subsequently became a Christian. A master of Ciceronian style, he had not mastered Christian thought when he wrote the *Divine Institutes* (304–313). Lactantius first derided Roman gods and Roman worship of the gods, citing Cicero and a few other philosophers in support of monotheism. Christians had used the same strategy, inherited from Judaism, many times before. The gods are only deified human beings who behave indecently, unwisely, and unjustly. The crass and materialistic way Romans try to worship them does them no honor. What good does it do, for instance, to carve statues in which the gods supposedly reside when they are impotent to prevent birds nesting there or leaving droppings on their heads. Far from Christians acting unreasonably in departing from the folly of their ancestors, the only sensible thing to do is to abandon the images and direct our gaze to the one true God.

Lactantius found fault not only with Roman gods and worship but also with the philosophies, even the Stoicism of his rhetorical model, Cicero. Cicero erred in assuming the eternal existence of matter. To posit that would be to posit two eternal principles—God and matter. If matter were eternal, it would not change. If it changes, it must owe its existence to God's creative work. God alone is impassible, immutable, and incorruptible (2.8). "Philosophy" per se received harsher treatment. Philosophy should entail a search for wisdom, but it doesn't, for it ends up only in speculations, something Zeno and the Stoics repudiated. The vast number of philosophical sects proves the unreliability of philosophy in a search for truth. Academicians (Platonists) lapsed into skepticism, physicists into positivism. Different schools fail to agree about what leads to a happy life; whom can we believe? None makes

God the highest good, not even Zeno, who sees living according to nature as the highest good, or Cicero, who opts for virtue as the highest good. Philosophers erred especially in seeking the highest good in the lowest, the earth, rather than in the highest, heaven. As a result, philosophy teaches neither virtue nor justice. If you are a philosopher, you will not live rightly or well, for you will not seek heavenly wisdom. All philosophies err on immortality. Epicureans make light of death. Stoics and Pythagoreans believe in immortality but do not base their belief on knowledge. Cicero and Plato thought it best never to have been born. Socrates "was a little more prudent than others," but many things about him are "not only not worthy of praise, but even most worthy of censure" (3.20). He, too, made light of heavenly things and taught sharing of wives. Simple observation proves how much more God's commands accomplish in human hearts. "Give an unjust, foolish sinner, and immediately he will be just and prudent and innocent, for with one washing all malice will be wiped out. . . . The font of God, very rich and exceedingly full, lies open to all, and this celestial light arises for all who have eyes" (3:20). What philosophers can claim this? The whole of human wisdom lies, rather, in knowing and worshipping God.

Daily Life of Christians

As both the anonymous author of the *Epistle to Diognetus* and Tertullian made clear, Christians of the second or third centuries could not separate themselves from their neighbors and live in ghettoes. They lived in the same cities and observed most of the same local customs regarding food, clothing, and the like (*Diognetus* 5.1-4; Tertullian, *Apology* 42). They did, however, try to distinguish themselves in substantive moral matters not only from pagans but from quasi-Christian sects such as Gnostics who, believing the flesh is evil, sought to commit every sin as a way of showing contempt for the flesh (Irenaeus, *Against Heresies* 1.25.4; 1.31.2). Early on, they relied on a Jewish ethic based on the Old Testament. Theophilus, bishop of Antioch, summed up the goal. Christians lived according to divine law taught by the prophets that prohibits idolatry, adultery, murder, fornication, theft, love of money, perjury, anger, and all licentiousness and uncleanness and teaches that "whatever a person does not want done to him/her, that person should not do to another" and that "thus a person who acts righteously may escape the eternal punishments and be judged worthy of receiving eternal life from God" (*To Autolycus* 2.34). Practice doubtless fell far short of theory, but the bishop proceeded to refute charges of sharing wives, incest, and cannibalism (3.4). Citing the ten commandments, he argued that Christians consistently taught justice, chastity, love and good citizenship. They were forbidden to witness gladiatorial combats or other shows. Far from committing sexual crimes, they practiced continence, observed monogamy, and guarded purity (3:15).

As more and more Gentiles entered Christian churches, Christians adapted their ethic to Stoic and Platonist modes of thought. The character of this adaptation depended to a considerable degree on social, educational, and cultural levels, just as it does today. Clement of Alexandria, for instance, opened the way for the wealthy to work out their salvation alongside the masses who possessed little. The rich, rather than despairing, need to realize that they have hope "if they obey the commandments" (3). They should put themselves under the Teacher, Christ, and make his New Testament their food and drink and the commandments their exercises. Jesus' words to the rich young man (Mark 10:17-31) must be understood "mystically" rather than literally. What Jesus commanded was stripping ourselves of the desires of the soul so that we can use money wisely in care for others. Salvation does not depend on external things but on the virtue of the soul. The call is: "Abandon the alien possessions that are in your soul so that, becoming pure in heart, you may see God" (19). If the rich can

free themselves from the power of wealth and exercise self-control, seeking God alone, such persons become "poor." They can fulfill the righteousness expected by Jesus' parable in Matthew 25:31-46. Love of God and of neighbor is the goal.

In *The Instructor* Clement laid out particulars of his Christian-Stoic ethic for the genteel more than for the hoi polloi. Those who have come to know the Teacher should "eat to live," that is, in moderation, and not "live to eat." They should eat plain and unpretentious meals that give health and strength. If they eat in moderation, something will be left over to share with the needy (2.1). Christians should drink wine also in moderate amounts and perhaps abstain altogether. There is no need to import exquisite wines, for this merely indicates self-indulgence. Wine ought to be drunk with proper decorum, sipped and not slurped like barbarians. Although he would not forbid drinking from alabaster cups altogether, Clement would forbid drinking from them alone as "overostentatious"(2.2). Drinking from gold, silver, or gem-studded cups would have no purpose but "fraudulent display." Christians should not own ostentatious glassware, couches made of silver, gold or silver dishes and utensils, ivory inlaid couches, and other luxurious items, for these exceed limits of moderation. Christian possessions should be "in keeping with a Christian way of life" (2.3). Christians should avoid drunken parties, sensuous songs, and gatherings that violate "the law" of Christ (2.4). They should observe propriety in speech, avoiding off-color jokes and unrestrained laughter (2.5), indecent talk, evil companions, sexual license (2.6), insults to others, immodest dress, rudeness in eating, brash speech or actions, whistling or spitting or violent coughing while eating (2.7). Christians need not use perfumes but neither should they fear to use some in moderation. So also garlands and oils (2.8). They should exercise temperance also in bedroom furnishings and in sleep, sleeping "half-awake" and not too long (2.9). Sexual intercourse is for the purpose of procreation. Thus Christians must avoid unnatural sexual practices such as sodomy and bestiality. They must not seek sex apart from marriage and exercise moderation and propriety within marriage. Christians ought to avoid expensive dress, ornamentation, cosmetics, and the like. Wives must dress in such a way as to enhance purity (2.10). Footwear should also be modest (2.11). Christians have no need of gems, pearls, and other ornaments (2.12). Rather than acquiring and bedecking themselves in outward things, Christian women should seek inward beautification and ornamentation (3.2). Men, too, should avoid frippery in hair styles, dyes, plucking beards, shameful public exposure, and debauchery (3.3). Christians should not possess too many slaves or servants in order to escape work or to aid immoral behavior (3.4). Women should not frequent the baths or cavort around naked (3.5). Christians should share their wealth generously, thus "laying up treasure in heaven" (Matt. 6:20), (3.6), setting an example of frugality (3.7), and developing discipline (3.8). They should not engage in baths for warmth or pleasure but only for cleanliness or health (3.9). Physical exercise is necessary and healthy, but it could be as easily obtained as a part of daily labor (3.10). Christians may wear gold and use soft garments in modest ways if they avoid indulgence. Clothes should be in keeping with a person's age, personality, place, character, and occupation. Posture, look, gait, and speech all need attention (3.11). In the end, Clement sums up, we must rely on the Teacher. He has laid out his "rule" in the law, the prophets, and the Gospels so as "to eliminate fear and free the will for its act of faith" (3.12).

If Clement deserves the title of a "liberal puritan," his contemporary in the West, Tertullian, might be described as an "illiberal" one. Although he admitted in an early writing that Christians differed little from their contemporaries as regards occupation and general condition (*Apology* 42), he sought more zealously than

Clement to put distance between Christians and Romans as regards moral behavior and outlook. Vows taken at baptism, Tertullian insisted, absolutely prohibit Christians from attending the spectacles, for they entailed renunciation of idolatry, the very essence of these activities with all of their religious trappings. Nonattendance is the Christian's chief badge among pagans, and those who remove this "openly deny their faith" (*Spectacles* 24).

In a treatise on *Women's Apparel* Tertullian emphasized modesty of dress that would set Christians apart from pagans. Since Eve brought sin into the world, a penitential garment is the suitable one for women. External beauty only incites lust, something Christians must avoid lest they cause others to sin. Wives should take care only to please their husbands, who ask that they be chaste. This is not to call for a lack of cleanliness or untidiness but only for what is natural and neat. What is natural is God's work, what goes beyond that is the Devil's work. To paint the face is to commit adultery in appearance. To dye the hair is foolish and shameful. To spend a lot of time arranging the hair is wasteful. Men as well as women must choose modesty over fashion regarding beards, dyeing hair, ointments, powders, etc. The dress of women should not detract from natural beauty. If wealthy and prominent women have to dress more elaborately for public functions, they should "temper the evil" of it. Although God provided wood to manufacture elaborate garments and gold to fit jewels, God placed them in the world to test the restraint of persons devoted to God. "All things are lawful, but not all things are fitting" (1 Cor. 10:23). Christian women have no reason to appear in public which requires fancy dress. They do so for serious purposes such as visiting the sick, attending worship, or hearing the Word of God. If anyone must visit a pagan friend, let her go "dressed in your own armor" (2.11). Fancy apparel is related to prostitution, and Christians must never cause others to sin.

The fact that Tertullian strains to find scriptural support for his views indicates that many women resisted his rigorism. As a Montanist, he would have found still stronger opposition. As more and more converts flooded the churches in the two long eras of peace (212–249, 260–304), the question of Christian lifestyle grew increasingly vexing. The large number of apostates during the persecution under Decius and under Diocletian illuminates the fact that many had not thought through their commitments. Fleshing out this point are canons of the Synod of Elvira in Spain held in 305 or 306. If the canons represent actual cases, as is likely, they point up the grave difficulties many converts, including clergy, had in sorting out what distinguished Christian from pagan even in elementary ways. Some upper class converts could not decide whether they could continue to function as *flamines*, offering sacrifices to the gods or preparing for public games. Divorce, adultery, fornication and sodomy were common. Parents sold their children into prostitution. Some intermarried with pagans, Jews, and heretics. Both clergy and laity exacted interest from borrowers. Some failed to attend church regularly. Others still kept idols in their homes. An adulterous catechumen conceived a child and had it killed. Some served as informers during the persecution under Diocletian. Such problems mounted higher and higher after Constantine as the constituency of the churches multiplied many times.

Chapter 14

The Struggle for Unity in an Age of Persecution

Persecution sometimes knit Christians together more tightly as they offered one another mutual support, assurance, and comfort. Bands of the faithful rallied around the martyrs as they bore testimony to the God they worshipped and tried to obey. During the persecution under Septimius Severus, for instance, two deacons, Tertius and Pomponius, bribed guards to obtain permission for the catechumens—Perpetua, Felicitas, Revocatus, Saturninus, and Secundulus—to go for a few hours to "a pleasanter part of the prison" where they could have more privacy (*Passion of S. Perpetua* 1). Pomponius carried messages to and from the martyrs to their families and friends. In addition, "many brethren," let in by a friendly soldier, visited "that both we and they might be mutually refreshed" (3). In an earlier chapter we noted the care deacons and laypersons extended bishops such as Cyprian and Dionysius in time of exile.

Christian leaders encouraged and exhorted martyrs and confessors through treatises and letters. Tertullian, Cyprian, Origen, and others composed exhortations to martyrdom. As one of his earlier (pre-Montanist) treatises, Tertullian's *To the Martyrs* reflects real sensitivity to the sufferings of victims of Severus's persecution. Though the flesh is in prison, the spirit is free. If ancient Romans could suffer for earthly things, how much more Christians for heavenly ones. Cyprian's *Exhortation to Maryrdom*, a treatise

prepared in response to the request of a person named Fortunatus, perhaps bishop of Tucca, collected scripture texts under a series of propositions designed to encourage faithfulness, the essence of which is that God will punish the unfaithful but protect and reward the faithful. Origen addressed his *Exhortation* to his friend and sponsor Ambrose when the Emperor Gallus summoned him to Gaul to answer for his Christian faith. Cyprian dispatched numerous letters of encouragement to confessors and martyrs not only of Carthage but also of Rome when that Church had no bishop during the Decian persecution. Letters from confessors to Cyprian acknowledged the solace and help the letters added to personal ministrations of minor clergy he had sent (cf. *Epp.* 31, 77, 78, 79).

Some letters indicate the strain persecution placed upon the most ardent Christians. Confessors themselves sometimes broke down as a result of their depressing circumstances, not only yielding to torture but behaving in reprehensible ways. In one letter, for example, Cyprian urged confessors of the Decian persecution to reprove, restrain, and correct some who got drunk and others who engaged in sexual license. One was released, returned home, and was put to death as a criminal. Some grew boastful, wrangled among themselves, and cursed their captors (*Ep.* 13). Yet such incidents paled alongside the controversy and division which wracked the churches everywhere over the question of readmitting the lapsed to communion.

Hippolytus's Schism

The first noteworthy schism of this period involved a Roman presbyter and learned theologian named Hippolytus. When Victor died in 198, Hippolytus evidently expected to succeed him, but Zephyrinus was elected instead. Although he spoke warmly of Victor, Hippolytus had little good to say about Zephyrinus. He called him "an ignorant and illiterate individual" who was "accessible to bribes and covetous" (*Refutation of All Heresies* 9.6), hinting that he was really a dupe of his successor, Callistus, of whom Hippolytus spoke still more harshly. Callistus, "cunning in wickedness and subtle in deceit," obtained the episcopate through fraud, Hippolytus charged, by catering to Sabellians as well as orthodox Christians. Whether Callistus was guilty of all the connivances Hippolytus told about him or not, the latter did make a strong case against him on both doctrinal and disciplinary grounds. He sincerely believed that Zephyrinus, perhaps unwittingly, and Callistus knowingly favored a modalist or Sabellian doctrine of the relation between the Father and the Son. Callistus charged Hippolytus with ditheism. Hippolytus also raised strenuous objections to changes of discipline that Callistus introduced: forgiving all sins, letting clergy who married two or three times retain office, allowing clergy to marry after being ordained, permitting wealthy women to marry their slaves, and sanctioning second baptisms. In defense of greater leniency Callistus cited the parable of the wheat and the tares (Matt. 13:30). The election of Callistus in 217 was the last straw for Hippolytus. He was elected bishop of Rome by a small but influential minority, drafting *The Apostolic Tradition* as a guide for his followers. According to early tradition, he was reconciled when Pontianus (bishop of Rome from 230 to 235), exiled with Hippolytus to

Sardinia, resigned the office. The Roman community then elected Anteros (235–236).

The Novatianist Schism

During the persecution under Decius, as noted earlier, large numbers of Christians lapsed. Individual offenses varied, however. Some hastened to obtain the certificates (*libelli*) by doing everything the decree required. Others, called *libellatici*, acted more circumspectly, getting certificates without actually offering incense, sacrificing, and eating the meat offered in the sacrifices. Still others, called *thurificati*, only offered incense. At the center of the controversy was whether all cases should be lumped together and treated as apostasy or whether they differed enough to require individual examination. Figuring prominently in the schism, however, were personal offenses and jealousies among the clergy in Carthage and in Rome.

When the lapsed in Carthage started to apply for restoration of communion as the persecution under Decius abated in 250, Cyprian, himself in hiding, refused to readmit any until a council of bishops could convene and decide how to handle the situation. In this he was standing fast on the traditional rigorous policy of the churches in Africa. The lapsed, however, eager to return, obtained some help from a disaffected group of clergy and from the confessors, who issued letters of commendation appealing for their readmission (*Ep.* 15). A faction headed by the deacon Felicissimus and including Novatus and five other presbyters, had opposed Cyprian's ordination as bishop and sustained an attack on him when he went into hiding during the persecution (*Ep.* 43). Cyprian evidently alienated some of his clergy further by appointing a commission, composed of three neighboring bishops and two presbyters of Carthage, to administer his diocese in his absence, contrary to the customary rights of presbyters (*Epp.* 41, 42, 43). Novatus took a lenient view about readmission of the lapsed. Cyprian had his commissioners excommunicate Felicissimus and other members of this faction, though not all of the presbyters, until a council could meet and decide formally how to deal with them. When the council convened in 251, it excommunicated Felicissimus and all five presbyters (*Epp.* 45, 59).

Meantime, another faction was developing in Rome. After Fabian, bishop of Rome, was martyred on January 20, 250, the see remained vacant for a considerable time because it was unsafe to elect a successor. In the interim presbyters, among whom Novatian was the most prominent, took the lead. Although the Roman clergy criticized Cyprian for going into hiding (*Ep.* 8), other letters penned by Novatian agreed with his policy concerning the lapsed (*Epp.* 30, 36). When the election of Fabian's successor finally was held, the Roman people split their vote between Novatian and another presbyter named Cornelius. They then appealed to the bishops of three other sees—Fabius of Antioch, Dionysius of Alexandria, and Cyprian—to help them decide. Responding promptly, Fabius voted for Novatian, Dionysius for Cornelius. Cyprian, evidently trying to see whom the presbyter Novatus might rally to his faction during a trip to Rome, delayed about three months. When he cast his vote, he did so in favor not of Novatian, who had supported his reinstatement as bishop of Carthage, but Cornelius. Novatus and Novatian thus proceeded to unite their factions to begin the Novatianist schism in 251, a surprising development considering the fact that they held opposing views on readmission of the lapsed until this time and one that illustrates the force of personal factors in the schism.

Novatian and his followers differed from the Catholic Church, represented by Cornelius and Cyprian, only on the matter of discipline and not on any basic doctrinal issues. Novatian, as a matter of fact, was one of the West's better theologians, writing, among other things, a widely used treatise on the Trinity that theologians could cite in opposition to Arians. In the two letters he wrote to Cyprian on behalf of the Roman presbyters he hinted at his rigorism not only in supporting Cyprian's opposition to readmission of the lapsed until a council could decide but also in the praise he lavished on vigorous discipline (*Ep.* 36). Indeed, according to Cornelius, Novatian had cultivated some partisans for this view among some of the confessors two or three months before the split (in Eusebius, H.E. 6.43). When Cyprian cast his vote for Cornelius, Novatian locked the door on his position.

When the council met in Carthage in May of 251, the bishops adopted what most persons today would consider a stringent policy. Although they feared that too great severity might cause many to give up hope altogether and fall back into paganism, they decided to impose lengthy penances and punish offenders proportionally according to their offenses. They differentiated, for instance, those who sacrificed voluntarily in some haste and those who did so involuntarily under torture or threat of it. *Libellatici* were also distinguished from *sacrificati*, the former to be reconciled immediately and the latter only after long penances (Cyprian, *Ep.* 52). In the Fall Cornelius assembled a synod composed of sixty bishops in Rome which confirmed the decrees of the Council of Carthage and excommunicated Novatian and his party. In May 252, spurred on by resumption of Decius's edict under Gallus, Cyprian convened a second synod at Carthage. This council decided immediately to restore to communion all who manifested genuine signs of repentance as a means of fortifying them for the new onslaught of persecution (Cyprian, *Ep.* 54).

Novatianists never gained a strong constituency, but they survived until the sixth century or after. Their support was welcomed by Nicaeans in the Arian controversy. In 410, however, the Emperor Honorius I included them in his effort to repress dissidents.

The Rebaptismal Controversy

The strong stand Cyprian took vis-à-vis Novatianists nearly precipitated a schism between Rome and Carthage over the question of readmitting or admitting Novatianists. Cyprian held that Novatianists would have to be rebaptized in order to enter the Catholic Church since they did not possess the Spirit. The Spirit can be conferred only in the Catholic Church which, by definition, is the church in communion with the bishop. No bishop, no baptism! For Cyprian it did not matter whether Novatianists had received baptism in the Catholic Church before they separated. If they left the Church, they cut themselves off from the Spirit, and they could not again receive the Spirit without baptism in the Catholic Church. Councils convened in Carthage, Iconium, and Synnada seem to have sustained this view in declaring baptism conferred by heretics invalid.

In Rome Stephen took the position that baptism administered with the Trinitarian formula, whether by heretics or schismatics, was valid. Towards the end of 253, he informed Helenus, bishop of Tarsus, and Firmilian, bishop of Casearea in Cappadocia, that he would not commune with them in the future because they rebaptized heretics (Dionysius of Alexandria in Eusebius, H.E. 7.5). In 255 a second council of Carthage, presided over by Cyprian, responding to an inquiry by eighteen Numidian bishops, decreed that schismatics and heretics should be rebaptized, "since no one can be baptized outside the Church" (Cyprian, *Ep.* 70.1). They sent a copy of this decision to Stephen with a letter of Cyprian that reinforced it, expressing a hope that Stephen would agree. Stephen, angered by it, refused to allow emissaries sent by Cyprian to appear before him or to communicate with them, forbade all Christians in Rome to give them hospitality, and called Cyprian "a false Christian, a false apostle, and a deceitful workman" (Firmilian to Cyprian, *Ep.* 75.25). He then informed the Africans, in a letter now lost, that they held an untenable position in opposition of his own. In September 256 the Africans responded with a third council devoted to the subject, eighty-seven of them in attendance. Cyprian polled each bishop, assuring them that none would be excommunicated for differences of opinion. They unanimously agreed on the necessity of rebaptizing schismatics and heretics.

Firmilian's letter to Cyprian upon receiving the report of this gathering reflects much greater bitterness and anger than Cyprian himself displayed. It is possible, however, that the rigidity of both Stephen and Cyprian would have pushed them toward a rupture of communion had not the Valerian persecution interrupted their rancorous debate in 257. Stephen died in August, 257. Cyprian was exiled to Curubis at about the same time. Evidently Stephen's successor, Xystus, smoothed over the ruffled feelings of Cyprian and other bishops, for Cyprian's biographer Pontius labeled him "a good and peaceable presbyter" (*Life of Cyprian* 14). September, 14, 258 Cyprian fell to the sword. His views about baptism lived on in Africa, however, in the Donatist sect, for they regularly cited him in defense of the rebaptism of Catholics.

The Donatist Schism

Timewise, the Donatist sect belongs to the next phase of Church history. Since the schism began in connection with the persecution under Diocletian, however, it would appear appropriate to discuss it at this juncture. Like the Novatianist schism, it too grew out of the contorted situation created by persecution. Once again, vast numbers of believers, wholly unprepared for the new onslaught, either fled or hastened to surrender copies of scriptures, as the first edict demanded, or to offer sacrifices. According to Optatus (*Against the Donatists*, 3.8), the temples of Numidia would not hold the crowds of apostates. In Milevis the bishop, Paul, summoned before the Curator of the city, gave up one copy of scriptures and said the readers had the rest. Brought before the authorities, the latter tried to cover for one another but finally yielded and brought not only copies of scriptures but also chalices, lamps, clothes kept for relief of the poor, and other objects.

One of those who took part in this, Silvanus, later became a Donatist bishop. When twelve bishops met after the death of bishop Paul to elect a successor, four admitted having surrendered copies of scripture, one actually throwing the Gospels in the fire, and a fifth having escaped by feigning blindness (Augustine, *Against Cresconius* 3.27, 30). On the other side of the picture, numerous Christians did remain faithful, some with fanatical zeal, especially in Numidia, where persecution was so intense. In Carthage some presented themselves to the authorities voluntarily, claiming to possess copies of scriptures which they refused to give up. Great crowds rallied outside the prisons where confessors were kept. As the persecution let up in March of 305 many fanatics fanned popular resentment of the *traditores* ("surrenderers").

Before Mensurius, bishop of Carthage, left for Rome to appear before Maxentius in defense of one of his deacons, he entrusted the valuables of the Church to the *seniores* or presbyters who were to preside in his absence. When he died before returning, the presbyters hastened to elect a successor, but they could not agree on two of their own, Botrus and Celestius, and the choice fell to the archdeacon Caecilian. Although publicly acclaimed by the citizens of Carthage, Caecilian was unpopular in the Church. He had alienated many as a result of his opposition to the cult of martyrs so popular in Africa at the time. One of those whom he offended was a wealthy Spanish woman named Lucilla, then resident in Carthage. In addition, the clergy did not like him because he forced them to turn over the gold and silver treasures they had hidden away. Then, of the three bishops who consecrated him, one,

Felix of Aptunga, was suspected of being a *traditor*.

Although Caecilian obtained the approval of other important sees, Numidian bishops led by Secundus of Tigisis and Donatus of Casae Nigrae contested the election on the grounds that Caecilian was personally unworthy and was consecrated by only three bishops rather than the twelve customarily required, one of the three a *traditor*. In Carthage they readily enlisted the support of opponents of Caecilian. Secundus, convinced Caecilian's installation was invalid, appointed an interim administrator, who was murdered. He then convened a council and invited Caecilian to attend, but Caecilian declined and instead asked Secundus to come to the cathedral to state his complaint. To have done so would have acknowledged the legitimacy of Caecilian's appointment, so Secundus proceeded to have Caecilian condemned in the council on the grounds that his consecration was invalid and that, as a deacon, he had denied food to the martyrs of Abitina. The council then elected Majorinus, a lector in the Church, as bishop and sent ambassadors to Rome, Spain, and Gaul and letters to the African provinces to report the action. The Numidians then returned home. Caecilian, as one would expect, refused to step down, so the schism began. Majorinus died soon afterward and Donatus, whose name the schism bears, was consecrated almost immediately (perhaps as early as the summer of 313). Donatus ruled for forty years.

News of the schism upset the Emperor Constantine when it reached Milan. Without waiting to hear the opposition's side, he decided in favor of Caecilian, ordering the financial officer in charge of the imperial estates in Africa to put money at Caecilian's disposal and lands seized in the persecution restored to the Church. He also ordered that any who made vile and base accusations against the church be brought before the magistrates (Eusebius, H.E. 10.6). In March or April 313 he exempted clergy supportive of Caecilian from municipal taxes.

The Donatists then appealed directly to the emperor. In their appeal they asked for judges from Gaul to investigate the case (Augustine, *Ep.* 88.2), taking the first step toward an alliance between Church and Empire. Although angered by the petition, Constantine required the proconsul, Anulinus, to send Caecilian with ten supporting bishops and an equal number of Donatists to Rome, where bishop Miltiades of Rome, an African, and a certain Marcus, plus three bishops from Gaul (Reticius of Autun, Maternus of Cologne, and Marinus of Arles)—were to serve as judges. The commission cleared Caecilian of charges against him and affirmed the validity of his consecration (Optatus 1.24). The Donatists, however, were not content to let the matter rest. They appealed again to Constantine, this time for a council. Although this request also distressed the emperor, he convened the Council of Arles on August 1, 314, installing Marinus, bishop of Arles, as president, with the understanding that the council's decision would be final. Despite their efforts to press the question of Felix of Aptunga's guilt, the Donatists lost again at Arles.

Like the Novatianist controversy, the Donatist schism entailed much more than personal jealousies. As W. H. C. Frend ably demonstrated in *The Donatist Church*, this dispute, more than any other, was fired by African nationalism and socioeconomic hostility to a Roman presence in Africa. Donatist support resided in the countryside among the Berber and Phoenician peoples who had controlled northern Africa before the Romans won the Punic wars. Donatist leaders came chiefly from the provinces of Numidia and Mauretania. Not surprisingly, the native populace never understood or accepted the decisions of Constantine's commission or the Council of Arles. The more fanatical of them, the Circumcellions or "hut haunters," carried on a guerrilla war.

Theologically the Donatists differed from the Catholic Church in much more basic ways than Novatianists. They conceived of themselves as a church of the "pure," *katharoi*. Whereas Catholics construed "holy" in terms of Christ's presence within a mixed body (*corpus permixtum*) of saints and sinners, the Donatists interpreted in terms of individual members. Because the Catholic Church tolerated *traditores* in its constituency, even among the clergy, they argued, it has ceased to be holy and the Spirit has fled from it. All of its ministrations—baptism, eucharists, ordinations—are invalid, for they depend on the worthiness of the minister. The Donatists, as Catholics constantly reminded them, could not back up their claim of purity in all constituents, but they pressed the point nonetheless.

Until the time of Augustine Donatists competed with Catholics for control of North Africa. In Numidia and small towns they held a clear numerical edge. A Donatist theologian named Tyconius (d.ca. 390), driven out of the sect by Parmenian, Donatist bishop of Carthage, rivaled Augustine for eminence, and Augustine relied heavily on his *Rules* of interpretation. Donatist influence dwindled, however, after the Council of Carthage in 411, where Augustine bested their best spokespersons in a debate. Where Donatists stressed that the holiness of the Church depends on the holiness of individual members, Augustine emphasized Christ. He distinguished between the validity and the efficacy or effectiveness of sacraments. Validity depends upon Christ and not on the administrator. The fact is no human administrator will be perfect. If baptism, eucharist, or ordination confer grace, therefore, they will do so as Christ's sacraments. Whether they are effective for salvation depends on the faith of the recipient and not on the administrator. Infants, for instance, are baptized "in hope." When they reach an accountable age, they must believe if they want to appropriate the benefits of the baptism conferred by the Spirit. The Donatists could be admired for their concern about the worthiness of ministers, but they nullified much of that by the way they acted toward Catholics.

One of the tragic by-products of the Donatist controversy was Augustine's rationale for the use of force to reconcile dissidents. Until 406 he opposed coercion against the Donatists. The violent way in which the Circumcellions pursued the Donatist cause, however, induced him to change his mind. In a letter to Festus, an official charged with implementing imperial decrees against the Donatists, Augustine urged the use of force, like parents use on children because they love them (*Ep.* 98). In 417 he reinforced his position in a letter addressed to Boniface, Governor of Africa under Honorius. By this time he had discovered that force worked and laid aside an earlier hesitancy, seeing that "many through the imperial decrees have been and are daily being converted, who now give thanks both for their conversion and for their deliverance from that raging destruction" (*Ep.* 185.7). Like patients cured by their physicians' harsh measures, they have discovered what great blessings they received while complaining of being persecuted. They persecute Catholics unjustly; Catholics persecute them justly (11). The argument supplied the rationale for the inquisition and crusade of the Middle Ages.

Although weakened, Donatists survived. They suffered along with Catholics as a result of the Vandal conquest and efforts to impose Arianism. In Proconsular Africa and also in Mauretania they seem to have lost ground, but they remained relatively strong in the villages of Numidia. The Byzantine reconquest of northern Africa returned Catholics to a position of ascendancy. Donatists were proscribed alongside Arians and Jews. Donatism evidently revived in the late sixth century, however, for Gregory I wrote a series of letters to bishops and Byzantine officials in Africa expressing grave concern that Donatism and Manichaeism had reared their heads again and that Catholics in Numidia needed help. In 593 the pope made a vigorous effort to have the movement crushed, urging the Praetorian Prefect Pantaleo to enforce antiheretical laws against them (*Ep.* 3.32) and goading Catholics to act.

There is some evidence for their survival to the very end of African Christianity as Moslems drew the shades on Christianity there.

The Meletian Schism in Egypt

During the persecution under Diocletian, Peter, the bishop of Alexandria, went into hiding. While he was absent, Meletius, the bishop of Lycopolis in Upper Egypt, visited the city and ordained two persons, Isidore and Arrius, as presbyters. He tried also through them to win over the presbyters to whom Peter had entrusted administration of his flock. When Peter learned of this, he instructed his people not to communicate with Meletius until he could investigate what was happening. Meletius may have acted out of genuine concern, but he violated established rules in invading another bishop's diocese and, worse still, ordaining presbyters in it. Peter, therefore, retaliated by deposing Meletius in a synod of bishops "for many lawless deeds and for sacrifice" (Athanasius, *Apology against the Arians* 59). The evidence is confusing, but it would appear that Meletius disagreed with Peter regarding readmission of the lapsed. Where Peter showed considerable leniency, Meletius adopted a rigorous stance. Soon after his deposition, he was sent by civil authorities to work in the quarries of the Thebaid and later to the mines in Palestine. He thus obtained credentials as a confessor. In Palestine and also upon his return to Egypt in 311 he ordained bishops, in effect initiating a Meletian Church fostering a rigorist image. In 325 Meletians claimed twenty-eight bishops. Although the Council of Nicaea set guidelines for readmission of Meletian clergy, the sect persisted and linked up with Arians in opposition to Athanasius.

Marginal Christianity

The groups discussed thus far in this chapter did not involve deviations from the Catholic Church on basic doctrines, even if many Church fathers refused to distinguish them from those that did. Although the Gnostic, Marcionite, and Montanist crises of the preceding era had already pushed the churches down the road toward more precise self-definition, there remained still much room for critical reflection and debate. Neither Christianity's relationship with Judaism nor its relationship with the Graeco-Roman world was settled. In the process of debating what constituted the essentials some groups found themselves on the margin, unable to identify sufficiently with these to retain affiliation with the mainstream. Most marginal groups in this period tended to pull Christianity back toward Jewish roots rather than Hellenistic.

This was true of the Encratites, a conservative sect whom Irenaeus (*Against Heresies* 1.28.1) attributed to Tatian. According to Hippolytus (*Refutation of All Heresies* 8.13), the Encratites agreed with the Catholic Church about God and Christ. Beyond that, they fostered an extreme asceticism involving rejection of animal food, intoxicating beverages, and sexual intercourse (Irenaeus, *Against Heresies* 1.28.1). Although the Church fathers ascribed the latter to Gnostic or Marcionite influences, they would appear to have been much closer to Essene customs admired by persons like Tatian and Hippolytus. After studying under Justin and teaching for a time in Rome Tatian made his way to Syria where he assembled his *Diatessaron*, a synthesis of the four Gospels. His ascetic tendencies would have fitted into the Syrian context quite well.

Inclination toward Judaism was also characteristic of different forms of what is known as Monarchianism. The name comes from the strong emphasis these groups placed on the single rule (*mon-arche* in Greek) of God. Until the early third century, actually, two christologies competed with one another. One of these, now usually called pneumatic (Spirit) christology, emphasized the indwelling of the Spirit in Jesus enabling him to perform miracles and ultimately to be raised from the dead. This christology dominated in Rome throughout the second century. The other,

Logos (Word) christology, stressed the preexistence and incarnation or enfleshment of the Eternal Logos in Jesus. It prevailed in Asia Minor where it perhaps originated in connection with a Johannine community of some kind.

Logos christology was seen by Monarchian Christians as a threat to Jewish monotheism. Some proponents of Logos christology—Justin and Origen, for instance—did not hesitate to call Jesus a "Second God." To avoid a charge of bitheism (of which Callistus accused Hippolytus), proponents of Logos christology framed a statement which appeared illogical and contradictory. (1) God is One. (2) Jesus is God, that is, a worshipful being. (3) Yet Jesus is other than the Father. Monarchians responded, "It can't be both ways. If God is One, either Jesus is God or He is other than the Father." In time the controversy tilted in favor of proponents of Logos christology, thanks especially to Tertullian and Hippolytus. In the late-second and early-third centuries, however, several marginal sects emerged and continued the tradition of pneumatic christology. Unfortunately their writings have not survived and opponents often distorted data about them.

Adoptionistic or Dynamistic Monarchians sought to get rid of the contradiction in Logos christology by saying that God is one and Jesus is other than the Father but denying that He is God. Several sects formed to advocate this viewpoint. One emerged in Asia Minor between 170 and 180 with the name *Alogoi*. The Alogoi vigorously opposed the Montanists and their prophetic claims, rejected the Gospel of John and the Logos concept it propounds as well as the Revelation of John, and objected to the term Logos as a Gnostic idea. Both Irenaeus and Hippolytus considered them schismatics rather than heretics, but nothing more definite is known of their christology. How long they existed or when, how, and why the churches of Asia Minor excluded them is not known.

About 190 Theodotus the tanner, a well-educated Christian of Byzantium, founded a party of dynamistic or adoptionistic Monarchians. Although Theodotus acknowledged at least partial orthodoxy in theology and cosmology, Victor excommunicated him because of christological errors. Influenced perhaps by the Alogoi, he taught a pneumatic christolology. Jesus was born of a virgin through the agency of the Holy Spirit according to divine plan. After living "promiscuously" and becoming "preeminently religious," the Spirit descended on him at baptism and acclaimed him as the Christ. From the Spirit he received power (*dynamis*) to fulfill his mission and to live a righteous life. Some Dynamists believed that Jesus became God by virtue of the resurrection, but others that he never did (Hippolytus, *Refutation of All Heresies* 7.23). Other notable features of this circle, which included Theodotus the Banker and a certain Asclepiodotus, were their admiration for Galen, use of textual criticism, and grammatical rather than allegorical interpretation of scriptures. After being excommunicated by Zephyrinus (199–217), this group made an abortive attempt to found a church at Rome, hiring Natalius, a confessor, to serve as their bishop, but he soon deserted them (Eusebius, H.E. 5.28).

Later writers ascribed to Theodotus the Banker the founding of a sect called Melchizedekians who based their christology on Hebrews 5–7. There appears to be distortion of their thought, however. Rather than elevating Melchizedek above Jesus, as Epiphanius (*Against Heresies* 55) charged, they regarded the Holy Spirit as the sole divine essence besides the Father and considered the Spirit identical with the Son. The Spirit appeared to Abraham. As in the Shepherd of Hermas, Theodotus viewed Jesus as a man anointed with the power of the Spirit but inferior to the Holy Spirit, who was the true Son.

A similar christology was propounded by followers of Artemas or Artemon. They also denied to Jesus the ascription "God," as some Theodotians did. The sect still existed in 268, for a synod of bishops at Antioch condemned Paul of Samosata for scorning the mystery of faith and strutting about "in the abominable heresy of Artemas" (Eusebius, H.E. 7.30.16).

The linking up of Artemas and Paul shifted the center of adoptionistic or dynamistic Monarchianism from Rome to the East where, as Origen's references make clear, many opposed Logos christology. Beryllus, bishop of Bostra in Arabia, apparently espoused the adoptionist christology until convinced of his error by Origen about 244 (Eusebius, H.E. 6.33). About 260 Paul of Samosata, bishop of the prestigious see of Antioch, began openly to oppose Logos christology and to propound a much more subtle form of the dynamistic Monarchianism than earlier exponents had. In explicit opposition to Johannine christology he denied the descent of the Son "from above" and instead asserted, "Jesus Christ is from below" (Eusebius, H.E., 7.30.11). The bishops, however, criticized him not just for his christology but for his haughtiness. He preferred the title of *Proconsular Ducenarius* of Queen Zenobia to that of bishop, they charged, and he acted more like a high public official than a servant of Christ. He behaved "like the rulers of the world" in church assemblies, rebuking people when they didn't applaud him sufficiently and assailing deceased preachers. He forbade singing psalms to Christ as "the modern productions of modern men" and trained women to sing psalms to himself. With support of Queen Zenobia of Palmyra, however, Paul proved a tough foe. It took three synods in Antioch before he was deposed and replaced by Domnus as bishop of Antioch. Even then, he retained office under Zenobia for four more years. When he refused to relinquish control of the church building, his opponents had to petition the Emperor Aurelian, who ordered the building given "to those to whom the bishops of Italy and of the city of Rome should adjudge it "(Eusebius, H.E. 7.30.19).

Modalistic Monarchians took the other route to elimination of the contradiction posed by

Logos christology, affirming that God is one and Jesus is God but denying that Jesus is other than the Father. In the West they were usually called Patripassians ("Father sufferingers"); in the East Sabellians. Modalism had considerable vogue in Western thinking generally from an early date, but it resulted first in a separate sect late in the second century. A major figure in the development of Modalism was Noetus, a teacher in Smyrna or Ephesus who was excommunicated for his views around 230. Epigonus (d. 200), a disciple of Noetus, came to Rome at the beginning of Zephyrinus's episcopate (199–217) and founded a separate Patripassian party based on Noetus's views. The party was first headed by Epigonus and then, after 215, by Sabellius. According to Hippolytus, who opposed them vigorously, the Patripassians rallied strong support in Rome, enlisting as allies both the gullible Zephyrinus and the wily Callistus (217–222). Callistus, however, trying to find a way out of an increasingly intense fight between two parties, excommunicated both Sabellius and Hippolytus and proposed a compromise formula that moved Roman doctrine in the direction of Logos christology. Sabellians or Patripassians survived for years in Rome. Their teachings reached Africa by way of Praxeas, who ran into a wall of resistance from Tertullian, was silenced, and forced to write a retraction.

In the East Sabellians stirred up a bitter battle lasting from about 220 until 270. Sabellius apparently developed far reaching relations with the East after his excommunication by Callistus. The key tenet of Sabellians was that Father, Son, and Holy Spirit are really different names for the same Being. Zealous to preserve monotheism, Sabellius called the one God the "Son-Father." God appears *successively* in the "modes" (thence modalism) of Father, Son, and Spirit and not simultaneously. From creation to incarnation God is manifested as Father, the Creator and Legislator; from incarnation to assumption as Son; and from the assumption on as Spirit. The Arian controversy in the East was, in many respects, a continuation of the debate between Sabellians and proponents of Logos christology. Indeed, Arius accused Alexander, bishop of Alexandria, of Sabellianism.

Whereas the preceding sects belong on the margin of Christianity, at least one known to the early Fathers, the Elkesaites, stepped beyond that point. This syncretistic Jewish Christian sect derived its central tenets from a mysterious book brought to Rome about 220 by Alcibiades of Apamea in Syria. Reputedly revealed by an angel who was the Son of God to Elxai in the third year of Trajan (101 C.E.), its contents were disclosed to no one except under oath of absolute secrecy. Among the distinguishing practices of the Elkesaites showing pagan influence were repeated ablutions in the name of the Father and the Son, not only to obtain forgiveness of sins but also to heal the sick. Elkesaites aligned baptismal days with the Zodiac. In line with their Jewish emphasis, on the other hand, they required circumcision and adherence to the law. They rejected sacrifices and parts of the Old Testament, however, as well as Paul's letters in the New. They viewed Christ as an angel and taught repeated incarnations, although they believed in the virgin birth. They used bread and salt in celebration of the Lord's supper. They forbade eating of meats but valued marriage. They allowed renunciation of faith in time of persecution.

In this era as in the preceding one the churches struggled to define who they were in an often bitterly hostile environment. In some ways persecution helped by forcing Christians to give serious attention to who they were and whether the price they were paying was worth it. In other ways, however, it added to the problem, to the extent that some viewed Christianity entirely through lenses ground by persecution. Dispute about what Christianity required led, as we have seen, to several grievous schisms and left the larger family always wondering whether they really remained faithful enough.

Chapter 15

Christian Spirituality

The age of the martyrs, costly and painful as it was, laid the foundations for Christian spirituality. Living under threat forced the faithful to strengthen and deepen their commitments to God. Critical in this was the formation they received through the catechumenate and baptism. Exhortations to faithfulness constantly harked back to the renunciation of Satan and the oath (*sacramentum*) uttered there. Given the ominous conditions under which they lived, it is not surprising that the catechumenate lasted up to three or more years and when it was compromised lapses of discipline increased. Even in less fearsome circumstances, however, lapses occurred, necessitating a shaping of more formal procedures to rescue the fallen and restore them to their commitment. Nevertheless, Christian spirituality depended then as now on a regimen of regular worship, frequent and fervent prayer, fasting, and other disciplines exercised both individually and corporately.

However much Christians might aspire to a high level of obedience to God on the part of all, they have had to reckon with the reality that some will honor their commitments more fully than others. In this era the martyrs set the standard, an artificially high one by virtue of the irregular demands exacted by persecution. When Gallienus opened the way to a long era of peace and persecution abated, the ideal of the martyrs inspired a few to seek solitary places like those the martyrs had had to flee to, or been exiled to,

during the persecutions. Anthony was not the first hermit, but his flight to the desert in 271 marks the beginning of a stream which, a century or so later, turned into a wide river. In this same confluence of circumstances, lived those, present in every era and realm of human existence, who sought more immediate and direct experience with God. This, quite clearly, was the goal of those now categorized under the Gnostic label. Although many of the Gnostic schools had fallen under the censure of the churches because of their dualism, there remained no small number of Christians, especially those of culture and education, who aspired to something more than "faith" defined as upright conduct and commendable demeanor. They, too, wanted knowledge, direct and intuitive knowledge (*gnosis*), of the living God. To such persons, Clement of Alexandria and Origen rendered a priceless service. So also did the desert monks, some of whom could report success in their most earnest endeavor to "see" God.

Christian Formation

Because both Hippolytus and Tertullian fall into the rigorist category, it is unlikely their demands would have been implemented in all of the churches during the early third century. Something similar to the formation process they describe, however, must have occurred everywhere churches lived under the shadow of persecution. According to the *Apostolic Tradition* of

Hippolytus, inquirers went through serious scrutiny before they were admitted to the catechumenate. They had to have confirmation of those who brought them "that they are competent to hear the word." If they obtained sufficient approval, they underwent an inquiry into their personal lives. The demon possessed could not be admitted until cleansed. Persons in numerous occupations had to relinquish them or be rejected: panderers, sculptors or painters of idols, actors or pantomimists, teachers of children in pagan schools, charioteers, gladiators, or their trainers or other persons connected with the combats, priests in the other cults, military commanders or public magistrates, astrologers, diviners, soothsayers, users of magic formulas, jugglers, clowns, amulet makers, keepers of concubines. Harlots, licentious men, eunuchs, and magicians were rejected outright.

Candidates normally spent three years as catechumens, but Hippolytus granted some concession to the zealous. After the instruction period catechumens had to withdraw and stay apart from baptized believers. After catechumens prayed the instructor laid hands on them and prayed, then dismissed them. Before baptism catechumens underwent a further examination to see "whether they have lived soberly, whether they have honored the widows, whether they have visited the sick, whether they have been active in well doing" (2.20). If they received a favorable report from sponsors, they were separated from other catechumens for a final phase of preparation for baptism. In this period they underwent daily exorcisms. As they approached baptism, normally on Easter Sunday, the bishop laid hands on them to exorcise demons and to determine whether he was personally assured of their purity. Those designated for baptism were instructed to wash themselves on Thursday for baptism on Sunday. All candidates fasted on Friday. On Saturday the bishop laid hands upon them and exorcised them a final time; breathed in their faces; sealed their foreheads, ears and nose with the sign of the Cross; and then raised them up. That night, they kept vigil, "listening to reading and instruction."

Baptism established a clear dividing line between the old life dominated by demons and the new life surrendered to God in Jesus Christ. At dawn prayer was said over the water to invoke the Holy Spirit to purify and empower it. Those to be baptized stripped off all clothing and other apparel for nude baptism (in private, of course). No one was to enter the water wearing "any alien object" such as rings, bracelets, hair combs, or jewelry. According to Hippolytus (A.T. 2.21), baptisms took place in the order of children, grown men, and then women. Those receiving baptism faced westward, the realm of darkness, and renounced Satan and "all his service and works" and were anointed with an oil of exorcism by a presbyter who, on applying the oil, declared: "Let all evil spirits depart from you." Turning around to face eastward, they took a trinitarian oath (*sacramentum*) pledging absolute loyalty. "I believe and bow to Thee and all Thy service, O Father, Son, and Holy Spirit," and entered the water. The bishop, presbyter, or deacon performing the baptism interrogated them and baptized them after each response.

Q: Do you believe in God, the Father Almighty?
R: I believe. [First immersion.]
Q: Do you believe in Jesus Christ, the Son of God, Who was born of the Holy Spirit and the Virgin Mary, Who was crucified in the days of Pontius Pilate, And died (and was buried) And rose the third day living from the dead, And ascended into the heavens, And sat down at the right hand of the Father, And will come to judge the living and the dead?
R: I believe. [Second immersion.]
Q: Do you believe in the Holy Spirit, in the Holy Church, and the resurrection of the flesh.
R: I believe. [Third immersion.]

Their baptism completed, the newly baptized received a second anointing, this time with an oil of Thanksgiving. They then dried, reclothed themselves, and joined the assembly of believers to receive the bishop's confirmation and to partake of the eucharist for the first time, both acts dramatically reinforcing their decision.

The bishop laid hands on the newly baptized, prayed for an infilling of the Holy Spirit "so that they may serve thee according to thy will" (*Apostolic Tradition* 2.22), "sealed" their foreheads with the sign of the Cross using an unguent, and gave the kiss of peace. In churches such as the Roman the new Christians partook not only of the bread and wine of the eucharist but also of a mixture of milk and honey symbolizing their entry into the promised land. At Rome, according to Hippolytus (2.23), they sipped three times from three cups—one of water, one of milk and honey, and one of wine—to emphasize their commitment to the Trinitarian God. Already at this early date, the bishop imparted secret instructions following baptism, anticipating instruction in the "mysteries" that became common by the fourth century.

Sustaining Commitment

The degree of commitment Christianity demanded of those who wished to enter distinguished it markedly from the competitors with the possible exception of the state itself. Sustaining such a level of commitment, however, was no easy matter, particularly as the churches incorporated large numbers in times of peace, as lapses during persecutions under Decius and Diocletion demonstrate. Here day to day discipline had to undergird and reinforce what transpired in the catechumenal/baptismal process. Exclusion and restoration of the "fallen" represented last resort efforts and not the normal means for sustaining commitment. Other measures were both more common and more crucial for the vast majority.

In addition to worship on Sundays, which will be discussed later, the churches relied on several practices. One of these was a regular regimen of prayer. Hippolytus directed believers to pray as prescribed by the *Didache* but also on arising in the morning, on retiring at bedtime, and at midnight. Treatises on prayer by Tertullian, Cyprian, and Origen reveal the central role they ascribed to prayer to sustain religious fervor. They viewed the Lord's prayer not only as a model for prayer but as "a compendium of the entire Gospel" (Tertullian, *Prayer* 1.6). Cyprian eloquently eulogized the prayer for supplying "foundations for building hope, supports for strengthening faith, nourishments for encouraging the heart, rudders for directing our course, helps for gaining salvation, which, as they instruct the minds of believers on earth, conduct them to the heavenly kingdom" (*The Lord's Prayer* 1). Cyprian argued strongly against private prayer and in favor of corporate, doubtless due to the problem of schism in his day, but all three treatises contain instruction regarding the way to pray.

In this era, persecution notwithstanding, Christians gathered early, as circumstances permitted, to receive instruction on other days besides Sunday. Hippolytus and Cyprian viewed corporate assemblies as the preferable practice, conscious probably of the supportive effect of the group.

> The God-fearing person should consider it a great loss if he or she does not go to the place in which they give instruction, and especially if he or she knows how to read.
> (Hippolytus, *Apostolic Tradition* 3.35)

Catechists receive help from the Holy Spirit, so it would be best "to go to the assembly to the place where the Holy Spirit abounds." On days when no assemblies met, however, the faithful were expected to "take a holy book and read in it sufficiently what seems profitable" (*Apostolic Tradition* 3.35.3). Gatherings such as these became increasingly common during the two long eras of peace before Decius and Diocletian, for both emperors aimed their repression at public meetings of Christians.

Fasting also contributed significantly to Christian discipline in this period. Besides the customary two-day fast prior to baptism and Wednesday and Friday fasts, Christians observed partial fasts during Holy Week in some areas, limiting their diet to bread, salt and water. Lenten fasting, however, probably did not begin until about 325. The Montanists, who distinguished themselves from Catholics by their frequent fasts, observed two weeks of partial fasts (xerophagies) during the year. In his Montanist period Tertullian accused Catholics of hating to fast whereas they faulted Montanists for teaching people to fast more often than to marry (*Fasting* 1.3).

The most important factor in sustaining commitment was the little bands of Christians themselves exhorting, encouraging, and inspiring one another. The fellowship meals, *agapes*, they shared symbolized the intimacy they developed. They helped one another financially. They provided work for the unemployed: some communities functioning as employment services for those who had to leave former occupations. Organized legally as burial clubs, they took care of the sick and dying and already deceased. Where possible, they visited the imprisoned and stood by the confessors and martyrs. They offered fellowship without regard to wealth or social status or education. Overall, they outstripped all competitors in charities and social aid, major factors surely in their system of support.

The Martyrs: Ideal Christians

Had there been no persecutions, Christian history would probably have turned out quite differently. Christian spirituality would certainly have been different, for some group other than the martyrs would have established the ideal, and the monks who emulated the martyrs would have looked elsewhere for their model. As the art of the catacombs shows at a glance, the martyrs continued the noble and heroic line of Daniel, the three children in the fiery furnace, and Jesus himself, crucified on behalf of others. Ninety-year-old Pothinus, bishop of Lyons, though weakened by age and disease, gave a noble testimony "as if he were Christ himself." Blandina, hanged before

beasts in the shape of a cross, appeared to other martyrs of Lyons as she exhorted them to be the Crucified Christ himself urging them on. "Although small and weak and greatly despised, she had put on the great and invincible athlete Christ," according to the *Letter of the Churches of Lyons and Vienne*, written just after this pogrom, "and in many contests had overcome the Adversary and through the conflict had gained the crown of immortality" (in Eusebius, H.E. 5.1). Perpetua and the other catechumens experienced visions, like Stephen had, of the victorious Christ urging them on in their confessions. When Felicitas cried out in pain brought on by advance of pregnancy, one of the guards asked, "What will you do when you come into the amphitheater if you cry out from such pains as this?" She replied, "Here I am being crucified; but there the Lord will suffer for me" (*Acts of S. Perpetua* 8.2). Eusebius, commenting on the martyrdoms in the persecution under Diocletian, observed in the confessors "the divine power of our Savior who has borne witness, Jesus Christ Himself, as it became present and manifested itself distinctly to the martyrs" (H.E. 8.7.2).

Reverence for the martyrs immediately left its mark on Christian thought. One notable effect was the cult of martyrs and relics visible already in the account of Polycarp's death in the second century. Not only the martyrs themselves but any object they touched was considered holy and spiritually potent to ward off diseases or to bring good fortune. To have a martyr touch handkerchiefs or scarves would assure certain power over the demonic. The remains of the martyrs themselves, then, would possess such power multiplied many times over and were thus interred in places, such as the catacombs, where the faithful could come and tap into it.

The influence martyrs wielded became clearly visible in letters of indulgence the lapsed or their families sought from confessors in order to secure restoration of communion. Cyprian had to plead with confessors during the Decian persecution to weigh carefully and cautiously all pleas for certificates reading, "Let so and so be received into communion with his own people," which would guarantee readmission (*Ep.* 15.3-4). He likewise had to caution his clergy regarding the "impudent manner" in which some confessors handed out commendations (*Ep.* 27). Paul, martyred in Carthage in 250, instructed the confessor Lucian to issue such certificates in his name to anyone who requested them after his death (*Ep.* 22.2) and Lucian persuaded all the confessors in prison with him to support the same policy.

Martyrdom was regarded as a second baptism. Where the first baptism washed away sins of the past, martyrdom wiped out all sins. "Only the baptism of blood makes us purer than the baptism of water," said Origen. Those who receive baptism in water may sin again, but those who suffer martyrdom can never do so. In baptism sins are removed; in martyrdom they are destroyed (*Sermons on Judges* 7.2).

Restoring the Fallen

Before proceeding to a discussion of the successors of the martyrs it will be useful to see how the churches attempted to deal with the repentant lapsed during the era when so many yielded to threats and harassment not only from popular sources but from officials. During the persecutions of Decius and Diocletian, the "fallen" included a vast constituency, thus forcing the churches to reflect more deeply on the question of discipline than ever before.

The churches, of course, carried over from the preceding era a variety of attitudes toward serious breaches of Christian discipline—apostasy, adultery, and murder. On the rigorist end of the spectrum stood the Montanists, Tertullian in his Montanist period supplying the information on their views, Hippolytus, Novatian and his followers, and, at the end of the period, the Donatists. As a Montanist, Tertullian assumed an extreme position in opposition to what he characterized as an "edict" of the "Pontifex Maximus,"

now thought by some to be a bishop of Carthage rather than Callistus of Rome. Whereas in his Catholic days Tertullian affirmed restoration of all offenders one time as specified by Hermas, in his treatise *On Purity* he denounced restoration of adulterers or fornicators as well as murderers and idolators, and labeled Hermas "the shepherd of adulterers" (10). God may forgive such sins, and offenders should do penance for that reason, but the Church cannot (11.21). Not even the martyrs can attain forgiveness for such sins as adultery save for themselves (22). Hippolytus took a similar stand against the leniency of Callistus, claiming to forgive all sins on the basis of the Parable of the Tares (*Refutation of All Heresies* 8.12).

When the Decian persecution decimated the ranks of the faithful, the Catholic churches showed they had not resolved polarities on the issue. Some, such as the deacon Novatus of Carthage, favored ready restoration of all who applied, whereas Novatian and his followers pursued a line close to that drawn by Tertullian and Hippolytus. Even the confessors disagreed on the matter. Cyprian and African bishops allied with him steered a middle course between these extremes, wanting to evaluate individual cases on their own merits but forced by the new onslaught of persecution under Gallus to adopt a more lenient position. By the time the smoke settled over the Novatianist schism the Catholic churches found themselves distinguishing degrees of penance according to the severity of the offense. Apostasy, adultery, and murder obviously required longer displays of remorse than drunkenness, brawling, or lesser offenses.

The barbarian invasions occasioned a further step in this direction. During an invasion of Cappadocia by the Boradi and Goths in 256–258, discipline among Christians broke down dreadfully. In the confusion created by the invasions some plundered hapless neighbors' property, claiming to "find" it; others took captive for their own use slaves who escaped; and still others joined the barbarians in murdering, informing on neighbors, and pillaging. In a canonical letter Gregory (Thaumaturgus), bishop of Neocaesarea, distinguished degrees of penance for various offenses. By about 300 the churches of the East had fashioned a full blown system of penance. According to a spurious article added to the canonical letter of Gregory, penitents were separated into five categories: "weepers," who remained completely outside the church grounds; "hearers," who listened to the sermon from the portico only until catechumens left; "fallers," who prostrated themselves inside the building proper during the sermon and left with the catechumens; "bystanders," who remained even during the eucharist but could not partake; and "restored penitents," who could again share the communion. After 300 church councils such as that at Elvira levied various penalties for infractions. The churches obviously strained to maintain commitment at an acceptable level as converts flooded the churches.

Monasticism

Several factors, some external and some internal, combined during the reign of peace initiated by Gallienus to foster a powerful movement of Christian asceticism. Externally, of course, Christianity inherited some ascetic tendencies from Jewish sects such as the Essenes, who carried their rigorism into the churches. A widespread dualism encouraged these further. In addition, some persons were naturally inclined toward a life of solitude, prayer, and self-discipline and found in it a counterweight to the dominance of the state. When persecution ceased, moreover, it left a vacuum for those who measured sanctity by the devotion of the martyrs. Men and women responded to Jesus' demand for self-denial and his appeal to the rich young man to sell his possessions and give the proceeds to the poor. They heard, too, Paul's exhortations to bodily as well as spiritual discipline and self-control and his expression of preference for celibacy in view of the expected return of Christ (1 Cor. 7). Many tried to emulate the example of the Jerusalem community in sharing goods and responded to the high moral standards set by the first generation of Christians.

Two different types of monasticism emerged during the late third and early fourth centuries, hermitic and coenobitic. Although Anthony of Egypt is often cited as the first hermit, he was not, for he himself sought guidance from other hermits. His popularity during a long career (270–356), however, gave impetus to the movement to the desert. Athanasius's biography, written just after Anthony died, further fueled the burgeoning movement. Born in Egypt of Christian parents, Anthony did poorly in school, avoided other children, and "desired only to lead a simple life at home" (*Life* 1). When he was about eighteen or twenty his parents died, leaving a younger sister to care for. Shortly afterwards, he was reflecting one day on the way the Apostles had forsaken everything to follow Jesus and how the early Christians of Jerusalem laid all their possessions at the feet of the Apostles. As he entered the church, he heard Jesus' words to the rich young man being read, took them to be directly spoken to himself, and, leaving the church, proceeded to give away all of his property to the poor except for a little he reserved for his sister.

Entrusting his sister to the care of nuns (virgins), he visited hermits and learned from each some of the secrets of the solitary life. Though he did some manual labor, he set himself to the difficult task of "praying without ceasing" (1 Thess. 5:17). A near illiterate, he memorized scriptures as he heard them read in the churches. In the desert Anthony did battle with demons which sought constantly to entice him away from his vocation and came out a victor. After living several years on the outskirts of a village, at age thirty-five he crossed the Nile and set out for Pispir, where he lived in an abandoned fort. His fame spread and great crowds came to see him. Spurred on by his example, many youth chose the monastic life.

As presented by Athanasius, Anthony viewed asceticism as a contest through which one could attain the prize of heaven. He was God's athlete overcoming the demonic. By prayer and fasting one could be made a better person day by day. For those who opened themselves to God's working, the Spirit would drive out vices such as avarice, malice, covetousness, and lechery and instill virtues such as wisdom, justice, temperance, courage (the Greek cardinal virtues), love, faith, meekness, and hospitality. The Devil and his hosts will do everything possible to subvert the faithful ascetic, but God's Power in Christ is sufficient to overcome them.

Like most monks, Anthony yearned for martyrdom and narrowly missed it during the persecution of Maximin Daia in 311 when he ministered to confessors in mines and prisons and encouraged others before the judges. When this persecution ceased, he returned to the "daily martyrdom" of the hermit—fasting, wearing a hair shirt and never bathing or even washing his feet. Again so many besieged him he had to flee to the Inner Mountains overlooking the Red Sea. There he guided other monks, performed miracles, saw visions, and did other things characteristic of a person utterly dedicated to God. He died at age 105.

Coenobitic or "common life" monasticism originated shortly after Constantine and Licinius issued the Edict of Milan and will therefore receive treatment in the next section. The way of desert, whether hermitic or coenobitic, was a way of holy obedience. The monks sought, first of all, to deny themselves, take up a cross, and follow Jesus (Luke 9:23). They wanted, above everything, to imitate Christ and the martyrs who had done so. Many were willing literally to meet the challenge of Jesus to the rich youth to sell all possessions and give the proceeds to the poor so as to follow him (Luke 18:22). A decision so radical as this made theirs, in the second place, a movement of protest both against Roman culture and against churches that allowed discipline to deteriorate. The more the churches accommodated the world, the louder their protest sounded. Like the martyrs, the monks lifted loud voices against alliance with a state whose very fabric was woven from the thread of religion. These latter-day martyrs still carried with them the early Christian suspicion of lives settled comfortably into customs shaped by superstition and idolatry. The earliest monks were rugged individualists, sometimes disdaining even the institutions of the Church in their quest for complete obedience to God alone.

The means for achieving such complete obedience were solitude, self-discipline, and prayer. The name *monachos* derives from the Greek word *monos*, alone. The object of the "solitary" was to confront the full mystery of the invisible God in silence. Even among coenobites, association with others was viewed as a barrier to this encounter. To be among other persons was to risk distractions. Solitude alone, however, will not assure centeredness on God. That requires discipline, especially the discipline of fasting. Here, to be sure, many monks fell under the spell of dualism, the idea that matter is evil and the spirit alone is good. Some literally attempted to destroy their bodies by starving themselves, wearing chains, disregarding personal hygiene, not bathing, and otherwise displaying contempt for the physical. In time such extremism gave way to more moderate disciplines designed to enhance the life of prayer.

The calling of the monk was, above all else, a calling to prayer. Their ultimate goal, of course, was the vision of God, like that experienced by Moses. Seeing God requires "purity of heart." Purity of heart is a product of God's transforming love at work in the lives of those who open themselves to God in prayer. Thus, in the words of Abba Isaac, a disciple of Anthony, every monk's aim was "continual and unbroken perseverance in prayer" with a view to attaining "an immovable tranquillity of mind and a perpetual purity" (Cassian, *Conferences* 9.2). Some prayed in simple ways, imagining God in human form, others prayed in more complex style. They recited the Lord's prayer as "the method and form of prayer proposed to us by the Judge himself" (6.24). They chanted the psalms, some attempting to recite all 150 psalms every day. They repeated the petition taken from Psalm 69:1: "O God, make speed to save me; O Lord, make haste to help me" as a kind of mantra designed to collect the mind in time of temptation. They developed "the prayer of the heart" or "Jesus prayer" which entailed reciting over and over: "Lord, Jesus Christ, Son of God, have mercy on me a sinner." The desert monks learned a lot about the psychology of prayer and how to induce moods which could facilitate intuitive experience of the divine. Abba Isaac depicted this experience as an enlightenment of the mind so that it "pours forth richly as from a copious fountain in an accumulation of thoughts and ineffably utters to God, expressing in the shortest possible space of time such great things that the mind when it returns to its usual condition cannot easily utter or relate" (9.25).

Christian Mysticism

The Christian mysticism that blossomed during this era had some of its roots in this kind of soil, others in the Old Testament psalms and prophets, others in the Pauline and Johannine writings of the New Testament, and still others in the experience of the martyrs. It was Platonism, however, that supplied the sunshine and rain to produce a luxuriant plant.

Platonism circulated in a variety of forms, some more or less closely affiliated with Christianity and some independent of it. Platonist preachers traveled around proclaiming the message of salvation found in the *Corpus Hermeticum*, a collection of materials dating from the second to the fourth centuries. In the main such popular promoters fell far below the level of Plotinus but they aspired to the same basic goals:

a return ultimately to unity with the One and, in the interim, "a flight of the alone to the Alone."

The Gnostics, who drew many ingredients for their hodge podge from Platonism, coveted immediate, intuitive experience of God. *Gnosis* meant for them not intellectual but spiritual "knowledge." According to *The Gospel of Truth*, a work sometimes ascribed to Valentinus himself, the Word, the thought and the mind of the Father, came forth from the Pleroma ("Fullness") in order to bring the gift of the knowledge of God. He enlightened the "perfect," that is, Gnostics, with true knowledge. Those who received such knowledge are "from above" and do the will of the Father. By knowledge they purify themselves from multiplicity and enter into unity with God.

Clement and Origen both walked the Gnostic path, distinguishing themselves from heterodox Gnostics by repudiating their dualism. This direction was quite likely worked out by Pantaenus, the "Sicilian bee" who founded the "school" of Alexandria. Clement, however, deserves credit for wedding biblical and hellenistic traditions to give birth to a Christian contemplative tradition. According to Clement, *gnosis* should combine three features: contemplation, fulfilling the precepts of Jesus (as the Word), and instruction of good persons (*Stromateis* 2.10.46). For Clement *gnosis* is a gift of the Teacher, Christ. In his *Address to the Greeks* he has the Logos cry out, "Freely I give you the Word, the knowledge of God, I give you this freely, in perfection, in myself" (120.3). How? By reading and explaining the scriptures to us. Philosophy may serve as a guide if we will use it wisely, but the starting point for *gnosis* must be the scriptures. Heterodox Gnostics erred by starting with philosophy. The ultimate goal of the Gnostic is to "know" or "see" or "possess" God. The way to the goal is prayer or contemplation. We can ascertain whether we have reached the ultimate goal when we love as God loves. "God is love and is knowable to those who love God." Clement was the first Christian theologian to characterize this as "deification." "The Logos of God became human so that you might learn how human beings can become divine" (*Address* 11). Like the Stoics, from whom he drew many ethical insights, Clement urged gnostics to strive for *apatheia*, a lack of desire by which disorders of fallen human nature are overcome and stability is attained. Love is the supreme motive.

Scholars debate today whether Origen should be credited as a cocreator of Neoplatonism with Plotinus. Both, it is now recognized, studied under Ammonius Saccas, who, like Origen, was born of Christian parents and evidently remained faithful to his upbringing. From early on Origen practiced what Eusebius called "the most philosophic life possible" (H.E. 6.3.7-10), an extreme asceticism which induced him to take literally Jesus' observation that some should become eunuchs for the kingdom's sake. From Clement he learned to put scriptures at the center of his quest for truth in a way that distinguished him from Plotinus, yet he went beyond his teacher in his contemplation of Christ in the scriptures. Origen has received much criticism for his handling of scriptures. He was obviously capable of commenting on them in the historical sense, but the higher "spiritual" or allegorical sense fascinated him far more precisely because it catered to his quest for *gnosis*. Since no item of scriptures had gotten there by chance, Origen had to find its spiritual nuances even when he did not dare do a literal interpretation. Unlike Clement, he manifested only a passing interest in the moral sense of scriptures.

Origen laid foundations for both asceticism and mysticism, which, in his mind, were closely connected. The soul must increasingly detach itself from the egoistic desires which enslave it in the world. This detachment takes place by following Christ and participating in his life. To follow him, however, brings the Christian into a fierce battle against demons, for they resist the indwelling Word with all their power. At the heart of Origen's mystical theology was the

action of the divine Logos who grows in the soul and to whom the soul is wed. Origen was the first to interpret the Song of Songs spiritually, either of Christ speaking to the Church or of Christ speaking to the individual soul. Like Clement, Origen distinguished the "gnostic" from the ordinary Christian, yet with concern for humility and awareness of human limitations. Origen's mysticism of the Logos extends into a mysticism of God, who is "beyond knowing."

Chapter 16

Life Together

Early Christianity distinguished itself from its competitors in a variety of ways, but no distinction stands out more clearly than its corporate consciousness and cohesiveness. Pagans as well as Christians discerned the difference. Whereas Mithra could claim conventicles scattered all over the Empire, Christianity possessed an Empire wide network bound together by a complex array of charities, worship, ministry, and doctrine. Not surprisingly, competitors often suspected something sinister in this. "They recognize each other by secret marks and signs and fall in love before they scarcely know each other," Minucius Felix quoted some pagans charging (*Octavius* 9.2). Some of the emperors, as noted earlier envisioned Christianity as "an empire within the Empire" that threatened the latter's control. When Constantine made his decision in favor of Christianity, it was its structured unity which apparently tipped the balances in its favor; this was the religion, he concluded, which could hold a tottering colossus together.

Charities and Social Aid

One of the strong links in the Christian chain was its charities and social aid offered with little discrimination. Although the Romans practiced largesse, as A. R. Hands has pointed out, they sought something in return, if not *quid pro quo* in the gift, then at least honor or friendship. Chris-

tians gave with expectation of "treasures in heaven."

Charities and social aid originated in local communities with giving of alms and foodstuffs for the clergy, the poor, and widows and orphans. Tertullian described the procedures ca. 200 C.E.

> Even if there is some kind of treasury, it is not accumulated from a high initiation fee as if the religion were something bought and paid for. Each person deposits a small amount on a certain day of the month or whatever that person wishes, and only on condition that the person is willing and able to do so. No one is forced; each makes his (or her) contribution voluntarily. These are, so to speak, the deposits of piety. The money from them is spent not for banquets or drinking parties or good-for-nothing eatinghouses, but for the support and burial of the poor, for children who are without their parents and means of subsistence, for aged persons who are confined at home; likewise, for shipwrecked sailors, and for any in the mines, on islands or in prisons. Provided only it be for the sake of fellowship with God, they become entitled to loving and protective care for their confession.   (*Apology* 39)

Cyprian's treatise on *Work and Almsgiving* indicates the accent churches increasingly placed on giving as a means of grace. After baptism those who slip can "safeguard salvation," through works of justice and mercy. Prayers and fastings have less potency when not accompanied by almsgiving. Those who fear losing their patrimony should fear more the loss of their salvation on account of covetousness and avarice. Besides alms contributed weekly or monthly, the wealthy sometimes gave huge sums.

Direction of charities and social aid in this period was entrusted to the bishops. The actual distribution, however, was done by deacons. Because of the vastness of the charities in the city of Rome, bishop Fabian appointed seven regionary deacons to oversee the work by districts. His successor Cornelius reported in 250 that, in addition to about a hundred clergy, the Roman Church supported 1,500 widows and indigents (Eusebius, H.E. 6.43). As the touching story of the deacon Lawrence, gathering the poor when commanded to assemble the Church's treasures, would demonstrate, this Church distinguished itself by the extent of its care. Yet it was not alone. Churches everywhere took care of widows and orphans; tended the sick, the infirm, and the disabled; buried the dead, including indigents; cared for slaves; and furnished work for those who needed it.

Three types of social aid attest the broad scope of Christian interknittedness. One involved care for prisoners incarcerated or forced to work in mines and for exiles during periods of persecution. The apologist Aristides reported that when Christians heard of anyone imprisoned, "they all render aid in that person's necessity, and if the person can be redeemed, they set him (or her) free" (*Apology* 15). Eusebius claimed that the youthful Origen not only stood by the side of martyrs during their imprisonment until their final condemnation but accompanied them to their execution (H.E. 6.3). To visit prisoners was a special charge of deacons, but many others joined them. So notorious were Christians in their care that Licinius, before the Edict of Milan, passed a law to the effect that no one was to supply food to prisoners on pain of imprisonment themselves (Eusebius, H.E. 5.8). Charity by no means remained at home. Cyprian related how in 253 Carthaginian churches quickly raised 100,000

sesterces to ransom Numidians captured by barbarian marauders, noting that "the captivity of our brothers (and sisters) must be thought of as our captivity" (Ep. 62.1).

A second entailed care for people in time of calamities. When a plague ravaged Carthage about 250 and Alexandria about 259 Christians in those cities risked their own lives to care for the sick and dying. During a widespread plague in the reign of Maximin Daia, they not only tended the sick but gathered all the hungry of the city to distribute bread to them (Eusebius, H.E. 9.8).

A third had to do with hospitality for strangers and aid to churches in poverty or peril. Rome owed much of its early influences to these two factors. About 170 Dionysius of Corinth commended Bishop Soter not merely for conserving the custom of hospitality but for extending it "by aiding the saints with rich supplies, which he sends from time to time" (Eusebius, H.E. 4.23.10). He went on to note that Rome had made a habit of "aiding all the brethren (and sisters) in various ways and of sending contributions to many churches in every city, thus in one case relieving the poverty of the needy or in another providing for brethren in the mines." Dionysius of Alexandria remarked in a letter to Stephen of Rome that the Romans had sent help "regularly" to the churches of Syria and Arabia (Eusebius, H.E. 7.5.2). With aid went letters encouraging and uplifting other churches and tying more tightly the cord which united them with one another. Cyprian's letter (62) to eight bishops of Numidia sent with money to ransom captives reveals the sense of intimate unity Christians felt for one another in spite of distance.

Fellowship Meals

Underlying the interknittedness of Christianity which helped it to withstand assaults was a fellowship preserved by tangible experiences of *koinonia* in *agape* meals. During the second century already, as mentioned earlier, these meals got detached from the observance of the eucharist. They continued, however, to be observed. In the Catholic Tertullian's day (ca. 200) *Agape* meals played a prominent role in Christian communal life in Carthage not only as fellowship but as worship. Tertullian outlined a kind of liturgy for the meals.

> Preliminary prayer
> Conversation "as if before God"
> The meal
> Ablutions
> Lights brought in
> Psalm singing
> Final prayer
> Distribution to the poor

To pagans who construed such gatherings in the worst possible light Tertullian retorted: "Our meal, by its very name, indicates its purpose. It is called by a name which to the Greeks means 'love.' Whatever it costs, it is gain to incur expense in the name of piety, since we comfort the needy by this refreshment, not as, among you, parasites contend for the glory of reducing their liberty to slavery for the price of filling their belly amidst insults, but as before God, greater consideration is given to those of lower station" (*Apology* 39.16). Clement of Alexandria spoke with similar feeling about the intended objectives of the meal. "One who eats of this meal, the best of all things, will acquire the kingdom of God, fixing his (or her) gaze even while here on the holy assembly of love, the heavenly *ekklesia*" (*Instructor* 2.1.4).

By the mid-third century the *Agape* meal had slipped from such a high pedestal, for Origen scarcely took pains to defend it against Celsus. Sects like the Carpocratians abused it in the way pagans imagined (Clement, *Stromateis* 3.2.10). As a Montanist, Tertullian derided Catholics for their continued observance. "At your house Agape is warmed up with saucepans," he charged with sarcasm, "faith is cooked up in kitchens, hope rests on dishes. But an *Agape* meal is all the more important, for there young men sleep

with sisters" (*Fasting* 17). Origen hinted at improprieties in the meals when he urged that the believer's kisses be chaste (*Commentary on Romans* 16:16). Cyprian, too, sounded cautious in urging "temperate festivity" with psalms or something "spiritual" (*To Donatus* 16). He denounced unfaithful bishops who "brought no aid to starving brothers and sisters" and others who neglected the offering for the poor (*The Lapsed* 6). Though the meals continued until the sixth century, they obviously looked more and more like pagan banquets and less and less like the charitable meals their name connoted.

Worship

The center of early Christian unity, in this era as in every other, was its worship of one God who had disclosed himself through the centuries to Israel and in a definitive way in Jesus of Nazareth. By the early third century the worship service was beginning to be separated into two parts, the first for catechumens and the second for the faithful. The second part, according to Hippolytus, was observed in connection with baptisms or ordinations as well as on Sundays in regular worship.

The service for catechumens was designed primarily to instruct new converts, but persons already baptized were exhorted to attend both the daily and the weekly instruction. The catechist, usually a presbyter, read scriptures and explained them. At the end of the sermon catechumens were dismissed. The formula *Ite! Missa est* ("Go, you are dismissed or sent!") may have been the source of the word "Mass."

The service for the faithful consisted still of the essential elements listed by Justin with some added details.

> Offerings (oblations) of bread, wine, oil, olives, cheese, etc. presented by deacons.
> Laying on of hands by the bishop and deacons on the offerings.
> Prayer of thanks offered by the bishops preceded by the *Sursum Corda* ("life up your hearts")

Bp. "The Lord be with you."
P.   "And with your spirit."
Bp. "We have them to the Lord."
P.   "Let us give thanks to the Lord."
Bp. "It is meet and right."

Bishop's prayer.

We render thanks to you, O God, through your beloved child Jesus Christ, whom in the last times you sent to us to be a Savior and Redeemer and the messenger of your will; who is your Word inseparable, through whom you made all things and in whom you were well pleased; whom you sent from heaven into a virgin's womb and who conceived within her was made flesh and demonstrated to be your Son, being born of the Holy Spirit and a virgin; who fulfilling your will and preparing for you a holy people stretched forth his hands for suffering that he might release those who have believed in you from suffering.

When he was betrayed to suffering on account of his own will that he might abolish death and break the bonds of the devil and trample on hell and enlighten the righteous and depict the end and manifest the resurrection, taking bread and giving thanks to you, he said, "Take. Eat. This is my body which is broken for you." Likewise also the cup, saying, "This is my blood which is poured out for you. When you do this, you make remembrance of me." Remembering his death and resurrection, therefore, we offer you the bread and the cup, giving you thanks because you have found us worthy to stand before you and minister.

Epiclesis (calling upon the Holy Spirit)

And we ask that you send your Holy Spirit upon the offering of your Holy Church, gathering into one all your saints who partake of the fullness of the Holy Spirit for the confirmation of faith in truth that we may praise and glorify you through your child Jesus Christ, through whom be glory and honor to you, the Father and the Son with the Holy Spirit in your Holy Church both now and forever. Amen.

(*Apostolic Traditions* 1.4.4-13)

Like the prayers of the *Didache*, these too emphasize thanksgiving (*eucharistia*). They hint, however, at the sacrificial teminology and thought which would be more evident by the mid-third century. "Remembering his death and resurrection, therefore, we offer you the bread

and cup . . . " contains the imagery of sacrifice. Cyprian did not hesitate to speak of "offering the eucharist," "offering sacrifice," "partaking of the sacrifice," or "altar" and "priest." In this he moved well beyond Hippolytus and Tertullian.

Wherever Christians traveled throughout the Empire, they would have found a two-part liturgy like this, the sermon featured in the first part, the eucharist in the second. Existence of these basic elements, however, did no preclude diversity in different areas—North Africa, Rome, Syria, Egypt, etc. Elaboration of this simple pattern and standardization, however, awaited the advent of Constantine and the entrance into the churches of more affluent and better educated persons who could appreciate elaborate and subtle ritual.

The Christian Calendar and Saints Days

This period witnessed also the elaboration of the Christian calendar. Observance of the Lord's Day, of course, was well established in the first century, and Christians overcame their reluctance to call it by the pagan name Sunday little by little in the second. In this period, however, Christians still observed Sunday as a day of worship and not as a day of rest, which it became in 321 by decree of the Emperor Constantine. In the mid-third century the Syrian manual entitled *Didascalia Apostolorum* (*Teaching of the Apostles*) revealed the importance of the day.

> Make not your worldly affairs of more account than the word of God; but on the Lord's day leave everything and run eagerly to your Church; for he is your glory. Otherwise, what excuse have they before God who do not assemble on the Lord's day to hear the word of life and be nourished with the divine food which abides forever?   (23)

Christians saw observance of Sunday as a law. When an assembly of 31 men and 18 women arrested in Abitina in 304 were interrogated by an official as to why they disobeyed the imperial edict, a presbyter named Saturninus responded, "We must celebrate the Lord's Day. It is a law for us." This day established a rhythm for the rest of the week. Wednesdays and Fridays Christians fasted, as in the first two centuries.

Easter was also well established in the Christian calendar by the beginning of this era. The festival consisted of three major observances. It began with a strict fast of one, two, or more days. "No one is to take anything at Easter until the sacrifice has been offered;" according to Hippolytus (A.T. 33) "anyone acting differently will not be considered to have fasted." Saturday night the faithful held an all night prayer watch consisting, in addition to prayers, of readings from the prophets, the Gospel, and the Psalms "until the third hour in the night after the Sabbath" (9:00 P.M.). At that hour they could break their fast and celebrate the Lord's supper (*Didascalia Apostolorum* 21). As noted earlier, the churches baptized new converts on Easter Sunday at dawn.

Following Easter, the churches celebrated fifty days until Pentecost, a Greek word meaning "fiftieth." According to Irenaeus and Tertullian, they regarded this as a single feast day during which fasting was forbidden. Judaism, of course, had observed Pentecost as a harvest festival. For Christians it assumed a quite different nuance connected with the resurrection. According to Tertullian (*Baptism* 19.2), baptisms were performed at this time just as they were at Easter. Near the end of this period, the Council of Elvira (305) prescribed special observance of the day of Pentecost, and, shortly after 332, Eusebius of Caesarea (*The Pascal Observance* 3) connected it with the ascension of Jesus. In the fourth century Christians added another nuance when they noted that the period consisted of eight Sundays, thus connoting resurrection in a special way.

Whether Lent, a forty-day fast prior to Easter, began during the third century is debated. The *Didascalia Apostolorum* attests that the churches of Syria held a less strict fast from Monday through Thursday before the strict fast started on Friday. The diet consisted of bread, salt, and water only. A forty-day fast independent of the Easter fast appeared in Egypt either in the late-third or early-fourth century. This fast extended the two days per week (Wednesdays and Fridays) when Christians fasted regularly. Lent did not begin elsewhere until later in the fourth century.

Christmas observances on December 25 cannot be dated earlier than the fourth century, perhaps about 330 in Rome. In the East, however, where January 6 was the day for feasts of the winter solstice, some Christians attempted to connect this date with Christ's life. According to Clement of Alexandria (*Stromateis* 1.21.146), the Basilidians celebrated January 6 as the date of Jesus' baptism, spending the preceding night reading. No clear evidence exists for observance of Epiphany ("Manifestation") before the fourth century.

Major expansion of the Christian calendar did not occur until the fourth century when the influx of vast numbers of converts necessitated some educative tool. From an early date, however, the "birthdays" of martyrs into the eternal realm were commemorated annually. Already by the mid-third century Christians prayed for the martyrs' intercession. Cyprian prescribed the keeping of a list of names of martyrs with the dates of their deaths and their burial sites. Only in the fourth century did the martyr cult expand to other saints, especially their successors the ascetics and bishops.

Art and Architecture

Christians met in the homes of members at the outset. Growth of their communities, however, necessitated adaptation of houses for use as church buildings. Fortunately one specimen of this type of architecture survived the destruction of the Roman fortress at Dura-Europos on the Euphrates River in Mesopotamia in 256. As was done in the case of the synagogue discovered there, a private house of medium size was reconstructed for use by a Christian community soon after 232. Externally it retained its previous appearance to allay suspicion among authorities. On the interior, however, walls were removed to make three rooms—a large oblong room with a seat for the presiding presbyter or bishop at the northern end, a second large room perhaps employed for *Agape* meals, or instruction of catechumens, and a small room turned into a baptistry.

The baptistry alone was adorned with paintings of a highly symbolical character. On the back wall of the baptistry were a painting of the Good Shepherd standing near his flock on an upper panel and, on a smaller scale, a painting of Adam and Eve, the tree of life, and the serpent on a lower panel. Christ has overturned the effects of the Fall. On the western side wall an artist had depicted on the upper panel two of Jesus miracles—the healing of the paralytic and the stilling of the storm—and on the lower panel a symbolic representation of the resurrection—the three Marys moving toward a tomb holding torches and vases filled with myrrh in their hands. On the short north wall opposite the baptistry the five wise maidens march in procession toward the left to meet the bridegroom. On the eastern wall between two doors the lower panel depicted David and Goliath and the Samaritan woman at the well as symbols of faith and hope. The objective was obviously to remind those who received baptism that they were participating in the power of the risen Christ to overcome evil and death.

A larger and more elaborate *titulus* or church center has been uncovered in Rome. Under a fifth century edifice of Saints John and Paul are the remains of at least four private houses, three of which date from the mid-second century, the other from the third. From the outside the three-storied house looked like an apartment building. On the first floor was a row of shops behind an arcade. On the upper floors, however, existed a room at least 50 feet by 40 to 60 feet, possibly two stories high. By the beginning of the fourth century this building was owned by Christians as frescoes with Christian symbols confirm. By that date it contained a room for storing relics and an altar. Evidently the long periods of relative peace permitted Christians to obtain title to property and to utilize it more or less openly. When persecutions broke out, of course, they risked confiscation or destruction of it until the time of Constantine, but the risk did not deter them.

Like their Jewish forbears, the first generations of Christians employed the medium of art with some reserve even as late as the Synod of Elvira in 305, and where they did use it, they followed in the same footsteps in depicting symbolically themes drawn from the scriptures, first of the Old Testament and then of the New. In the Graeco-Roman world of the third century this led to some rather curious specimens, for Christians often had to employ pagan artists who would not understand what they were depicting and would incorporate a vast array of pagan symbolism alongside the Christian. At the same time, in periods of persecution, Christians had to use Christian symbols such as the Cross sparingly not only for fear of detection but also because of popular distortion and misunderstanding. What happened, therefore, was that Christians attached their own interpretations to pagan symbols. The peacock represented immortality, the dove the Holy Spirit, and the palm of victory the triumph of martyrs. In one of their boldest reinterpretations Christians depicted Christ as the Unconquered Sun driving his chariot across the sky. They construed the vine of the burial cult of Dionysius in terms of Jesus' words about the vine and the branches (John 15:1-3). They depicted Jesus' the Good Shepherd as a Greek Hermes, the Ram carrier (Criophorus).

In time, however, more distinctively Christian symbolism began to prevail. On an early tombstone a Christian artist scratched an anchor, the shaft of which is a cross, with fish hooked to each end of the anchor. From Tertullian we know that Christians were using the Greek word for fish ICHTHYS as a cryptogram, "Jesus Christ, Son of God, Savior." In the catacombs, underground cemeteries cut into the soft tufa beds outside of Rome, Christian painters expressed their faith in imagery drawn from the scriptures in a manner similar to the scenes at Dura-Europos. Christian art emphasized deliverance from and victory over evil.

It is important to recognize the symbolical nature of early Christian art. Christian artists did not attempt to depict biblical or other scenes literally. Although they depended on both oriental and Roman art forms and techniques, therefore, they sought nothing less than to use symbolism to bring the mystery of Christ's redemptive work and his Church in its transcendent character nearer to the earthly realm.

Holy Orders

In this critical period of Christian history the churches relied heavily on authorized leadership to coordinate, educate, inspire, and guide a growing and increasingly diverse constituency. Although the main lines of Christian organization and understanding of ministry were in place by 180, significant new developments occurred in the period which followed as a consequence of rapid expansion, challenges posed by persecution and upward mobility of both leaders and constituency.

At the local level the threefold office of bishop, presbyters, and deacons existed nearly everywhere. The roles which each played, however, varied considerably. In Asia Minor and North Africa, where there were large numbers of bishops, bishops obviously played less significant roles than in Rome and Italy or Alexandria and Egypt, where there were few. On the other hand, where bishops had extensive responsibilities, as in Italy and Egypt, presbyters and deacons assumed greater importance; where bishops had smaller charges, as in Asia Minor or North Africa, presbyters and deacons figured less

prominently. The fact is, presbyters of Rome and Alexandria and their surrounding territories had responsibilities equivalent to bishops of small towns in Asia Minor or North Africa. Indeed, according to the *Didascalia Apostolorum*, composed in Syria about 250, deacons had considerably more importance than presbyters. Presbyters held more or less honorific places, whereas deacons discharged extensive ministries under the direction of the bishop. Roman regionary deacons appointed by Fabian to supervise the extensive charities of the city had no counterpart elsewhere.

Local offices were also extended, in part to bear the growing weight of ministry and in part to provide support for the needy. About 215 Hippolytus listed among the unordained: confessors, widows, readers, virgins, subdeacons, and exorcists. The *Didascalia* deleted virgins and exorcists but added deaconesses. Cyrian referred to acolytes. The confessor, Hippolytus directed, was to be permitted to minister as a deacon or presbyter without ordination, "for he has by his confession attained to the dignity of the presbyterate" (*Apostolic Tradition* 10). Readers, selected by the bishop, read scriptures during the worship service. Subdeacons assisted deacons. Exorcists did not require laying on of hands, Hippolytus said, "because the fact is evident" (15). Acolytes assisted in the eucharist.

The role of women requires special comment. Widows were classified as an "order," though an unordained one. Tertullian explicitly indicated this. Church orders regularly listed widows after the three ordained orders, and Clement and Origen listed widows several times in a quadrumvirate of clergy. Some widows seem to have performed a highly regarded function. Although Hippolytus excluded them from performing a liturgical role, he noted that they had a special duty to pray. The *Didascalia* directed, likewise, that widows do nothing but pray for those who gave alms and for the whole Church. Hippolytus did not mention women deacons or deaconesses, but the *Didascalia* listed their role separate from that of widows. Deaconesses were to perform the same ministry to women that deacons did to men—visiting the sick and tending their bodily needs, anointing persons being baptized with the oil of exorcism and the oil of thanksgiving, and teaching the newly baptized how to keep "the seal" of baptism pure and unbroken (16). Like Tertullian, the *Didascalia* forbade women to baptize, but Tertullian himself went beyond others in constricting the role of women. He was scandalized that in some of the sects women taught, debated, exorcised, and "maybe even baptized" (*Prescription against Heretics* 41.5). Even after joining the Montanist sect, which the prophetesses Priscilla and Maximilla had led alongside Montanus, Tertullian still refused women the right to teach, baptize, or offer the eucharist, for such duties belong to males (*The Veiling of Virgins* 9.1). Women prophetesses could speak, but not during the regular worship.

At the regional level the churches gradually accommodated their structures to conform to Roman dioceses and provinces. Although the Council of Nicea formalized this arrangement in 325, the trials of the second and third centuries accelerated the need for joint decision making by bishops. The first synods addressed the Montanist crisis in the late-second century and the debate regarding the observance of Easter about 196. Apart from these, the custom of convening synods of bishops and other clergy to resolve debated issues seems to have caught on in the first half of the third century. Unfortunately little data about the earlier conventions have survived: A synod held in Carthage between 218 and 222, for instance, dealt with the question of rebaptism of heretics. Two synods at Alexandria in 228 and 231 censured and excommunicated Origen because of his ordination in the diocese of Caesarea and perhaps because of his theology. A synod which convened in Iconium in Asia Minor under Firmilian of Caesarea in Cappadocia about 230–235 declared baptisms by heretics invalid.

Ninety bishops of Numidia gathered to condemn Privatus, bishop of Lambese, as a heretic. In 244 a synod convened at Bostra in Arabia to watch Origen overwhelm Beryll, the bishop of Bostra, but no record of the actual debate has survived. Much deeper insight into the function of synods comes from those which dealt with the problem of the "lapsed" during the Decian persecution, where the interaction of bishops on these complex matters illustrates the growth of episcopal collegiality.

As can be seen in the action of these councils, the bishops of churches in metropolitan centers such as Carthage, Rome Alexandria, or Caesarea in Cappadocia possessed respect and influence based on the size and preeminence of their churches. In the synods dealing with affairs in the Roman province of Africe, for instance, Cyrian presided as *primes inter pares* ("first among equals"). Dealing with the sticky issue of rebaptism in 255, Cyprian took pains to poll each bishop in attendance with assurance that none would be penalized for dissenting from the majority and his own opinion. He then reported the action not only to Stephen, bishop of Rome (*Ep.* 72) but also to the bishops of Numidia (*Ep.* 70). He also corresponded with Firmilian, bishop of Neocaesarea in Cappadocia, and obtained his affirmation. Firmilian's opening greeting supplies an interesting confirmation of the sense of a universal-bonding the bishops experienced. The bishop of Caesarea thanked God and said

> that we who are separated from one another in the body are so joined in the Spirit as if we were not only occupying the same region but dwelling together in the very same house. And it is right to say this because the spiritual house of God is one.
>
> (Cyprian, *Ep.* 75.1)

Stephen should be thanked, too, because as a result of his opposition, "we have found in brethren situated so far away so great a unanimity of faith and of truth with us" (75.3). The fact that such "unanimity" did not include Stephen demonstrates the sense of equality among bishops of major sees.

Having said that, we must also recognize that, in the West, the bishop of Rome as well as the Church of Rome held a position of prestige and perhaps authority not accorded to any other see. Irenaeus pointed to this standing in his often quoted but much debated statement that "every church must agree (*convenire*) with this Church (of Rome) on account of its more powerful origin (*propter potentiorem principalitatem*)," that is, as "founded and constituted by the two most eminent Apostles Peter and Paul" (*Against Heresies* 3.3.1). Such a respectful attitude, however, did not preclude the bishop of Lyons from remonstrating Victor when the latter threatened to excommunicate or did excommunicate the Christians of Asia for their retention of the Jewish date for breaking the fast at Easter. In the initial edition of his treatise on *The Unity of the Catholic Church* Cyprian almost certainly acknowledged Roman primacy, as Tertullian did, based on succession from Peter. In a revision made during the rebaptism controversy, however, he modified his statement to demonstrate that all bishops equally hold a succession from Peter.

In the battle against heresies of one kind or another succession lists of certain churches undoubtedly enhanced their standing. Churches, such as Rome, Antioch, or Ephesus, which could trace succession from apostles occupied enviable positions. When Irenaeus, although claiming to be able to cite numerous other succession lists, illustrated with the Roman list above, he elevated the Roman claim above all others and assured it a permanency no other see could match, despite the unreliability of some of his information.

In this crucial era occurred another landmark change, in this case in the understanding of the role of the ordained clergy. The clergy had already begun to be sharply distinguished from the laity as early as Clement of Rome. Although the process of differentiation moved steadily forward during the second century, however, some sense of the oneness of the whole people of God persisted. Tertullian, for instance, insisted that laymen could baptize, dispensing what they had received (*Baptism* 17). Origen pointed out that baptism was the lay person's ordination. On preference for virginity, moreover, Tertullian thought lay persons should abide by the same rule as the clergy, asking, "Are not even we lay persons priests?" (*Exhortation to Chastity* 13.4).

What pushed the distinction forward was the gradually increasing tendency to interpret the Lord's supper or eucharist as a sacrifice. The process, however, advanced more slowly in some areas than in others. Whereas Irenaeus still identified bishops as presbyters. Hippolytus thought of them as "high priests to propitiate your countenance without ceasing and to offer you the rights of your holy church, and by the Spirit of the high priesthood to have authority to forgive sins according to your commandments" (A.T. 3.5-6). Both presbyters and deacons fell far below this level. Likewise, the *Didascalia* acclaimed bishops as "high priests" and "kings," whereas presbyters and deacons are "priests" and Levites" (9), both chosen by bishops. Cyprian did not distinguish so sharply between bishops and presbyters, but he sounded a far more priestly note in the way he construed the offices. Since they are dedicated to the service of the altar, they must avoid all uncleanness (*Ep.* 67.1). They must receive honor due the priestly estate, for Jesus taught due respect for all true priests (*Ep.* 3.2). In a letter to a fellow bishop, moreover, he argued that water must be mixed with wine in the communion cup on the grounds that "the priest who imitates what Christ did and then offers the true and full sacrifice in the Church of God the Father, if he thus begins to offer according to what he sees Christ himself offered, performs truly in the place of Christ" (*Ep.* 63.14).

The Alexandrians, deeply rooted in a teaching tradition, did not distinguish clerical grades as sharply as Hippolytus and Cyprian. The "gnostic" is the true presbyter. "That persons is in reality a presbyter of the Church and a true minister of the will of God, if he does and teaches what is the Lord's," Clement wrote, "not as being ordained by human beings, nor regarded righteous because a presbyter, but enrolled in the presbyterate because righteous" (*Stromateis* 6.13). Clement decisively distinguished his "gnostics" from heretical ones in "maintaining the apostolic and ecclesiastical correctness of doctrine" (7.16), but he saw the improvement of persons through study of scriptures as their vocation. Origen distinguished the order of bishops, presbyters, and deacons more clearly than Clement and could say that bishops offer to God the sacrifices of propitiation just like the high priest of ancient times (*Homily 5 on Leviticus* 4). Because of his painful experience with Demetrius, however, he directed some harsh words at abuses of power by bishops, surpassing the worst secular rulers. Like Clement, he insisted that presbyters must live worthily of their vocations. In Alexandria presbyters elected bishops and installed them until the fourth century.

Throughout this critical era the power and importance of bishops increased steadily. At the beginning of the period Irenaeus, Tertullian, and Clement of Alexandria still thought of bishops as presbyters, albeit presbyters in a class by themselves. As the chief witnesses and guardians of apostolic tradition, bishops were those most eminently qualified to hold the title of presbyters. By the middle of the century bishops had supplanted teachers such as Clement and Origen as the trustworthy conservers of the faith. The action taken by Demetrius, bishop of Alexandria, against Origen in 228 and 231 doubtless signified the triumph of the episcopal office over the teaching office. Not surprisingly, as a presbyter in Caesarea, Origen stressed that the bishop is a servant and not a ruler of the church (*Homily 6 on Isaiah*, 1). At this point he might have saved his breath. Church councils, once including others besides bishops, were becoming episcopal councils. Bishops resolved in them not only doctrinal

but moral issues of importance in their dioceses. Cyprian put it quite plainly. Whoever is not in communion with the bishop in a diocese is not in the Church (*Ep.* 66.8). As head of the clergy, the bishop exercises a real primacy over the Church and the locus of its unity. That is why there can only be *one* bishop. Just as there is one God, one Christ, and one Holy Spirit, so must there be only one bishop (*Ep.* 49.2). The bishop is the rock on which the Church is founded. In cases where false claimants arise a bishop will receive confirmation from other bishops of the universal Church.

In circumstances so contorted as those of this era ordination also assumed increased importance. Election of bishops involved the laity, but ordination by laying on of hands was restricted to the clergy. Bishops alone, convened normally from churches in the same province, laid hands on bishops. The bishop of a particular diocese evidently appointed and laid hands on presbyters as a sign of ordination, but other presbyters also laid hands on those being ordained; presbyters could dispense what they had received. The bishops alone appointed and ordained deacons, according to Hippolytus (A.T. 1.9), since they were "not ordained to the priesthood but to serve the bishop and to carry out the bishop's command." By the mid-third century Cyprian was speaking of ordination as a "promotion" from one "degree" (*gradus*) to another. He defended the election of Cornelius, for instance, on the basis of his "having been promoted through all of the ecclesiastical offices" (*Ep.* 55.8). Ordination obviously favored the episcopate.

Chapter 17

First Principles

Christianity confronted its most serious challenges during the period extending from Clement of Alexandria to Constantine. Nowhere does the challenge stand out more clearly than in the efforts of Christians to express their faith in a context radically different from the one in which they began. For some still, deviations from an essentially Jewish understanding posed a severe threat. For others, Christianity served more to legitimate what they had already absorbed from the Graeco-Roman milieu. Church leaders of this period had to wind their way between these extremes, on the one hand remaining faithful to Christianity's inheritance from Judaism, but at the same time, on the other hand, accommodating to the culture and thought patterns of the Roman world sufficiently to make Christianity intelligible and appealing.

Against such a background as this it would be too much to expect anything like a systematic theology. The closest anyone came to that was Origen's *First Principles*, composed about 220, in which the brilliant Alexandrian set forth the items he counted essential to the Church's faith and beyond which theologians could speculate with considerable freedom. Others, too, struggled to establish a pattern of truth that could guide the churches through a veritable jungle of ideas without getting lost completely. At the center of their efforts they framed what most called "the rule of faith," a summary related to but not exactly equivalent to the baptismal confessions, and sought further to define the canon. It will be useful here to examine these two developments and then look at some of the leading writers and their ideas in order to discern how the churches established some guiding principles. The contribution of the episcopate in this was discussed earlier.

The Rules of Faith

During the late second and third centuries theologians regularly invoked what they called "the rule of faith" or "the rule of truth" in response to the claims of heretical teachers. What they seem to have cited in a rather general way were the baptismal confessions employed in local churches which they adapted and filled out according to specific circumstances. It is obvious from the use Irenaeus, Tertullian, and Hippolytus made of them that they did not feel bound to exact formulations, indicating that these creeds had not yet attained a fixed form. Sometimes, for instance, they cited them as two part (Father and Son), at other times as three part confessions, consistently highlighting christology. In his *Prescriptions against Heretics* Tertullian summarized "the rule of faith" as

> The belief that there is only one God, and that (God) is none other than the Creator of the world, who produced all things out of

nothing through His own Word, who was first sent forth; that this Word is called (God's) Son and under the name of God was seen "in diverse manners" by the patriarchs, heard at all times in the prophets, at last brought down by the Spirit and power of the Father into the Virgin Mary, was made flesh in her womb, and, being born of her, went forth as Jesus Christ; thereafter he preached the new law and the new promise of the kingdom of heaven, performed miracles; having been crucified he rose again the third day; having ascended into the heavens, he sat at the right hand of the Father; sent in his stead the power of the Holy Spirit to lead such as believe; will come with glory to take the saints to the enjoyment of everlasting life and of the heavenly promises, and to condemn the wicked to everlasting fire after the resurrection of both shall have happened, together with the restoration of the flesh.(13)

Despite this rather free summary, Tertullian elsewhere spoke as if the form was more precisely established, although, in this case, without mentioning the Holy Spirit.

> The rule of faith is one everywhere, alone incapable of alteration and reform—the rule which teaches us to believe in one God almighty, creator of the world, and His son Jesus Christ, born from the Virgin Mary, crucified under Pontius Pilate, raised on the third day from the dead, taken up into heaven, now sitting on the Father's right hand, destined to come to judge the living and the dead through the resurrection of the flesh.
>
> (*Veiling of Virgins* 1)

Taken together, the evidence shows that Tertullian could not have known a fixed creed, even a local one, yet he did know some kind of formularies. Not long afterwards, Tertullian's contemporary Hippolytus attests the use of a formal and fixed baptismal confession in Rome, which

J. N. D. Kelly calls "semiofficial" at this juncture.

When he composed the *First Principles* about 220, Origen thought still in terms of a summary of faith drawn from scriptures as his basic guides. His "summary" of what "has been transmitted in a clear manner by the apostolic preaching" went far beyond the normal trinitarian confession of baptism—the soul, free will, the devil and his angels, creation and destruction of the universe, inspiration of scriptures, and the angels of God. Interspersed with these items are notations about points of disagreement or divergence. Origen noted, for example, that nothing "is clearly handed down about the sun, moon, and stars, whether animate or inanimate" (*First Principles* Pref. 9). He obviously felt free to explore beyond the parameters established by the "rule of faith." On some issues this resulted in real danger for him. By the time he had moved to Caesarea he hinted at what appears to have been a formal creed whose articles "in being believed, save the person who believes them" (*The Gospel of John* 13:16). Here he underlined that the Christian must achieve all of the articles and not pick and choose between them. Contemporary study had demonstrated, too, that Origen attached great importance to the ecclesiastical tradition.

By the mid-third century the baptismal questions had acquired official recognition in a settled form. In a letter to Cyprian Firmilian of Neocaesarea in Cappadocia spoke of an "ecclesiastical rule" of baptism, of an "established and ecclesiastical interrogation," and of "the customary and established words of the interrogation" (Cyprian, *Ep.* 75.10-11). Several factors undoubtedly pushed this process forward—the needs of the instruction of converts for baptism, the battle to define faith in the midst of threats of heresy and schism, use of confessions for liturgical purposes, and recitation by confessors in time of persecution. The churches, nevertheless, did not reach the level of precision mandated by ecumenical councils in the fourth century and after.

Canon of the New Testament

Although the basic nucleus for the New Testament formed in the preceding era, important facets of the formation process occurred in this one. The four Gospels, of course, had a firmly established place by the end of the second century. Irenaeus and the Muratorian Canon, a list now usually dated about 175 or 180, confirm this for the West, although a lacuna at the beginning of the latter caused omission of Matthew. Countering Gnostic claims of inspiration for other Gospels, the bishop of Lyons declared it "impossible that the Gospels be either more or fewer in number than they are." Christ "has given us the Gospel under four aspects, but bound together by one spirit." Invoking Revelation 4:7, Irenaeus depicted Matthew as a lion symbolizing Christ's "effective working, leadership, and royal power"; Mark as a calf depicting Christ's "sacrificial and priestly order"; Luke as a human face describing Christ's advent as a human being; and John as an Eagle pointing to the gift of the Spirit hovering over the Church. Four Gospels replicate "the four catholic covenants" given humankind: under Adam, under Noah, under Moses, and under Christ (*Against Heresies* 3.11.8). Tatian's *Diatessaron*, a collation of the four Gospels, demonstrates their fixed place in Syria and the East at this time. Like Irenaeus, Clement of Alexandria appealed to tradition to confirm the four Gospels.

The Pauline corpus of thirteen letters also had attained universal recognition. The author of the Muratorian Canon knew of spurious letters under the name of Paul, but he singled out the thirteen now in the canon as authentic. Although Irenaeus did not list them as he did the Gospels, he cited all thirteen. It was evidently customary to view the Apostle's letters in two blocs—to churches and to individuals—a fact that accounts for the current arrangement. Tertullian listed all of Paul's letters in opposition to Marcion. He also noted that Catholic Christians "generally ascribe Luke's narrative to Paul" in order to sustain a claim to apostolic authorship (*Against Marcion* 4.5). In the East Clement cited all except Philemon.

Acts, 1 John, and 1 Peter had attained general acceptance as well, Acts in connection with the Gospel of Luke. The author of the Muratorian Canon described Acts as "the Acts of all the apostles." Irenaeus, Clement, and Tertullian cited all three writings liberally. At this period the Revelation also was employed in public worship in many churches, but the Montanist crisis soon made such usage controversial. According to the Muratorian Canon, the Roman church received "both the Revelation of John and the Revelation of Peter, though some of us don't want them to be read in the church." Irenaeus, Clement, and Tertullian, however, cited Revelation favorably. Yet it remained in the disputed category for two centuries more.

The other writings now a part of the modern canon vied with several other works for universal acceptance. Clement of Alexandria, for instance, included Barnabas and the Revelation of Peter with the books now recognized (Eusebius, H.E. 6.14). Others cited 1 Clement and Hermas. Though of disputed authorship, Hebrews had strong support among the Alexandrine scholars if not in the West. Clement ascribed the writing to Paul but theorized that Luke translated into Greek a Hebrew original composed by the Apostle. Origen, although acknowledging that Hebrews was "not inferior" to Paul's other writings, knew the Apostle could not have written it. While some speculated about authorship by Luke or Clement of Rome, he concluded that God alone knows (Eusebius, H.E. 6.25). In north Africa Tertullian quoted Hebrews only once as the work of Barnabas and evidently placed it below apostolic writings, though above Hermas, despite its support for his rigorous views on discipline (*Modesty* 20). Cyprian explicitly rejected Pauline authorship of Hebrews and never quoted from it. In line with this, no western writer before Hilary (d. 368) quoted it as an Epistle of Paul.

Both Clement and Origen were aware of differing attitudes towards James, Jude, 2 Peter, 2 and 3 John, and the Revelation. In a sermon Origen referred, among other things, to the "twofold trumpet" of Peter's epistles, James, Jude, and John "in his epistles and Revelation" (*Homily on Joshua* 7.1). Elsewhere, however, he labeled 2 Peter "doubtful" and reported that not all considered 2 and 3 John authentic, though he did not question common authorship of the Gospel, the Revelation, and 1 John (Eusebius, H.E. 6.25. 7-10). In the West Tertullian revealed no acquaintance with James, 2 Peter, or 2 and 3 John, but he quoted from Jude as an authoritative writing. Cyprian evidently did not refer to any of these disputed writings. Tertullian frequently quoted the Revelation as the work of the same author as the Gospel. Every other Latin writer after Tertullian—Cyprian, Commodian, and Lactantius—also quoted it as authoritative, perhaps especially so in time of persecution. Irenaeus, too, constantly cited the Revelation as the work of the Apostle. Although he quoted from 2 John, he never cited James, Jude or 3 John. Hippolytus, who quoted from all universally acknowledged books except Philemon and 1 John, also made much use of Revelation, writing a commentary on it, but he evidently did not cite other disputed writings.

Interpreting the Scriptures

The early Christians obviously sought to do theology on the basis of the revelation found in the scriptures, initially the Old Testament but by this period increasingly the New. Although they differed somewhat in their theories of inspiration, they all subscribed to some kind of verbal theory. The real author of the scriptures is the Holy Spirit. Every jot and tittle, therefore, must have meaning because God would not go to the trouble of speaking idle thoughts. Herein rested the crux of the problem of interpretation. How do we wrest from the scriptures the message God has placed within them?

By the late second century allegorical exegesis was beginning to prevail throughout the Christian world, not only among Gnostics but among orthodox writers as well. Now that the New Testament had achieved a firmly established place alongside the Old, the allegorical method was beginning to be applied to it too. The hererodox Gnostics evidently initiated this process. The Valentinians, for instance, cited the parable of the laborers in the vineyard to sustain their theory of thirty aeons. Others confirmed the five senses from the parable of the foolish virgins. Valentinians had a special interest in allegorizing the Gospel according to John. Catholic writers countered with allegorical interpretations of their own. Irenaeus allegorized the parable of the good Samaritan as the fall of the human race among evil demons and their rescue by the Holy Spirit (*Against Heresies* 3.18.2). Origen gave a similar exposition (*Homily on Luke* 34). Tertullian tried hard to avoid allegory, but even he lapsed into it occasionally. Origen, of course, sometimes outdid the Gnostics in his creative interpretations.

The Gnostics contributed one other important item to early Christianity, the commentary. The earliest commentary known was a *Commentary on the Gospel of John* by the Valentinian scholar Heracleon, which Origen cited frequently in his commentary. Hippolytus wrote soon after a *Commentary on Daniel*, perhaps more expository sermons than commentary. Origen expanded the commentary effort immensely.

The western fathers used allegory cautiously, clinging still to the typological approach they inherited from Judaism. Irenaeus, conservative here as in most matters, often lapsed into allegory, but he tried hard to find the simple and obvious meaning of texts or, where that proved difficult, types. Tertullian exhibited still greater restraint. Wary of Gnostic abuses, he preferred the literal sense of Jesus' words and did not allegorize even Old Testament dietary laws. He formulated the rule that it is better to find less rather than more meaning in the text. Hippolytus continued along the line of caution in preferring typology to allegory, owing much to Justin and Irenaeus. Cyprian, likewise, manifested real restraint, usually prooftexting or finding "types" to sustain certain views.

The eastern fathers, inspired by Philo, showed far less caution. Clement of Alexandria, to be sure, acted with greater restraint than Origen by virtue of a special interest in the moral sense of scripture, often prooftexting ethical views by quotations of Jesus' words. Origen, however, felt deterred only by his own scholarly gifts. He had no peer in exposition of the texts in the literal sense. But no one was more conscious than he that, taken literally, many texts, especially of the Old Testament, caused extreme perplexity and offense. Some problems could be solved by typology, but many others could not if one assumes that every iota of scripture is equally as inspired as every other. So Origen raced from literal to spiritual or mystical interpretation. Every detail had meaning because it had a counterpart in the invisible world. Origen's influence prevailed everywhere in the East until the Antiochene school began to challenge it during the fourth and fifth centuries.

The most accurate way to depict theological thought in this somewhat fluid period will be to look at individual contributors.

Irenaeus, Bishop of Lyons

Born around 130, Irenaeus (ca. 130–202) grew up in Smyrna, where he sat at the feet of the saintly Polycarp (martyred ca. 155), drawing from him his penchant for biblical theology. Present in Rome during Polycarp's debate with Anicetus, Irenaeus studied in the school of Justin, from whom he gained much in apologetic methods but diverged in preference for biblical theology over Platonism. Moving to Lyons sometime after 164, he was ordained a presbyter. He narrowly missed martyrdom in 177, when Pothinus, the ninety year old bishop, sent him to Rome

with a letter for Eleutherius (175–189). On his return to Lyons after the pogrom there he succeeded Pothinus as bishop. We know little of his activity as bishop apart from his theological writing. He interceded with Victor (189–199) when the latter rashly excommunicated Christians of Asia because they refused to observe the Roman custom concerning Easter. According to Gregory of Tours, Irenaeus died as a martyr in 202, but the late date of Gregory's writing (576) makes this tradition suspect.

Two major works of Irenaeus—*Refutation and Overthrow of Knowledge Falsely So-Called* (usually entitled *Against Heresies*) and *Proof of the Apostolic Preaching*—have survived. Unlike Justin, Irenaeus had few kind words for nonbiblical writers. He placed his confidence, rather, in the Old Testament and in writings beginning to be collected as a New Testament. Against Marcion and some of the Gnostics, he argued that the same God inspired both. He considered the Septuagint inspired in its entirety. What he included in the New Testament beyond the four Gospels and thirteen letters of Paul is uncertain. Although Irenaeus criticized the Gnostics for allegorical exegesis, he employed it freely himself even in his interpretation of the New Testament, the first orthodox leader to do so. To solve problems posed by the Old Testament, he proposed a theory of progressive education of humankind. In the last analysis, he relied for his authority on the tradition committed to the churches by the apostles.

Against Gnostic and Marcionite dualism Irenaeus affirmed Jewish monotheism. One God created *ex nihilo* and not by emanations. Through the Son and the Holy Spirit God acted directly in creation and not through intermediaries and continues to act in inspiration or revelation. Where his teacher Justin thought of Logos as the hypostatized Divine Person, Irenaeus viewed the Logos as the Word of John 1:1-14, not a "second God" but the one God self-disclosed. Biblical and Pauline also in his concept of Redemption, he developed what is known as the theory of recapitulation in which Christ reversed the effects of Adam's fall. Whereas Adam disobeyed, Christ obeyed and thus overcame the powers that hold humankind captive—sin, death, and the devil. To establish fully his theory that Jesus did this in every stage of human life—infancy, childhood, youth, adulthood—he argued that Jesus lived to age fifty on the basis of John 8:57. Alongside the recapitulation theory, Irenaeus also developed the Greek concept of divinization in a modest way. "He became man," Irenaeus said, "in order that we might become divine."

Much debate has occurred about Irenaeus's doctrine of free will. In opposition to the gnostic division of persons into material, spiritual and psychic, the bishop of Lyons insisted on survival of free will even after the Fall. Although the fall affected the "likeness" of God, it did not mar the "image." Despite the fact that every person is born in sin, therefore, human beings still can and must choose between good and evil; they do not inherit guilt.

Although Irenaeus drew much of his thinking about the Church from Paul, he did not develop the Apostle's principal imagery of the Body of Christ. He thought instead of the Church as the People of God under a new covenant. He presupposed adult baptism, though one passage related to his recapitulation theory has been used to support infant baptism. He said little about the eucharist, which evidently played a limited role in his thinking. It was "the antidote of life" and "no longer common bread." He preferred the phrase "new oblation of the new covenant." His view of ecclesiastical authority has been hotly debated among Protestants and Catholics. His statement that "every church must agree or come together with (*convenire*) this Church of Rome on account of its more powerful authority or greater antiquity (*propter potentiorem principalitatem*)" remains very uncertain because the Greek original has been lost. On eschatology Irenaeus was millenarian.

Tertullian

Little is know of the life of Tertullian (160?–225?), the first theologian to write extensively in Latin. Probably born and reared in Carthage, he received an excellent education. He was converted to Christianity around 193 to 195 and immediately assumed a position of leadership in the church of Carthage. A rigorist on matters of discipline, he joined the Montanist sect around 206, yet continued his leadership in the defense of Christianity against Gnostics and Marcionites. After several years he separated from the Montanists and formed a sect named Tertullianists after himself. Throughout his career he belonged to the literary circles of Carthage. The exact date of his death is uncertain.

Thirty-one of Tertullian's writings have survived. These cover a variety of issues but may be grouped into three categories: apologies for Christianity, treatises on the Christian life, and works composed in opposition to heresies. Shortly after conversion Tertullian addressed apologetic treatises *To the Nations* and *Against the Jews*. Subsequently he revised the former and published it as the carefully argued and finely crafted *Apology*, his best known work. Later he elaborated a purely psychological argument developed in one chapter of the *Apology* under the title of *The Testimony of the Soul*. In 212 he summarized his apology for Christianity in a treatise directed *To Scapula*, the proconsul of Africa.

Tertullian's treatises on the Christian life reflect a rigoristic mentality that conversion to Montanism reinforced. In treatises *On the Shows* (196 or 197), *On Idolatry*, *On the Dress of Women*, and *To the Martyrs* he left little room for accommodation to customs of contemporaries. Christians should be different. So too in treatises or sermons *On Baptism*, *On Prayer*, *On Repentance*, *On Patience*, and *To His Wife*. Those who came for baptism should already have "*ceased sinning.*" Some stiffening of these views is evident in treatises written as a Montanist, particularly in a work *on Modesty*, in which Tertullian condemned second marriages as fornication, and in a treatise absolutely forbidding *Flight in Persecution.*

In antiheretical writings, too, Tertullian displayed a separatist mentality. Like Irenaeus, he argued that heresy represented a departure from the truth that Christ delivered to the apostles and they to the churches they founded. He regularly condemned heresy as a consequence of influence of philosophy, despite the fact that he owed much to Stoicism. In a treatise *On the Soul* he characterized philosophers as "patriarchs of the heretics." Although he could admit begrudgingly at times that some philosophers stumbled onto the truth, he insisted on obtaining truth from revelation, including visions granted Montanist seers.

Defending Christianity from the culture of his day, Tertullian accentuated the authority of "the rule of truth" and of the Bible interpreted more or less literally but with reference to context and his own situation. He also invented ecclesiastical Latin. No match for Irenaeus in his grasp of biblical theology, he drew many of his basic presuppositions from Stoicism and thus laid a foundation for a distinctive Latin theology. Stoicism influenced his concept of the corporeality of both God and the soul. From this assumption he deduced that sin is transmitted by seminal generation so that every human soul inherits characteristics of Adam's soul. He did not, however, take the step Augustine took in connecting guilt with transmission of sin.

Tertullian secured the victory of the Logos christology of the apologists and Irenaeus over modalism. Whereas Praxeas held that one God is successively Father, Son and Spirit, Tertullian insisted that the one God, for whom he coined the word *Trinitas*, is simultaneously Father, Son and Spirit. His formula for this was "one substance in three persons." Anticipating later debate, he also insisted that the divine and human natures were not mixed or confused during the incarnation so as to produce a *tertium quid.*

Montanism influenced Tertullian's eschatology as it did his disciplinary views. According to this view, the dawning of the age of the Paraclete promised in John 14:16 signaled a time of new revelations and of more rigorous Christian discipline—increased fasting, absolute prohibition of second marriages, and willingness to suffer martyrdom. In some ways, given the influence of Montanism, it is remarkable that Tertullian had such a great impact on later theology, testimony perhaps of his basic orthodoxy and ability to coin apt theological phrases.

Clement of Alexandria (ca. 160–211/216)

For this period the most creative and daring efforts at relating Christian faith to contemporary culture took place in Alexandria and, thanks to Origen's removal there, Caesarea in Palestine. The origins of the "school" at Alexandria are obscure. Some scholars argue that the school grew out of catechetical classes for new converts, others that it developed out of private initiative, perhaps that of Pantaenus, the first headmaster of note. Pantaenus, unfortunately, left no written works. He did, however, train a worthy successor in Clement, who admired and emulated him.

Born of non-Christian parents, probably in Athens, as a Christian Clement visited lower Italy, Syria, and Palestine before settling in Alexandria. It is uncertain whether he was ever ordained. The first Christian to attain some distinction as a scholar, he fled Alexandria in 202 or 203 during the persecution under Septimius Severus. He died between 211 and 216.

Three of Clement's major writings have survived: *Protrepticus pros Hellenas* or *Address to the Greeks*, an apology for Christianity; *Paidogogos* or *The Instructor*, how new converts should conduct themselves; and *Stromateis*, how more advanced Christians can grow still more. In addition, Clement left behind a sermon discussing how a rich person can be saved, a collection of gnostic texts, some exegetical notes, and fragments of several other works.

Unlike Tertullian, Clement held Greek philosophy in high esteem. Both the Hebrew prophets and the outstanding philosophers, especially Plato and the Stoics, served as pedagogues leading to Christ. Apparently unaware of the contradiction, Clement held both that the divine Logos inspired Greeks who attained truth and that the Greek greats plagiarized from Moses. The truth became incarnate in Jesus of Nazareth. Like Justin, Clement argued that Christianity was a species of philosophy far superior to Greek mystery religions. In support of this he cited hundreds of classical texts, perhaps taken from popular manuals. Walking a careful line between those who insisted on "faith alone" and the Gnostics, he concurred with the latter on the need for *gnosis*, spiritual knowledge, but rejected both their negative view of creation and their ethical attitudes which led at times to libertinism and at other times to extreme asceticism. He also endorsed marriage and strongly advocated free will in opposition to Gnostic dualism.

In typically Alexandrian fashion, Clement employed allegorical exegesis. Scriptures, he thought, have three senses: literal, moral, and spiritual. In practice Clement showed greater interest in the moral than in the other two senses. *The Instructor* is primarily a guide to the Christian moral life centered around the Stoic ideal of temperance. He aspired, however, to guide Christians beyond mere ethical rightness to self-control and impassibility and ultimately to *gnosis*, a term he was not prepared to relinquish to the Valentinians or other Gnostics.

Origen

The most eminent theologian prior to the conversion of Constantine, Origen (ca. 185–ca. 254) was born in Alexandria of Christian parents. His father, Leonides, taught him Greek literature and the Bible. Following his father's martyrdom in 202 during the persecution under Septimus Severus, he became a teacher and then the headmaster of the school of Alexandria. As the school grew, he assigned introductory lessons to his pupil Heraclas and confined himself to the teaching of more advanced students. Between 215 and 220 he began writing, publishing his famous work *On First Principles*. He traveled widely—to Rome, Arabia (modern Jordan), and, at the invitation of the governor, Antioch. In 231 he passed through Palestine on a trip to Athens and was ordained at Caesarea by Theoctistus and Alexander. Angered by this, Demetrius, bishop of Alexandria, gathered a synod of Egyptian bishops which ordered Origen out of Egypt and a second which defrocked him, an act rejected by Palestinian bishops. In Caesarea Origen attracted many bright and earnest seekers such as Gregory of Neocaesarea in Cappadocia and his brother Athenodorus. Acquiring a high reputation as a theologian, he received frequent invitations to defend the faith. During the Decian persecution he was imprisoned and tortured severely, but remained resolute. His health impaired by this, he died in 254 or 255.

Origen desired, above all else, to be an orthodox Christian and interpreter of the Bible. His writings, many of which have perished, consist chiefly of commentaries, sermons, and brief notes on texts of scriptures. While still in Alexandria, Origen began, but did not complete, the *Hexapla*, the Old Testament in six parallel columns—Hebrew, a Greek transliteration, the literal version of Aquila, the slightly freer version of Symmachus, the Septuagint with diacritical marks to indicate deviations from the Hebrew, and the still freer version of Theodotion. Only fragments have survived. During his Caesarean years, Origen wrote several important works in addition to homilies and commentaries: a treatise on *Prayer*, an *Exhortation to Martyrdom*, his *Dialogue with Heraclides*, and, most significant of all, his reply to the *True Discourse* of Celsus.

Origen surpassed all contemporaries as exegete, spiritual writer, and theologian—elements he mingled in all of his works. Like Clement, he ascribed three senses to scriptures—corporeal or literal, psychic or moral, and spiritual or mystical. Unlike Clement, however, he rarely dwelt long on moral application. Rather, he used his unsurpassable gifts for explaining the literal sense to open the way for his real love—the spiritual sense. Convinced that every jot and tittle of scriptures was inspired, he hastened to find everywhere the manifestation of Christ in them. All scriptures prophesy of Christ both as a whole and in details.

As a spiritual writer, Origen sought to ground his spirituality in scriptures. Although Platonism clearly furnished him with the basic framework for his thought, he would not have considered himself a Platonist but a Christian and a Bible expositor. One of the chief architects of the language and themes of Christian spirituality, Origen interpreted the bride of the *Song of Songs* as either the church or the individual soul. Origen also laid groundwork for Christian asceticism, soon to burgeon in the eastern church.

As a theologian, Origen anticipated and, some would say, precipitated much of the debate which took place after the conversion of Constantine. His early treatise *On First Principles* (220) notwithstanding, he was not a systematic theologian but a Christian who earnestly sought to answer questions raised by persons like his friend and patron Ambrose. This philosophical foundation of his thought was the Middle Platonism of his teacher Ammonius Saccas—a combination of Platonism, Stoicism, and a little Aristotelianism. Speculative ideas for which later generations condemned Origen included his doctrine of the preexistence of souls, *apokatastasis* or final restoration of all things, and subordination of the Logos. Christian teaching on these matters, however, had not reached a definitive form. All of the outstanding theologians of the fourth century owed him a massive debt: Athanasius, Basil, Gregory of Nazianzus, Gregory of Nyssa, and Didymus the Blind in the East; Hilary of Poitiers, Ambrose, Jerome, and Rufinus in the West. Not until the turn of the fifth century did attacks on him begin. His thought was condemned at Constantinople in 553, rendering it suspect in the East. Yet westerners continued to study Origen until the thirteenth century. Today he and Augustine are the most studied of the Church Fathers.

Hippolytus

Born before 170, perhaps in the Greek East, Hippolytus (d. 235) was ordained a presbyter under Victor (189–198). Strongly influenced by Irenaeus, under whom he may have studied, he was a vigorous proponent of Logos theology and opponent of the modalism of Noetus, Sabellius, and Cleomenes. As noted earlier, his efforts brought him into conflict with Zephryinus (198–217). The accession of Callistus, whom he accused of both Sabellianism and lax discipline, led him to separate from the Church of Rome. In 235 both Hippolytus and Pontian were exiled to Sardinia. Resignation of the office by the latter opened the way for Hippolytus's reconciliation and the ending of the schism. His remains were returned to Rome in the third century and Hippolytus was revered as a martyr.

Several of Hippolytus's writings have survived: the *Philosophumena* or *Refutation of all Heresies*, *The Chronicle*, *The Apostolic Tradition*, a number of exegetical and homiletical works, and fragments of others. Like Tertullian, Hippolytus attributed heresies to the influence of pagan ideas. In opposition to modalism, he subordinated the Logos to the Father and distinguished, with Theophilus of Antioch, between the Unspoken (*endiathetos*) and Spoken (*prophorikos*) Logos. Indeed, he believed that, if God wished, God could make a man God (*Refutation* 10:33). Callistus, accordingly, charged him with Ditheism. Hippolytus also represented a rigorist stance on matters of discipline.

Novatian

Although Novation withdrew from the Catholic Church and formed a separate sect in 251, he deserves mention as the next important theologian after Tertullian to write in Latin. Four of his writings survived under the name Tertullian or Cyprian: treatises on *The Trinity, Jewish Foods, The Shows*, and *The Good of Modesty*. In *The Trinity* Novatian repudiated Marcion, the docetists, the adoptionists, and the modalists, arguing for the unity of the Creator God and the Son as true God and true man, who is, nevertheless, distinct from the Father. On discipline, of course, he assumed a rigorous stand similar to Tertullian's. In *The Shows* he also forbade attendance. In *The Good of Modesty* he listed three stages: virginity, continence in marriage, and faithfulness in marriage.

Cyprian

As a theologian, Cyprian (d. 258) cannot be ranked alongside his mentor Tertullian or his eastern contemporary Origen, but he merits comment for his ecclesiastical leadership and views about the unity of the church. Born at Carthage about 200 to 210 of affluent parents, he became a rhetorician (lawyer). Converted to Christianity by Caecilian, a Carthaginian presbyter, in 248 or 249 he was installed as bishop of Carthage. During the persecution which erupted soon after this, he went into hiding, an act which complicated his leadership in the Novatianist controversy. When a fearful plague struck Carthage in 252 or 254, Cyprian organized a heroic ministry to the sick and dying that favorably impressed fellow citizens. He and Stephen of Rome nearly precipitated another schism as a result of their controversy over rebaptism, but the Valerian persecution interrupted the debate, claiming the lives of both. Cyprian was beheaded outside of Carthage on September 14, 258.

Although a fine Latin stylist, Cyprian lacked the depth and creativity of Tertullian, whom he called "the master." His views on the Church, however, exerted an immense influence on later Christian thinking, especially among the Donatists. The Church is both one and universal. It is one because its founder is one. In order for it to retain its unity while spread throughout the world, said Cyprian in the first edition of his treatise on *The Unity of the Church*, he gave the primacy to Peter. All of the apostles shared in the same power, but unity derived from Peter. In a later edition of this writing Cyprian deleted this point and insisted that the rock of Peter is faith. The unity of the Church depends upon agreement among the bishops in synods. On a local level Cyprian believed unity would be achieved through the common bond of all the people, both clergy and laity, with the bishop. Like Ignatius of Antioch, Cyprian insisted that anyone who was not with the bishop was not in the Church. Yet he never acted without consulting the community on important matters.

For Cyprian salvation depended on the Church. The Church is the bride of Christ. Therefore, "no one can have God as a Father who does not have the Church as a mother" (*The Unity of the Church*, 6). The Holy Spirit is active only within the Church and not in conventicles of heretics or schismatics, between whom Cyprian recognized no real distinction. Consequently "outside the Church there is no salvation" (*Ep.* 73.21). The Church alone is the ark in which one can safely travel. Sacraments—baptism, eucharist, ordination—are validly administered only in the Church. When schismatics or heretics enter the Church, therefore, they must receive baptism, a major element of Donatist doctrine.

Part 4

Christianizing an Empire, 313–400 C.E.

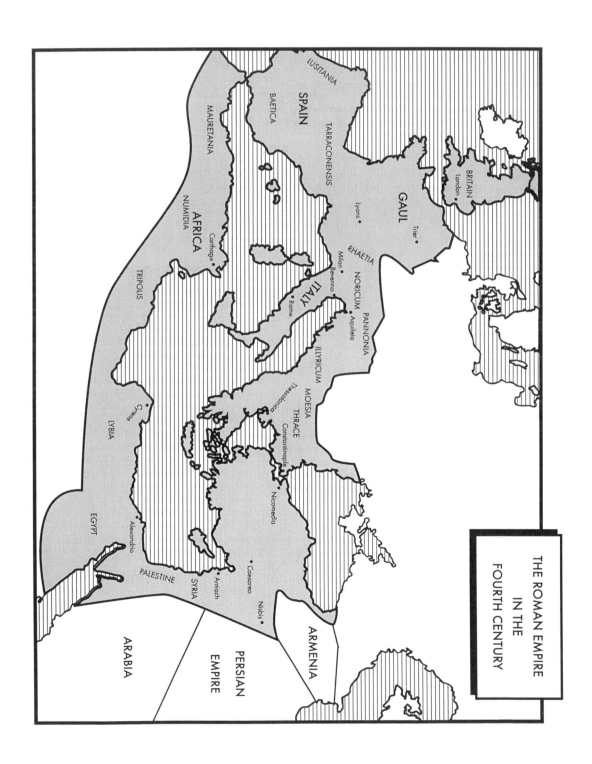

THE ROMAN EMPIRE
IN THE
FOURTH CENTURY

Chapter 18

Constantine

Christians can scarcely be faulted for the enthusiasm with which they celebrated the conversion of Constantine and the beneficent era of peace he inaugurated. From the perspective of later history they might have viewed more circumspectly some of the aid he gave the churches, but for most it must have appeared like the arrival of the Millennium. To the eyes of Eusebius, Constantine had redrawn the scheme of the history of salvation: once Abraham to Moses to Christ, now it was Abraham to Christ to Constantine. Christians could truly sing the "new song" of the psalmist (98:1-2) and exult in the things martyrs longed to but did not see. Constantine had vanquished a "whole race of God-haters" and signaled a bright and glorious new day for Christianity. He had freed all humankind from the tyranny of oppressors and led all in confessing faith in the one true God. Not only so, he was raising up magnificent new edifices to restore those razed by the tyrants, sending bishops letters and gifts and honors, and, in other ways, showering the churches with favors. Eusebius, Christianity's first church historian, could not find phrases adequate to depict the first Christian emperor—"almost another Christ," "the only true philosopher," "vessel of the divine Logos."

Constantine himself envisioned his own role in much the same way before he died in 337. In 330, when he moved the capital of the empire from Rome to Byzantium out of disappointment

that he could not convert its pagan aristocracy, he erected a church in honor of the twelve apostles. Between twelve coffins he had set up to serve as pillars, he placed a thirteenth for himself; he was the thirteenth apostle (Eusebius, *Life of Constantine* 4.60). He called himself a "bishop ordained by God to oversee whatever is outside the church" and, as Eusebius noted, took his charge seriously (4.24). In reality he did not hesitate to act as a "bishop" directing affairs inside the church either, especially in the Arian controversy. In front of his imperial palace in Constantinople he had a large placard erected depicting a huge serpent into whose back Constantine and his sons triumphantly thrust daggers. Satan had at last been cast down.

Some modern historians would concur with Eusebius and Constantine in the importance they ascribe to the latter in the Christianization of the empire. "What made the Roman world Christian is what Eusebius and others said made it Christian: the conversion of Constantine," Robert M. Grant has remarked. "The triumph of Christianity in a hierarchically organized society necessarily took place from the top down" (*Early Christianity and Society*, 11). How one defines "Christian" here will obviously interject some qualifications into this conclusion. Others, including the author, would emphasize more strongly than this the effectiveness of Christianity at the grass roots. Yet there can be little question that Constantine radically improved the situation of the churches vis-à-vis competitors in the evangelization of the empire. From his conversion until about 324, when he took up the fights against Licinius, Constantine extended tolerance to other religions and displayed limited favoritism to Christianity. From 324 to 330 he adopted a harsher attitude toward paganism and leaned ever more heavily on the churches. After 330 he dropped all pretense of toleration and did all he could to eliminate paganism as well as divergent forms of Christianity.

Constantine's Conversion

Constantine's "conversion" has been the subject of immense debate for more than two centuries. According to Eusebius's *Life of Constantine*, as the emperor prepared his army for the deliverance of Rome from the usurper Maxentius, he prayed fervently for a sign. About noon he saw a cross of light in the sky above the sun bearing the inscription "By this conquer." His whole army witnessed the miracle. That night Christ appeared to him with the same sign and commanded him to make an image of it as a safeguard in all engagements with his enemies (*Life* 1.28-29). Eusebius himself, much more rationalistic than the superstitious Constantine, reported this as an account declared "long afterwards" by the emperor himself. It should be noted that Eusebius did not include it in his earlier account in which he presented Constantine as favorably disposed to Christianity from the beginning. If any doctoring occurred, it was done by the emperor himself and not by the bishop of Caesarea.

On the basis of somewhat mixed evidence some historians have contended that Constantine adopted Christianity only for political reasons and never became a genuine Christian. Jacob Burckhardt believed Eusebius intentionally concealed the real Constantine in his *Life of Constantine* and based his account of the vision on an earlier encounter Constantine had with Apollo in the Gallic sanctuary in 310. Other scholars contend that Constantine integrated the Christian God into the Roman pantheon in support of his claims to a universal monarchy. Still others consider his conversion and thus his efforts on behalf of Christianity authentic. Much depends, of course, on the weight placed on this single experience. If the whole of Constantine's efforts on behalf of Christianity is taken into account, one can hardly deny that he thought he was a Christian, but the experience at the Milvian bridge cannot have done more than start a process of conversion consummated in a deathbed baptism.

Constantine's Favors, 313–324

Long before his defeat of Maxentius, Constantine favored Christians with toleration on his full accession to power, though no ancient author labeled him a Christian at the time. Directly after the capture of Rome, he proceeded beyond mere toleration. In a letter written to Caecilian of Carthage in the winter of 312 to 313, he promised provision for expenses for a stated number of "the servants of the lawful and most holy Catholic Church" in Africa, Numidia, and Mauretania, mentioning Hosius, bishop of Cordova as his adviser. He instructed Caecilian to request more if needed. He also arranged for Anullinus, the proconsul of Africa, to prevent "persons of turbulent character" (the Donatists) from distracting the Catholic Church. In one letter to Anullinus he commanded him to restore property seized from the Catholic Church and given to private persons. In another he directed that Anullinus and his staff "provide personal service to this holy worship in the Catholic Church over which Caecilian presides" and keep them "immune from all public burdens of any kind whatever, . . . " since "their conduct of the greatest worship towards the Divinity will in my opinion bring immeasurable benefit to the common wealth." In this latter letter a new attitude has emerged wherein worship of the Christian God is considered vital to the well-being of the empire.

Following Licinius's defeat of Maximin on April 30, 313, Constantine and Licinius issued the Edict of Milan on June 15. In this edict they granted "both to the Christians and to all others free power of following whatever religion each individual wished, in order that whatever Divinity there be in the heavenly seat can be appeased and propitious to us and to all who are placed under our rule." As the entire document makes clear, the main object was freedom for the Christian religion. To repeated assertions of "free and absolute liberty" for Christians to practice their religion, the emperors appended orders for restoration of places of worship and other property and compensation where these had been sold so as to assure that "the Divine favor toward us, which we have experienced in such great events, will prosperously continue for all time, to our success and the public happiness." Evidently, as A. H. M. Jones has argued, it was Licinius who insisted on impartiality here. In his battle with Maximian he evidently adopted Constantine's advice to rely on the Supreme God of Christians with some reservation and dragged his feet when his co-Augustus pressed for recognition of Christianity alone. Early conclusions of both Eusebius and Lactantius that Licinius was also a convert to Christianity proved ill founded. On the other hand, both pagans and Christians evidently believed Constantine had opted for Christianity. The Roman Senate, for instance, omitted any reference to the gods in the inscription they placed on Constantine's triumphal arch. The only negative evidence is the coins Constantine minted during the years after Milan from which he failed to remove images and inscriptions referring to the gods. The treasury minted coins in honor of Hercules the Victorious, Mars the Preserver, Jupiter the Perserver, and, until 323, the Unconquered Sun, the Companion of the Augusti.

Until 323, then, Constantine displayed his Christianity with reserve. He evidently sought to integrate in some way the leading religious competitors—the religion of the Unconquered Sun and the religion of Jesus Christ. In 321 he declared *Sunday* a legal holiday, construing it in Christian terms. Christ was a manifestation of the Unconquered Sun. For his Labarum he did not feature a Cross but the Chi Rho. Yet he did not hesitate to show partiality toward the church. In 318 he permitted bishops to rule in civil suits. In 321 he legalized bequests to the church and gave full legal recognition to many missions performed by bishops. He probably built the Basilica Constantiniana with its baptistry in the Lateran and endowed them. He endowed other churches in Italy, Sicily, and Africa and, to a lesser extent, in Gaul and Greece. In 316 he forbade branding of prisoners on the face. In 320 he repealed Augustus's laws against celibates and childless married couples. He sided heavily with Catholics in North Africa against the Donatist church.

Constantine set this earlier caution aside after defeating Licinius, Augustus in the East, in a series of battles between 314 and 323. Although married to Constantine's half-sister Constantia, Licinius viewed his rival with suspicion from the start. The final conflict was precipitated by Constantine's appointment of his sons, Crispus and Constantine II, as consuls without Licinius's consent. When Constantine trespassed on the latter's dominions in a campaign against the Goths, Licinius protested and, when Constantine refused satisfaction, went to war. Behind the conflict lay more than ambition. The two emperors diverged increasingly on religious matters. The more Constantine favored Christians, the more Licinius looked upon them with suspicion and hostility. Eventually he initiated a series of retaliatory measures against the churches in his territory. He forbade councils and prohibited bishops from visiting one another's cities, an act designed to prevent ordination of new bishops. he enjoined worship of men and women in the interest of morality and ordered meetings to take place outside rather than inside the city gates on pretense of concern for public health. He purged his court and later the whole civil service by requiring public sacrifices as a test for office. Christian reaction led to arrests of a number of bishops and some executions and demolition of church buildings in some cities. This new outburst of persecution gave Constantine the pretext for undertaking a crusade against Licinius under auspices of the Christian God. Until the outbreak of this war in 324, Constantine's coins still bore the legend "To the Unconquered Sun" or "To the Sun, the Companion of our Augustine." Thereafter, even this token of religious ambivalence ceased.

Constantine called on Christian bishops to assist him in his preparations for war. He picked fifty troops voted for their piety to guard the Labarum. He gave Christian soldiers leave to attend church on Sundays and marched pagan soldiers off to a parade where they had to recite a prayer to the Highest Divinity, acknowledging God as the only God. Licinius was thus cast in the roles of defender of the ancestral gods. Although Licinius commanded a larger army and fleet, Constantine dealt his opponent a devastating blow at Hadrianople on July 3, obliging him to retreat with heavy losses to Byzantium. Crispus, whom Constantine put in charge of his fleet, bottled up Licinius's fleet in the Hellespont and inflicted a crushing defeat, sinking 130 ships. Licinius, at first holding fast at Byzantium, had to flee across the Bosphorus to Chrysopolis. There, on September 18, Constantine administered the second and decisive blow ending the war. Although he spared his enemy momentarily on the pleas of his half-sister, Constantine soon had Licinius executed for fear of insurrection. Thus, Eusebius exulted, did Constantine unite again the Roman Empire into a single united whole under a peaceful rule.

More Favoritism, 324–330

Following his triumph over Licinius, Constantine issued a decree directing that all injuries and losses inflicted upon individual Christians or churches during the persecution be remunerated. He proceeded to place the blame for the wars, famines, and other calamities on those who had formerly blamed Christians for them. He depicted himself as the instrument chosen and empowered by God to see "that the human race might be recalled to the worship of the august law, schooled by my agency, and that the blessed faith might be increased under the hand of the Almighty God" (Eusebius, *Life of Constantine* 2.28). He went on to enumerate measures he enacted to redress injuries to Christians": release of exiles; return of confiscated property; freeing of Christians deported to the islands and those forced into servitude; granting of property of martyrs to their next of kin or, if there were none, to the churches. The edict closed with an exhortation to all to worship the Almighty God who had effected so signal a victory over Licinius and his evil cohorts. Soon afterward, Constantine promulgated two new laws prohibiting the erecting of images,the practice of divination, and the offering of private sacrifices and providing for the erection or restoration of churches at public expense under direction of the clergy.

Few of Constantine's actions display his increased determination to advance the cause of Christianity more clearly than patronage of church edifices and the construction of a new capital at Byzantium. In a letter written to Eusebius after his victory over Licinius he lamented the ruinous state of church edifices and determined to change it. Liberty restored and "that serpent driven from the administration of public affairs by the providence of the Supreme God and our instrumentality," he wanted all to "see the efficacy of the Divine power" and thus directed Eusebius to "admonish all to be zealous in their attention to the buildings of the churches, and either to repair or enlarge those which at present exist, or, in cases of necessity, to erect new ones." He empowered the bishop of Caesarea to demand whatever he needed from provincial governors and the praetorian prefect. The same letter went to other bishops (Eusebius, *Life of Constantine* 2.46). The emperor and his mother Helena sponsored erection of new church buildings to commemorate Jesus' burial and resurrection in Jerusalem, his birth in Bethlehem, and his ascension from the Mount of Olives. Later Constantine himself commissioned another church to be erected near the Oaks of Mamre. In a letter to Macarius, bishop of Jerusalem, he interpreted discovery of the tomb of Jesus as an act of divine providence connected integrally with his victory over Licinius that called for the erection of an edifice surpassing all others in beauty (Eusebius, *Life of Constantine* 3.29-32). Outside of Palestine, he ordered churches constructed in Nicomedia, where he had compelled Licinius to surrender, Antioch, Heliopolis in Phoenicia, and other cities. In Rome he added basilicas dedicated to the Apostle Peter and to the Apostle Paul, endowing them with extensive eastern estates. He completed erection of a church also in Cirta, capital of Numidia, in 329. When Donatists seized it, he promptly commissioned a replacement.

Dismayed that he could not convert ancient Rome, in 326 he turned his gaze toward Byzantium as a "new Rome," naming it Constantinople in honor of himself. It was to be a fully Christian city. There he commissioned the building of a church on a grand scale in honor of the martyrs and purged the city's pagan temples of sacrifices. He ordered the erection of a second church in honor of the apostles and the installation of a Cross on the ceiling of his personal apartment in the imperial palace. The "new Rome," however, differed from the old in that it had no sacral significance as *dea Roma*, "the goddess Rome." In his capital Constantine supervised the construction himself, turning nothing over to the bishops.

The bright hopes Constantine attached to Christianity were diminishing somewhat even as he announced these grand plans. Strife had been fracturing the churches of Alexandria and Egypt for several years in the form of the Meletian controversy. On top of it came the Arian conflict that spread like wildfire from Egypt to other parts of the empire. Not one to stand idly by as a divided church threatened to disrupt his efforts at uniting his empire, Constantine immediately dispatched

a letter to Alexandria by a specially chosen emissary, Hosius, bishop of Cordova. Addressing both Alexander and Arius, he expressed dismay that their controversy added to that of the Donatists, threatened to thwart his twofold objective—worship of the same God throughout the world and restoration of world order. He pointed an accusing finger directly at Arius but minimized the importance of the dispute. The debate involved "small and very insignificant questions" over which two Christians should not wrangle. Not all can be of one opinion on everything (Eusebius, *Life of Constantine* 2.63-72). As might be expected, however, neither the letter nor the bishop of Cordova halted the bitter dispute.

Constantine then ordered a general council, inviting bishops from all over the empire and putting at their disposal the means of transportation. At Nicaea, a city not far from his soon to be established capital, the council convened in the central edifice of an imperial palace. Waiting until all the bishops took their places, the emperor then proceeded, according to Eusebius, to pass through their midst in his splendid regalia "like some heavenly messenger of God" (*Life of Constantine* 3.10) and then waited for the bishops to give a signal to sit down. In his opening address delivered in Latin, he impressed upon them his earnest desire for their "unity in a common harmony of thought" and his conviction that "intestine strife within the church of God is far more evil and dangerous than any kind of war or conflict." News of this dispute distressed him enough to convene the council. The bishops, therefore, must "begin from this moment to discard the causes of that disunion which has existed among you and remove the perplexities of controversy by embracing the principles of peace" (Eusebius, *Life of Constantine*, 3.12). Constantine then guided the debate until he secured a consensus, himself proposing the highly disputed word *homoousios* ("of the same essence") to describe the relation of the Son to the Father. Soon after the Council of Nicaea, he sent a handwritten letter to the churches explaining the decisions reached there and indicating that his first objective was "that unity of faith, sincerity of love, and community of feeling in regard to the worship of Almighty God, might be preserved among the highly favored multitude who compose the Catholic Church" (ibid., 3.17). The decrees of the council were to be regarded as "indicative of the Divine will" (3.20). He also warned the bishops before they departed to be flexible and avoid any further contention. When the Egyptians continued the controversy, he again sent them a warning.

The decision reached at Nicaea, achieved under a considerable amount of imperial duress, did not bring harmony. Although nonsigners such as Arius and Eusebius, bishop of Nicomedia, were sent into exile, they did not remain inactive and quiescent. By 330 the Arians regained ascendancy as Constantine himself shifted the weight of his support from Nicaea.

Religious Intolerance, 330–337

Constantine ordered the building of his new capital immediately after his victory over Licinius at Chrysopolis on September 18, 324. His predecessor Diocletian had already begun to shift his administrative headquarters from Rome to Nicomedia, for the ever-growing demands on the monarchs necessitated an Eastern center. According to Lactantius (*Deaths of Persecutors* 7.8.10), Diocletian "aimed to make Nicomedia as great as Rome" and accelerated the building process. Constantine knew well the plans of his predecessors and carried his own designs in his head for a long time, frequently changing them—first thinking of Sardica (modern Sophia in Bulgaria), then Thessalonica, before deciding on Byzantium. After his victory at Chrysopolis, realizing he no longer had to rely on Western forces, he made his decision quickly. Tied to this was recognition that Old Rome remained pagan to the core. Although he celebrated his vicennalia (twenty-year festival) in Rome in 326 with dazzling

games, he was not prepared to settle with the Senate for anything less than complete submission to the Christianization of the city. But the Senate and people of Rome repulsed his efforts.

Constantinople first appeared on coins as the rival to Rome in 330, the year Empress-mother Helena died. From this point Constantine's policy changed to one of intolerance. He now loudly proclaimed his support of Christianity, rewarded pagans for conversion, and undertook the suppression of paganism, stopping short only at the uprooting of the imperial cult that might erode popular loyalty. So many religious practices intersected with devotion to the state, even Constantine could not abolish all of them and had to be content with stripping them of their most objectionable features.

Constantine's severest attacks on paganism were restricted to the East. Even there, modern research into inscriptions has shown that the effect was far less devastating than some Christians or embittered pagans reported. Actually the old religions had been hearing a death knell for a long time; Constantine merely hastened the process. Other emperors had laid hands on temples before, though none intended to destroy them as Constantine did. Between 330 and 337 began the destruction of the chief centers of the pagan cult. In its first phase it involved robbery of treasures—gold and silver, bronze, and art masterpieces—to enrich Christian churches or the new capital. Next followed the actual demolition of buildings such as the temple of Asclepius at Aegae in Cilicia and others at Apheca and Heliopolis in Phoenicia that offended Christians by their rites of sacred prostitution. In the West, however, Constantine failed to bring paganism down despite the fact that his laws applied equally to both spheres. He may have framed a general prohibition of sacrifice, but death prevented him from enforcing it.

May 17, 330 Constantine dedicated his new capital, thus giving his Christian empire one center free from any touch of paganism. Although some scholars have questioned how "Christian" the new capital was, coins struck at the time show the globe set on the cross of Christ on the scepter of the "Tyche," the goddess of Fortune, who personified the city. A solemn mass accompanied the dedication. Constantine, however, could not escape the dominance of mythology connected with ancient Rome, interpreting Constantinople accordingly. The City of Constantine was, as it were, anti-Rome. The emperor had to create there even a Senate, like that which had given him so much trouble in old Rome. He lured some aristocrats from old Rome by erecting grand houses for noble families, evidently mostly Christian, and began to celebrate the presence of Romans by placing the ancient inscription *populus Romanus* on coins in 335. He freed citizens of Constantinople from the burden of taxation. He called it "the second Rome," subordinating it to the ancient capital. Rome itself continued down the road it had always traveled. When Constantine died, his sons had to agree to allow the Senate to apotheosize him in the old manner (Eutropius 10.8.2). After his death the pagan aristocracy in the old city still fought for their rights.

Shortly after the Council of Nicaea, the emperor issued a severe edict against heresies and schisms in the East—Valentinians, Marcionites, Montanists (Cataphrygians), and Paulianists (followers of Paul of Samosata)—depriving them of all meeting places. Later he retracted the decree against Novatianists. He did not mention Arianism, for the council had supposedly killed it. When he discovered three months later that Eusebius, bishop of Nicomedia, and Theognis, bishop of Nicaea, still clung stubbornly to Arius's views, he exiled them and ordered an election of bishops. When the Nicomedians demurred, Constantine personally replied, denouncing Eusebius and warning that they were approaching high treason. The Nicomedians and Nicaeans finally bowed and elected Amphion and Chrestus as successors. Meantime, the emperor kept up efforts to get Arius to retract, inviting him to come to the

imperial court. Arius and his followers submitted a confession that satisfied the emperor but not Alexander, bishop of Alexandria, who resisted his efforts to force a reconciliation. In 327 Constantine reassembled the Council of Nicaea to readmit Arius to communion. Eusebius of Nicomedia and Theognis petitioned for readmission also on the basis of complete submission to the original decision, including *homoousios*. The bishops accepted their pleas and restored them to their sees.

Although the apparent reconciliation elated the emperor, the controversy did not abate. Anti-Arians refused to recognize Arius and pressed their case against bishops who leaned toward Arian theology. When Marcellus, bishop of Ancyra, and Eustathius, bishop of Antioch, made accusations against Eusebius of Nicomedia and Eusebius of Caesarea and Narcissus of Neronias, all Origenists, they themselves ended up being condemned in a council at Constantinople and sent off into exile. Constantine was now obviously shifting his support from the rigid Nicaeans led by Athanasius, newly elected bishop of Alexandria, toward Arians or semi-Arians. Athanasius proved to be a thorn in Constantine's side for the rest of his life, for he would not yield an inch to any position but his own whereas the emperor's efforts mandated compromise, something in which Arians proved more to his liking. "Unlike the emperor," A. H. M. Jones has remarked (*Constantine and the Conversion of Europe*, 183), "he preferred the truth to concord." In 332 Athanasius responded to an imperial summons to the Palace of Psammathia to answer charges made against him the preceding year by four Meletian bishops, where the court acquitted him of the charges. Not content to let the matter drop, the Meletians accused him of the murder of a Meletian bishop named Arsenius, producing a severed hand as all that remained of the victim. Athanasius disproved the accusation promptly by producing the supposed victim. Constantine, furious at the way the Meletians had made a fool of him, wrote Athanasius a letter denouncing them. At this time, Arius, still barred from Alexandria by Athanasius, entreated the emperor demanding "to be received back" and claimed all the people of Libya were on his side. This petition only infuriated Constantine, however, and caused him to write a denunciation of Arius and his views in violent terms.

Growing more and more anxious to effect a reunion of divided Christians, in 334 Constantine ordered the convening of a Council at Caesarea under the presidency of Eusebius "for the purification of the holy Christian people." Although summoned by the emperor, Athanasius refused to attend because he saw it as a tool of the two Eusebiuses to get Arius reinstated. A year later, Constantine ordered the convocation of another council to meet at Tyre and issued a threat of deposition against any who refused to attend. This time Athanasius yielded with reluctance, expecting condemnation on formidable charges. Clearly outvoted, Athanasius and the Egyptian delegation withdrew, leaving the council free to condemn Athanasius in absentia and to examine and accept an orthodox confession of faith sent by Arius. Before this decision reached Egypt, however, Athanasius hastened to Constantinople to intercede with Constantine. The emperor wavered in his presence, but finally decided, after a visit from the two Eusebiuses, to exile Athanasius to Treves in Gaul. The latter departed Constantinople on November 7, 334, to spend the first of five periods in Exile. What probably tipped the balances was Athanasius's threat to prevent shipment of grain from Alexandria, which Constantine interpreted as confirmation of intransigence. He now viewed Athanasius as the chief obstacle to Christian unity, although he refused to allow election of another bishop to take his place. Egyptian bishops still declined to restore communion to Arius, so that the emperor ended up recalling him to Constantinople, where he had to order Bishop Alexander to give Arius communion. The day before that momentous event was to take place, however, Arius suddenly dropped dead. Hopes for restoration were thwarted again.

Although Constantine concentrated much of his help within the churches, he tried also to fulfill his promise to be a bishop for those outside the church and a thirteenth apostle. In 331, after his oldest surviving son Constantine defeated the Goths on the Danube, the Sarmatians begged for admission into the empire. Not long afterwards, the Goths themselves were converted by the great Arian missionary Ulfilas. In the East Iberia (Georgia) officially adopted the Christian faith during Constantine's reign. After conversion of the queen, the king sent an emissary to Constantine to ask for instructors to teach his subjects. The kingdom of Axum (Abyssinia or Ethiopia) also adopted Christianity through the agency of two Roman boys, Aedesius and Frumentius, captured and made slaves of the king. Constantine probably worsened the situation of Christians in Persia, however, by writing a letter to Sapor I, reminding him of all the disasters which befell emperors who persecuted Christians, notably Valerian, who died as a prisoner of the Persians. Up to this point Christians had been tolerated. Now they were suspected of being agents of the Romans. A few years before Constantine's death, Sapor opened hostilities and later started persecution. Constantine signed a friendly treaty with Armenia, the first Christian kingdom, and took up the offer of the Armenia nobility to rule their kingdom in exchange for defense against the Persians, who had occupied it in 334. He was preparing for a Persian war when he died.

A Mixed Blessing

Constantine's contribution to the evangelization of the Roman Empire and even beyond was an immense but not an unmixed blessing. Increasing assistance he supplied the churches tipped the scales for Christianity over against all competitors, even the syncretistic solar monotheism attractive to many of the emperors as they sought to unify their fragmented and far-flung empire. Constantine moved from tolerance of all cults to favoritism for Christianity to open intolerance and efforts to make Christianity the religion of the empire. Not only so, he sought also to effect unity among Christians since, in his view, the unity and well being of the empire depended on the concord in common faith and worship of all its citizens. Here he set Christianity on the track of persecution that has cast a shadow on its history ever since. Christians had themselves experienced fearsome persecution at times, but even that did not equal the pain they inflicted on non-Christians and even on other Christians as they gave religious sanction to the state's coercive powers. By the time of Theodosius I intolerance had become a public virtue.

The irony of the blessing Constantine bestowed is evident in his deathbed baptism. Exactly why he delayed baptism is uncertain. He may have done so for political reasons, to avoid offending the predominantly pagan populace; for personal reasons, because he felt unworthy and, early on, unsure of his faith; for theological reasons, wanting to be sure he would receive full remission of sins and not wanting to undergo the rigors of penance at this time; or for a combination of these reasons. However, that my be, when he fell ill shortly after Easter 337, he withdrew from Constantinople to a nearby spa with thermal springs and then to Helenopolis, where he prayed in the church his mother had built in honor of Lucian of Antioch and other martyrs. He then traveled to Nicomedia, where he convened a group of bishops and told them he had wanted to receive baptism in the Jordan River, but now he could not. he then asked for baptism and, donning the white robe of a catechumen, he received baptism at the hands of Eusebius of Nicomedia, whom he had once sent into exile for Arian sympathies. He died at Pentecost. Though buried in Constantinople in the Church of the Apostles, the Roman Senate honored him by deification. It remained for the sons of Constantine—Constans, Constantine II, and Constantius—to continue

Christianizing an empire already divided and only superficially touched by Christian faith.

Chapter 19

Church and State after Constantine

Constantine inaugurated an era of bright hopes for the churches and his sons followed the same policies. Only the emperor Julian seriously threatened to reverse the tide set in motion by Constantine's energies on behalf of the churches and against paganism. The brevity of his reign, however, diminished his efforts to supplant Christianity with a revived paganism. The next several successors, all Christians, resumed support and favors intended by Constantine. Although Jovian, Valentinian, and Valens exhibited considerable tolerance toward paganism, they did not extend it to Christian sects. Gratian and Theodosius brought an end to all tolerance. Under Theodosius the catholic church was defined legally in terms of communion with Damasus, the bishop of Rome, and Peter, the bishop of Alexandria. Constantine's vision had finally become reality.

Not all Christians, even those within the orthodox sphere, were incognizant of the dangers lurking in Constantinianism. The churches would easily become a pawn of the powerful state. One of Constantine's own sons, the Arian-leaning Constantius, ruler in the East (337–361), pointed up the risks, as Constantine himself had, when a ruler cannot remain content with ecclesiastical decisions. For the West, therefore, there emerged a less optimistic and more realistic theory separating the spheres of church and state, articulated with particular force by Ambrose, bishop of Milan, and Augustine, bishop of Hippo.

Constantine's Sons and the Church, 337–361

After a three-month interregnum during which potential claimants to the throne were disposed of, the rule of the empire was divided between Constantine's three surviving sons. Constantine II, the oldest, ruled Britain, Gaul, and Spain and held a certain precedence; Constans took charge of the rest of the West as far as Thrace; Constantius II controlled the East. In 340 Constantine II, charging his younger brother with flouting his authority, invaded Italy and was killed at Aquileia, thus leaving two-thirds of the empire in the latter's hands. In January 350 Constans was overthrown by an officer of German descent named Magnentius. After obtaining support of Vetranio, another claimant crowned by his troops, Constantius defeated Magnentius at Mursa on September 28, 351 and, after Magnentius's final defeat in the summer of 353, reunited the empire under a single Augustus.

All three sons, reared as Christians, followed faithfully in the footsteps of their father, stepping up his late attacks on paganism, extending favors to the churches, and intervening at will in ecclesiastical affairs. As ruler in the West, where Nicene orthodoxy had strong support, Constans applied pressure on behalf of Nicaeans. In 342 he arranged the Council of Sardica, which cleared Athanasius, Marcellus of Ancyra, and Paul of

Constantinople. In 345 he prevailed upon Constantius to reinstate Athanasius after the latter's second exile. He also used military force to crush Donatism, by this time a powerful socioeconomic rebel movement in North Africa.

In the East, where sympathy for Arianism was strong, Constantius leaned in a different direction on this divisive matter. He sought counsel of Eusebius, of Nicomedia and Constantinople, and later Eudoxius, bishop of Constantinople, as his court bishops. Although he did not favor the overtly Arian bishops who said the Son was "unlike" (*anomoios*) the Father, he sided with those who advocated abandonment of unbiblical terms such as *homoousios* ("of the same essence") or *homoiousios* ("of like essence") and use of the simple and biblical *homoios* ("like"). Accordingly, he intervened in the appointment or deposition of more and more bishops and summoned others to his court to browbeat them into conformity, as he did in the case of Tiberius, bishop of Rome, and Hosius of Cordova. In 355 he transferred the Council of Milan from the church to his palace so as to force the bishops to choose between condemnation of Athanasius and their own exile. When the bishops protested that the emperor's action violated the church's canon, he replied, "My will is the canon," appealing to Arian bishops to sustain him (Athanasius, *History of the Arians* 4.8). The culprit in Constantius's eyes was the intransigeant Athanasius, who would not go along with a neutral, conciliatory formula such as *homoios*. Peace and harmony must take precedence over theological considerations. When the opponents objected, Constantius took refuge in his success: Had he not defeated the usurper Maxentius?

Both Constans and Constantius continued their father's war against paganism. In 341 Constans issued a law decreeing the cessation of all sacrifices. In 356 Constantius ordered the closing of temples and the cessation of sacrifices under penalty of death. Although some temples were closed, it would appear that authorities enforced these decrees rather lightly, for no pagans suffered martyrdom.

Constantius extended the privileges of the clergy, exempting them from all supplementary taxes and from requisition of animals for postal service. Although the clergy were not satisfied with exemptions from regular taxes and asked for more, he granted immunity only for church lands, a concession revoked by Julian. Otherwise he exempted from personal taxes only those clergy scraping out a bare living. He relaxed some rules of Constantine preventing ordination of men of curial family only if they surrendered their fortunes.

Julian and the Restoration of Paganism, 361–363

Born in 331, Julian was the son of Constantine's brother Julius Constantius and Basilina, Julius's second wife. The family to which Julian's mother belonged included both pagans and Christians, and her faith was apparently mixed, shaped somewhat by Eusebius of Nicomedia but also by a classical heritage. She died, however, when Julian was very young. His father was executed when Julian was only six years old, a victim of the struggle to assure Constantine's sons complete control of the empire. Two uncles and seven cousins of Constantius also were put to death. It is suspected that the person responsible for their deaths was Constantius II, although early Christian accounts attribute them to the armies rather than to Constantius. Directly after elevation to the imperial rule, Julian blamed Constantius in a *Letter to the Senate and People of Athens* (3). Had he been older, he too would have met the same fate. Christians evidently whisked him away to a church, where he received asylum (Gregory Nazianzen *Oration* 4.19). Constantius deprived both Julian and his twelve year old stepbrother, Gallus, of their property. He sent Gallus into exile for a time and kept an eye on the education of Julian, directing him to Eusebius of Nicomedia. When the latter was transferred from Nicomedia to Constantinople (338–342), Julian followed and was baptized during this period. The education in which he reveled, however, he received at the hands of the eunuch Mardonius, who had taught his mother. As a child, he loved the shows and games which many Christians denounced. He loved Greek and Latin literature that Mardonius taught him in complete independence of any Christian ideas. About 343 or 344 Constantius reunited Julian and his brother Gallus, now seventeen, and imprisoned them in the imperial domain of Macellum in Cappadocia. Julian spent seven or eight unhappy years there "severed from any serious study" and isolated from the people of the area as well as friends. He did resume study of Plato and Aristotle with Mardonius after a time. At some point he acquired a knowledge of scriptures as well, but he never allowed them to touch him personally.

Julian's brother Gallus remained a Christian despite experiencing the same kind of treatment at Constantius's hands that Julian did, perhaps because he was six years older. In 351 Contantius released Gallus and Julian from exile at Macellum and elevated Gallus, now twenty-six, to the dignity of a Caesar, adopted him as his stepbrother, and entrusted to him the rule of the East. Julian was brought to Constantinople where he took further studies under the eye of Mardonius. At this stage he evidently leaned toward the philosophy of a cynic with a definite penchant for monkish austerity. After four years Constantius's suspicions about the kind of education Julian was receiving at Constantinople prompted him to send the latter to Nicomedia again. But it was there that he made his sharp turn toward paganism under the influence of the celebrated rhetorician Libanius, who despised all things Latin and detested the Christian church. Run out of Constantinople, Libanius became astonishingly popular and successful in Nicomedia. At this time Julian also found himself attracted by the occultism that was so powerful in the province under the leadership of the theurgist Edesius and the

Neoplatonist Maximus, who combined divination and theurgy. Maximus converted Julian to Neoplatonism. Where Neoplatonism later became Augustine's bridge to Christianity, for Julian it led to his complete break with Christianity.

Following Gallus's execution by order of Constantius in 355, Julian spent seven months being taken from one prison to another, yet allowed considerable freedom. Empress Eusebeia intervened to save him from a capital sentence, defending him personally against accusations and arranging an audience with the emperor. Although Julian wanted to retire to Bithynia or Ionia, Constantius exiled him to Athens. This suited his cultural desires exactly. Yet he remained there only three months—July to September of 355. Athens was still a largely pagan city with more idols than any other city. Most teachers there were pagan and Julian frequently let them know his desire to revive the ancient religion. He developed a fascination for the hierophant of Eleusis, the ancient mystery religion of Greece, and made him his religious guide. Although some scholars speculate that he was initiated into the cult of Eleusis, evidence for that is not adequate. He was initiated into the Mithra cult centered in devotion to the Unconquered Sun. Along with worship of the Sun, he especially honored Jupiter, Mercury, Minerva, and Cybele.

In September 355 Constantius ordered Julian to leave Athens and go to Milan and then elevated him to the role of Caesar at the urging of Eusebeia. Although Julian at first wanted to decline the honor, he finally accepted and took Helen, sister of the emperor, as his wife, perhaps under pressure from Constantius. Julian led very effectively on the frontier in Gaul and along the Rhine. By 360 he had reestablished Roman control on the frontier against the Alemanni, Franks, and other tribes long threatening. Popular both with the people of the area and the troops, Julian aroused fears of Constantius, who directed Julian to dispatch troops to aid in the war against the

Persians. The soldiers rebelled and acclaimed Julian Augustus in February 360. When Constantius refused to accept compromise, Julian marched East ready to engage Constantius in battle. Before he reached Constantinople, however, the emperor died in Cilicia on November 3, 361.

Whatever his early religious opinions, Julian had been forced up to this time to hide them except on occasion among his troops. On his accession he immediately ordered the opening of the temples, offering of sacrifices to the gods, and restoration of the pagan cultus. Assembling Christian bishops, he directed them to lay aside their differences and each observe their own beliefs in the conviction that freedom would increase dissension, "knowing as he did from experience," according to Ammianus Marcellinus (22.5.4), "that no wild beasts are such enemies to humankind as are most of the Christians in their deadly hatred of one another." Pagans exploded with joy. In Rome the pagan party reestablished the Altar of Victory ordered torn down by Constantius in 357. In many places, of course, the temples had never closed, but where they had, they now were quickly reopened and revived. Julian himself saw to it that a pagan temple and altar were erected in Constaninople and, with great pomp, imolated victims at the foot of a statue of Fortuna erected by Constantine in the chief basilica of the city. Reversing the favoritism of his predecessors, he restored pagan priests to their ancient honors, privileges, exemptions, and rents. Twenty years of Christian hegemony, however, had taken a toll of the priesthood and Julian had a major challenge. Julian also sought to revive occult practices, himself assisting in a seance (Ammianus Marcellinus 22.7).

Wise enough not merely to restore the pagan cults materially, Julian undertook a thoroughgoing reform. He developed a hierarchy in imitation of Christianity's, in effect founding a pagan church similar to the one planned by Maximin Daia (Eusebius, H.E. 8.14; Lactantius, *Deaths of Persecutors* 36). He installed a priest over each province, similar to a metropolitan; on whom the *flamen* in each city (a kind of bishop) would depend, and charged them to enroll priests and lower clergy. The emperor himself was the sovereign pontiff (*pontifex maximus*), having power to designate leading dignitaries, deprive and punish them, fix the law and theology and design the religion. Julian himself wrote pastoral letters to his priests. The provincial priests not only offered sacrifices and presided over provincial assemblies or festivals, they also governed the clergy of the province, deriving their authority from the *pontifex maximus*. Julian demanded that priests, their wives, their children, and their servants set "an example of respect toward the gods" or be deprived of their "sacred ministry" (*Ep.* 49). Under the provincial priest were priests in each city who supervised others serving local temples. On one point Julian's plan differed from the Christian, that is, in admission of women to the priesthood to serve certain deities.

Julian organized temple activities along Christian lines also. He ordered prayers to be offered at set times, especially morning and evening. Psalms were sung and musicians trained in psalm singing. He appointed teachers and readers to give instruction in pagan doctrines and exhortations. A great weakness here, however, lay in a lack of scriptures or tradition to sustain preaching.

Julian introduced penitential discipline, although it is difficult to see how it could function effectively given pagan mores. He evidently placed much emphasis on clerical morals, wanting his priests to rival the most exemplary members of Christian clergy in zeal and morality. He chose for the priesthood only persons of strictest moral repute without regard to social class, whereas up to his day priests only guarded purity. While they served the altar, Julian considered them priests at all times and thus bound to be pure at all times. He instructed them to pray three times a day, offer sacrifices once a day, observe exact continence, nourish themselves by readings and philosophical meditations, and to avoid contact with the public except in performance of ministry. Not only did he expect them to avoid evil, they were not to contemplate evil or engage in doubtful pleasantries or read literature offensive to the gods or frequent the theater or taverns or circuses. In short, Julian propounded a puritan sense of behavior.

Julian paid Christianity another compliment in imitating its charities. He instructed his high priest in Galatia to establish numerous hostels in each village so that strangers could have the care they needed. The Jews take care of their own. Pagans take care of nobody. But "the impious Galileans (Christians) take care not only of their own but ours as well" (*Ep.* 49). Thus the latter win all the converts. To sustain his charities, Julian put the necessary funds at the disposal of the provincial priests, directing that a fifth be used for priests and the rest for strangers and the needy. Yet he realized that pagans themselves would need to learn how to give as Christians did. According to Sozomen (5.16), Julian especially admired the letters bishops wrote to commend poor travelers to care of other Christians. He also wanted the priests to match the church in burial of the dead, discerning in this again a key to Christianity's success. He even counseled his priests, with some reluctance, to assist prisoners.

Julian's revived cultus shocked well-educated pagans not only by the extent of sacrifices but by its occultism. Julian constantly searched entrails of animals sacrificed for clues to the gods' plans. "Julian tried particularly to profane his hands," Gregory of Nazianzus theorized, "in order to erase every trace of the nonbloody sacrifice (of the eucharist) by which we commune with Christ, in his sufferings and in his divinity" (*Oration* 4.52). He constructed a sanctuary dedicated to Mithra in the palace at Constantinople and participated in the mysteries there as a priest as well as devotee. Yet he did obeisance to all the gods—those of ancient mythology, the asiatic deities, the Egyptian deities Isis and Osiris.

Above all, he considered himself "a servant of the Sun god" (*Oration* 4) which he often identified with Jupiter. This allowed him to maintain a compromise between absolute polytheism and absolute monotheism and, at the same time, incorporate Platonism. The Supreme God created the universe and distributed control over various nations and cities to lesser gods. Thus we have differences of customs, laws, and moral codes.

Julian did not try to attack Christianity outright so much as he sought to disrupt it. Late in 361 or early in 362 he issued an edict recalling exiles banished by Constantius. Most of these were Nicaeans: Athanasius, Meletius of Antioch, Eusebius of Vercelli, and Lucifer of Cagliari. Some, however, were semi-Arians: Basil of Ancyra, Eleusis of Cyzicus, Sivanus of Tarsus and Eustathius of Sebaste. Others included the Sabellian Photinus and the Arian Aetius. Under guise of concern for freedom Julian fanned the flames of controversy in the churches, favoring heretics where he could. Athanasius had scarcely returned in triumph to Alexandria before Julian exiled him again. When Alexandrians protested, Julian wrote a long dissuasive against Christianity and in behalf of his reform; yet he had some difficulty chasing Athanasius out of the city.

As another measure for restricting Christian influence, Julian excluded Christians from civil and military service and thus won some converts to his cause, for many held to Christianity by a thin thread anyway. He placed a great price on the conversion of scholars and people of letters. One such convert was Caesarius, brother of Gregory of Nazianzus and son of the bishop. At the same time he barred Christians from teaching pagan literature, in effect, excluding them from the schools since such literature comprised the curriculum, on the grounds that they could not do so honestly. Christians, however, could attend public schools. Julian thus put parents in the difficult position of deciding whether they would give their children adequate education. He retracted exemptions from public duty granted Christian clergy by his predecessors to dampen the appeal of ministry for the wealthy. Although he denied that he wished "Galileans" killed or harmed in any way, he declared unequivocally his preference for "the god-fearing," that is, pagans. After riots in Edessa in 361 or 362 Julian confiscated ecclesiastical possessions and forbade further feuding.

Julian also composed a treatise *Against the Galileans*, published sometime early in 363. For his material he turned to earlier polemicists such as Celsus and Porphyry, pupil and successor of Plotinus. From what has survived it is possible to see the main lines of his attack: discrepancies between the Old and New Testament, Christian abandonment of Jewish customs, introduction of new customs such as the cult of martyrs, the superiority of pagan savior-gods such as Heracles or Asclepios to Jesus, and Christian persecution of pagans and other Christians. Although Julian wanted this to be his greatest work, he did it hurriedly and, due to his death a few months later, it made little impact. Ironically, he modeled his revived paganism after Christianity in many particulars—hierarchy, charities, hospitals and orphanages, even monasteries and convents.

Julian touched off a crisis in Antioch in October 362 when he ordered the remains of Babylas, a bishop of Antioch martyred during the persecution under Decius (249–251), removed from a church built in front of the temple of Apollo. A crowd of Christians gathered to sing psalms. A few made threatening gestures. Julian, losing control of himself, ordered ringleaders arrested and punished. A few days later, the temple caught fire and burned. Julian retaliated by closing the Great Church of Antioch Constantine had built and confiscated its golden vessels. Thereafter he stepped up his efforts to repress Christianity. He dealt with cities according to their Christian affiliation, depriving some of rights because they were Christian, granting others special favor because they showed zeal for the old religion. Once again he banished Athanasius, who had just re-

turned to the city of Alexandria, thus raising the level of hatred for the emperor. Before he left Antioch in March 363 the city found itself at complete loggersheads with him.

Fortunately for Christianity Julian did not live long enough to implement his plan for supplanting Christianity with a revived syncretistic religion of the state. In the spring of 362 he evidently decided to resume the war on the eastern front abandoned by Constantius. Inspired by the exploits of Alexander the Great, he led his army to the walls of the Persian capital, Ctesiphon. Unfortunately by this time summer heat had set in, discouraging efforts to capture the city. Fearful lest the Persians seize his ships and use them against the Roman troops, Julian ordered them burned. He then had to lead a demoralized army overland. On June 25, 363, they engaged a large Persian force. Julian valiantly raced in an out among his troops to spur them on. Leaving himself so exposed, however, had fatal consequences, for a spear, whether Persian or Roman is uncertain, pierced his side and claimed his life a few hours later.

From Julian to Theodosius

The morning after Julian's death, his generals met to elect Jovian as his successor. When Jovian protested that he could not lead a largely pagan army because he was a Christian, the generals replied, "We are all Christians here." Jovian led the battle for several days until Shapur, fearful of a full-scale war with the Romans, opened the way for a thirty-year peace treaty. Part of the price of peace was the surrender of Arsaces, the King of Armenia, whom Shapur arrested and blinded. The Romans also ceded five provinces on the left bank of the Tigris. As they passed by Tarsus on the way west, they buried the corpse of Julian just outside the city walls. Tarsus, ironically, was the home town of the Apostle to the Gentiles.

Jovian (363–364) inaugurated a period of toleration and noninterference which his successor, Valentinian I, continued. According to pagan historian Ammianus Marcellinus, he did not disturb anyone nor cause any to worship this or that nor issue threatening edicts forcing others to worship as he did (*Rerum gestarum libri* 30.9.5). He repulsed efforts of Arians to prevent the recall of Athansius to Alexandria.

Early in his reign Valentinian (364–379) shared his rule with his brother Valens, consigning the East to him. Both feared religious practices that would work to their political disadvantage. Thus they forbade haruspicy for harmful purposes, although they did not consider it criminal. Similarly they forbade bloody sacrifices without putting a clamp down on other forms of pagan worship. Valens, however, did not maintain Jovian's policy of noninterference. He returned, rather, to a policy similar to that of Constantius, leaning toward a modified form of Arianism and threatening opponents with harassment and exile. Jointly the emperors barred wealthy citizens from entering the priesthood to avoid public service.

Gratian, who began a joint rule with Valentinian and Valens in 367, did not pave the way for Theodosius. During his reign, he refused the title Pontifex Maximus, took away the endowment from the sacred colleges, and removed the Altar of Victory from the Senate House. Whether he did these things before Theodosius came to the throne, however, is unlikely. It appears that he did nothing spectacular against paganism until 379. The fact is, he continued Valentinian's policy of nonintervention in church matters so long as peace prevailed. In Africa he confiscated property of Donatists in 376. When confronted with Arianism for the first time in 378, he turned to Ambrose for advice. For a time thereafter he continued his policy of toleration, banning only Eunomianism, Photinianism, and Manichaeism in an edict issued after Valens's death in 378. When bishops in a Roman synod asked him to exile a bishop condemned by the pope or by the synod and to free the pope from jurisdiction of any court except the emperor's. Gratian reluctantly granted the first request for bishops under the pope's jurisdiction but evaded the second with vague language.

A Fully Christian State

Theodosius himself, therefore, deserves credit for turning the empire into a fully Christian state. Invited by Gratian to share the rule in 379, he did not take long to act. In February, 380 he issued the edict *Cunctos populos* commanding all the peoples under his rule to follow the form of religion handed down by the Apostle Peter to the Romans and followed by Damasus, bishop of Rome, and Peter, bishop of Alexandria. In sum, that would mean to believe "in the doctrine of Father, Son, and Holy Spirit, one deity of equal majesty and pious trinity." Those who adhered to such faith could call themselves Catholic Christians, but others must be designated demented and barbarian and heretical and be stricken first by divine vengeance and then by imperial action in accordance with the will of heaven. (*Theod. Cod.* 16.1.2.) Theodosius genuinely believed he had received power from heaven to establish the one true form of religion as represented by Rome and Alexandria. A Spaniard, he shared the Western views on Nicea. Another experience, however, may have added to the vigor with which he pursued his pro-Nicene policy. While most emperors from Constantine on delayed their baptisms until their deathbed, an illness forced Theodosius to receive baptism at the hands of Ascholius, bishop of Thessalonica, a Nicene with strongly Western affinities. Shortly after his arrival at Constantinople, at any rate, Emperor Theodosius began to remove Arians and replace them with bishops who accepted the Nicene Creed. In Constantinople itself, Arianism had gotten a strong grip and Theodosius had to weather a popular storm against his replacement of Demophilus with Gregory of Nazianzus. Soldiers had to protect the saintly Gregory on his way to the Church of the Apostles. The empire still unsettled by controversy between Arians and

Nicenes, Theodosius convened the Second Ecumenical Council at Constantinople to ratify conclusions he had already reached. In a special rescript in January, 381 he denied heretics any place to celebrate the mysteries and prohibited their assembly. The name of the one supreme God alone was to be celebrated everywhere in accordance with the Nicene faith. Photinians, Eunomians, and Arians were specifically condemned. The edict even defined Nicene faith. Any who disturbed the true churches were to be driven from the walls so that the Catholic churches could again achieve unity in this faith. (*Theod. Cod.* 16.5.6)

The emperor proceeded with energy to stamp out heresy. In 372 Valentinian I had already forbidden Manichaean assemblies and ordered confiscation of their property. In 381 Theodosius tightened up further by ordering that no Manichaean of either sex could bequeath or inherit (16.5.7). He levied a death penalty against Encratites, Saccofori, and Hydroparastatae (16.5.9), the first time the death penalty was prescribed for heresy! The decree also introduced inquisitors and informers into the churches. By 383 laws against heresy reached a peak, as he summoned a synod to deal with all heresies. Only Novatians and Luciferians escaped.

Theodosius was evidently not hostile to paganism from the beginning of his reign, for legislation against it was mild until 391. The emperor did his best to protect legitimate rights of pagans, restraining the cutting of trees in sacred sites and protecting pagan art works and temples. He played no part in its disestablishment. He even appointed pagans to high office. According to Libanius (*Oration* 30.18), he allowed libations but not sacrifices to be offered. Christians, however, used existing laws to rally against paganism. Cynegius, Praetorian Prefect of the East from 384 to 388, a crony of the emperor, led the attack. In February 391 he ordered an end to sacrifices, directing judges to fine even onlookers (*Theod. Cod.* 16.10).

On June 16, 391 Theodosius signaled the beginning of a new era by application of his decree against sacrifices of 380. In this year Christians destroyed the Serapeum in Alexandria, though not on imperial command. Official policy was to close but preserve edifices. In the West the campaign against paganism sought to eradicate all traces. Eugenius, elevated to the purple after the death of Valentinian II in August, 392, entered into an alliance with the pagan aristocracy of Rome. Later in the year, Theodosius openly attacked paganism by legal action, forbidding every type of pagan religious practice—blood sacrifice, incense, family devotion, etc. Pagans rallied behind Eugenius, who crossed the Alps in 393 and joined in the effort to restore the Altar of Victory to the Senate. War was inevitable. Theodosius, accompanied by his two sons, left Constantinople in May 394 and reached enemy territory in September. Although victorious in an early engagement, he was nearly overwhelmed in a second. A sudden storm evidently arose and saved him and his army. Resistance collapsed. Eugenius was killed. Arbogast, a barbarian general, committed suicide. Thereafter, Theodosius inaugurated a full blown antipagan policy in the West.

One incident during Theodosius's reign offers a good look at the emperor's commitment to the Catholic Church. In 390 citizens of Thessalonica rioted in protest of the imprisonment of a favorite charioteer and killed the Gothic officer named Butheric whom he had tried to rape. In Milan Theodosius immediately ordered a massacre. Before the troops arrived he sent a second messenger to countermand the first command, but the message did not arrive in time to avert the slaying of thousands. Ambrose, bishop of Milan, was horror-stricken when the news reached him. A week or so later, however, he dispatched a private letter to Theodosius, demanding that the emperor do penance, just as David had after the killing of Uriah the Hittite. Although initially recalcitrant, he consented to his pastor's demand.

For a whole year he put on sackcloth and ashes and went through the process to be restored. Many viewed it as a victory of church over state, priest over king. Obviously the emperor wanted to be convincingly Catholic.

Theodosius died January 17, 395 at the height of success. During his sixteen-year career, he brought closer to completion the christianization process inaugurated by Constantine. Unquestionably the Nicene party in the church benefited the most, for Theodosius assured its triumph within the empire. The Apostle to the Goths, Ulfilas (?311–381), however, had planted the Arian seed well enough among barbarians that it would take centuries of mission effort and the help of numerous other rulers to secure the victory of orthodoxy. The churches would have been wise to take a closer look at Theodosius's gifts, however, for in subsequent centuries they would exact a high price, not the least part of which came in the form of persecution.

Chapter 20

Christianizing the Roman Empire and Evangelizing the World

The conversion of Constantine, however interpreted, opened a new chapter in Christian history. Instead of representing a despised and persecuted minority, Christianity now became the fad and Christian leaders found themselves with the enviable task of trying to Christianize the masses who knocked on church doors trying to get in, erect new and grand buildings to replace those destroyed under Diocletian and his cohorts, and expand existing structures to reach into every nook and cranny of the empire with the gospel of Jesus Christ. Small wonder Eusebius and other Christians would think the millennium had arrived.

Church Structure and Conversion of the Empire

From this point on there was a concerted effort, in councils of bishops as well as by observant missionary bishops like Ambrose of Milan, to increase the number of congregations and episcopates. Attentive leaders sensed the moment had arrived to bring the whole empire under the Christian banner in fact as well as in name. In Gaul, for instance, there is evidence for the existence of only a dozen episcopal sees before Constantine; by the end of the sixth century they had grown to 119. In north Africa, although episcopates numbered nearly a hundred already at the time of Cyprian (248–258), by the fifth century the three provinces of Africa, Numidia, and Mauretania counted an estimated 632 to 768 bishops. Similar evidence could be cited for other parts of the empire.

Christianity expanded, as noted early, as an urban religion. Churches planted in the cities assumed responsibility for evangelizing the suburbs and, eventually, the surrounding countryside. Sometimes claims overlapped, creating tensions. As a consequence, councils of the Constantinian and post-Constantinian period decided to bring the jurisdictional areas into approximate line with the dioceses and provinces of the empire. In 325 the Council of Nicaea made the political province (equivalent to an American state) the basic unit for the churches' larger divisions. By 341, the Synod of Antioch in Encaeniis, the Eastern churches had adopted the diocesan divisions (roughly equal to American counties) within a province as well. The Council of Constantinople in 380–381 strongly reaffirmed the diocesan and provincial patterns. A parochial system probably began to develop during the late fourth century also, perhaps first in Gaul, but the evidence is by no means clear. Expansion of urban churches to surrounding areas probably supplied the main impetus for the development of parishes, the actual implementation of which required several centuries.

The evangelizing of rural areas, so long neglected in the process, occurred in a more irregular manner than that of the cities. Planting of churches by the clergy usually followed several patterns. (1) Sometimes a bishop or group of bishops consecrated another bishop and sent him to evangelize and to organize a group of Christians into a church. For the period under study, for example, Eusebius of Nicomedia and other bishops consecrated the great Arian missionary Ulfilas in 341 and sent him to work among the Goths (Philostorgius, *Church History* 2.5, 6). (2) Sometimes a bishop sent presbyters or deacons to start and organize a Christian community. After Constantine the role of presbyters at the local level increased in significance in many areas. (3) Sometimes the bishop or bishops nearest at hand gathered with an already existing congregation and instructed them until they could elect a bishop or presbyter who would be consecrated or ordained. (4) Sometimes a bishop himself evangelized and instructed converts until he had prepared a suitable candidate to carry on after him. In Gaul, for instance, Martin (d. 397) served as a kind of itinerant bishop planting churches and monasteries.

Local Communities and Conversions

Constantine, his mother Helena, and other wealthy patrons increased markedly the appeal of Christianity through the erection of opulent edifices attractive to a cultured clientele. With nudgings of various kinds inquirers came, many reluctantly and many willingly, to find out what Christianity offered. In the *First Catechetical Instruction*, composed at the request of a somewhat disheartened deacon assigned the task of talking to inquirers, Augustine outlined procedures he thought helpful. Catechists should examine the motives of those who came—whether from fear or love of God or for temporal advantages or to escape some personal loss. In response they should accentuate love throughout their presentation. They should adapt their message—the history of salvation from Genesis to Revelation—to the hearers' capacity and powers of comprehension. Certain classes would require special handling, especially the well educated and students. Catechists must treat them indulgently and patiently, like a mother hen tending her chicks, repeating when necessary and prodding the indifferent and slow learners. Indicative of the variety of persons coming at this time (ca. 400), they must adapt what they did to the needs of hearers, whether "learned or dull, a citizen or a foreigner, rich or poor, a private citizen or one honored and appointed to some public office, a person of this or that race, or this or that age or sex, from this or that sect, or coming from this or that popular error" (23.4).

Many who came from imperial insistence doubtless hesitated and only reluctantly opted for Christianity. Constantine met stout resistance to his pressures in ancient Rome, enough to prompt him to turn his attention toward the East and a new Rome (Constantinople). In the time of Theodosius many persons of the upper classes deferred baptism, perhaps following the example of the emperors themselves, but more likely resisting joining the church. The very demands of discipleship inhibited many. Some doubtless felt genuinely that the expectations were greater than they could meet, but the hesitancy of many others seems to have been more mundane. Baptism was an insurance of forgiveness of all past sins as they continued to live according to prevailing lifestyles. Persons of higher social station particularly faltered on the way to the baptistry simply because they were not prepared to surrender many of the pleasures and privileges and duties which their wealth enabled them to enjoy or demanded that they discharge. Although the emperor Theodosius took away the option of not becoming a Christian, the wealthy and powerful could defer baptism until they stood at death's door and thus continue to enjoy life in a more secular mode. The clergy had to chide and cajole. Gregory of Nazianzus poked fun at some who delayed because they did not have the right clothing for baptism which would make them "worthy of notice," as if grace would be diminished thereby.

> A bishop shall baptize me,—and he a Metropolitan,—and he of Jerusalem (for the Grace does not come of a place, but of the Spirit)—and he be of noble birth [Gregory satirized some saying], for it would be a sad thing for my nobility to be insulted by being baptized by a man of no family.
>
> (*Homily* 12.23-25)

The Christian Argument and Appeal

Vast numbers, however, did find the appeal of Christianity strong enough to lure them into the churches. Apologists of this day, just as earlier ones, used a wide array of arguments to convince the unconverted. Some made much of the superiority of Christian baptism to Jewish baptism and circumcision. The latter were only "shadows" and "types" which wash away filth of body but do not cleanse the soul. They contrasted the weakness of Greek philosophy with the power of baptism to effect actual change in human lives. "Give me an unjust, foolish sinner," Lactantius boasted, "and immediately he will be just and prudent and innocent, for with one washing all malice will be obliterated." Philosophy cannot change character. "But the few commands of God so change the whole person and render one new when the old has been put off that you do not recognize that person to be the same person" (*Divine Institutes* 3.26). Such brash claims shocked educated pagans like the Neoplatonist philosopher Porphyry (ca. 232–ca. 303) and Emperor Julian (361–363). The latter caricatured the Christian appeal: "Let whoever is a seducer, whoever is a murderer, whoever is sacrilegious and infamous approach without fear: For with this water will I wash and will immediately cleanse that person" (*Symposion* 336B). At the same time the emperor paid Christian baptismal

procedures the high compliment of incorporating them into his plan for reviving paganism.

Apologists ridiculed the materialism of both pagan and Jewish worship and argued the superiority of Christian worship. According to Lactantius, a teacher of rhetoric appointed by Diocletian but converted around 300,pagans poured all their energies into temples, altars, sacrifices, libations, and images but gave little thought to manner of life (*Divine Institutes* 31). By contrast, Christian worship focused on one God without deference to subordinate creatures, even *divine* ones, and worshipped in a spiritual manner. Arnobius, bishop of Sicca (d. 330), among many others, defended the spiritualization on the grounds that divine beings do not need physical temples, images, altars, shrines, sacrifices, incense, and libations; indeed, they are offended by such things. Or, from another point of view, Eusebius contended that Christ's once-for-all sacrifice needed to be remembered in the "the bloodless sacrifice" of the eucharist. Ultimately, however, the apologists pointed to Christian charity and behavior as the final confirmation of authentic worship. Christians offer positive proof of the superiority of their worship by exhibition of justice, Lactantius insisted. Innocence toward God and mercy toward humankind satisfy the perfect justice of Plato.

Christian discipline supplied Christians with their strongest case, both in answering critics and in establishing the superiority of Christianity as a philosophy. By the fourth century pagans rarely invoked the slanders they used earlier such as cannibalism, incest, etc., though they often blamed Christians for calamities befalling the empire. In his campaign to reestablish pagan religion the emperor Julian did deride "the Galileans" as "impious" and "corrupt" and "depraved," but he meant by these mainly their "atheism," that is, refusal to believe in the gods of Greece and Rome. He also put them down for drawing their converts "from the baser sort—shopkeepers, tax-gatherers, dancers, and libertines" (*Against the*

Galileans 238E). Once again, however, he paid the high compliment of trying to imitate Christian discipline in his revived cult. For his clergy he wanted only "the noblest," "the most reverent," and "the most philanthropic" without class distinctions.

Christian apologists turned the tables on enemies. They ridiculed myths about the gods and the terrible moral examples they offered, which even allegorical exposition of Homer could not rehabilitate. They treated philosophers more gently, for they could often enlist them, especially Stoics and Platonists, in their critique of pagan morality, religion, and life. Yet even the philosophers failed to live up to what they themselves taught. Though they lauded courage, justice, wisdom, and temperance—the cardinal virtues— Lactantius argued, they seldom practiced them (*Divine Institutes* 5.13-15). What distinguished Christians from philosophers was the way they lived, like the philosophers said people should live. This argument attracted a considerable number of persons otherwise contemptuous of Christian thought, such as the noted Roman Neoplatonist Victorinus, whose conversion helped steer Augustine into the Christian fold. Another Neoplatonist, Alexander of Lycopolis, explained what exercised such a pull. As he saw it, Christianity "gives most of its attention to moral preparation" and presents its truths in such a simple way that the masses "give themselves diligently to the pursuit of virtue and the stamp of godliness is set on their behavior" (*Against Manichaean Views*). Alexander, who apparently did not become a Christian, objected to Christian reliance on scriptures rather than reason, but he admired Christian behavior.

Scriptures supplied apologists, evangelists, missionaries, and others their fundamental documents for defending and propagating the faith in this era as in earlier ones. Even though church and synagogue were irreparably divided by this time, apologists could not ignore the Jews. In some parts of the empire Jews continued to rep-

resent a significant minority as Christianity toppled its competitors. Sadly, missionary bishops like Ambrose of Milan displayed no tolerance for them, and Christian exhortations often resulted in outbursts of violence and persecution. John Chrysostom and Augustine composed violent sermons and treatises against the Jews. The most basic contention was that scriptures predicted the cessation of the old law (Isa. 8:16-17) and covenant and the institution of a new law (Micah 4:2-3; Isa. 2:3-4) and covenant (Jer. 31:31-32). The success of Christianity proved God's intention for the church. Jerusalem had fallen, the Temple been destroyed, the Jews scattered while Christianity prospered and became a universal faith.

Use of scriptures in apology to Gentiles required greater subtlety than that to Jews, as apologists of this day recognized. Lactantius (*Divine Institutes* 5.4) gently rebuked those who tried to prooftext their arguments from scriptures. Arnobius constructed his case *Against the Nations* almost exclusively from hellenistic writings. Lactantius himself considered it best to give proofs from philosophers and historians and then add testimonies from scriptures. Where they cited scriptures, however, apologists allegorized in order to find in scriptures the best in Greek philosophy, poetry, or other literature. Like their predecessors, they still had to argue the superiority of truth found in scriptures based on inspiration and antiquity. Whatever truth the Greeks received, they got either through the divine Logos who spoke in the prophets or by plagiarizing from Moses, author of the Pentateuch and "the founder of all barbarian wisdom." Arnobius made light of charges of novelty against Christianity. Nothing is older than God, who created everything (*Against the Nations* 2.71-72)! Eusebius went to the trouble of compiling a list of Greek notables who showed familiarity with the Jews (*Preparation for the Gospel* 9.1ff.). In addition, the apologists argued that the scriptures offered greater consistency of content than the disparate corpus of Greek and Roman literature or even some of its commendable expositors such as Plato (Eusebius, *Preparation for the Gospel* 14.4).

Such arguments posed obvious problems in the effort to reach both Jews and Gentiles, but, with imperial encouragements and enticements, they persuaded some. Ambrose recorded specific accounts of conversions among Jews in which he had played a role (*Explanation of the Psalms* 36.80; *Sermons on Luke* 6.65). In his treatise *Against Julian* (2.3-7) Gregory of Nazianzus related an apocryphal story of the conversion of many Palestinian Jews when some sort of miracle hindered their rebuilding of the Temple. Winning of Gentiles depended more heavily on clothing scriptures in a hellenistic philosopher's toga by allegorical exegesis to overcome their alien character. At least one element in Augustine's conversion, at any rate, was Ambrose's skillful use of allegory to soften offensive aspects of the Old Testament. Augustine first went to hear Ambrose because of his rhetoric, but he gradually latched onto something deeper.

Christians and Persecution of Pagans

During their first three centuries, Christians had ample reason to cry out for toleration and did so eloquently. In the mid-second century Justin Martyr pleaded powerfully for the freedom to believe without restraint. Religious liberty, Tertullian insisted, "is a fundamental human right, a privilege of nature, that every person should worship according to his or her own convictions. One person's religion neither helps nor harms another person." He went on to say, "It is not in the nature of religion to coerce religion, which must be adopted freely and not by force" (*To Scapula* 2). Lactantius, tutor of Constantine's son Crispus, declared that "nothing is so much a matter of free will as religion, and no one can be required to worship what one does not will to worship. One can perhaps pretend, but one cannot will" (*Divine Institutes* 54).

As Constantine and his successors arranged a marriage between the church and the state,

however, Christian memory of pleas for toleration faded. Even before, many were not prepared to extend the freedom they asked for themselves to those they considered heretics. Tertullian, for instance, insisted that "Heretics may properly be compelled, not enticed, to duty. Obstinacy must be corrected, not coaxed" (*Scorpion's Sting* 2.1). Following Constantine's conversion, this kind of logic could be expanded as zealous Christians sought to impose their faith upon everyone in the empire. Evidently because of their tenacity in adhering to their faith, Jews usually received less favorable consideration in sermons or treatises than Gentiles. Ambrose, bishop of Milan, for instance, lashed at them for unbelief, self-righteousness, and obstinacy. He called them "mindless," "worse than lepers," and spoke of Judaism as "the most empty Jewish superstition" and "the evil Jewish fire" which burns but does not warm. Chrysostom characterized the large Jewish populace of Antioch as "wretched" and "good-for-nothing." He counted them enough of a threat to the church to deliver a series of harsh sermons against them, as Augustine also did. Ambrose rebuked Emperor Theodosius when he forced the Christian citizens of Callinicum, a town on the Euphrates, to make reparations for a Jewish synagogue they had destroyed in a rage against "unbelievers."

Christian tolerance toward Gentiles decreased as their victories increased with imperial assistance. Preachers regularly exhorted the unconverted to respond with an openness and enthusiasm they could not have manifested before Constantine. Sometimes their zeal led to excesses. Augustine, for instance, let the ardor of the moment carry him away in a sermon delivered at Carthage in June, 401. Against the background of a series of edicts by Honorius he inflamed the passion of his hearers against idols. God had wished, ordered, and predicted the wiping out of every pagan superstition. The Romans had pulled down the idols in that stronghold of paganism. Would that Carthaginians would shout, "As in

Rome, so also in Carthage!" If the Romans tore down the Roman gods, then why do they still stand here (*Sermon* 24.5-6)? Such incitements sometimes produced disasters for Christians as well as pagans. In Sufes, Byzacena, probably in 399, pagans massacred sixty Christians as a reprisal for toppling a stature of Hercules.

In more reflective moments the clergy cautioned against the use of violence and left the liquidation of paganism or heresy to the state. Though Chrysostom urged monks to destroy idol temples, he refused to coerce anyone to believe. Christians never made war on anyone; rather, they sought "to effect the salvation of persons by persuasion and word and mildness" (*Saint Babyla* 3). Quite clearly, however, something was happening to Christian perceptions as Christians smelled victory over all competitors. The churches demanded freedom for themselves they would not think of conceding to others. When the Arian Empress Justina demanded one church building in Milan in which she might exercise her faith, Ambrose responded, "Palaces belong to the emperor, churches to the bishop" (*Letter* 20.19). At the same time he constantly urged imperial action against heretics, schismatics, or pagans. Optatus, bishop of Milevis (ca. 370), was the first to advocate the death penalty for Donatists. In 406 Augustine laid the foundation for the medieval inquisition as he justified the use of force against the latter.

Evangelizing the Empire

Evangelization of the Roman provinces proceeded at an uneven pace after Constantine's conversion. Antioch and Syria, Asia Minor, Alexandria and parts of Egypt, Rome and it environs, and parts of North Africa represented already strong Christian constituencies. Elsewhere, imperial encouragement notwithstanding, paganism offered stout resistance.

In parts of Syria and Palestine Semitic faiths held on tenaciously. By this time, few Jews voluntarily accepted Christianity. In Phoenicia

and sections of Syria various Semitic cults did not disappear until the sixth century. Anti-Christian riots occurred during Julian's reign. When Marcellus, bishop of Apamea, ordered the demolition of temples in the city and villages, a group of pagans seized him and burnt him alive while soldiers he had enlisted were preoccupied with carrying out his command to destroy the temples (Sozomen, *Church History* 7.15). Even in Antioch, perhaps the first large city to become predominantly Christian, paganism remained strong enough in the sixth century to claim a recognizable head. Throughout Asia Minor, moreover, pagans still constituted cults during the second half of the fourth century and as late as the sixth.

In Greece Christianity overwhelmed the old faiths without struggle. Athens, however, was still viewed by Christians as a corrupter of youth. In 529 Emperor Justinian eliminated the last source of offense by closing the schools there. To the north of Greece Christians carried on the christianization process in Dalmatia and in the Danubian provinces.

Although Alexandria boasted a strong Christian contingent, even among non-Greek-speaking persons, by the time of Constantine, much remained to be done both there and in the rest of Egypt. During the late fourth century, an energetic and zealous bishop decided to flaunt the victory of Christianity over its competitors. Converting a temple of Dionysus into a church, he removed the statues and paraded objects used in the mysteries through the streets of the city. Pagans retaliated by killing many Christians, wounding others, and turned the Serapeion into a temporary fortress. They held out steadfastly and rallied enough public support that the emperor granted them a pardon in hopes that this would entice them to become Christians. Such clemency evidently failed to convince many, but the emperor proceeded thereafter to demolish all pagan edifices in the city (Sozomen, *Church History* 7.15). Evangelization of the rest of Egypt took place gradually. Upper Egypt developed an inclusive episcopal organization during the fourth century. The bishop of Alexandria evidently directed the process of placing bishops in every important city in Egypt. Yet pagan cults still hung on in outlying areas well into the sixth century, as they did elsewhere.

In North Africa, a stronghold of Latin Christianity at the time of Constantine's conversion, Christianity extended its reach outward from important cities little by little. Paganism, however, held on tenaciously there too. First the Donatist controversy, which began in 311, and then Arianism, imported by the Vandals in the fifth century, weakened Christian witness noticeably. In Augustine's day (bishop of Hippo 395–430) paganism still thrived. The temple of Caelestis in Carthage was not closed by imperial order until 391. Until 398 most rulers were pagan. Small wonder, then, that bishops like Augustine sometimes grew impatient and cried out for vigorous action.

As strong as Christianity became in Rome even before Constantine, pagan cults continued there long after this era. Many of the aristocracy risked much in defense of the ancient religions of Rome. Quintus Aurelius Symmachus (d. 410), a notable orator in a family prominent in public affairs for over a century, openly and vigorously opposed removal of the Altar of Victory from the Senate by Emperor Gratian. As Perfect of Rome, Symmachus headed a deputation of the Senate to Gratian in 382, a second to Valentinian II in 384, a third to Theodosius and Valentinian II in 392. All proved unsuccessful. Eugenius, in his brief reign, restored the Altar, but Theodosius removed it again after defeating Eugenius and Arbogastes. Indicative of his tenacity, Symmachus tried again in 403 or 404. Ambrose lifted up a strong voice in opposition to restoration of the altar in a letter to Valentinian. Such an act could be conceived as nothing less than a resumption of persecution of Christians by pagans and a sacrilege (*Letter* 17.9).

Outside of Rome, paganism persisted in the villages and countryside. Christianity registered its greatest success in northern Italy where Ambrose pressed for the triumph. In Milan he battled Empress Justina and the Arians for control of the area. In 396 he hinted at many churches, though pagan enclaves still dominated areas around Turin in the fifth century. A large part of the populace of Ravenna still remained faithful to the ancient deities. South of Rome paganism survived at least until the time of Gregory the Great (590–604).

Although Christianity gained a stronghold in Spain early on, it overwhelmed paganism slowly. The Visigoths who invaded Spain during the fourth century brought an aggressively Arian faith, regarding it as the national Gothic faith, and attempted to win others to it. The Suevi, who invaded Spain in the fifth century, initially adopted the Catholic faith but then were converted to Arianism.

By the time of Constantine Christianity had barely penetrated north of the Pyrenees and the Alps into the provinces of Gaul and Germany. After Constantine, however, it spread rapidly, especially in the cities. In the cities many prominent members of the upper classes entered the church. The most heralded missionary was Martin of Tours (d. 397). Serving in the Roman army, he divided his cloak and gave half to a beggar on the road near Amien one day. A vision of Christ impelled him to receive baptism and take up the monastic life. After obtaining a discharge from the army he traveled some and then in 360 joined Hilary, bishop of Poitiers. Shortly afterwards he founded the first monastery in Gaul at Ligugé. About 372 he became bishop of Tours. There he encouraged the spread of monasticism and building of churches around Tours possibly introducing a rudimentary system of parishes. Victricius (ca. 330–ca. 407), bishop of Rouen and also a soldier who had renounced his military profession, undertook mission work as far as Flanders, Hainault, and Brabant.

When and how Christianity developed in the British Isles is uncertain. Since most Roman contacts at this time came through Gaul, it is reasonable to infer that Christianity entered through such contacts. Substantial evidence exists for at least two lines, one Anglo-Saxon and the other Roman. The clash between the two reached a high level in the seventh century and resulted in a Roman victory. Precise data on Christianity in Britain do not appear until the fifth century.

Beyond the Boundaries of the Empire

Although the adoption of Christianity as the religion of the Roman Empire represented Christianity's most notable triumph, it did not stand alone. The powerful missionary impulse of the first three centuries continued to propel it outward beyond the boundaries of the empire.

The northern barbarians began to enter the church in vast numbers, lured in part by admiration of all things Roman. The first barbarians to opt for Christianity in large numbers were the Goths. They probably heard of Christianity through captives they took as they laid waste to Moesia and raided the coasts of Greece and Asia Minor in the third century, then moved into Dacia, which the Romans had abandoned. Exposed initially to three types of Christianity—Catholic, Arian, and Audian—most became Arians as a consequence of the work of Ulfilas (ca. 311–383). Catholicism evidently reached the Goths first. Constantine himself overcame Gothic invaders who then, terrified by their defeat, embraced the Christian religion (Socrates, *Church History* 1.18). A Gothic bishop name Theophilus attended the Council of Nicaea (ibid. 2.41). Audius, a Syrian bishop charged by fellow bishops with teaching anthropomorphism, won numerous converts among the Goths and developed an extensive organization with monasteries and bishops. Ulfilas, however, born among the Goths, was far better equipped to reach them than the others. Consecrated a bishop by Eusebius of Nicomedia about 341, he spent the remainder of his life among the Goths, at first beyond the empire and then in Moesia II. He translated all of the Bible except the four books of Kings into Gothic, refusing to do these because they were too warlike.

Although Armenia formally opted for Christianity around 300, paganism there still survived in mountainous areas. During the fourth century, Armenian literature appeared, including an Armenian translation of the Bible and other religious books. Nerses (d. ca. 373), a direct descendant of Gregory the Illuminator, undertook to reform the Armenian church after his election as Catholicos around 363. His criticisms of the monarchs, however, resulted in exile and then in his death. When Armenia fell under Persian rule in the fifth century, Christians were severly persecuted.

Christianity arrived in Georgia in the late third or early fourth century through the efforts of a Christian captive name Nino or Nonna. Nino won over the queen after performing a healing in the name of Christ. The king, Mirian, reputedly became convinced when he got lost during a hunting trip and found his way out by calling on the name of Christ. The people soon followed the king, who sent to Constantinople to ask for an alliance and for clergy (Socrates, *Church History* 2.7). Mirian's son and successor zealously supported the church. Until the Persian invasion of the fifth century, Christianity continued to thrive.

Constantine's conversion did not prove a boon for Christianity in Persia. So long as it remained illegal in the Roman Empire, Persian authorities seldom molested the church. When Constantine adopted it, he wrote a letter to Sapor II (320–381), the Persian king, commending to him in strong terms the Christian religion and indicating his affectionate interest in Christians all over Persia (Eusebius, *Church History* 4.13.9-13). Sapor, a Zoroastrian, evidently took alarm at the note, for he soon initiated a pogrom throughout his kingdom that extended even to Armenia. Despite severe persecution, Christianity survived among the Syriac-using members of the population. Sapor first ordered Christians to pay double taxes collected by their bishops. When one bishop refused, he was martyred. In Julian's day persecution diminished, but resumed under his Christian successors. Sapor's successors proved more tolerant.

Christianity may not have reached India and Ceylon until the fifth century, unless one accepts early legends about the Apostle Thomas. Whenever it did reach India, it probably spilled over from Persia. One bishop at Nicaea signed himself "John the Persian of all Persia and Great India," but whether India refers to the present country or to Southern Arabia is uncertain. Emperor Constantius sent a "Theophilus the Indian" on a mission to Southern Arabia and Ethiopia. The same person proceeded to "other parts of India," but again this may have meant Southern Arabia. Persecution in Persia may have caused Christians to flee to India.

By the reign of Valens, Christianity was represented among people east of the Jordan. A dowager ruler of the "Saracens" required the consecration of a monk of her choice as bishop as a condition for peace after her forces defeated the Romans. The monk, named Moses, informed the Romans that he knew well the Roman creed. He and others proceeded thence to win converts among this people. One of these was a tribal chieftain named Zocomus, impressed by the prayer of another monk that his wife would bear a child (Sozomen, *Church History* 6.38). A synod meeting at Antioch in 363 or 364 included a "bishop of the Arabs" (Socrates, *Church History* 3.25). Christianity arrived early, too, in southern Arabia. Pantaenus's "India" may have meant southern Arabia; if so, it would confirm Christian presence there in the second century. The Theophilus dispatched by Constantius was reported to have worked among the Himyarites in southwest Arabia. Constantius supported his work even with gifts for native rulers and churches designed both for Roman travelers and traders and natives. Ordained a bishop, Theophilus erected three churches there (Philostorgius, *Church History*

3.4-5). Refugees from Persia may have started other work there as well.

The earliest knowledge of Christianity in Abyssinia or Ethiopia is connected with the arrival of Frumentius and Edesius, two Roman youth taken captive. According to Sozomen, these youth were returning with their mentor Meropius, a philosopher of Tyre and also a relative, from "India" when they were taken captive at a port where they stopped for water. The Abyssinian king made Edesius his cupbearer and Frumentius, the older boy, administrator of his house and treasures. Because they served him faithfully for long years, the king freed them. At the request of the king's son, however, they did not return to Tyre as they wished but remained behind to direct the affairs of the kingdom. Frumentius, on inquiring, discovered Christians in Abyssinia, assembled them, and built a church. When the prince attained adulthood, he granted Frumentius and Edesius freedom. Although Edesius returned to Tyre, Frumentius went to Alexandria, where he asked Athanasius to appoint a bishop over the Abyssinians. After consulting his clergy, Athanasius consecrated Frumentius himself, who spent the rest of his life evangelizing his adopted people (Sozomen, *Church History* 2.24).

By the end of the fourth century Christianity stood in a position very different from the one it held at the beginning of it. Within the Roman Empire, with imperial backing, it had become, at least nominally, the religion of the majority. The memory of persecution of Christians had faded. Now other cults experienced the lash, most soon to pull a curtain of secrecy over their religious activities or abandon them altogether. Whereas Christianity survived three centuries of intermittent harassment and persecution, most others, Judaism excepted, faded fast. Beyond the boundaries of the empire Christianity was also experiencing success. Outside, Armenia alone adopted Christianity as the state religion, but Christianity was registering smartly in virtually all areas contingent to the Roman Empire. To some extent the conversion of the Roman colossus helped, for as Rome went, so went many other peoples living in Rome's shadow. In at least one area, Persia, however, Constantine's and his successors' intimations of their hopes for Christians led to persecution. Yet even that did not deter the remarkable advance of the Christian faith. What would hurt far more would be internal dissension and strife.

Chapter 21

A People Rent by Strife

As noted concerning earlier periods, Christianity inherited diversity from its Jewish parent and added to it as it incorporated more and more diverse peoples. What astounded Christian watchers like Constantine was Christianity's ability to hold together, not only in spirit but visibly, so many divergent elements. However scholars may judge Constantine's conversion, he obviously discerned in Christianity a unitive capability the solar monotheism of Mithraism or any of Christianity's other competitors could not claim. Although all of them boasted local societies that offered many of the same things Christianity did, none had an empire-wide network and structure that joined the local groups in a worldwide fellowship and mission. Constantine hoped earnestly and with reason that his newly adopted faith would cement together the whole sprawling colossus he governed in a manner never seen before. If he guaranteed peace and offered help, how could the church fail to assist him in the attainment of that goal?

Sad to say, the church soon disappointed. Anyone who had looked at its earlier record should not have been surprised or shocked, for it had experienced fragmentation almost from the beginning, as earlier chapters have made clear. The Donatist controversy greeted Constantine even before his conversion. Both parties vied for his favor. The Donatists, perhaps naive in invoking any kind of imperial help to promote their cause, lost. Constantine, at any rate, sustained the Catholic party which had the support of Christians outside of north Africa and which would have been more likely for that reason to help him unite his empire. Constantine and his sucessors, therefore, with the exception of Julian, vigorously sought to herd the Donatists back into the Catholic fold.

On the heels of the Donatist controversy came a second, precipitated by an Alexandrian deacon named Arius. Despite the feverish efforts of Constantine to impose a settlement which would preserve unity in both church and empire, this was only the beginning. At first focused on the relationship between Christ as the divine Logos and God the Creator and Father, it gradually shifted to a debate regarding the relationship between human and divine in the person of the Son, the incarnate Logos. Sectional or regional rivalries played a major role in the controversy. The "schools" in Alexandria and in Antioch approached the doctrine of Christ quite differently, Alexandria doing it "from above," that is, emphasizing the divine, Antioch "from below," that is, accentuating the human. Imperial efforts at reconciliation by force merely exacerbated the tensions; they did not diminish them. As a result, the Arian controversy and its sequel boomed thunder and lightning throughout the century.

Arius and His Teaching

According to Epiphanius (*Against Heresies* 69.1), Arius was born in Libya and was already an "old Man" (69.3) when the controversy erupted about 318. Whether he studied under Lucian of Antioch or represented Antiochene theology is debatable. The first clear evidence for his story locates him in Alexandria as a presbyter and pastor of the church of Baucalis, where the remains of Mark were thought to have been interred, with a reputation for popularity as a preacher and for asceticism. He probably took that influential post about 313, the year Alexander assumed the episcopate, although Sozomen (*Church History* 1.15, 32.20–33.2) alleged that he took part in the Meletian schism in 306, a point not confirmed by other writers. The new bishop had his hands full with an ultra-ascetic group led by a certain Hieracas of Leontopolis, who questioned the doctrine of resurrection, urged celibacy, and denied that baptized children who died in infancy could enter heaven since they had not done righteous works (Epiphanius, *Heresies* 67). Persecution also had left some after effects.

In the circumstances Alexander evidently acted with considerable suspicion toward his presbyters, demanding specimen sermons to see if they were orthodox. At this point, about 318, the conflict between Arius and Alexander came to the surface. The two publicly repudiated the other's theology, and Arius blithely rejected his bishop's authority. Alexander complained of Arian congregations meeting for worship in the city. Among his fellow presbyters Arius evidently had strong support, for some were already resisting the bishop for other reasons. Alexander's denunciations of Arius, therefore, did not have the desired effect of uniting a sorely divided clergy, but he did secure Arius's formal condemnation by an Alexandrian synod about 321.

Arius left Egypt, but he did not give up. He appealed to Eusebius, bishop of Nicomedia, and perhaps also Eusebius of Caesarea. Synods in both Bithynia and Palestine rallied Arius's supporters. Alexander replied by issuing a series of letters setting forth not only the charges against him but also against his followers, then convened another synod in Alexandria in 323 to condemn the renegade presbyter, as the dispute reached its height. At this point the emperor began to take an interest in the affair. He sent Hosius, bishop of Cordova, to Alexandria in the winter of 324/5. Alexander welcomed his help in restoring some semblance of unity to the Alexandrian church. Hosius probably informed Constantine of actions he took, but the emperor had decided already to convene a general council to resolve the growing dispute. Bishops assembled in Antioch assumed the meeting would take place in Ancyra, but Constantine wanted it to occur close to his own watchful eye.

There is considerable uncertainty regarding Arius's own views, for his lengthy poem entitled *The Banquet* (*Thalia*) has survived only in part and his opponents may have distorted what he said. Although scholars once assumed he drew his idea of Christ as a "created Logos" from Lucian of Antioch, the consensus now is that Arius was more Alexandrian than Antiochene. Following in the footsteps of Origen, he directed his salvos against an *Exposition of Faith* by Gregory Thaumaturgus. Arius had an intense concern about the *unity* of God. To safeguard the single rule (*monarche*) of God, he insisted on subordination of the Son not merely in role but in nature. Only the Father exists from all eternity. The Logos, therefore, is created. "There was a time when he was not," Arius insisted. To be sure, he existed before everything else, "the firstborn of all creation," yet he belongs to the order of creation. Like Apollinaris later, Arius believed that the Logos united with the flesh (*sarx*) of Christ, so that he did not have a human soul. The Logos took over the function of the rational soul, which would explain why Christ did not sin, i.e., disobey God, whereas all other humans do.

The Council of Nicaea in 325

Constantine, alarmed by the disruption of the "peace" of the church, did not wait long to take action. He arranged for the bishops to travel to the council by imperial post and entertained them at his own expense. How many attended is uncertain, despite the traditional 318 cited by Athanasius. Recent research confirms only about two hundred names, so that Eusebius of Caesarea's estimate of 250 may be fairly accurate (*Life of Constantine* 3.8).

Arius had some supporters, though probably not as many as the twenty-two the Arian Philostorgius (*Church History* 1.8) claimed. He did have the backing of Bithynian bishops Eusebius of Nicomedia, Theognis, and Maris as well as Syro-Palestinian and Cilician bishops. Eusebius of Caesarea leaned toward Arian Christology. Arius evidently felt enough support that he could state his position boldly at the outset. He had already taken a stand against the use of the term *homoousios*, "of the same substance or essence," in a letter he wrote to Alexander and in his *Thalia*. "For he is not equal to God," he wrote, "nor yet is he of the same substance (*homoousios*)." Eusebius of Nicomedia backed him up on this contention.

The majority was not sympathetic. Eusebius of Nicomedia rashly began with what the Arians considered nonnegotiable and thus put themselves in an impossible position when the council settled on the disputed term. Eusebius of Caesarea attempted to make peace by proposing the use of a Palestinian baptismal confession. The majority rebuffed this, however, for the creed did not address the key issue, namely, whether the Son was "of the same essence" as the Father or was a lesser being, which in one fell swoop thrust aside the Arian cliches that the Son was "a thing made," "a creature," and that "there was a time when he was not" and that "he is mutable by nature" (Athanasius, *Epistle to the Africans* 5). The Arians kept weaseling their way around all the other terms, but they could not escape the implications of this one. The original creed of Nicea has not survived. What is usually cited as the Nicene Creed is the one adopted at Constantinople in 381.

The Arians entered one more protest, objecting that the term could not be found in scriptures. Constantine, however, settled the matter by defending the use of the term against their objections and interpreting it in such a way even Eusebius of Nicomedia could accept. The council then proceeded to condemn Arius's views and person, excommunicate him, and degrade him from the presbyterate. He and three others—Secundus of Ptolemais, Theonas of Marmarica, and the deacon Euzoius—were sent into exile by Constantine. The combination of civil and religious penalties held ominous implications and sowed the seeds for years of bitter wrangling as emperors changed their minds on such matters.

The bishops assembled at Nicaea attended to some other matters of importance before they departed. As noted earlier, they resolved the controversy over Easter by adopting the Roman custom of observing it always on Sunday. The emperor himself reinforced the decision by circulating a letter applauding the decision to observe *one* day lest "in so holy a thing there should be any division" (Eusebius, *Life of Constantine* 3.18-20). Not all Easterners, however, acceded to the decision. The council also condemned the Audians and Meletians and issued several rules relative to matters of discipline, including questions about readmission of Novatianists and members of other sects.

The Sequel to Nicaea

Tough as its actions were, the Council of Nicaea did not attain the unity the emperor desired so fervently. Immediately after the council, the Nicaeans retained Constantine's confidence. The emperor promptly removed Eusebius of Nicomedia and Theognis of Nicaea, who had signed the statement about *homoousios* but refused to approve Arius's exile, when they approached him and admitted they had signed only for prudential reasons. He exiled them to Gaul. Continuing dissension in Egypt, perhaps from Libyan bishops, forced Constantine to meet again with them. Evidently a local Egyptian synod approved the sentence against Eusebius and Theognis. In 326, however, Eustathius of Antioch got into a heated debate with Eusebius of Caesarea. Some tactless remarks he made during a visit by Constantine's mother Helena led to charges of heresy and immorality and his removal from office, probably in 327. Arians seized on this opportunity to plead for the return of Arius, Eusebius, and Theognis. In November 327, Constantine invited Arius to his court at Nicomedia. Arius and Euzoius presented a kind of noncommittal creed to the emperor and his advisers which was silent on *homoousios*, but it satisfied him. Constantine, backed up by a synod in Bithynia, then instructed Alexander, bishop of Alexandria, to restore Arius to communion. Alexander refused. Eusebius of Nicomedia promptly assembled a synod in Nicomedia which confirmed the restoration of Arius and formally anathematized Eustathius and Alexander. On April 17, 328, before all of this happened, Alexander died. Athanasius, elected to succeed Alexander despite substantial opposition, embarked on a stormy career as the leader of the Nicaeans. Eusebius of Nicomedia, restored to his see, led the Arians right up to the moment of his death in 341. The synod of Nicomedia appealed to Athanasius to reinstate Arius, but he refused and disregarded Constantine's threats. Meantime, by 330 the Meletians allied themselves with the Arians against Athanasius. United with Eusebius, they initiated a fierce campaign which dominated church affairs for the next ten years.

Born of non-Christian parents in Alexandria around 295, Athanasius converted to Christianity at an early age. Educated in the school of Alexandria, he became a deacon and a secretary to Alexander and attended the Council of Nicaea

with him. Before 318, while still in his twenties, he composed his short treatise on *The Incarnation*, in which he explained how, by the incarnation of the divine Logos, God restored the image of God in fallen humanity and overcame death, the consequence of sin, by his death and resurrection. Hurled into the center of the Arian controversy at the beginning, he suffered exile five times as a result of his tenacious defense of the Nicene formula: (1) Constantine exiled him to Treves at the end of 335. He returned to Alexandria November 23, 337. (2) Constantius ordered him into exile from March 19, 340 until October 21, 346. (3) After synods at Arles and Milan condemned his views, Constantius again exiled him from February 9, 356 until February 21, 362. (4) Julian, seeking to foment trouble in Catholic churches, exiled him from October 24, 362 until September 5, 363. (5) Finally, Valens removed him from office and sent him into exile from October 5, 365 until February 1, 366. He died May 2, 373.

Athanasius resisted all pressures to abandon the Nicene formula. In 332 or 333, Arius evidently feared his friends at court had abandoned him and boldly protested directly to the emperor. Emphasizing the strength of his support in Libya, he aroused the suspicion of Constantine that he was threatening schism, what the emperor most wanted to avoid. As a result, Constantine wrote an extraordinarily severe letter dissecting Arius's theology and finding it incompatible with Nicaea. He proceeded to order Arius's works burned, like those of the anti-Christian polemicist Porphyry. Anyone who refused to surrender copies was to be executed. The emperor concluded by inviting Arius to make a defense at court. Arius evidently did well enough in this to be invited to defend himself two years later at a major gathering of bishops in Jerusalem. Composed mostly of Syro-Palestinian and Cilician bishops sympathetic with Arius, the bishops met first at Tyre to condemn Athanasius. The synod of Jerusalem in September 335 proceeded to clear Arius and notified Athanasius of its action, together with Constantine's approval. Athanasius, before receiving this letter, set out secretly for Constantinople to appeal personally to the emperor. This turned out to be a disaster, resulting in his first exile in November, 335. When Arius returned to Alexandria, he met a volatile reaction and was refused communion. Constantine summoned him back to the capital, where friends at court defended him before the emperor against charges of fomenting discord in Alexandria.

The position of the Nicene party continued to deteriorate. Arians capitalized on the refusal of Marcellus, bishop of Ancyra and a strong Nicene supporter, to participate in the synod of Jerusalem. A new synod met in the summer of 336, deposed Marcellus on the charge of holding the heresy of Paul of Samosata, and demanded that Alexander, bishop of Constantinople, admit Arius into communion in the capital. In a meeting with the emperor Arius subscribed to the Nicene Creed. As a consequence, Constantine ordered Alexander to admit him to communion. As Arius proceeded to the Hagia Eirene Church where he was to receive communion, however, he stopped at a public toilet and died there of some kind of internal hemorrhage. His death may have changed the course of Western history.

Arian Ascendancy, 335–361

Arius's misfortunes notwithstanding, thanks to the shift in Constantine's sentiments, Arians remained more or less ascendant from 335 until the death of Constantius in 361. At his death in 337, Constantine received baptism at the hands of Eusebius of Nicomedia. Athanasius returned from exile immediately, but he did not remain long. In 339, he had to flee to Rome, taking with him some monks and thus importing that institution to the West. By intervention of Constans, the Western emperor, he returned to Alexandria in 346 over objections of Constantius. After the death of Constans, he was again vulnerable to Arian attacks. Consequently in 356 Constantius suc-

ceeded again in driving him from his see. He remained in hiding near Alexandria until Julian took the throne in 361, but Julian sent him packing once more in 362. His last exile, under Valens, lasted only a few months (365–366).

Four different positions emerged during this period: (1) Nicaeans, led by Athanasius, insisted that the Son is "of the same essence" (*homoousios*) with the Father. If the Son were not true God and true man, Athanasius argued, then humankind would not have been restored again to the divine image. "Nor again would humankind have been deified if joined to a created being, or if the Son were not true God, nor would humankind have come into the Father's presence unless he who took on a body were by nature and in truth his Logos" (*Second Oration against the Arians* 70). (2) On the opposite extreme, thoroughgoing Arians contended that the Son is "unlike" (*anomoios*) the Father. He is a created being, above humans but not truly God. Between these two positions stood (3) those who were prepared to say that the Son is "like" (*homoios*) the Father according to the Scriptures but not "of the same essence," and (4) those who tiptoed toward the Nicene position by saying that the Son is "of *like* essence" (*homoiousios*) but would not go so far as to concede the Nicene position. Arians made much of the fact that the term *homoousios* cannot be found in scriptures. Athanasius replied by pointing out that, while not in scriptures per se, it expresses what scriptures intend.

During Constantius's reign, Nicaeans did not win many victories. In 341, bishops assembled at Antioch affirmed the Nicene formula but deposed Athanasius. In 343, a synod meeting in Sardica cleared Marcellus of Ancyra and Athanasius of charges of heresy, but a counter synod held at Philoppopolis repudiated its actions. Three synods convened at Sirmium (351, 357, 358) and others held at Arles (353), Milan (355), Antioch (358), Ancyra (358), Constantinople (360), and Alexandria (362) favored the Arian party. Arian ascendancy reached its peak in 357 at the second synod at Sirmium. This synod proscribed the use of terms such as *ousia* (essence), *homoousion*, and *homoiousion* as unscriptural and distinctly denied the true divinity of the Son.

Apollinaris: Nicene Overkill

One of the most vigorous advocates of the Nicene formula and bitterest opponents of Arianism was Apollinaris (ca. 310–ca. 390), who became bishop of Laodicea in 360. A staunch ally of Athanasius, receiving him on his return from exile in 346, Apollinaris sought to give a definitive answer to the question: Why did Christ not sin, that is, disobey God, despite the fact that all human beings do so? The answer lay in the way the divine Logos united with the human. Whereas human beings consist of body, soul, and spirit or rational soul, in Christ the divine Logos replaced the spirit, thus making him incapable of moral error. Arius had thought of him as less than God; Apollinaris, reacting against this, thought of him as less than human.

In 362, a synod meeting in Alexandria condemned teaching similar to this. Apollinaris, however, explained himself to the satisfaction of other Nicaeans. As his views became better known, he himself came to the attention of other synods. Roman synods condemned Apollinaris by name between 374 and 380. Both Apollinarianism and Arianism were condemned at the second ecumenical council held in Constantinople in 381.

The Great Cappadocians

The controversy grew increasingly complex, especially after the death of Constantius. Many sought a middle ground between the Nicene *homoousios* and the Arian *anomoios*. Basil of Ancyra, after about 356, gathered around him a group of bishops who favored the term *homoiousios* and received a favorable nod from the synod of Alexandria in 362 and from Athanasius. Strict Arians looked with much less favor on this. When Macedonius, successor of Eusebius of Nicomedia as bishop of Constantinople (342–362),

came out strongly on the side of Basil, the Arian-dominated Synod of Constantinople in 360 deposed him.

Meantime, a group known as *Pneumatomachoi*, who affirmed the full divinity of the Son but doubted that of the Holy Spirit, appeared. Possibly the Tropici mentioned by Athanasius in one of his letters written between 355 and 361, the Pneumatomachoi came to the forefront in 373 when Eustathius of Sebaste broke with his friend Basil of Neocaesarea (the Great). Pope Damasus condemned them in 374. They reached their peak about 380 on the eve of the Council of Constantinople, which condemned them along with Arians and Apollinarians.

Leadership out of this morass came from three bishops known today as "The Great Cappadocians"—Basil of Neocaesarea (ca. 330–379), Gregory of Nyssa (ca. 330–ca. 395), his brother, and Gregory of Nazianzus (329–389). Educated at Caesarea in Cappadocia, Constantinople, and Athens in the finest culture of the day, both pagan and Christian, Basil forsook the world and became a hermit in 358. In 364, he left his seclusion, after Emperor Julian had unsuccessfully tried to lure him to court, and took up a defense of the Nicene position against the Arian emperor Valens. In 370, he became bishop of Neocaesarea, where he served the rest of his life. This brought him into the thick of the battle against the Arians, the Pneumatomachoi, as well as Damasus of Rome and Athanasius of Alexandria, who refused to recognize Meletius as bishop of Antioch. Basil had unusual gifts as an organizer. He framed two rules for monks which helped to draw monasticism closer to the institutional church. He developed hospitals and hostels for care of the poor, for whom he organized a system of relief.

Gregory of Nyssa, Basil's younger brother, temporarily became a rhetorician but then entered a monastery founded by Basil. Consecrated bishop of Nyssa around 371, he supported the Nicene Creed warmly. Deposed by Arians during the reign of Valens (376–378), he returned to his see and played a major role in the Council of Constantinople in 381. A theologian of great originality and a mystic, he was much in demand as a preacher.

Gregory of Nazianzus, son of the bishop of Nazianzus, studied at Athens at the same time Basil did. He too took up the monastic life and only reluctantly accepted ordination as a priest in the village of Sasima about 372. He assisted his father at Nazianzus until the latter's death in 374, then retired to Seleucia in Isauria. In 379, Theodosius called him to Constantinople, where his eloquent preaching did much to establish the Nicene faith and to prepare for the Council of Constantinople. During the Council, he was appointed bishop of Constantinople, but he withdrew after only one year and spent the remainder of his life at Nazianzus or on his own estate.

The Cappadocians came up with a redefinition of the Nicene formula which was acceptable to moderate Arians as well as Nicaeans. Fear of Sabellianism or Modalism still possessed many, who were convinced that the term *homoousios* would obscure the distinctness of persons within the Trinity. In response to this problem, the Cappadocians interpreted the word *homoousios* with the formula: *Mia ousia kata treis hypostaseis* ("one substance in three persons"). Such an interpretation required a redefinition of the word *hypostasis*. Previously it had meant "substance." Basil explained the distinction between *ousia* and *hypostasis* by using an analogy. For Athanasius Father, Son, and Spirit are one being living in a threefold form or in three relationships, as, for example, one person may be at the same time a father, a son, and a brother. For Basil Father, Son, and Spirit are three like or equal beings sharing a common nature, as, for example, different persons share in the common nature of human beings. Both views conserved Christ's divinity. The East generally has followed the Cappadocians, the West Athanasius. The West has always tended toward Modalism.

The Council of Constantinople, 381

Theodosius I, the Great, an ardent supporter of Nicaea, convened the second ecumenical council at Constantinople in 381. Only 150 Nicene and 36 Arian bishops, all Easterners, attended. Meletius, bishop of Antioch, opened the council but died during the course of it. Gregory of Nazianzus and then Nectarius of Constantinople succeeded him as presidents. Since the Nicene Creed was lost in the interim, the bishops had to draft an essentially new statement into which they inserted the *homoousios*. At the same time, they condemned a long list of "heretics": Eunomians or Anomoeans, Arians or Eudoxians, Semi-Arians, Pneumatomachians, Sabellians, Marcellians, Photinians, and Apollinarians. Against the Pneumatomachoi, the Council asserted the full divinity and elaborated on the doctrine of the Holy Spirit, barely mentioned in the Nicene Creed. The Council also established Constantinople as the second see after Rome "because it is new Rome" (canon 2) and laid down some rules for receiving persons from various sects or factions (Arians, Macedonians, Sabbatians and Novatians, Tetradites—those observing Easter on the Jewish Passover, Apollinarians to be received by laying on of hands; Eunomians, Montanists, and Sabellians to be rebaptized).

Further Controversy

Emperor Theodosius put his stamp of approval on the Council shortly after it concluded its business. He directed that all churches be surrendered to supporters of the Niceno-Constantinopolitan formula tested by communion with selected bishops (*Theodosian Code* 50.3). Even this powerful action, however, in no way ended the divisions and controversies. Arianism, it is true, no longer dominated within the empire thereafter, but it held sway among the Goths, Vandals, Lombards, and Burgundians during the next couple of centuries, only gradually rooted out by the efforts of Catholic missionaries.

The martyr of the protracted controversy may have been Origen. Quoted by both Arians and Nicaeans, his teaching became the subject of controversy and eventually condemnation nearly three hundred years after his death. Even before the Arian controversy broke out, Methodius of Olympus, bishop of Lycia (d. 311), attacked Origen's doctrines of creation and resurrection, maintaining the identity of the resurrection body with the earthly one. Pamphilus (ca. 340–309), a disciple of Origen and a later director of the school at Caesarea, prepared a defense of his mentor with the help of Eusebius of Caesarea during his imprisonment in the persecution of Maximinus Daza. Eusebius later supplemented this *Apology*.

Origen's followers included many of the notables of the fourth century. Besides Pamphilus and Eusebius of Caesarea, there were genuine Origenists like Didymus of Alexandria, Athanasius, the Great Cappadocians, Hilary of Poitiers, and, for a time, Jerome. There were also slavish Origenists like the "tall brothers," monks of Nitria—Dioscurus, Ammonius, Eusebius, and Enthymius. The main opposition to Origen came from the anthropomorphites, monks of the desert near Scete in Egypt headed by Pachomius, father of communal monasticism.

Epiphanius, bishop of Salamis (ca. 315–403), touched off the fuse in 394 by condemning Origen publicly at Jerusalem. John of Jerusalem and Rufinus (ca. 345–410), translator and editor of many of Origen's works, defended him. Jerome, though previously a disciple heavily dependent on some of Origen's biblical works, now condemned him. The controversy grew so bitter that Rufinus had to flee Palestine and take refuge in Aquileia in northern Italy. Through free translation he sought to vindicate Origen and conserved many of his writings.

In Egypt, meanwhile, Theophilus, patriarch of Alexandria (d. 412), inaugurated a fierce campaign against Origenism, which lasted from 399 until 403. When the "tall brothers" refused to deliver church funds to him, they had to flee to Chrysostom in Constantinople for protection. Theophilus then turned his guns toward Chrysostom, using the dissatisfaction of a group which included Empress Eudoxia to have him condemned at "the Synod of the Oak" in 403 and again at Constantinople in 404. Although Chrysostom was cleared, the dispute over Origen continued. Justinian (527–565), forced to take sides, convened a synod at Constantinople in 544 that condemned fifteen propositions of Origen. The Fifth Ecumenical Council (Second Council of Constantinople) in 553 reiterated the condemnation. Only in modern times have any dared to take the great scholar's side again.

Chapter 22

Changing Churches

Converts crowding to get in required changes in the churches of the Roman Empire. The most obvious indication of the new era was the restoration and erection of buildings large enough to accommodate the influx of new members and grand enough to suit the taste of the wealthy and cultured who came with the flood. Less visible but no less important, the churches adjusted their practices in admission of new members, shortening the process to incorporate them more rapidly. They elaborated their liturgies so as to effect a higher level of culture. They reinterpreted and restructured the ministry to mirror the prevailing social pattern in a hierarchical society. In the meantime, the incorporation of so many persons with such limited formation placed a heavy demand on the churches' disciplinary procedures.

Buildings! Buildings!

The persecution under Diocletian (303–311) left few Christian edifices erected during the long reign of peace from Gallienus (260–268) to Diocletian intact. House churches, of course, often escaped, but others did not. After the conversion of Constantine, therefore, the churches had to build in frenzied fashion simply to provide for persons already members. Within a few years they had to make room for vast numbers of new converts imperial pressures sent bounding in their direction. Cities such as Rome, Antioch, Alexan-

dria, Carthage, and Constantinople, where there were heavy Christian constituencies, or Jerusalem, revered for its history, soon became centers of church architecture, adorned with buildings constructed in the grandest possible style. On a smaller scale, however, churches appeared everywhere.

Constantine commissioned churches for many important centers. In Rome St. John the Lateran, the episcopal see; St. Peter's; St. Paul's Outside the Walls; San Lorenzo; and Saints Peter and Marcellinus. In Jerusalem the Church of the Holy Sepulchre, the Church of the Holy Cross, the Church on the Mount of Olives, and another at the traditional site of the Ascension. In Bethlehem the Church of the Nativity. At Mamre, where Abraham was believed to have entertained the three strangers. In Constantinople churches dedicated to Holy Wisdom (Hagia Sophia), Holy Peace (Hagia Eirene), and the Holy Apostles. In Nicomedia a church replacing one destroyed by Diocletian in 303. At Antioch the famous Golden Church, which his son Constantius completed. Others in smaller towns outside the capital.

Two styles prevailed, the rectangular basilica and the circular, convergent martyrium. The churches avoided the ornate style of temples adorning the typical Greek and Roman forum and imitated instead the common public buildings called basilicas. Basilicas consisted usually of a rectangular room, divided into three sections by rows of columns parallel to the longer walls. At one end there was a niche (apse), at the other the entrance. The roof extended in tiers like a layer cake with the higher part in the center and the lower part over each side aisle. Windows on both the upper and lower levels allowed light to fill the sanctuary. This style dominated for several centuries.

Initially employed as memorial chapels enclosing the tomb of a martyr or hallowing a place associated with Jesus, in the East, the convergent style became popular for worship connected with the saints. During the late fourth and the fifth century, Christians often erected grand martyria and relocated the relics of a martyr or saint. Notable in this style of building was the dome, like that in the Roman pantheon. These buildings resembled tombs. Many were built octagonally to symbolize the "eighth day," that is, the day of resurrection. Convergent churches normally consisted of two parts distinguished by a row of columns, a center and an aisle running around the walls. Like basilicas, they had a layered roof so that the dome would rise much higher than the roof over the aisle and windows on both tiers would allow light to illuminate the whole building. Saint Stefano Rotondo in Rome dates from the fourth century. The greatest of the domed churches was Hagia Sophia in Constantinople, dedicated December 26, 537 by Emperor Justinian, which is today a mosque.

From the mid-fourth century on, churches were constructed with the apses facing East, since prayers were said facing in that direction. This evidently represented a reversion to an earlier custom, attested in the "house church" at Dura-Europos. In the age of Constantine, churches had apses in the west end, probably as a consequence of Constantine's predilection for Sun worship. It was he who made the "Day of the Sun" a legal holiday in 321 and probably established December 25, the festival in honor of the Unconquered Sun, as the date of Christ's birth. Few churches, however, had a true East-West longitudinal axis.

Inside churches, the altar or communion table claimed the center of attention. In some it stood at the back of the apse, in others where the apse joined the sanctuary, and in others near the center of the sanctuary. Altars were wooden tables of varied sizes and shapes upon which the people placed their "offerings." Gradually stone replaced wood and the Synod of Epaon in Gaul in 517 prohibited wooden altars altogether. As the focal point of worship, altars were often constructed of costly materials. Constantine, for instance, presented the Church of St Peter with a silver altar "inlaid with gold, decorated with green and white jewels and jacinths on all sides," four hundred jewels weighing three hundred fifty pounds altogether (*Liber Pontificalis*, Life of Sylvester). Justinian also studded the golden altar of Hagia Sophia with precious stones. During the fourth century, churches also began to place canopies, called *ciboria* ("cups"), over the altar, once again enhancing the importance of the altar. Early on, too, five or six columns were placed around the altar to adorn the apse in which the presbyters sat. This feature later gave way to the iconostasis, the screen dividing the choir from the nave or sanctuary. The chair of the bishop, *cathedra*, stood at the back of the apse on a higher level than the benches for presbyters. Because its location made it difficult for people to hear, some bishops had portable chairs or else preached from the *ambo* or pulpit, which stood nearer the congregation, sometimes in the middle of the nave. Ambos were often elaborately carved.

Churches usually had other buildings attached such as a house for the clergy, a hostel to care for travelers, a bath, a *diaconia* where deacons distributed charities, and a baptistry. Early on, baptisms probably took place in streams or rivers or other bodies of water. The earliest mention of a separate building for baptisms concerns a new church erected at Tyre in 314. Like martyria, in the West, baptistries were usually octagonal or circular with an inner octagon of eight columns surrounding a sunken font and supporting a domed roof. In the East baptistries were rectangular or square. The font, normally recessed into the floor, was sometimes octagonal, sometimes cruciform. Since most baptistries averaged only two to four feet in depth, affusion rather than immersion may have been practiced in most places. Indeed, catacomb art uniformly depicts the candidate standing in water just above the ankles having water poured on the head. Candidates, however, may have kneeled and had their heads pushed face forward into the water. Because baptisms were nude, baptistries usually had an adjoining dressing room and some a whole complex of rooms.

By the end of the fourth century Christians began to do something they resisted earlier, that is, to convert pagan temples into Christian churches. Some obviously no longer felt a need to guard themselves against all things pagan as they had previously. Instead of razing the temples, therefore, they put them directly, with some modification, to Christian use. San Clemente in Rome, for instance, incorporated walls of what may have been a factory building and covered a sanctuary of the Mithra cult with its apse.

Art

Like architecture, Christian art took an upward turn during the fourth century as more affluent, cultured, and well educated persons entered the churches. In earlier centuries, of course, some Christians appreciated and used art, the earliest surviving specimens being those in the catacombs of Rome. Christians used the style of the declining cosmopolitan art of Rome, early on relying on pagan artists, but they shifted from the realistic to a symbolic style and drew themes from the Bible just as their Jewish forebears had. From the very first catacomb art featured the theme of deliverance. The early gallery of the Catacomb Domitilla represented this with paintings of the Good Shepherd, Daniel between two lions, and Noah in the ark receiving the returning dove. Fourth century painters added to these Moses smiting the rock to slake the thirst of the Israelites in the wilderness, the three Hebrews in the fiery furnace, Abraham restrained in the sacrifice of Isaac, the healing of the woman with the hemorrhage, the healing of the paralytic, the three Magi presenting the gifts to the Christ child, and others. Among all the catacombs the most popular was Jonah being tossed overboard, swallowed by a mythical sea monster, and luxuriating under a vine in Nineveh. Frequent, too, were symbolic depictions of baptism and Lord's Supper, the sacraments of salvation. Alongside biblical scenes like these, artists depicted hope with symbols such as the anchor, the dove, the vine of immortality, and the orant, a person with hands uplifted in prayer. The paintings reveal clearly the reliance on popular Greco-Roman forms and Jewish-Christian stories.

Christians also adorned sarcophagi with art. In the West they inherited from second and third century ancestors the frieze-type coffin on which they depicted a series of scenes without division by space such as the Raising of Lazarus, the Healing of the Blind, the Paralytic, Jairus's Daughter, or Old Testament subjects. In the East, after persecution ceased, Christians could bury their dead above ground in more elaborate tombs with vastly improved art. In these columnar sarcophagi artists could separate scenes by panels and thus depict them with far greater effectiveness. One of the finest specimens is the sarcophagus of the Roman prefect Junius Bassus, who died in 359. In ten separate panels the artist has depicted such central biblical scenes as Abraham's sacrifice of Isaac, Adam and Eve, Daniel in the Lion's Den, Jesus and the Samaritan woman at the well, the Zacchaeus story, and the arrest in the Garden of Gethsemani.

Christian art of the fourth century reflected clearly the process of accommodation to culture taking place at the time. The earliest Christian vault and wall mosaics discovered thus far are located in a small mausoleum under St. Peter's in

Rome. Built during the second century for the Julii family, the mosaics probably date from the middle of the third century and after. A mosaic in the center of the vault depicts Christ as the Unconquered Sun driving his chariot across the sky, the nimbus around his head shooting out like the arms of the cross, and bearing in his left an orb. The pagan Sun God has been transformed into the risen Christ, triumphant over death and Lord of the universe! Constantine himself, it must be remembered, furthered this process with adjustments in the Roman calendar.

Church art in this period did not achieve the splendor it attained in the next two centuries, but at Constantine's urging it improved rapidly. Constantine complained about the lack of artisans to do skilled work and directed that some youth be given leisure to learn their art. Although little of the art of Constantine's churches has survived, the *Liber Pontificalis* describes how the interior of St. Peter's looked. A gold mosaic decorated the apse. Gold and precious marbles adorned Peter's shrine. The altar was silver gilt set with four hundred precious stones. On top of it was a solid gold cross. A large golden dish served as the offertory. Before the Apostle's tomb was a crown of light and four large candlesticks. Thirty-two silver candelabra lit the sanctuary. The emperor wanted the churches, at least some of them, to assume some of the glamour of the imperial court. Though St. Peter's held a special place among Christian shrines, its furnishings were not exceptional among churches in important urban centers.

Baptistries, like churches, often had elegant furnishings and art. The well preserved Orthodox Baptistry at Ravenna, constructed and furnished between 400 and 450, featured figures of prophets in each of the eight niches on its walls. On a second tier friezes of sixteen minor prophets adorned the arcades on each side of the windows. The dome represented in three rings empty thrones and altars, apostles, and Christ's baptism. The mosaics were extraordinarily rich in color.

Wealthy Christians also brought Christian symbolism into their home, depicting the story of faith on wall panels, places and vases, lamps, or other objects of art. Constantine and his mother Helena led the way in this christianization process.

The Liturgy

The dramatic change in the church's situation in the Roman world opened the way for significant additions to its worship. Like the edifices now erected with imperial support and sanction, the liturgy too grew more elaborate and took on some of the pomp and ceremony of the imperial court. No longer the despised and persecuted minority fighting for their lives, Christians could speak about their "mysteries" in language they formerly rejected as the language of the "world." Similarly, they took over calendar observances from that world and transformed them into Christian "moments" by some theological sleight of hand as they sought to christianize a vast new constituency.

The Sunday liturgy remained the mainstay of Christian worship in this era, and the first part, the service for catechumens, changed little. This service consisted still chiefly of prayers, readings from both Old and New Testaments, and the sermon as the key means of instructing converts. An added feature, influenced by Christian monasticism, was more and more extensive singing of Psalms. As in earlier periods, sermons were mainly verse by verse expositions of scriptures but, as time passed, with greater rhetorical polish by persons like Ambrose, Gregory of Nazianzus, Augustine, or John Chrysostom, who were skilled in the art. The last studied under the famous Antiochene rhetorician Libanius and gained such fame himself as to be nicknamed *Chrysostomus*, "golden mouth."

Hearers stood during sermons, which were often long. They also came and went and interacted with the preacher. In the absence of amplification systems used in modern church buildings, many doubtless had difficulty hearing unless preachers had well-developed voices. Some did and some did not. Augustine, for instance, although captivating as a speaker, had a weak voice.

The second part of the liturgy, the mass of the faithful, still reflected the regional diversity of early Christian worship, but there were pressures toward uniformity. Changes took the form chiefly of elaboration in the eucharistic rite by way of fixed forms. According to Cyril of Jerusalem, around 350 the eucharistic liturgy of the church of Jerusalem consisted of the following elements.

As a symbol of purification, presbyters and the bishop washed in a laver passed by a deacon.
The deacon cried aloud: "Receive one another, and let us kiss one another."
The bishop and people repeated the *Sursum corda*:
    B. "Life up your hearts."
    C. "We lift them up to the Lord."
    B. "Let us give thanks to the Lord."
    C. "It is fitting and right."
A confession was recited as a "spiritual hymn."
Next, the bishop recited a prayer entreating God to send the Holy Spirit on the gifts laying before Him so as to make them become the Body and Blood of Christ.
This "spiritual sacrifice" was offered.
Prayer was lifted up "for the common peace of the churches, for the welfare of the world, for kings, for soldiers and allies, for the sick, for the afflicted" and "for all who stand in need of help."
A litany commemorated the "saints of all the ages": patriarchs, prophets, apostles, martyrs, the holy fathers and bishops, and all the other dead.
The Lord's prayer or "Our Father" was recited.
The congregation said, "Amen!"
The cantor invited the worshippers to partake of the communion with the words, "O taste and see that the Lord is good."
Worshippers said, "Amen!" as they received bread and wine.
The liturgy concluded with a benediction.

Egeria, a pilgrim who visited the East between 381 and 384, depicted for that city a much more elaborate celebration both daily and on Sunday. Morning worship on Sunday began at full daylight and lasted until about eleven o'clock in the Martyrium and then continued in the Church of the Resurrection, a practice reflective of the tendency to focus on sacred places and events. The Jerusalem liturgy influenced worship customs throughout the Roman Empire.

The Calendar

The Christian calendar underwent major development during the fourth century as the Holy Land once again opened for pilgrims. As converts poured into the churches by thousands, a calendar marking "great moments" in the history of salvation served a crucial educational function, enabling the newly baptized to "act out" in daily, weekly, or yearly observances the story they had chosen as their own. Some of these observances already had fixed places in the calendar, but many others were added at this time.

For daily worship Constantine's conversion widened Christian options immensely. Where the faithful had had to gather clandestinely in family or small groups, they could now flock to the churches for early morning hymns; minor prayer services at 9:00 a.m., noon, and 3:00 p.m.; and evening hymns. By the late fourth century in many areas companies of monks set the standard of faithfulness by assembling before daylight to sing Psalms and throughout the rest of the day to maintain the daily regimen of prayer.

The weekly calendar, already largely in place, became more fixed. Concerned to set themselves apart from Jews, especially in areas where the latter represented sizeable minorities, Christians no longer hesitated to claim Sunday as the Christian day of worship. They fasted Wednesdays and Fridays, marking them with afternoon eucharists. They also held special eucharists on Saturday mornings. Christians never fasted on Saturdays even during Lent.

According to Egeria, whose depiction of the liturgy in Jerusalem reveals its future direction, the Easter cycle constituted the major feature of the Christian year. Candidates for baptism began daily instruction and all began fasting eight weeks before Easter. This culminated in Holy Week, the week just prior to Easter. Observance of Easter lasted seven full weeks, reaching its conclusion at Pentecost. Following Pentecost, the faithful resumed Wednesday and Friday fasts which they had given up at Easter. At this time Jerusalem observed only two other special days, Epiphany and the Dedication of the Church of the Holy Sepulchre. Other sources, however, recounted a whole row of saints' days on which the churches celebrated the Lord's supper.

In Egeria's time, Lent lasted eight weeks rather than forty days that became traditional later on. During Lent, the faithful as well as catechumens fasted all days except Saturdays and Sundays. They also attended a number of extra services added to the normal cycle, including a Friday night vigil which lasted until the celebration of the Saturday eucharist before sunrise. The amount of preaching also increased. During Lent, fasters gave up not only oil and fruit but even bread. Some even maintained a complete fast from Sunday eucharist until the breaking of it on the next Saturday, but such rigorism was not required. Others ate each evening or at least at noon on Thursdays.

Holy Week began with a vigil on Friday evening a week before Easter Sunday. Observers proceeded on Saturday to Bethany, the house of Lazarus. On Sunday they observed normal services in the morning. In the afternoon, however, they held special services at the Eleona and Imbomon on the Mount of Olives and then proceeded down the Mount of Olives carrying palm branches and made their way through the city to the Church of the Resurrection for evening prayers at a late hour. On Monday, Tuesday, and Wednesday the faithful observed the usual prayer services but added a four-hour service beginning at three in the afternoon in the Martyrium. On Thursday they maintained the usual observances until noon. At two o'clock they began a continuous round of services which lasted until dawn the next day, save for a short break for an evening meal. These focused on the betrayal by Judas. The nighttime services took place on the Mount of Olives. On Friday people gathered at seven o'clock at Golgotha *behind* the cross and at noon proceeded to the *front* of the cross. That night the young and vigorous who had sufficient stamina kept a vigil at the Church of the Resurrection. On Saturday there was no celebration of the Eucharist.

Easter was the center of the Christian calendar. The paschal vigil began on Saturday night. Candidates received baptism and shared in their first communion about midnight. The following week, the bishop instructed them each morning in the "mysteries," that is, baptism and eucharist. On five of the eight days of Easter Week Christians celebrated the eucharist in buildings on Golgotha. On Wednesday they observed it at the Eleona and on Friday at Sion.

The period from Easter to Pentecost differed from the rest of the year because of the absence of fasting, the whole period being a time of rejoicing. Filling out the biblical frame, the churches began to mark the Ascension of Jesus on the fortieth day after Easter. According to Egeria, this feast took place in Bethlehem rather than Jerusalem. Pentecost, "fiftieth," continued the celebration of Easter. No all night vigil preceded it. Rather, the festival entailed a full round of observances, lasting, in Jerusalem, until midnight.

The fasts of Encaenia or Dedication and Epiphany were also recognized in the late fourth century with eight-day celebrations, which symbolized resurrection. The Feast of Dedication commemorated annually the erection of the Church of the Holy Sepulchre. Epiphany, January 6, involved a vigil at the Church of the Nativity in Bethlehem, a midnight celebration of the eucharist, and then a trek to Jerusalem. The festival continued for eight days with daily eucharists in various holy sites. The Presentation of Christ in the Temple was commemorated forty days after Epiphany, according to Egeria, with services similar to those observed at Easter.

Christmas entered the calendar in the West during this period, where Epiphany was unknown. The earliest evidence for December 25 as the date of Christ's birth appeared in the Philocalian Calendar drawn up at Rome in 336. According to John Chrysostom, in a sermon delivered in 386, it was not introduced in Antioch until around 375. Egeria did not refer to it for Jerusalem. Alexandria did not adopt it until about 430. At Constantine's urging Westerners evidently adopted the Roman festival of the Unconquered Son, December 25, and christianized it by attaching it to a "great moment" in Christian history of salvation. This suited perfectly the emperor's strategy. As the custom moved eastward, it left a serious problem in that Epiphany, universally recognized in the East, also commemorated Christ's birth. The solution was to make January 6 represent the visit of the Magi or the baptism of Jesus.

Celebrating the Saints

The cessation of persecution quickened interest in martyrs and saints. By the end of the fourth century Christians had erected martyria all over the empire and lovingly transferred their remains or relics there. Pilgrims traveled thousands of miles in the most difficult conditions to visit holy sites, first those in Palestine but also those in other places consecrated by the blood of saints. The churches also expanded the calendar to commemorate these exemplary Christians who inspired others by their living and by their dying.

In a funeral oration preached for his brother Basil of Caesarea in 379 Gregory of Nyssa recalled festivals in honor of Stephen, Peter, James, John, and Paul during the period between Christmas and January 1. Numerous later sources confirm the custom in the East, but local calendars differed widely. Rome, for instance, honored only John in December, Peter and Paul in June. A festival in honor of Mary did not appear until the sixth century in Gaul, the seventh in Rome.

Numerous other festivals began locally, primed by special interest. From a very early date the churches remembered their martyrs by special celebrations. Later on, others adopted the same and incorporated them into their calendars.

Christian Discipline

Beneficial as it was in many ways, the membership explosion that came with Constantine's conversion heavily taxed Christian discipline. Vast numbers now had minimal comprehension of what it meant to be Christian. The Synod of Elvira (Illiberris) in Spain about 306 illustrated the breakdown of basic morality in its severe canons. After declaring themselves Christians some continued to function as *flamines*, priests offering sacrifices as public officials, and to offer pagan sacrifices. Other canons dealt with murder, adultery, abandonment of spouses, using children as prostitutes, usury, lighting candles to placate spirits, incest, augury, sodomy, false witness, intermarriage with Jews or Gentiles, gambling. A few years later, the Synod of Arles in Gaul indicted gladiators, charioteers, actors, userers, and others who violated well established Christian standards.

In some areas the churches took strong and decisive action. Churches in the East developed what appears in retrospect to have been a highly legalistic system of discipline and one which eventually proved unworkable. Originally put together in response to the breakdown of Christian discipline in the late third century, it assumed more fixed features in the era of peace inaugurated by Constantine. Rather than excommunicating serious offenders permanently, bishops now graded penalties to fit the offense. As in the earlier period, they distinguished five grades: "mourners," "hearers," "fallers," bystanders," and "restored penitents." Penalties varied from synod to synod until some standardization occurred late in the fourth century. In 314 the Synod of Ancyra in Galatia, for instance, required persons forced to offer sacrifices and doing so willingly to spend one year as "hearers," three as "kneelers," and two as "bystanders" before restoration to communion. It required persons found guilty of "bestiality" (having sexual intercourse with animals), if under age twenty, to spend fifteen years as "fallers" and five as "bystanders," if over twenty, to spend twenty-five years as "fallers" and five as "bystanders." It stipulated that persons indulging in magic or other pagan customs would have to do three years as "fallers" and two as "bystanders." In some cases it levied penances without gradation—seven years for adultery, ten years for abortion or child exposure, five or seven years for unpremeditated murders and lifetime excommunication for premeditated.

By the late fourth century, though the system remained in force, bishops quietly phased it out. Even with threat of government enforcement hanging over their heads, many persons would not endure the humiliation of long penances. To avoid having to undergo them, they covered up and persuaded friends to cover up for them. In canonical letters written in 374 and 375 Basil of Caesarea threatened to place those who covered up for others under the same penalty the guilty party deserved (Canon 74). About the same time, John Chrysostom, realizing how difficult it was to impose discipline upon the easygoing populace of Antioch and repulsed by the mechanical character of the whole system, openly opposed long years of discipline and developed several alternative modes of repentance. No sin, he declared, is outside God's mercy, and God accepts even imperfect repentance. Length of repentance doesn't matter a whit; what matters is sincerity. Repentance must be voluntary. It is enough to confess privately. "If you have condemned your sin, you have put off the burden of it" (*Lazarus* 4). Alternatives to the system, Chrysostom observed

elsewhere, include simple confession, contrition, humility, almsgiving, prayer, and forgiveness of others (*The Devil as Tempter*, Hom. 2).

In the West the churches never developed grades or degrees to differentiate offenses and penalties. As in earlier times, the *exhomologesis* (public confession) required public displays of remorse such as weeping, wearing dishevelled hair, soiling of face and neck, and donning of sackcloth. Restoration as described by Jerome (*Dialogue against the Luciferians* 5), entailed a priest's offering of an oblation, laying on of hands, invoking the return of the Holy Spirit, and inviting prayers of the people for restoration of the penitent. Catholics repudiated the rigorism of the Novatianists or Donatists. The church, Ambrose insisted, has the power to forgive all sins. God has granted priests the power to forgive all. God, of course, does the forgiving; human beings only exercise the ministry of God's forgiveness. Yet, Ambrose went on to note, the rule of a single repentance following baptism still applies. He displayed the authority of a strong bishop to demand public confession in his excommunication of Emperor Theodosius for the slaughter of seven thousand citizens of Thessalonica. Only grave and notorious scandals necessitated public confessions; prayer sufficed for minor sins, Augustine said (*Sermon* 351, *Repentance*).

A Royal Priesthood

Rapid influx of new Christians created a crisis of leadership for the churches. Understandably but unfortunately, many Christian communities laid hands too hastily on some of the new and more cultured converts, indiscriminately ordaining neophytes, the lapsed, and persons of questionable reputation. Canon 2 of the Council of Nicaea summed up the dilemma succinctly, noting that

> many things, either by necessity or otherwise by human pressures, happened contrary to the ecclesiastical rule, so that persons recent-

ly converted from Gentile life to the faith, after a very brief instruction, were baptized and almost immediately thereafter were promoted to the episcopate or presbyterate.

Such haste opened a pandora's box of moral, educational, and theological maladies for which key leaders subsequently struggled to supply remedies. Many of the newly ordained, like Synesius of Cyrene, conscripted forcibly to be bishop of Ptolemais and metropolitan of the Pentapolis in 410 C.E., lacked both motivation for and understanding of their offices. Others had a poor sense of the boundaries which separated Christian from pagan, even on basic matters not involving subtle cultural distinctions. Fourth century councils and other documents have left ample evidence of various kinds of debauchery which injured badly the church's reputation. The powerful jaws of superstition still held many clergy fast, for they indulged in sorcery, magic, and astrology and wore amulets and magical charms. Some dressed and acted like dandies. They indiscreetly frequented the pubs, bathed with women in public baths, had strange women living in their houses, and acted carelessly in their relations with virgins and widows. Some continued to participate in pagan wedding rites, to attend the shows and games and to share in such other customs as the churches had once uniformly denounced as idolatrous. Some sought and used their offices for the sake of personal gain—buying and selling offices, taking usury, always seeking better appointments, and engaging in secular enterprises on the side. Married clergy often let family problems damage their witness.

Many disciplinary canons of fourth century councils addressed these problems head on. As a matter of prime importance, the bishops sought to halt indiscriminate ordinations by establishing certain age limits (50 for bishops, 30 for priests), insisting on adequate training, careful examination of background and reputation, prohibition of clerical "tramps," issuing letters of commendation for both clergy and laity, and, in the East, eliminating popular elections. In line with increased care in selection, they turned increasingly to the monks as models of piety, conscripting many of them for the clerical ranks. The bishops also sought to remove or render innocuous in other ways unworthy or disreputable clergy. Since high views of ordination prevented outright withdrawal of orders, removal from duties was customary in the case of such serious offenses as lapsing in persecution, adultery or fornication, simony, usury, or other forms of avarice. The councils likewise laid down rules for clerical behavior in relations with women, attendance at public functions, and the like, and absolutely banned all forms of sorcery, magic, and astrology.

The drive to sustain and improve the moral worthiness of the clergy in a lascivious age carried with it an additional impetus toward celibacy. Essentially the same factors that produced the monastic movement were at work here. Wiser heads tried to steer clear of extreme forms of asceticism such as self-mutilation, but at the same time they sought to sound a clear note against the licentiousness and otherwise lax morality of the age. Specifically with reference to the clergy, concern for purity expressed itself in several ways. In both East and West nonmarriage *after* ordination became the general rule by the early fourth century. There was strong opposition to second marriages and to marriage to widows. Within marriage clerical continence was practiced widely in both East and West, but it became a "binding rule" only in the West, first by order of Pope Siricius (384–399). Even there, some braved the papal wrath by opposing the view openly—Bonosus, bishop of Sardica, and the layman Helvidius, condemned at Capua in 389; Jovinian, condemned at Milan in 390; and Vigilantius, condemned by Pope Innocent I (402–417). A celibate clergy, however, played a significant part in the evangelization of Europe.

In connection with the struggle to conserve its integrity, the distinction between clergy and laity became more and more pronounced. In a treatise on *The Priesthood*, composed about 373 when the bishop of Antioch tried forcibly to ordain him, John Chrysostom placed the office well above mortal competence or worthiness. To preside over the church or to undertake the care of souls is so exalted, all women and the majority of men fail to qualify. This office, he wrote, may be "discharged on earth, but it ranks among heavenly ordinances" (3.4). Priests, therefore, must be as pure as angels. In administering the eucharist, they represent God to humankind and thence have an authority not even given to angels. In baptizing, they not merely pronounce the removal of spiritual uncleanness but "actually and absolutely take it away" (3.6). Even beyond baptism, they "have authority to forgive sins," and they bear fearsome responsibility to care for the needy and to teach and preach the gospel.

Not all carried so exalted an image of the office and few could implement it. In this era, nonetheless, the clergy, especially bishops, often exercised immense social and political power. As a bishop, Ambrose of Milan (374–397), for instance, administered not only baptism, the eucharist, and penance, but he in effect functioned as a public official. He superintended extensive church charities to relieve the poor, care for the sick and imprisoned, entertain strangers, pay debts of persons unable to meet their liabilities, maintain and educate orphans, and meet other needs. He defended widows and orphans against public seizure of their estates. He heard and adjudicated civil disputes. He confronted emperors and empresses regarding both beliefs and behavior. As metropolitan of northern Italy, he supervised the dioceses of the entire province of Aemilia-Liguria. He stood as a bulwark against Arianism, even that of Empress Justina. He played a significant role in urging on the final defeat of paganism throughout the empire.

Official investment of the episcopate with public responsibilities of necessity reshaped it. Whereas early on bishops presided over small flocks like shepherds, some, especially in areas where there were few episcopates, now became powerful executives whose main duty was to direct other clergy and to represent their churches in the public arena. Yet by the end of the fourth century many did exceedingly well in these new roles as Christianity became the public faith. Basil of Caesarea as well as Ambrose, for example, managed to combine pastoral and public duties with remarkable skill. This new cadre, drawn from the very best of society, lifted Christianity to a new plateau. Although it may have stumbled momentarily in its effort to assimilate vast numbers, it recovered its stride in this period and went on to become truly the religion of the empire.

Chapter 23

The Call of the Desert

What began as a trickle in the late third century became a flood in the fourth as thousands of young men and women fled to the desert. Many withdrew to escape from the intolerable burden of public taxes and service, but many others sought literally to fulfill the call of Christ to self-denial, cross bearing, and discipleship. The martyrs had inspired pagan and Christian alike by their examples. Since the era of peace prevented actual martyrdom, some elected a martyrdom of fasting and prayer in battle against the forces of evil. They confronted demons in their main habitats, that is, the desert.

Egypt was not the only locus for the monastic experiment. Monasticism may have developed independently in Syria, for Syrian monasticism assumed a character of its own, being far more austere than Egyptian. From these two places the movement spread all over the Roman Empire, first in the East and then in the West. As it grew, it changed character. The hermitic type persisted, but it yielded ground to the less austere communal type of monasticism initiated by Pachomius. Wise ecclesiastical leaders, in the meantime, rescued it for the organized church by pulling the monks closer to the churches and putting them at the service of the church. Monasteries served as centers of charity. Monks sustained bishops in their theological battles. In the West they bore the main burden for the evangelization of Europe.

Egypt

The rapidly increasing flow of hermits to certain parts of the Egyptian desert assured that they would not remain in isolation from one another very long. Associations of hermits developed at different locations. The first was at Pispir, not far from the Red Sea, where Anthony had fled to escape the crowds who wanted to imitate his holy life. In his *Life of Anthony* Athanasius described cells in these mountains "filled with holy bands of men who sang psalms, loved reading, fasted, prayed, rejoiced in the hope of things to come, labored in almsgiving, and preserved love and harmony with one another" (44). Anthony left the privacy of his "Inner Mountain" about every five to twenty days to give them help and advice (89). Anthony's disciples included Hilarion, the founder of monasticism in Palestine (ca. 310); Macarius the Egyptian, who initiated a settlement at Scete (ca. 330); as well as others who remained at Pispir.

Associations sprang up elsewhere. At Chenoboskion, where the famous Gnostic library was discovered in 1945, a monk named Palaemon headed a group of hermits who lived nearby, shared his style of life, sought his advice, and cared for him in illness. The most famous of his pupils was Pachomius, usually regarded as the father of coenobite or communal monasticism.

Pachomius remained at Palaemon's side until the latter died. After burying him he founded the monastery at Tabennesis.

Huge bands of monks gathered in a valley about sixty miles south of Alexandria and established three communities. Monasticism at Nitria was initiated by Amoun, whose wealthy and cultured parents died when he was twenty-two. Already married, he persuaded his wife to lead a life of continence from the day of their marriage. After eighteen years they separated, and Amoun went to Mount Nitria (ca. 320–330), where he spent the remainder of his life. By the end of the fourth century about five thousand monks, according to Palladius, inhabited the area. Monks here still lived under no rule and pursued the solitary life, working and praying alone but gathering on Saturdays and Sundays in the large church. They supported themselves by weaving linen, but they included physicians, confectioners, wine sellers, and bakers. They attached great importance to memorization of scriptures and some could reputedly quote all of both Old and New Testaments. They valued work and obliged even guests to join them in it after a limited time there.

Not far from Nitria, six hundred monks lived in a place called Cellia, "the cells" (Sozomen, *Church History* 6.31). Like the hermits at Nitria, they also assembled on Saturdays and Sundays for worship, but they did not maintain as close contact otherwise. They built their huts far enough apart that they could not see or hear one another. Among the most famous monks to reside there was Macarius the Alexandrian, who had cells also in Scete, Libya, and Nitria. He astonished even other monks by his fasting and lived to be nearly a hundred (died ca. 393). Evagrius of Pontus in Cappadocia spent two years in Nitria and fourteen in Cellia. His writings on prayer influenced markedly Eastern theology and practice of prayer.

At Scete a monastic colony sprang up under the leadership of Macarius the Egyptian, or the Great, about 330. A disciple of Anthony until that time. Macarius dug a tunnel a half mile long between his cell and a cave in order to escape visitors (Palladius, *Lausiac History* 17). Many of his sermons, letters, and sayings have survived. Like monks at Nitria and Cellia, those at Scete attended faithfully on Saturdays and Sundays one of the four churches in the community. Life was harsh not only because of self-imposed austerities, but also because of lack of water and food. The community maintained a strict discipline. Like those at Nitria, they combined work and prayer, trying to memorize all of the scriptures. Cassian gained much of the material for his *Conferences* and *Institutions* at Scete from such famous monks as Paphnutius and Serapion.

Other colonies of hermits formed near Alexandria, Rhinoccorura, Babylon and Memphis, Heracleopolis, Phoenice, Oxyrhynchus, Achoris, the Arsinoite regions, and the Thebaid. Some of these numbered in the thousands. Palladius, for instance, counted two thousand in a colony near Alexandria (*Lausiac History* 7). All subsisted on simple diets, usually one meal a day, which they varied according to individual age and strength (Cassian, *Conferences* 2.22). They tried to avoid extremes in asceticism. They slept only a short time before dawn (ibid., 7.34). Younger monks confessed faults to older and experienced monks.

Associations like these evolved naturally into coenobite monasticism of Pachomius. A monk named Aotas had tried to establish a community but failed (*Life of Pachomius* 77). Pachomius, born about 292 of pagan parents in the Upper Thebaid, first came in contact with Christians while serving in the army raised by Constantine. There he witnessed the application of Christian charity in food and drink brought to soldiers by Christians and thus decided to become a Christian. Upon release from the army he went to Chenoboskion to receive instruction in the faith and be baptized in the village church. Hearing about Palaemon, he joined him, sharing his dwelling and working with him. One day, he went to

Tabennesis on the eastern bank of the Nile, where a celestial voice instructed him to remain and build a monastery (*Life* 7). With Palaemon's assistance he built a cell there. His brother, John, soon joined him, but he wished to live as a hermit. Others, however, followed, and within a short time the community numbered a hundred. When the monastery at Tabennesis overflowed, he built another at Pabau or Proou which also grew rapidly. Not only individuals but colonies of monks came. Pachomius directed some of them to set up new communities at Chenoboskion, Monchosis, Thebeu, Tase, Tismenae, Panopolis, and Pachnoum. Pachomius himself changed his residence from Tabennesis to Pabau, which then became the head monastery of the Pachomian system. In 346 disease ravaged the monasteries, claiming the lives of over a hundred monks, including Pachomius'. Before he died, Pachomius named Petronius, superior of Tismenae, to succeed him, but he died two months later. Petronius appointed Orsisius, superior of Chenoboskion, to succeed him. Under him the Pachomian communities thrived, but their material prosperity led to controversy over management. In 350 Orsisius solved the problem by appointing Theodore as his coadjutor and leaving the control to him. Theodore ruled the complex of monasteries wisely for eighteen years. Little is known of the monasteries after Theodore's death except that they evidently continued to prosper and spread. According to Palladius, there were 3,000 monks during Pachomius's life and 7,000 when he wrote (around 420) (*Lausiac History* 7).

Pachomius gradually developed rules for his monks which became more and more precise as the communities overflowed. At the beginning Pachomius evidently admitted new monks after a preliminary examination. In time, however, he required a three-year probation and admitted strange monks with some caution. Pachomian communities consisted of numerous buildings within a walled enclosure: a church, assembly hall, dining hall, library, kitchen, food pantry,

bakery, infirmary, various workshops, and houses for members of the community. According to Jerome, they numbered from thirty to forty. Each dormitory housed twenty-two to forty monks in individual cells and contained a common meeting room. Near the monastery gate was a hospice for visitors, who included women.

A superior general or archimandrite held supreme power over the monasteries. He appointed heads for each of them and visited them regularly. A superior and an assistant governed each monastery. Monks were assigned to houses usually according to their work. Each house was ruled by a head and an assistant. Monks were ranked according to seniority. Twice a year the monks gathered at Pabau—to celebrate Easter and for administrative purposes on August 13. During the latter meeting, superiors reported on the work of their monasteries during the year and each monk forgave others for the wrongs done to him by others.

The Pachomians admitted all except a few whose earlier lives made them unsuitable, requiring willingness to obey the rules of the community. Even children entered. New applicants remained outside for several days while doorkeepers taught them prayers, psalms, and the rules.

The monks gathered in their houses several times a day for prayers: at dawn, noon, evening, before they went to bed, and at night. On Saturdays and Sundays they celebrated the eucharist. Twice a week, on fast days, monks received instruction in Christian doctrine and scriptures with emphasis on memorization. Those who could not read had to learn. Most monks wove mats and baskets, but some did more specialized work required by the communities. During work, monks observed the rule of silence and were expected to meditate constantly on scriptures. Pachomius recognized the importance of work not only to maintain the monasteries but also for its spiritual values. Monks normally ate two meals a day, at noon and in the evening, in silence. Food consisted of bread, cheese, herbs, olives, fruit, and certain green vegetables but neither wine nor meat. Monks fasted on Wednesdays and Fridays. During Lent, they ate only uncooked food and some ate only every two or five days. If monks fell ill, they were cared for in the infirmary, where they could take wine and eat meat. Monks could choose how long they wanted to sleep, but many tried to spend most of their time in prayer. They were not permitted to speak to one another after they retired to their cells in the evening.

Monastic discipline was severe. Monks underwent constant surveillance and correction. If they spoke or laughed during psalmody or prayer, they were required to stand before the altar and be rebuked by the superior of the monastery. If they arrived late, they would undergo the same humiliation and stand during the next meal in the refectory. If they committed more serious offenses such as lying or disobeying, the superior would determine punishments. Repeated offenses could lead to demotion, corporal punishments, and expulsion. Yet Pachomian rules avoided excesses. Pachomius, for instance, allowed fires in cold weather and permitted monks to visit sick relatives, attend funerals, or receive visits from relatives. The main object of obedience was harmony and spiritual growth for the community.

Not far from the Pachomian community at Panopolis, Schenoudi developed a different type of cenobite monastery. As a young boy, he joined his maternal uncle Bgoul, head of the White Monastery, and earned such a reputation for piety that he succeeded him as head of it perhaps around 385. He remained in that position until his death around 451, reputedly at 118 years of age. The monastery grew rapidly, requiring him to add many buildings. he also established a monastery for women. Unlike Pachomius, Schenoudi was noted for strictness and harshness, once flogging a monk so severely he died.

Early writings mention other coenobite monasteries besides these. Deserving of special mention are communities of women which developed alongside those for men. Some women as well as men lived as hermits. Palladius, for instance, reported that a serving woman named Alexandra left the city of Alexandria and lived in a tomb for ten years, spinning flax and praying or recalling scriptures (*Lausiac History* 5). Pachomius founded the first community. This began with a cell built for his sister, Mary, at Tabennesis. Soon many other women came and placed themselves under Mary's direction. Pachomius himself laid down the rules for the community, his monks did the building. When this community overflowed, Pachomius built a second near the monastery at Tismenae. Later on, Theodore formed a third convent near Pabau. Palladius reported that one of the monasteries housed four hundred women (*Lausiac History* 33). The convent established by Schenoudi was still larger, reportedly consisting of eighteen hundred nuns. Convents appeared elsewhere, too. At Antinoe there were twelve, according to Palladius (*Lausiac History* 59), one with sixty nuns presided over by an eighty-year-old ascetic named Amma (mother) Talis. Chrysostom referred to associations of virgins in Egypt (*Hom. in Matt.* 8). The anonymous *History of the Monks* (5) reported that there were very many nuns at Oxyrhynchus.

Syria

Monasticism sprang up in Syria during the last quarter of the third century evidently without direct connection with Egyptian. The earliest known figure was Jacob, consecrated bishop of Nisibis around 300, who took up the anchorite life about 280 or shortly before in the mountains of Nisibis. Still more famous was Juliana Saba, whose fifty-year career Ephrem Syrus celebrated with a poem. Since he died in 367, he must have taken up the life of a hermit about 317. Syrian monks lived in both Roman and Persian territories in Mesopotamia.

Syrian monasticism distinguished itself from monasticism elsewhere in its severity, primitivism, mortification, and individualism. Gregory of

Nazianzus spoke with astonishment about Syrian monks who fasted for twenty days at a time, wore iron fetters, slept on the bare ground, and stood motionless with hands outstretched in prayer in the rain, wind, and snow (*Historic Poems*, col. 1455). Theodoret of Cyrus recorded that Jacob of Nisibis dwelt in the solitude of the highest Mountain tops and in the thickets of the forests. During the summer, he sought no shelter; in the winter he lived in a cave. He wore no clothing, lit no fires, and built no dwelling. He rejected work and ate no food earned by work, sustaining himself by eating herbs and fruits (*Religious History*, col. 1293-94; Voobus, I:151). A letter of Ephrem depicted a monasticism whose devotees abandoned their communities and assumed a life not far removed from that of animals. They lived with animals, ate grass, and perched on rocks like birds. They shunned work and spent their time exclusively in prayer. Contemptuous of life, they took no precautions against savage animals and snakes. A poem of Ephrem depicted emaciated persons looking more like eagles than like human beings. In another writing he noted several groups of monks unwilling to die a natural death and seeking either to starve themselves or to kill themselves by some kind of hideous torture. Arthur Voobus has ascribed the severity of Syrian monasticism to Manichaeism, which dominated in Mesopotamia during this period.

When coenobitism reached Syria is uncertain. An inscription attests the existence of a monastery at al-Hit in Hauran in 354 and Ephrem Syrus (ca. 306–373) left hints of others in his poems. Manichaeism also had something to do with the founding of coenobite communities. According to Jerome (*Life of Hilarion*), Hilarion, a discipline of Anthony, settled in Majuma ca. 306. Syria did not have any monasteries before that.

Ephrem Syrus deserves considerable credit for the shape and influence which monasticism took in northern Mesopotamia. Hearing the call in youth, he spent much of his life in the vicinity of Nisibis, moving to Edessa about ten years before he died. An admirer of Jacob of Nisibis, he favored anchoritism over coenobitism and a severe form over the milder Egyptian form. Through poems, sermons, and other writings he promoted the anchorite model vigorously. After him, however, the flux of youth toward solitude changed the character of the movement. Hermits established residences and moderated the wild features of Syrian monachism. The churches exerted pressures here, too, for many did not regard animalistic practices of some monks as Christian. Even the government stepped in to put a stop to excesses. An inward consolidation gradually brought the monks into closer contact with Christian communities and effected further changes. Many monks became bishops.

Despite reservations of the earlier generations, therefore, coenobitism gradually increased. According to the *Acts of Ephrem* (10), Edessa had already become something of a center of monasteries before Ephrem arrived there around 357. *The Pilgrimage of Etheria*, however, dated about 385–394, shows that monasteries did not dominate the mountains around Edessa. Coenobite communities would have been small. Syrians established predominantly coenobitic communities in Armenia. When Theodoret composed his *Religious History* around 444, he reported that there were thousands of coenobite monasteries not only in Syria but in all of the East. By this time the size of communities also increased.

Palestine

The Holy Land had drawn pilgrims from at least the third century on. The conversion of Constantine increased opportunities. The holy sites especially attracted hermits who wanted to spend their lives.

Monasticism in Palestine began with Hilarion. Born of pagan parents about 291 near Gaza, he was converted and educated in Alexandria. Attracted to the Egyptian desert by the example of Anthony, he returned at age fifteen to Palestine, gave away his inheritance, and settled down to a solitary life near Majuma, south of Gaza, on the Egyptian model. About 330 others joined him in the founding of a monastery. To escape the crowds which flocked to him on account of his reputation and miraculous gifts, he returned to Egypt around 353. Later he moved to Libya, Sicily, and finally to Cyprus, where he died in 371. His disciples included Epiphanius (ca. 315–403), who founded a monastery near Eleutheropolis, halfway between Jerusalem and Gaza, around 335. In 367, however, the bishops of Cyprus consecrated him their metropolitan as bishop of Salamis. In that capacity he played a major role in theological controversies in support of the Council of Nicaea.

A new wave of enthusiasm for the monastic vocation followed the return of Athanasius from exile in 346 and the publication of his *Life of Anthony* in 356. Basil of Caesarea, baptized in 357, toured monastic sites in Palestine and Egypt. Hilary of Poitiers (ca. 315–367) and Eusebius of Vercellae (d. 371) carried stories about the Egyptian monks to the West. Rufinus (ca. 345–410) visited the monks of Egypt about 372. There he met Melania the Elder (ca. 342–ca. 410), an aristocratic Roman woman who brought three hundred pounds of silver for Pambo, Abbot of the Pachomian monastery in Nitria. After six years at Nitria Rufinus proceeded to Palestine in 381 and, with Melania's help, founded a monastery for men like the one she had founded in 373 for women on the Mount of Olives. He returned to Italy in 392.

Palestine's most famous monk was Jerome (ca. 342–420). Born at Strido near Aquileia in Italy, he studied in Rome and received baptism there. He then returned to Aquileia to devote himself to an ascetic life. About 374 he set out for Palestine but stopped on the way in Antioch. He then spent four or five years as a hermit in the desert of Chalkis. Ordained a presbyter at Antioch, he spent some time in Constantinople and returned to Rome, where he served as secretary to Pope Damasus and taught scriptures and fostered asceticism especially among wealthy and cultured Roman women. Forced to leave Rome after the death of Damasus in 385 he toured Antioch, Palestine, and Egypt with Paula and Eustochium, two women of the Aventine Circle he had met with in Rome. Finally, in 386 he settled at Bethlehem, where he spent the remainder of his life, studying and presiding over a monastery. Funding for the monastery came from the wealthy Roman matron Paula, who, with her daughter Eustochium, took up residence in Bethlehem also in 386.

John Cassian (ca. 360–435), one of the chief architects of Western monasticism, joined a monastery at Bethlehem as a young man, but he left it about 385 to study monasticism in Egypt. Etheria traveled at this time through Palestine, Sinai, and Syria in search of holy sites.

Sinai

The desert around Mount Sinai became one of the choicest spots for monks because of its connection with Moses. When Etheria visited Sinai in the late fourth century, she found a flourishing community of anchorites not only on the mountain but all around it. Monks constructed a church on top of the mountain and at the site of the Burning Bush where St. Catherine's now stands. The monks delighted in guiding pilgrims and were amply rewarded for it.

Prominent in the development of monasticism in Sinai was Silvanus, a Palestinian, who had headed a community at Scete before moving to Sinai about 380. Living first at Sinai, he later founded a large monastery in the Wadi Ghezzeh, near Gerara, in the Gaza area. His disciple Zacharias succeeded him about 415 as leader of the community there (Sozomen, *Church History* 6.32).

Cappadocia

By the late-fourth century the monastic seed was planted in virtually every area where Christianity penetrated. In Cappadocia Macrina (ca. 372–379) and her brother Basil of Caesarea (ca. 330–379) took the lead. Macrina exerted a major influence over both Basil and Gregory of Nyssa, another of the brothers in this eminent family. She lured Basil away from a promising secular career to the Christian priesthood and toward the monastic life. With her mother she established a monastery for women on the family estate in Pontus. With former servants they practiced koinonia in goods and work. In his *Life of Macrina* Gregory reported that Macrina gave away all of her possessions and followed the rule of apostolic poverty. She gained quite a reputation for healing miracles. Basil imitated his sister.

After receiving the best classical education possible at Caesarea, Constantinople, and Athens, Basil responded at the urging of Macrina to the monastic call. He visited monks in Syria and Egypt in 357 and then assumed the role of a hermit on the Iris River near Neo-Caesarea. He framed the monastic Rule that bears his name between 358 and 364. Set out in a shorter (55 items) and a longer (313 items) form, Basil's Rule avoided the extreme asceticism of the hermits. He preferred the model of Eustathius, bishop of Sebaste, to the Egyptian or Syrian models. Asceticism is to be a means to perfect service of God attained in communal life under obedience. Basil clearly preferred the communal to the anchorite type of life. The main objective of the monk is to love God and neighbor; it is better achieved in community. Monks too should seek to unite in the one Body of Christ. The communal life is far safer and more practical. Questions posed and answered by the Rule point up the social context which contributed to the call of persons to the monastic life. Married persons, slaves, and children were among the applicants. Basil favored the entrance of children because more pliable. Unlike some hermits who tried to devote themselves exclusively to prayer, Basil required a combination of prayer and labor. Monks should choose trades which would allow

for a tranquil life and aim at simplicity and frugality, farming perhaps preferable. They should perform their services for those who are in need. Decisions about vocation, however, should be made by the community and not by the individual. Individuals must obey them.

Basil probably saved monasticism by putting it in service of the church. Stripped of some of its severity, especially in the Syrian model, and equipped with broader purposes, it attracted some of the brightest youth, including Basil's brother Gregory. Gregory of Nyssa (ca. 330–ca. 395), Basil's younger brother, entered a monastery founded by his brother. Consecrated bishop of Nyssa around 371, he took an active role in support of the Nicene faith. In addition to numerous theological treatises, Gregory composed many works on spirituality: a treatise on Christian perfection entitled *The Life of Moses*; sermons on the Song of Songs, the Lord's Prayer, and the Beatitudes; treatises on virginity; and a *Life of Macrina*, his sister. In *The Life of Moses* he depicted the mystical journey as a progression from light to darkness and laid the foundation for apophatic (negative way) theology characteristic of Orthodoxy. We can only say who God is not; we cannot say directly who God is.

Basil also drew Gregory of Nazianzus (329–389) toward the monastic life. Son of the bishop of Nazianzus in Cappadocia, Gregory met Basil at the university of Athens. Soon thereafter he opted for the contemplative life. Ordained against his will, he was installed in the see of Sasima around 372. He served as an associate (suffragans) to his father until the latter's death in 374 and then withdrew to a hermitage in Seleucia in Isauria. In 381 he was appointed bishop of Constantinople, but he resigned after less than a year and retired first to Nazianzus and then to his own estate.

The West

The West had had its ascetics in earlier centuries, but it turned its gaze eastward in earnest when Athanasius brought two Egyptian monks, Ammonius and Isidore, to Rome in 338 during his first exile. Later he went to Trier and Gaul. His *Life of Anthony*, composed in 356, soon circulated in a Latin translation in the West. By the late fourth century the names of the more famous Egyptian monks had become household words in Rome. Women especially played a seminal role in the development of asceticism there.

At the center of the women ascetics in Rome stood Marcella (325–410). After the premature death of her husband she took up a life of devotion. In her palace on the Aventine Hill she gathered other notable women—her sister Asella, Fabiola, Lea, Paula, Eustochium—for intensive study of scriptures, charitable activities, and prayer. Her mother Albina joined the circle of pious women who gathered around her. When Jerome came to Rome in 382, she enlisted him to assist in the study of scriptures. By his own admission, she constantly pressed him to go deeper in his interpretation of them. When Jerome and others took flight to Palestine in 385, she remained in Rome at the helm of the movement. She died in 410 as a consequence of abuse suffered at the hands of the Gothic invaders of Rome.

On the death of her husband and two sons, Melania the Elder, a wealthy Roman aristocrat, took up the ascetic life at age twenty-two. In 372 she placed her only surviving child in the care of Christian friends and set out for Egypt, where she visited monks in the Thebaid, Nitria, and Scete and left rich gifts. She defended orthodox (Nicene) monks in court against Arian accusers and, when many of them were banished to Palestine, followed them there. With the help of Rufinus, she founded a double monastery on the Mount of Olives. At the heighth of the Origenist controversy, which pitted Rufinus against Jerome, she returned to Italy about 399 or 400. When the Goths invaded Italy in 408, she fled with other members of her family and returned to Jerusalem, where she died around 410.

Paula (347–404), another eminent member of the Aventine Circle, took up the ascetic life at age thirty-three following the death of her husband. According to Jerome, she could trace her lineage back to Agamemnon and her husband's back to Aeneas. Two daughters, Blesilla and Eustochium (ca. 370–419), joined her in her devout life, but Blesilla died, possibly as a result of excessive austerities. Jerome's letter to Eustochium, then only fifteen, on virginity created such a storm that she and her mother fled the city behind Jerome. When she finally arrived in Bethlehem, Paula and Eustochium founded a monastery for men and a much larger one for women which Paula ruled. Subsequently a granddaughter named Paula joined her grandmother and aunt to be reared under her grandmother's direction. Eustochium succeeded Paula as head of the monastery.

Another distinguished member of the Aventine Circle was Fabiola (d. 399). A member of the famous *gens Fabia*, she had violated church custom by divorcing her first husband and remarrying. After the death of her second husband, she distributed much of her immense wealth to the poor and devoted herself to care of the sick. In 395 she joined Paula and Eustochium in Bethlehem, but she returned to Rome on account of her discomfort with the Origenist controversy, the isolation of the monastery, and threat of invasion of Palestine by the Huns. There she joined Pammachius, son-in-law of Paula, in erecting a hospital in Portus.

Many males in these powerful Roman families resented and opposed the contemplative life. So too did the masses. In 384 they blamed the death of Paula's daughter Blesilla on the monks and called for their expulsion from Rome. The poet Rutilius Numatianus ridiculed monks for their "fear of the evils of fortune." Yet some of the nobility dared to offer support. Pammachius (ca. 340–410), a Roman senator of the Furian family and husband of Paulina, another of Paula's daughters, admired Jerome. After Paulina's death he embraced the monastic life and devoted the fortune he had inherited from her to care for the indigent. Among other things, with Fabiola he erected a hospital for pilgrims at Portus and the Church of Ss. Giovanni e Paolo. What he found offensive was excesses and not the ascetic life itself. Although Jerome dedicated several works to him, Pammachius did not hesitate to criticize Jerome's intemperance in his attacks on Jovinian because of the latter's views on virginity and on Rufinus because of his support for Origen. Pammachius died during the Gothic invasion of Rome in 410.

Challenges to the ideal of virginity evoked sharp replies from Jerome, Ambrose, and Augustine. A Latin theologian named Helvidius, evidently concerned to defend marriage against growing preference for celibacy, met vigorous opposition from Jerome for denying the perpetual virginity of Mary. Jovinian (d. ca. 405), a monk, was attacked by both Jerome and Augustine and condemned by synods at Rome and Milan for denying that virginity was a higher level of Christian life than marriage and that abstinence as such was better than eating. In 402 Pope Innocent I made celibacy an "indissoluble rule" for the clergy.

The monastic life also caught on in Gaul. Hilary of Poitiers (ca. 315–367) and Eusebius of Vercellae (d. 371) got a taste of it during their exile to Phrygia (356–360) and passed on some of their enthusiasm to Martin of Tours (d. 397). A soldier in the Roman army and already a catechumen, Martin had a vision of Christ which impelled him to receive baptism and take up the religious life. In 360, after resigning his commission, he joined Hilary of Poitiers and founded the first monastery in Gaul at Ligugé. Later he established the famous monastery at Marmoutier. After his appointment as bishop of Tours about 372, he promoted the spread of monasticism throughout Gaul as a means of evangelization.

Looking to the Future

As twilight settled over the West, the ascetics prepared themselves for the immense challenges that lay ahead. No longer marginal to church and society, as the early hermits had been, the monastic tradition had taken sufficient institutional shape to equip monasticism not only to survive but also to serve the churches in remarkable ways. In the East Basil's Rule assured that the monasteries would help the churches, administering relief to the poor, operating a hospital for lepers, visiting the sick, and educating the deprived. In the West Cassian's Rule, although favoring the Egyptian model, also guaranteed a more amenable working relationship between church and cloister. So, too, would a model developing at Lérins. In the traumatic times which followed, the churches turned to the monks to see how Christians should respond when their world crashed around them. In both East and West they prevailed on monks like Basil, the Gregorys, Martin, Paulinus, and a host of others to assume the highest offices of the church. The most crucial days, however, lay ahead for the monks as they carried the Christian message to the barbarians pressing southwards into the Roman Empire. Theirs would be the strategic role in the evangelization of Europe.

Part 5

Dividing Worlds,
400–600 C.E.

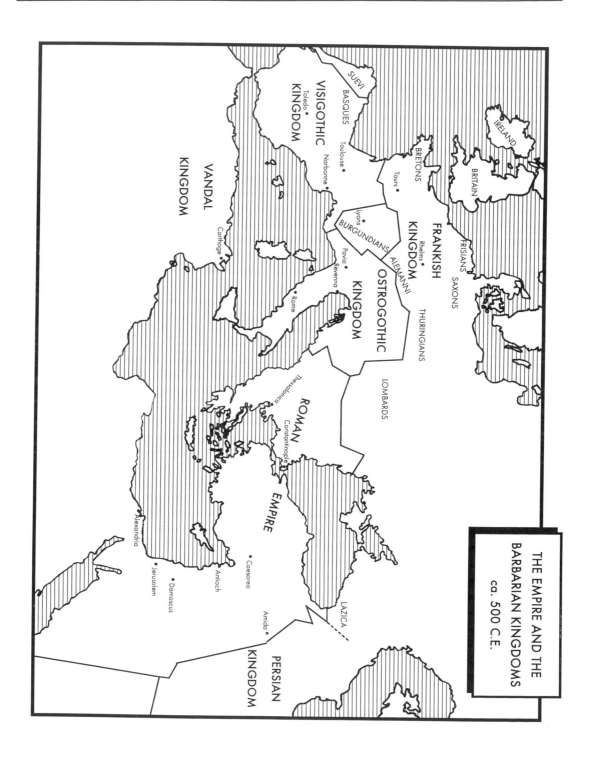

THE EMPIRE AND THE
BARBARIAN KINGDOMS
ca. 500 C.E.

Chapter 24

The Barbarian "Invasions"

What moderns usually call the barbarian "invasions" had little resemblance to what we would call invasions. They represented, rather, gradual migrations southwards until the "barbarians" finally controlled most of the territory that had belonged to the western part of the Roman Empire. During the third century, the Romans managed to hold back the tide of northern Europeans who constantly pressed southwards seeking warmer climates and more hospitable places to live. They invited some to settle as *coloni*, farmers, within the confines of the vast empire. Pressures persisted, however, as more and more tribes sought the benefits of living within the Roman Empire. Meantime, internal decay rendered Roman resistance increasingly ineffective. As early as Constantine, removal of the capital from Rome to the East represented growing alarm at the decline of the Western empire. Diocletian planned to move the capital to Nicomedia. Constantine simply selected a site he could Christianize more readily, the obscure village of Byzantium. By the late fourth century the emperors had virtually abandoned the West, turning over the control of the army to a succession of barbarians. In 476 Odovacer, no longer willing to serve the emperor's lackey in the West, Julius Nepos, returned the symbols of office to Emperor Zeno (474–491). For a long time already Western leaders had not been able to stem the tide of incursions by first one and then another tribe.

The churches suffered severely on the extremities of the empire, in some areas virtually disappearing altogether. In Rome, Vandals and others notwithstanding, things did not change radically, partly because, as Augustine pointed out, many of the barbarians had already been converted to Christianity. What began to occur was a gradual process of cultural deterioration which the churches helped to retard but could not prevent altogether. The barbarians envied Roman culture, but they lacked the means to conserve what they admired. The one institution which possessed some capability for holding on to the past and giving directions for the future was the Roman church. Skillful popes managed to step into the political and cultural vacuum created by the "invasions" and enhance the influence of the church. The so-called Donation of Constantine, composed in the eighth century as Frankish rulers challenged papal claims, was fictitious but not entirely erroneous in depicting the bishop of Rome as the successors of Constantine in the West. From about the mid-fifth until the mid-eighth century the bishops of Rome functioned in fact as the major political as well as religious leaders in the West. The barbarians were too divided among themselves to establish the kind of hegemony the Carolingians would later hold.

The Barbarian Migrations

The initial wave of people pressing southwards consisted of German peoples east of the Rhine and north of the Danube. Slavs came later, during the sixth century. Originally located in southern Scandinavia, Denmark, and adjacent lands, the German tribes drove the Celts, who occupied lands west of the Elbe to the Rhine, farther and farther westward. By about 200 B.C.E. West Germans had pushed the Celts to the Rhine and as far south as the Main. A century later, they had occupied southern Germany and attempted to flood Gaul but were halted by Julius Caesar. Subsequently another migration followed from Scandinavia. It consisted of a different group of Germans usually designated East Germans. Whereas the West Germans evolved from a race of hunters and shepherds to one of farmers by the early Christian era, the East Germans remained migratory. Pressures from the latter forced the West Germans to seek settlements in Roman territory. The major tribes included the Alemanni, the Franks, the Saxons, and the Thuringians. The Alemanni, a composite of Suevian tribes, settled along the upper Rhine, the Franks along the lower Rhine, the Saxons between the Weser and the Elbe, and the Thuringians south of them. During the fifth century, the East Germans, consisting of the Goths, the Vandals, the Gepids, the Burgundians, and the Lombards effected the occupation of the Roman Empire in the West. By the third and fourth centuries they had already moved southwards as far as the Black Sea and the Danube.

The Goths. The major movement began with the Goths during the second century C.E. Never a united people, the Goths eventually formed two great divisions—Ostrogoths and Visigoths—along geographical lines. Their attacks on the Roman Empire began soon after the reign of Alexander Severus (d. 235). In 251 they dealt the Roman army under Decius a devastating blow near the mouth of the Danube, killing the emperor himself. Although Claudius I retaliated in 269 and secured peace with them south of the Danube, they had their way north of the Danube in the Roman province of Dacia. In 270 Emperor Aurelian withdrew Roman garrisons from the province. Constantine secured Roman control to the south of the Danube with a line of fortresses and a treaty making the Visigoths *foederates* ("allies") of the empire.

The Goths themselves were threatened with the advent of the Huns during the reign of Emperor Valens (373–379). A people of Mongolian origin, the Huns moved westward into Europe from their pastureland near the Caspian and Aral Lakes. Fierce fighters, they terrified the Ostrogoths, Heruls, and Alans, who occupied Dacia. Following defeat of the Ostrogoths, the Huns advanced against the Visigoths, who then fled for protection into the Roman Empire. In 376 Emperor Valens reluctantly admitted about 80,000 of them. This precipitated a violent reaction as the Visigoths entered southern Moesia, a war lasting nearly two years and culminating in the battle of Hadrianople on August 9, 378. Valens's impatience and underestimation of Gothic strength resulted in an ignominious defeat. The German cavalry proved far superior to Roman infantry. Despite their victory, however, the Goths could not capture Hadrianople itself. Subsequently Theodosius (379–395), coemperor with Gratian, concluded a treaty which permitted them to settle in the territory as *foederates*, supplying troops as needed by the empire. He also worked out a settlement with the Ostrogoths, not locating them near the Visigoths but in Phrygia of Asia Minor. Realizing the seriousness of the Gothic threat, Theodosius was unremitting in efforts to conciliate the Goths and win their support. After his death in 395, however, the Goths no longer trusted the Romans and elected Alaric their king. He turned out to be a bitter enemy of the empire. Defense of the empire fell to Stilicho, a German, as master of the armies of both East and West under Theodosius's incompetent sons, Arcadius in the East and Honorius in the West. Faced with far greater strength in the East, Alaric turned westward. For some strange reason Stilicho did not follow up on a defeat of Alaric at Pollentia in northern Italy on Easter day in 402. Although he made no concessions to barbarians outside the empire, he treated the *foederates* within it, of which he himself was one, with considerable deference and evidently thought of Alaric as a potential ally. Faced with a crisis in Italy, Emperor Honorius recalled troops from the Rhine, thus leaving it exposed to invasion by Vandals, Suevi, and Alans. As a consequence of a false accusation of treason, Stilicho was executed in 408, eliminating one of the strongest pillars in the West.

The death of Stilicho opened the way for Alaric to attain his double goal of establishing a permanent place within the diocese of Italy or Illyricum for his people and obtaining a high military command for himself. In pursuit of these designs he marched on Rome. After a siege he obtained a hefty amount of gold and a treaty, but the Roman Senate balked at some demands. Twice more Alaric besieged the city, sacking it in 410. Among captives taken at that time was Emperor Honorius's sister, Galla Placidia. Alaric, however, did not live long enough to enjoy his victory, dying at the end of the year. His brother, Ataulf, who succeeded him as king, changed from a vigorous opponent of all things Roman to a "Restorer of the Roman world." he persuaded Galla Placidia to marry him, contrary to the wishes of her brother. She later became the ruler of the West. Ataulf was slain by a hostile servant in 415. Under his successor, Wallia, the Goths moved into Spain, where they fought and subjugated the Siling Vandals and the Alans. A remnant of Alans fled to Gallaecia to unite with the Asding Vandals under Gunderic. As a recompense, Emperor Constantius III rewarded the Goths with the gift of Aquitania Secunda in Gaul, rather than territory in Spain. Roman proprietors relinquished two-thirds of their estates to Visigoths, thus easing the transfer somewhat.

The Vandals. By the time of Honorius's death in 423 three German kingdoms existed in Gaul: the Visigoths in the southwest, the Burgundians in the southeast, and the Salian Franks in the northeast on the lower Rhine. In Spain the Suevi commanded the northwest, Gallaecia, and the Vandals, merged with the Alans, the south, Baetica. Meantime, Galla Placidia enlisted the help of Boniface, military commander in Africa, to take control of the Western crown for her son Valentinian III. Boniface overcame forces led by Aetius in support of a civil servant named John, but evidently held imperial ambitions himself. When Galla Placidia attempted to recall him, he refused to come and defeated an army sent to oppose him as an "enemy of the Republic." When faced with another army under leadership of a Goth named Sigisvult, he invited the Vandals to come to his aid. Under Gunderic, "King of the Vandals and Suevi," the Vandals had already made incursions into African Mauretania. Following Gunderic's death in 428, his brother Gaiseric responded with enthusiasm to Boniface's proposal that they divide Africa between them. In May 429 the combined nation of Alans and Vandals, numbering an estimated 80,000, crossed over into Africa. The Vandals killed and plundered with abandon, not sparing even the churches. Galla Placidia worked out a plan of reconciliation with Boniface, but he proved no match for Gaiseric, who defeated him at Hippo. New forces sent from Italy and Constantinople under command of Aspar were no more effective. Only Carthage and Cirta held out against the Vandal forces. Meantime, in Italy Aetius, against the wishes of Galla Placidia, forced himself into a position of power as Valentinian III reached age sixteen in 437. In 442 he concluded a new treaty with Gaiseric which was far more favorable to the Romans than one entered into in 335. By the terms of the new treaty the empire took back the two provinces of Mauretania and ceded most of the rest of Africa to the Vandals, including Carthage, which had fallen to Gaiseric in 439.

The Anglo-Saxons. As the Vandals took charge of Africa, the Anglo-Saxons conquered Britain. During the reign of Honorius, Britain suffered raids from Picts and Scots. The Anglo-Saxon occupation began about 428 and reached its goal with the withdrawal of Roman administration in 442.

The Huns. The Huns under Attila dominated the next phase of European history until 454. Aetius had cultivated relationships with the Huns in his effort to install John as emperor. In 433 Rugila, the Hun king, subdued the Burgundians. In appreciation Aetius surrendered another part of Pannonia in exchange for the province of Valeria where they had resided for forty-five years. Attila succeeded Rugila as king of the Huns. Although still a nomadic people, the Huns had abandoned some of their earlier customs and taken on others more useful in Pannonia. Attila reached the height of his influence and power between 445 and 450 and turned his eyes enviously to the West.

Ambitions of Honoria, sister of Valentinian III, played directly into his plans. When her brother discovered a plot to overthrow him, he put her lover Eugenius to death and arranged a marriage with someone he knew would not assist her in her ambitions. She appealed to Attila in a manner which he construed as a proposal of marriage. Attila responded by addressing a letter to Emperor Theodosius II (408–450), who directed Valentinian to accede to Attila's demand for the hand of Honoria and half of the Western empire as dowry. Shortly thereafter, however, Theodosius died and his successor, Marcian, refused any longer to pay an annual tribute to the Huns. Consequently, Attila turned his war machine toward Gaul in 451. His forces included not just Huns but Gepids under Ardaric, Ostrogoths under their three chieftains (Walamir, Thiudemir, and Widimir), Rugians, Scirians, Heruls, Thuringians, Alans and others. Burgundians joined them when they reached the Rhine. The Romans and their allies—Salian Franks, Ripuarian Franks, Burgun-dians of Savoy, and Celts of Armorica—needed the help of the Goths under Theodoric to turn Attila and his forces back for Orleans; whether after a siege or not is uncertain. The allies overtook Atilla's army at Troyes. The battle proved costly to both sides, but it accelerated the departure of the Huns from Gaul. It also dealt a mortal blow to Attila's prestige. A year later, Attila, still demanding Honoria's hand, invaded Italy. He leveled Aquileia and seized Verona and Vicentia. Ticinum and Milan had to buy their way out of destruction. The way to Rome stood open, Aetius not able to muster enough of an army to halt the Huns' march. The savior of the city turned out to be Leo I, the bishop of Rome, whom the emperor sent along with two Roman senators to negotiate. Although considerations offered are unknown, Attila retreated without his bride. The main deterrent may have been a plague that broke out among his troops as an army sent by Emperor Marcian arrived from the East. Attila died a year later.

The Huns scattered after his death when the Gepids, Ostrogoths, Rugians, Heruls, and other vassals united to defeat the Huns at Nadao in 454. Some Huns remained in the West, but most fled to the regions north of the lower Danube. Emperor Marcian rewarded the Gepids by assigning control over all of Dacia, the Ostrogoths with settlements in northern Pannonia as *foederates* of the empire, the Rugians with new homes on the north banks of the Danube opposite Noricum as *foederates*, the Scirians and Heruls with territory farther east. From all of these the Romans drew heavily to keep the armies up to strength.

Roman Decline. During the next forty years, the power of the Romans steadily declined in the West while that of the Germanic peoples increased. In north Africa the Vandal kingdom lasted a century, until overwhelmed by the Byzantines under Justinian I. Gaiseric built up a fleet which regularly raided the coasts of Italy and prevented the Romans from offering effective resistance to Germanic peoples in Gaul and

Spain. Roman government itself fell to pieces. After the murder of Valentinian III in 455 a series of emperors held brief tenures. The real power behind the throne was the Suevian general Ricimer, who succeeded Stilicho and Aetius as defender of the empire. Because the legitimate imperial line ended with Valentinian, Ricimer became an emperor maker, of course, consulting with Emperor Leo I (457–474) in Constantinople. When he died in 472, he left a power vacuum filled a few years later by Odovacer, a Scirian or Rugian. Odovacer had become a Roman officer elevated virtually to the position of *magister militum*. Unlike Ricimer, he no longer wanted to prop up the weak emperors but to rule Italy under the imperial authority of Constantinople unhampered by a second emperor. The problem was, Constantinople had already appointed Julius Nepos (473–480). When Emperor Zeno declined to do more than bestow on him the title of Patricius, Odovacer accepted that title but claimed another, the title of king, thus giving himself the double office of imperial officer and German king. The death of Julius Nepos in 480 regularized his position further.

The Ostrogoths. Odovacer's independence prompted Zeno to seek a counterweight in the West through the Ostrogothic chieftain Theodoric. Born about the time of the battle of Nadao (454), Theodoric was sent as a boy to Constantinople, where he learned to appreciate Roman culture and institutions. Returning home in 470 or 471, he was elected King of the Ostrogoths. Immediately thereafter, his father Thiudemir and Theodoric led their people southwards into the Balkan peninsula and forced Emperor Leo to grant them new settlements in Macedonia. After eliminating another rival of the same name, in 483 Theodoric received the coveted title of *magister militum*. In that role, however, he quarreled with Zeno and marched on Constantinople. Realizing that the Ostrogoths would be a constant source of trouble, Zeno dispatched them to Italy to conquer and displace Odovacer. Theo-

doric started for Italy in 488 but did not reach it until August 489. Within a year, however, the Ostrogoths, with the help of the Visigoths, decisively defeated Odovacer. After a major victory on August 11, 490, the Roman Senate declared Theodoric master of Rome, Southern Italy, and Sicily. Although defeated three times, however, Odovacer still held out in Ravenna, necessitating a two-year siege by the Goths. Early in 493 the bishop of Ravenna negotiated a treaty in which the two principals agreed to rule Italy jointly, and Theodoric entered the city on March 5. Ten days later, he slew his rival on the allegation that he was plotting against him. His troops proceeded to massacre what remained of Odovacer's army. Theodoric's reign in Italy lasted until 526. During this long reign, Romans filled the office of consul but Goths the army. Theodoric himself evidently continued as *magister militum*. Goths were also excluded from the Roman Senate, although it had no political power. Theodoric served as deputy governor of the emperor. He could issue edicts, but he could not pass laws. He did continue to hold the title of kind assumed by Odovacer. Noted for tolerance, Theodoric sought to keep peace between Goths and Romans and other peoples living in his realm. He did, however, attempt to convert Jews to Christianity. Ten years after his death in 526, the control of Italy returned to the empire under Justinian. Both Vandals and Ostrogoths ceased to have corporate identity after the victory of Justinian in north Africa and in Italy.

The Visigoths. The Visigoths enjoyed their great day during the reign of Euric (466–484) in the kingdom of Toulouse. Euric expanded the Visigothic frontiers to the Loire and the Rhone rivers. He gained control of Arles and Marseilles. In 481 Odovacer conceded to him the whole of Provence. Under his leadership the Visigoths captured Aquitania Prima. They also ventured into Spain against the Suevi and eventually extended Visigothic sway over all of Roman Spain except a few places on the coast. Roman power in Gaul, however, had not ceased entirely. Aegidius, a native of Gaul, preserved some strongholds after succeeding Aetius as *magister militum* in 454.

The Franks. The European spotlight turned next on the Franks. The Franks did not enter this picture until 451 when the Salians sided with Rome against the Huns. Led by Childeric, they again aided the Romans at Orleans, where Aegidius defeated the Visigoths in 463 or 464, and at Angers against the Saxons. Childeric died in 481 and was succeeded by his son Clovis (481–511), greatest of the Merovingian kings and the one responsible for the Christianization of the Franks. Clovis succeeded his father in 481. His first major achievement was to defeat Syagrius, the representative of Emperor Zeno in the West after the death of Aegidius, at Soissons in 486. With this victory his power extended to the Seine. Subsequently he extended it to the Loire. From the point of view of Clovis's relations with Christianity, however, his marriage to Clotilda, niece of King Gundobad of Burgundy, held even greater importance, for it was she who was largely responsible for his conversion. In 496 the attack of the Alemanni on the Ripurian Franks gave Clovis the pretext he needed to attack them. His conquest opened the way for a march to the East.

Following his victory over the Alemanni, Clovis opted for the Catholic faith of his wife Clotilda, notwithstanding the Arian dominance among most of the neighboring barbarian peoples—Visigoths, Ostrogoths, and Burgundians. He evidently took this step because he sensed the enormous help he might receive from the Catholic Church, the one cohesive Western organization, and his victory over the Alemanni convinced him of the power of the Christian God. He probably received baptism in 496, either at Rheims or at Tours, a city he had recently captured from the Visigoths. At any rate, his conversion gave him a further reason for his continuing conquests. For a time the Ostrogothic king Theodoric preserved peace among the barbarians in the West, but in 507 Clovis launched an attack on the Visigoths near Poitiers, routing them and killing Alaric. He then sent his son Theodoric to subdue the entire Visigoth kingdom as far as Burgundy. He himself seized Alaric's treasure at Toulouse and transferred it to Bordeaux. His conquest united all of Gaul under the Franks except Septimania, Burgundy, Provence, and Armorica. Afterwards Clovis was soon elected king by the Ripuarian Franks. Emperor Anastasius I (491–518) recognized Clovis's kingdom as within and not outside the empire and, according to Gregory of Tours, conferred on him an honorary consulship. Clovis died in 511.

The Lombards. The next people to figure prominently in the barbarian migrations were the Lombards. Residing originally near the mouth of the Elbe between the East and West Germans, they migrated southwards during the second century into the areas now known as Austria and Hungary. Emperor Justinian (527–565) permitted the Lombards to enter the Roman provinces as *foederates* or allies. In 565, the year of Justinian's death, they united with the Avars in crushing the Gepids. Under Alboin they vacated Pannonia to the Avars and began their conquest of Italy with several allies, chiefly the Saxons. They never succeeded in conquering all of Italy, however. After the death of Alboin in 572 they remained chiefly in the north until the rule of Agilulf early in the seventh century. They expanded again about forty years later under Rothari. In the late seventh century they captured the heel of Italy. Meantime, the Roman Empire held onto territory in the northeast from Venice to the south of Ancona, in the center around Rome, and, in the south, Naples and the toe. Ravenna continued to function as the seat of government of the exarch, the imperial governor of Italy. Unlike earlier invaders, the Lombards entered without any pretense of alliance with the empire. They subsequently treated the Romans as "guests" in their kingdom in the class of freemen. They set up a system altogether independent of the Roman. The Code of Rothari exhibits no Roman influence, but considerable Christian influence. Issued in 643, it began, "In the name of the Lord. . . . " Rights of the churches appear in several, for instance, in prohibition of sacrilege. Under Liutprand the code underwent further modification between 713 and 735, manifesting growing Christian impact on the Lombards. The code identified Liutprand as "the most excellent Christian King of the Lombards." It elevated the status of women and slaves and deferred to the bishop of Rome in decisions about marriage.

Christians in the Barbarian Migrations

The migrations of peoples during this period obviously changed the situation of the Roman Empire and its people, including Christians, radically. It is well known that Christianity gradually won over the migrants. Although this may seem somewhat surprising, Christianity had several factors in its favor for doing exactly that. In his *History of the Expansion of Christianity*, Kenneth Scott Latourette listed four: First, the migrants admired Roman civilization and culture and took over many of its features, including Christianity. Second, the religions most of the invaders espoused offered feeble opposition to more advanced religions such as Christianity and, later, Islam. Third, Christianity had already accommodated itself to Greco-Roman culture in ways which would make it attractive and helpful to the barbarians, above all, in the battle against the powers of evil. In addition, Christianity contained within itself a powerful missionary vitality not dampened by the invasions. As Latourette points out, however, in this period "professional" missionaries figured far more prominently. Initially Arian Christianity dominated among the Goths and, through them, other barbarian peoples. Later on, thanks especially to the Franks, Nicene Christianity gained the ascendancy.

The effects of the barbarian migrations varied markedly from area to area. On the edges of the empire, where Christianity had not had opportunity to get deeply rooted, the invasions virtually obliterated the churches, necessitating reevangelization. The Romans had developed Pannonia (modern Hungary), Noricum (modern Switzerland and Austria), and Rhaetia (modern Bavaria) mainly to buffer the northern boundaries of the empire. In such places Christianity had to be brought back by missionary activity from the seventh century onwards. Christianity also nearly went out of existence in the Flemish plain (modern Holland) and the British Isles.

Closer to the center of the empire, the churches suffered less severely. In most of Gaul, for instance, the invasions disorganized the life of the churches, but they did not obliterate them. Modern ecclesiastical archaeology has turned up evidence of continuing Christian activities at Strassbourg, Treves or Mainz, and Xanten as well. Here it would be difficult to overestimate the importance of monastic communities and leaders who could negotiate with the barbarians.

The invasions had their least effect in some other areas where activities continued much as they had before the invasions. Families carried on as they had in the fourth century, not as in the heyday of the empire but in its diminishing years. They held steadfastly to their Christian heritage as an integral part of their cultural inheritance. In Italy the Ostrogoths conserved the Roman legacy when they conquered it (489–493). The Visigoths did much the same in South Gaul (413–507) and later in Spain. The Burgundians gained a reputation for gentleness. Even the Vandals left the western part of Africa unconquered, and while the region lapsed into barbarism, Christianity did not disappear. The Vandals envied Roman society and romanized. Few of the conquerors, as a matter of fact, escaped Christianization of some sort. The chief struggle had to do with brand of Christianity, Arian or Nicene. Arians attempted to impose the Arian faith, Nicenes the Nicene. The Vandal kings Genseric, Huneric, and Thrasamund rallied people to Arianism and fiercely persecuted dissenters. In Carthage, Genseric drove Quodvult-deus from his see and kept it vacant for twenty-four years (456–480). Such policies finally failed, however, increasing Catholic hostility and determination rather than diminishing it. Africans welcomed Byzantine troops under Belisarius as liberators in 533. Unfortunately the controversy as well as the invasions greatly weakened African Christianity. On the Catholic side, Clovis became the champion after his baptism, imposing the Catholic faith on the Visigoths in 507, the Burgundians in 532–534, and the Ostrogoths in 536.

Many bishops played significant roles in mediating with the invaders to avert far worse consequences than could have occurred. Although feats claimed for bishops have suffered from embellishment, some have the ring of truth. During the Visigothic invasion of Gaul under Wallia in 406, for instance, Exuperius played a major role in the defense of Toulouse as the invaders ravaged one city after another. Germanus, bishop of Auxerre (418–448), led a contingent of Britons threatened by a combined raid of Saxons and Celts from Scotland. His enthusiasm inspired them to victory.

In 451, as noted earlier, Leo I (440–461) served as an emissary to negotiate with Attila, though the latter's withdrawal probably was inspired by other pressures. The most effective protector was doubtless Severinus, the apostle of the Danube, whose devout life and miraculous powers awed the Rugians, Alemanni, Thuringians, Heruls, and other invaders of Noricum in the late fifth century. After spending some years as a monk in the East, he came to Noricum about 453 and established two monasteries. Although never consecrated a bishop, he gained the confidence of Odovacer. His influence at least tempered some of the cruelty of the invaders. The intercessions of Genevieve of Paris (422–502) were believed to have diverted the Huns from the city in 451.

The churches themselves offered places of sanctuary for the frightened citizens. Although the invaders did not always honor sanctuaries, most of the barbarians had undergone sufficient Christianization to respect Christian places and things. Gregory of Tours, for instance, recorded that, when Clovis defeated Syagrius at Soissons, Remigius of Rheims sent a plea that he preserve a beautiful vessel belonging to him. Clovis, not yet a convert, gave orders to save it, but one of his troops, declaring that the king should not have more than his legal share, smashed it to pieces. At this time Clovis did not retaliate. Later, however, when reviewing his troops, he found fault with this man's arms and threw one of them on the ground. As the soldier stooped over to retrieve it, Clovis smashed his head with an axe, saying, "So you did to the vessel of Soissons." A century later, the Lombard laws included some items on sanctuary in the churches.

Twilight in the West

Civilization diminished slowly as a consequence of the barbarian "invasions" and not suddenly as has often been assumed. Cities like Ravenna illustrate the continuance of art and architecture of commendable quality. The imperial residence from 402–404, Galla Placidia (423–450) chose it as her official residence. The Ostrogoth Theodoric and his successors made it the capital of Italy from 493 to 535. After 540 it came again under Byzantine rule. Rome, repeated sackings notwithstanding, still continued to build impressive churches and to furnish them with fine mosaics and frescoes under Popes Sixtus III (432–440) and Felix IV (526–530).

The Western churches went on with the task of evangelization. The fall of Rome in 410 revived oft-repeated charges that Christianity was responsible for the calamities because Christians had abandoned the gods who had made Rome great. Augustine spent thirteen years (413–426) writing his classic apology, *The City of God*, in response. Pope Gelasius had to protest the revival of the Lupercalia about 495, and pagans constantly threatened to revive past celebrations as popular anxieties mounted with new threats.

Much depended on leadership of dedicated clergy and monks. In Gaul outstanding bishops like Caesarius, bishop of Arles from 503–543, assisted in the transition. Caesarius exercised most of his ministry under Arian Gothic kings in a city and country where the population included Catholics, Arians, Jews, and pagans. In his sermons he addressed a wide array of people interested in the good life. He left no aspect of life untouched by his criticisms as superinspector. He urged memorization of the scriptures, their letters from heaven. He depicted life as a battle between Christ and the devil. Each person must decide which way to go. The Devil uses paganism to lure them away from Christ. Traps included ritual bathing on St. John's day, bacchanalian orgies among rural people, vows to trees, prayers to fountains, pagan alters and idols, women refusing to weave on Thursday because of deference to Jove, consultation with soothsayers and healers about omens—all customs well known in antiquity. Caesarius warned against taking drugs to have or not have children, buffoonery in daily life, and selfish use of money. He appealed to the charity of his flock. He expected to exercise a control over the lives of his people he could not have, but the Franks discerned accurately the importance of dealing with bishops like Caesarius. Bishops such as he forged Christian communities which Clovis and others could use as a basis for holding their kingdoms together. Their work, at any rate, supplied the foundation on which medieval Europe would be built.

Chapter 25

The Ongoing Task

Christianity had made great strides within the Roman Empire during the fourth century. The whole Mediterranean sphere covered by the Roman Empire had become Christian in name if not in fact. The church had organized by provinces and dioceses to assure that every nook and cranny would have some kind of Christian witness. Grand new edifices dotted the landscape once graced by pagan temples, statues, and other reminders of a devout religious past. Masses of people crowded into the churches and martyria and joined with enthusiasm in the worship of the cult which had survived centuries of intermittent persecution.

However significant this progress, nonetheless, in 400 C.E. much remained to be done to effect major changes in the lives of individuals and in the shape and character of a whole society. Perusal of the sermons or letters of John Chrysostom in the East or Augustine in the West will show that Christianity had not supplanted the old cultus or the oriental mysteries or the philosophical religion of the Roman people. It had registered its most noteworthy success in the cities, the target of its first mission efforts. Yet even there, the old religion held on in cities such as Rome, especially among the Roman aristocracy. The upper classes did not yield readily even to imperial pressures to convert to Christianity. In rural areas, moreover, paganism held on tenaciously during the next two centuries, for Bene-

dict of Nursia and Gregory the Great both complained about the remnants of it in Italy. The word pagan, as a matter of fact, derives from the Latin word *paganus* meaning "farmer." If the survival of ancient religious commitments did not cause enough problem in and of itself, the barbarian "invasions" confronted the church with an added challenge. Although most of the invaders had had exposure to some sort of Christianity, they knew it in the form of Arianism which, in some ways, suited better their polytheism, for Arianism implicitly gave encouragement to belief in multiple divine beings. Much of the mission task, therefore, focused on winning Arians to the Nicene faith of the Catholic Church.

The East Roman Empire

Already by the time of Constantine the vital center of the Roman Empire had shifted to the East. Constantine's removal of the capital to Byzantium simply took note of reality and gave in to the inevitable. Although the Romans continued some kind of nominal rule in the West, the empire itself existed in the East, and it was there that Christianity steadily embraced the entire body politic or was embraced by it. Since the East was more Greek than Roman, it is best to speak about the development of a hellenistic Christian society, for, as Werner Jaeger has artfully established, Christianity took on the form of Greek *paideia*.

With the exception of Julian (361–363) emperors after Constantine (d. 337) believed that God had entrusted to them the task of Christianizing the Roman Empire. Theodosius I (379–395) brought Constantine's vision of a Christian empire to a new level when, in 391, he ordered the Praetorian Prefect to prohibit all sacrifices and visiting of pagan holy places, declared marriage of Christians to Jews a form of adultery, and deprived apostates from Christianity of all honors and hereditary rank as well as the right of inheritance and of bequests of property. Theodosius's sons, Arcadius in the East (395–408) and Honorius in the West (393–423), were much less resolute than their father and ran into roadblocks. In the East Arcadius and Honorius renewed prohibition of ancient holidays in the calendar, proscribed the visiting of temples and the celebration of sacrifices, withdrew privileges enjoyed by pagan priests, and ordered destruction of temples still standing in rural areas.

In the West Honorius, still very young, had to yield to Stilicho, the Vandal who headed the army and who became his father-in-law. Although Stilicho did not rescind statutes against paganism, he treated them lightly. The Roman aristocracy, led by the Senator Symmachus, held out strongly for the old religion and blamed Christianity for the fall of Rome. Stilicho permitted pagan gatherings and the continuance of temples in Africa. He did, however, burn the Sibylline books. In 410 Rome fell into the hands of Alaric and the Goths. Alaric, although professing Christian faith, set up Attalus as a rival to Honorius for a time, but he soon withdrew support, opening the way for the demise of pagan political power in Italy. After Stilicho was executed in 408, Honorius stiffened the policies of the government in the West. He ordered the income of pagan temples devoted to the army, remaining images destroyed, the temples devoted to public purposes, pagans excluded from civil offices and the army. Had it not been for the barbarian migrations, Christianity might have had the same success in the West that it did in the East.

Bishops deserve credit for the zeal with which their flocks sought to make Christianity the sole religion of the empire. In the East John Chrysostom, bishop of Constantinople from 398 to 404, constantly urged his people to live lives of such commendable piety that others would want to imitate them by becoming Christian. He discouraged the use of coercion. If Christians lived like they should, they would not have to force conversions. In sermons addressed to members of his flock in Antioch, however, he overstated the Christian case *Against the Jews* in ways that laid the foundation for persecution in later centuries. Like most others of this period, he was caught up in a mass movement to victory and did not see where boundaries needed to be set. Without such zeal, however, it is hard to explain how Christianity could have won the East Roman Empire as it did.

Persistence of legislation against paganism as late as Justinian (527–565) demonstrates that the old cults had not ceased by that time. Although authorities registered greater concern about heretical Christian groups, they could not ignore the pull of paganism. Legislation of this period forbade bequests for maintenance of pagan cults, prescribed the death penalty for baptized Christians engaging in pagan rites, ordered pagans to go to churches for instruction, exiled and confiscated the property of those who refused baptism, required baptism of pagan children, and confiscated property of pagans who had received baptism in order to serve in the army but had made no effort to convert their families. Such strong legislation, requiring baptism of all adherents of the old cults, confirms that the battle for religious commitment remained vigorous. As Justinian directed his energies to the imposition of uniformity of belief, he made a virtue of intolerance. Christianity did not persecute pagans as severely as the latter had persecuted Christians in the first three centuries, but persecution did occur. In the main Christian violence toward competing cults took the form of destruction of temples and idols or, in the case of Jews, synagogues, and repressive legislation.

The West Roman Empire

Although the same legislation applied to both East and West, the winning of the West Roman Empire proved far more difficult than the winning of the East. During the career of Ambrose as bishop of Milan (373–397), four types of pagan religion still exerted appeal: the traditional public religion, the animism prevalent in rural areas, the mystery religions, and Neoplatonism as the religion of the educated. Although it is debatable how strong the appeal of the old state cultus was generally, the Roman Senate kept it alive. The Pontifical College still carried on as it had in the past. The Vestal Virgins still occupied their place at the foot of the Palatine. The temples still stood open to the public and performed their customary sacrifices to the gods. Many pagan festivals still went on as usual. Statues of the Olympian and other gods dotted the Forum. The Romans, convinced that Rome had become great not merely because of the gods but because of their *devotion* to the gods, did not surrender the ancient worship easily.

The strength of the old religion became quite manifest in the battle three distinguished Roman nobles—Praetextatus, Symmachus, and Flavian—fought to save the Altar of Victory in the Senate House. Toward the end of 382 Emperor Gratian issued a strong edict confiscating revenues allocated by the Senate for the maintenance of sacrifices and ceremonies, diverting monies paid to the Vestal Virgins to the State Post, appropriating lands bequeathed to the Vestals and the priests by the Treasury, and abolishing all exemptions from public burdens previously enjoyed by pagan religious functionaries. Subsequently, in a second edict, he ordered removal of the Altar of Victory from the Senate. The Pagan Party promptly rallied private maintenance for the traditional reli-

gion. Symmachus led a deputation to the emperor petitioning for a repeal of the decrees. Thanks to a strong letter from Ambrose and a counterpetition from a minority of Christian senators, Gratian refused Symmachus and his party a hearing. When Gratian was murdered in 383, the pagan party revived their hopes again. In the summer of 384 Symmachus presented a brilliant "Memorial" pleading for a return of the Altar of Victory and "the restoration of that condition of religion under which the State has so long prospered." He argued so forcefully that even Christians wavered. This time, Ambrose pulled out all the stops to prevent the thirteen year old Emperor Valentinian II from granting the petition. If Valentinian granted Symmachus's petition, he would wrong God, his father, and his murdered brother, Gratian. The emperor yielded to his pastor's pleas. Subsequently Ambrose wrote a point by point refutation of the "Memorial." The Altar of Victory did not return to the Senate and the priests and Vestal Virgins did not regain their privileges.

The old religion held on still more tenaciously in small towns and rural areas usually untouched by authorities. The tenaciousness of the old in such areas was clearly manifest in Africa during Augustine's day. June 1, 408, Honorius issued stern edicts intended to eliminate the last vestiges of the old religion. Shortly afterwards, as reported by Augustine, the citizens of Calama held a pagan festival "without interference from anyone." Pagan dancers paraded in front of the church right up to the door and, when the clergy tried to stop the performance, stoned the church. A week later, after the bishop of Calama had informed authorities about the violation of the imperial edicts, pagans stoned the church a second time. The next day, they struck again, this time not only stoning the church but setting it afire and killing one of the clergy. For hours, from four p.m. until late at night, the mob raged, forcing the bishop to hide to save his life. None of the authorities intervened. The only person who offered Christians help was a stranger. When Augustine himself went to Calama, he had little success in securing amendment or conversion. As a matter of fact, a former official named Nectarius wrote to Augustine to entreat him to intercede for the offenders whom he thought the authorities punished too severely (Augustine, *Ep.* 90). Eight months later, not convinced by the bishop of Hippo's response, he wrote again to protest the penalty (*Ep.* 103).

The task of evangelizing the western part of the empire was complicated immensely by the barbarian invasions, as Augustine's career attests quite well. Himself a convert from Manichaeism, a dualistic sect with strong appeal in North Africa, Augustine took the same strong stand against paganism his mentor Ambrose of Milan had. Although early in his career as bishop of Hippo he had opposed the use of coercion, he discovered in the case of the Donatists that force worked; consequently, after about 406 he favored it as the means of Christianizing the empire, specifically the portion over which he himself had special responsibility. In his response to the pleas of Nectarius of Calama he made light of any effort to defend the old religion. How could one argue the morality of the old when it painted, carved, wrote, danced, and sang of Jupiter's adulteries? If Nectarius really wanted to help his fatherland, as he claimed, then he would let people "be converted to the worship of the true God and to a chaste and religious life." Christians, after all, had acted with mildness. He, as bishop, had always tried to prevent too severe a penalty. He strove to obtain pardon not only for Christians' sins but for those of others, but pardon cannot be obtained without amendment of life, and amendment can come only by conversion.

The sacking of Rome by the Goths led by Alaric in 410 complicated the Christian apologetic task. Christians had been arguing the superiority of the Christian religion on the basis of victories it secured. The fall of Rome, the Eternal City, proved what many pagans and reluctant

converts to Christianity had suspected all along. Abandonment of devotion to the gods who had made Rome great had caused earthquakes, floods, and other disasters. Now it brought the worst of all disasters, the fall of Rome. And on the heels of this came the Vandal invasion of North Africa. In 413 Augustine began what many consider his greatest work, *The City of God*, in response to this charge. In 417 he urged Paulus Orosius, a native of Braga in Spain who had migrated to Africa ahead of the Vandals, to write his *Seven Books Against the Pagans*. In *The City of God*, completed in 426, Augustine first reviewed history to show that the world had not gotten worse because of the advent of Christianity. The fact that the Goths were Christians had caused them to mitigate the harsh treatment barbarians meted out in pre-Christian times. Contrary to what pagans thought, moreover, Rome had not become great because of the gods. Its expansion had occurred through the use of brute force. The gods had often proven impotent, for instance, to prevent the sack of Troy. It is the true God who determines who will win and who will lose. Here an eternal struggle has existed between the earthly and the heavenly cities.

The Vandals were laying siege to Hippo during the last months of Augustine's life (d. 430). The Donatist schism had weakened Christianity in North Africa, and many Donatists evidently joined the Arian Vandals against Catholics. The Vandals expropriated Catholic churches, exiled clergy and lay leaders, and sentenced some bishops to hard labor in the interior. Not until Belisarius, the Byzantine general, recaptured North Africa in 533 and 534 could Catholics again relax. Thereafter, Catholics proceeded to apply repressive measures against Arians and Donatists. Christianity made some progress among the native Berbers, but it must not have had a firm grip, for it disappeared when Islam swept across North Africa early in the seventh century.

In parts of Italy the old religion still remained vital during the fifth and sixth centuries.

Despite Ambrose's effective work in the provinces of Aemilia and Liguria, many educated persons still honored the old gods in Turin during the fifth century. According to Maximus of Turin (d. 408–423), moreover, paganism dominated the surrounding countryside. When Benedict of Nursia went to Monte Cassino around 529, he found a temple to Apollo with its statue and altar on which people still placed their offerings. Gregory the Great complained that paganism survived in Sicily, Sardinia, and Corsica at the end of the sixth century. Arianism, however, posed a more serious challenge than the remnants of a dying paganism.

In Spain the Synod of Toledo in 589 lamented growing idolatry. As in Italy, however, Arianism offered more competition. The Suevi converted from paganism to Catholicism and then to Arianism. The Visigoths were Arians. Usually tolerant of Catholics, in 580 King Leovigild convened a council at Toledo and persuaded it to convert Catholics, accepting them without rebaptism. A year before, his son, Hermenegild, married a Catholic wife and converted, but he was killed in an insurrection against his father supported by Spanish-Romans. Under another son, Recared, Catholicism triumphed. In 589 Recared declared himself a Catholic. Eight Arian bishops, many Arian priests, and a number of nobles followed in his train. Others, however, refused and rebelled. Although Recared succeeded in suppressing the opposition, his successor died in an Arian rebellion.

In Gaul Christianity had taken huge strides during the fourth century, especially in the cities. Martin of Tours (d. 397) contributed significantly. So too did other bishops such as Victricius of Rouen (ca. 330–ca. 407), like Martin a former soldier. In the late fourth and early fifth centuries prominent members of the Gallo-Roman upper classes entered the church and advanced its cause. Among the most eminent was Paulinus (353/4–431), who became bishop of Nola in 409. Born into a noble and wealthy family of Bor-

deaux, he received a good education. After a brief public career and a few years of leisure, he received baptism at the hands of Elphinus, bishop of Bordeaux, in 390 and, with his Spanish wife Therasia, took up the ascetic and contemplative life and began to distribute his fortune to the church and the poor. Ordained a priest at Barcelona in 394, he and his wife founded a home for monks and the poor at Nola and lived lives of great austerity. He corresponded with some of the most eminent churchmen of his day—Martin of Tours, Ambrose, Augustine, and Pope Anastasius I—and is ranked alongside Prudentius as one of the foremost Christian poets of the patristic period.

Thanks to the organized effort of Martin of Tours, Victricius, Paulinus, and others, Christianity reached into the countryside of Gaul, where the invasion by barbarians had less impact than it did in the cities. Attila and the Huns left great devastation when they swept through Gaul early in the fifth century. Although Romanized, other barbarians did the same. Nonetheless, Christianity survived. Some bishops courageously rallied their flocks. Lupus held the see of Troyes together for more than fifty years (427–479). Sidonius Apollinaris (ca. 423–ca. 480), a member of an aristocratic family of Lyons and son-in-law of Emperor Avitus (455–456), was elected bishop of Clermont in 469, probably while still a layperson, to protect the city against the Goths. He exerted himself strenuously but unsuccessfully to avert the occupation of Clermont by the Visigoths under Euric in 475. After a period of imprisonment he returned to his episcopate, where he spent the last few years of his life writing letters. Despite the disruption, the conversion of Gaul continued. In the mid-fifth century a synod at Arles labeled bishops neglectful if they had not stamped out worship of idols in their territory and legislated penalties for landowners who permitted idolatry on their lands.

Although the barbarian invasions disrupted the churches in Gaul as they did other aspects of civilization, they did not obliterate it. Monasteries such as that at Lérins survived and produced a succession of notable bishops for churches throughout southern Gaul. These included Honoratus (ca. 350–429) and Hilary (403–449), Archbishops of Arles; Maximus (d. 405/423) and Faustus (ca. 408–ca. 490), bishops of Riez; Eucherius (d. ca. 449), bishop of Lyon; and Caesarius (ca. 470–542), Archbishop of Arles. In many parts of Gaul Arian Christianity dominated with the entry of the Goths. Burgundians who moved south of the Rhine adopted the Catholic faith which they found in that area, but they then converted to Arianism. The Franks under Clovis (ca. 466–511), however, chose the Catholic faith and helped to expand it throughout Gaul by the sword. If Gregory of Tours (ca. 540–594) reported accurately, however, the level of Gallic Christianity at the end of the sixth century (591) had fallen rather low. What helped it was an infusion of new blood with the migration of the Celtic peoples from southwest Britain to Armorica. The immigrants brought with them the more disciplined Christianity of the British Isles and Celtic monasticism.

The British Isles

Evidence of Christianity prior to the Anglo-Saxon invasion of the British Isles is slim. By the end of the fourth century many leading families in Roman Britain had accepted Christianity. According to Theodoret, Christianity in the Isles was Catholic. Most likely, the source of it was Gaul. In 429 two Gallic bishops, Germanus of Auxerre and Lupus of Troyes went to Britain to dampen the influence of Pelagianism. There Germanus preached to considerable crowds in churches and elsewhere. Although Christianity spread rapidly throughout the islands during the fifth century, the Angles and Saxons began to establish permanent settlements and virtually to obliterate all traces of it in the east during the last half of the century. The churches survived in the western part into which the invaders did not penetrate. From the west, especially from Ireland, emerged a powerful impetus for the winning of the Anglo-Saxons and the reevangelization of the continent.

A major figure in the survival and spread of Christianity was Patrick (ca. 390–ca. 460), "the Apostle of Ireland." Born in Britain and reared as a Christian, Patrick was captured at age sixteen by Celtic pirates and spent six years as a pig herdsman in a district of Ireland called Tirawley. He escaped and made his way to the southeast coast of Ireland where he persuaded sailors to give him passage to Gaul, where he spent some time in the monastery at Lérins founded shortly before by Honoratus. Returning to his family, he dedicated himself to the church. He undertook training for the ministry, however, at Auxerre in Gaul, from whence he was sent to Ireland, where he spent the rest of his life as a kind of itinerant bishop evangelizing local chieftains, educating their children, ordaining clergy, and establishing monasteries for men and women. What his relationship was to a certain Palladius ordained around 431 by Pope Celestine I (422–432) "for the Scots believing in Christ" and sent "as the first bishop" is uncertain, but he made a lasting mark on Christianity in Ireland during a career extending about thirty years.

Another person of major importance for the evangelization of the British Isles was Ninian (ca. 360–ca. 432). Son of a converted chieftain of the Cumbrian Britons, Ninian received instruction in Rome as a youth. Consecrated a bishop in 394, probably by Siricius I (385–399), he returned to Scotland by way of Tours, where he met Martin, to whom he dedicated the church he founded at Whithorn called Candida Casa. The latter became a center from which Ninian and his monks set out to convert the Britons and Picts and a seat of training for Welsh and Irish missionaries.

Celtic Christianity had a quite different character than that found on the continent during this period. It lacked territorial organization under diocesan bishops and featured a strongly monastic character. Bishops often played subordinate roles to abbots. Celtic Christianity also differed from Roman in such customs as the date of celebrating Easter and the form of the tonsure. In the sixth century Irish monasteries had a reputation for scholarship and religious vitality. Around them developed a Christian celtic culture which they carried to other peoples.

The most famous and influential of the Irish missionaries was Columban (ca. 543–615). Born about 543 in southeast Ireland, now Leinster County, and reared by a devout mother, Columban heard early on the call to an ascetic life and, despite his mother's pleas, left home to pursue it. After studying scriptures with a certain Sinell, he entered the monastic community of Bangor in Ulster County. Several years later, around 590, he led a band of twelve to Brittany and into Merovingian territory. Eventually he and his companions took up residence in a ruined castle at Annegray in the Vosges. The attraction of many to the community forced Columban to find another place for a monastery, a former fort, Luxeuil. Still expanding, the monastery established another at Fontaines. Columban's monasteries followed a rule much more severe than Benedict's. The rule called for absolute obedience to the head of the monastery, as much silence as possible, a minimum of food, early rising, and more rigorous penance for sins. The alien character of this form of Christianity aroused strong opposition. Columban had to defend himself before a Gallican synod in 603 and at Rome. Although the bishops did not close the monastery, Columban aroused the hostility of Brunhilda, grandmother of the Burgundian King Theuderich in whose territory he resided. Theuderich proceeded to force his deportation in 610. The monks began work at Bregenz on Lake Constance among the Alemanni, but in 612 the Burgundian king extended his dominions to that area also and forced further migration. Columban and his followers then settled in Bobbio, Italy, where they established a community noted for its learning. Columban died in 615.

Although forced out of Gaul, Columban's stern monasticism made a deep impression on the Merovingian lands in the way of Christian ideals. Eventually the custom of imposing specific penances for individual sins became a part of accepted Gallic practice. From the point of view of Christian missions the boost Columban's monasteries gave to evangelization was of still greater importance. From Luxeuil missionaries proceeded northwards. Most famous of his companions was Gall, whose name was given to the town near the head of Lake Zürich where he worked with zeal in destroying pagan idols.

Ireland sent numerous other *peregrini* besides Columban to carry out the evangelization of Europe. Another seminal figure was Columba (ca. 521–ca. 597), founder of a kind of missionary training center on the island of Iona. Born in Donegal, Ireland, in 521 of royal parentage, Columba received his early education under a Bishop Finnio. Early on, he dedicated his life to a monastic vocation. Although ordained a priest, he never was appointed a bishop. In 562 or 563 he took twelve companions to Iona, where they built a monastery in which they could train missionaries. From Iona Columba ventured many times into Scotland as a missionary to non-Christians, witnessing and winning Picts, Druids, and others. Although Ninian and Kentigern (d. 603) may have won over many of the Picts and Scots in the period preceding, contemporary evidence seems to indicate that Columba had plenty to do.

The Barbarians

The evangelization of the Germanic peoples immigrating into the empire has been mentioned numerous times already in discussing the winning of the Roman Empire. The fact is, it proceeded in somewhat the same gradual way the invasions themselves occurred. Since most of the barbarians admired Roman culture, they tended to take over all things Roman, including religion, but they did not assimilate either culture or religion without adapting it to their own needs and outlook. Barbarians recruited for the Roman army took over the faith which dominated the army, but, at the same time, they changed it. Thence, there remained a considerable task of deepening and strengthening the understanding of Christianity.

The first of the invaders to adopt the Christian faith in considerable numbers were the Goths. Some of the Goths opted for the Catholic faith first, for, according to Socrates, one Gothic bishop attended the Council of Nicaea. Augustine reported persecution of Gothic Catholics, and John Chrysostom strove hard to win converts among the Goths, consecrating a bishop to send to them. Other Goths became Audians. The Audians formed a separate rigorous sect in Syria led by Audius, a person of commendable piety but questionable theological views. Constantine banished them to Scythia. During the mid-fourth century, Audius won many converts among the Goths, but the latter suffered severe persecution at the hands of the pagan Goths about 370. Most Goths, however, became Arians as a result of the extraordinary mission work of Ulfilas (ca. 311–383). During Ulfilas's lifetime, the Christian Goths suffered severe persecution at the hands of Athanaric, a native chieftain, evidently in revenge for mistreatment by the Romans. Another chieftain, Frithigern, solicited Roman help and defeated Athanaric and then adopted Christianity, the faith of the Romans, which at the time was Arian in the court of Constantius II. When harassed by the Huns, Frithigern and his followers obtained permission to cross the Danube. A dispute erupted between this mass of settlers and the peoples of the area and led to a conflict. The Goths defeated imperial forces at the battle of Adrianople in 378. Nevertheless, they seem to have passed on their faith to the Ostrogoths, Gepids, and Vandals, although evidence on this is conflicting.

As strong as Arianism was among the Goths, it did not have an equally strong chance of winning the battle of faiths even in the West. The majority of Westerners were Catholics. The Catholic Church had far stronger organization which even the invaders admired. Gothic rulers, moreover, were not as intense in their loyalty to the Arian faith as were Catholic rulers. Not many of them at any rate, persecuted. With the conversion of Recared in Spain in 589 the last of the Gothic Arians officially went over to the Catholic faith. The Franks soon assured the triumph of the Catholic faith over Arianism in the heart of Europe.

Outside the Empire

Christianity continued to spread not merely within the Roman Empire but beyond its boundaries as well during the fifth and sixth centuries. As a matter of fact, the chief factor in slowing or halting its advance to the East was the rise of Islam in 622. Nestorian Christianity came to dominate the church in the Persian empire toward the close of the fifth century. Monophysite Christianity spread rapidly in the East during the sixth.

In *Armenia*, the first nation officially to adopt Christianity, the instruction of the populace in Christian faith continued steadily throughout the fourth century. The Bible was translated into Armenian near the end of the fourth or beginning of the fifth centuries. Under Nerses (d. ca. 373), the sixth Catholicos of the Armenian church, a reform took place deepening the Christian impact on the country. In the fifth century, however, Armenia fell under control of the Persian empire. Although Persian rulers at first seemed satisfied to interfere in and control church affairs, later they propagated Zoroastrianism and persecuted Christianity as a hereditary enemy. The persecution did not let up until near the end of the century.

In *Georgia* Christianity arrived late in the third or early in the fourth century. As in Armenia, Georgian Christianity also suffered from Persian dominance after making steady progress during the fourth century. In the second half of the fifth century, however, Vakhtang I (446–499), drove the Persians out, purged the country of Zoroastrianism, built churches, and established bishoprics. Whereas Armenian Christianity chose the Monophysite tradition, Georgians remained Chalcedonian except for a brief period during the sixth century. Originally dependent on the patriarchate of Antioch, the Georgian church became autocephalous during the eighth century.

In the *Persian Empire*, as indicated in an earlier chapter, Christians became suspect when Constantine adopted Christianity as the religion of the Roman Empire and tried to obtain favorable standing for Christians in Persia. With strong centers in Edessa and Adiabene Christianity extended itself throughout the Mesopotamian area over which the Persians extended their control. During the fifth century, Christians carried the faith to the east of the Tigris-Euphrates valley. Severe persecution in Persia lasted throughout the long reign of Sapor II (310–379) but subsided under Sapor III (383–388), Bahram IV (388–399), and Yazdegerd I (399–420). The change of policy opened the way for the conversion of prominent nobles. In 410 Christians formed a national organization headed by the bishop of the capital city Seleucia-Ctesiphon, who received state recognition. The Catholicos was made responsible for the behavior of the people. The state tolerated Christianity and gave it a certain national recognition which tempered suspicions, although it did not prevent occasional persecution. After the condemnation of Nestorius a strong Nestorian tradition developed at Edessa under leadership of Ibas. Following the Council of Chalcedon in 451, harassment and persecution caused many Nestorians to migrate to Persia, where a school at Nisibis gradually supplanted the one at Edessa as a Nestorian center. Several Persian rulers from the mid-fifth century on, especially Peroz (457–484), actively supported them. Severance of ties with the Roman Empire after their expulsion from Edessa by the emperor Zeno in 489 helped to improve their situation in Persia. The Nestorian church distinguished itself

from the early sixth century on by its mission work in Arabia, India, and east Asia.

How early Christianity arrived in *India* is uncertain, but the evidence for it is strong by the end of the fifth century. Cosmas Indicopleustes reported in the middle of the sixth century the existence of Christians on what is thought to have been Ceylon, in Inner India, in Male, and in Kallina, the last two probably on the west coast of India. Christians in Kallina, he said, were led by a bishop consecrated in Persia. Commercial contacts with India could have led to the planting of Christianity in a number of locations and from southern Arabia as well as Persia.

Evidence for Christianity in *Arabia* is fragmentary but more definite than that for India. By 500 Christianity spread itself widely, coming chiefly from the Roman Empire and Mesopotamia through merchants, officials, professional missionaries, and hermits who sought refuge in the deserts of northern Arabia. It owed much also to contacts with Abyssinia or Ethiopia. Although the emergence of Islam put a stop to Christian expansion in the area, the ruler of Hira, southwest of Babylon near the Arabian edge of Mesopotamia, may have been a Christian in the last part of the sixth century. Cosmas Indicopleustes reported the presence of Christians in Arabia Felix and among the "Homerites" (Himyarites?).

Christianity also spread extensively to the north of Persia, east of the Caspian Sea and west and east of the Oxus River. although it never had great strength in the area, *Merv* had a bishop from 334 through the fifth and sixth centuries and a metropolitan in the sixth, tenth and eleventh centuries. *Herat* had a bishop in the sixth century. Christians existed among the *Hephthalite Huns and Turks* toward the close of the fifth century.

In summary, Christianity continued its vital mission thrust during the fifth and sixth centuries. Within the Roman Empire a now highly organized church continued the task of converting the unconverted. Although vestiges of the old religious cults and practices remained throughout the period, the appeal of the old diminished as imperial legislation increasingly worked in the church's favor against competitors. The countryside yielded last. As this process continued, however, the barbarian invasions posed a new challenge not so much to conversion to Christianity as to which brand, Arian or Orthodox. Since most barbarians had been exposed first to Arianism, the Catholic Church, especially in the West, had to work hard to gain the upper hand in areas colonized by those of Arian persuasion. In this instance greater zeal for Nicene orthodoxy worked in its favor as it won first one and then another of the barbarian leaders. A tragic sidelight of Christianity's success was growth of intolerance toward pagans, Jews, and other Christians which would result in violence as a style of mission which reached its consummation in the crusades of the Middle Ages.

The connection of Christianity with the Roman Empire doubtless aided it immensely in winning the barbarians, most of whom envied Roman culture. Although the invaders often wreaked havoc on the cities and peoples they conquered, they absorbed much of the culture and with it the religion. In consequence, Christianity not only survived the transition from Roman to barbarian, it gained from it. In some other areas, however, the Roman connection proved a disadvantage for Christianity. In Persia, for instance, it resulted for a time in fierce persecution. In many areas of the East it perhaps gave an alien cast which impeded evangelization. Yet even in these Christianity planted its seed and saw plants sprout and grow. Few areas bordering on the land of Christianity's birth were lacking a Christian witness by the year 600.

Chapter 26

Solitude the Rage

During the fifth and sixth centuries, the contemplative life became the rage in both East and West. Husbands and wives, sometimes entire families, and the best and brightest youth took up the ascetic way as the ideal philosophical/religious life. The reasons for the popularity of the monastic vocation would have differed in the two areas. In the East monasticism rode the wave set in motion during the preceding century first in the form of hermitic and then in that of coenobitic solitude. Although both types remained vital, Basil of Caesarea assured the triumph of the coenobitic type and, with his Rule, corralled the monastic movement for the institutional church. Monasteries dotted the landscape. So many developed in cities such as Constantinople and Antioch that some emperors went on the attack to disperse them. The monks, however, won the battle and played significant roles in the theological controversies which racked the Eastern churches during these two centuries and in the iconoclastic controversy in later centuries.

In the West monasticism, carried westward by several routes, started late but caught fire immediately in an age of extreme cultural disruption brought on by the barbarian invasions. People witnessing the end of civilization as they had known it found in the hermitic or coenobitic life a means of survival. The contemplative way conditioned them for repeated shock waves and prepared them for death. The nobility in Italy, Gaul, Ireland, and elsewhere got caught up in a movement of detachment from this world and contemplation of the world to come. In Ireland a more disciplined monasticism emphasizing *peregrinatio*, exile, ignited a movement for the evangelization of the British Isles and the continent of Europe. Monks and monasteries took on an immensely important social role as kings and princes, especially in Merovigian Gaul after the conversion of Clovis (ca. 496), promoted and used them not only to Christianize their realms but to effect order.

The East

Eastern monachism had reached maturity by about 400 and underwent little significant change thereafter. Some extreme forms of hermitism still existed, especially in Syria. The Boskoi grazed like cattle. Dendrites lived in trees. Catenati loaded themselves with chains to prove the triumph of mind over body. The Stylites erected pillars and raised them higher and higher toward heaven. First and most famous of the Stylites was Simeon (ca. 390–459) who was also a catenatus. Born on the Syrian border of Cilicia, he first lived the life of an anchorite in the monastery of Eusebona (between Antioch and Aleppo) and then at Telanissos, which was nearby. After several years he built a pillar and gradually raised it to a heighth of sixty feet. There he lived more than thirty years, fascinating admirers with athletic feats such as standing all night motionless with his hands raised upward to heaven or touching his forehead with his feet 1,244 times in succession. He attracted a stream of pilgrims and inspired many imitators. According to his admiring biographer, he exerted much influence—converting pagans, advising kings and princes, reconciling enemies, and upholding the cause of Chalcedon.

Thanks to the influence of Basil of Caesarea's Rule, drafted in two forms between 358 and 364, the majority of monks in the East opted for the communal (coenobite) style of monasticism. Drawn from the Pachomian pattern in Egypt, the Rule eliminated many of the extremes of hermitic monasticism, although it was still severe. It put asceticism to work in communal obedience. It established set hours for liturgical prayer, manual labor, and other tasks and imposed the rule of poverty and chastity similar to that adopted later in the West. Basil's Rule also arranged for education of children and for care of the indigent in connection with the monastery.

Lauras (converts) sprang up in great numbers all over the Byzantine world. In Egypt, the cradle of monasticism, strong communities composed of hundreds of monks—both men and women—continued at Nitria, Scetis, Oxyrhynchus, Faou, Tabennesis, and Thebes. The Gnostic library uncovered in the 1940's belonged to a monastery at Chenoboskion or Nag Hammadi.

Near what was thought to have been the location of Mount Sinai, monks formed a community at Wadi Faran, an oasis well supplied with water. Faran was an episcopal see in the fourth century. About 389 Etheria found a considerable number of men and a church at the foot of Jebel Musa on what they thought to be the site of the Burning Bush. In the sixth century some of these monks appealed to Emperor Justinian (527–565) for protection against Bedouin tribes. Always interested in securing the boundaries of his empire, the emperor erected the cloister which still stands there and sent troops to protect it. In the tenth or eleventh century the relics of St. Catherine, an Alexandrian saint martyred early in the fourth century, were brought to the monastery and her name attached to it.

In Palestine monasteries continued to spring up near many of the holy sites. The two monasteries erected by the Roman matron Paula (347–404) continued under the direction of her daughter Eustochium (370–ca. 419) and then her granddaughter Paula (d. 439) at Bethlehem. Sabas (439–532), a native of Mutalaska in Cappadocia, founded a large laura (the present Mar Saba) in 478 in the desolate Wadi en-Nar between Jerusalem and the Dead Sea. In 492 the patriarch of Jerusalem made him superior of all the hermits in Palestine.

The monastic life had great appeal in the East. The diocese of Constantinople had sixty-eight and that of Chalcedon forty monasteries during Justinian's day. The power of the monks and their independence troubled the Byzantine emperors. The Arian emperor Constantius (337–361) burned monasteries and monks in Egypt who persisted in support of Athanasius. Valens (364–378), also an Arian, massacred monks at Nitria, where they numbered 5,000, and sent others to the mines. In 376 John Chrysostom wrote his passionate defense of monasticism *Against the Adversaries of Monastic Life*. In 390 Valentinian II (383–392), alarmed at the increase of monastic influence, decreed that all monks should leave towns and go to the desert. Theodosius I (379–395), however, canceled the order.

Independence of monks must also have troubled bishops during the fifth and sixth century theological controversies. Egyptian monks favored the doctrine of one nature in Christ (monophysitism), monks of Palestine and Constantinople that of two natures (dyophysitism). As proposed by Emperor Marcian (450–457), a Chalcedonian, the Council of Chalcedon ruled that monasteries were not to be built thenceforth without approval of the bishop of a diocese and that monks, whether in town or country, should submit to episcopal authority under penalty of excommunication. Monks, however, must not haven taken the decrees too seriously because later councils had to reiterate the threat.

Eastern monasticism paid a high price for its involvement in theological controversy. One of the earliest in which they took part was the controversy over Origen's teaching. Origen had stout defenders in the fourth century—Pamphilus, Athanasius, Basil of Caesarea, Gregory of Nazianzus, and Didymus the Blind. Jerome belonged in the Origenist camp until 395, when Epiphanius, the chief anti-Origenist, visited Jerusalem and attempted to obtain a condemnation from John of Jerusalem. The controversy flamed so high in Egypt that the Origenists had to flee to Constantinople to take refuge with John Chrysostom. It flared again during the sixth century, when monks of the New Laura, near Jerusalem, propagated Origen's views again. Palestinian opponents stirred controversy anew. Justinian convened a council at Constantinople in 543 which condemned a long list of Origen's "errors." Origenist monks split into two factions. The continuing controversy led to a final condemnation of Origen's teaching at the Council of Constantinople in 553.

Monks played a role in the condemnation of Nestorius at the Council of Ephesus (431–433) and at Chalcedon (451). When he became patriarch of Constantinople in 428 Nestorius disputed the term "Mother of God" (*theotokos*) as applied to Mary. The extreme reverence in which monks held Mary led immediately to attacks on Nestorius. Their substantial numbers carried great weight, and they readily enlisted the support of the patriarch of Alexandria, Cyril (412–444), always ready to recoup some prestige lost to upstart Constantinople.

The West

The savaging of Rome early in the fifth century resulted in the relocation of the center of Western monasticism. Many fled to Africa and to Palestine ahead of the Goths and Vandals. When Melania the Elder fled Rome in 408, her daughter, Albina, her granddaughter, Melania the Younger, and her husband, Pinian, accompanied her on her flight from Italy. The wealthy ascetic couple founded two monasteries at Tagaste, Augustine's home town, where they remained for seven years. Later they entered convents at Bethlehem founded by Paula and Eustochium. After Pinian's death in 431 Melania the Younger founded another monastery on the Mount of Olives.

In the West monasticism found stout defenders and promoters in Ambrose (ca. 339–397) and Augustine (354–430). Ambrose lauded monastic self-denial and supported a monastery on the outskirts of Milan. At the request of his sister Marcellina (ca. 330–ca. 398), once a member of the Aventine Circle in Rome who later lived with Ambrose in Milan, he composed a treatise on *The Virgins*, in which he sought to allay parental fears of the ascetic life.

Africa

Augustine doubtless had more to do than anyone with the monks becoming models for the clergy in the West. At Cassiciacum near Milan before his conversion he already participated in a quasi-monastic group, one certainly interested in asceticism. The crucial experience leading to conversion was the narration by Ponticianus of a story about two young Roman noblemen who left their finances and became hermits after hearing the story of Anthony of Egypt. Augustine recorded dramatically in his *Confessions* how this took him from behind his back where he had hidden himself and made him see how defiled and deformed he was in his sexual indulgence. On his return to Africa he formed an ascetic community. After his ordination at Hippo he established a monastery. Although he cannot be given credit for the rule which bears his name, he set an example which later generations returned to repeatedly by founding a monastic community for the clergy of his diocese.

The monasteries of Africa, as other aspects of church life, suffered severely as a consequence of the Vandal invasions. The experience of Fulgentius (468–533 or ca. 462–527), bishop of Ruspe and a devoted Augustinian, was probably a common one in the fifth and sixth centuries. A Roman civil servant, he took up the monastic vocation in which he suffered constant persecution at the hands of the Vandal King Thrasamund, an Arian. Soon after his installation as bishop of Ruspe, around 502 or 507, he was banished to Sardinia with about sixty other Catholic bishops. Although allowed to return about 510–515, he was banished a second time two years later. After the death of Thrasamund, in 523, Hilderic permitted Fulgentius to return. Persecution later drove many monks from north Africa to Spain.

Gaul

Monasticism had more lasting success in Gaul. From a seed planted there by Athanasius during his exile in Trier in 336 monasticism grew into a thriving plant. The person largely responsible for popularizing it everywhere in Gaul, however, was Martin of Tours (d. 397). Sulpicius Severus (ca. 360–ca. 420), an Aquitanian noble converted to the ascetic life about 394 by the example of Paulinus of Nola (353/4–431), popularized Martin as the model monk, bishop, and missionary even before he died. The contribution of monasticism to the evangelization of Gaul enhanced its place in the Frankish kingdom during the fifth and sixth centuries.

The ascetic movement appealed to many of the nobility. Two monasteries in particular—Lérins and St. Victor at Marseilles—attracted eminent persons who then played a major role in shaping the Frankish church. The monastery of Lérins was founded by Honoratus, later Archbishop of Arles, about 410. A member of a consular family, Honoratus (ca. 350–429) had set out after his conversion to visit holy sites in Syria and Egypt. Following his brother Venantius's death in Achaia, he took the advice of Leontius, the bishop of Fréjus, and settled on the island of Lérins. He continued to direct the monastery even after his election as Archbishop of Arles in 426. Hilary (403–489), a relative of Honoratus, succeeded him as Abbot of Lérins and Archbishop of Arles.

Lérins laid claim to numerous other eminent figures in this period. Vincent (d. before 450) framed the often quoted definition of Catholic faith as "what has been believed always, everywhere, and by all." Salvian (ca. 400–ca. 480), whose name is usually associated with Marseilles, came originally to Lérins from a noble family of Cologne. Eucherius (d. ca. 449) left a wife and family to enter Lérins and later served as bishop of Lyon (from 434 on). He actively promoted the ascetic life. Lupus (x. 383–479), bishop of Troyes (429–479), entered Lérins after seven years of marriage to Pimeniola, sister of Hilary of Arles. Caesarius (ca. 407–542), Archbishop of Arles (502–542), entered Lérins in 489. With the help of Alaric II and Theodoric the Great, the Gothic rulers, he succeeded in making Arles the primatial see of Gaul.

Rivalling Lérins in influence during the fifth and sixth centuries was the Abbey of St. Victor at Marseilles founded by Cassian in 415. Western monasticism owes its shape in great part to John Cassian. Born in Provence or, more likely, Dobrudja, Scythia Minor of the Roman Empire, Cassian (ca. 360–435) entered a monastery in 382 near the cave of the nativity at Bethlehem accompanied by Germanus. In 385 he and Germanus moved to Egypt in search of "perfection" and soon became enamored with Egyptian hermitic ideals. Thereafter, neither felt comfortable any longer in Bethlehem.

They spent time at three different locations: the salt marshes near Panephysis, the desert of Scete, and in the region of Diolcos and Panephysis. At Scete they joined a community headed by

Macarius (ca. 300–ca. 390), then over ninety. In 399 or 400 they had to bring their stay to an abrupt halt when the Origenist controversy erupted. Breaking a pledge to return to Bethlehem. Cassian turned up next in Constantinople, probably because of his Origenism. John Chrysostom welcomed Origenists, one of several things alienating the clergy of the city from him.

Sent by Chrysostom on a embassy to Pope Innocent I (402–417) around 405, Cassian developed a friendship with Leo, later Pope Leo I (440–461). Some years later, he founded twin monasteries at Marseilles, one for women and one for men, dedicated to the martyr Victor. The barbarian invasions provided a kind of apocalyptic stimulus to the monastic movement. Within a short time St. Victor and other houses associated with it claimed 5,000 monks. Cassian supplied the guidance which the movement needed through the publication of his *Institutes* and *Conferences* between 425 and 430. He died in 435.

In some contrast to Basil of Caesarea, Cassian looked upon the hermitic as the most mature form of monasticism. The coenobium is for beginners, the hermitage is for the mature. He did not depend on Pachomius for his rule, advising rather than ordering and differing in many details. His special contribution lay in development of the daily hours of prayer. In Egypt, according to his own account, the monks observed two formal prayer times—nocturns and vespers—in which they chanted twelve Psalms and kept the rest of the day for silent meditation. Cassian felt that monks needed more and added three others traditionally observed in the churches: the third, sixth, and ninth hours. In the sixth century Benedict of Nursia added three more. Monks in Cassian's monasteries lived a moderately austere life. They slept three or four hours a day. Their diet consisted of two large buns, soaked beans, and fresh vegetables. On Saturdays and Sundays they received more cooked food. A group of elders governed the monastery. Younger monks were to obey older ones and confess to them.

Cassian derived many of his ideas from Evagrius Ponticus (346–399), whom he met at Nitria, although he made critical changes. Evagrius devised the classification later known as the "seven deadly sins" (greed, lust, avarice, melancholy, anger, accidie, and vainglory or pride) and explained how monks could fight them through recitation of the Psalms, study of the scriptures, manual labor, and remaining in one's cell. Eventually monks can attain *apatheia*, the key Stoic virtue. *Apatheia* produces charity and charity leads to *gnosis*. Cassian opposed excessive mortification. He emphasized scriptures, understood first literally and then spiritually, as the key source for filling and conditioning the mind. The goal is purity of heart, attained by praying without ceasing. Cassian depended to some extent on Augustine for his doctrine of grace, but he shared the Eastern concern for free will.

During the turbulent and unsettled period of incursions by the Goths, Burgundians, and Franks, monasteries sprang up throughout Gaul. Germanus (ca. 378–448) may have founded the abbey which bore his name at Auxerre. Moutier St. Jean, son of a senator of Dijon, founded the Abbey of Reome, which later bore his name, about 450. Two brothers, Romain and Lupicin, founded Condat high in the Alps at Jura on the border between France and Switzerland, also in the middle of the fifth century. Condat affected an Eastern style. Under its fourth abbot, Eugende (496–510), it developed a school which supplied education to the people of the area. The monastery had considerable influence on the Burgundians as they extended their rule to the area. The Burgundian King Sigismund, after renouncing Arianism, rebuilt the monastery at Aguane and brought monks from Condat and Lérins to inhabit it between 515 and 522.

The Merovingian line which began with Clovis took an active interest in the promotion of monasticism. Although Clovis (ca. 466–511) himself did not found any monasteries, he gave large gifts to the monasteries of Martin of Tours and Hilary of Poitiers (ca. 315–367). The next two generations of Merovingians established and endowed numerous monasteries. Childebert I was a friend of monks, and Chlotar I, though by no means a saintly person, was associated with Radegundis in the founding of St. Croix.

Queen Radegundis (518–587), daughter of a prince of Thuringia, had married Chlotar around 540 rather reluctantly. When the latter murdered her brother about ten years later, she fled and persuaded Medard, bishop of Noyon, to ordain her as a deaconness. Shortly thereafter, she founded a monastery for women outside Poitiers and spent the last thirty years of her life in it. Adopting the rule framed by Caesarius of Arles, she emphasized charity and peace and urged her nuns to pray for all rather than be preoccupied with their own salvation. Merovingian monasteries evidently did not make too much use of the Rule of the Benedict at this period.

Why did people of power and wealthy found monasteries? Some did so out of hope of winning salvation through relief of poverty, the good work of good works. Others wanted to ensure perpetual prayer on their behalf and for their families. Monks were professional pray-ers. Others valued the fact that the monasteries guarded relics of martyrs and holy persons, and those which could claim important relics prospered—Tours, Poitiers, Lyon, Trier, Autun. Some others recognized in the founding of monasteries a way to save family properties, otherwise easily seized or lost, and continue to exert some influence over their use. Individuals entered monasteries, of course, to find salvation, to have more security than the world offered, and to give themselves to the life of prayer.

Ireland

In Ireland monasticism assumed a character quite distinct from earlier forms. Although it antedated his arrival in 432, its development depended heavily on the promotion of it by Patrick. As noted in an earlier chapter, Patrick fostered monasticism in his evangelization of Ireland. In Ireland, as a matter of fact, monastic institutions overrode episcopal organization and captured the imagination of the people. When kings or chieftains converted, they often became monks and abbots of monasteries, which sometimes numbered in the thousands.

Women also got caught up in the ascetic movement. The most famous of the Irish monastic founders was Bride or Brigid (d. ca. 523), credited with founding the first women's convent at Kildare.

What especially distinguished Celtic monasticism was its austerity. Love of God, in the Celtic view, required "application and toil." Physical penances such as fasting and plunging into cold water were encouraged to kindle service to God. Key figures in defining Celtic monasticism were Columba (ca. 521–597) and Columban (ca. 543–615). Columban's rule called for moral perfection achieved by thorough self-scrutiny, confession, and doing appropriate penance. Penance was therapeutic rather than punitive. Accordingly, Columban required private confessions before eating and going to bed.

Italy

By the sixth century monasteries were scattered all over Europe poised to carry out the task of evangelizing and reevangelizing. Although they shared a common heritage, they existed in great variety often determined by their founders. No rule dominated in the way Basil of Caesarea's Rule prevailed in Eastern monasticism. Only larger monasteries would have had copies of that Rule in Rufinus's translation or the Rule of Pachomius in Jerome's or Cassian's *Conferences* and *Institutes*. The solution to the problem came from Italy in the concise, temperate, and appropriate form framed by Benedict of Nursia. Although Benedict's Rule did not gain immediate widespread acceptance, it gradually caught on and overwhelmed all competitors, including the influential but more stringent Rule of Columban.

Benedict's background is obscure. Born at Nursia around 480, he was educated at Rome. The licentiousness of the city, however, caused him to withdraw about 500 and take up a hermit's life in a cave at Subiaco. A community gradually formed around him and he established twelve monasteries with twelve monks each. The jealousy of some monks, however, caused him to flee Subiaco. Around 525 he took a small group of monks to Monte Cassino, where he remained until he died, probably in 547. Here he composed his first Rule.

Benedict's Rule addressed one of the central problems of the turbulent sixth century in Italy as first the Ostrogoths and then the armies of Justinian and later the Lombards created havoc. As a matter of fact, the Lombards ravaged Monte Cassino in 577, and it was not rebuilt until 717. In the midst of such an insecure situation, the Rule focused on stability and orderliness. It provided for a community ruled by an abbot elected for life and supported by agriculture. Within the walls of its enclosure the monks could raise all the food the community required and provide for all other necessities. The community existed for nothing else than to arrange an orderly life for those within it, although, like other families, it did extend hospitality to outsiders and relieved the needs of the people around it. The monks wanted simply to serve God without distractions from the world.

Under the Rule of Benedict monks ordered their day around three activities. They spent about four hours a day in liturgical prayer, four in meditative reading (*lectio divina*) and six or more in manual labor of some kind. Benedict wanted nothing to take precedence over the *Opus Dei*, "Work of God." Seven times a day, usually beginning about 2:00 a.m., the monks gathered to recite the Psalms. Whereas some desert monks sought to recite all 150 Psalms every day, Benedict arranged for their recitation once a week. The spiritual reading consisted solely of scriptures, early monastic literature, and the writings

of the church Fathers, although, in three or four hours a day, monks may have ventured beyond that diet from time to time. Manual labor would not have consisted only of farm activities because Benedictine monasteries employed *coloni* to do heavy manual labor. Monks, therefore, probably engaged in domestic arts and crafts.

The monastic movement also drew women. Benedict's twin sister Scholastica (ca. 480–ca. 543) established a convent at Plombariola, a few miles from Monte Cassino. According to Gregory the Great, brother and sister met annually outside the monastery to compare notes. Scholastica died before Benedict and was buried in the tomb he had prepared for himself. He was buried beside her.

The Rule of Benedict gained ground slowly after the death of its framer. Cassiodorus (ca. 485–ca. 580), a Roman senator who eased tensions between Romans and Goths, founded two monasteries along Benedictine lines at Vivarium and became a monk in one of them around 540. After trying in vain to establish a school at Rome along lines of the Alexandrian, he turned his monastery into a kind of academy which encouraged both secular and religious learning. He collected a huge library and required the monks to spend time in study. A disciple of Benedict, Placidus, the son of a wealthy senator, founded a Benedictine monastery at Messina in Sicily around 534. Shortly thereafter, he and his sister Flavia and two monks were slain by Moorish pirates. In Sicily most monasteries followed the rule of Basil. Martyrdom of monks assisted in the dissemination of the movement.

The most ardent advocate and promoter of Benedictinism, however, was Pope Gregory I (590–604), the Great, who, in his *Dialogues*, turned Benedict into a legend and set an example for others in living the monastic life. The son of a Roman senator, in 573 he relinquished his role as perfect of the city of Rome, sold his vast properties, and distributed much of his wealth to the poor. He founded seven monasteries, six in

Sicily and one in Rome, the Monastery of St. Andrew, into which he himself entered. After serving seven years as *apocrisarius* to the court at Constantinople (578–585), he became abbot of St. Andrew's. Reluctantly he assumed the papacy in 590. About 593 he composed the *Dialogues*, which highlighted the lives of Benedict and other early Latin saints. Although it is not certain that even the Monastery of St. Andrew followed the Rule of Benedict in Gregory's time, his promotion of Benedict as the saint par excellence obviously weighted the scales in favor of the Rule thereafter.

With Gregory Western monasticism stood at the threshold of its golden age. He valued the monastic vocation in itself, not simply as a means to an end. He exempted certain monasteries from episcopal control. He sharply separated the monastic from the clerical life and insisted that clergy give up clerical functions when they entered monasteries. He did his best to raise the monastic life to its highest possible level, and he vigorously opposed Emperor Maurice's (582–602) prohibition of soldiers or public officials entering monastic communities. He entrusted monks such as Augustine, head of St. Andrew's in Rome, with the task of evangelizing the British Isles. From this point on, the monks would play an increasingly important role in the life of the church.

Chapter 27

East Is East and West Is West

One of the striking developments of the fifth and sixth centuries was the expansion of the cleavage between the East and West. The barbarian invasions consummated in the fifth century hastened and widened the breach, for they constricted exchanges between the two areas. The separation, however, had more basic roots even than barbarian control of the West. The two areas had different histories and cultures. Although differences in language would have been an obvious sign of separation, they signaled something deeper in cultural differences. The Roman East was not, after all, really Roman. Actually it was not Greek either, even though Hellenism spread itself widely throughout the ancient world. The course of several controversies shows that the East was not homogeneous. There was a Greek East, to be sure, but there were also an Egyptian East and a Syrian East. Consequently the emperors had constantly to struggle to hold a disparate people together. All of these areas inherited and sought to live by some of the same ideas, but they appropriated and applied them differently. It is not surprising, therefore, to find Christians of East and West taking different paths during these centuries.

The divergencies appeared in a number of areas. For one, Easterners and Westerners developed different models for church and state. Practical realities forced Westerners to temper the fourth-century Eastern vision of a Christian empire. In conjunction with that, they also conceived of the church in different ways, Easterners far less ready to accept Roman authority and more concerned for regional autonomy.

Although heirs of the same liturgies, moreover, Easterners and Westerners had quite different concepts of worship and used different styles and liturgies. In the East, of course, the imperial court impacted worship more heavily than in the West, for, after Constantine's removal of the imperial capital to Byzantium, Westerners had limited exposure to imperial ways. Not only so, in the East the churches benefitted from imperial largesse to a far greater extent than in the West, where only a few places, such as Milan or Ravenna or Rome, had significant contacts with the powers that be.

In this period of transition which was so significant for shaping the Western church, furthermore, Christian culture underwent a "barbarization" not experienced in the East. The "Dark Ages" did not descend on the East as they did on the West. Although Justinian (527–565) closed the last hellenistic school at Athens in 529, Eastern culture did not go into a nosedive as Western culture did. Yet it would not be correct to assume a complete disintegration of Western culture. What was happening was a resynthesizing of Roman culture, itself a synthesis, with that of the Germanic peoples who now took control of the territory formerly within the Roman Empire.

Contrasting Temperaments

Formally the East and the West maintained their historic ties up to 1054 except during the brief Acacian schism, 484–528, and during the Photian schism, 869–879. It does not require special insight, however, to see the widening of the distance between the two halves of Christendom. The truth of the matter is that Easterners and Westerners had fundamentally different temperaments. Easterners were imbued far more deeply with the spirit of hellenism than Westerners. They used the Greek language while even cultivated Westerners such as Augustine scarcely knew or desired to know it. Easterners delighted in speculative thought just like the ancient Greeks. By this period certainly the average Easterner had a better education than their Western counterparts which, in the church, enabled lay persons as well as clergy or monks to take an active part in theological discussion and debate. Although this had a downside in a near obsession for theological precision, it precluded the dominance of theology by ecclesiastical authorities such as happened in the West. From it, moreover, derived the Eastern preference for a conciliar approach to settling matters of debate. This approach, unfortunately, did lend itself to wrangling and division, for minorities seldom conceded the majority opinion in theological matters.

Westerners, on the other hand, had a more practical bent than Easterners. Trying to survive in these turbulent centuries, they could not afford the luxury of speculative thought in which Easterners engaged so heartily. The number of Western bishops who participated in the first seven ecumenical councils could be counted on two hands. How to help the faithful overcome temptation, sin, and guilt was of far greater moment than whether Christ was *homoousios*, *homoiousios*, *homoios*, or *anamoios* with the Father. Consequently, Westerners expended far more of their energies fashioning a system of pastoral guidance than they did engaging in speculative theology.

The barbarian invasions increased the penchant for the practical. It is not surprising that it was Celtic monks who fashioned the penitential system as a means of introducing converts to the bare rudiments of Christian life.

Church and State

East and West quite clearly went in different directions in their understanding and acting out of the relationship between church and state. Constantine set the pattern for the East, or, perhaps more accurately stated, perpetuated the ancient Roman pattern. Eusebius, as Constantine's *alter ego*, envisioned the emperor as God's representative in all affairs of the empire, including religious affairs. Although the church may assist him in discovering God's will, he alone has universal authority and is the ultimate reference in religious matters. To disobey the emperor would be to disobey God. Confirmation of the theory can be found in Constantine's handling of the Donatist and Arian controversies. In the latter he even proposed the controverted term *homoousios* to describe the relation of the Son to the Father, probably at the suggestion of Hosius of Cordova. Except for Julian, Constantine's successors followed in his footsteps. In the fifth century the emperors increased their use of the church for political purposes. This tendency reached its peak in the sixth century under Justinian.

Justinian not only summoned councils, he took control of each step of the proceedings. When he learned that African bishops opposed his condemnation of the "Three Chapters," he excluded them from the Fifth Ecumenical Council in 553 designed to effect that goal. His wife, Theodora, who leaned toward Monophysitism, secured the removal and possibly the death of Pope Silverius (536–538) and installation of Vigilius (538–555) on the basis of a promise that he would help negotiate the condemnation of Chalcedon. Justinian then forced Vigilius, against conscience, to condemn the "Three Chapters." Although some scholars have objected to characterization of Eastern church/state concepts as caesaropapist, in Justinian's case this would seem appropriate.

Justinian dealt harshly with persons not considered orthodox. He deposed, excommunicated, and sometimes banished Nestorians and Eutychians. Depending on political circumstances, he vacillated in his treatment of Arians, being somewhat lenient until his forces won Africa from the Vandals in 534. He placed Manichaeans under the death penalty. He took harsh action against Montanists and Gnostics. He placed Samaritans and Jews under severe restrictions, albeit not as repressive as those against heretics. His legislation punished apostasy from Christianity with death and required baptism of all citizens. They also denied pagans the right to education and forbade their public worship. On closing the school at Athens in 529 Justinian offered professors the option of baptism or exile. Seven chose exile.

Justinian's *Code* even legislated theology, worship, and structure of the church. One title included four laws "On the Highest Trinity and on the Catholic Faith and That no one dare debate about these matters publicly." Others dealt with legacies to churches, bishops and the clergy, heresy, apostasy, repression of paganism, sanctuary, and manumission. The later "Novels" focused on such specific matters as the number of clergy which could minister in Hagia Sophia, disposal of land belonging to the Church of the Resurrection in Jerusalem, erection of a see at Justinian's birthplace, clerical discipline, and regulation of monasteries. In a "Novel" issued March 16, 535, Justinian stated his own theory of church and state. Priests and emperors should work in harmony, the priests offering prayers and the emperors ruling.

In practice Justinian followed the arrangement set up by Marcian at the Council of Chalcedon in 451 to assure a free imperial hand in the guidance of the whole Eastern church through the patriarch of Constantinople. "New Rome" was "to have the same advantages in the ecclesiastical

order" as Old Rome "and be second to it" so that the patriarch would "alone consecrate metropolitans of the diocese of Pontus, Asia, and Thrace and the bishops of parts of these dioceses occupied by the barbarians." Patriarchs thenceforward spoke often of themselves as "ecumenical" patriarchs. When John the Faster tried to formalize it, Pope Gregory I (590–604) indignantly denounced the idea. The emperor, likewise, took pains to assure control of monasteries.

What made many wary of the Constantinian model of a Christian empire was the Arianism of Constantius II (337–361), successor of Constantine in the East. Athanasius quickly learned that he would have to pay a price for steadfastness in adhering to Nicene orthodoxy. It was the Western church and not the Eastern, however, which came to his aid. When the emperors Constans and Constantius jointly convened the Council of Sardica around 343 to settle the issue of Athanasius's orthodoxy, Eastern bishops refused to attend on the ground that Westerners regarded Athanasius as a member of the assembly. Westerners met anyway under leadership of Hosius of Cordova and cleared Athanasius. A letter of Western bishops to Emperor Constantius subtly questioned the use of secular force against orthodox bishops and suggested that the emperor's task was to ensure "most precious liberty" to all his subjects. Hilary of Poitiers (ca. 315–367), who preserved the letter, went on to develop the principle of freedom in religion. God does not ask for and will refuse a coerced confession. The Western Council of Sardica (canon 3) sought to buttress its position by constituting the bishop of Rome as a court of appeal for bishops in certain cases.

With the backing of Constans the Council of Sardica brought temporary relief for Nicene supporters in the East and even the restoration of Athanasius. Ironically, however, in the meantime Constans persecuted Donatists, evoking from Donatus the query, "What has the emperor to do with the church?" After the death of Constans in 350 Constantius resumed his repression of Nicene bishops. When Western bishops insisted at the Council of Milan in 355 that they would violate canon law if they obeyed his directives, he declared that the imperial will was the same as canon law! He also sent for Pope Liberius (352–366) and forced him to break with Athanasius. When Liberius refused, Constantius banished him from Rome until he signed an Arian formula. When Hosius of Cordova (ca. 257–357), then nearly a hundred, declined to sign a statement against Athanasius, Contantius banished him to Sirmium. Hosius penned a courageous letter propounding a two kingdoms theory. God has entrusted the earthly kingdom to the emperor but the church to the bishops. Constantius had better watch out lest he offend God. At the Council of Sirmium in 357, nevertheless, the emperor forced the aged Hosius to sign the "Blasphemy," an agreement to communicate with Arians, before he could return to Cordova. Before he died, Hosius repudiated his signing.

The firmness of the Constantinian model's grip on Eastern thinking is evident in the hesitancy of Athanasius to speak other than obediently and respectfully of Constantius. Not until 358, in his *History of the Arians*, did he break that pattern. Some emperors—Jovian and Valentinian I—professed the dualistic theory, but it came to its most forceful expression in Martin of Tours (d. 397) and Ambrose of Milan (ca. 339–397). Martin argued against the trial of Priscillian, a Spanish bishop who founded an aberrant ascetic sect which went by his name, in the imperial court at Trier on a charge of witchcraft, a capital offense. A secular judge should not try an ecclesiastical case, he insisted. After Martin left the city Priscillian was tried and executed.

Ambrose, as noted in an earlier chapter, pressed the theory of separate jurisdictions to the maximum in 385 in his conflict with Empress Justina over the use of the basilicas of Milan for Arian worship. "Palaces belong to the emperor, churches to the bishop," he declared. Ambrose, however, did not contend for completely separate

realms. The emperor has a *duty* to suppress paganism and heresy and can call and ratify councils, of course, at the request of the church. Here, Ambrose tended toward a theory of church ascendancy over the state.

From this point on in the West the papacy became the bulwark for the liberty of the church. The Council of Sardica had pointed in the direction in which the popes from Damasus on (366–384) would steadily move. As will be seen subsequently, the confused political situation in the West aided the papacy in its struggle to emancipate itself from dominance by the emperors. Yet where the church obtained too many favors from the established powers, whether in East or West, it ran the risk of subordination to them. Like Ambrose, the popes tried to guard against this risk by placing the church in the ascendant position. In the West this policy had a certain feasibility in the fifth and sixth centuries as the invasions created a power vacuum. Bishops intervened in cases of capital punishment. They received appointment as financial officers of cities. They sat in judgment on the morality of emperors and other officials, as Ambrose had in requiring Theodosius I (379–395) to do penance for the massacre of the citizens of Thessalonica in 388.

In 494 Pope Gelasius I stated the two kingdoms theory in its classical form in a letter to Emperor Anastasius I (491–518). Of the two realms the priestly is the more weighty, for the priest must render an account to God in the judgment. In actual practice, however, neither the emperors nor the rising Frankish kings in the West, beginning with Clovis (481–511), took that doctrine seriously. Frankish kings played about the same hand as the emperors did. In 549 the Council of Orleans recognized as much when it laid down the rule that bishops would be elected "with the consent of the king (*cum voluntate regis*)." Although a pope as powerful as Gregory the Great (590–604) often objected to imperial decrees, he taught that to offend God's anointed was to offend God. When Emperor Maurice (582–602) ruled that soldiers could not become monks, his objections notwithstanding, Gregory obeyed the ruling. Subsequent history is full of the Western church's struggle to liberate itself from secular control, both Western and Eastern.

Worship

East and West also took different paths in the evolution of their worship practices during the fifth and sixth centuries as Christian worship entered the third major phase of its development. In the first phase, prior to Constantine, it took on everywhere the basic features characteristic of Christian liturgical practice which it inherited from Judaism and early Christianity. The major elements taken from the synagogue were sermons, psalms, prayers, and a calendar. To these the first Christians added the observance of the Lord's supper or eucharist and distinctively Christian hymns. By the late second century the Christian calendar included two fast days, the Lord's day or Sunday, Easter, and Pentecost, plus some days commemorating martyrs.

In its second phase, during the fourth century after Constantine's conversion, Christian worship assumed other features under the influence of the imperial court, the availability of buildings specially designed for worship, and the Jerusalem liturgy. From the imperial court came a decided preference for dramatic ceremonies and a system of entrances and processions and for the chanting of the service. To fit the new context of worship, liturgical materials had to be amplified. At the same time the Jerusalem liturgy provided the push away from the eschatological toward the historical and mystical shape of worship. In the fourth century the liturgical year added a nativity cycle and a wide range of secondary feast days and cycles.

In its third phase, beginning in the late fourth century, Christian worship in the East was impacted heavily by monasticism, the rage of the fifth and sixth centuries. At the heart of the monastic devotional regimen was the chanting of the psalms. Since the people looked to the monks as teachers, spiritual guides, and guardians of orthodoxy, it is not surprising to see a blending of the monastic devotional routine with the liturgy current in the great sees—Constantinople, Antioch, Alexandria, and Jerusalem—where monasteries abounded. In the West the monastic impact came later after the liturgies had solidified, but it was telling there too.

Up to the fourth century the liturgy retained a uniform outline throughout Christendom, but it was still fluid and subject to alteration in details. By the second half of the century fluid uniformity had given way to fixed liturgies representing different geographical areas. The fixing of worship forms was doubtless necessitated by growth in the size of congregations and the demand for greater splendor to suit the tastes of more cultured and affluent constituencies. In addition, constantly increasing concern for theological precision, especially in the East, mandated more exact formulation of prayers and other elements of the service. Certain centers, especially the patriarchal sees, crystallized local liturgies and set the pattern for the churches in their sphere of influence. Variations in language in different regions, moreover, assured that the liturgies of East and West would diverge still further.

Language accounts for one of the most self-evident ways in which Eastern and Western worship differed from one another. In the West Latin quickly established itself as the language of the liturgy, and the liturgy was not translated into other languages. In the East, although Greek was the *lingua franca* of the empire and thus spread over a wide sphere, the churches did not fix Greek as the liturgical language but rather encouraged translation into the vernacular. Early on, Syriac-speaking Christians fashioned their own liturgy which later came under influence of the Greek liturgy of Antioch. In the patriarchate of Antioch the Greek liturgy was also translated into Syriac, the prevailing popular language. Elsewhere the Greek liturgy appeared in the language of the people—Coptic in Egypt with some admixture of Greek, Armenian, Georgian, and, later, other languages.

More basic in distinguishing the worship of East and West was the relative importance of the liturgy in the two areas. The liturgy had much greater significance in the lives of Christians in the Byzantine sphere than it did in the lives of Western Christians. It was the central expression of church life, far more important than the sermon, catechetical instruction, almsgiving, or any other organized church activity. To participate in the liturgy was to take part in the drama of salvation with the saints of all the ages and the heavenly hierarchies. The writings of Pseudo-Dionysius, probably composed in Syria about 500, gave eloquent expression to the mythology of the liturgy. According to Pseudo-Dionysius, the liturgy of the church models itself, in Platonic fashion, on the heavenly. God in essence, the Godhead, cannot be known, for God is "beyond essence" and "beyond knowing." Christ, however, God incarnate, can communicate Light to us through the heavenly hierarchies in a kind of downward spiral. The hierarchy is a "sacred order" whose goal is "to enable beings to be as like God as possible and to be one with God" (*Celestial Hierarchy* 3.2). Thus the higher ranks (seraphim, cherubim, and thrones) transmit wisdom to the middle (dominions, powers, and authorities), and the middle to lower (principalities, archangels, and angels). At this level the celestial hierarchy matches up with the ecclesiastical hierarchy, which also has three levels. The ecclesiastical hierarchy communicates the divine revelation through the mysteries (sacraments)—baptism (called the Illumination), eucharist, ordination, and anointing of the dead. As Jesus communicates through the celestial hierarchy, so also he, as it were, assimilates the earthly hierarchy "to his own light" (*Ecclesiastical Hierarchy* 1.1) and bestows the power of the sacred priesthood. This hierarchy belongs, therefore, to the noumenal and not merely to the phenomenal world. Because by its nature it encompasses all sacred elements in itself, it can be the means of divinization and, as the ultimate goal, union with God. God "has bestowed hierarchy as a gift to ensure the salvation and divinization of every being endowed with reason and intelligence" (1.4).

By way of contrast, Western Christians made far more of the reception of the eucharist or Mass itself. In the East the eucharist took place only as the people assembled for worship and churches thus had only one altar. In the West, as the number of priests multiplied in monasteries to serve the needs of people for forgiveness of sin and masses for the dead, the number of altars in the churches multiplied, usually by creating altars in the side aisles.

Paralleling differences in liturgy were differences in church architecture in the three major geographical areas of Christendom—the Latin West, the Greek East, and the Syriac-speaking area from Palestine eastward. Byzantine church architecture took a major turn during the reign of Justinian (527–565). Up to this time, the basilica had dominated in both East and West and it would continue to prevail in the West. In the East, however, Justinian deliberately broke with tradition in favor of vaulted centrally planned church buildings used since the third or fourth century in palace halls, funerary structures, baths, garden buildings, and, to a limited extent, churches or martyria. Although this type of edifice appeared more frequently around 500, not until Justinian did architects make it the rule, thus deliberately setting out in a different direction from the West. The major impetus for the change probably came from the liturgy, for the centrally planned structure was ideally suited to performance of a service wherein the liturgy dominated everything else. Foremost of Justinian's churches was Hagia Sophia in Constantinople, constructed between 532 and 537 after the original basilica erected in 360 was burned in the Nike revolt.

Outside Constantinople itself, only San Vitale in Ravenna, completed between 546 and 548, imitated the plan of Hagia Sophia closely. As the imperial capital in the West, of course it stood within the court circle, and Justinian and Theodora attended the dedication. Elsewhere the style was more sober and less daring, based on older architectural principles.

Culture

Christian culture declined in both East and West during the fifth and sixth centuries but for quite different reasons. In the East theological disputes consumed the energies of the best scholars and, in time, created a climate of intimidation in which they feared to express themselves. In the sixth century Emperor Justinian was the boldest theologian as well as the fashioner of a political and cultural renaissance, for he was one of few who did not have to fear his own censure. In the West the barbarian invasions took their toll. It is possible, nevertheless, to cite some outstanding examples of continuing cultural vitality in some ways stronger than in the East.

The "Golden Age" of Greek Christian literature came to an end during the first half of the fifth century. Besides the copious polemical literature written in the heat of combat over Christology by advocates of Monophysite and Dyophysite traditions, the Antiochenes produced some outstanding exegetical works—John Chrysostom's (347–407) homilies and Theodore of Mopsuestia's (d. 428) commentaries being notable examples. Socrates Scholasticus (ca. 380–450), Sozomen (early fifth century), and Theodoret of Cyrus (ca. 393–ca. 466) extended the *Church History* of Eusebius, which ended in 323, into the early fifth century. The most creative literature, however, came from the pens of ascetics such as Hesychius of Jerusalem (d. after 450), Nilus of Ancyra (d. ca. 430), Diadochus of Photice in Epirus (mid-fifth century), and Pseudo-Dionysius (ca. 500). The last, as noted earlier in discussion of the liturgy, exerted massive influence on Christian

spirituality of both East and West in subsequent centuries. Although early use by Monophysites aroused some opposition to the writings, acceptance by Leontius of Byzantium in the first half of the sixth century, Gregory the Great, Sophronius of Jerusalem (d. 638), and Maximus the Confessor (d. 662) banished fear of them.

Justinian also encouraged literary arts. The most noted writer was the historian Procopius, author of a *History*, a treatise on *Buildings*, and *Anecdota*, which satirized Justinian, Theodora, and practically all other persons of importance in Constantinople. Leontius of Byzantium ranked high as champion of Chalcedonian orthodoxy against Nestorianism and Eutychianism (ca. 543–544). John of Ephesus (ca. 507–586) represented the Monophysite cause in his *Ecclesiastical History* and *Lives of Eastern Saints*. Evargius Scholasticus (ca. 536–600), a lawyer by profession, preserved valuable sources in his *Ecclesiastical History*, covering the period from the Council of Ephesus in 431 to 593.

Better indexes of the renaissance which occurred under Justinian were his contributions to art and law. After the Nike revolt destroyed the public buildings in Constantinople Justinian rebuilt the city on a more lavish scale than Constantine had originally planned. He sought to make works of art not only of churches but also of palaces, the Senate, monasteries, public baths, theaters, the aqueduct, and even fortifications. Outside the capital, he had erected at the foot of the traditional site of Mount Sinai the famous monastery later devoted to St. Catherine, and he scattered mosaics all across the Roman world, the most notable being in Ravenna. Unfortunately, Justinian's extravagances in war and in building nearly bankrupted the imperial treasury.

Justinian's famous *Codex*, issued first in 529 and reissued in 534, compiled and harmonized and Christianized the laws of the Roman Empire. In his legislation Justinian sought to achieve what he attempted to do everywhere, that is, to make the whole conform to the ideals of a Christian commonwealth. Accordingly, the Code began with a confession of faith and anathemas against heretics. Other legislation tried to humanize, for example, by improving the lot of slaves although it did not prohibit slavery.

After Justinian's death in 565 the external security of the empire deteriorated rapidly. The barbarians grew bolder. Meantime, pressure from Turkish tribes caused the Slavs to seek settlements within the empire. First settling on the north coast of the Black Sea and possibly to the south of the Danube by 300, they stood ready in the sixth century to move into the Balkans. In 562 the Avars launched their first attack on the empire. Thereafter, Slav and Avar raids occurred frequently, almost exterminating the old population north of the Balkans. In 577 an estimated Slavic population of 100,000 entered Thrace and Illyricum. Emperor Maurice (582–602) strove desperately to hold back the combined Avar-Slav forces, but by the end of his reign Slavs had settled throughout Macedonia and around Thessalonica. Whether they reached Greece is debated. Under Heraclius (610–641) the Slavs made further advances into the Balkans. Meantime, a more dangerous and damaging threat rose in the East. In 608 the Persians conquered Syria and Palestine and ravaged Armenia, Cappadocia, and Galatia. In 619 they captured Egypt. Imperial policy framed by Justinian had so offended Syrians and Egyptians that they either offered no resistance or else aided the Persians. Heraclius recovered Syria and Egypt, but at tremendous cost. He had to obtain a loan from the church to finance his Persian expedition. Meanwhile, he failed to see the Islamic threat on the horizon which would soon sweep away all the Eastern and North African lands still held by the empire. Had it not been for its sea power, the Byzantine empire might have disintegrated all at once.

Although the West experienced this radical disruption far sooner, it would be erroneous to posit a complete break with the Latin past and a total disintegration of culture. The barbarian invasions dealt a devastating blow to culture and learning on the edges of the empire, but, even there, they survived, thanks especially to the monasteries and the churches. Monks copied and illuminated precious manuscripts. Monasteries built up libraries to preserve the treasures of the past, both classical and Christian. Monastic schools perpetuated the tradition of learning. At the beginning of the sixth century cathedral or episcopal schools appeared. Caesarius of Arles conducted one in Provence during his episcopate (503–542). In 527 a Spanish council at Toledo set out careful plans for episcopal schools. The institution spread thereafter. Steady barbarization led the second Council of Vaison in 529, the year Justinian closed the school at Athens, to direct the churches to give Christian education to young children admitted as readers. This type of school spread rapidly because of pressing need. Gregory of Tours (ca. 540–599) received his education from his uncle Gallus, bishop of Auvergne, and his great-uncle Nicetius, bishop of Lyons. In 599 Pope Gregory I reproached Didier, bishop of Vienne, for teaching grammar. Although the exact point is uncertain, the letter would seem to indicate that Didier had to undertake the most elementary instruction, whereas in Rome the level of culture had not fallen so low.

Quite clearly, there was a downward spiral in the West from the early fifth until the renaissance of learning in the eighth century. In the first half of the fifth century the West boasted some of its most illustrious names. Jerome (ca. 342–420) had no peer even in the East in biblical scholarship. Augustine (354–430), though not apt at biblical languages, excelled as a theologian. Through his *Conferences* and *Institutes* John Cassian (ca. 360–435) made a contribution to Western monasticism exceeded only by Benedict of Nursia's *Rule*. In one area, poetry, the West surpassed the Greek East, which produced no important poet other than Gregory Nazianaus, although the Syrian church excelled also in poetry. Latin poetry flowered in the fourth century with the Spanish priest Juvencus (ca. 330), the noble Roman woman Proba (ca. 360), and the nominal convert to Christianity Ausonius (ca. 310–ca. 395), teacher of Paulinus of Nola (353/4–431). Paulinus composed thirty-five poems, but they lacked creative power. Greatest of the Latin Christian poets was Prudentius (348–ca. 410), a lawyer who had a distinguished career in civil administration.

From the late fifth century on, Westerners had to struggle to conserve the remains of their classical heritage as the invasions took their toll. Yet even here, in Italy and Gaul, both classical and Christian traditions survived throughout the sixth century. In Italy Boethius (ca. 480–ca. 574), the son of a Roman consul, became a friend and adviser of Theodoric, the Ostrogothic chief, and, in 510, himself a consul. He planned to translate all of Plato and Aristotle into Latin, but his premature death prevented realization of that task. He wrote commentaries on several of Aristotle's works and on Victorinus Afer's translation of Porphyry's *Isagoge*. He composed original works on arithmetic, geometry, and music for the quadrivium. Extended debate on his relationship to Christianity has recently settled in the affirmative with the authentication of a treatise he composed *On the Holy Trinity*. He penned his most famous work, *The Consolation of Philosophy*, during his imprisonment awaiting execution for treason, a charge incurred during his defense of an ex-consul named Albinus on the same charge. *The Consolation* became very popular in the Middle Ages. King Alfred translated it into Anglo-Saxon, Chaucer into English.

Cassiodorus (ca. 485–ca. 580) was, like Boethius, a member of a Roman noble family. He held several high civil offices—quaestor (507), consul (514), chief of civil service (526), and praetorian prefect (533). In 540 he founded two monasteries under the Rule of Benedict at Vivarium and retired there. His writings included *The Institutions of Divine and Secular Letters*, in which he urged a union of sacred and profane studies in Christian education, and the *Historia*

Ecclesiastica Tripartita, which combined the histories of Socrates, Sozomen, and Theodoret. The latter served as the chief textbook of church history in the West during the Middle Ages.

Rome's worst days probably came when Justinian reestablished Roman rule over Italy. The Ostrogoths resisted the Byzantine advance fiercely for twenty years (535–555). When King Totila realized he could no longer hold Rome, he deported the entire population to Campania. For forty days the city remained desolate. The Lombard invasion followed in 568 close on the heels of this devastating experience. Yet, although the Lombards threatened, they did not take Rome itself, and it seemed somehow to come back from the dead each time. Its vitality in this arduous time can be seen in the life and work of Gregory the Great.

Gregory, too, belonged to a wealthy and prominent family. From his parents, Gordian and Silvia, he inherited immense properties in both Italy and Sicily. Emperor Justin II (565–578) named his Praetor of Rome, an office which could not have held the importance it once did in a city whose population had dwindled from about a million to 40,000, but it entailed the civil administration of the city. On receiving his inheritance at the time of his father's death, around 575, Gregory founded six monasteries in Sicily in the diocese of Palermo, on his mother's estate, and a seventh, St. Andrew's, on the Caelian Hill in Rome. Bequeathing the remainder of his fortune to the poor, he himself entered the latter, though he may not have taken monastic vows, for Pope Benedict I (575–579) appointed him as one of the seven regionary deacons of Rome. An unusually gifted person in an age when the gifted were in short supply, in 578 the pope appointed him *apocrisarius* or *nuncio* to the imperial court at Constantinople, where he served under Tiberius II (578–582) and Maurice (582–602). In 585 or 586 he returned to Rome to the Monastery of St. Andrew. Given the dearth of competent persons at the time, however, Pope Pelagius II

(579–590) could not do without him, and he selected Gregory as his personal secretary. Like many other devout persons of this era, he coveted solitude rather than high office, but when Pelagius fell victim to a plague on February 7 or 8, 590, the cry went up for Gregory.

Gregory could not match Boethius or Cassiodorus in scholarship. By his own confession he knew no Greek, which is perplexing by virtue of his years in Constantinople. He also lacked their knowledge and appreciation of classical culture. Where he excelled was in personal piety and practical wisdom. As a popularizer and transmitter of Augustine, he laid the foundations of medieval Western theology. Although he understood his mentor imperfectly, he handed on his central teachings in a lucid style which people of limited education could grasp. More importantly, he set a noble standard for his office as *servus servorum Dei* ("servant of the servants of God") and stabilized the church in one of its most trying eras.

In Gaul as in Italy, the classical tradition was decreasing as the Bible, the Fathers (especially Augustine), and hagiography were increasing. One would err to conclude from this, however, that learning ceased and culture vanished. As noted earlier, great monasteries like those at Lérins and Marseilles were turning out a succession of outstanding leaders of high intelligence, good family background, and substantial education who were creating a new cultural synthesis. Gregory of Tours and Venantius Fortunatus reflect in their writings how at the end of the sixth century the shift was taking place.

Gregory (ca. 540–594) belonged to a Gallo-Roman senatorial family which produced several bishops. Elected bishop of Tours in 573, he, like others of the same era, preached and wrote, above all, to encourage faith. In that pursuit it is not surprising to find a mixing of fact and fantasy. In his chief hagiographical work, *Eight Books of Miracles*, he displayed extreme credulity and said little of real historical value. In his *History of the Franks*, which he began in 576, by contrast, he depicted accurately the parts of the story on which he had firsthand information. As earlier chroniclers had done, he began with a confession of faith and sketched history from creation to 397. In books 2–4 he related Frankish history to 575 based on well-selected sources. In the main part of the work, books 5–9, he narrated events as they happened between 575 and 591. Without his account historians could scarcely reconstruct the history of the period.

Venantius Fortunatus (ca. 530–ca. 610) was not a native of Gaul but of Treviso (near Venice) in Italy. Educated at Ravenna, where Eastern influence still lingered, about 565 he undertook a pilgrimage to the shrine of Martin of Tours in appreciation for the cure of an eye ailment. Flattering poetry won him a good reception at the court of Sigebert of Austrasia at Metz, where he stayed until 567. As the Lombards overran northern Italy, he decided to stay at Poitiers. There he became acquainted with Radegunde, the former queen who had by then become a nun, and Agnes, Abbess of the monastery. Meantime, he befriended Gregory of Tours, who encouraged him to publish his poetry. In the late sixth century he was elected bishop of Poitiers. Educated in classical form and style, he is remembered chiefly for his long metrical life of Martin of Tours, but he also composed prose lives of Hilary of Poitiers, Germanus of Paris, Radegunde, and other notables. Some have characterized him as "the first of the medieval poets."

Especially noteworthy in this period of transition was the substitution of hagiography for history. In the circumstances it is not hard to understand why this happened. The first concern had to be to give people overwhelmed by tragedy some sign of hope. Biblical miracles lived again in the saints, bishops, monks, and, here and there, rulers who sometimes did something extraordinary. The church produced saints' lives which could offer examples not so much of what had been as of what ought to be. Local holy persons set a living example of a pattern called for by the Bible.

Christianity has often been criticized for what happened here, and some criticisms are doubtless deserved. In reaching for some straw of hope, Westerners simply papered over reality by resorting to hagiography which often must have misled those it was designed to help. Admitting that point, however, one must recognized that the churches were the only Western institutions stable enough to do anything in a time of severe crisis. They may have undertaken too much when they tried to fill the humongous void created by the barbarian invasions. The maintenance of civilization was a subordinate part of the church's task of spreading the gospel, converting, and Christianizing. It took time for enough of the latter task to be achieved that the churches could contribute more to the broader aspects of society.

Chapter 28

Imperial Power and Right Doctrine

Imperial intrusion into ecclesiastical affairs routinized by Constantine and his successors proved increasingly costly in subsequent centuries. The more the emperors tried to effect unity by imperial mandate, the more they drove wedges between the churches and the peoples of the empire and the wider they made the gap between East and West. The East developed an obsession for orthodoxy, as if the mystery of God might somehow be encompassed in a neat formula. The monks especially were inflexible. "God is an exacting Judge who demands adherence to the appropriate formulas. Anathema on those who don't agree!" In consequence, bitter wrangling shattered the empire itself, with the Egyptians heading in one direction, the Syrians in another, and the Greeks in another.

John Chrysostom

Nothing illustrates better the costliness of misguided imperial politics than John Chrysostom's battles with Empress Eudoxia during his brief tenure as bishop of Constantinople (398–407). Elected to the office over his own protest, he immediately undertook the daunting task of reforming the court, clergy, and people of Constantinople, a task his easygoing predecessor Nectarius (381–397) had left untouched. Zealous that Christianity present an attractive front to a still unconverted society, Chrysostom rebuked pride in wealth, wanton luxury, profligate spending, pagan customs at weddings and funerals, superstitious reliance on amulets and magic charms, lack of seriousness about baptism, and numerous other popular vices. The empress, unfortunately for their relationship as pastor and parishioner, interpreted much of his preaching as a personal affront. His clergy, too, whose level of commitment had sagged badly under Nectarius, resented his efforts to upgrade their performance by deposing two deacons and refusing communion to other clergy as well as preaching reform. As he proceeded to take active measures to reform churches under his patriarchate, he ruffled other feathers. Three bishops in the latter group finally found a leader in Theophilus of Alexandria (385–412), who had consecrated Chrysostom to the see of Constantinople but who had himself coveted the office. The club Theophilus used to strike was Chrysostom's support of Origen and protection he offered Origenists.

In 401 three of the "Tall Brothers," Origenist monks from Egypt, and about fifty other Origenists sought refuge in Constantinople. Chrysostom received them with caution, writing to Theophilus to check their standing. In 403, however, Epiphanius, bishop of Salamis and bitter anti-Origenist, appeared in the capital and refused to commune with Chrysostom unless he condemned Origen and expelled the Tall Brothers. Chrysostom replied that he would leave the matter to a synod already scheduled. Epiphanius abruptly left

Constantinople on May 16 and died en route home. A month later, Theophilus arrived with an Egyptian entourage determined to depose John, knowing he had Eudoxia's support and that of many other clergy. The synod of thirty-six bishops assembled at the Oak, a suburb of Chalcedon, in July 403 and, after hearing twenty-nine charges against Chrysostom, deposed him. In a letter to the emperor the bishops urged his banishment for treason in calling the empress a Jezebel. His exile, however, lasted only a few days, for the people of Constantinople mobbed the imperial palace and demanded his recall. As he returned, they hoisted him triumphantly on their shoulders, carried him back to his episcopal throne, and would not leave until he preached a sermon *ex tempore*. A rival council composed of sixty bishops gathered later to annul the proceedings of the Synod of the Oak. Patriarch and empress lavished compliments on one another.

The reconciliation, however, did not last long. Within two months another occasion arose for the great preacher to offend his powerful parishioner. When licentious dancing accompanied the erection of a silver statue in honor of Eudoxia, he could not refrain from criticism which quickly reached the empress's ears. His old enemies proceeded to convoke another synod at the end end of 403. The synod dragged on for some time until Chrysostom's opponents persuaded the emperor to prevent him from celebrating the Easter rites on April 16, 404 on the grounds that he had unlawfully returned to his see. As he prepared to baptize about 3,000 candidates, troops attacked the congregation, arrested him, and confined him to his palace. This time, even the outcry of the people failed to prevent his exile first at Nicaea and then at Cucusus in Lesser Armenia, where he died on September 14, 407. In his place Emperor Arcadius appointed first Arsacius (404–405) and then Atticus (406–426), the two who had taken the lead in plotting against Chrysostom. In his exile he received comfort from a noble matron and deaconess

named Olympias, with whom he shared a special friendship during the time he resided in Constantinople. Olympias did not allow imperial threat of confiscation of her property to interfere with her faithfulness to a friend.

Nestorianism

The liability of imperial intrusion is visible also in the continuing competition between the sees of Alexandria and Antioch and their Christologies. Both the *Logos-sarx* Christology of Alexandria and the *Logos-anthropos* Christology of Antioch had valid points to make, the former doing Christology from above and the latter from below. Imperial anxiety to force a common formula on all, however, created a rigidity which denied the validity of alternate views and encouraged constant criticism and one-upsmanship, a tendency clearly illustrated by the Christological controversies of the fifth and sixth centuries.

The condemnation of both Arius and Apollinarius in the first two ecumenical councils had exposed the weakness of Alexandrian *Logos-sarx* Christology, its inclination toward effacement of the human nature by the divine. Although Apollinarius meant to correct Arius's subordination of the Logos-Son to the Father in his essential nature, he fell into the same trap as Arius when it came to the human nature, for both attributed Christ's sinlessness to the Logos's replacing of the human mind. Christ could not have sinned, viz. disobeyed God, as we do, because he did not have a human mind, the source of such disobedience. It was precisely the devaluing of the human which most concerned the Antiochenes and their *Logos-anthropos* Christology, surfacing especially when Nestorius, himself a heresy hunter, became patriarch of Constantinople in 427.

Behind Nestorius stood Diodore, head of the so-called school of Antioch and bishop of Tarsus from 378 to 394, and Theodore, bishop of Mopsuestia in Cilicia (392–428). Diodore was both anti-Arian and anti-Apollinarian. Concerned to preserve Christ's complete human nature, he emphasized strongly the distinctiveness of divine and human. The Logos should not be thought of as Son of Mary. Rather, the Logos, born of the Father, made a temple for himself of the man born of Mary. Although Diodore verbally maintained the unity of the person of Christ, he came fearfully close to the separation of persons charged, probably unfairly, to Nestorius. The Son of God only *indwelt* the son of David. Although a far more astute and discerning theologian, Theodore leaned in the same direction. A friend and fellow student of Chrysostom, he shared the Antiochene concern to safeguard the human nature. In Jesus God dwells "as a Son," which means that the human and divine natures remain distinct but are united in will and operation so as to remain indissoluble. In correcting Apollinarius, Theodore too came near to propounding a doctrine of two persons. His analogy for the union of natures was the biblical image of the conjugal union of husband and wife, two persons united as "one flesh." In his scheme Mary could be called *Theotokos*, "Mother of God," only insofar as she was the mother of the man assumed by God.

The deficiency of Antiochene Christology came out clearly in the theology of Nestorius. The first to deny publicly that Mary was *Theotokos* was not Nestorius but his domestic chaplain, Anastasius, whom Nestorius brought with him from Antioch. In a sermon preached in the capital on November 22, 428, Anastasius argued that, since Mary is only human, she could not be Mother of God, for "it is impossible for God to be born of humankind" (Socrates, H.E. 7.32.2). The sermon aroused such a storm that, on Christmas day, Nestorius launched a series of sermons in support of Anastasius. The imperial court stood by Nestorius, but monks, clergy, and most of the people either opposed him or stood by in silence as a lawyer named Eusebius, later bishop of Dorylaeum (ca. 448–451), led the protest. When the archimandrite Basil brought a group of monks to the episcopal palace to remonstrate, Nestorius had them remanded to prison.

The opposition, however, increased. On Lady Day (March 24), 429, Proclus, bishop of Cyzicus, delivered a panegyric "On the Virgin Mother of God" in which he contended that salvation required that God be born of a woman. Nestorius, who was present, asserted his right as the patriarch to reply. Although Proclus succeeded him as Archbishop of Constantinople, at this point a more formidable opponent appeared in the person of Cyril, patriarch of Alexandria (412–444) and nephew of Theophilus, nemesis of John Chrysostom.

Anxious like his uncle to make the most of every opportunity to put Constantinople in its place, Cyril first responded to the sermons of Nestorius against the *Theotokos* in an encyclical *To the Monks in Egypt* about Easter 429. For him it was a simple question as to whether Mary's Son was God or not. In June Cyril wrote Nestorius his first letter informing him that inquiries of Pope Caelestine and complaints of the churches forced him to seek Nestorius's correction. Early in 430, Cyril sent a second letter reinforcing his case against Nestorius. Nestorius replied to both, contending still that *Theotokos* was "pagan" and that it was better to call Mary *Christotokos*. He ended his second letter by noting that their imperial majesties were happy with what was being taught in the capital. Cyril, quick to pick up on the last point, proceeded to address a treatise to Theodosius II (408–450) *On Right Faith*, a second to his sisters Arcadia and Marina, and a third to Pulcheria and Eudocia, the elder sister and wife of Theodosius. On this he miscalculated, for the imperial household prided itself on its orthodoxy. However, Cyril gained help from another direction, Pope Caelestine (422–432).

Caelestine had written Cyril immediately after receiving copies of Nestorius's Christmas sermons attacking the use of *Theotokos* early in 429 and asked Cyril whether they really were Nestorius's. After he had received letters and a treatise from Nestorius, he had had them translated into Latin and turned them over to Cassian

(360–435) for a reply. Cassian responded with a treatise *On the Incarnation of the Lord against the Nestorians*, 430–431, contending that Pelagianism naturally leads to Nestorianism, that Mary must be called *Theotokos* rather than *Christotokos*, and that there must be an essential rather than moral union. In April 430, in the meantime, Cyril replied to Caelestine's inquiries and sent further writings against Nestorius. He also tried to enlist other supporters in the East, but he found reactions mixed because John, the patriarch of Antioch (428–441), did not wish to worsen the controversy involving his friend Nestorius, even though he agreed about *Theotokos*.

Councils in both Rome and Alexandria in 430 sought to secure the submission of Nestorius. After the Synod of Rome Caelestine wrote seven letters. In one addressed to Cyril he asked him to act as his proxy, but not, as sometimes thought, at the Third Ecumenical Council, plans for which had not yet formed. In a letter to Nestorius he threatened separation from the college of bishops and excommunication if Nestorius did not conform to Cyril's teaching. In the other letters—to the clergy and people of Constantinople and to Eastern bishops—he warned of Nestorius's teaching. Nestorius, however, simply stiffened his resolution, confident of imperial backing.

In November 430 Cyril assembled the Synod of Alexandria to execute the commission of Caelestine. The synod demanded that Nestorius anathematize his "impious tenets." After reviewing the theological points in question, the bishops appended a list of *Twelve Anathemas* to which Nestorius was to assent. The Apollinarian cast of the latter enabled Nestorius to effect a breach between Cyril and John of Antioch. When the four bishops bearing the letter and anathematisms arrived in Constantinople on December 5, 430, they learned that Emperors Theodosius and Valentinian III had summoned a universal council to convene at Ephesus by Pentecost 431. Emperor Theodosius intervened because the welfare of the empire, in his mind, was "bound up with the worship of God." He blamed Cyril for fomenting the troubles, but he was ready to forgive, he said, if Cyril would hurry to the council.

Both Nestorius and Cyril rallied their forces in anticipation of the council. Nestorius's main allies included John of Antioch; Andrew, bishop of Samosata (431–434), and Theodoret, bishop of Cyrus (423–458), one of the notable apologists of the Antiochene school and author of an *Ecclesiastical History* covering the period from Eusebius to the outbreak of the Nestorian controversy (323–428). Both Andrew and Theodoret composed critiques of Cyril's *Anathemas*. Cyril countered Andrew in an *Apology against the Orientals*, Theodoret in an *Apology against Theodoret in Behalf of the Twelve Chapters*, and Nestorius in a treatise *Against the Blasphemies of Nestorius*. He also wrote Caelestine to ask whether or not the council should accept Nestorius's recantation, if offered. During the fortnight before the council opened (June 7-21, 431), Cyril busied himself with the strengthening of his support. Meanwhile, some of Nestorius's supporters tried, without success, to get him to concede.

Unfortunately, for Nestorius and the conduct of the council, John of Antioch and the pro-Nestorian contingent did not arrive until after the council opened. Cyril refused to delay any longer, even though he knew he had a clear majority in his favor. This decision proved costly, for it overrode the will of the imperial High Commissioner, Count Candidian, as well as Nestorius's supporters. The 198 assembled bishops presided over by Cyril, claiming to represent Pope Caelestine, quickly arrived at their decision—to depose and excommunicate Nestorius. On June 26, however, John and the Orientals arrived. Without taking time to change clothes, they convened a second council composed of forty-three bishops and, after hearing Candidian's report on what had transpired deposed Cyril and his main supporter, Memnon, bishop of Ephesus, and excommunicated all of their adherents unless they should repudiate the *Twelve Anathemas*.

Although the belated arrival of papal legates with instructions to support Cyril shifted support in the capital to his side momentarily, he did not have long to celebrate. Count Candidian and the Nestorians blocked the access of Cyrillians to the imperial court for a time. As now one and now the other party gained Theodosius's ear, the emperor finally decided to treat Cyril, Memnon, and Nestorius as alike deposed and sent a new commissioner, John, to the council. In August, 431 the new commissioner arrived at the council with a letter from Theodosius noting that he had accepted the deposition of the three prelates "as intimated to us by your piety." The commissioner placed Cyril and Nestorius and later Memnon under arrest.

The Council of Ephesus did not itself arrive at a doctrinal statement acceptable to those who attended. What is known as the *Formula of Reunion* originated, rather, with the Orientals and was largely the work of Theodoret of Cyrus. Although it affirmed the use of Theotokos, the statement favored the Antiochene rather than the Cyrillian position. Theodosius finally dissolved the council, sending Nestorius to a monastery in Antioch and Cyril back to Alexandria. He appointed an old friend of John Chrysostom, Maximian, patriarch in place of Nestorius (431–434). There remained still, however, the task of reconciling the two camps headed by John of Antioch and Cyril. Skillful negotiations on the part of John led in 433 to acceptance of the *Formula of Reunion* by Cyril with the proviso that Nestorius would be sent into exile. This agreement rankled many. Theodore, for instance, refused to consent to Nestorius's deposition. Alexander, his metropolitan, would neither accept the latter nor communicate with Cyril. The hierarchy in Cilicia excommunicated Cyril and withdrew from communion with Antioch.

After four peaceful years in Antioch Nestorius was banished to Petra and then to Egypt, where he finally died about June, 451. When his writings were banned, his followers circulated those of Diodore of Tarsus and Theodore of Mopsuestia, translated into Syriac, Armenian, and Persian. Harsh imperial action against the Nestorian school in Edessa forced the removal of most Nestorians to Persia.

Eutychianism

The imperial solution to the Christological controversy which swirled around Nestorius did not pacify supporters of Cyril either, exile of Nestorius notwithstanding. Cyril himself had to make far too great concessions to Antiochene thinking to put at ease the anxieties of his followers who still clung to the formula "one incarnate nature of God the Logos." In their minds the *Formula of Reunion* of 433 was dyophysite. They could say two natures *before* the union, but they insisted that there was only one *after* it. At Alexandria the Monophysites were led by the ambitious Dioscurus, Cyril's successor (444–451); at Constantinople by Eutyches, for thirty years archimandrite of a large monastery near Constantinople, and his godson Chrysaphius, minister of Theodosius. The influence of the eunuch Chrysaphius with Theodosius from 441 until the latter's death as a result of a fall from a horse on July 28, 450, assured for a time the triumph of Eutyches.

Leading the opposition to Eutychianism was Theodoret of Cyrus. In a work written in 446–447, *The Beggar or Polymorph*, Theodoret described the Eutychian theology as a collection of old Gnostic rags and argued (1) the unchangeable character of the Lord's divinity, (2) the nonmixture of divinity and humanity, and (3) the impassability of his divinity. The Eutychians soon responded with a counterblast against Irenaeus, bishop of Tyre and friend of Nestorius; Ibas, bishop of Edessa (435–457), who had interpreted Cyril's acceptance of the *Formula* as a retraction and blasted his own bishop, Rabbula, as a tyrant and turncoat; and Theodoret. Through connections at court the Eutychians secured the deposition of Irenaeus and consecration of Photius in his place as bishop of Tyre (448–451); the deposition and banishment of Ibas with imprisonment in as many as twenty different places; and the confinement of Theodoret to his own diocese—all by imperial decree.

The tide began to turn against Eutyches soon thereafter, however. In November, 448 he was hailed before Flavian, Archbishop of Constantinople, at a synod on charges brought by Eusebius, bishop of Dorylaeum (448–451) and the leader of the opposition to Nestorius twenty years before. Eusebius had tried to divert his friend Eutyches from the path of error but had failed. At first Eutyches declined to attend the synod but sent a letter in which he confessed his belief in "one nature" of God incarnate and argued that a doctrine of "two natures in one Person" could not be found in the Fathers and, even if it could, he would not believe it. When he did finally attend, he refused to admit two natures in the incarnate Lord. The synod proceeded to condemn him not only for Apollinarianism but also for Valentinianism. He then appealed to the synods of Rome, Alexandria, Jerusalem, and Thessalonica.

Eutyches did not delay in appealing to Rome. Flavian did. In the meantime, Eutyches used his court connections to advantage, and on March 30, 449, Theodosius summoned a council to meet at Ephesus on August 1, which has gone down in history as the "Robbers' Synod." Pope Leo was a bit late in issuing his *Tome* to head off a council which he considered unnecessary, and the *Tome* and his legates received a very rough and impolite treatment at the council.

As a prelude to the council, Emperor Theodosius ordered Flavian to produce a written statement of his faith. Flavian complied willingly, affirming his agreement with Nicaea, Constantinople, and Ephesus and acknowledging belief in "two natures in one person" after the incarnation. Meantime, Chrysaphius and Eutyches invited Dioscurus to attack Flavian. Chrysaphius also made sure the council would consist of as few opponents of Eutyches as possible. Theodosius himself assured Dioscurus that Theodoret would not attend. He summoned Pope Leo I, who sent three legates bearing the *Tome*, which favored the dyophysite views of the *Formula of Reunion* and Flavian.

Meeting in the same church the earlier Council of Ephesus had met in under the presidency of Dioscurus, the "Robbers' Synod" proceeded in a predictable fashion. Dioscurus relegated forty-two prelates who had taken part in the condemnation of Eutyches to the status of spectators. He refused to allow the papal legates to read Leo's *Tome*. When the council heard the minutes of the council which condemned Eutyches read, they cried out for the burning of Eusebius of Dorylaeum, his accuser, and acclaimed Eutyches' confession of one nature in the incarnation. They reaffirmed Eutyches' orthodoxy and restored him to his office as presbyter and archimandrite. They then proceeded to depose Flavian and Domnus, Archbishop of Antioch. Troops rushed to force signatures against Flavian and to arrest Flavian and Eusebius. Flavian later died as a result of kicks and blows he received from some of the monks. The bishops then reinforced imperial decisions against Irenaeus, Ibas, and Theodoret and ratified Cyril's *Twelve Anathemas*.

Reaction against the proceedings set in immediately. Theodoret, Flavian, and Eusebius of Dorylaeum all appealed to Rome. Receiving these appeals at a synod in Rome celebrating the anniversary of his consecration, September 29, 449, Leo wrote seven letters of protest against the "Robbers' Synod," urging Easterners to "stand fast" against this injustice. He persuaded the Western Emperor Valentinian III, his mother Galla Placidia, and his wife Eudoxia to intercede with Theodosius. Theodosius, however, ignored all entreaties, and the situation did not change until he died on July 28, 450. His sister Pulcheria (450–453) and her husband Marcian turned the tide against the Monophysites.

Chalcedon

Pulcheria's first act was to have the eunuch Chrysaphius, who had exerted such strong influence over her brother, put to death, thus depriving the Eutychians of their chief secular support. She then wed Marcian, a senator and soldier held in high esteem and as committed to the dyophysite position as she was. Together the monarchs proceeded to reverse the effects of the Synod of Ephesus in 449, bringing Flavian's body back to Constantinople, recalling Theodoret and other exiles, and restoring relations with Rome. Before responding to letters of Leo placing blame for the situation on Dioscurus and other bishops who aided him and suggesting how the issue could now be dealt with, the regents issued a summons to the bishops on May 17, 451 to meet in an ecumenical council at Nicaea on September 1. Although Leo still did not favor a council, he appointed two legates on June 24 and supplied them with a copy of his *Tome* and other instructions. He also send letters addressed to Emperor Marcian, the patriarch Anatolius, Julian of Cos, and the Council. Leo's main concern was the restoration of those deposed for faithful adherence to the Catholic faith as set forth in his *Tome*.

Although the emperor originally designated Nicaea, he had to shift the site closer to the capital, the suburb of Chalcedon, for fear of the Huns in Illyrica. When many of the 520 bishops, all Easterners except the two papal legates and two Africans, hesitated lest the monks of the capital disrupt their proceedings, Marcian issued a decree forbidding disturbances. Empress Pulcheria added to this a letter expelling all monks, clergy, or lay persons in the vicinity except those present by imperial orders or to aid their bishops. Thus secured, the council opened at Chalcedon on October 8 and lasted until November 1. Imperial Commissioners headed by Patriarch Anatolius took charge in the absence of "the believing Emperors" who "presided for the sake of order."

As the council opened, supporters of Dioscurus, Juvenal of Jerusalem, and Anastasius of Thessalonica—bishops of Egypt, Palestine, and Illyricum—lined up on one side and supporters of Leo on the other, to the left and right of the nineteen imperial commissioners. The commissioners ordered Dioscurus to defend himself and directed that Theodoret, excluded from the "Robbers' Synod," be invited in. The appearance of Theodoret as the accuser along with Eusebius of Dorylaeum set off a round of cheers from backers of Leo and a chorus of boos from backers of Dioscurus. The commissioners had to take a firm hand to silence the raucous assembly. When secretaries reviewed the proceedings of the "Robber's Synod"—how it had forbidden the reading of Leo's *Tome*, rehabilitated Eutyches, and condemned Flavian—many bishops present at that meeting hastened to offer excuses and apologies for their part in it. Review of the minutes of Flavian's Council of Constantinople and his declaration of faith brought forth a general exclamation that he had "rightly explained the faith." At this point Juvenal, the patriarch of Jerusalem, and all of the bishops of Palestine crossed over to the Leonine side. Next followed the bishops of Illyricum, except for Atticus, bishop of Nicopolis (446–451) and Metropolitan of Epirus Vetus, who claimed illness and left the hall, and even four Egyptian bishops. Dioscurus remained almost alone save for the rest of the Egyptians. Before concluding the first day's session, the bishops attributed the evils of Ephesus in 449 to Dioscurus, Juvenal, Thalassius, Eusebius of Ancyra, Eustathius of Berytus, and Basil of Seleucia and declared them deposed.

Two days later, at the second session, without Dioscurus and the deposed bishops present, the bishops set about the task of framing a satisfactory doctrinal statement. In turn they reviewed the Creeds of Nicaea and Constantinople, Cyril's second letter to Nestorius and his letter to John of Antioch, the *Tome*, and some extracts Leo had collected from Hilary of Poitiers, Gregory of Nazianzus, Ambrose, Chrysostom, Augustine, and Cyril. The *Tome* forcefully argued against Eutyches the doctrine of two natures without confusion in one person. The majority of the assembly simply ignored the *Twelve Anathemas* of Cyril and acclaimed the *Tome*, saying, "Peter has spoken through Leo." Some, however, found three passages in the *Tome* sounding a bit too Nestorian. At the request of Atticus of Nicopolis, who had now returned, the commissioners granted a five-day recess to allow a committee headed by Anatolius to examine the *Tome* and prepare a response to the doubters.

After reaffirming the deposition of Dioscurus in a session he refused to attend, in its fourth session the council reiterated its acceptance of Nicaea, Constantinople, Ephesus (431–433), and Leo's *Tome* as "in harmony with the Creed." The imperial government, however, pressed for a precise doctrinal formula acceptable to all. A statement drawn up by the committee headed by Anatolius sounded acceptable to some but not to others. When the commissioners inquired of the emperors how to break the deadlock, they were instructed either (1) to put the committee back to work, or (2) to let each bishop, one by one, express his belief through his metropolitan, or (3) to hold a synod in the West. Since the last two options were unthinkable, the bishops declared their determination to come up with a definition. The committee, therefore, went to work once more and came out with the formula of Chalcedon. The critical clause affirmed *Theotokos* while rejecting both Eutychianism and Nestorianism.

Following therefore the holy Fathers, we all teach, with one accord, one and the same Son, our Lord Jesus Christ . . . who for us and for our salvation, according to his humanity, was born of the Virgin Mary, *Theotokos*, one and the same Christ, Son, Lord—only-begotten, confessed in two natures, without confusion, without change, without

division or separation. The difference of natures is in no way denied by reason of their union; on the other hand, the distinctness of each nature is preserved, and both concur in one Person and one *Hypostasis*.

Although the language was Cyrillian, the substance was basically Antiochene and Leonine. Discerning observers could easily foresee disaster looming on the horizon.

In the first place, the emperors pressed for a more precise formula than the six hundred plus signers could subscribe to in good conscience. Just as Constantine had done at Nicaea, moreover, they forced acceptance of a Western formula when, in fact, nearly all of the signers were Easterners. The majority doubtless favored Cyril's and not Theodoret's or Leo's definition. The only happy subscribers, therefore, were either the adherents of the imperial court or Nestorians, who hailed the definition as a vindication of their exiled leader. Armenians, Syrians, and Egyptians, never comfortably a part of the empire anyway, returned home convinced Monophysites. As if this were not enough by itself, Marcian laid a heavy hand on the churches by proposing three canons designed to limit the growing assertiveness of the monks, the increasing secularity of clergy and monks, and clerical migration and by insisting on elevation of the status of the patriarchate of Constantinople to jurisdictional level equal to that of Rome in the West. The latter proved extremely offensive to the papacy, but the assembled bishops chose not to pay serious attention to the protests of the papal legates. Leo did his best to have the canon overturned, but he finally had to approve the Council's decision regarding faith without withdrawing his protest about Canon 28. Emperor Marcian himself had his hands full defending the theological formula. February 7, 452 he issued a decree making it illegal for "cleric or soldier or person of any condition" to raise disputes in religious matters. Few, however, paid any attention to that or several other decrees designed to quiet the opposition to Chalcedon.

Monophysitism

The Cyrillians soon displayed their numbers and strength in Palestine, Egypt, and Syria. Dropping Eutyches' doctrine, which suggested absorption of the human nature by the divine in the incarnation, the Monophysites now proposed, in line with Cyril, a coalescence of divine and human natures in a single theanthropic ("divine/human") nature. They saw in Leo's resistance to Canon 28 of Chalcedon a glimmer of hope that he, too, might reject the Council's decisions, but that hope proved false.

In *Palestine* a former monk named Theodosius stirred up the large body of monks there against the Council of Chalcedon as having rehabilitated Nestorius and defamed Cyril by deposing his successor, Dioscurus. Theodosius did not find it difficult to rally the support of such illustrious pilgrims as Empress Eudocia, widow of Theodosius II, whose definitive council was the so-called Robbers' Synod of Ephesus in 449. When Juvenal of Jerusalem returned to his see, he found the gates of the city closed to him and had to flee to Constantinople as Theodosius proceeded to place Monophysites in the bishoprics of Palestine. The emperors first wrote to the monks to defend Chalcedon and then took action to arrest Theodosius, who fled to Mount Sinai, and to restore Juvenal. Leo also sought further information and wrote to the monks to explain the *Tome* and to Empress Eudocia to point out that Chalcedon opposed both Nestorianism and Eutychianism. Tragedies in her family evidently encouraged the empress to return to the Catholic fold. The capture of Theodosius by imperial police and his death in a monastery in Constantinople in 457 put an end to the Monophysite rebellion in Palestine.

In *Egypt* the Monophysites mounted a more determined and permanent challenge. Although the Alexandrian populace regarded Dioscurus as their patriarch until he died at Gangra in Paphlagonia September 4, 454, the Prefect of Egypt proceeded to install Proterius immediately after the Council of Chalcedon on orders from the emperor Marcian. Mob riots broke out against Byzantine imperialism and had to be suppressed by troops dispatched from Constantinople. On the death of Marcian and election of Leo I (457–474) as his successor in 457, Timothy Aelurus ("the Cat") seized on the occasion of the absence of the general in command to take control of the patriarchate. When Proterius secured a measure of revenge by having the general remove Timothy, his partisans hunted him down, murdered him in the church baptistry, dragged his remains around the city and burned them, reputedly after cannibalizing them. They then appealed to Emperor Leo to overturn Chalcedon. Prompted by Pope Leo I, who declared the proposal to be a work of the Antichrist, the emperor exiled Timothy "the Cat" to Gangra and ultimately to the Crimea, where he remained until after the emperor's death. The Chalcedonians elected another Timothy, Salofaciolus ("the Little Capmaker"), to replace him (459–482). Pope Leo wrote his last three extant letters to the Patriarch Timothy Salofaciolus.

Timothy Aelurus, however, was not finished. After the accession of Leo (474–491) the usurper Basiliscus (475–477) bid for the support of the Monophysites of Egypt by recalling Timothy from the Crimea after eighteen years of exile (458–476). In a decree called the *Encyclical* he sanctioned the two councils of Ephesus (431–433 and 449) and denounced both the errors of Eutyches and the "novelties" of Chalcedon. He required all bishops to sign, making deposition the penalty for refusal. Timothy got a cold shoulder from the Patriarch Acacius in Constantinople, but he repaid him by summoning a synod at Ephesus to reinstate Paul, a bishop whom Acacius had deposed. He had no trouble returning to Alexandria carrying the remains of Dioscurus in a silver casket. Timothy Salofaciolus retired to a Pachomian monastery.

In *Syria* Monophysitism also had a strong supporter in Maximus, an ardent Cyrillian. To the faithful throughout Syria Monophysitism alone could guarantee the divinity of Christ. Leader of the Monophysite forces was Peter the Fuller, who had once belonged to the community of Acoeme-tae, ardent Chalcedonians, but had split with them and become head of a monastery at Chalce-don. In 468 he accompanied Zeno to Antioch, where he served as commander-in-chief of "the East." There he led the Monophysites in driving out Martyrius, Patriarch of Antioch (460–470), and succeeded in having himself installed as Mar-tyrius's successor. Martyrius appealed to Gen-nadius, patriarch of Constantinople (460– 471), and secured Peter's exile. Basiliscus restored him to the throne of Antioch (475–476), but Zeno banished him once more when he regained control of the empire in 477. Monophysites murdered the Chalcedonian Stephen (478– 482). Acacius installed Calandion as a compromise candidate (482–485), but Peter the Fuller ascend-ed the throne a third time (485–488).

The Monophysites reached the pinnacle of their power under Basiliscus, who obtained the signatures of three of the four Eastern patriarchs to his *Encyclical*—Alexandria, Antioch, and Jerusalem. Only Acacius of Constantinople held out, drawing support from the monks of the capital, especially the Stylite Daniel, who de-scended from his pillar to rouse the populace in support of Chalcedon and to predict the return of Zeno. The prediction so overawed Basilicus that he issued an *Anti-Encyclical* negating the *Encyc-lical*, but the move did not save him. Zeno reentered Constantinople in July 477 and restored the *status quo* as it existed before Basiliscus. Receiving congratulations from Pope Simplicius (468–483), the emperor and the Patriarch quickly proceeded to remove Timothy Aelurus, Paul of Ephesus, Peter the Fuller, and his protege John of Apamea. In Egypt, however, the removal of

Timothy did not end the schism, for Monophy-sites replaced him with one of their own, Peter Mongus ("the Stammerer" (477–490), despite the fact that the Catholic Patriarch Timothy Salofaci-olus was still living. Zeno sent orders to the Prefect of Egypt to put Peter Mongus to death, but Timothy interceded to have the sentence commuted to exile. He ruled five years (477–482). By virtue of a political *faux pas* on the part of John Talaia, Timothy's elected successor, however, which offended the Patriarch Acacius, Peter Mongus returned to the throne. Zeno sent instructions to banish John Talaia. he also ad-dressed to the bishops of Egypt the *Henoticon*, which he intended to resolve the controversy by shifting imperial favor to the Monphysites.

Shifting Balances

The object of Emperor Zeno in issuing the *Henoticon* is quite clear. Hopes for recovery of the West extremely dim after Odovacer returned the symbols of the office in 476, he must now concentrate on uniting the populace in the East, most of whom favored Monophysitism. Deliber-ately sidestepping the issue of Chalcedon's legiti-macy, the *Henoticon* focused on the Creed of Nicaea, reaffirmed at Constantinople and at Ephe-sus by those who opposed Nestorius, as an ade-quate basis for union. It denounced Eutyches, approved Cyril's *Twelve Anathemas* and, summa-rizing the faith in an unexceptionable way, anathematized all who believed anything to the contrary. Zeno's successor, Anastasius (491–518), pursued the same policy in hopes of conciliating Syria and Egypt. In 496 he secured confirmation of the *Henoticon* at a Council of Constantinople. He removed Euphemius from the patriarchate of Constantinople and installed Macedonius II (496–511), who, though Chalcedonian, did not quibble about the *Henoticon* for a time, but, when he did, Anastasius replaced him with Timothy, a Monophysite.

No real change of policy occurred under Justin (518–527) and his able nephew Justinian

(527–565). The *Henoticon*, although not formally revoked, was allowed quietly to disappear. Immediately after Justin's accession on July 15, 518, the populace of Constantinople cried out for confirmation of Chalcedon, expulsion of the Monophysite Severus from the patriarchate of Antioch, and reconciliation with Rome, but they could not force a major shift. Justinian made only a token turn toward Chalcedon, for he needed still to unite the empire. Empress Theodora, moreover, favored Monophysitism.

Justinian, an astute lay theologian, took a keen interest in theological matters. Three controversies gave him an opportunity to shape the doctrine of the churches—Theopaschitism, 519–533; Origenism, 531–543; and the "Three Chapters," 544–553. The Theopaschite controversy originated from an addition of the phrase "who was crucified for us" to the Trisagion: "Holy God, Holy strong, Holy immortal, *who was crucified for us*, have mercy on us." A Monophysite clause emphasizing the doctrine of one nature in Christ, its addition precipitated riots in Constantinople when introduced on November 6, 512 by the Monophysite Patriarch Timothy. Later, however, with the backing of Emperor, a modified form, "One of the Trinity was crucified in the flesh," became acceptable, notwithstanding the opposition of radical Chalcedonians such as the Acoemetae. By its use Justinian hoped both to dissociate himself from Nestorianizers and to aid understanding of Monophysites. The phrase not only received approval at the Fifth Ecumenical Council in 553, Justinian himself embodied it in a hymn. He argued that if one of the Trinity did not suffer in the flesh, He could not have been born in the flesh and Mary could not be called *Theotokos*.

Origenism, so hotly contested about 400, again became an object of debate early in Justinian's reign when the New Laura near Jerusalem secretly became the center for Origenism, triggering the wrath of Saba, Abbot of the Old Laura. In 531 Saba went to Constantinople to demand that Justinian expel the Origenists. Saba died in 532 before Justinian could take any action. Subsequently, however, two monks of the New Laura gained the emperor's ear and in 537, appointment to important sees, so that it was not until 543 that the papal *apocrisarius* at the imperial court, Pelagius, managed to turn Justinian's opinion. In 543 Justinian issued an edict or letter to Menas, Patriarch of Constantinople (536–552), condemning the Origenists. Soon afterwards, the Home Synod under Menas gave spiritual sanction to the condemnation. Included in the errors of Origen were: his overstatement of the subordination of the Son, his theory of preexistence and fall of souls, his universalism, and his doctrine of successive worlds. In 553 the Fifth Ecumenical Council included Origen in the list of persons condemned for heresy. Thereafter, Eustochius, Patriarch of Jerusalem (552–564), quickly put an end to Origenism in the monasteries of Palestine.

Justinian's condemnation of the "Three Chapters" arose out of a suggestion of Empress Theodora that the Monophysites might be more conciliatory if he were to condemn the Nestorianizers. In 544 Justinian issued an edict condemning the "Three Chapters," which meant originally certain propositions but later came to mean the person of Theodore of Mopsuestia, the letter of Ibas of Edessa to Maris, and the writings of Theodoret of Cyrus. Somewhat reluctantly, the Eastern bishops subscribed to the condemnation. Pope Vigilius (538–555), however, resisted until brought to Constantinople and browbeaten for a year; even then, Western bishops repudiated him for capitulating. Byzantine recovery of Rome from the Ostrogoths at precisely this time, however, left the pope without options, and Justinian would let no one stand in his way.

The Council of Constantinople, opening May 5, 553, brought Justinian's main theological concerns together for final disposition. So anxious was he to get on with it that he published in anticipation in 551 a *Confession of Right Faith against the Three Chapters*, thus breaching his agreement with Pope Vigilius. At the Council Vigilius bravely declined to condemn Theodore, although he agreed to censure his language, or to dishonor Theodoret and Ibas. Justinian exploded. He revealed the secret oath Vigilius had taken to aid in the condemnation of the "Three Chapters" and ordered his name removed from the diptychs on the grounds that he had revealed himself a Nestorian by refusing to condemn them. The assembled bishops had only to assent to Justinian's will in the matter. All 164 signed. The pope's capitulation led to a rift with Western bishops which, in some cases, lasted a century and a half. He could hardly have done otherwise.

Justinian's successors deviated from the conciliatory route he had taken. Justin II (565–578) and Tiberius II (578–582) both favored Chalcedon and persecuted Monophysites. In both instances the Patriarchs—John III Scholasticus (566–577) and Eutychius (577–582)—played a strong role in determining ecclesiastical policy under weak monarchs. With the support of Justin and Sophia John III launched a severe persecution of Monophysites in 571. Eutychius began to persecute them in 580. Maurice (582–602), although not super-Orthodox, aligned himself with John the Faster, Patriarch of Constantinople from 582–595, in his quest to make the see of Constantinople an "ecumenical patriarchate" equal to Rome. Once more, doctrine conceded to politics without solving a problem. Compromise and coercion could quell dissent momentarily, but they could not effect unity either of the church or of the empire.

Chapter 29

Being Christian in a Collapsing World

In the West Christians confronted a radically different world in which they had to live out their faith than Easterners knew. During the fifth and sixth centuries, they had to wrestle with the reality of life and death in a collapsing world. By temperament, of course, Latins also differed significantly from Greeks. As their absence from the ecumenical councils would indicate, few of them had an obsession for the crucial phrases describing the relationships of the Son to the Father or of the human to the divine nature in the incarnation. Beset by matters much more urgent, they wanted to have some *raison d'être* for the fall of the Eternal City and to hear some word of encouragement when the very wrath of heaven seemed unleashed against them.

Two quite different sets of answers came to their ears, one from the monk Pelagius and the other from the bishop of Hippo, Augustine. Pelagius gave an answer for the few, the strong: Augustine for the many, the weak. This evil, Pelagius insisted, is a consequence of human failure to live up to their God-given potential. Consequently, the answer lies in discipline, doing the good which nature equips us to do. For Augustine, long one of the weak himself, such an answer failed to take into account the awesome power of evil and the frailty of humanity. People needed more than self-discipline, strong wills: they needed supernatural grace, the Holy Spirit,

God's presence and power to strengthen them in their weakness.

Over the long run, neither Pelagius nor Augustine won the debate, although Pelagius's reputation suffered far more damage than Augustine's. Christians of the West claimed Augustine as their theologian *par excellence*, and his thought shaped Western thinking more than any other. Nevertheless, it would be naive indeed to assume that a rapidly barbarized civilization understood and appropriated his ideas without significant alteration. Far from it, while acclaiming him, they also modified what they took from him, tempering his thought to fit their own experience and point of view. In a society on its way to domination by monks like Pelagius, the Synod of Orange in 529 sprinkled Augustine with a few dashes of modified Pelagianism to make him more savory to medieval taste.

Augustine

Augustine's own life (354–430) and work mirror in many ways the tumultuous times through which Western civilization was passing. A child of ambitious middle class parents, he received the best education their meager resources would allow—first at Thagaste, then at nearby Madaura, and finally at Carthage. As a matter of fact, he had to delay his study at Carthage one year while his father, Patricius, found money to send him. Although his parents agreed about education, they did not agree about religion. Patricius was pagan until converted near the end of his life, Monica a devout and puritanical Christian. Their conflicting desires in religion for their son probably had much to do with an extended and tortuous process of conversion.

At Carthage the seventeen year old Augustine abandoned what little Christianity he possessed. "In love with love" (*Conf.* 3.1.1.) he entered into a common-law marriage which lasted fifteen years to a woman he never named but who bore him a son named Adeodatus ("Given by God"). At age nineteen he experienced what some have labeled his "first conversion" on reading Cicero's *Hortensius*. The *Hortensius* changed his "feelings" and directed his energies toward God and a search for Wisdom for its own sake. He turned to the Bible to find Wisdom, but its crude style disappointed someone so geared to style. It may also have heightened a sense of guilt kept ever before his mind by his mother Monica, for he turned to the Manichaean sect then attractive to so many students. The Manichaeans helped him to solve the problem of scriptures by rejecting the Old Testament and allegorizing what they did accept and by explaining that evil was an eternal substance and thus unavoidable. He was doing what he was doing because he *had* to and should not feel badly about it. He remained a Manichaean "hearer," equivalent to a catechumen in the Catholic church, for nine years.

Tragedy, however, broke the grip of Manichaeism on Augustine's life, a death of a dear friend. Manichaean theology could neither account for the tragedy nor assuage the grief and pain Augustine felt. When he returned from Carthage to teach in his hometown, he renewed a friendship with this friend of his youth. They became exceedingly close. During an illness, his friend received baptism at the urging of his family and recovered momentarily. Augustine tried unsuccessfully to win him back to Mani-

chaeism. Then, while Augustine was out of town, his friend died. Grief overwhelmed him. He could think of nothing but death. So he tried the geographical solution and went back to Carthage.

At Carthage Augustine experienced success as a teacher of rhetoric, but he found the students rowdy and undisciplined. By 382, moreover, he had grown disillusioned with Manichaeism, after a conference with Faustus, the leading Manichaean theologian, failed to solve his theological conundrum. Encouraged by his friend Alypius, an administrative lawyer who had gone on ahead of him, he decided to go to Rome. When Monica, grief stricken at the prospect of his leaving, insisted on accompanying him, he lied to her and sailed without her. His guilt at deceiving her, an illness, and students who did not pay their tuition shortened Augustine's stay in Rome, and he welcomed the Perfect Symmachus's invitation to become professor of rhetoric in Milan, site of the imperial court in the West and, more importantly, the bishopric of Ambrose. Monica, not easily put aside, later joined him at Milan.

Augustine initially went to hear the famous bishop Ambrose out of curiosity regarding the latter's rhetorical skills. Open to being taught at this critical juncture of his life, however, he gradually reached beyond rhetoric to substance. Through allegorical exposition Ambrose helped the struggling catechumen to transcend the rough exterior of scriptures and to discover there the Wisdom for which he longed. Ambrose was less "soothing and entertaining" than Faustus, but "far more learned" (*Conf.* 5.12.23). He could defend the Old Testament against the Manichaeans. When Monica arrived, she reinforced her son's growing reliance on Ambrose as a spiritual guide.

More prominent at this juncture than Ambrose, however, was a circle of friends, ten in all, who rallied around Augustine in Milan, among them his common-law wife, until he sent her back to Africa and arranged an engagement to a ten year old girl at Monica's insistence; his son, Adeodatus; his mother Monica; and his African friends Alypius and Nebridius. They loved Augustine enough to pool their resources to support the search for truth in which they engaged. They became the midwives of his rebirth.

The first stage in the process, in the summer of 386, entailed a transition from what remained of Manichaean thought to Platonic, particularly on the question of evil. Whereas Manichaeism propounded a radical dualism, ascribing to evil an eternal existence, Neoplatonism taught that evil is the absence or perversion of good. For Augustine this translated into a radically different explanation for his seeming inability to control his sex drive. He was not doing what he was doing because he *had* to, as the Manichaeans said, but because he *wanted* to, as the Neoplatonists said. He had free will and he must exercise it.

It was precisely at this point, however, that Augustine would see the need to go beyond Platonism and would, in the future, make a signal contribution to Western thought. Though in his mind he agreed with the Platonists, he still found himself a captive of two wills, so that, like the Apostle Paul, he still did not do the good he wanted to do. And it was in Paul, over whose writings he had been poring, that he found the answer, viz., in the grace of God. Hearing from his Platonist friends about the conversion of Victorinus, a noted Neoplatonist philosopher, eased his mind. If Victorinus found Christianity respectable, he too could find it so. But he still had to face up to himself.

Self-confrontation occurred at Cassiciacum, a villa near Lake Como where the little band had gathered to pursue Wisdom, in a strange way but one perfectly suited to Augustine's struggle of soul. Ponticianus, an imperial agent visiting Cassiciacum, related the story of the conversion of two young Roman noblemen who, on hearing the story of Anthony of Egypt's conversion, left their fiancees and took up the ascetic life. The story struck Augustine at the core of his being. As he graphically depicted his experience, through it God took him from behind his own back and made him look at himself, how vile and deformed and unclean he was. It brought him back to where Cicero's *Hortensius* had put him at age nineteen. So distraught was he that he hastened to a secluded garden with Alypius on his heels. He knew the problem lay in his will. Within himself he kept praying, "Let it be now," but he did not yet achieve what he sought. The voice of continence kept challenging. More and more distressed, he tore himself away from Alypius's side and threw himself down in a flood of tears. There he heard a child's voice urging, "Take up and read. Take up and read." Interpreting this as a divine command, he returned to where Alypius was sitting and picked up the scriptures he had thrown down in exasperation. They fell open to Romans 13:13: "not in rioting and drunkenness, not in fornication and wantonness, not in contention and envy, but put on the Lord Jesus Christ and no longer take thought for the flesh and its concupiscences." He did not need to read further.

In September, 386, abandoning plans for marriage, Augustine took up a semimonastic "leisure" at Cassiciacum under patronage of Romanianus, to whom he dedicated a treatise *On the Happy Life*, to sort out his Christian philosophy. Unlike Ambrose and many Christians of earlier generations, he did not regard philosophy negatively, and he needed time to heal. By the end of his stay he was searching deep within himself for answers. "Teach me to know myself. Teach me to know You," was the urgent entreaty of the *Soliloquies*. He was discovering both the God of the philosophers and the God of Paul, the God of grace. He received baptism at the hands of Ambrose on Easter (April 25), 387.

Shortly thereafter, Augustine, his mother, Adeodatus, and his friend Evodius headed back to Africa. Monica died at Ostia before they set sail for Carthage, but not before she and her "son of tears" shared a vision of Wisdom together (*Conf.* 9.10.23-25), a remarkable mystical experience. After returning to Rome for a time to wait for the lifting of a blockade of the port, Augustine finally arrived in Carthage late in 388.

On his return to Africa Augustine formed around himself once again a semimonastic community on the family estates in Thagaste, where Alypius later became bishop. Very soon, he had to take up the pen against the sect of Manichaeans. He wrote first a commentary *On Genesis* against them and then summarized his position in a treatise *On True Religion*. Subsequently in a treatise *On Free Will* he set forth a Neoplatonic view which Pelagius would later cite in support of the central tenet of his own system. Augustine's thinking gradually shifted, however, from a rational to a dogmatic stance.

Making a signal contribution to the African church in his anti-Manichaean writings, he found himself pulled increasingly into its official life. In 391, having recently lost his friend Nebridius and his son Adeodatus, he went to Hippo Regius in search of a site for a monastery. As he stood in the congregation, the bishop, Valerius, spoke of the urgent needs of the church for priests. The congregation turned to Augustine and pushed him toward the apse where the bishop and priests sat. A Greek who could not speak Latin well, Valerius tiptoed around custom to insist that Augustine preach. In 395 he asked the Primate of Carthage to consecrate Augustine as his coadjutor, also in violation of church canons, this time Nicaea's. With Valerius's blessing Augustine secured the monastery he had sought, but for the clergy of Hippo rather than for a circle of select friends.

Very soon, Augustine found himself engaging not only the Manichaeans but also the powerful Donatists. Donatism had had great success in Numidia, particularly in small towns and the countryside, and was in Augustine's day the established church. One Donatist, Tyconius, was the leading African exegete from whom Augustine himself borrowed heavily, though eventually excommunicated from his own church. Drawing on the discontent of people in rural areas, the Donatists, especially the most radical group

called the *Circumcelliones*, employed violence against Catholics and fostered violence in return. Augustine viewed his role as bishop as protector of the people. Accordingly, he dealt with Donatists heavy handedly and became the recognized leader in the push to put down the Donatist revolt. When Augustine arrived in Hippo, Catholics were a minority, so the vigor with which he preached against Donatism was understandable. He showed none of the tolerance for which other Catholic bishops were known. He caricatured Donatists in popular tracts. He applauded imperial efforts of Honorius, a devout Catholic, to put an end to the schism as well as suppress paganism. In his long treatise *Against the Epistle of Parmenian* he argued early on that Christian emperor had a right to punish impieties. When in 405 Emperor Honorius issued the *Edict of Unity* branding Donatism a heresy, the bishop of Hippo viewed it as an act of providence. Seeing that force worked, thereafter he developed a full justification for the state's suppression of non-Catholics. Fallen human beings require constraint, *disciplina*, he argued. After 405 he busied himself disposing of property of Donatist churches, drawing up lists of Donatists, receiving Donatist converts, and seeing that laws were enforced. In June 411 he personally headed the Catholic bishops at Carthage in the final confrontation with Donatist bishops. The imperial legate, Flavius Marcellinus, a devout Catholic, ruled that the Donatists had no case against imposition of the *Edict of Unity* of Honorius. Thenceforward, Donatism was repressed, although some vestiges survived underground until the seventh century.

The sack of Rome on August 24, 410 by the Goths under Alaric opened a new phase in Augustine's eventful life. Rome, symbol of civilization and of the endurance of civilized society, had fallen. Immediately the great bishop addressed lengthy sermons to the fears, griefs, and anxieties of his people and wrote letters to leading refugees, many of whom fled to Africa ahead of the invaders. He had to help them make some sense of the political collapse which had taken them by surprise and to find in it some ray of hope. His answer, spun out over thirteen years, became his indisputably greatest work, *The City of God*, a response to renewal of pagan charges blaming Christians for the fall of Rome. The word of hope on which he drew this work to a close was that, amid evils all around, there still flows, "as in a vast, racing river" (*City of God* 22.24.11), a wealth of good—in the human body, in human intellect, in nature—which remind us of the greater good of eternity.

It was this same tragic set of events which furnished the setting for the advent of Pelagius and the controversy which would occupy so much of Augustine's energies during his last years and which held a central place in later impressions of the theology of Augustine. Because the controversy will receive extended treatment below, however, brief note should be taken of Augustine's remaining years. He continued, of course, to fulfill the increasingly important role of bishop. He not only tended the faithful in this own flock, he also exercised a paternal care for the body politic to which they belonged. He kept pressure on public officials to extirpate the last vestiges of paganism and heresy and to unify Christians in the Catholic church. In his last years after the fall of Rome he had to minister also to an array of prominent refugees such as Melania the Younger and her husband Pinian, who fled Rome ahead of the Goths, and to answer inquiries of notables such as Paulinus of Nola and his wife Therasia on how best to live the Christian life in such circumstances. Augustine's significance as a theologian, of course, brought him to the notice of scholars such as Jerome, who could point up the great African's deficiencies in biblical interpretation even as Augustine could point up Jerome's as a theologian.

On September 26, 426, Augustine appointed his successor, Heraclius. Although preoccupation with the Pelagian controversy had caused him to neglect intellectual matters at home, he composed

his treatise *On Christian Doctrine*. As he aged, he modified some earlier views. Whereas in 390 in his treatise *On True Religion* he had negated continuance of miracles after the apostolic age, in the last book of *The City of God* he gathered a panoply of miracle stories. he made room for the unexpected. His health failing, he had to stand by helpless as he watched Roman Africa give way to the Vandals. In the spring of 430 they overran Mauretania and Numidia. In August Augustine fell seriously ill and died on August 28. Shortly afterwards, the Vandals set siege to the city, which was evacuated and partly burned. Fortunately, his library escaped.

Pelagianism

Little is known about Pelagius apart from the controversy he precipitated. According to early accounts, he was a British monk noted for his learning and piety. He spoke both Latin and Greek. He arrived in Rome at least as early as the pontificate of Anastasius I (399–401) and was held in high esteem by the group Jerome had shepherded in the 380s. Around 405 he made contact with Easterners, who shared his more optimistic view of human nature. He may have been influenced by Theodore of Mopsuestia (392–428), "the Interpreter," in writing his commentary on Romans. His own views, however, were shaped chiefly in reaction against Manichaeism and in debate with Augustine.

About 405 Pelagius became indignant when he heard a bishop quote with approval a statement from Augustine's *Confessions* (10.40): "Lord, you have commanded continence. Give what you command, and command what you will." Pelagius concluded that this kind of deterministic thinking was the source of moral laxity among Roman Christians. In his mind all that is required is the exercise of human capacity for free will, *natural* grace.

Pelagius began to gather disciples. The most notable of them was Caelestius, who equalled

Pelagius in ability and exceeded him in outspokenness. More emphatically than Pelagius, Caelestius rejected the idea of a "Fall" of humankind. Human beings in every age are in the same state as Adam at creation. They are free to will or not to will the good.

Pelagius and Caelestius might never have come to the attention of Augustine had it not been for the Gothic invasion of Italy. About 409, as the Goths approached Rome, they departed for Sicily and Africa. Staying in Sicily only long enough to plant some seeds of their theology, they proceeded to Hippo and then to Carthage, where, in 411, Augustine occupied himself with the Donatists. Pelagius pushed on toward Palestine, but Caelestius remained in Carthage, where, on seeking ordination, he found himself accused of heresy before the bishop, Aurelius, by the then deacon Paulinus, later bishop of Nola, resident in Carthage as an agent of the church of Milan and writing a biography of Ambrose.

In 411–412 Aurelius summoned a council and Paulinus outlined Caelestius's errors: (1) Adam was created mortal and would have died whether he had sinned or not. (2) Adam's sin injured only himself and not the whole human race. (3) Newborn infants are in the same state as Adam before he sinned. (4) Adam's sin and death did not cause the death of all humankind, nor does Christ's resurrection cause the resurrection of all. (5) The Law brings people into the kingdom of God just as the Gospel does. (6) Even before Christ came, there were those who did not sin. In the course of the examination Caelestius insisted in reference to the second point that the transmission of sin was an open issue, but on the third point he claimed that he had always affirmed that infants needed baptism "for forgiveness of sins." The council condemned him, and he proceeded to Ephesus, where he again sought ordination.

Although Augustine did not attend the council, he soon entered the fray in sermons and treatises to refute Caelestius's views as destruc-

tive of the doctrine of redemption. At the request of Marcellinus, Emperor Honorius's high commissioner, Augustine wrote in 412 his first major anti-Pelagian treatise *On Merits and the Forgiveness of Sins and the Baptism of Infants*. Yes, he admitted, Adam was created mortal, but he would not have died had he not sinned. Here already he seized on the mistranslation of Romans 5:12, "Adam, in whom (*in quo*) all sinned," to make the point that Adam's sin afflicted all his descendents. Sin is more than imitation of Adam. Infants would not require baptism unless they were spiritually sick. In baptism they received forgiveness of original sin and not their own misdeeds. Though by the grace of God and our free will we can be without sin, no one save Christ ever lived a sinless life.

As he completed this response, Pelagius's *Commentary on Romans* came into his hands with a further argument against original sin, that is, that if Adam's sin works against those who do not sin, Christ's righteousness is efficacious for those who do not believe. In a letter to Marcellinus Augustine replied that infants, too, are believers and benefit from what parents and sponsors do for them. When Marcellinus had trouble understanding how, if it were possible to be without sin, as Augustine conceded, none had been sinless, Augustine wrote another treatise, *On the Spirit and the Letter*, pointing out that scriptures cite many examples of things God can do which have never happened. To live without sin depends on grace, that is, the Holy Spirit working in the soul, and not on free will. The will is set free only by grace.

The views of Pelagius and Caelestius found ready acceptance in Africa. Their appeal prompted Augustine to deliver a stern warning to a Carthaginian congregation on June 25, 413 about the novelty of saying that infants are baptized in order to enter the kingdom rather than to have sins forgiven. Unbaptized infants, he echoed Cyprian, are damned. One of the notables attracted to Pelagius was Demetrias, daughter of Olybrius, consul in 395, who had fled to Carthage with her mother Juliana and her grandmother Proba as the Goths approached Rome. Her wealthy mother and grandmother arranged a marriage to an affluent protector in exile, but on the eve of the wedding Demetrias chose the life of virginity, gave her possessions to the poor, and took the veil. Jerome wrote to congratulate and encourage her and to give advice. So, too, did Pelagius in 414. In his letter he emphasized the "strength" of human nature characterized especially by free will. Even non-Christians have done good deeds; how much more should Christians, trained to better things and aided by divine grace. Many—Abel, Joseph, Job—lived saintly lives under the Law; how much more worthily should we live under grace. Everything turns on the will. We can merit grace! Augustine wrote Juliana in 417 or 418 to warn lest Demetrias think she could attain spiritual riches by her own merits.

Early in 415 Augustine responded to Pelagius's treatise *On Nature* at the request of two youths of good birth and education, Timasius and James, whom Pelagius had persuaded to take up the ascetic life and to embrace his views, with a work entitled *On Nature and Grace*. Against Pelagius's theory of the sufficiency of the "grace of nature," the bishop of Hippo argued a case for supernatural grace. Grace is not contrary to nature, but nature, vitiated by sin, must be delivered and governed by grace.

By this time the center of attention shifted from Africa to Palestine, where Jerome was already doing battle with Pelagius. Pelagius had gained the ear of John, the Patriarch of Jerusalem (386–417). In a letter to an inquirer and in his *Dialogues against the Pelagians* (415) Jerome argued much as Augustine had against the Pelagian concept of natural grace by which one can live sinlessly. In the meantime, John invited Orosius, a young Spanish refugee from Bragada in Gallaecia, to relate what he knew of the Pelagian controversy to the diocesan synod of Jerusalem on July 28. When Orosius concluded, the Patriarch in-

vited Pelagius in and asked him if he held opinions Augustine, Jerome, and others attributed to him. To the surprise of Orosius, when he said yes, the Patriarch did not let that become a cause of condemnation. Instead, he asked if Orosius and his fellow presbyters wanted to file a formal charge. When they declined, finding it increasingly difficult to communicate because of language barriers, John accepted Orosius's suggestion that the matter was Latin and should be referred to Pope Innocent I (402–417). Several weeks later, when Orosius went to pay his respects to John, the latter accused him of saying that no one could live without sin even with God's help. To clear himself, Orosius wrote his *Apologetic Book on Free Will*, which he addressed to the priests of Jerusalem.

Subsequently two refugee bishops from Gaul, Heros of Arles (409–412) and Lazarus of Aix (409–412), drew up formal charges against Pelagius and presented them to Eulogius, bishop of Caesarea (404–417) and Metropolitan of Palestina I. Eulogius summoned the Synod of Diospolis to meet on December 20, 415 at Lydda. Thirteen bishops, including John of Jerusalem, attended, but Heros and Lazarus did not because one of them was ill. With a decided advantage in Greek language Pelagius easily defended himself on the propositions cited before a panel of Eastern bishops inclined, like John Chrysostom, to emphasize free will themselves. The synod acquitted him. Pelagius now set about to repay Jerome. In a treatise *In Behalf of Free Will* addressed to Jerome he acknowledged the need for grace, but, as Augustine charged, he never accorded it its full Pauline significance. It meant: (1) nature with free will, (2) forgiveness of sins, (3) law and teaching, (4) inward illumination, (5) baptismal adoption, and (6) eternal life, but not the Holy Spirit present to empower. A year later, Pelagius received a major boost from Theodore of Mopsuestia's five books *Against Those Who Say People Sin by Nature and Not by Their Own Will* directed at Jerome. Some Pelagian thugs also raided Jerome's monastery at Bethlehem, and he barely escaped with his life.

The scene shifted after this, 416 to 418, to Rome and Africa. In the summer of 416 Orosius, returning to Africa, delivered a letter of Heros and Lazarus to a council of Carthage presided over by Aurelius. The council addressed a letter to Pope Innocent I asking him to place the weight of the Apostolic See behind their condemnation of Pelagius and Caelestius. A council at Mileve in Numidia, with Augustine among the sixty-one bishops present, seconded the request. Augustine and four other bishops backed this up with a private letter to the pope, revealing the level of anxiety in Africa about Rome's handling of the cause in view of known sympathies in Rome for Pelagius and Caelestius. The Synod of Diospolis, they explained, cleared Pelagius only because he admitted grace, but it did not realize that he had not accorded it its full meaning, viz. the help of the Holy Spirit. Innocent replied to each of the letters, indicating that he had excommunicated Pelagius and Caelestius for having denied the need of grace and expressing his own doubts about the Synod of Diospolis. The pope's replies, among his very last acts, brought great joy to the Africans.

The rejoicing, however, did not last long. In 417 Caelestius reappeared in Rome, where he obtained clearance from Innocent's successor, Zosimus (417–418), a Greek, by presenting a confession of faith which glossed over the points of dispute. At a local synod in September, 417 Caelestius deftly persuaded the gullible Zosimus of his own orthodoxy and of the haste of the Africans in condemning him. Zosimus assured Aurelius of Carthage that Caelestius's faith was "completely satisfactory" (*Ep.* 2.6). Pelagius also obtained the pope's approval, sending a doctrinal statement and letters from himself and Praylius, Patriarch of Jerusalem (416–425), who had succeeded John. Zosimus did not have sufficient theological acumen to catch in Pelagius's letter

the subtle point that Christians, "by using their free will correctly, *merit the grace of God* and keep His commandments," a point Augustine noted immediately. It was not enough for him to say, "We confess free will but hold at the same time that we stand continually in need of the divine assistance." The question was: "What kind of assistance?" Zosimus summoned another synod to clear Pelagius. He blamed Heros and Lazarus for fomenting trouble. He also directed Paulinus of Nola to come to Rome and defend his accusations against Caelestius, but he declined on the grounds that the judge had already declared for his adversary.

Aurelius of Carthage quickly assembled a few bishops at Carthage who proposed that Zosimus leave things stand as they had been under Innocent, "until he should become better informed about the case." In November, 417, 214 bishops gathered and sent a second letter reiterating that they would adhere to Innocent's decision against Pelagius and Caelestius until they should come to the proper understanding of grace. Zosimus backpedaled. While boasting that his decisions were not subject to review, he conceded the need for further deliberation and assured the Africans that things would stand as they were under Innocent. Meantime, the Africans turned to the imperial court, where they obtained a rescript from Honorius banishing Pelagius and Caelestius from Rome and threatening confiscation and exile for their followers. In 418 a council convened at Carthage, with 215 bishops representing all five African provinces, to lay down the Catholic doctrine of original sin and the need of grace. Zosimus had no option but to condemn Pelagius and Caelestius. Surprisingly, the contorted handling of the case did not lead to a breach with Augustine or the Africans. Rome smoothed the ruffled feelings of the Africans with letters to Valerius and Augustine composed by the presbyter (later pope) Sixtus and carried by the acolyte (later pope) Leo.

Pelagius's Friends

The victory at Carthage in 418 did not signal the demise of Pelagianism. Pelagius still had prominent and influential friends, including the Roman exiles to Africa Pinian, his wife Melania, and her mother Albina. They tried to persuade Pelagius to condemn the propositions alleged against him. In a letter he assured them that he believed in the necessity of grace and in "baptism of infants for forgiveness of sins." A bit suspicious of his assurances, Pinian consulted Augustine. The bishop of Hippo replied in two treatises, *On the Grace of Christ* and *On Original Sin*, calling attention to the subtle way in which Pelagius steered around the main point. He affirmed grace with reference to the possibility of *choosing* good or evil but not with reference to *willing* or *being* good or evil. In his view grace is *natural* and not *super*natural He was really a masterful advocate of free will. At the same time he contradicted himself when he spoke of baptism of infants for forgiveness of sins and yet denied that Adam's sin affected the whole human race. Augustine assured Pinian that Pelagius and Caelestius merited the condemnations they had received.

What must have troubled thoughtful lay persons as well as monks and clergy about Augustine's views is evident in a long letter (*Ep.* 194) Augustine wrote to the Presbyter Sixtus, later Pope Sixtus III (432–440), late in 418. The chief problem was the obvious arbitrariness of God in the Augustinian theology. Sympathizers with Pelagius wanted to know: (1) If we do not will anything good without God's direct help, as Augustine said, do we have any free will at all? (2) If God "has mercy on whom He will" apart from some kind of antecedent merits, is God not arbitrary, a "respecter of persons"? (3) Is God not unjust to punish one person and to reward another when they are of the same merit? (4) Is there no grace of creation, viz., natural grace? (5) If we have not received grace to live well, how can we

be blamed if we live badly? (6) If we ascribe evil to an inheritance from Adam and think of all humankind as a "condemned lump" (*massa perditionis*), is God not arbitrary to blame one and bless another? (7) Would it not be better to say that God acts according to merits foreseen? (8) How can parents pass on to their children what was forgiven them when they received baptism? (9) When sponsors say for children being baptized that they believe in the forgiveness of sins, is it not for the sins the infants have committed? Augustine's replies, defending the "inscrutable will of God," anticipated the uncompromising stand he took in treatises written in 426–427 *On Grace and Free Will* and *On Reproach and Grace*. In these Augustine stopped just short of double predestination, that is, God's choice of some for salvation and of others for damnation. Because all humankind is a "condemned lump," God must have condemned all. By grace, however, God elected some for salvation. This grace is irresistible, as certain as the end to which it points.

Leader of the opposition to Augustine's more pronounced anti-Pelagian views was Julian, bishop of Eclanum (417–454), whose family had once had close ties with Augustine. Immediately after the death of Innocent I, who had consecrated him, Julian took up the cudgels against views he feared would be fatal to divine justice and human responsibility and would alienate cultured people by superficial piety. He first attacked Pope Zosimus (417–418), then Augustine, and finally Pope Boniface (418–422).

In 418 Zosimus sent his *Tractoria* condemning Pelagius and Caelestius to all the principal sees of both East and West. Although none in Africa refused to sign, nineteen bishops in Italy led by Julian did and added a memorial in which they set forth the Semi-Pelagian position. The grace of Christ cooperates with free will and "will not follow those who refuse it." Whether one is good and another bad is due to persons and not the will of God. Both grace and baptism are necessary. Yet there is no "natural (original) sin." In disagreement with Pelagius, however, the document affirmed that the whole human race died in Adam and has been raised in Christ. In one of two letters he sent to Zosimus Julian repudiated three propositions attributed to Pelagius and Caelestius: that humankind did not die in Adam or rise again in Christ, that newborn infants are in the same state as Adam, and that Adam was created mortal and would have died whether he had sinned or not. Zosimus excommunicated and deposed all nineteen bishops. Emperor Honorius banished them. Not daunted by this action, Julian and his friends sought a new synod to rehear their case. When blocked in that, they turned to Rufus, bishop of Thessalonica (410–431), and Atticus, Patriarch of Constantinople (406–426), for help. From there they tried to gain a hearing at Alexandria, Antioch, and Jerusalem, but in vain. Only Theodore of Mopsuestia, who was of the same mind, offered refuge about 423.

Julian, a self-confident and haughty person, next took up the pen against Augustine, whom he, like Pelagius, suspected of Manichaeism. Augustine supplied the occasion with the first book of a treatise he wrote *On Marriage and Concupiscence* in 419 in reply to a Pelagian cavil that he implicitly condemned marriage as the means of transmission of sin. In this treatise he affirmed that marriage is good, but noted that concupiscence entered into it by way of Adam's sin and is the reason even those born in wedlock from Christian parents are not born children of God and thus need grace. Concupiscence remains in the baptized, though not its guilt, so that they are still inclined to sin. Julian attacked Augustine's doctrine in "four thick books" (Augustine, *Against Julian* 1.2). Augustine responded hastily to some inaccurate extracts of Julian's work in the second book of *On Marriage and Concupiscence* and, when the full treatise came into his his hands, in a full length treatise *Against Julian the Pelagian* in 422. In the latter, among other

things, he gave his rejoinder to the five Pelagian arguments against the doctrine of original sin: (1) It makes the devil the author of human birth. (2) It condemns marriage. (3) It denies that all sins were forgiven in baptism. (4) It charges God with injustice. (5) It makes human beings despair of perfection. Around 424 Julian retaliated with a lengthy critique of the second book of Augustine's *On Marriage and Concupiscence*. Augustine began but did not live to complete a further response to Julian in 429–430. Although Julian handled opponents such as Augustine so crudely that he did not find many personal sympathizers, some of the extreme aspects of Augustinianism, for example, the condemnation of unbaptized infants and the irresistibility of grace, made his protest quite intelligible.

Julian also came to the attention of Pope Boniface I in 420 through two letters, one Julian himself addressed to Rome charging Catholics with Manichaeism and the other he and the eighteen exiles directed to Rufus, bishop of Thessalonica (410–431), seeking help. At the instance of the pope, Augustine wrote a substantial treatise *Against the Two Epistles of the Pelagians* defending (his own) Catholic teaching. From this point on, the Pelagians lost ground. Atticus drove Julian and his cohorts out of Constantinople. In 424 Theodotus of Antioch banished Pelagius from Jerusalem. Pope Caelestine exiled Caelestius from Italy, and in 429 he was forced out of Constantinople. The Council of Ephesus in 431 condemned both Pelagius and Caelestius. Julian, hounded from town to town finally ended up teaching at a school in Sicily, where he died in 454.

Semi-Pelagianism/Augustinianism

Revered and respected as Augustine was, questions about the extremer forms of his teaching persisted, especially in monastic communities, for his emphasis on grace seemed to undercut the life of prayer to which monks devoted themselves. In 426 African monks of Hadrumentum, reading Augustine's letter to Sixtus for the first time, thought it annihilated free will and sought clarification from Augustine himself. In response he sent them his treatise *On Grace and Free Will* (427), in which he affirmed the need for preserving both but depicted the will as so debilitated by the Fall that only supernatural grace can overcome its effects. The monks understandably raised the question as to why they should be censured for wrong if they had no more freedom than Augustine allowed. When Augustine learned of their objection, he sent them the treatise *On Reproach and Grace*. In it he answered that they deserved reproach because of their depravity as a part of the "condemned lump," just as unbaptized infants did. The elect persevere because predestined to do so. Why they are elect belongs to God's inscrutable will. Although all should receive instruction because we do not know who is among the predestinated, the elect need and receive more help than Adam, the help of *irresistible* grace.

As this exchange was taking place, the original Pelagianism experienced some revival in Gaul and in the British Isles. In Gaul a monk named Leporius combined Pelagian and Nestorian emphases on free will to depict Jesus as an ordinary man who used his free will to live a sinless life. Gallic bishops forced Leporius to flee Gaul and take up refuge in Africa, where he came under Augustine's influence and retracted his views. In Britain, homeland of Pelagius, Pelagius's ideas found fallow soil among the laity. In 429 a large synod in Gaul sent Germanus, bishop of Auxerre (418–448), and Lupus, bishop of Troyes (427–479), to the British Isles to combat Pelagianism. A major confrontation took place at Verulamium (now St. Albans). The fact that Germanus returned in 447, accompanied by Severus, bishop of Treves (446–455), to finish the job, attests the tenacity of Pelagian ideas among lay persons there.

More subtle and difficult to counteract was the modified form of thought known as Semi-Pelagianism. As originally defined by a Carthaginian monk named Vitalis, Semi-Pelagianism ascribed the initial act of faith to the movement of the will unaided by grace but insisted on the need of grace thereafter. In an extended response (*Ep.* 217) Augustine countered that, if Vitalis's view was true, the church should stop praying for conversion of the unconverted, regeneration of catechumens, and perseverance of believers, for prayer depends on the grace of God taking initiative preveniently. If we don't believe that when we pray, we only pretend to pray. Only when the will is transformed by grace does it become free. In short, God effects through grace what we will. Whether Vitalis discerned his "error" and subscribed to the "Twelve Articles" of Catholic teaching Augustine outlined for him is unknown, but Augustine did not convince the monks at the two leading centers in south Gaul, Lérins and Marseilles.

Cassian, founder of the two monasteries at Marseilles, thought Augustine pressed too far the idea of prevenient grace. Hilary, Abbot of Lérins and bishop of Arles (429–449), agreed with him in that. Both believed that Augustine's theology undermined human responsibility. Therefore, they stressed that nature can take the first steps toward its own recovery without the aid of grace. Though underscoring the need of grace, they differed from Augustine at two points—denying the need for prevenient grace and the concept of irresistible grace. Informed by Prosper of Aquitaine (ca. 390–ca. 463), an ardent Augustinian, and a monk named Hilary about the situation in Gaul, Augustine composed his treatises *On the Predestination of the Saints* and *On the Gift of Perseverance* in 428 and 429, setting forth his views in their most pronounced form.

In his treatise *On the Predestination of the Saints* Augustine took note of the difference between Semi-Pelagians and Pelagians, i.e., in their emphasis on unaided free will only in the *initial* step of faith. He had himself, erroneously, once held that view, before becoming a bishop.

Now he recognized that faith is a gift too in its beginning as well as in its perfection. Predestination prepares for grace. Grace is predestination taking effect. That is seen clearly in infants, some saved and some not. It is seen also in the incarnation, for Jesus did nothing to deserve it. Some are called not *because* but *in order to* believe. No foreseen piety leads to their calling. It is all of grace.

In the supplementary essay *On the Gift of Perseverance* Augustine sought to prove that perseverance is also a gift of God. As proof, he invoked the Lord's Prayer and the prayers of the church for faithfulness. Why do some and not others persevere? That too is a part of God's inscrutable will. Predestination is nothing other than God foreknowing and preparing to bestow the divine favors on some while leaving the rest of humankind in the "condemned lump." Thus, perseverance is pure gift. Sensing the harshness of such a doctrine, Augustine warns against preaching it to a congregation. One must always speak to the latter as a part of the predestined. The damned should only be referred to in the third person. These were Augustine's last words in the Pelagian controversy except for a brief summary in his treatise *On Heresies*, an unfinished work.

Post-Augustinianism

Although Augustine's last treatises satisfied Prosper and Hilary, they exasperated the Semi-Pelagians, who circulated excerpts from them. After a futile attempt to defend his hero, Prosper took refuge in Rome around 431. In Rome, however, he found little sympathy for pronounced Augustinianism, for both Caelestine (422–432) and Leo (440–461) held Semi-Pelagians in high esteem. Leo, as a matter of fact, called on Cassian to reply to the Nestorians in 430–431. Try as he might, therefore, Prosper could not evoke from Caelestine or Sixtus III (432–440) or Leo a denunciation of Semi-Pelagians. Although Cassian declined to let Prosper draw him into a battle

over his thirteenth *Conference* in 433–434, Vincent of Lérins did take up the challenge in his *Commonitorium* in 434,wherein he established the rule of Catholicity as "what has been always, everywhere believed by all." Under Leo, both as Archdeacon and as pope, a whole series of writings emerged from Rome praising Augustine and yet repudiating extremes of Augustinianism. These agreed with Augustine's emphasis on the need for supernatural grace, but they either rejected or remained silent regarding his doctrines of predestination and irresistible grace.

The controversy remained muted until it flared up again about 475 under the leadership of Faustus, bishop of Riez (459–ca. 490). Probably British, Faustus was a monk in the Abbey of Lérins. In 433 he succeeded Maximus as abbot and in 459 became bishop of Riez. When one of his clergy, Lucidus, began to teach Augustine's doctrine of predestination, Faustus forced him to retract his teaching. At the request of the Synod of Lyon in 474 he wrote also *Two Books on Grace*, in which he argued vehemently against the doctrine of prevenient grace. When Scythian monks inquired of Pope Hormisdas (514–523) what weight to attach to the name of Faustus, he replied in August 520 after some delay that Faustus was "not received" in Rome and that Catholic teaching would be found in Augustine. Provoked by Hormisdas's delay in responding, the Scythian monks wrote some refugee bishops from Africa residing in Sardinia. One of them, Fulgentius, bishop of Ruspe (507–533), a convinced Augustinian, picked up the pen against Faustus around 523, endeavoring to crush the influence of his Semi-Pelagianism. Although Faustus had died more than thirty years before, his impact lived on in south Gaul.

The long contorted issue was finally brought to a point of resolution at the Synod of Orange in 529 through the skillful guidance of Caesarius, Archbishop of Arles (502–542) and the most outstanding preacher of the Latin church at the time. Even though educated at Lérins and thus well acquainted with the distaste for Augustinianism, Caesarius had learned to love Augustine's "Catholic sentiments." His preaching of grace aroused the suspicion of some fellow bishops in south Gaul and they invited him to clear himself before the Synod of Valence (527–528). Illness prevented him from attending, but he sent a message by Cyprian, bishop of Toulon (524–549), emphasizing the need for prevenient grace. Immediately thereafter, he secured the approval of Pope Felix IV (528–530) of a series of propositions which he presented for approval at the Synod of Orange on July 3, 529. Although only fourteen bishops attended, the added approval of the pope assured its unusual importance in history.

The Synod of Orange essentially upheld the Augustinian viewpoint. In its first two canons it affirmed Augustine's doctrine of the Fall against Pelagianism. The Fall affected human nature as a whole, soul as well as body. Not only death but also sin was transmitted to the human race. In canons 3 through 8 the Synod rejected Semi-Pelagianism, insisting on the need for prevenient grace. Grace evokes prayer, prepares the will, initiates faith, encourages seeking, and aids our weakened nature. The remaining canons (9–25) also underlined the importance of grace, but they made no mention of predestination or the irresistibility of grace. Augustine's central teachings but not his extremes had survived. Monasticism, so significant already in the churches of Gaul, did not lose its *raison d'être*. Quite to the contrary, the foundations of the Middle Ages were well laid.

Chapter 30

The Emergence of the Papacy

Rome attained special importance in the church at a very early date because it was the capital of the empire and because it was there that both Peter, the Apostle to the circumcision, and Paul, the Apostle to the Gentiles, had died. The eagerness of the Apostle Paul to go to Rome and to be sent by the Roman Christians to Spain (Rom. 15:24) indicates the importance he attached to the Roman church. At the end of the first century the Roman presbyters assumed that they had not only a prerogative but a responsibility to offer fraternal counsel to the Corinthians who had risen up and deposed their elders. In his letter to the Romans Ignatius, on the way to martyrdom in Rome, bore witness to the prestige of the Roman church, addressing the Roman church as one "which presides in the place of the region of the Romans" and describing this as "a presidency of love." As Dionysius of Corinth noted in a letter to Soter, the bishop of Rome from 175 to 182, Rome attained distinction for its charities "to many churches in every city" (Eusebius, H.E. 4.23.10). Clement (96 C.E.) and Ignatius (110–117), moreover, both cited Rome's connection with Peter and Paul. Toward the end of the second century Irenaeus carried this a step further when he spoke of Rome as "the greatest and most ancient and universally known church, founded and established at Rome by the two most glorious apostles Peter and Paul" (*Against Heresies* 3.3.1) and proceeded to cite the list of Roman bishops up to

his own day with the comment that "every church must agree (*convenire*) with this church on account of its greater preeminence (*principalitatem*)" (3.3.2). Although Irenaeus's main point was that churches of apostolic foundation like Rome should serve as measuring rods for all of the churches, the very fact that he cited the Roman list rather than that of other churches attests Rome's special importance.

Rome took a giant step forward in the early third century with the appearance of the theory that Rome derives its authority from the bishop of Rome as Peter's successor. Curiously the idea manifested itself with the brilliant renegade Tertullian. Borrowing Irenaeus's succession theory, Tertullian demanded that heretics produce their lists as Smyrna or Rome could, proving respectively that John appointed Polycarp and that Peter appointed Clement. Here Irenaeus's distinction between the apostles and their successors gave way to the establishment of Roman primacy by citing Peter as the first bishop of Rome. The two rivals for the Roman episcopate in 217, Callistus and Hippolytus, both relied on this theory and backed it up by citing Matthew 16:18-19. Neither, however, claimed *papal* but only *episcopal* authority.

That step was taken by Stephen (254–257) in his debate with Cyprian of Carthage over the question of heretical baptisms. Cyprian took the position that heretics and schismatics could not administer baptism at all because they did not possess the Spirit and therefore had to receive baptism, Stephen that they only needed to have hands laid on them. Stephen appealed to the Petrine text as the basis of his authority and, according to Cyprian (*Epistle* 75.17), "boasts of the seat of his episcopate and contends that he holds the succession from Peter, on whom the foundations of the church were laid." Although Cyprian evidently acknowledged the special role of the bishop of Rome, he maintained strongly that all bishops are successors of Peter. When African synods took Cyprian's side, Stephen warned against "innovations" and threatened excommunication. He not only claimed authority for the Roman usage but magnified his office as successor of Peter and occupant of Peter's chair, which, he insisted, gave the bishop of Rome authority over other bishops. Had the persecution under Valerian not claimed the lives of both Cyprian and Stephen, there would likely have been a schism.

During the late third and fourth centuries, the churches centralized around several great sees—Rome, Alexandria, Antioch, and later Constantinople. Dionysius, bishop of Rome (259–268), after consulting with a Roman synod, issued a mild rebuke to his namesake in Alexandria regarding his tendency to subordinate the Son to the Father too much. Of great importance here was the fact that Dionysius was responding to an appeal from Dionysius of Alexandria's opponents, initiating the custom exploited to advantage by Roman bishops in subsequent centuries. In 325 the Council of Nicaea (Canon 6) specifically mentioned, however, the rights of Rome in Italy, Alexandria in Egypt, and Antioch in the East. The emperors, moreover, strongly asserted their authority in ecclesiastical matters in ways that limited the claims of the bishops of Rome. First Constantine and then his sons, especially Constantius, exercised the role of the Roman Pontifex Maximus. Under Liberius (352–366) the Roman episcopate recovered some

of its prestige in conflict with Constantius II. Constantius, an Arian, forced an Arian settlement on the Synods of Arles (353) and Milan (355). When Liberius refused to acknowledge their decision, Constantius tried bribes and threats and then banishment to Beroea. Liberius did yield, but the intemperance of the Arians turned sympathies in favor of supporters of Nicaea. Liberius led the repentance of Western bishops. The major leader, however, was Athanasius, bishop of Alexandria, so that Liberius stood chiefly as the leader of Nicene Orthodoxy in the West.

Damasus

Roman primacy took another major step during the pontificate of Damasus (366–384). Damasus had to fight to gain control of the see to which he was elected on September 24, 366. Rapid growth in the wealth of the Roman church made headship of it a special prize worth seizing. Consequently a minority gathered the same day and elected and consecrated Ursinus. Followers of Damasus, who was not yet consecrated, attacked the followers of Ursinus in Santa Maria Maggiore and killed 137 of them. Although the claim of Damasus was upheld, Ursinus continued to pursue the case until Gratian (375–383) intervened and banished him to Cologne and cleared Damasus. Damasus convened a Roman council in May and June, 382, which made two requests of the emperor: that he confirm the privilege of the bishop of Rome to try cases of recalcitrant bishops so that no bishop would have to appear before a secular court, hearing both cases of the first instance and appeals; and that he shelter the bishop of Rome from accusers. In response Gratian extended two new powers to the Roman see: (1) He made the pope master of the process for trying all accused metropolitans throughout the West. (2) He provided for appeals to the pope for bishops tried by local synods. None of this, however, extended beyond the West, and Damasus and his successor framed a theory which would support its extension to the East as well.

The attitude of bishops such as Basil of Caesarea (370–379) was disdainful. In the Meletian schism Basil and most Eastern bishops supported Meletius as bishop of Antioch against Paulinus, whom Damasus and Athanasius upheld.

Damasus did not have an easy time establishing Roman primacy during the reign of Emperor Theodosius (379–395). The emperor himself recognized two centers of Christianity—Rome and Alexandria—in his edict *Cunctos populos*, issued in February 380. At the Council of Constantinople in 381, later recognized as an ecumenical council, moreover, upstart Constantinople was accorded a rank just after Rome as "new Rome" and ahead of Alexandria, Antioch, and Jerusalem. Damasus responded by convening a Roman synod which, among other things, set forth the first official definition of papal claims. With obvious reference to Constantinople, the synod based Roman claims "on no synodal decisions" but on Christ's promise to Peter recorded in Matthew 16. It proceeded thence to establish a Petrine hierarchy without Constantinople—Rome, Alexandria, and Antioch. Although the theory has obvious weaknesses, it was taken for granted by the successors of Damasus and put in classic form by Leo the Great (440–461).

From Damasus to Leo

Papal primacy did not reach beyond the West during the pontificates of Damasus's successors. Siricius (384–399) extended his authority over Spain, Illyria, Italy and Africa. In a decretal addressed to Himerius, bishop of Tarrangona, February 10, 385, he urged circulation of his judgments to the bishops of Carthagena, Baetica, Lusitania, Gallaecia, and neighboring provinces and added, "No bishop is at liberty to ignore the decisions of the Apostolic See, or the venerable decrees of the canons." In other letters he threatened excommunication of any bishop who ordained without the knowledge of the Apostolic See of the Primate of Africa. At this juncture Rome obviously placed itself above the episcopate, but the East still went its own way not worried about being out of communion with the West, as the case of Flavian, bishop of Antioch from 381 to 398 indicates. Although Western bishops accorded Rome special recognition, they also held Milan in high regard during Ambrose's time (374–397). Rufinus, in a letter to Anastasius (399–401), declared his consensus in faith with Rome, Alexandria, his own church at Aquileia, and Jerusalem.

Innocent I (402–417) clearly asserted Rome's authority, but his letters indicate some of the same restrictions on it. Although the West generally acknowledged it, Africa expressed some reservations. Chrysostom welcomed Roman help in his defense, but he relied too on the decisions of Nicaea. In the West Innocent confirmed Anysius (388–410) and his successor Rufus (410–431), bishops of Thessalonica, as his vicar throughout the provinces of Illyria, checking a pull toward Constantinople. He handed out advice to Victricius, bishop of Rouen (395–415), and Exuperius, bishop of Toulouse (405–415), cultivating referral to Rome. In a letter to Decentius, bishop of Eugubium (Gubbio), Innocent expressed shock at the intrusion of non-Roman liturgical practice into his metropolitanate and insisted on observance of Roman customs "everywhere" throughout Italy, Gaul, Spain, Africa, Sicily and the neighboring islands. To follow foreign customs is to desert the head of the church.

During the Pelagian controversy, Africans sent Innocent three letters asking his support. In the first of his replies, addressed to the Council of Carthage (416), Innocent congratulated the council for referring the matter to the judgment of his see, "the source of the whole episcopate." He made similar assertions in reply to the Synod of Mileve and to a letter from Augustine and fellow bishops. At this point the Africans rejoiced at the support they received from the pope. The statement "Rome has spoken, the case is settled" ascribed to Augustine does not represent his response accurately, however. What he actually said was that reports of the two councils (Carthage and Mileve) had been sent to the Apostolic See and that Rome had sent rescripts so that the case is settled. African independence would shine through clearly when later popes glossed over the Pelagian problem.

Chrysostom's appeal to Rome should not be overstated either, for he sent identical letters to Venerius, bishop of Milan, in 408 and to Chromatius, bishop of Aquileia, in 407. Not only Rome but Milan and Aquileia represented leading prelates. Innocent replied to appeals from both Theophilus of Alexandria and Chrysostom saying that he would require a council to settle the matter, meantime maintaining relations with both. Obviously Innocent had not yet elevated his claims to the level of a general council, a view Chrysostom would have held also.

Zosimus (417–418) blundered badly in trying to assert his authority. His most serious error was his patronage of Caelestius and Pelagius. In a letter to the African bishops in September 417 he declared Caelestius's faith "completely satisfactory" and the furor needless. In a second letter he confirmed both Pelagius's and Caelestius's faith. African bishops promptly let Zosimus know that he was misinformed. He had the good sense to back away from his earlier decision and affirm the actions taken by Innocent I. The Africans then proceeded to get a rescript from Emperor Honorius banishing Pelagius and Caelestius. Zosimus then condemned the Pelagians.

Boniface I (418–422) did not make the same mistake regarding the Pelagians and he had occasion to advance further the claims of Rome. When the bishops of Illyricum refused to confirm the election of Perigenes as bishop, despite popular approval and Boniface's confirmation, and obtained a decree from Emperor Theodosius II in which he directed that such matters could be settled by an assembly of bishops but not without the intervention of the bishop of Constantinople, Boniface leaped forward to defend the authority

of his see against this "innovation." In the first of three letters he appealed to the authority of Peter personified in his see. In the second, addressed to the bishops of Thessaly, he reiterated the Petrine claims and appealed to the Council of Nicaea's affirmation of Roman primacy and to the words of Jesus in Matthew 16. In the third letter he added an appeal to precedent: once Rome has decided, what other bishop would need to call an assembly? Here he corrected Cyprian by saying that, while all bishops hold the same episcopal office, they must recognize the need for subordination for the sake of ecclesiastical discipline. Boniface stood in easy reach of Leo's concept of the papacy.

Coelestine (422–432) had little difficulty maintaining Roman authority in areas where it was already unquestioned, for instance, in Illyricum, but he had problems in areas less directly under his control and where conciliar organization was better developed, as in Africa and the East. Especially damaging to Roman standing in Africa was the case of Apiarius, a priest of Sicca Veneria in Proconsular Africa whose bishop, Urbanus, had deposed and excommunicated him around 417. Apiarius went to Rome and obtained help from Zosimus, who threatened Urbanus with deposition if he did not restore Apiarius and sent three legates to settle the issue. Legates were an innovation borrowed from imperial practice and, before they arrived, a council met at Carthage on May 1, 418, and forbade appeals from "presbyters, deacons, and inferior clergy." At a small synod held at Caesarea Maurentania on September 30, 418, the legates upheld the right of appeal to Rome by bishops and to "neighboring bishops" by "presbyters and deacons" and directed that Urbanus be excommunicated or sent to Rome if he would not cancel his decision against Apiarius. To back up his *commonitorium* Zosimus mistakenly cited the fifth and fourteenth canons of the Council of Sardica as canons of Nicaea. The issue remained unresolved when Zosimus died. When it resumed under Boniface I, at the

Council of Carthage on May 25, 419, the Africans affirmed their acceptance of Nicaea and, in a letter to the pontiff, indicated that they would abide by such canons if proven Nicene and observed in Italy, but they objected to the arrogance of the papal legate Faustinus. In the meantime Apiarius had assumed a position at Tabraca, near Hippo, repeated conduct that had led to his deposition, and been excommunicated again. When he appealed to Rome, Coelestine restored him to communion without hearing his accusers and sent him back to Africa accompanied by Faustinus, the overbearing legate despised by the Africans. In a council held at Carthage around 426 the latter pressed for acceptance of the pope's decisions on the basis of "the privileges of the Roman church." The Africans, however, after three days of inquiry, obtained a full confession from Apiarius and proceeded to entreat the pope to make fuller inquiry before restoring someone like Apiarius to communion and to point out that hearing cases of lower clergy violates the canons of Nicaea, which granted this right to local bishops. They were willing to recognize Roman primacy but not a primacy of jurisdiction.

Coelestine ran into similar resistance in the East in the Nestorian controversy. Eastern bishops resorted to Roman primacy when it suited them, but they could ignore it when they found it convenient to do so. At the Council of Ephesus in 431 Cyril of Alexandria presided, "holding also the place of the archbishop of the church of the Romans." When the Roman legates arrived, the assembled bishops heard and acclaimed Coelestine's letter. They placed Cyril and Coelestine on the same level, hailing the latter "as of one mind with the Council." The legates interpreted in reverse as the adherence of the bishops to their head, but the bishops paid no attention. Cyril also ignored the assertion of papal claims by the legate Philip and asked the legates, "as representing the Apostolic See and the bishops of the West," to subscribe to the decree against Nestorius. Coelestine's successor, Sixtus III

(432–440), was left the task of reconciling the see of Antioch. This happened without too much papal involvement, however, in the agreement of Cyril of Alexandria and John of Antioch to the Formulary of Reunion of April 433.

Leo

Leo I (440–461), the Great, laid down the theoretical base and established the primacy of the Roman see. In a series of sermons preached to bishops of his metropolitanate on the anniversary of his consecration and in several letters he put forth a clear and comprehensive statement which the papacy has since operated on with little alteration. (1) Jesus bestowed supreme authority on Peter, as Matthew 16:18-19, Luke 22:31-32, and John 21:15-17 prove. (2) Peter was the first bishop of Rome. (3) Peter's authority has been perpetuated in his successors. (4) This authority is enhanced by the continuing mystical presence of Peter in the see of Rome. (5) Thence, the authority of other bishops does not derive directly from Christ but is mediated to them through Peter and Peter's successors. (6) Further, while other bishops' authority is limited to their own dioceses, the bishop of Rome has a *plenitudo potestatis* ("fullness of power") over the whole church and a responsibility to govern it.

Leo had much greater success in implementing these claims than most of his predecessors. His bold leadership during the Hunnic invasions doubtless added to his personal mystique. Once again, however, the West acknowledge Roman primacy much more readily than the East. In the West even Africa now accepted Leo's authority as the synodical structure collapsed in the wake of the Vandal invasions. In Gaul, however, Leo ran into stiff resistance when he tried to discipline Hilary, Archbishop of Arles (429–449). Hilary, accompanied by Germanus of Auxerre (418–448), had assembled a council and removed Celidonius from the bishopric of Besancon because of two irregularities—marrying a widow while he was a layman and giving judgment in capital cases. Celidonius appealed to Rome and obtained Leo's support. Hilary crossed the Alps in midwinter to protest, insisting that the Roman see had no right to review decisions of a Gallic synod, the point made earlier in the case of Apiarius by African bishops. Leo, annoyed, dismissed charges against Celidonius and restored him to his see. He then wrote a letter to bishops of the province of Vienne stating the prerogatives of the Apostolic See, condemning Hilary's arrogance and rude language, his encroachment on provinces not under him, and his recourse to the secular arm. Leo then declared Hilary deposed and his rights transferred to the bishop of Vienne and procured a rescript from Valentinian III, dated July 8, 445, which decreed that it was unlawful for bishops of Gaul or other provinces "to do anything without the authority of the Venerable Pope of the Eternal City." In short, the pope created a papal autocracy in the West. Hilary sought to conciliate Leo somewhat after a time, but in the end he remained as inflexible as Leo until his death on May 5, 449. Relations with Rome improved under Hilary's successor Ravennius (449–455) as Leo sought to rally Western backing for his *Tome*.

Eastern reaction to the *Tome* reflects quite clearly the continuance of Eastern reservations about Roman claims. Both Eutyches and his opponents appealed to Leo for support. Leo sought further information from Flavian, Patriarch of Constantinople (447–449) and Emperor Theodosius II (408–450) for more information. Flavian obliged. On June 13, 449, Leo dispatched the *Tome*. The latter had hardly left Leo's hand before Flavian sent a second letter negating a council and saying that the matter only required Leo's "weight and support." Leo agreed, but the council later known as the "Robbers' Synod" was already set to meet at Ephesus in August 449 by order of Theodosius. Leo appointed three legates and sent with them a batch of letters including the *Tome*. Dominated by Dioscurus, the Monophysite Patriarch of Alexandria (444–451), with

armed force at his disposal, the synod set aside the papal letters, reinstated Eutyches, and deposed Flavian. The legate Hilary barely escaped to return to Rome and give Leo a report. Flavian, Eusebius of Dorylaeum, who had also been deposed, and Theodoret of Cyrus all made appeals to Rome but not in the language Leo himself would have used. In fact, Theodoret based his plea on Rome as the locus of the tombs of "our common fathers and teachers of the truth, Peter and Paul." Receiving the letters during a synod in Rome, September 29, Leo wrote seven letters to protest the proceedings at Ephesus and enlisted the Western Emperor Valentinian III, his mother Galla Placidia, and his wife Eudoxia to write the Eastern rulers. All based their claims for Rome on the Council of Nicaea. Theodosius II, however, sent cold rebuffs to all, saying essentially that the Easterners could look after their own affairs.

What turned the situation in Leo's favor was Theodosius's death on July 28, 450, when thrown from his horse. His successor, Marcian (450–457), zealously supported the position of Leo in the *Tome*. With the backing of both Western and Eastern emperors Leo acquiesced to Marcian's summoning of a council for the fall of 451. At the first session of the Council of Chalcedon the Roman legates presided, dealing with procedural matters. At the second session on October 10 the assembled bishops acclaimed the *Tome*, crying "Peter has spoken through Leo," but Cyrillians found traces of what they thought was Nestorianism which they asked some time to consider. When the council reconvened five days later, it deposed Dioscurus. In the next session, October 17, the bishops assented to the statement of the legate Paschasinus which confirmed "the rule of faith as contained in the Creed of Nicaea, confirmed by the Council of Constantinople, expounded at Ephesus under Cyril, and set forth in the letter of Pope Leo when he condemned the heresy of Nestorius and Eutyches." As they construed it, Leo's *Tome* was in accord with the

Nicene Creed. Over the determined opposition of the Roman legates, moreover, on November 1, the Council reaffirmed the decision of Constantinople in 381 concerning the privileges of the Patriarchate of Constantinople, as second only to Rome, and decreed that the Patriarch of Constantinople would consecrate metropolitans for Pontus, Asia, and Thrace. Although this was not an innovation but a statement of current practice, it offended the legates, but they tried in vain to block it. Honorific titles and flattering letters to Leo did not appease him on this point. He feared a rival to his own see and foresaw subordination of the church to the State. He based his appeal on the decision of Nicaea—Rome, Alexandria, Antioch—but it fell on deaf ears. He finally had to declare his acceptance of the faith of Chalcedon without being required to withdraw his protest over the departure from Nicaea.

The Struggle for Integrity

From the Council of Chalcedon on, the papacy struggled to preserve its integrity against encroachments by the patriarchs in Constantinople and dominance by the emperors. Elevation of Constantinople at Chalcedon represented an imperial effort to assure that they would have more direct control over the entire church. Leo's successors resisted mightily. Ironically two rather tragic happenings intruded to liberate them from Constantinople. One was the Lombard invasion of Italy in 568 which brought an end to Justinian's reestablishment of Roman control in Italy. From this point on, popes had to negotiate with other secular powers, eventually establishing an alliance with the Franks. The other was the Islamic invasion of Palestine and North Africa which began in 632 and finally came to a halt a century later at the battle of Tours. The struggle which the papacy went through during this period gave it the basic shape which it retained throughout the Middle Ages.

The first major test for the papacy as defined by Leo arose soon after his death during the pontificates of Simplicius I (468–483) and Felix III (483–492) when Emperor Zeno issued the *Henoticon* in 482, an edict whose object was to restore religious unity throughout the Byzantine empire. The intentional vagueness of the decree offended both Monophysites and Chalcedonians. Apprised of the problem by the Patriarch Talaja of Alexandria, who had been deposed because he refused to acknowledge the *Henotikon*, Felix immediately demanded recognition of the Council of Chalcedon. Unfortunately his legates sent to Constantinople permitted themselves to be intimidated and entered into communion with the Patriarch Acacius, adviser to Zeno in the affair, and with other Monophysites. At a synod in Rome Felix deposed his legates and excommunicated Acacius. Acacius promptly retaliated by removing the pope's name from the diptychs and severing all connections with Rome. Although his successors attempted repeatedly to restore connections, the schism lasted from 484 until 519.

Felix III was the first pope not ascended from the lower classes and knew the mindset of the ruling classes. He also benefited from the able assistance of Gelasius as head of the chancery. Together Felix and Gelasius, who succeeded him as pope (492–496), challenged the policy pursued by the imperial government in Constantinople. During his brief pontificate, Gelasius continued the policy which he had helped Felix III frame to clarify the function and standing of the emperor within the church. In a letter addressed to Emperor Anastasius (491–518) he set forth a doctrine of two powers, priestly and royal. The priestly is more weighty, he said, for priests have to take responsibility at the judgment even for kings. Moreover, even the emperor, though ruling humankind, had to bow his head and receive the eucharistic salvation from the hands of priests. If priests submit to the emperor in the civil realm, lest they obstruct the course of secular affairs, then the emperor should submit to them in religious matters. If such obedience is owed ordinary priests, how much more obedience is owed "the bishop of that see which the Most High ordained to be above all others." In 495 a Roman synod elaborated the main point: "The apostolic See holds the *principatus* over the whole church as the Lord Christ delegates it." The emperor's function in a Christian society is to learn, not to teach, what is Christian. He must find out from those who are qualified what is Christian, that is, from the pope, who alone holds the *principatus* over the divine community. The pope's powers are the same as Peter's. Emperors, therefore, should not order priests about but submit their actions to ecclesiastical superiors. Those who do so merit the title "Catholic." In a somewhat indirect fashion Gelasius was telling Anastasius that the part he played in the Acacian Schism severed him from the church, a bold position in a time of burgeoning caesaropapism.

Two important pieces of literature supplemented the Gelasian scheme of papal monarchy. One was the writings of Pseudo-Dionysius entitled *The Heavenly Hierarchies*, in which the unknown author depicted a divinely ordained order of ranks in ecclesiastical and heavenly societies necessitating different faculties and functions, the other was the fictitious *Legend of St. Silvester* composed around 480 to 490 which stood behind the eighth century *Donation of Constantine*. The *Legend* detailed the conversion of Constantine and explained how he had moved the capital to Constantinople. The main point was to highlight Constantine's contrition before Sylvester, prostrating himself to receive the pope's forgiveness and to be reinvested with his imperial symbols and garments.

Although it did not bear fruit immediately for the papacy, the conversion of Clovis, probably in 496, was to have immense importance in the eventual liberation of the papacy from imperial control. In the West Clovis and his successors played the role which Constantine had played within the Roman Empire and within the church. By the time of Pippin III (751–768) the Franks became the vital instruments for protecting and

assisting the papacy without posing the threat to its integrity which the Byzantine emperors posed.

At the very time daylight began to break through in understanding of relationships between church and state, however, the papacy itself was shaken by factions in the election of a successor to Anastasius II (496–498). A majority favored Symmachus (498–514), who advocated strict adherence to the principles laid down by Leo and Gelasius. A minority of some size, however, backed Laurentius, who wanted to accommodate the imperial viewpoint and who was not entirely opposed to a modified *Henotikon* as a means of restoring unity within the church. Both parties appealed to the Gothic King Theodoric the Great, an Arian, who declared Symmachus pope. When Laurentians made serious charges against Symmachus, Theodoric convened a council which investigated the charges and concluded as he had. Of special significance, the council ended with the declaration that the apostolic see could be judged by no one. Yet it took the firm hand of Theodoric to deliver all Roman churches to Symmachus's charge and to end the schism. A whole row of forgeries appeared to back Symmachus's claims and to place the papacy above criticism. The *Liber Pontificalis* ("Papal Book") also began to appear at this time, mixing narrative and interpretation of papal history up to the time of writing. Entries preceding the pontificate of Anastasius II have little correspondence to what actually happened, but those made after about 500 reflect growing self-awareness of the papacy itself.

Relationships between Rome and Constantinople remained strained throughout the reign of Anastasius (491–518) because of his severe attitude and acts of violence against supporters of Chalcedon until a rebellion led by Vitalian forced him to open negotiations with Hormisdas (514–523). Because Anastasius refused to condemn Acacius, however, the negotiations proved fruitless until Justin, an ardent supporter of Chalcedon ascended the throne in 518. Justin received papal legates with honor, accepted the papal formula for unity, and struck the names of Acacius, Emperors Zeno and Anastasius, and other Monophysites from the diptychs. The improvement of relations with the East, however, aroused the suspicions of Theodoric, whose hegemony had already suffered a blow by the alliance of the Vandals with Byzantium after the death of their ruler, his brother-in-law Thrasamund. Theodoric tried a number of Roman nobles, including the scholar Boethius, for treason. When Justin revived the ancient laws against heretics to extirpate all traces of paganism and Arianism, Theodoric hailed John I (523–526) to his palace in Ravenna and forced him to lead a delegation to Constantinople to demand revocation of violent measures against Arians. The first pope to set foot in the imperial capital, John received a warm welcome, "as though he were Saint Peter himself." Justin backed away from some measures, allowing Arians to retain their churches, but this did not pacify Theodoric. He ordered John I imprisoned, where he died a few days later on May 18, 526.

The Formula of Union ending the Acacian Schism in 519 referred to the Roman church as the one apostolic church which, according to Christ's promise in Matthew 16:18f., had always preserved the true and pure catholic faith. Although this seemed like a victory for the papacy, it represented a well calculated move by Justinian, who already guided his uncle Justin. In his mind the Roman church had an integral role to play within the empire under his own direction. In a revived Roman Empire the city of Rome would rank higher than other cities and, correspondingly, the bishop of Rome would rank higher than other patriarchs. But Justinian never intended for the pope to hold *jurisdiction*. When he ascended the throne in 527, Justinian soon made clear that he would not tolerate any other ruler to claim final authority in matters he considered necessary for the well being of the empire. His was a refurbished Roman imperial concept

Christianized. The emperor holds responsibility for religious matters because these are a part of public law. During Justinian's long reign (527–565), the papacy faced a real challenge to its integrity, for the whole Eastern church fully supported the imperial viewpoint. At Constantinople in 535 the assembled bishops declared that nothing could happen in the church without the consent and approval of the emperor himself.

The papacy did not have a happy experience with Justinian. In 536 Silverius (536–538?) was charged with treasonable liaison with the Ostrogoths when he tried to negotiate with them to prevent unnecessary bloodshed, deposed, and sent into exile by a military court. He died shortly after resigning his office as a consequence of deprivations suffered during his exile. Vigilius (538–555), elevated to the office by Belisarius, Byzantine conqueror of Italy, ran afoul of Empress Theodora, a Monophysite, when he stated his adherence to the formula adopted at Chalcedon and repeated the condemnation of the Monophysite Patriarch Anthimus. He also incurred the disfavor of Emperor Justinian when he refused to condemn the "Three Chapters"—the person and writings of Theodore of Mopsuestia, and the writings of Theodoret of Cyrus and Ibas of Edessa. To compel Western acceptance, the emperor ordered Vigilius removed and brought to Constantinople, where, under pressure, he acquiesced in the action and then vacillated as the West raised a storm of protest. He died on the way back to Rome in June, 555. This celebrated case was a clear sign that the Byzantine government would go to any lengths to secure the agreement of the Roman church in favor of "Roman" policy.

Dominance of the papacy by Justinian continued under Vigilius's successor, Pelagius I (556–561), chosen after an interval with Justinian's approval. Papal *apocrisarius* to the imperial court under Agapetus (535–536), he served Vigilius's vicar at Rome during the latter's trip to Constantinople. He voluntarily sacrificed his personal fortune during Totila's siege of the city to relieve the famine of the inhabitants. He held the Western view about the "Three Chapters" and at Constantinople in 551 he persuaded Vigilius to oppose condemnation of them. From prison he vehemently attacked Vigilius's vacillation, but, in the end, he too capitulated to the emperor and approved their condemnation, perhaps because of his prospect of being elected pope. His wavering alienated many in the West and caused him to issue a solemn declaration of his commitment to the first four ecumenical councils, especially Chalcedon, and to take an oath that he had not been responsible for the harsh treatment and death of his predecessor. Although these acts reassured the bishops of Gaul and King Childebert of Paris, they did not satisfy the bishops of Milan, Aquileia, and Ravenna.

The Byzantine control dropped precipitously as a result of the Lombard invasion of Italy in 568, and the papacy now found itself in a position to reconsider its own Roman past and to reassert itself. Once the exarch took up residence in Ravenna, the emperor had little power and authority to direct the Roman church. The popes now had to act as intermediaries between the Lombards and Constantinople and, where they had to, they often negotiated independently with the invading armies with little fear of interference from Constantinople. Unlike earlier Germanic conquerors, the Lombards did not envy the Roman Empire. Rather, they sought to destroy it and to replace imperial administration with their own. The founded duchies in both north and south and looked on Rome itself as a duchy nominally related, like Naples and Sicily in the south, to the Byzantine empire. Although most were originally pagans, by the eighth century they had accepted the Catholic faith. Meanwhile, the papacy collected patrimonies all over Italy and in Dalmatia, Gaul, Africa, Sardinia, and Corsica to become by the end of the sixth century the largest single landowner in Western Europe. All of these it governed after the Roman model. They furnished revenues to support the impoverished population of Rome as well as monasteries and the papal household itself.

Gregory I, the Great

As the sixth century came to a close, therefore, the Roman church found itself in a very different position than the one which existed in the time of Justinian. The church now served as a link between diverse peoples and not just the constituency of the Roman Empire. The Visigoths in Spain, the Franks in Gaul, the Lombards in Italy all figured prominently in the larger picture and opened the way for some adjustments in the theory of the papacy.

Insight concerning this came from Spain, where in 589 the Visigothic King Recared had converted to the Catholic faith. Isidore, Archbishop of Seville (ca. 600–636), whose brother, Leander, had become an intimate friend of Gregory during their stay in Constantinople, perceived a way to forge a link between the Roman and Germanic nations through the church. He contended that, since the church is the one Body of Christ, it is composed of a plurality of nations within which the different princes function. Because there is only one Body, there can be only one rule, the pope's. The king's function, as a member of the church, is to strengthen priestly directives, that is, to use "princely terror" to support the word of priests. The king must use coercion to assure a just society. He assists where the priestly word proves inadequate.

Gregory I (590–604) united the Gelasian and Isidorean theories. His predecessor, Pelagius II (579–590), had already had to protest assumption of the title of "universal patriarch" by the Patriarch John IV (582–595). Gregory reiterated the protest, noting that the claim imposed on the Roman *principatus*. Rome alone, he argued, holds the *principatus* over the People of God, the society of the Christian republic. This society was composed of nations outside the frame of the Eastern empire. Rome would provide the basis for the unity of the diverse peoples of the West. Although Gregory addressed the emperor in a quite different tone than Western rulers, the emperor as "dominus" or lord and the others as "sons," he went on to insist that priests are superior to laypersons. Only if this is recognized can Christendom assume some kind of order. Just as heaven is hierarchical, so also the society of the Christian republic.

Gregory is rightly acclaimed for the farsightedness of his policy. He recognized better than any of his predecessors the importance of the Germanic peoples to the future of the church. He had spent enough years in Constantinople as the *apocrisiarius* to know the dangers posed by the emperors. Certainly he could see that Rome could expect no help from the struggling Eastern empire. Taking office just after the conversion of Recared, on the other hand, he could exploit his friendship with Leander, bishop of Seville (ca. 584–ca. 600), to cultivate relationships with the now Catholic Goths. In Gaul he established regular communication with the Merovingians and with the bishops, making the bishop of Arles his vicar. In Italy he maintained pleasant relations with the Lombard Queen Theodelinda, laying the groundwork for the eventual conversion of her people. To England he dispatched Augustine, Abbot of St. Andrew's monastery in Rome, in 596 to win the Anglo-Saxons. He already had a point of contact through Bertha, wife of the King of Kent and daughter of Charibert, King of the Franks.

Part 6

The Church in Time of Transition 600–850 C.E.

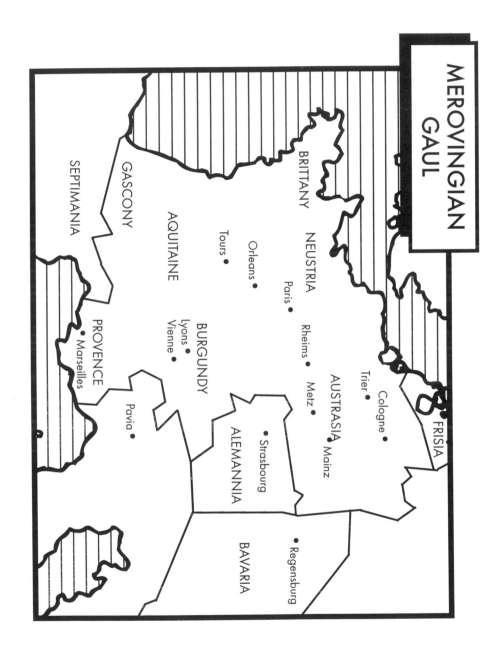

MEROVINGIAN GAUL

SEPTIMANIA

GASCONY

BRITTANY

AQUITAINE

Tours

Orleans

NEUSTRIA

Paris

PROVENCE

Marseilles

Lyons
Vienne

BURGUNDY

Rheims

Metz

AUSTRASIA

Trier

Cologne

Mainz

FRISIA

Pavia

ALEMANNIA

Strasbourg

BAVARIA

Regensburg

Chapter 31

The Continuing Drive

How Europe was evangelized or reevangelized is a very complex story not easily told because of the constant shifts in population and corresponding changes in religious affiliation. The significant thing to observe throughout this period is Christianity's continuing drive to win all and sundry to the Christian faith. Incorporation of the barbarians in the Christian fold, however much it may have altered the understanding of Christianity and the ways in which it was expressed, did not deplete the energy of Christians to share the good news of Jesus Christ. Arians seem to have had the same amount of mission energy as Nicene Christians.

Unfortunately, this high motivation often resulted in persecution, especially as the churches allied themselves with the state, or in this case with various peoples. The Frankish kings, first the Merovingians and then the Carolingians, aided the churches in achieving their goals, but they also used them to attain the state's goals. All too often, the sword helped spread the word, and at a price. The converts under coercion resented the faith they had accepted and, when opportunity appeared, repaid those who had brought it. The use of force against pagans extended naturally to the use of force against other Christians. Much of the mission work in Europe, as a matter of fact, entailed in this period the triumph of the Catholic faith over the Arian or some other versions. Most of the converts probably did not and could not

understand what the debate was all about, but they yielded to threat and intimidation to opt for one or the other.

It will seem curious to many persons today that monks deserve the major credit for the evangelization of Europe. They had help, to be sure. Kings and princes and people in all walks of life offered land and funding and other kinds of support. but the monks, both men and women, were willing to run the risk of going into the areas overrun by the barbarians and establish monasteries as centers in which they could propagate the gospel and from which they could go out to the surrounding countryside. Not tied down by tightly controlled organizations, they could adapt to the contexts and to the people among whom they worked. In time, of course, Rome tied them more closely to the ecclesiastical hierarchy, but not before they had succeeded in planting seeds and watching their crop come up and grow. When they obtained too much land and wealth which the faithful lavished upon them at times, they lost much of the effectiveness they had when all they could offer was holy lives.

Evangelization during this period (600–850) was confined largely to Western Europe, the Byzantine Empire, and to the east of the latter. The fact that the Byzantine Empire had become Christian at least in name by the end of the fourth century undercut somewhat the motive for mission, but it did not eliminate it. The East, too, had to respond in some way to the continuing migration of peoples from northern Europe and the East.

Western Europe

The impetus for the evangelization of Western Europe came chiefly from two sources. One was Pope Gregory I (590–604), who sought vigorously to tie the evangelization of Europe to Rome and the hierarchy. He was fortunate to select able persons who both respected Rome and knew how to win the people among whom they worked. The other was Celtic Christianity in the British Isles. A more rigorous and disciplined type than that found on the continent, it elevated the level of Christian commitment wherever it went and, with that, raised the motive for mission. Pope Gregory managed to a considerable degree to harness the thrust of the Celtic mission to his efforts through the agency of Augustine of Canterbury and other monks.

England

Celtic Christianity bore fruit first in England. The missionary training center on the island of Iona figured prominently in the evangelization. Aidan (d. 651) was a monk of Iona when Oswald, King of Northumbria, following his rout of Caedwalla about 633 or 634, summoned help from Iona to complete the mission work of Paulinus in his kingdom. The first person sent could not handle the assignment, so Aidan was dispatched. Oswald set up a headquarters for him on the island of Lindisfarne, where he developed an intimate relationship with the bishop. After Oswald was slain by Penda, the pagan ruler of Mercia, an Anglo-Saxon kingdom, his brother Oswin continued support of Aidan's mission work in Northumbria.

Iona appointed Finan as Aidan's successor. Finan baptized Peada, son of Penda, when the King of Northumbria refused to allow him to marry his daughter unless he became a Christian. After Penda's death in battle Christianity grew rapidly in central England. The King of Northumbria sent priests to revitalize the faith of the East Saxons in Essex. Eventually one of them was ordained a bishop at Lindisfarne. Cuthbert also came from Iona to extend Christianity in the north and the reawaken the faith of those who relapsed into paganism.

From Lindisfarne came the surge of effort which brought the last of the Anglo-Saxons into the Christian fold. Wilfrid (634–709), who had a stormy career as bishop of York, spent the years 681 to 686 working in Sussex among the South Saxons. In the wake of conquest of the Isle of Wight by the King of Wessex in 686 Wilfrid directed work there as well, though the actual work was done by his nephew. Wilfrid's more significant contribution, however, lay in the efforts he put forth to connect Christianity in Great Britain with Rome. Dissatisfied with Celtic Christianity, he studied at Canterbury and Rome. After three years in Lyon, he received the Roman tonsure. Returning to England, he became abbot at Ripon, where he introduced the Rule of Benedict. At the Synod of Whitby in 664 he played a major role in the triumph of the Roman party on the date for observing Easter. Consecrated bishop of York at Compiegne by twelve Frankish bishops, he found his see occupied by Chad on his return in 666 and retired again to Ripon. Theodore of Canterbury restored him to the see in 669. Several times subsequently he found himself in trouble and had to appeal to Rome.

Iona was not the only source of Celtic mission work in Britain. Celtic efforts, moreover, were supplemented too by continental missionaries. Gallic Christianity had deteriorated too much in the sixth and seventh centuries to offer much help. Pope Gregory the Great, however, launched a major mission effort not only in England but also in Germany and Scandinavia. According to Bede, Gregory's interest in England was pricked by seeing boys of fair hair and complexion offered for sale on a Roman market. Asking who they were, he was told they were Angles. He responded, "Right, for they have angelic faces and it is right such should be coheirs with the angels in heaven." Before his selection as pope, Gregory wanted to go as a missionary himself, but the populace of Rome did not want to lose someone so critical to the city's survival. When he became pope, he selected a group of thirty-nine monks. Under leadership of Augustine, abbot of the Monastery of St. Andrew, they set out in 596 to win Britain to the Catholic faith. In Gaul the monks became so frightened that they sent Augustine to Rome to ask Gregory's permission to abandon the mission. Gregory sent Augustine back with a letter ordering them on. In England the mission proved extraordinarily successful, first in Kent, whose ruler, Ethelbert, was married to a Frankish princess named Bertha. Bertha worshiped at Canterbury. After a delay of several days Ethelbert received them and promised freedom to preach and to receive converts. They selected Canterbury as their residence and place of worship. Although success came slowly at first, they obtained still greater freedom and traveled widely, baptizing tens of thousands. Gregory dispatched reinforcements and sent vestments, sacred vessels, relics, and manuscripts. He authorized Augustine to appoint twelve diocesan bishops and to place a bishop at York who could also ordain twelve bishops.

Since the Celtic mission was in full swing at the same time, a potential conflict emerged with the introduction of the Roman hierarchical system. Gregory handled the situation with sensitivity, however, and the missionaries confined their activities largely to the south of England. Augustine never consecrated twelve bishops as authorized by the pope and did not establish a second metropolitanate at York. He died shortly after Gregory did. In 616 Ethelbert died. After him a pagan reaction surfaced immediately with his successor, Eadbald. Eadbald, however, was converted and gave vigorous support to Christianity. The Roman mission got a further boost through the marriage of Ethelbert's daughter to Edwin,

King of Northumbria. To obtain her hand, Edwin had to agree to allow his queen and her entourage freedom to worship as Christians. She chose to take Paulinus with her as bishop. At the urging of Pope Boniface V, Edwin received baptism together with other notables and a large part of the population of the kingdom. The baptism took place at York, where Paulinus became bishop. Edwin's influence aided the evangelization in East Anglia.

The West Saxons were won over by a missionary sent by Pope Honorius I (625–638). Consecrated bishop by the Archbishop of Milan, then residing in Genoa, Birinus was assigned an episcopal seat near what is now Oxford. Among the Anglo-Saxons, however, the faith suffered frequent reverses. Altogether, the conversion of the Anglo-Saxons took nearly a century.

The conflict between the Ionan and the Roman missions came to a head in Northumbria, where Wilfrid championed Rome. At the Synod of Whitby in 664 the King listened to the argument of both sides and decided in favor of Rome. Theodore, Archbishop of Canterbury from 668 until his death in 690, extended the continental system and the authority of Rome throughout England. Although sixty-six years of age when appointed, he traveled everywhere consecrating bishops and establishing new dioceses. The Celts made one last attempt to regain control of Britain, reducing the prestige of Canterbury, but Wilfrid restored the authority of Rome in York. It took longer, however, for Rome to establish itself outside the Anglo-Saxon domain. In Scotland the Roman system did not prevail until the twelfth century.

Where Irish Christianity inspired changes in Gallic, Christianity of the British Isles had much to do with the conversion of peoples in the Netherlands, Germany, and later Scandinavia.

Belgium and Holland

Parts of Belgium had been evangelized before the fifth century as a part of Roman Gaul, but the barbarian invasions wiped out most of the Christian communities. After the invasions the first missionaries to people in the area came from Ireland. The most famous of the early missionary monks was Amandus, a Gallo-Roman from Aquitaine. After a visit to Rome he felt called to preach. Commissioned about 625 by King Clotaire II and ordained a bishop, but without a fixed see, he centered his activities at Ghent. He obtained the support of Clotaire's successor, Dagobert, to make baptism compulsory. Popular outcry against that caused him to leave Ghent. For a time he tried to do mission work among the Slavs on the Danube, but he soon returned to Ghent. Although he fell out with Dagobert and was banished, he returned again to the realm and worked among the Franks, founding a number of monasteries in the area around Arras. In 647 he was appointed bishop of Maastricht, but his penchant for creating controversy forced him to leave again and work among the Frisians. Later, he forsook this task and went to preach among the Basques. Amandus was succeeded in 641 by a far more effective missionary, Eligius or Eloi, who received appointment as bishop of Noyon. In what is now northwestern France and western Belgium he traveled incessantly, preached, and founded churches and monasteries.

Wilfrid, the bishop of York, landed in Friesland in 678 during one of his many trips to Rome seeking support in time of conflict. He received permission of Aldgisl to preach. He evidently led many prominent persons to faith and baptized thousands. Egbert initiated a more successful work later, for his efforts captured the imagination of Willibrord, the Apostle to the Netherlands. Reared in the monastery founded by Wilfrid at Ripon, Willibrord went to Ireland. Inspired by tales of Egbert and Wictbert, who had preached in Frisia two years, in 690 he took eleven monks with him, landing near the mouth of the Rhine. At Utrecht they evidently got a chilly reception, so Willibrord went to Pippin of Heristal, Mayor of the Palace under the Merovingians. Pippin

welcomed him as an ally in extending his sway over the Frisians. Going to Rome to obtain authorization, he returned with relics and a papal blessing. In 695 or 696 he went again to Rome to receive consecration as archbishop and returned to receive from Pippin a Frankish fortress at Utrecht which would serve as his headquarters. Willibrord labored among the Frisians for forty-four years. Although he did not witness the conversion of all Frisians, he did help to root Christianity firmly in Frisian soil. Following the death of Pippin in 714, the Frisian King, Radbod, who apparently never converted to Christianity, won back some territory lost to the Franks and restored paganism. When Charles Martel secured control, he drove back Radbod and showered favors on Willibrord, having him baptize his son Pippin the Short and restoring his cathedral city, Utrecht. Since Radbod's successor, Aldgisl II, was a Christian, he opened doors for the English mission, but he later reverted to paganism as he tried to drive out the Franks. Charlemagne soon turned the tables on him.

Germany

The evangelization of the area north and east of the Rhine emerged as an offshoot from Willibrord's work in Frisia. Among Willibrord's younger aides was Winfrith, later known as Boniface, the Apostle of Germany. Born at Crediton in Devon about 680 of an Anglo-Saxon family, he expressed a desire early to become a monk. Although his father at first opposed this, a severe illness caused him to change his mind. Winfrith acquired a reputation for learning, Christian character, skill as teacher, and administration. Ordained at age thirty, he chose to become a missionary. His venture into Frisia in 716 turned sour because Radbod refused opportunity to preach. Returning to England, he declined an abbacy of a monastery. Two years later, he went to Rome to seek papal sanction for his missionary endeavors. Pope Gregory II (715–731) did not give immediate approval, but Winfrith won him over. In 719, given the name Boniface ("Doer of Good"), he headed north toward Thuringia. Hearing of the death of Radbod, he redirected his steps toward Frisia, where he spent the next three years assisting Willibrord, who wanted him to be his own successor. Boniface, however, declined and asked instead to be sent back to Germany. Gregory II demanded that he come again to Rome and from that time on gave full support. On his return to Germany his courage in felling the Oak of Thor at Geismar, near Fritzlar, won him instant success. As he hacked away at the tree, a strong gust of wind blew it down. The fall burst it into four sections. Pagan bystanders saw in this a confirmation of the power of Christianity. Immensely successful in Hesse, Boniface felt he could move one year later to a new territory, this time to Thuringia. In the latter he was challenged chiefly to reform a politically divided and decadent Church. In this he won support of Charles Martel as well as the papacy. He also had a capacity for enlisting support of many other helpers, bishops and abbots and abbesses and other missionaries from England. Missionary helpers included a trio from one family—Willibald, his brother Wunnibald, and their sister Walpurga. Boniface's strategy was to win first the upper classes and then watch as the masses followed their leaders. He established monasteries which could serve as centers of evangelization. One of the most famous of these was the monastery at Fulda. One new feature of his approach was the place he gave women in the work. Besides Walpurga, he employed a relative named Leoba, who had been trained on the Isle of Thanet, as head of a religious house for women at Bischofsheim. From Thuringia Boniface moved to Bavaria. Although consecrated Archbishop of Mainz in 747, he functioned as an itinerant missionary throughout his life. After the death of Charles Martel in 741, Carloman and Pippin the Short commissioned him to reform the whole Frankish Church. His influence dominated decrees of synods intent on raising the moral and religious level of Christian communities. In his last few years he returned to Frisia, site of his first mission effort, and this time enjoyed marked success. In June 754, however, pagans attacked a camp where Boniface was confirming neophytes and slew him along with the others. Surprisingly, Boniface never felt he had succeeded in what he intended to do.

Further extension of Christianity in Germany depended on the powerful support of Charlemagne (768–814). Under him was completed the conversion of the Frisians. Charlemagne forcibly baptized the Saxons after his thirty-two year campaign against them.

The Saxons

Except for the Scandinavians, the Saxons held out longest against the advance of Christianity among the Germanic peoples. Located on the outer reaches of the Frankish kingdom, they did not yield easily. They martyred two English priests who went among them as missionaries. Boniface himself wanted to undertake a mission and received a letter from Pope Gregory II authorizing him to do so in 722. Lebuin, an English missionary among the Frisians, made a fruitless effort to win converts around 775. It remained, then, for Charlemagne to do what others failed to do through conquest and missionary instruction. Beginning his combined effort in 772, he did not complete it until 804. In the interim Saxons joined the Christian fold and later revolted against it. After 804, however, the "conversion" seems to have held, for the Saxons remained steadfastly Christian from then on. Among the conquerors only one voice, that of Alcuin, questioned the method.

Central Europe

Both the Roman Catholic and the Orthodox churches took part in the evangelization of central Europe. Largely as a result of geography, this process began later, in the eighth and ninth centuries. Although the work had some of the same characteristics as that in Western Europe, it also differed in some respects. As in the West, conversions usually took place *en masse*, monks doing much of the work and Rome offering support. However, the evangelization entailed greater use of coercion than in the West. The story is organized around peoples rather than territories.

The Avars

A terror during the seventh and eighth centuries, the Avars met stout resistance from Charlemagne. Thereafter, they scattered among the Slavs and came to Christianity mostly in connection with them. In 795 and 796 one group of Avars, defeated by the Franks, agreed to receive baptism.

The Slavs

The Western Slavs received the faith from Italy, the Eastern from Constantinople, leaving an area of conflict where jurisdictions overlapped. Pressing into the Balkans and the eastern section of the Alps in the sixth and seventh centuries, the Slavs virtually eradicated Christianity. Italian missionaries converted many Serbs and Croats in the seventh century. During the late eighth century, some Slavs sought Bavarian protection against the Avars, thus coming under the Franks and accepting baptism. Virgil, bishop of Salzburg (767–784), consecrated a bishop and a number of clergy for them. Following the submission of the Avars to the Franks in 796, other Slavs entered the Christian fold.

German dominance during the ninth century aided the expansion of Christianity. Colonists poured into the East especially in the tenth century, strengthening Latin Christianity further. The most important gains among Slavs were in what is now Austria, Hungary, and Czechoslovakia. More remote from Constantinople than the Balkans, these areas gave the Roman Church an advantage. Louis the German, son of Louis the Pious and grandson of Charlemagne, actively sought to extend the church in his domain east of the Rhine during his long reign (825–876). He pressed for the adoption of Christianity of the Latin variety in Bohemia and Moravia, but the Moravians appealed to Constantinople between 861 and 863 to counteract German influence. Emperor Michael III responded by sending two experienced missionaries, the brothers Constantine and Methodius. Before the latter left Constantinople they devised an alphabet for writing Slavonic and began translation of the Gospels. After arriving in Moravia they translated the liturgy into Slavonic. They then obtained approval for their work from the pope, perhaps because of fear of an extension of eastern influence. While in Rome, Constantine became a monk and took the name Cyril. He died in Rome February 14, 869, and was buried in the Church of San Clemente, Methodius returned to work among the Slavs.

The German princes did not look with favor on the work of Methodius. In 869 or 870 they expanded their sway in Central Europe, subjugating the Slavic princes—Svatopluk, Ratislav, and Kocel. German bishops summoned Methodius to a synod and, finding him at fault for infringing on the territory of Salzburg, confined him to a monastery for two and a half years. Pope Adrian II (867–872), however, intervened and ordered him reinstated and restored to his diocese. Meantime, military defeats forced the Germans to recognize the autonomy of Moravia. The Moravians welcomed him as their archbishop, but German clergy continued to agitate. In 879 Pope John VIII summoned him to Rome to answer charges of heresy and of use of Slavonic in the liturgy and cleared him completely, even permitting use of Slavonic earlier denied. He died in 884 or 885. In 900 the Magyars crossed the Danube from the East and occupied Lower Pannonia. In 906 they destroyed Moravia. Driven out of Moravia, the disciples of Cyril and Methodius carried Christianity to Slavs in the Balkans and to the Bulgarians.

Christian Missions from the East

Christianity spread less vigorously from the East than from the West. As K. S. Latourette has suggested, there were a number of reasons for this: (1) geography, (2) the spread of Islam, (3) the close relationship of church and state in the East, (4) the lesser role allotted to Christianity in the East. Christianity spread in several varieties from the East: Arian, Monophysite and Nestorian as well as Orthodox.

Justinian I

Justinian sought unsuccessfully to extirpate paganism within the empire and, as seen earlier, to reclaim much of the empire in the West. Driving the Vandals out of north Africa, he sought to extend Christianity among the Berbers. He initiated an expansion of Christianity in Nubia, the Sudan, and Ethiopia. The first serious attempts to introduce Christianity to Nubia came in Justinian's reign. Both Orthodox and Monophysite missionaries worked among the Nubians. Due to Monophysite dominance in Egypt, the latter had greater success in the area.

Ethiopia or Abyssinia adopted Christianity in the fourth century. In the fifth century the church there became Monophysite. In close contact with Egyptian monasticism, the Monophysites prospered in the sixth and seventh centuries. What happened between the seventh and the thirteenth centuries is very obscure. Some kind of revival took place in the thirteenth century through contact with Coptic Christians of Egypt.

The Slavs

The Slavs and Avars who moved into the Balkans and Greece slowly assimilated Orthodox Christianity in areas where it remained strong. Constantinople considered the Balkans and Greece an inseparable part of the empire and Christianity integral to it. Most of the "invaders," largely Slavs, accepted baptism. Use of them in the military structures hastened their assimilation.

Although a few bishoprics lapsed in some areas, the transition did not threaten the existence of the church as a whole. Some Slavs rose to high office in state and church. Nicetas I became patriarch of Constantinople (766–780). The Byzantine Church did not need more explicit efforts, for example, in the dispatching of Cyril and Methodius to work among the Slavs of central Europe. In the main, however, the conversion process went on unspectacularly.

The Bulgars

The most dramatic work of conversion from the East in the ninth century was that of the Bulgars. In the first half of the century the Bulgars under Krum handed the Byzantine forces one defeat after another. In 811 Emperor Nicephorus (802–811) was killed in battle and his skull used as a drinking cup by the victor. Nevertheless, the Bulgars began to assimilate Greek culture and religion. The process reached a climax with the baptism of King Boris in 864 or 865 after his defeat at the hands of Louis the German. Rather than accepting the Latin form of Christianity, however, Boris turned to the Greek probably because the Byzantines invaded Bulgaria as the Bulgarian army fought the Germans. Although his nobles resisted, Boris proceeded with the evangelization of his people. Greek and Armenian missionaries poured into the country. When the patriarch of Constantinople, Photius (858–857, 878–886), refused to establish a Bulgarian episcopate, Boris appealed to Rome and to Louis the German for clergy. He got them, and Rome immediately began baptizing and instructing converts. Once again, however, Boris did not feel satisfied with Rome and turned again to Constantinople. In 870 Patriarch Ignatius (867–878) selected a Bulgar to become archbishop of Bulgaria and sent ten bishops and many priests with him. The Latin clergy returned home to the West. Rome continued to appeal the decision and got the backing of the emperor, but Boris quietly continued ties with Constantinople. For his evangelizing efforts Boris was fortunate to have the literature developed by Cyril and Methodius and some of those they had trained as missionaries, who had been exiled from Moravia. In 889 Boris himself gave up his throne and entered a monastery founded near his capital. His son Simeon continued his efforts, following a brief reaction by another son, Vladimir. From Bulgaria Christian Slavonic literature spread to other countries.

Christianity East of the Byzantine Empire

Information on Christianity east of the Byzantine Empire is scattered and incomplete. Besides Orthodox Christians there were many other types. considerable missionary vitality seems to have existed in the area, especially on the part of Nestorians.

Persian Empire

The conversion of Constantine did not help Christians in the Persian Empire, for the Sassanids suspected that Christians were subversive. Severe persecution often occurred. Toward the latter part of the sixth century, however, Chosroes II, whose wife was Christian and who owed his throne to Byzantine help, favored the churches and proclaimed liberty of conscience. He, however, showed preference for the Jacobites, Monophysite Christians from Syria, and hostility to the Nestorians. Chosroes was the ruler who invaded the Byzantine Empire early in the seventh century and conquered Jerusalem and Alexandria. After Heraclius finally turned him back he persecuted both Jacobites and Nestorians. Nestorians made some converts among the upper and probably also the lower classes, but Christians definitely belonged to a minority. When Islam replaced Zoroastrianism in the eighth century, Christians continued to exist as separate bodies with their own organization and civil status. In some ways Christians had improved status, for Arabs accorded protection, toleration, and assistance in repairing their churches. They also chose Christians for

high civil offices. Although persecutions sometimes broke out, they were never as severe as under the Persians. Missionaries were more active than in any other land in which non-Christians ruled. Two reasons have been cited for this: the large number of merchants among Christians and the number of contacts they made with pagans as a result.

Arabia

Christianity spread to Arabia early. By the fifth century Christian communities existed in most areas of the peninsula. The rise of Islam in the seventh century put a stop to Christian expansion and slowly eliminated most of the churches. The ruler of Hira, however, may have been a Christian in the last part of the sixth century. As late as 676, Nestorians held a synod in the land of the Katars in southeastern Arabia. Christianity won the island of Socotra, near the Gulf of Aden, but the manner and date are uncertain.

Central Asia

Christianity spread extensively to the north of Persia, east of the Caspian Sea and west and east of the Oxus River. Its strength varied from time to time. Merv had a bishop from 334 through the fifth and sixth centuries and Herat in the sixth and a metropolitan in the sixth, tenth and eleventh centuries. Samargand was the center of a Nestorian ecclesiastical province in the eleventh century. Christians were known among the Hephthalite Huns and Turks toward the close of the fifth century. About 781 the Nestorian Patriarch Timotheus reported success among the Turks. Until Islam penetrated the region in the eighth century, Christianity seemed to have had good prospects of becoming dominant in the area between the Caspian and what later became Chinese Turkestan. Christianity's chief rival in the area was Manichaeism, but the Moslem rulers opposed it more than they did Christianity. Christianity appeared strong during the ninth through eleventh centuries. The final contest between

Islam and Christianity took place in the thirteenth and fourteenth centuries, to Islam's advantage because of its political force.

China

The large number of merchants among Nestorians gave Christianity a vehicle for expansion into China. Although not active missionaries, the merchants offered loyal support to churches and monasteries. There were Christians in present-day Sinkiang or Chinese Turkestan in the ninth century. Converts were made among nomads of the area in the early eleventh century. In the thirteenth century the Onguts, a Tartar people living north of the great northern bend of the Yellow River, and some of the Uighurs were Christians. Christians may have worked in Tibet in the later eighth century.

The earliest date of Christian entrance into China is 635, recorded on an inscription on a monument erected in 781 in or near Ch'angan, then the capital of China (now Hsianfu). The inscription claimed that Emperor Kao Tsung had adopted Christianity and founded monasteries in each department of his realm. However, Christianity probably did not preempt the native religions, Confucianism and Taoism, but evidence of its existence in the eighth and ninth centuries is substantial. Buddhism certainly had more monasteries. In the eleventh and twelfth centuries Christianity was all but unknown in China.

India

Christianity had greater success in India than in China. Coming into existence in the first few centuries of Christian history, Christian communities continued throughout the Middle Ages. Geography favored Christianity in this because it opened more commercial contacts. Yet the route through which Christianity came is unclear. Evidence favors a Persian source. Although Christians passing through India in the thirteenth and fourteenth centuries recorded the presence of Christians, Christianity remained somewhat alien to the culture. Manichaeism also gained some foothold in India.

ANGLO-SAXON ENGLAND
IN THE SEVENTH CENTURY

PICTS

DALRIADA

STRAITH-
CLYDE

Lindisfarne
Bamborough
BERNICIA

PICTS

NORTHUMBRIA

Hexham

Jarrow

Whitby

York

MERCIA

LINDSEY

GWYNEDD   Chester

NORFOLK

EAST ANGLES

SUFFOLK

Lichfield

WALES   HWICCE

DYFED

MORGAN-
WYG   Gloucester

EAST
SAXONS

London

Canterbury

WEST
SAXONS   Winchester

SOUTH
SAXONS   KENT

WEST
WELSH

Chapter 32

The Churches of Western Europe

The churches rather than the Church is used deliberately here to indicate that, despite efforts of Rome, Christians did not experience unity in the West any more than in the East. As a matter of fact, one of the major concerns of the papacy was to effect some semblance of unity among disparate groups. In England Celtic mission work created a more independent approach to Christianity which the Synod of Whitby in 664 only began to resolve. In France and later in the so-called Holy Roman Empire the monarchs dominated church life and, as often as not, the papacy. Meanwhile, within those vast areas existed separate peoples who challenged the Frankish and the Germanic rulers to bring them under some kind of common order. Of course, the process by which national churches came into existence differed in different parts of Western Europe and, even as Rome exerted its influence, often too quite different forms. It also defies neat periodization, as if the same things happened everywhere at the same time.

In a comprehensive history it is not possible to look at all of the areas individually. Some of the dynamics can be presented, however, through discussion of selected examples: the Church is in the Merovingian and the Frankish Kingdoms, 604–888, the Church in England during the Anglo-Saxon period up to the time of Alfred the Great, 663–847 and the Church in Spain from about 600 to 859. In each instance the story is tied inseparably to developments in other spheres of life.

The Church in the Merovingian and the Frankish Kingdoms

The history of Christianity in the Merovingian and Carolingian kingdoms divides into four segments: the period of transition from the old Gallo-Roman to other patterns of church life (604–711), the period of disintegration of church life under the Mayors of the Palace (711–751), revival of church life under Pippin III (751–768) and continuing reform under Charlemagne and his successors (768–888).

Transition under the Merovingians

The Frankish churches entered the seventh century on a low note. According to Gregory of Tours, not only princes and nobles but even the clergy, including bishops, presented a sad spectacle. Monasteries suffered from excessive wealth and property and the clergy from domination by the upper classes. The Merovingians supported the churches, but they also ruled them. They appointed and removed clergy, a practice which became increasingly threatening to the churches during the tenth and eleventh centuries. Simony, the buying and selling of ecclesiastical offices, became common. Bishops conducted themselves like secular rulers, vacating their offices at will. The Gallic Church lost its zeal for evangelization except insofar as it fit into plans of their rulers for conquest.

At this crucial period in the history of the Merovingian Church the entrance of Columban had a major impact. As indicated earlier, Irish monasticism introduced an element of discipline that Gallic monasticism had lacked. When Columban and his company entered Merovingian lands, he took care to obtain permission from King Guntram and later solicited land from King Theudebert, help from Theuderic, and protection from Childebert for his monastery at Luxeuil. His intense missionary concern must have touched some buttons with them. What strikes the reader of his monastic rules and the piety of the Merovingian Church, as J. M. Wallace-Hadrill has pointed out, is its focus on God and the relationship of God with man rather than upon relics and patronage of local saints. His religion was personal rather than institutional. His monastic rule called for moral perfection achieved by thorough self-scrutiny, confession, and doing appropriate penance. Penance was therapeutic rather than punitive. Thence, he required private confession before eating and going to bed. Through his agency confession and penance became part of daily life. About 650 the Council of Chalon officially judged private penance "of use to all."

The impact of Columban and Irish Christianity will appear somewhat surprising in view of the fact that he had to exit Burgundy and ended up at Bobbio in northern Italy. The answer to that poser rests in his influence on Frankish gentry who helped found monasteries in the tradition he represented. One example is the founding of a pair of monasteries on the family estate of Chagnoald, a monk of Luxeuil, one for men and one for women, the latter by Chagnoald's sister Burgundofara (later Ste. Fare). The latter's will called for disposal of immense properties to her convent. Another is the founding of several monasteries by the sons of Authar following a visit by Columban to bless the brothers Ado and Dado (later Audoen and Ouen, bishop of Rouen).

Columban's *Rule of Monks* reflected already some influence of the Rule of Benedict. His successors at Luxeuil increasingly tempered Columban's with the gentler rule of Benedict to create a mixed rule, perhaps with other influences as well. Columban's rule suited monks, but it was too harsh to guide people outside the monastery.

Thanks to patronage of Merovingian royalty, especially Dagobert I, his son Clovis II, and Clovis's wife Balthildis, monasticism thrived. Dagobert endowed the famous St. Denis in Paris and cofounded Solignac with Eligius, bishop of Noyon. Balthildis, once an enslaved Anglo-Saxon, founded the influential monastery at Corbie, north of Paris, and the women's convent of Chelles, both on royal property. The founding of these houses had much to do with the powerful missionary thrust of the Merovingians toward the north. The monasteries did spadework for Willibrord in the Netherlands.

The Merovingian Church had passed well beyond the age when Christians still felt comfortable with classical literature. Merovingians loved the Bible not so much as the source of doctrine as for personal edification, that is, as hagiography. They came to know it especially through the liturgy. From the lives depicted in its many books they sought to develop an image of the ideal Christian and to incorporate it into the lives of Merovingian saints. At the end of the sixth and the beginning of the seventh centuries Gregory of Tours and Venantius Fortunatus had produced a considerable corpus of such lives. The Merovingian Church sought to extend that to its own work: enhancing popular devotion, defining the model Christian life, and keeping the cult of holy persons within the framework of the church. The lives took on a very stereotyped form with sameness as a proof of authenticity. Above all, the saint had to perform miracles. In the seventh century the impact of Irish monasticism on Gallic Christianity added a moral element to the concern for the miraculous. Jonas of Bobbio's *Life of Columban* highlighted ways in which the saint confronted moral turpitude, especially among royalty. Where in the sixth century Gregory had written about saintly bishops and monks, his successors in the seventh focused on political bishops martyred for the sake of the church. Some also heralded the Merovingians themselves. Three Merovingian queens—Chrotechildis, Radegundis, and Balthildis—attained honor as saints, although none of their husbands did. What gave them such distinction was protection of church property, fighting the church's battles, and supporting its bishops. Kings often came out with mixed records.

From Clovis onwards, the Merovingians meant to control the Church in their territory. They did this through councils, canons of over twenty of which survive. Clovis himself assembled the first of these in July 511 just after his defeat of the Visigoths of Aquitaine and specified its agenda and approved its decisions. From subsequent records it is clear that the Merovingian kings viewed their people as a Christian people entrusted to their care. Although bishops sometimes displayed some independence, they could not contest royal prerogatives and could easily lose their lives if they did. Councils in 614 and 626, however, convened under Chlotar II (613–629) reveal the Merovingian Church in a time when the bishops took courage in numbers and had a king sympathetic to the Church. Yet even here, they recognized the ascendancy of the King over themselves and the Church. Late in the Merovingian period, however, neither kings nor bishops had much control. All sorts of abuses occurred: dividing of church property, laymen administering parishes, bribery widespread, and use of lay patronage to circumvent bishops. Boniface wrote to the pope in 742 that Carloman wanted to restore ecclesiastical discipline trampled on for sixty or seventy years. Although some discipline had been exercised in the interim, it was not impressive. The Church stood in need of serious reforms undertaking by Carloman, Pippin III, and Charlemagne.

Gallo-Roman bishops generally had good relationships with Rome, but they did not hesitate to remind the popes about their rights as local churches. They looked to Rome as the exponent and defender of orthodoxy. Clovis and his sons, moreover, sent a votive crown to Rome as a symbol of respect, and Gregory of Tours described Clovis as the "New Constantine," connecting his reign with the papacy. The Franks did not learn about the primacy of Rome from others, they knew what it meant themselves. From Rome's side, too, the ties were clear. Gregory the Great directed a number of letters to the Merovingian kings expressing his expectation that they would see to the proper ordering of the Church. He also wrote bishops, pressing his concern about the low moral state of things, particularly the practice of simony. Both kings and bishops seemed to react with no negative feeling. Roman influence also showed in the Frankish liturgy. The influence increased in the eighth and ninth centuries. Not only the sacramentary, a liturgical manual, but practical guides to performance of the liturgy, came from Rome. The advent of the Carolingians increased ties with Rome.

Decline under the Mayors of the Palace

Monarchical rule slipped badly during the late Merovingian period, from about 670 onwards, and with it the Merovingian Church. A series of inept kings left the running of affairs to their Mayors of the Palace—Pippin of Heristal (d. 714), Charles Martel (688/689–741), and Pippin III (714/715–768). Pippin of Heristal concluded a pact with the Anglican missionaries (Willibrord, Ewald, Suitbert) to the north and sent Willibrord to Rome to secure ties with the papacy. This step laid the groundwork for the Carolingian Kingdom's religious policies.

The Christian West owes Charles Martel (688/689–741) immense thanks for stopping the advance of Islam at the battle of Poitiers (not Tours) in 732, but his attitude toward the Frankish Church has evoked criticism. Like his predecessors, Charles continued Carolingian rule under Merovingian shadow kings (Chilperich II, Chlotar IV, and Theuderich IV) as he secured control of both Austrasia and Neustria and enlarged the kingdom through his repeated battles with Frisians, Saxons, Alemanni, Bavarians, and Aquitanians. Although he favored mission work in the territory on the borders of the kingdom, he made no room for the reform efforts of Boniface within the Frankish Church itself. Hard pressed to secure recompense for those who assisted him in his military exploits, rather, he seized church lands and monasteries. In effect, Charles laicized control of the Church and, if the new owners gave anything back to the monks, they doled out bare subsistence.

Charles's tactic is easy enough to understand when one considers the vast holdings the churches and monasteries had accumulated from Roman times on. Before the Franks ever appeared, the churches had become wealthy proprietors and the Merovingians extended their wealth further. In 584 King Chilperic complained that his treasury was depleted because the wealth had gone to the churches. Not only land, but money, laborers, and relics counted in the wealth. Estate surveys of the Carolingian era confirm that in the wealthy region of Aquitaine the Merovingians set an example for bishops, monks, and missionaries in willing estates to the churches. Dagobert (d. 580) lavishly endowed the famous monastery of St. Denis in Paris, assuring that it would become the royal burying place. In addition to giving extensive lands, he rebuilt and embellished the abbey church. He instituted an October fair for the abbey. Then he gave it his own body. His son, Clovis II, and the latter's wife, Balthildis, placed the Abbey under the Mixed Rule and accorded it immediate royal protection. So much royal favor put St. Denis in a position to receive better treatment from Charles Martel than most others, but even here he both gave and took away. He secularized some of the Abbey's vast estates, but he gave it the remainder of the great villa of Clichy

and sent his son Pippin III there to receive his education. He too was buried there. That he created anxiety among the monks is evident in the fact that the monastery did not openly espouse the Carolingian cause until after Charles's death.

Although the Frankish Church had lost much property during the reign of Charles Martel, it was still rich when he died. The huge establishments like St. Denis, of course, fared the best. In theory, the Church probably owned nearly a third of the cultivated land of Gaul, though in practice it could not have done so. Better days, however, lay on the horizon with the advent of Charles Martel's sons, Carloman, who inherited Austrasia, and Pippin III, who inherited Neustria. Although their military commitments precluded immediate restoration of church properties, they did restore to any church or monastery which could prove poverty the land they had to have.

Revival of the Frankish Church under Pippin III

Charles Martel's sons, Carloman and Pippin III, inherited their father's missionary concern. Serving still as their predecessors had as Mayors of the Palace, they gave no overt signs of a coup until 750. In 750 Pippin sent two emissaries to Rome, one an Anglo-Saxon and the other a Frank, to ask whether a ruler bearing no power deserved still the title of king. Pope Zacharias (741–752), well aware of what was going on in the kingdom, replied that it was a matter of power, in effect, declaring the Merovingians obsolete. Thence, Pippin quietly retired the king and queen to an area where they could cause no trouble.

Further help for securing the throne came from Rome. Pope Stephen, who succeeded Zacharias in 752, called on Pippin to deliver Rome from the Lombard threat. Pippin arranged to meet the Pope at Ponthion near Chalons January 6, 754. There, with an oath, Pippin committed himself and his sons to the defense of Rome. When the Lombards refused to negotiate, he mounted a campaign against them, anointed by the pope before he set out bestowing on Pippin, Carloman and Charles the title of "Defender of the Romans." Twice Pippin defeated the Lombards led by Aistulf. Although Rome did not feel secure until 759, the victories marked the beginning of the Papal States and the popes as temporal as well as religious rulers.

Pippin clearly meant to rule the Frankish Church through its bishops. What he began, his son Charles carried to its completion during his long and eventful reign. Under Pippin, however, the reins of leadership fell into the hands of Chrodegang, Archbishop of Metz. Born about 712 of aristocratic background, he was reared in the court of Charles Martel. Shortly after Charles's death in 741, he received appointment to the see of Metz just as Boniface's reforms got underway in Austrasia. In 748 he founded the monastery of Gorze with support of Pippin. Accompanying Pope Stephen to Francia, he became in effect the successor to Boniface as the dominant figure under Pippin in the Frankish Church. His thought had a clearly Roman slant. He envisioned his monks as strict followers of the Rule of Benedict and not as missionaries with pastoral duties in the area around the monastery. Monks had duties quite different from secular priests. The object of trained clergy was to celebrate the Divine Office correctly and regularly.

Continuing Reform under Charlemagne and His Successors

What Pippin III began, Charlemagne continued. He extended the Frankish domain and with it Christianity. For him every campaign had a religious aspect. The longest and most difficult of his conquests was that against the Saxons. In his first campaign against them he had penetrated deep into Saxon territory and destroyed the Irminsul, the tree trunk believed to support heaven, and engaged in mass baptisms that resulted in all kinds of reprisals against Frankish mission posts. Charlemagne took severe measures against those who still resisted. After he subdued Widukind, he

subjected the Saxons to draconian measures, imposing the death penalty for any kind of attack on a church, for ignoring Lenten regulations, for killing a clergyman, for refusing or avoiding baptism, for plotting against Christians, or for breaking faith with the king. In 803 Charlemagne deported whole Saxon communities to areas where they could undergo constant supervision. Surprisingly, after this the Saxons settled down and did not again contest Christianization. Like the Franks themselves, they thought of themselves as a part of the *populus Christianus*.

Charlemagne also continued Pippin's conquest of the Lombards. By 774 he had subjugated Desiderius and, unlike his father, remained to see that his control held. He assumed the title of "King of the Franks and Lombards." The pope received him as a protector and ratified all previous contracts entered into by his predecessors. In 781 he bestowed on Charlemagne's two younger sons, Pippin and Louis, the titles of King of Italy and King of Aquitaine respectively. Although he expected to have no more trouble with the Lombards, in 786 he had to subdue the southern Lombard duchy of Benevento. On the death of Pope Hadrian in 795 he expressed to Leo III (795–816) a statement of his task "everywhere to defend the Church of Christ" and also of the pope's "to raise your hands to God like Moses to ensure the victory of our arms." When disaffected Romans manhandled the pope in 799, he had to appeal to Charlemagne. The latter arrived at St. Peter's in late December 800 and held a formal inquiry into charges against the pope. Assembled clergy affirmed his self-avowed innocence. On Christmas Day, a grateful Leo placed a crown on Charlemagne's head as he rose from his knees during the mass. The congregation chanted, "Charles, most pious Augustus, crowned by God, great and peace-loving emperor, life and victory!" Charlemagne may have been surprised, as Einhard reported, but the action did little or nothing for his status outside of Rome. It probably tied the crown more closely to Rome. After 800 his capitularies and other pronouncements did become noticeably more religious. He felt an obligation to care for the Christian people committed to him and to watch over the clergy. His concern was his and the people's salvation.

Charlemange's reform efforts entailed numerous points. At court he developed something like a university to which he drew some of the best scholars of the day such as Alcuin. He developed a library, sending out a circular asking for books in 780. Although interest in scriptures and the fathers persisted, classical texts grew more numerous. When in 794 Charlemagne decided to make Aachen his capital, he thought of it as in some sense a New Rome. The object of study and education was primarily the furtherance of Christianity at home and abroad. Alcuin, the Northumbrian educated at York and brought to Charlemagne's court in 782, taught liberal arts to equip young men to read and understand the Bible.

In the religious sphere Charlemagne required the Frankish Church to put its house in order. He tightened the grip of the monarchy on the clergy in 779. Ten years later, he issued his first capitularies regarding the Church, composed of eighty-two articles directing special representatives of the crown to accompany bishops in remedying abuses. Although about two-thirds of the articles repeat legislation from an earlier collection of canons, the others address specific points, stressing preaching as the prime obligation of the clergy and the need for observation of the way the clergy celebrate mass, administer baptism, chant the Psalms, and explain the Lord's Prayer. In short, Charlemagne made the clergy responsible to himself for the religious and moral life of the people. Subsequent legislation indicates that the level of Charlemagne's frustration with the effects of his directives increased rather than decreased. To the very end, he continued to send letters and issue directives. His kingdom was not becoming what he had hoped it would be by the time of his death in 814.

Louis the Pious (814–840) sought reform by a monastic rather than an episcopal route, relying especially on Benedict of Aniane, initiator of a reform movement according to the Rule of Benedict, and Helisachar. Although none doubted his religious zeal and piety, this approach aroused sharp opposition due to its intense attention to detail in monastic life. Matters did not improve under Louis's successors—Louis the German, Lothair, and Charles and Bald. The Viking invasions disrupted life in the kingdom, divided in 843 by the treaty of Verdun, hastening the breakup of order and the onset of feudalism. The most notable reform may have taken place in the area controlled by Charles the Bald in Gaul, thanks especially to the efforts of Hincmar, Archbishop of Rheims. An associate of Charles from 834 on, when he witnessed the deposition and restoration of Louis the Pious, Hincmar first reformed the Abbeys of Compiegne and St. Germain-de-Flay at Beauvais. Elected Archbishop of Rheims in 845, he took an active part in opposing the invasion of West Francia by Louis the German in 858. Later he contested Lothar II's efforts to divorce Teutberga and marry Wildrada, a matter which brought him into conflict with the papacy. The two main problems he faced regarding reforms of the church had to do with clerical orders and control of church property. He approached these as a lawyer, citing canon law against priest, pope, and king.

The Carolingians and Theological Controversies

Before concluding this study of the Merovingian and Carolingian Church, some word should be added about the involvement of Charlemagne and his successors in resolution of doctrinal controversies. Hardly anything confirms the extent of their interest in and control over the Church along Constantinian lines more clearly than this. Three controversies involved Charlemagne himself: iconoclasm, adoptionism in Spain, and the addition of *filioque* to the creed by the Western Church. Two others arose during the reign of Charles the Bald: over predestination and interpretation of the eucharist.

The iconoclastic controversy originated in the Byzantine Empire during the eighth century when some of the stronger emperors tried to dampen Muslim fervor against Christians by removing one of the ostensible reasons: the use of icons, especially on the outside of the churches. At the seventh ecumenical council, Nicaea in 787, eastern bishops affirmed the use of images in worship. Shortly thereafter, Charlemagne had the *Caroline Books* issued in his name and with his authority to combat the decisions of that council, although they also condemned iconoclasm. In 794 he convened a Synod at Frankfort which also condemned the adoration and service of images.

Adoptionism, the view that Christ was God's Son by adoption rather than by incarnation, surfaced again in Spain during the eighth century, first in the Spanish liturgy. From about 780 Elipandus, bishop of Toledo, and subsequently Felix, bishop of Urgel, defended adoptionism on the basis of its use in the liturgy. In 792 the Synod of Regensburg forced Felix to recant. The next year, Alcuin took up the pen against him and in 799 he refuted Felix at Aix-la-Chapelle or Aachen, the capital.

The *filioque* controversy was precipitated by the insertion into the Creed of Constantinople the added phrase "and from the Son" after the words "and in the Holy Spirit, who proceeds from the Father" by Western churches without consulting the Greek Churches. The addition first appeared at the Third Council of Toledo in 589, evidently against Arianism dominant among the Visigoths. It spread from Spain to France, where it had attained general usage by the time of Charlemagne. In 809 two monks from Charlemagne's court made a pilgrimage to the Holy Land, where hermits on the Mount of Olives condemned them for their use of *filioque* when they said the creed. Shortly afterwards, Charlemagne convened a Synod at Aix-la-Chapelle to sanction use of the term. Pope Leo III refused to incorporate the term formally into the creed, but the Photian schism opened the way for that.

Controversy over Augustine's doctrine of predestination sprang up in the middle of the ninth century, when Gottschalk, a monk in the monastery of Orbais, near Rheims, carried Augustine's doctrine to its logical extreme: Everything, he insisted, is foreordained of God—evil as well as good, condemnation as well as salvation. Gottschalk's views were condemned at the Synod of Mainz, convened by his abbot, Rabanus Maurus, in 848, and again at the Synod of Quiery, convened by Hincmar, Archbishop of Rheims and metropolitan superior, in 849. The latter ordered Gottschalk, who did not want to be a monk, imprisoned in a monastery dungeon the rest of his life (d. 868/869). Gottschalk had some distinguished supporters—Ratramnus of Corbie, Prudentius of Troyes, Lupus of Ferrieres, and Archbishop Remigius of Lyons—as well as opponents, and the controversy continued after his death.

The eucharistic controversy involved two monks from the famous monastery at Corbie. In 844 Paschasius Radbertus composed a treatise *On the Body and Blood of the Lord*, in which he made two affirmations: (1) that the bread and wine are changed mystically into the body and blood of the Lord as a literal interpretation of the words "This is my body" would imply, and (2) that the eucharistic and the historical body of Christ are identical. At the request of Charles the Bald Ratramnus countered both points, insisting that (1) the change is a spiritual one and that (2) the eucharist is called the "body" of Christ because it is the Spirit of Christ. This issue also remained moot until 1215 when the Fourth Lateran Council affirmed the views of Radbertus.

The Church in England

The story of the Church in England after the Synod of Whitby (664) and up to the Norman Conquest in 1066 was disrupted by the Viking invasions, beginning in 793, which brought church life to a virtual standstill. These developments suggest division into three major periods: that of the organizing of the Church with connections to Rome, 664–793, that of the disruption brought on by the Vikings, 793–900, and that of the rebuilding of the English Church in the tenth and eleventh centuries, in part with assistance of Danish rulers.

Building with Roman Connections

King Oswy settled the issue brewing in Northumbria concerning the direction in which the English Church would go by accepting the latest Roman way of establishing the date of Easter. Queen Eanfled, Oswy's wife, may have tipped the scales, for she had been brought up in Kent, where the Roman date was already observed. The noted Celtic missionaries readily accepted the decision. Tuda, a southern Irishman and the new Northumbrian bishop, conformed. So did Eata, the Abbot of Lindisfarne, an Englishman trained under Aidan. Implementing the Roman model, however, remained the major task of Theodore, appointed Archbishop of Canterbury after a five year vacancy.

Theodore (ca. 602–690) was born in Tarsus and educated there and at Athens. After spending most of his life in the East as a monk, he moved to Rome to teach. When two other Roman monks declined to replace Wighard as Archbishop of Canterbury, one of them, Hadrian, an African, recommended Theodore. Pope Vitalian consecrated him in 668, but fearful lest his long years in the East might have corrupted his perceptions, he sent Benedict Biscop and Hadrian to England with him. During his twenty-two years at the see of Canterbury, he did a remarkable work of organizing the churches of England under Canterbury and advancing in the process of evangelization. He arranged the first council affecting the whole of the English Church to meet at Hertford in 673. Although his plan to have annual councils ran into too many difficulties because of travel, he convened a second at Hatfield in 680 at

which, at the request of Pope Agatho (678–681), the bishops drew up and forwarded to Rome a declaration of orthodoxy. Theodore divided dioceses and extended the episcopate. He also issued canons to regulate church life, deposed unworthy bishops, and rendered moral decisions. His division of the diocese of York into three parts resulted in a rift with the volatile Wilfrid. When he died, however, the English Church's relationship with Rome had been secured.

Pope Vitalian's decision to send Benedict Biscop (ca. 628–689) with Theodore proved of great consequence too. A Northumbrian of noble birth reared at the court of King Oswy, after two journeys to Rome he entered the monastery of Lérins in 666. At Canterbury he became abbot of the Monastery of St. Peter and St. Paul (later St. Augustine's). In 674 he founded the Monastery of St. Peter at Wearmouth and in 682 that of St. Paul at Jarrow. An enthusiast of art and learning, he brought paintings, relics, and manuscripts from Rome on five trips there. An enthusiastic advocate of Roman practice, he secured the services of John, archcantor of St. Peter's in Rome, to teach the chant in England. He is reputed also to have introduced use of glass windows and churches built of stone to England. His pupils included Bede, entrusted to his care at age seven.

Bede (ca. 673–735) brought English scholarship and culture to a level it had not known before. Sent first to Wearmouth, he was transferred to Jarrow, probably when it was founded. Perhaps indicative of his gifts, he received ordination as a deacon around 692 at age nineteen and as a priest at age thirty. He visited Lindisfarne and York but probably never went outside of Northumbria. He devoted himself to study of the scriptures and to teaching and writing, gaining fame for scholarship within his own lifetime. Bede's writings reflect a resurgence of the classical tradition of education which Charlemagne later instituted in the Frankish kingdom. He wrote works *On Orthography* and *On Metric Art* for pupils in the monastery, a treatise *On Times* for the clergy to use in calculating Easter according to the Roman dating, and another treatise *On the Nature of Things*, a cosmography based on Isidore of Seville and supplemented from Suetonius and the younger Pliny. He composed a number of biographies, including one on Benedict Biscop, but his greatest writing was *The Ecclesiastical History of the English Nation*. Unlike so many medieval writers, Bede knew the difference between history and hagiography. He collected and evaluated evidence meticulously. He also wrote poetry. Less than a century after he died, he was being honored with his title "Venerable" and in 1899 Pope Leo XIII entered his name among the "Doctors of the Church."

Other notable scholars appeared on the scene at the same time, though none matched Bede. Iona's most distinguished was Adamnan (ca. 625–704). Probably a native of Donegal County, Ireland, he was elected abbot of Iona in 679. A visit to Wearmouth led him to accept the Roman dating of Easter, which he furthered in Ireland on three visits. He is probably remembered best for the "Canon of Adamnan," a rule he persuaded the Synod of Tara to adopt in 697, prohibiting the taking of women and children as prisoners of war, and his *Life of St. Columba* which he wrote between 688 and 692. Although hagiographical, the latter contains much valuable data. Aldhelm (d. 709), the first bishop of Sherborne, also established a reputation as a scholar and was held in high esteem as a poet. A near relative of Ine, King of Wessex, he became Abbot of Malmesbury around 675. He took part in the reform work of Theodore, and when the old see of Wessex was divided, he became bishop of the newly created diocese of Sherborne. King Alfred considered him the best of the Old English poets.

The Anglo-Saxons distinguished themselves by their poetry. From a religious standpoint *The Dream of the Rood* (Cross) stands out. Evidently written before 750 because parts of it were carved on the Ruthwell Cross near Dumfries, it presents the Cross recalling the story of the crucifixion. Now that Christ has risen, however, the cross is honored with gold and jewels and adored by angels. From a more secular point of view *Beowulf* is far better known. Although not explicitly Christian, the poem was the work of a Christian author, for he alluded to the Creation, Cain and Abel, the Flood and the Judgment and denounced reliance on pagan gods. Most likely, *Beowulf* was the creation of a minstrel entertaining the Mercian court of King Offa. Early in the ninth century, an otherwise unknown poet named Cynewulf wrote four poems: on *Christ*, *Juliana* the martyr, *Elene* about the finding of the true cross by Helena, and *Faces of the Apostles*. *Elene* is considered the classic.

The point was made earlier, but it is worth underscoring that the Anglo-Saxon Church was intensely missionary. The English did not remain content with evangelization of their homelands. Exemplary here was the remarkable missionary family of Willibald (700–786). Related through his mother to Winfrid (Boniface), Willibald received his education at Waltham Monastery in Hants. In 722 he undertook a visit to Rome with his brother Winnebald and his father Richard. From Rome he went to the Holy Land via Sicily and Cyprus, returning through Tyre to Constantinople. In 730 he retired to Monte Cassino, where he spent ten years. In 740 Pope Gregory III (731–741) challenged him to join his brother Winnebald and his sister, Walburga, in Germany as a missionary. There Boniface appointed him bishop of Eichstatt in 742. With the help of Winnebald he founded the double monastery in Heidenheim, Württemberg, where his sister became abbess after Winnebald's death. Willebald had much to do with consolidating the Church in Francia.

A New "Dark Ages"

The Viking invasions brought a rude end to the English renaissance of the seventh and eighth centuries. First raiding the coasts, where they wasted the monasteries on Lindisfarne and at Wearmouth and Jarrow, the Vikings extended their raids ever farther inland with little to hold them back. From 835 on, the raids increased yearly. In 851 a fleet of 350 Viking ships anchored in the Thames. The Danish army burned Canterbury and London. In 866 the Danes overthrew the rival kings of Northumbria and forced Mercia to pay a ransom, called Danegeld. In 870 they moved to Reading. Although King Aethelred I and his brother Alfred won one battle, the West Saxons lost others. After succeeding his brother, Alfred was forced to buy off the Vikings. The accession of Alfred the Great (871–899), however, provided a turning point in the sorry story.

The Church in Spain

The Church in Spain enjoyed a renaissance of sorts in the seventh century, but it saw its gains rudely wrenched away in the early eighth century by the advance of Islam. Stronghold of the Visigoths, Spain remained predominantly Arian until the late sixth and early seventh centuries, when the distinguished brothers Leander and Isidore of Seville helped to turn the tide in favor of the Catholic Church.

Leander (ca. 550–600 or 601) and Isidore (ca. 560–636) belonged to a noble family of Cartagena. When the city was destroyed, the family fled to Seville, where Isidore was born. In 582 Leander, the older brother, went on an embassy to Constantinople, where he became a friend of Gregory the Great. On his return, probably in 584, he was appointed bishop of Seville. He spent his energies chiefly fostering Catholic Orthodoxy in Spain against the Arian Visigoths. In 589 he presided over the famous Synod of Toledo which incorporated the *filioque* clause into the Nicene Creed. King Recared publicly accepted the Catholic faith at the same time.

Isidore, the far more widely known of the two, was educated at a monastery under tutelage of his brother. Encyclopedic in his learning, he used it to further two aims—to check Arianism

and to eliminate barbarism in Spain. Around 589 he entered a monastery either as a monk or as a cleric and continued his studies. Around 600 Gregory I appointed him Archbishop of Seville. Thenceforth he devoted his energies to the spread of the Catholic faith through founding schools and convents and working for the conversion of Jews. He wrote extensively on a variety of subjects. In his *Etymologies* he collected the knowledge of his day on such subjects as grammar, rhetoric, mathematics, medicine, and history, as well as theology. His *Three Books of Sentences* are a manual of Christian doctrine and practice, making generous use of Augustine and Gregory. In a treatise *On Ecclesiastical Offices* he supplied information on the Mozarabic liturgy used in Spain as well as on church orders. In his *Chronica Majora* he traced history from creation to 615, borrowing from Julius Africanus, Eusebius, Jerome, and others and adding original material on the history of Spain. His *History of the Kings of the Goths, Vandals, and Suevi* supplies most of the information now extant on those peoples, especially the Visigoths. Noted for his learning, piety, and charity, Isidore was canonized in 1584 and made a Doctor of the Church in 1722.

The Council of Toledo in 589 established an alliance between Church and state similar to the one Constantine implemented in the Roman Empire. Through the general councils the king tended not only to affairs of the Church but also of the state. He convened the councils, set the agenda, and presided so that they became an invaluable instrument in the effecting of his aims. Without the Church's binding authority the king's authority was in danger. On the Church depends the security of the state.

Conversion of the Jews was of special concern. At the Fourth Synod of Toledo in 633 Isidore of Seville spoke strongly against the forcible conversion of Jews. Under pressure from the king, however, later councils decreed that Jewish children should be separated from their parents in order to free them from their influence and lead them to baptism. They also decided to give all Jews a choice of emigration or conversion. In the Gothic Kingdom there was to be no place for any except the Catholic faith.

Spanish Christianity took keen interest in liturgical reform during the seventh century. Councils gave much attention to the establishment and propagation of one uniform rite for the mass and for offices. Under Isidore, for instance, the fourth council of Toledo called for "one rite of prayer and psalmody, one manner in solemnities of the masses, one in vespers and matins." The Mozarabic Liturgy, in use in Spain until the reconquest during the eleventh century, had some peculiarities: prayers sprinkled with scriptures, strong preference for theological instruction, an explicit sense of the value of the symbolic acts, active participation of the community. Major figures in its expansion, besides Isidore, were the three metropolitans of Toledo—Eugenius (d. 657), Ildephonsus (d. ca. 669), and Julian (d. 690).

Due to the controversy over Priscillianism in the fourth century and after, monasticism did not have a good reception in Spain until the conversion of the Visigoths to Catholicism. Leader in that was Leander, bishop of Seville. Under his leadership the third council of Toledo ruled that a bishop might make one of his parish churches into a cloister. That decision opened the way for the forming of seventy-seven dioceses with monastic centers. Increasing regard for monasticism accounts for the large number of abbots who participated in the legislative work of the councils.

The Muslim conquest of Spain radically disrupted the life of the churches in 711–713. Many Christians converted to Islam. Many churches were turned into mosques. However, some—nine in Toledo, more than ten in Cordoba, four in Merida—remained open for worship. Only Toledo, Seville, and Merida retained metropolitans, however, and the number of bishops

was reduced from sixty-nine to eighteen. Christianity's chief bulwark was the many cloisters which Muslims made into charitable centers to serve Muslims as well as Christians. Indicative of the decline of Christianity is the loss of name theologians or church leaders. The one name that does stand out in the late eight century was that of Elipandus, Archbishop of Toledo, who revived adoptionism and suffered condemnation along with his follower Felix of Urgel in Carolingian synods. Elipandus evidently wanted to accommodate the ruling Muslims on a point of faith.

The difficulties of the Christian situation surfaced in the middle of the ninth century when a fanatical group of Christians banded together in search of martyrdom. They persuaded Eulogius, bishop of Cordova (ca. 800–859), to take on the role of apologist for them. Educated for the priesthood, he became a deacon and later a presbyter of the Church of St. Zoilus in Cordova and adopted an ascetic life. Brought up by his grandfather as a hater of Islam, he had grown more advanced in his hostility through the influence of his teacher Speraindeo, Archbishop of Cordova, and his intimate friend Alvar. The tolerant Emir Abdal-rahman II (822–852) sought to check the movement with the support of an Archbishop Reccafred. He imprisoned Eulogius for a time, but freed him and did not restrict his writing. When he was chosen to succeed Archbishop Wistremir of Toledo (d. 858), the emir Mohammed I refused to ratify the appointment. Deeply disappointed, Eulogius sought and attained martyrdom on March 11, 859. Alvar later glorified him in hymns and a life.

One section of Spain, the mountainous region in the far northwest, held out against the Islamic tide. Asturia and Gallicia gradually increased in size and strength. Under Alfonso I (739–757) it developed into the Kingdom of the Asturias which provided a jumping off point for the reconquest of Spain by Christian forces in the eleventh century.

Chapter 33

Eastern Christendom, 610–867

In the East, as has been noted more than once, emperors assumed responsibility for the churches as well as for the state. Sometimes that worked to the churches' advantage, but at other times it created severe problems. Patriarchs often functioned as agents of the emperors rather than in the best interest of the Church. Only rarely did they challenge rulers. For the period now under discussion monks proved more independent. They demonstrated decisively in the iconoclastic controversy that the Church could challenge the state effectively, if not on the short run, at least on the long one.

The story of the Byzantine Church during this period can be divided according to the two dynasties which ruled the empire at the time: that of Heraclius, 610–717, and that of the Isaurians, 717–867. The first period was marked by continuing controversy over the formula adopted at Chalcedon and the loss of much of the empire to the Muslims, the second by Isaurian successes against Islam and other enemies of the empire, the iconoclastic controversy, and growing tensions between East and West leading to the Photian schism.

The Dynasty of Heraclius

Heraclius (610–641) halted the Persian advance between 622 and 629 after suffering a series of defeats at their hands. No sooner had he stopped the Persians, however, than he had to watch helplessly as Islam ripped first one and then another province from the empire. Not until 678 did the Byzantine forces under Constantine IV (668–685) succeed in checking the Muslims with a naval victory off Syllaeum in Pamphylia. After the latter's reign, however, the dynasty slipped downhill under the repressive regime of Justinian II (685–695), opening the way for its overthrow in the "First Anarchy" (695–717).

The Monothelete Controversy

Heraclius's need for unity in the face of the Persian threat prompted him to seek some formula for reconciling the Monophysites. Severus, patriarch of Antioch (512–518), had come up with a proposal a century before which might reconcile the Monophysites to the doctrine of two natures in the incarnate Christ propounded at Chalcedon. He spoke of one "theandric operation (*energeia*)." In Alexandria around 600 some spoke of either one "operation" or one "will." According to Sergius, patriarch of Constantinople (610–638), the formula again came into play during the Armenian campaign of Heraclius in 623, when the emperor himself tried to win converts to Monenergism, unsuccessfully until he consulted Sergius. In 630 the emperor appointed Cyrus to the vacant see of Alexandria with instructions to win the Monophysites over to the doctrine. Cyrus succeeded in 633 in reuniting them to the Byzantine Church.

Success here proved short-lived, however. Two influential monks, Sophronius and Maximus the Confessor (580–622), stated their opposition. Sergius managed to calm the opposition of Maximus, but he could not do the same for Sophronius, elected patriarch of Jerusalem in 634. For the moment he seems also to have enlisted Pope Honorius. In 638 Sergius promulgated the *Ecthesis*, as the controversy waxed hotter, forbidding the use of either "one operation," as tending toward Monophysitism, or "two operations," as suggestive of opposing wills in Christ and concluding with the alternative phrase, "one will of our Lord Jesus Christ, the true God."

Easterners generally accepted the *Ecthesis*. Upon the death of Pope Honorius (625–638), however, Westerners raised fierce objections. The Byzantine government tried for years to beat down opposition. In 648 Emperor Constans II issued the *Typos*. Unlike the *Ecthesis*, the *Typos* spoke of "will" rather than "operation" and did not profess to be a *symbolum* or doctrinal formula. It was simply an edict forbidding citizens "to raise any sort of dispute . . . over the one will and energy, or over two wills and two energies" and to go back to where things stood before the controversy. It threatened severe consequences for those who violated the prohibition. One of the unfortunate victims of the *Typos* turned out to be Pope Martin I, elected just shortly after it appeared. In October 649 he convened a Lateran Synod which condemned Monotheletism and affirmed "two natures" and "two wills" and repudiated both the *Ecthesis* and the *Typos*. Pope Martin communicated the decisions to the rest of Christendom and to the emperor. Constans sent the Exarch of Ravenna to seize and carry off the pope in June 653. Later he brought him to Constantinople in September, 654, where, after brutal treatment, he died September 16, 655. Constans ordered Maximus the Confessor mutilated. He died in 662.

Imperial pressures continued for ten years under Constantine IV, but the major victory over

the Muslims in 678 and the signing of a treaty with the Saracens took away imperial concern to reunite the Monophysites. Thereafter, Constantine reversed his policy and sought to obtain political cooperation with the West. August 12, 678, he addressed a letter to Pope Agatho (678–682), who, at the emperor's request, convened a Synod at Rome on Easter, 680, which again condemned Monotheletism. The emperor proceeded to convene a Council to meet at Constantinople, the Sixth Ecumenical council, which agreed with the pope and the Roman Synod and with the Council of Chalcedon, Leo's *Tome*, and other pronouncements in affirming two wills and two natures. The Council condemned Monotheletes—Sergius, Cyrus, and others. Honorius, who had seemed to agree with Sergius, may also have come under this censure.

The Islamic Invasions

Islam devastated the empire in the seventh century, and it is not surprising that the emperors sought to unify all forces to meet the threat. The Islamic forces came like a hurricane. Within a century of the death of Muhammed (ca. 570–632) they had overwhelmed the Persian Empire (636–640), conquered Syria, Mesopotamia, Egypt, and swept across North Africa and stood at the threshold of Gaul, where Charles Martel halted their advance at Poitiers. Heraclius, worn out from fighting the Persians, could do no more than rescue the True Cross from Jerusalem. His forces suffered a decisive defeat at the Yarmuk in 636. Adding to the threat, the Saracens overran southern Asia and Armenia (651–654) and set siege to Constantinople itself for five years, 673–678. Fortunately, a storm and the newly invent "Greek-fire" united to destroy most of their ships, enabling Constantine IV to crush what remained at Syllaeum.

The Council in Trullo

Some word should be added about the famous Council in Trullo, convened by Emperor

Justinian II in 692 to supplement the Fifth and Sixth Ecumenical Councils. The name derives from the domed hall (Trullus) of the imperial palace in which the bishops met. The Council elevated the place of Constantinople in the East and intensified the rivalry with Rome. It issued many rules concerning the clergy, perhaps strong evidence of serious problems. It forbade the clergy to have anything to do with inns, horse racing, theaters, dice, brothels. It also reiterated rules for monks. No one was to take vows before age ten. Monks and nuns must not wander away from their convents. It laid down some directions for lay persons as well regarding theaters, clothing, observance of heathen festivals, impersonation of women by men, and many other things. It set forth penalties for absenting worship three Sundays in a row and laid out numerous regulations on baptism, penance, marriage, and the eucharist.

The Isaurian Dynasty

The Isaurian dynasty lasted a century and a half, 717–867. Its first two Emperors—Leo III (717–741) and Constantine V (741–775)—were strong military figures, but they precipitated fierce opposition when they sought to strengthen their situation vis-à-vis the Muslims by restricting and then prohibiting the use of images in worship. After the brief reign of Leo IV (775–780), who pursued the same policy, a wave of reaction was led by Empress Irene, who succeeded her son Constantine VI (780–797), after acting as his regent. After her death in 802 a "Second Anarchy" set in, lasting from 802 to 820. Emperor Leo V (813–820) waged another campaign against the use of images which carried over into the reigns of Michael II (820–829) and Theophilus (829–842), the most vigorous of the iconoclasts. On the latter's death, however, his wife, Theodora, inaugurated the final phase of the controversy, restoring the use of images during her regency with her son Michael III (842–867).

The Iconoclastic Controversy

The use of images in worship gained recognition very slowly in the early Church. As late as 400, Christian theologians expressed strong reservations about the practice as a violation of the second commandment. Such scruples were breaking down in the fourth century, however, as more and more persons of wealth and culture entered the churches. Veneration of sacred objects such as relics of martyrs and saints grew increasingly common. In the sixth century appeared pieces of the true cross, the veil of Veronica, and images of Jesus and his Mother. By the eighth century the use of images in worship had reached the point of extremes.

Leo III had the support of several bishops who preached against images and relics, and some pious lay persons were shocked at the extremes. In Isauria, where Leo came from, there were many Muslims and Jews, both of which found the practices highly offensive to their monotheism. The Paulicians also, who considered matter evil and thus objected on different grounds, existed in considerable numbers there. Add political reasons and one can see the motives underlying the campaign against the use of images in worship. In the army Leo had virtually unanimous backing. His most vigorous opposition came from the monks.

Leo issued his first edict calling for the destruction of images in 725. In 726 he began to enforce the edict. Greece and Egypt, already disaffected because of heavy taxation, rebelled. Although the reaction was quickly brought under control in Greece, in Italy it united the papacy and the people in opposition to the Exarch of Ravenna. Meantime, Patriarch Germanus (715–730) led resistance at Constantinople. Leo simply removed him and installed Anastasius (730–754), who immediately countersigned and gave ecclesiastical sanction to the edict. Authorities removed images, mosaics, and paintings from the churches and whitewashed the walls.

Distinguished churchmen put forth the case for the use of images in worship. Most notable of these were Patriarch Germanus, Pope Gregory II (715–731), and John of Damascus (?676– ?756). Germanus rejected the claim based on Jewish and Muslim opposition by noting that both broke the second commandment and argued that images were intended only to inspire people to imitate what they represented. In his *First Oration in Defence of the Images*, published in 727, John, holder of high office at the Court of the Caliph in Damascus, based his case for the use of images on the incarnation. Images repudiate a docetic view of Jesus' human nature. Iconoclasts, he argued, have adopted a Manichaean view and will end up in docetism. Worship is not paid to images per se but to what they represent. Since the incarnation broke the second commandment, Christians should not return to the bondage of Judaism. Anyway, iconoclasts are inconsistent, for they adore the Cross, why not images? Images, moreover, are the same as sacraments. Pope Gregory III, succeeding to the chair of Peter in 731, convened a Roman Council which excommunicated all who destroyed or defiled images. Although the emperor attempted to retaliate by dispatching a fleet to Italy, it was wrecked in the Adriatic and all he could do was to seize papal estates in Sicily and Southern Italy. From this point on, Rome turned to the Franks for help and away from the Exarch of Ravenna.

Despite heavy opposition, Constantine V, more a theologian than his father, pressed the policy against images. In 753 he convened a council to meet in the Palace of Hieria, across from Constantinople, to oppose both veneration of images and the intercession of saints. Though Rome, Alexandria, and Antioch refused to send representatives, 340 bishops attended and carried out Constantine's directives. The eucharist is the only lawful representation of Christ. Image worshipers are idolaters. Leo and Constantine are rescuing the Church from idolatry. The Trinity had deposed the three great defenders of images.

Appointing an iconoclast, Constantine II (754–766), to the vacant see of Constantinople, the emperor took extreme measures against monks—torturing them, putting them to death, and turning monasteries into barracks. His successor, Leo IV, applied the iconoclastic measures more mildly while his wife, Irene, maintained a secret devotion to images.

During the minority of her son, Constantine VI, Irene turned the policy around after a few years. In 784 she removed Patriarch Paul IV (780–784), appointed a layman, Tarasius (784–806), in his place, and renewed relations with Rome. Although Hadrian I (772–795) did not like the appointment of a layman to the see of Constantinople, he responded favorably to her proposal for a council to settle the issue, sending two legates. Dispersed by soldiers when they first assembled, in August 786, the bishops reassembled at Nicaea in 787, becoming the Seventh Ecumenical Council. The Council repudiated the Council of Hieria of 753 and replied to its arguments one by one. In its *Definition* it declared that icons could receive "greeting and reverential worship" but not "the adoration which belongs to God alone." It then anathematized the chief iconoclasts and declared that the Trinity had made "glorious" three great defenders—Germanus, John, and George.

Iconoclasm remained powerful, however, despite the efforts of Empress Irene. As a matter of fact, her personal ambition, realized in the dethroning of her son in 797 to become the first ruling Empress in Roman history, proved costly. The Caliph Harrun Arraschid forced her to conclude a peace treaty and pay tribute. In the West, meanwhile, she suffered a blow when the pope crowned Charlemagne Roman emperor on Christmas Day 800. Following the "Second Anarchy," a second period of iconoclasm began in 813. A military revolution was precipitated by the defeat of Emperor Michael I (811–813) at the hands of the Bulgars, which soldiers interpreted as a consequence of iconolatry. When Patriarch Nicephorus (806–815) refused to convene an ecumenical council to overturn Nicaea of 787, Emperor Leo V, the Armenian, removed him and placed an iconoclast, Theodotus I (815–821), in his place. Theodotus immediately called a council, which overturned Nicaea and reinstated Hieria. Persecution of icon users was resumed. Although Michael II (820–829) let up on persecution, his son Theophilus (829–842) imprisoned monks, scourged bishops, banished image worshipers from Constantinople, and suppressed the painting of pictures there. The vigor with which he pursued his policy, however, prepared the way for the restoration of the use of images in 843. The empress regent, Theodora (d. 867), convened a council that reaffirmed the decrees of Nicaea and excommunicated all iconoclasts.

East-West Tensions

Three developments impaired the prestige of the empire shortly after 800. One was Charlemagne's effort to obtain recognition for his coronation as emperor. When hostilities broke out over Venice, Emperor Michael I agreed to send two ambassadors to Aachen to recognize Charlemagne as joint ruler of the empire. Actually, there were now two empires. Another was a series of disasters inflicted by the Bulgarians. In 811 Krum slew Nicephorus I. Two years later, the Bulgarians overwhelmed his son, Michael I, and laid siege to Constantinople. Emperor Leo V annihilated them, however, at Mesembria in 817. A third was the loss of Crete in 825 and Sicily in 827 to the Saracens. The situation turned around, fortunately, under Theophilus (829–842).

The ending of the iconoclastic controversy effected a certain amount of unity as Leo V and Theophilus redirected the antipathy toward the Paulicians, who had taken a strongly iconoclastic position. Many Paulicians fled to Saracen territory and from there made raids on the empire for fifty years. Empress Theodora put 100,000 of them to death and drove out large numbers. Meantime, mission efforts improved. After Mi-

chael III (842–867) subjugated the Slavs of the Peloponnese, founding of churches and monasteries led to their rapid Christianization. Cyril and Methodius, meantime, undertook their notable work in Moravia about 864. Subsequently their disciples evangelized Bulgaria. It was in part this mission work which precipitated the schism between Pope Nicholas I (867–878) and Patriarch Photius. Photius resented Latin missionaries in a country converted by Greeks and denounced their invasion in a letter to three eastern patriarchs. East-West tensions came clearly into the open in the last ten years of Michael III's reign (842–867).

The Photian Schism

The immediate cause of the schism between Rome and Constantinople was the removal of Patriarch Ignatius and the installation of Photius in his place. Ignatius was the fourth child of Emperor Michael I. When Leo V overthrew his father, he mutilated and banished Ignatius. Ignatius chose to become a monk, founding monasteries in the Islands of the Princes, where he served as abbot and sheltered refugees from Constantinople who were banished for using images. When Methodius died in 846, Empress Theodora remembered Ignatius and appointed him patriarch. When she fell from power, Ignatius ran afoul of her brother Bardas, minister to her son Michael III and Caesar (862–866), by refusing to serve him communion on Epiphany, 858, because he divorced his wife and married his daughter-in-law. Later he added to his offense by refusing to force Theodora and her daughters to enter convents. On November 23, 858 Ignatius was seized and banished, though he refused to resign. Emperor Michael III and Bardas selected Photius (800–891) to replace Ignatius in violation of canonical regulations prohibiting the filling of sees not vacant.

Photius, brother of the patriarch Tarasius (784–806) and related through his mother to Empress Theodora, was the abler of the two, a professor of philosophy at Constantinople. Among his widely applauded writings was the *Bibliotheca*, extracts and abridgements of 280 volumes of classical authors, mostly historians and theologians. He also began a *Lexicon*, which his students completed. In his *Amphilochia* he collected three hundred questions and answers on points of scripture. Photius also gained distinction in imperial service as First Secretary of State. In the latter he became a favorite of Bardas. Since he was a layman, he had to be raised step by step through the lower Orders to the rank of bishop. On Christmas Day, 858, Gregory Asbestas, Archbishop of Syracuse consecrated him.

The conflict here was not between Ignatius and Photius but between styles of ecclesiastical politics, one claiming independence for the Church and the other subservient to the state. The monk Ignatius took the former line, the scholar Photius the latter, just as most other patriarchs did. Popular feeling sided with Ignatius.

Early in 859 Photius sent letters to Alexandria, Antioch, and Jerusalem and a letter and embassy consisting of an Imperial Spatharius and three bishops to Rome announcing his enthronement. Photius explained his reluctance to accept the office pressed on him by the emperor and the clergy and declared his adherence to the faith of the seven ecumenical councils. He ended with a request for the pope's prayers. The Imperial Spatharius explained what had happened to Ignatius, that he had voluntarily withdrawn after a council had deposed him for neglecting his flock, and invited Pope Nicholas I to send representatives to a synod which was to clear up details of the iconoclastic controversy. The pope seized on the occasion to assert a jurisdiction which would preserve the independence of the Church of Constantinople.

Nicholas dispatched two legates on September 25, 860 with powers to investigate and report on the affair and with replies to both the emperor and the patriarch. Asserting that the rights of the pope had been violated in the deposition of Ignatius "without reference to the Roman pontiff" and that the offense was made worse by appointment of a layman, he denied his consent to Photius's consecration until his legates brought a report. If the emperor would show his devotion to the Roman see by restoring the Vicariate of Thessalonica and the papal patrimony in Calabria and Sicily and the right to consecrate the archbishop of Syracuse, they might reach a compromise, *ecclesiastica utilitas*. In a briefer note to Photius, Nicholas censured him for receiving consecration without having first served in lower Orders and declined to approve until his legates brought a report on his behavior and commitment to *ecclesiastica utilitas*.

Although the emperor and Bardas were inclined to accept the proposed arrangement, Photius persuaded them not to do so, for it would have cost him half of his jurisdiction. When the Roman legates arrived, they met stern resistance. Photius prevented them from hearing Ignatius's side, giving them costly presents, and the emperor induced them to take Photius's side by threat. Thence, at the Council of Constantinople in May, 861, they affirmed the deposition of Ignatius and sanctioned the appointment of Photius. When in the fall the pope heard of these happenings, he renounced the action of his legates. In March, 862 he took up the cause of Ignatius and denounced Photius. He informed the three eastern patriarchs that Ignatius had been illegally deposed and a wicked person installed in his place, something Rome would never tolerate. They must see to it that Photius was deposed and Ignatius was restored. He informed the emperor and Photius of the supreme authority of the Roman See.

In 862 Theognostus, exarch of the monasteries of Constantinople, presented a *Libellus Ignatii* to the pope and pleaded for papal support. Nicholas responded. In a Lateran Council in April 863 he deposed and excommunicated Photius and reinstated Ignatius. When the emperor finally responded in August, 865 to assure him that his efforts on Ignatius's behalf were in vain, requir-

ing him to withdraw his sentence, the pope
reiterated that the Roman See alone was the final
court of appeal in Christendom. With tempers
rising over control of the Church in Bulgaria at
the Council of Constantinople in Lent of 867
Photius condemned the Latins for errors they
introduced into Bulgaria and recounted complaints he had heard of papal tyranny in the
West. He proceeded then to excommunicate
Nicholas. Unfortunately for him, however, he lost
his major supporters—Bardas, murdered in 866,
and Emperor Michael, assassinated September 24,
867. Basil I (867–886), realizing that public
opinion favored Ignatius, banished Photius and
reinstated Ignatius. On the death of Ignatius in
878, however, Basil restored Photius. In a Synod
of Constantinople, November of 879 to March of
880, legates of Pope John VIII (872–882) concurred in the affirmation of Photius as a "legitimate" occupant of the see. The pope, however,
disowned his legates for this and finally anathematized Photius. On the death of Basil I, his son,
Leo VI (886–912) deposed him and sent him into
exile in Armenia.

Chapter 34

The Papacy, 604–867

Papal history from Gregory I (590–604) to Gregory VII (1073–1085) has few bright spots. Gregory II and III (715–741), Nicholas I (858–867), and Sylvester II (999–1003) stand out against a bleak background of many popes who had brief tenures. Twenty popes ruled from 604 to 701, twenty more between 816 and 900, and twenty-three between 900 and 1003, an average of five years. Save for the few eminent figures, the popes of this period left scant records of their activities. Moreover, the most embarrassing part of papal history occurred at the end of the period, what has been characterized as "the Great Pornocracy" (900–962). Later a papal schism led to the deposition of three contenders and the installation of a new pope at the Synod of Sutri in 1046.

In the period under study in this chapter the history of the papacy features in great part a struggle to establish a working relationship with the powers that then existed as they constantly changed. From 604 until 715 the popes detached themselves little by little from dependence on the emperors in the East and their exarchs in Ravenna. As the Carolingians displaced the Merovingians in the Frankish kingdom after about 715, pontiffs linked the future of the papacy inseparably to the former, especially under Pippin III. The coronation of Charlemagne on Christmas day, 800, marked the beginning of a new epoch lasting until the end of the Carolingian era. There-

after, with the resuscitation of a German kingdom from the ruins of the Frankish, popes had to fight a new battle to hold on to the *principatus*.

Detachment from Byzantine Control

In the first period (604–715) the papacy still depended on the emperor in Constantinople or his representative in the West, the exarch of Ravenna, to protect it and to back up its directives throughout the West. Rome's experience with Constantinople had not been happy, however, and it is not surprising to see the popes looking increasingly toward Western powers before the period ended. In 536 Silverius (536–537) was charged with treasonable liaison with the Ostrogoths as he tried to negotiate with them to prevent unnecessary bloodshed and deposed and sent into exile by a military court. He died as a consequence of deprivations he suffered before his successor took office. Vigilius (538–555) ran afoul of Empress Theodora, a Monophysite, when he stated his adherence to the formula adopted at Chalcedon and repeated the condemnation of the Monophysite Patriarch Anthimus. He also incurred the disfavor of Emperor Justinian when he refused to condemn the "Three Chapters"—the person and writings of Theodore of Mopsuestia, and the writings of Theodoret of Cyrus and Ibas of Edessa. To compel Western acceptance, the emperor ordered him removed and brought to Constantinople where, under pressure, he acquiesced in the action and then vacillated as the West raised a storm of protest. He died on the journey back to Rome in June 555. Gregory the Great (590–604) also had strained relations with Emperor Maurice because of his direct negotiations with the Lombards to lift the siege of Rome in 593.

The fact of the matter is, the Byzantine emperors from Justinian on proved increasingly powerless to aid the West. Justinian's costly reconquest was the last valiant effort to reconstitute the Roman Empire. The popes now needed to look elsewhere for help. Although they could not afford to ignore Constantinople, neither could they count on Constantinople to support the Roman *principatus*.

Honorius I (625–638) took upon himself much of the civil administration of Italy when the Byzantine government failed, directing the work of Byzantine officials. He jealously guarded Roman primacy in both East and West. He beclouded his record, however, by the way he handled the proposal of Patriarch Sergius to end the Monophysite opposition to the doctrine of two natures in Christ adopted at Chalcedon. Unwisely, when Sergius addressed a letter to him on the subject, Honorius did not attempt to inquire more fully into the matter, consulting with opponents such as Maximus or Sophronius, but labeled the whole controversy a war of words and declared: "We confess *one* will of the Lord Jesus Christ." When he at last received the *Synodikon* of Sophronius, he did not change his position but triggered Emperor Heraclius's *Ecthesis*, forbidding use of the phrase "one or two energies in Christ" and asserting instead one will. Although Honorius probably could not be classified as a Monothelete, he earned an anathema from the Council of Constantinople in 680–681 by incautious action.

Honorius's successors certainly made up for any error on his part, for one after another they condemned the *Ecthesis*. Martin I (649–655), however, paid a high price for his boldness in opposing an imperial decree. Emperor Constans II (642–668), grandson of Heraclius, abandoned the *Ecthesis* and issued the *Typos* with severe threats forbidding discussion of the issue of one or two operations or one or two wills in Christ. Indicative of the difficulty of harmonizing both imperial and papal claims, the pope convened a council at the Lateran which condemned the *Ecthesis* and *Typos* and asserted the doctrine of two wills and two operations in Christ and reaffirmed agreement with Chalcedon. Constans immediately ordered the Exarch Olympius to seize Martin on the grounds that he was illegally enthroned since the emperor had not approved his election. Olympius, frightened, allied himself with the pope, who declared himself independent of the empire and had troops to back him up. In June, 653 the new exarch took him captive and removed him to the Island of Naxos and later to Constantinople. Shamelessly abused and then exiled to Cherson in Armenia, he died on September 16, 655.

Vitalian (657–672) maintained friendlier relations with Constantinople but took care not to compromise himself. In 663 Emperor Constans II made the first imperial visit to Rome in two hundred years, but his visit did not suffice to prevent the separation of Italy from the empire, for he could not expel the Lombards. When Constans was assassinated in 668, Vitalian supported Constantine Pogonatus (668–685), the lawful heir to the throne. With the Islamic threat diminished by a victory at Syllaeum in 678 Constantine remembered the pope's support as he moved to bring the Monothelete controversy to an end. Imperial legates brought a doctrinal letter which quoted the Lateran Council of 649 affirming the doctrine of two wills in Christ. Then, on November 7, 680, the emperor opened the Council that condemned Monotheletism and its authors and defenders, including Honorius. Pope Leo II (682–683) ratified the decrees of the Council after altering the one in which it condemned Honorius. The more cordial relations brought by this action led to revocation of the edict of Constans in 666 which declared Ravenna independent. The emperor, however, reserved for himself the confirmation of papal elections, thus creating a very awkward problem of protracted vacancies in Rome. When a full year elapsed before the election of Benedict II (685–685), this decision was rescinded, and confirmation of papal elections returned to the Exarch of Ravenna.

Although relations between Rome and Constantinople appeared to improve with the election of Sergius I (687–701), the improvement did not last long. Emperor Justinian II (685–695) was not happy with the outcome of the Fifth and Sixth Ecumenical Councils and convoked the supplementary council known as the Council in Trullo, which adopted one hundred and two disciplinary canons animated largely by hostility to Rome. When word got out that Justinian intended to seize Sergius, the militia of Ravenna and Pentapolis hurried to Rome and joined the people to protect him. The imperial legate took refuge in the pope's quarter and had to flee to the city in disgrace. Justinian could not avenge the insult. In 695 he was himself deposed and sent into exile.

The era ended on a more favorable note. Constantine I (708–715), on better terms with Justinian II during his second term (705–711), journeyed to Constantinople, accorded royal honors along the way. It was the last time a pope went so far East until the modern era. The emperor confirmed all of the Roman Church's privileges on the condition that the pope would accept the decisions of the Council in Trullo which agreed with Western customs. Under Philippicus Bardanes (711–713), who deposed and assassinated Justinian for the second time, Monotheletism had a brief revival which resulted in a rupturing of relationships between eastern and Western churches. The West no longer recognized the emperor, dated no documents according to his reign, and did not set up his image in the churches as in previous times.

Alliance with the Franks

In the next period (715–768) Rome cast its lot with the rising power in the West, the Franks. Whereas relations with the dynasty begun by Heraclius experienced ups and downs, those with the Isaurians plunged downward in a hurry. Pope Gregory II (715–731), one of the ablest holders of the office since his namesake, reacted quickly to Emperor Leo III's (717–741) imposition of higher taxes on church property in Italy to support his military engagements and his iconoclasm. The pope led the people in opposition to increased taxes and resisted imperial efforts to remove him. He refused Leo's demand that the West accept his edict regarding images through action of a Roman synod. In a letter to the emperor, Gregory rebuked his meddling into theological matters, declaring it intolerable, and called on people in the West to be watchful regarding the impiety rising from the East. The militia of Pentapolis and Venice hastened to Rome to protect the pope, expelling the imperial *duces* and proposing election of another emperor. Gregory, however, moved more cautiously, fearing an imperial attack on Rome and encouragement this step might give the Lombards. The Lombards proved untrustworthy in opposition to Leo III. Although Liutprand initially placed himself at the head of the revolt against the emperor's edict, he reversed himself, joining the exarch of Ravenna in a siege of Rome. Although Gregory succeeded in arranging a peace, he had once again to submit Rome to imperial control through the exarch. Gregory saw greater peril in Lombard control, however, than he did in Byzantine.

Here is where the Frankish alliance took shape. Rome already had ties all over the Germanic world. Of special significance was the connection with Boniface, the Apostle to the Germans. In 718 Wynfrid came to Rome to visit the tomb of Peter and to ask the pope to give him another mission, since his venture into Frisia had proved abortive. Gregory, calling him Boniface ("Doer of Good"), commissioned him to work in Thuringia. In the fall of 722 Gregory recalled him and consecrated him a bishop. Subsequently Boniface not only evangelized the German people, he also inaugurated the reform of the Church in the Frankish Kingdom at the bidding of Pippin III.

Papal efforts to halt iconoclasm were unavailing. Gregory III (731–741) convened a synod in Rome which anathematized iconoclasts. The emperor replied by having the papal legates carrying the decision jailed in Sicily. He dispatched a fleet to Italy, but it suffered shipwreck. Not deterred, he proceeded to confiscate the Roman Church's holdings in southern Italy and Sicily and to transfer control of the dioceses of those areas as well as bishoprics east of the Adriatic in Illyria to the patriarch of Constantinople. Gregory III's situation was made more precarious by the Lombards. Uniting forces with the dukes of Spoleto and Benevento, he reinforced the walls of Rome, fortified Civita Vecchia, and acquired the Tuscan castle of Gallese. Liutprand, however, proved too strong for the allies and advanced to the very gates of Rome itself. In these extreme circumstances the pope appealed to Charles Martel to come to the aid of St. Peter. Although the latter treated the pope with deference, he did not send help, even after further pleas. At the time he found it prudent not to interfere in Italy. A lasting alliance would come later, under Zacharius (741–752) and Stephen II (752–757).

Zacharius, a Greek and a native of southern Italy, modified papal policy toward the Lombards and concluded a twenty-year truce with Liutprand and, later on, with Ratchis. At the same time he used the good offices of Boniface to strengthen ties with the Franks. The climax of Boniface's reform efforts in the Frankish Church came in 747, when, in a synod, all the bishops agreed to be obedient subjects of St. Peter and his successor, the bishop of Rome. Meantime, Pippin III, still Mayor of the Palace under the Merovingians,

gave Zacharius a brilliant opportunity to endear himself to the rising Carolingians by asking whether title or power determined the legitimacy of a king. And Zacharius did not fail to seize the moment. He spoke the words Pippin wanted to hear: "It is a matter of power."

Almost immediately Zacharius needed Pippin's assistance to meet the threat posed by Aistulf, recently enthroned successor to Ratchis, who took Ravenna and the surrounding area and marched on to Rome. At this critical point, however, Zacharius died, and it remained for Stephen II to secure help as Aistulf's army stood at the gates of the city. To lift the spirits of the despairing Roman populace, Stephen marched through the streets barefoot at the head of a procession, carrying a highly venerated icon of Christ. Secretly he sent a message to Pippin asking for safe conduct into his realm. Pippin received him with the highest honors at Ponthion in January, 754. The pope pleaded for the protection of Pippin and received an assurance in the form of a decree in which Pippin promised St. Peter with an oath to protect the Roman Church and the prerogatives of the See of Rome. Although the Frankish nobles showed some reluctance to approve, Pippin persuaded them to do so at the diets of Braisne and Quiersey in April, 754. The results took the form of a decree known as the "Donation of Pippin." Although the text no longer exists, it is believed to have included a promise not only to protect the Roman Church and her possessions but also certain other parts of Italy against the Lombards. What was happening was that the Franks were replacing the eastern emperor and the exarch of Ravenna as the protector of the papacy and the pope was overstepping the bounds by allying permanently with a foreign power. The relationship came to expression in the title *Patricius Romanorum* conferred by Stephen on Pippin and his sons, Charles and Carloman. July 28, 754, Stephen solemnly crowned Pippin, his wife, and the two sons at St. Denis in Paris. In a short time Pippin made good his promises in the defeat of Aistulf, not once but twice. In 756 he formally presented to the pope territories captured in central Italy known later as the Papal States.

The famous *Donation of Constantine* apparently made its appearance in the midst of these negotiations. Obviously a fabrication, the *Donation* purports to be a recognition of the primacy of Rome by Constantine after Pope Sylvester I cured him of leprosy by baptizing him. A grateful emperor not only confirmed the primacy, he also invested him with imperial privileges and prerogatives and ceded to him and his successors the Lateran palace, the city of Rome, and all the provinces of Italy and the West. The document goes on to explain that Constantine moved his capital to Constantinople because the earthly rule should not be located where the King of Heaven has established the ruler of the Church. The object of this was the Byzantine Empire and not the Franks.

Stephen's successors steered along the line he laid out. The Lombards remained a threat under Desiderius (757–774), but Frankish power prevented it from reaching serious proportions. Symbolic of strong support for Rome, Pippin III held a synod at Gentilly in 767 which sanctioned the use of images in worship, an implied condemnation of the policy of Constantine V (741–775) and refusal to enter diplomatic and political negotiations.

The election of Paul I (757–767) signaled the beginning of a new problem—the interference of the Roman nobility in papal elections. Paul's election entailed group opposition, and during Paul's final illness, "Dux" Toto approached Rome at the head of an army to sway the election to his brother Constantine (767–768). Thirteen months later, Christopher, the "Primicerius" of the Roman Church and his son Sergius deposed Constantine with Lombard assistance. Toto was assassinated. The Lombards proceeded to elevate a monk named Philip to the papacy, but Christopher forced him to return to his monas-

tery. After more than a year, then, Stephen III (768–772) was legally elected. Stephen immediately put in a request to Pippin to send Frankish bishops knowledgeable in canon law to take part in a synod at the Lateran early in 769. Pippin died before the letter reached him, but Charles and Carloman fulfilled the request. The Synod decreed that thenceforward no layman could be elevated to the papacy and that the laity would have no vote in an election but could only acclaim and ratify it.

The Papacy and the Carolingians

The transition from Pippin to his sons created a momentary crisis for the papacy as the Queen Mother Bertrada, a powerful figure at court, sought to unite the Franks and Lombards through marriage. The detente enabled Desiderius to avenge himself on leaders of the anti-Lombard party, Christopher and Sergius. No longer able to count on the Franks, Stephen made peace with Desiderius, but it proved short-lived. Charles divorced his Lombard wife, for unknown reasons, and she returned to her father, Desiderius. The wife of Carloman also went to the Lombard court. Thereafter, the latter counted Charles his bitter enemy. Desiderius then asked the newly elected Pope Hadrian I (772–795) to crown the sons of Carloman, who died December 4, 771, leaving Charles sole ruler.

Hadrian, however, refused to be drawn into the Lombard plan and adhered to the policy inaugurated by Stephen. Renewal of attacks and threats by Desiderius forced him to appeal to Charles. The latter quickly crossed the Alps and struck decisive blows against the Lombards, whose Kingdom collapsed. On Easter, 774 he entered Rome. Frightened, Hadrian demanded assurances of security from Charles and his nobles before he would let them enter. On April 6, King and pope met in St. Peter's to hear the Donation of Pippin read. Charles then added new territory to the papal domain, signed the decree with his own hand, and laid it on the tomb of St.

Peter. Both he and his nobles swore to execute its provisions. The same year, Charles began to use the title *Patricius Romanorum* bestowed upon him as a child.

Charles, however, did not view himself as an underling of the pope but as a suzerain over the patrimony of Peter. He refused the pope's plea to take action against Archbishop Leo of Ravenna, who assumed an independence similar to that the pope himself exercised in the Duchy of Rome. He interfered at will in the internal administration and jurisdiction of the Papal States and refused repeated requests to turn them over to the church. Not until 481, when Charles made his second visit to Rome, did the two enter into a settlement. The pope baptized the four year old son Pippin and conferred on him the title King of the Lombards and on Louis the title King of Aquitania. Charles further enlarged the Papal States, but at the price of Hadrian relinquishing claim to other parts of the erstwhile Lombard Kingdom. In 787 Charles added other territories. He showed his own mind most clearly in 794 in issuing the *Caroline Books*, which rejected the Second Council of Nicaea of 787 and condemned the use of images in worship. He then made the humiliating demand that Hadrian sanction the iconoclastic views of those writings.

Ties between the papacy and the Frankish Kingdom attained a new strength during the long pontificate of Leo III (795–816). Immediately on election, Leo sent the protocol of his election to Charlemagne to recognize his overlordship over the Papal States. In a mosaic he ordered to be crafted for the Lateran, Peter is depicted bestowing the pallium on the pope with his right hand as he hands the banner of the City of Rome to Charles kneeling before him. And Leo soon needed help.

Charged with perjury and adultery by a powerful opposition party, he was waylaid during a procession in 799, mistreated, and imprisoned. Escaping with the help of faithful followers, he fled to Charles's court. On advice of Alcuin

Charles had the pope returned to Rome and, in order to settle the matter, he went to Rome himself in November, 800, and examined the charges against Leo. The bishops agreed with Alcuin that no human being could judge the Apostolic See. They decided that Leo could cleanse himself with a solemn oath and condemned his opponents as rebels. Two days later, Christmas Day, 800, Leo crowned Charles Emperor.

What this act meant will give reason for speculation from now on. It may well be that the act took Charles by surprise, as his biographer Einhard said, because Leo had the most to gain by it. Considered in light of the *Donation of Constantine*, it would have created the impression that the pope was founding or refounding an empire. Bestowing the imperial crown elevated his position above that of other metropolitans. In actuality, however, at the time he was the emperor's subject, dating papal bulls according to the reign of "Our Lord Charles."

After Charlemagne's death in 814 the popes began to strive for greater independence and to regain the ascendancy of Rome. As the empire fell apart, they did not have to try too hard. In 817 Pope Paschal I (817–824) and the emperor signed an accord in which Louis the Pious relinquished the right of confirming the election of a new pope before his consecration and agreed that future papal elections should take place according to canon law without governmental interference, a policy already followed in the preceding two elections. When bitter quarrels accompanied the election of Paschal's successor, Eugenius II (824–827), Lothaire, sent to Rome to investigate, reimposed the imperial suzerainty over Rome which his father had relinquished.

Gregory IV's pontificate (827–844) bore the burden of the feuds between Louis the Pious and his three older sons (Lothair, Louis, and Pippin) over a change of succession in favor of Charles the Bald. At Lothair's request the pope intervened to try to restore peace and concord. Defying threats from bishops around Louis, Gregory insisted that all must obey him as Vicar of Christ, even if the papal decrees ran counter to the imperial will. Since the government of souls is greater than that of mundane affairs, the papacy was superior to imperial power. The pope's efforts notwithstanding, in June, 833 the sons forced Louis to surrender unconditionally at Colmar and enter a monastery to perform an ecclesiastical penance. Later, however, this was lifted and Louis returned to the throne.

When the grandsons of Charlemagne divided his empire into three parts by the Treaty of Verdun in 843, they effectively freed the papacy from the secular power, for they could not control it in a united way. When Lothair sent his son Louis to Rome to safeguard imperial rights at the election of Sergius II (844–847), the pope did not permit him to enter St. Peter's until Lothair assured him that he came with pure intentions and in the best interests of both Church and state. When Saracens sailed up the Tiber in August, 846 and plundered the treasures of Sts. Peter and Paul, however, Lothair again sent Louis at the head of an army which had a few minor victories. He then ordered a collection from his kingdom to pay for the restoration of St. Peter's. Leo IV (847–855) built a wall around the Vatican to secure St. Peter's against such raids in the future and built a navy to protect against the Saracens. He personally went with his army and navy to Ostia, where they routed the Muslims in 849 and destroyed their fleet.

During the years 847 to 852, another document appeared which propounded an elevated view of papal authority under the name of Isidore of Seville. The first part of the *Pseudo-Isidorian Decretals* consists of spurious documents of popes up to Melchiades (311–314) and the so-called Apostolic Canons. The second part includes canons of a numbers of councils from Nicaea in 325 to the thirteenth Synod of Toledo in 683 and the *Donation of Constantine*. The third part contains both genuine and spurious decrees from Sylvester to Gregory II. Although

the editor pretended to collect canonical documents, his purpose was to free bishops from civil authorities in the Frankish Kingdom and from the power of metropolitans and provincial synods. The pope is the protector of bishops and the judge of all matters relating to them.

The most effective holder of the papal office in this period was Nicholas I (858–867). Elected with the strong backing of Emperor Louis II, he established the *principatus* of the papacy in a manner not seen since Gregory I. The pope is the vicegerent of Christ on earth and he speaks with the authority of God. He holds the office of supreme teacher, judge, and lawgiver. Papal decisions have the force of law for all. Councils are only means for executing papal decrees. As the highest authority on earth, the pope's decisions are final and irrevocable. No one may sit in judgment on the pope, not even the emperor. This exalted conception led Nicholas to oppose both Frankish and Byzantine rulers. Both spiritual and secular authorities must keep to their proper spheres of activity. Princes should not take part in founding and organizing churches or in the appointment or election of bishops. They should not participate in ecclesiastical synods. Since spiritual authority is higher than secular, the Church must sometimes exercise direct influence over the state, but not the reverse. The state exists to support the Church.

Predictably such an exalted view was easier to frame as theory than to put into practice. His struggles with Patriarch Photius were reviewed earlier. Nicholas also ran into difficulty with Western bishops, but successfully exerted Roman claims. Although Archbishop John of Ravenna had the backing of Emperor Louis, Nicholas forced his complete submission on charges of oppressing papal subjects at a Synod held in Rome in November, 861. He also brought Hincmar, the powerful Archbishop of Rheims, to heel when the latter withdrew power from Rothad, bishop of Soissons. Nicholas reinstated Rothad and some other clergy of Rheims deposed by

Hincmar because they were ordained by his predecessor.

In a contest between prince and priest Nicholas also won, forcing Lothair II, King of Lorraine, to take back his wife Teutberga, whom he had divorced to marry a former consort, Wildrada. Although Lothair had obtained the agreement of two papal legates at the Synod of Metz, Nicholas disagreed and called a Synod in Rome to reverse Metz. Emperor Louis, uncle of Lothair, sent an army to besiege Rome to no avail. Lothair took Teutberga back.

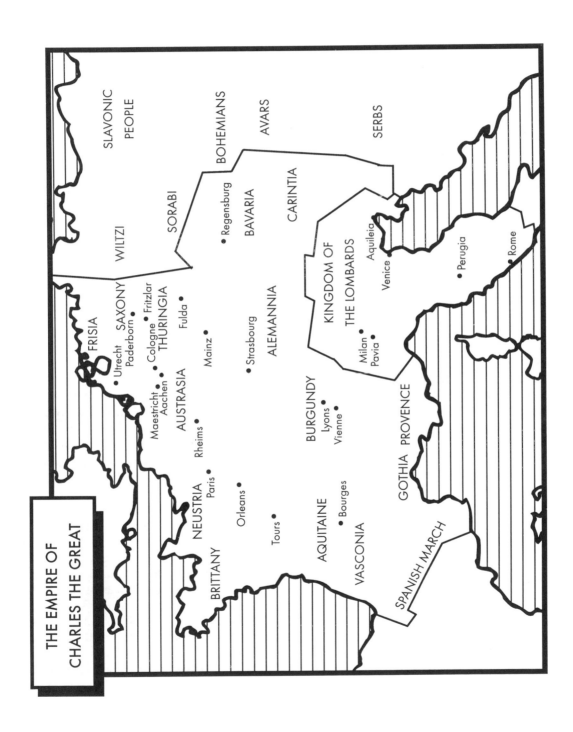

Chapter 35

The Golden Age of Monasticism, 604–1153

It should already have become evident that monasticism played a central role in the drama of Christianity during the middle Ages. In the longer drama the period from the death of Gregory the Great to the death of Bernard of Clairvaux merits the characterization of a golden age. Thereafter monasticism waned in importance as the universities, themselves products of monastic learning, took center stage and then, about 1300, the Renaissance shifted attention from the other world to the present one.

During this period, monasteries enjoyed unparalleled influence in society. Monks set the example of piety. They preserved learning. They served as the wellspring for the revival and reform of the Church, particularly the papacy. Their service to church and society evoked rich gifts from the wealthy and powerful. By the twelfth century monasteries controlled vast amounts of land throughout Europe. They erected grand churches and cloisters. In their very success, however, lay the seeds for their decline as they departed from their original vocation to poverty and prayer.

From Gregory to Charlemagne

The Benedictine tradition did not catch on immediately. The Monastery of St. Andrew on the Coelian hill in Rome which Gregory the Great founded and in which he lived for a time did not operate under the Rule of Benedict.

Nevertheless, his *Dialogues* indicate deep saturation and appreciation for Benedict and had much to do with the spread of the Benedictine form of monasticism. As a consequence of his affection for the Rule, it became the source supreme for subsequent legislation on monasticism. Although monasteries after Gregory still operated all over Europe under different rules, the Rule of Benedict gradually became the best known, first through Roman and then through Anglo-Saxon influence, especially that of Boniface in German territory.

By the time of Charlemagne many monasteries grew into huge institutions with immense economic and political impact. As a result, they modified Benedict's vision in two ways: (1) with the idea that the monks should normally become clergy, and (2) with the disappearance of manual labor, especially farming, as a monastic custom. The sending out of monks as missionaries probably had much to do with the first, but the growth of monastic wealth accounts for the second. Under the Merovingians and Carolingians in Gaul, for instance, the monasteries received immense gifts of land and other material goods. Consequently the donors looked to them for intercession, learning, and social order. In England, as noted in an earlier chapter, monasteries at Wearmouth and Jarrow triggered the remarkable revival of learning which Charlemagne drew from in support of his renaissance. Monasticism no longer represented a flight to the desert away from the world but one of the institutions integral to society.

The competition of traditions is quite visible in English monastic history. The earliest monks came from Ireland to Iona, bringing with them the powerful missionary impulse and more rigorous form of Christianity with its emphasis upon self-examination and penance. From Iona the Celtic tradition spread to Lindisfarne and took hold in Northumbria. Not long afterwards, however, Gregory the Great sent Augustine and a group of monks from the Monastery of St. Andrew, none of whom probably knew yet the Rule of Benedict. Introduction of the Benedictine Rule came by way of Wilfrid, who had been brought up at Lindisfarne but had become familiar with the Rule of Benedict in several trips to Gaul on his way to Rome, and Benedict Biscop, who had spent two years at Lérins, where the Rule was followed. Wilfrid probably gave the Rule to Ripon and Hexham, Biscop to the Monastery of Saints Peter and Paul at Canterbury and to the new monasteries he founded at Wearmouth and Jarrow. At the same time, however, it is clear that the Rule of Benedict was not the sole guide for any of these monasteries. For a time monasticism thrived in Anglo-Saxon England, and, as it did, it changed its character. The Viking invasions, however, brought it to a sudden end. Although Lindisfarne and Jarrow survived sacking in 793–794, the Danish invasion of 867 to 870 extinguished almost entirely what monasticism survived. It did not revive again until the late tenth century.

The person responsible for the dominance of the Rule of Benedict, at least in Frankish and German territories, was Charlemagne. In the last years of his life he desired to reform and unify monasteries throughout his domain under the Rule of Benedict. Although he died before he could effect the reformation, his son, Louis the Pious, picked up on the plan and enlisted the services of the reformer Benedict of Aniane.

Benedict of Aniane (ca. 750–821) served under Pippin and Charlemagne as a soldier. In 773, however, he became a monk in the monastery of Saint-Seine near Dijon and a few years later, 779, retired to his family estate at Aniane, where he founded a monastery which became the center of reform for French houses. Initially embued with the more rigorous style of the desert, he soon converted to the Rule of Benedict. After the death of Charlemagne, Louis the Pious built for him the Abbey of Inde, later known as Cornelimunster, which was to serve as the model for monasteries throughout the empire. Benedict could visit all the monasteries and order them to do whatever he thought appropriate. In 817 the Synod of Aachen officially approved his plan to systematize all monasteries under the Rule of Benedict. Benedict made a collection of all known monastic rules to serve as support for his own legislation and for that of Benedict of Nursia. In three respects he innovated on Benedict of Nursia: (1) recognizing agricultural work as extraordinary for monks, (2) prohibition of all teaching by monks except those entering the communities, and (3) expanding the liturgical prayer of the Rule of Benedict. Although the reform collapsed as the empire disintegrated, the impact of Benedict of Aniane continued in later foundations such as Cluny, Gorze, and Brogne and in the revival led by Dunstan in England.

Cluny

The viking raids in the second half of the ninth century dealt a devastating blow to monasteries not merely in Anglo-Saxon England but elsewhere. The malaise that struck the papacy was symptomatic of decline everywhere. Help, however, came soon in the founding of Cluny in 910, and simultaneously in the refounding of the Abbey of Gorze near Metz (ca. 933) and the founding of the Abbey of Brogne, near Namur (ca. 920). Cluny made a spectacular contribution to the reform of the church, especially the papacy, under Hildebrand (Pope Gregory VII).

Land for Cluny was the gift of Duke William of Aquitaine, whose only son had died and who was personally burdened with guilt because of a murder he had committed years before. In 910 he consulted Berno, Abbot of Baume and Gigny, and gave the land free of any overlord. The charter specified that "the monks shall form a congregation there, living under the Rule of Benedict." Duke William not only guaranteed free election of their own abbot, he also put the monastery under direct authority of the pope, an arrangement which helps to explain the role it took in ecclesiastical reform.

Berno, abbot from 910 until 927, set out the basic plan: faithful observance of the Rule of Benedict as interpreted by Benedict of Aniane and independence of the individual monastery but interconnected with other monasteries sharing the Cluny ideal for reform. Although Cluny had only local influence at first, its impact expanded under Odo (927–943) as the reform spread. Under his leadership the reform fever caught on at other monasteries in Burgundy—Aurillac, Lezat, Romainmoutier, and Sarlat. The influential monastery at Fleury remained independent of Cluny, but it too became a center of reform. With the backing of Pope Leo VII (936–939) Odo extended reform activities to Italy. Reform continued under Majolus (954–994), Odilo (999–1048), and Hugh (1049–1109). Odilo formed a union in which monasteries came under Cluny's direction. Hugh brought the union to its highest point of influence with more than 1,500 houses connected with Cluny. Monasteries related to Cluny in several different ways: (1) as priories directly under the abbot of Cluny, (2) as a part of the Cluniac system but under their own abbots, appointed by the abbot of Cluny, (3) as associates of Cluny open to inspection and direction by the abbot of Cluny, and (4) as independents following Cluniac usages and customs and joined by a bond of friendship. The abbot of Cluny acted as a suzerain over "vassal" houses.

Cluny greatly increased liturgical prayer, which the monks of Cluny considered the heart of the monastic life. It also added to the solemnity and splendor of the liturgy and ritual and ornamented church building accordingly. Cluny itself built one of the most massive and ornate churches in all Europe, something which invited criticism from the Cistercians, notably Bernard of Clairvaux, in the twelfth century. The demands of the daily schedule did not lighten the demands on monastic asceticism. Monks did Vigils at 12:30 a.m., Matins at 4:00, prime at 6:00 with brief naps in between.

The Impact of Cluny

There is some debate about the effects of the Cluniac reforms, but they seem to have touched the monasteries at Brogne founded in 919 by Count Gerard and at Gorze refounded by Abbot John in Metz in 933. Both of these houses based their work on the Rule as interpreted by Benedict of Aniane. Broyne spread the reform to twenty other monasteries in Flanders. Gorze attracted the support of German bishops and spread its impulse throughout Germany. Fleury transmitted the Cluniac reform to other parts of France. Fecamp and Bec in Normandy aided it there. In Italy the most noted monastery to come under Cluniac influence was Monte Cassino.

Cluny inspired other reform movements. In Italy it gave birth to a hermitic trend. Romuald (ca. 950–1027), a nobleman of Ravenna, entered the Abbey of Sant'Apollinare in Classe as a consequence of his revulsion that his father killed a man in a duel. He was elected abbot in 988 but, some time later, resigned and retired to the marshes to practice a more rigorous asceticism. In later years he founded the Camaldolese Order, which imitated the anchoritic ideal of eastern monks. Peter Damian (1007–1072), a son of poor parents of Ravenna, entered a Benedictine hermitage at Fonte Avella in 1035. Elected prior in 1043, he founded new monasteries and reformed old ones for the next ten years. In 1057 he was appointed cardinal bishop of Ostia against his will, but he played a leading role in the reforms of Hildebrand. John Gaulbert (985–1073), initially a Benedictine monk at San Miniato in Florence, joined Romuald at Camaldoli. In 1036, however, he decided to found a monastery at Vallombrosa, which he hoped to turn into "a kind of hermitage" with prayer, quiet contemplation, and continuous silence. Nilus of Rossano in Calabria (910–1005) lived in various monasteries in central and southern Italy under the Rule of Basil of Caesarea and then for a time in the Monastery of St. Alexius in Rome and at Monte Cassino. He then decided to become a hermit of Valleluce near Gaeta and later near Frascati, where he founded and became the first abbot of Grottaferrata.

In Germany, where monasteries had not suffered from the Viking raids, the reform was boosted by bishops and emperors. In Cologne, for instance, Archbishop Bruno, the brother of Otto I, founded St. Pantaleon and promoted monastic life in other ways. Both Otto I and Henry II championed the Cluniac reforms. Under Henry IV, Archbishop Anno of Cologne fostered them. The older abbeys, however, such as Fulda, Corbey, Reichenau, and Hersfeld dragged their feet on Cluniac "innovations," but imperial pressures pushed them toward the reform anyway. The Monastery of Hirsau in the Black Forest, founded in 1050 by monks from Einsiedeln, was the greatest single channel for Cluniac reforms in Germany. Monks from Hirsau went to Cluny to live in order to study customs there and bring them back to their own monastery. Hirsau soon founded thirty other monasteries and exerted influence on more than a hundred others.

In Spain the older monasteries still followed eastern traditions. Because most monasteries in northern Spain were destroyed in the tenth century by the Moors, monasticism began anew when Christians began to reconquer Spain. Here the Rule of Benedict shaped the life of outstanding monasteries like Montserrat, many of which had French connections. King Sancho of Navarre (d. 1035) sent monks to Cluny to learn the pattern of life there. Cluny established twenty-five houses in Spain as a part of its federation, but many others depended on the Cluniac way.

The revival of English monastic life in the late tenth century under the leadership of Dunstan (909–988), Ethelwold, and Oswald took place under the Rule of Benedict, but the impact of Cluny was more indirect than on the Continent. A comprehensive "Monastic Agreement" adopted at Winchester in 970 drew from many different sources, including Cluny. Unlike some others, the English revival did not attempt to return to the Rule but to blend a number of ideas, especially from Fleury and Ghent. The monastic life was viewed as a means for the "perfection of the clerical life" and for bringing strength and order into the Church in England. Special features of the "Agreement" included encouragement of daily communion, a special connection between the monks and royalty, and provisions for monks in cathedral cloisters to elect bishops. English monasteries again played a significant role in society as they had in the eighth century during the period from 960 to 1066.

The Cistercian Reform

By 1100 the Rule of Bendedict had become the common property of monasteries throughout Europe, but interpretation of the Rule was not uniform. Reactions against Cluniac usages began to arise in both Italy and France, calling for a return to the more literal interpretation of the Rule and questioning the liturgical extravagance of Cluny. By its very success Cluny had strayed far from the simplicity of the original Rule. Abbots often lived apart from the rest of the community and fraternized with the nobility of the area. Sometimes local princes filled the office of abbots. Peter Damian, John Gaulbert, and numerous others sought a return to the more simple days.

The Cistercian reform was a part of the return to earlier ideals. The origins of the movement are obscure. It would appear to have originated with a small band of hermits in Burgundy who invited Robert, Abbot of Saint-Michel de Tonnerre, to lead them. After securing papal permission, Robert led the community to Molesme around 1075. When an influx of new members created division, one group, led by Stephen Harding and Alberic, persuaded the abbot to follow their interpretation. Robert then led a group of twenty-one to Citeaux in 1098. When monks at Molesme protested the departure of their abbot, Pope Urban II (1088–1099) ordered him to return to Molesme. He obeyed, and Alberic became abbot of Citeaux (1099–1109), Stephen Harding prior and the next abbot (1109–1134). Citeaux did not do well until Bernard, a young nobleman, appeared at the abbey in 1112, bringing with him thirty young noblemen, many of whom were close relatives.

The objective of the new order was to return to the early simplicity of the Rule of Benedict. To attain that, they tried to pare away all superfluous wealth and luxury, not only in money but in food, clothing, buildings, etc. Food and clothing were to be as simple as possible. The Cistercians omitted all foods not mentioned in the Rule, particularly meats. They dressed in undyed wool habits, and thus were called "white monks" by contrast with the Benedictines, who wore black. They simplified liturgical practices and accoutrements. They refused income from ecclesiastical possessions and renounced feudal sources of wealth such as mills, fairs, bakeries, and the possession of serfs. They emphasized renunciation of the world by building monasteries as far from human habitation as they could. To sustain the community with food and other necessities, they introduced a system of lay brothers, called "Tertiaries." The latter did the heavy farm labor and freed "choir monks" for the liturgy and other work.

The monks of Citeaux also simplified the liturgy and other internal matters. They threw overboard the liturgical accretions of several centuries and returned to the threefold division of the day found in the Rule of Benedict: the *Opus Dei*, *lectio divina*, and manual labor. They also recovered the one full year of novitiate and would permit no one to enter before age sixteen or seventeen. They thus no longer operated schools. Writing books required permission of the general chapter at first, but this soon went by the board as a consequence of Bernard of Clairvaux's prolific writing.

Stephen Harding's *Carta Caritatis*, issued in 1119, spelled out the administrative machinery required by an organization which soon spread all over Europe. Although Cluny made the power of the abbot supreme, he lacked a system to enforce his directives and could never have supervised monasteries as far flung as those involved in the Cluniac movement. The *Charter of Love* obtained uniformity by supplying a complete directory for the liturgical and disciplinary life. To see that the norm was followed, it required (1) an annual visit to each abbey by the abbot of the founding monastery and (2) an annual gathering of abbots at a general chapter at Citeaux. Where earlier monasteries had had visitation, for example, by local bishops, the Cistercian provided for visits by monastic superiors with a detailed set of regulations to gauge what happened in the monastery.

Bernard and his companions put in their appearance at a fortuitous moment for the floundering monastery at Citeaux and helped the movement to gain wings. When he died in 1153 the order tallied more than 340 houses and European-wide influence. Clairvaux alone, under Bernard's leadership, founded more than sixty monasteries in France, Germany, Spain, Italy, England, Ireland, and other countries. Within a few years after its founding Clairvaux and not Citeaux had become the heart of the movement, attracting people from all walks of life.

Bernard of Clairvaux

Born at Fontaine, just two miles from Clairvaux, in 1090 of noble and saintly parents, Bernard inherited a strong religious inclination. His father, Tescelin, was an experienced knight; his mother, Aletha, a saint. When he went to Citeaux at age twenty-two, he took four brothers in the group of thirty. In 1115 Stephen Harding selected him to found a new monastery at Clairvaux. Clairvaux grew so rapidly that, within three years, it sent out its first colony. Bernard ruined his health by excessive work and rigorous ascetic practice. Yet his fame as a preacher, miracle worker, and theologian spread. He soon commanded the respect and confidence of popes, and in 1145 a member of his own order became Pope Eugenius III (1145–1153). The latter called on Bernard to preach the second crusade at Vezelay in 1146, something Bernard would regret deeply as the crusade turned out to be a fiasco. He died August 20, 1153 and was buried at Clairvaux.

Other Monastic Groups

Cluny and Citeaux represented only two of a whole panoply of monastic groups in this period. Not all groups followed the Rule of Benedict. The Augustinian Canons originated in northern Italy or southern France in the middle of the eleventh century. They received official approval of the Lateran synods of 1059 and 1063. By 1100 they had adopted the Rule of St. Augustine, which Augustine did not compose but may be the work of a disciple, and become known as the Canons Regular. The Augustinian Canons sought to live a life of poverty, chastity, and obedience patterned after that of the earliest Christians.

The Victorines, Canons Regular of the former Abbey of St. Victor in Paris, was founded by William of Champeaux, teacher of Peter Abelard, under sponsorship of King Louis VI. They drew up their customs under influence of Bernard of Clairvaux. The movement never caught fire, but it produced some notable scholars—Adam, Hugo, Richard, and Walter of St. Victor.

The Premonstrants, who also followed the Rule of St. Augustine, were called White Canons because of their dress. The order was founded by Norbert of Xantes, one of the celebrated preachers of his day, in 1119. In 1126 the Premonstrants gained papal sanction and received special papal privileges. They grew rapidly, spreading from Great Britain to Palestine, and once claimed a thousand houses. Among peculiarities were a simple diet consisting of only two dishes, religious instruction confined to prayer, and prohibition of books.

The Carthusians, whose name derived from the site of their first convent at Chartreuse or Cartusium (Latin), southeast of Lyon, were founded by Bruno, Chancellor of Rheims cathedral (d. 1101). In 1151 they claimed fourteen houses. Eventually they founded 168. Alexander III (1159–1181) formally recognized the order in 1170. The Carthusians have been known from the beginning for the severity of their religious life. At first monks lived in cells of two, later one. They divided their time between prayer, silence, and work, mostly copying of books. They practiced rigorous self-mortification, wore austere dress, subsisted on a meager diet, and bled themselves five times yearly for hygienic purposes.

The Carmelites or the order of the Blessed Mary, the Virgin of Mount Carmel, originated in 1156 during the crusades. Their original rule paralleled that of the Carthusians for its severity. In 1245 they adopted the practice of subsistence by begging after witnessing the success of Franciscans and Dominicans.

Several other orders appeared in this period but did not attain much success: the Antonites, sanctioned first by Pope Urban II in 1095; Font Evraud, founded by Robert d'Abrissel (d. 1117) with both men and women in one monastery headed by an abbess; the Order of Grammont, founded by Stephen of Auvergne in France (ca. 1054–1124) around 1143, popularly called Bons

Hommes; the Trinitarians, founded in 1198 in Meaux by John of Matha (1160–1213) to redeem Christian captives from the Saracens; and an obscure group known as Brothers of the Sack or "Bushmen" because of their success in begging. In these one can see the change beginning to take place in monasticism. At the beginning of the thirteenth century the golden age of cloistered monasticism would have given way to new forms to meet the exigencies of the times.

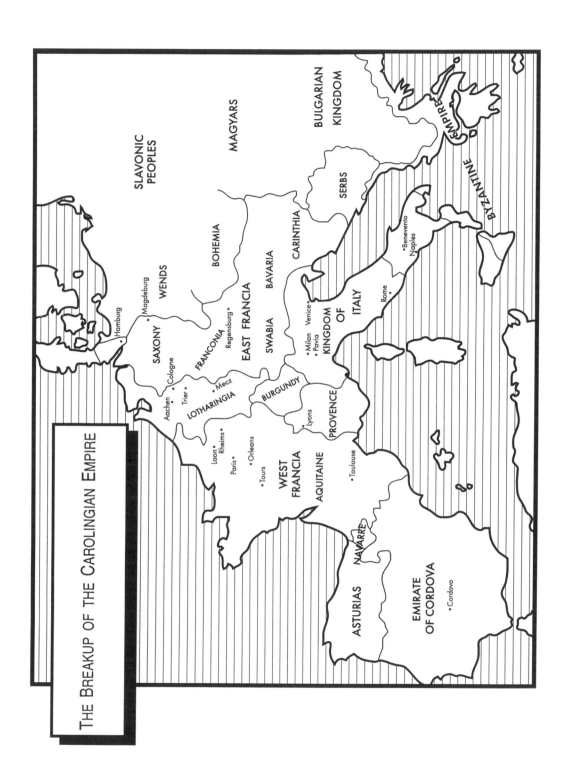

THE BREAKUP OF THE CAROLINGIAN EMPIRE

SLAVONIC PEOPLES

MAGYARS

BULGARIAN KINGDOM

SERBS

CARINTHIA

BYZANTINE EMPIRE

Benevento
Naples

BOHEMIA

WENDS

Magdeburg

Hamburg

SAXONY

Cologne

FRANCONIA

Regensburg

EAST FRANCIA

BAVARIA

SWABIA

Venice

Milan
Pavia

KINGDOM OF ITALY

Rome

Trier

Aachen

Mecz

LOTHARINGIA

BURGUNDY

PROVENCE

Lyons

Laon
Rheims

Paris

Orleans

Tours

WEST FRANCIA

AQUITAINE

Toulouse

NAVARRE

ASTURIAS

EMIRATE OF CORDOVA

Cordova

Chapter 36

Early Medieval Theology, Penance, Canon Law, and Spirituality

The early Middle Ages will be remembered more for their spirituality than for their doctrinal contributions. Yet it would be a mistake to gloss over the debates and developments which did take place, for they laid a foundation for later thought and institutions. Furthermore, theology and spirituality were interconnected in ways which modern observers might overlook. The great concern of these centuries was to effect a Christian society. As seen in the preceding chapter, monks took the lead in this, and their example carried over into everyday life, even into discussions of doctrine, most of which had a quite practical import.

Some issues have already received attention in other contexts: the use of images or icons in worship, a matter which concerned chiefly the East but also spilled over into the Frankish Kingdom, the adoptionist controversy in Spain, the controversy over the addition of the *filioque* to the Niceno-Constantinopolitan Creed, the eucharistic controversy, and the predestinarian controversy touched off by the Augustinophile Gottschalk. All had important repercussions in subsequent centuries. Here it will be worthwhile to look at some noted theologians in both West and East—Alcuin, John Scotus Erigena, and John of Damascus—who anticipated the medieval schoolmen. An item which will require serious

consideration also if one is to understand and appreciate what was happening in the life of the Church in this period and afterwards is the practice of penance which led in time to the system of indulgences. Related to it is the development of canon law, a carry over from early Christian history which took on increased importance in the Christianizing of Europe.

Some Theologians of Note

Despite the heavy blows Western culture suffered from the barbarian invasions, revival of learning did take place, particularly during the Carolingian era. As noted earlier, the chief channels for this resurgence were monastic and cathedral schools. Cassian founded a school in the Monastery of St. Victor at Marseilles in 404, and such schools continued to exist throughout the Middle Ages. It was Charlemagne and his successors, however, who boosted learning to a new level by requiring monastic schools to expand their curricula and to open their doors to persons other than monks and by bringing outstanding scholars such as Alcuin and John Scotus Erigena to his court.

One eastern theologian deserves special mention at this point because he has had an importance in Orthodox theology similar to that of Thomas Aquinas in the West. John of Damascus (ca. 675–ca. 749), born at Damascus of a rich Christian family, succeeded his father as *Logothete*, Intermediary of Christians to the Caliph. About 716 he had to abandon that role and withdrew to the Monastery of St. Sabas near Jerusalem, where he received ordination as a priest. He played a major role in the iconoclastic controversy at the time of Leo III (717–741), arguing the appropriateness of using images. He collected scriptural and patristic texts on the Christian moral and ascetic life and wrote commentaries on Paul's letters, but his most important work was *The Fountain of Knowledge*.

The Fountain of Knowledge consists of three parts: a treatise on philosophy, another on heresy, and a third, the most important, on *The Orthodox Faith*. In the last John reflects heavy dependence on Aristotle but with some admixture of Plato transmitted by Maximus the Confessor. *The Orthodox Faith* is a comprehensive presentation of the teaching of the Greek Fathers on the main Christian doctrines: the Trinity, Creation, Incarnation, Sacraments, Mariology, and Images. John argues for the existence of God on the basis of the contingency of creatures and the orderliness of the universe. On the Trinity he developed the Cappadocian doctrine of *perichoresis* or mutual indwelling of the whole of the Godhead in each person. For his doctrine of angels he relied on Gregory of Nazianzus, his favorite theologian, and Pseudo-Dionysius. On the incarnation he synthesized a number of Greek theologians. With Leontius of Byzantium he insisted on an interpenetration of divine and human natures in hypostatic union. In line with his support of the use of images he had a fully developed mariology. On the eucharist he propounded a real presence in the Greek sense of transelementation rather than the later Latin transubstantiation. Translated into Latin (though rather poorly) at an early date, *The Fountain of Knowledge* influenced Peter the Lombard and Thomas Aquinas. In 1890 Pope Leo XIII honored John of Damascus by naming him a Doctor of the Church.

Alcuin (ca. 735–804) was born in Northumbria. A relative of Willibrord, he was educated at the famous cathedral school of Archbishop Egbert of York under Ethelbert. During several trips to Rome, he became acquainted with Frankish monasteries and monks. He succeeded Ethelbert as head of the cathedral school at York. In 781 he met Charlemagne at Parma. After a brief return to England, he accepted the invitation of the latter to develop an educational program at his court. In 796 Charlemagne invested him with the Abbey of St. Martin near Tours, where he set up an important school and library, as well as several other monasteries. He died at Tours May 19, 804. Among his famous pupils were Amalarius of Metz and Rabanus Maurus.

Alcuin was not an original thinker, basing his thought heavily on Jerome and Augustine, but he combined ecclesiastical learning with classical. His writings range over a number of areas. They include a work on the Trinity; commentaries on Genesis, the Psalms, the Song of Songs, John, and other New Testament writings; a revision of the Vulgate text; classical works on grammar and orthography; poems and hymns; lives of Willibrord, Vedastus, and Richarius; devotional and ethical treatises. In the Frankish Kingdom he established a reputation in the controversy with Felix of Urgel, the Spanish adoptionist.

The most original Western theologian in this period was John Scotus Erigena (ca. 810–ca. 877). Born in Ireland, he won fame as a scholar early, and around 845 Charles the Bald summoned him to his court and placed him at the head of the palace school of Laon. He took a prominent part in the eucharistic controversy initiated by Paschasius Radbertus and in the predestinarian controversy precipitated by Gottschalk. He apparently continued at the court until he died, but reports of his later life are obscure.

Although often classified with the schoolmen, Erigena anticipated them by three centuries and differed in his strong leanings toward Neoplatonism, which he sought to integrate with

Christian thought. In his *Periphyseon* or *De divisione naturae* (*On the Divisions of Nature*), he adapted the Neoplatonic theory of emanations to the Christian concept of creation. According to his theory, the universe continually develops. All things come out of God and find their way back to God. Thence, nature consists of four parts: (1) that which creates and is not created—God; (2) that which is created and creates—the world of ideas or primordial causes; (3) that which is created and does not create—the phenomenal world of space and time; and (4) that which is neither created nor creates—the return of all to God from whence all came. The latter happens through Christ. In his own day Erigena came under no censure, but the *Peri Physeon* was condemned at Paris in 1210 and at Sens in 1225.

Like Pseudo-Dionysius, whose works he translated, Erigena believed that God is unknowable. One can know *that* God is, but not *what* God is. But his real interest lay in the immanence of God, so much so that he was charged with pantheism. Yet the pantheism is not thoroughgoing, for God is also *above* all creatures. As a Platonist, Erigena emphasized that evil is simply the absence of good and sin the failure to rise to higher things. Eventually evil will disappear entirely. In the future consummation all will enjoy the blessings of God's presence, but the saints will also enjoy forever the contemplation of truth.

Penance

The system of penance developed in the early church proved too rigorous and broke down by the end of the fourth century. Indeed, the West never adopted the system of grades and degrees of offenses used in the East. Discipline rested with bishops even in the East and to a still greater degree in the West. The result was a vast variety in the way churches handled serious offenses among their members. Sometimes they imposed such severe penalties that, as the Synod of Toledo in 693 reported, offenders sought relief in suicide. Most penitents, however, simply deferred their repentance to their deathbeds.

There is ample evidence of a widespread breakdown of discipline in the fifth century and after as the barbarian invasions disrupted all social life. Salvian of Marseilles (ca. 400–ca. 480) portrayed a decadent society in which the only form of penance was on death bed. Gregory of Tours, likewise, gave a gloomy portrait of society in which brutality, treachery, intrigue, and corruption afflicted princes, nobles, clergy, and common people. The worst atrocities appeared to pass without punishment. Few displayed any signs of sincere penitence. In the late fifth century the *Statuta antiqua* represented an effort to restore discipline in southern Gaul, and Caesarius of Arles (d. 543) insisted on "lowly and compunctious penance" for a mass of daily offenses, but he made exceptions for young persons, allowing them to do private penance.

A change in the practice of penance came by way of Celtic monasticism. Like the Pachomian monasteries in Egypt, Celtic monasteries practiced confession of faults to an abbot or superior as an element of spiritual direction. Because Ireland hardly knew bishops, monks acted as spiritual advisers to lay persons and began to impose on them the same penalties for faults as existed in the monasteries. Gradually they accumulated penitentials.

Some penitentials date from the time of Patrick (ca. 380–ca. 460) and Finnian of Clonard (early sixth century). In Wales and Ireland the application of this rigorous confessional method produced a revival. From there it spread to England and to the Continent. The early penitential books became models. Clear evidence exists to demonstrate that penitentials were in use in Frankish territory in the late sixth century, in England in the late seventh, in Italy in the late eighth, and among the Visigoths in Spain in the early ninth. In societies desperately in need of Christianization these proved remarkably effective.

Theodore of Tarsus, Archbishop of Canterbury (668–690), adopted essentials of the Celtic model. In the Frankish Kingdom efforts of Columban provoked reaction against the more severe Celtic approach and attempts to suppress the penitentials. The reaction led to revival of the canons of ancient councils. By the Carolingian era, however, penitentials came into their own as the clergy felt a need for books of reference. Nonetheless, many still lamented lack of standardization in the books themselves. At the Synod of Chalon-sur-Saone in 813 the bishops denounced the "books called penitentials, whose errors are certain and authors uncertain." At Paris in 829 they ordered a search for such books to be burned "that through them unskilled priests may no longer deceive people." This campaign did not succeed, public discipline had little success among the Germanic peoples, and a system allowing private confession caught on.

The penitentials provided for the administration of a strictly private penance. Confession was made in private to a qualified person, usually a priest. However, monks and even women ascetics served this purpose. The importance of confession was underscored. Acts of satisfaction were also ordinarily private, though not always secret. Some penances probably could not be kept secret. If the penance involved excommunication, the reconciliation was sometimes granted in private.

Whereas the older system forbade second penances, this one allowed for repeated lapses and restorations. Repentance and confession came to be thought of as normal for Christians. It is not hard to see, therefore, why efforts to restore the old system did not succeed. Although public penance was never suppressed and occasionally practiced in the later Middle Ages, it was associated chiefly with Lent. Penitents often were excluded on Ash Wednesday and readmitted on Maundy Thursday. Sometimes offenders did "solemn" penances marked by formal exclusion from the church and wearing of sackcloth and ashes.

The penitential books prescribed a variety of penalties, most influenced by monastic discipline and sometimes extreme. Prescriptions included: recitation of Psalms in a variety of ways; fasting with stress on abstinence from meat, butter, or delicacies; vigils accompanied by bodily exercises to cause discomfort; flagellation or flogging; taking a monastic vow in the case of serious offenses; exile or pilgrimages; and temporary exclusion. Societies sometimes imposed legal penalties, for example, payment to relatives in satisfaction for murder or injury. Penitential books encouraged money satisfactions, and penitents probably preferred them to lengthy fasts or other impositions. Very often, the two were combined. The severity of the offense determined the amount of satisfaction required.

The way in which the penitentials combined Christian with contemporary culture bears strong witness to the purpose served by the new form of penance. Once again, as in the Roman Empire after the conversion of Constantine, Christianity found itself laden with the task of Christianizing an entire society. Wiping out all traces of "paganism" had not worked in the Roman Empire and it did not work here either. The writers of penitential books took up the task of laying out enforceable directives which simple converts could follow. They addressed such issues as belief in vampires and witches, eating horse flesh and drinking the blood or urine of animals or humans, sacrificing to demons, placing a child on a roof or in an oven to cure a fever, diabolical incantations, auguries, and many other things. The penitentials are replete with information on folklore of Celtic, Anglo-Saxon, and Germanic peoples. They also attest the mingling of Christian and pagan in the emerging societies.

The penitential books took over from medicine of the first several centuries the principle that a disease must be cured by its opposite. Thus Abbot Finian insisted that patience should replace anger, kindliness envy, restraint impulsiveness, joy dejection, and generosity greed. The authors

strove to reconstruct the personality of the offender, of course,with the aid of supernatural
grace. They wanted to rehabilitate and to guide
offenders toward a harmonious relationship with
the Church, society, and God. The penitentials
obviously exerted a powerful influence in the
West. They helped their societies rise to a higher
stage of moral culture which must be acknowledged even as one recognizes abuses which
inevitably entered with the system of indulgences.

Canon Law

Closely tied to the development of the
system of penance was the collection of ecclesiastical canons on various aspects of Christian life,
a process which took on increased importance in
reform of the Church under Gregory VII. Although in the East imperial legislation and codification diminished somewhat the need for separate
codes of ecclesiastical canons, since they covered
every aspect of both religious and civil life,
private collections did occur. A number of bishops—Dionysius of Alexandria and Gregory Thaumaturgus in the third century, Basil of Caesarea
and Amphilochius of Iconium in the fourth— had
made collections before the codes of Theodosius
II (438) and Justinian (529–533) were promulgated. Later the most notable collection was that of
John Scholasticus (d. 577), who enriched his
selection of ecclesiastical canons with some items
from the Novellae of Justinian.

The first Western collection to gain wide
usage was that of Dionysius Exiguus (ca.
500–550), a Scythian monk who lived in Rome.
It included the so-called Apostolic Canons; the
canons of the councils of Nicaea, Ancyra, Neocaesarea, Gangra, Antioch, Laodicea, Constantinople, Chalcedon, Sardica, and Carthage in 419;
and forty-one papal decretals from Siricius
(384–398) to Anastasius II (496–498). In Spain
bishops met regularly in a series of synods and
produced a *Hispanic Collection* also known as
Isidorian but not the work of the great scholar

Isidore of Seville. This collection included far
more sources than Dionysius.

Wide diversity of practice and division over
the use of penitentials in the Frankish Kingdom
caused Charlemagne to turn to Pope Hadrian I
for direction. Hadrian sent a copy of Dionysius
Exiguus in an enlarged version, which Charlemagne promulgated at Aachen in 802. During the
middle of the ninth century, however, the *Pseudo-Isidorian Decretals* appeared with an obvious
concern to free the bishop from the power of
princes and metropolitans. Subsequently numerous other collections appeared, all of them including the false decretals. Of these the most
influential was the *Decretum* of Burchard, bishop
of Worms, composed between 1008 and 1012.
Burchard was striving to free the church, but, as
a friend of Otto III and Henry II, he propounded
an ambivalent doctrine. On one side, he claimed
papal supremacy; on the other, he undercut the
power of the papacy and conceded the power of
princes to appoint bishops.

In the next generation canon law took another turn as the reform of Hildebrand encouraged
search throughout the archives of Italy for papal
and conciliar pronouncements bearing on the
question of papal prerogatives, the freedom of the
Church, and clerical celibacy. A series of compi-
lations appeared: *Collection in 74 Titles* (ca.
1050), others by Anselm of Lucca (ca. 1083),
Cardinal Deusdedit (ca. 1087), Bonizo of Sutri
and Piacenza (ca. 1085), all belonging to the
Gregorian reform. Opposing collections also
appeared, authored by Lanfranc, abbot of Bec, for
instance.

With Ivo of Chartres (1091–1116) the essentially polemical purpose of collections gave way
to moderation. Issuing his *Panormia* about 1095,
he urged mutual respect and cooperation between
Church and state, meaning willingness to compromise on nonessentials. As the study of civil
law also advanced rapidly, the way lay open for
more scholarly study of canon law. The key
figure here was Gratian, the "father of canon

law," who issued his *Decretum* about 1140, containing nearly 4,000 patristic texts, conciliar decrees, and papal pronouncements.

Worship and Spirituality

Medieval spirituality was primarily liturgical spirituality. For most Christians devotion consisted of corporate worship in churches conducted by priests according to prescribed rituals. Not all, however, worshipped in a uniform or standardized way. Although Christians of this era inherited from their forbears in earlier centuries certain common elements such as the bipartite structure of the Liturgy of the Word and the Liturgy of the Upper Room, a lectionary, a calendar, and hymns, the radical transition created by the barbarian invasions added to the diversities of their inheritance on a considerable scale.

In the East Christian worship had already undergone most of its evolution by the seventh century. The conversion of Constantine and his magnificent gifts to the Church in buildings, financial support, access to holy sites, and ideas opened the way for rapid and radical changes in existent liturgies in the fourth century. Services increasingly took on features of the imperial court, just as the new places of worship did, for the King of kings deserved at least as much honor as the ruler of the Roman Empire, his servant par excellence. The liturgy became a grand drama replete with appropriate dress, setting, and pomp and circumstance. From the sixth century on, images began to enhance the service as well.

In the East, just as in the West, growth of the liturgy in the fifth and sixth centuries resulted in further variations. Liturgical scholars today single out two major families, named after the patriarchates of Antioch and Alexandria. To the Antiochene family belong the Byzantine rite with its two major liturgies—St. Basil and St. Chrysostom—and the Jerusalem rite with which the liturgy of St. James, all other Syrian rites, and the Persian or Nestorian rites have some connection.

To the Alexandrian family scholars ascribe the Liturgy of Serapion, the Liturgy of St. Mark, and all other Egyptian and Ethiopic rites. Among Orthodox Christians the Liturgy of St. Chrysostom was and is used as the normal rite; that of St. Basil as the rite for part of Lent, the midnight celebrations on Christmas and Epiphany, and on St. Basil's day (January 1); and the Liturgy of the Presanctified (preconsecrated bread) on Good Friday.

Notable changes in the eastern liturgies after the fourth century included the following: (1) A service of private preparation of the clergy, called the *Prothesis*, was added at the beginning. It consisted of prayers said while the minister put on vestments and prepared the elements. (2) Special prayers and songs were inserted before the reading of the scriptures. By this time the lectionary had become fixed. (3) During the sixth century, the Creed entered the liturgy. Previously it had been recited only at baptism. (4) Several things gave the whole service a more mystical quality. A railing and later a curtain were added to separate the apse from the nave of the Church. Subsequently, the curtain gave way to the icon screen, shutting off the sanctuary from the people. At the same time priests began uttering prayers in a subdued tone, only raising their voices at special points, to emphasize the mystery. (5) From the fifth century on it became increasingly uncommon for people to take communion every Sunday. (6) Music expanded. Choirs replaced one or two cantors of the earlier period. (7) Reading of the Gospel and the Offering of the eucharistic elements took on more pronounced ceremonial form. Processions passed through the doors of the icon screen for the reading of the Gospel (the Little Entrance) and for offering the Host (the Great Entrance). (8) The method of administering communion was changed from giving the people both bread and wine to dipping the bread in the wine with a spoon and placing it in the mouth (intinction). Done in the vernacular, these lengthy liturgies sought to engage participants in an experience of the mystery of redemption.

In the West, as one would expect, the liturgy also went through a process of extensive revision. For a time two rites—the Roman and the Gallican—competed with one another, but by the end of the ninth century the Roman rite gained the ascendancy. Two other rites—the Mozarabic (Spanish) and the Milanese—continued in usage but they never gained a wide acceptance. Both had some ties with the Gallican liturgy.

The origins of the Gallican rite are obscure, but fairly definite evidence demonstrates its existence about the middle of the fifth century and argues for an indigenous origin rather than Roman or Milanese. It differed from the Roman rite in being more colorful, elaborate,and flamboyant. In Merovingian times it allowed for spontaneity in composition of prayers, perhaps each Sunday, and its many responses and musical parts involved the people more in the worship. The rite was more dramatic and flexible than the Roman. Pippin III and Charlemagne prohibited its use, assuring the triumph of the Roman rite.

Although its early history is also obscure, the Roman rite evidently took shape in the early fourth century when the Church began to enjoy respite from persecution and then some security with the conversion of Constantine. Freedom to celebrate the eucharist publicly wrought immediate changes in the solemnity and splendor of the ceremonial. The Roman rite underwent substantial revision in the next several centuries. The most significant change occurred under the impact of the Gallican rite in the late eighth and early ninth centuries. Charlemagne requested a copy of a liturgical handbook from Pope Hadrian I about 790 to assist in promoting uniformity in worship as well as creed and canon law. Hadrian sent the *Gregorian Sacramentary*. Since it lacked provisions for much of the Christian year, however, scholars at Charlemagne's court had to make up for them with selections from the *Gelasian Sacramentary*, a manuscript of which survives from the mid-eighth century, which arranges feasts for the entire year. The Roman Missal had its origins in the combination of the two liturgical handbooks.

Others also assisted in the promotion of the Roman rite. In England Benedict Biscop did his best to assure the spread of the Roman music and liturgy at Wearmouth and Jarrow. Not surprisingly, Boniface, coming from the Anglo-Saxon Church, strove to spread its use on his mission field in Germany. Amalarius of Metz (ca. 780–ca. 850), one of Alcuin's most distinguished pupils, worked zealously to promote the Roman liturgy. In a treatise *On Ecclesiastical Duties* he made a detailed allegorical examination of it. In 831 he went to Rome to ask Pope Gregory IV (827–844) to supply him with an authorized Roman antiphonary. When Gregory felt unable to do so, Amalarius returned home to fashion his own. Later he used his powers as Archbishop of Lyons to bring changes in the liturgy, arousing considerable hostility and censure.

The Roman liturgy differed from the Byzantine at several points. It was more simple and practical, although addition of elements from the Gallican rite made it more and more of a spectacle with the focus on visible action rather than the words. Communion became less and less frequent for the laity. By the sixth century church councils legislated communion at least three times a year—Christmas, Easter, and Pentecost. The Fourth Lateran Council in 1215 reduced that to Easter. The Nicene Creed was not introduced into the Roman liturgy until the eleventh century. Whereas in the East the liturgy was translated into the vernacular, in the West it remained Latin, even though only scholars and diplomats used the language, except for a small vernacular service inserted after the Gospel, called the Prone. The Prone usually consisted of bidding prayers, the Epistle and Gospel, the Creed, sermon, exhortation, and the Lord's Prayer simultaneously, participation of the people decreased as elaboration of music reduced psalmody.

The number of masses said in the West greatly exceeded that in the East as separate masses conducted by each priest replaced the practice of communion or concelebration. Each mass was viewed as a propiatory sacrifice, so the more the better. Masses were designed to meet specific objectives. Special masses for the dead, for instance, increased beyond calculation. There were also masses for going on a journey, for recovery from illness, for capture of thieves, for rain or fair weather, or for release of captives, even for the death of persons, though the Synod of Toledo in 694 forbade these. Proliferation of masses naturally required redesign of churches so that several priests could offer mass at the same time. Westerners met the need with side chapels and chantries, collegiate churches, and placing of altars in the bays of the naves of cathedrals and abbey churches. Finally, whereas in the East the accent fell on the resurrection, in the West it fell more heavily on the death of Christ.

Spiritual Guidance

For the average Christian of these centuries spiritual growth depended also on pastoral guidance of an increasingly private and personal kind. The Irish had a word for the priest or monk who heard confession and counseled them, *amchara*, which is translated "soul friend." In the sixth century appeared a popular adage that "Anyone without an *amchara* is like a body without a head." The Celts expected everyone to have a spiritual guide. As indicated in the previous chapter, the practice of private confession and direction spread from Ireland to Gaul, England, Germany, and Italy. In Ireland confession could be made to lay persons, men or women, as well as monks and clergy, but this custom gradually gave way to a more sacerdotal one. Columban, whose early biographer reported that he had once confessed to a woman and acted on her advice, required laymen guilty of certain offenses to "confess to a priest" in his Penitential. Theodore, Archbishop of Canterbury, explicitly excluded women from prescribing penance on the grounds that this is an exclusively priestly function.

The items on which the penitential books legislated would indicate that monks and clerics had to offer spiritual guidance of a very elemental sort, especially in earlier centuries. Nevertheless, even these writings designed to create more equitable standards made room for variations of age, sex, economic status, education, and other factors. Spiritual guides were expected to act with sensitivity in treating grave offenses such as murder, adultery, sacrilege, theft, and perjury, as well as less serious ones such as gluttony and drunkenness. The penitentials did not gloss over the realities of everyday life either, and in time the system helped to establish new patterns of behavior. Burchard of Worm's *Corrector*, compiled between 1008 and 1012, at any rate, dealt still with many gross offenses cited earlier, repeating Irish and Anglo-Saxon as well as Roman canons, but it prescribed more reasonable penalties than earlier penitentials. Indeed, Burchard underlined the image of a "physician" treating the sick.

It is not hard to understand, of course, why opposition to penitentials arose in France. Besides the competition they offered to the older practice of public confession, John T. McNeill has cited the wide variety of penalties prescribed in different documents, the fact that they came into existence without ecclesiastical authorization or agreement except that of the author, the moral debatability of some provisions such as that allowing money substitutes for penances or commutation into briefer and more tolerable penalties. From the last came the practice of indulgences. Yet the penitential system did offer a more practical means for spiritual guidance than public penance which earlier Christianity had shown would not work. However loudly bishops may have fulminated against the practice, therefore, the private approach had a better chance of success than public penance, which itself had never been uniform. By 813 the bishops of one province virtually conceded the point when they adopted a single penitential book. Although strong protests continued down to the eleventh century, when Peter Damian sarcastically noted in *The Book of Gomorrah* (1051) that penitentials were thorns and false sprouts having no confirmed authors and no authority, there was no turning back.

Lay people responded eagerly to some who gained reputations as confessors. Columban had to turn people away. They did not respond well to others, who had to threaten and cajole. By the time of Burchard, however, it had become the goal of every priest to "be able to bring help to every person, ordained or unordained; poor or rich; boy, youth or mature man; decrepit, healthy or infirm; of every age and of both sexes" (Decretum 323). The humane provision for repeated confession and repentance made room for much more sensitive guidance than public penance. In their best form, as in the so-called "Roman Penitential" of Halitgar, dated around 830, the penitentials urged bishops and presbyters "to humble themselves and pray with moaning and tears of sadness, not only for their own faults, but also for those of all Christians, so that they may be able to say with the Blessed Paul: 'Who is weak and I am not weak; who is scandalized and I am not on fire'." Burchard's *Corrector* gave thoughtful directions for the whole process, obviously involving the director at every step in the pain of the directee. As open to criticism as the whole enterprise was, therefore, one must conclude with John T. McNeill that "these manuals must have helped to redeem them from superstition, inhumanity and vice, and to set their feet on the pathway of spiritual and moral advance."

Monastic Models

Helping to guide the masses down a more genuinely Christian path and serving as models of piety were monks, both men and women. In the Benedictine tradition, which gradually established itself as the dominant form of monasti-cism, piety was, above all, affective and practical. The Benedictines eschewed the speculative approach of Pseudo-Dionysius and, later, the schoolmen. They aimed to effect acts of love rather than to have debates on the nature of love. They wanted to experience the mystical union without having to explain the experience. Benedictine spirituality was also liturgical, nourished on celebration of the *Opus Dei*. Chanting the Psalms seven times a day established a rhythm in the monks' lives. Observance of the Christian calendar fixed their attention on the principal events in the life of Christ—birth, ministry, passion, resurrection, and ascension. Meditation on the scenes from the life of Christ gave birth to a devotion on the humanity of Christ, which Pierre Pourrat has called "one of the most remarkable characteristics of Benedictine spirituality" (*Le spiritualité chrétienne* 2.3). The Benedictine nuns of Helfta developed a special devotion to the crucified Christ and, toward the end of the thirteenth century, to the heart of Jesus. Unlike some other forms of monasticism, moreover, Benedictine spirituality encouraged freedom which opened the way for significant contributions to the life of prayer.

The Benedictines undoubtedly brought deep personal piety to expression in their communities throughout the Middle Ages, but they did not have significant articulaters of their mystical piety until the end of the eleventh and beginning of the twelfth centuries, in Anselm of Bec and Canterbury and Bernard of Clairvaux. Although both come at the end of the period under discussion, they summed up the best in the tradition—Anselm speaking more forcefully for the speculative and rational, Bernard for the affective side of spirituality.

Anselm, abbot of Bec (1078–1093) and archbishop of Canterbury (1093–1109), stands at the head of the scholastic tradition and will receive further treatment in that context, but he also merits comment here because of his affective piety. Unlike many other speculative theologians, he did not let his head overwhelm his heart and dry up his spirituality. Instead, he united intellectual energies with prayer of the heart. In his *Eleventh Meditation on Redemption* he prayed that he might taste by love what he tasted by cognition and sense with the heart what he touched with the spirit. Over and over, he pleaded that God might introduce him into the sanctuary of divine love. "You who made me ask for this grace also make me receive it," he insisted. Although Anselm applied reason relentlessly in defense of the truths of faith, he took the same position as Augustine on faith and reason. Faith precedes reason. "I believe in order to understand." And his personal piety did not lose its affective quality.

Bernard of Clairvaux (1090–1153), unlike Anselm, did not like speculative theology. He favored practical knowledge which helps us to know and serve God, which gives human beings knowledge of themselves and love of virtue. There is no need to search for sources of his ideas in great mystical scholars. He took most of them directly from the scriptures and the Latin Fathers—Ambrose, Augustine, Cassian, Gregory the Great. The major elements of his spirituality coincided with the teachings of contemplatives who preceded him. He expressed them anew in simple and profound ways.

Perfection in love, he insisted, depends on grace. Grace enables us to avoid evil and do good so long as the will yields to its impulses. Bernard, however, a practical realist, did not expect anyone to attain perfection in this life. Human beings never conform totally to the divine will while on earth. Better, therefore, plan on indefinite progress in good. The place to start is with a recognition of our imperfection. Admission of imperfection should inspire humility, the foundation on which the Christian life must rest. "Unless it stands on the foundation of humility," he declared in a *Sermon on the Song of Songs* (36.5), "no spiritual building can stand at all." Humility and self-knowledge go hand in hand on the way to perfection. Humility gives birth both to an awareness of our own need and of the divine power available to help. In humility we abandon ourselves to receive the grace of God. "God resists the proud but gives grace to the humble" (1 Pet. 5:5).

If humility opens the door, love pulls us through it. Bernard considered love a natural affection. In his four stages in the love of God, therefore, he insisted that human beings must begin with love of self. We begin to believe in God, aided by grace, because of the benefits we receive. On the same basis we proceed to the second stage, love of God for self's sake. Even unbelievers ought to go this far. Little by little, experience of God's love may move us to a third stage, love of God for God's sake. To some, that might seem the pinnacle, but not to the practical Bernard. The highest stage is love of self for God's sake, something human beings cannot attain in this life. Human loves always have an admixture of selfishness, even the love of martyrs. We see it only in Jesus.

The means of perfection, according to Bernard, are prayer, meditation, examination of conscience, discretion, and spiritual direction. Once again distressingly realistic, Bernard reminded that the journey to spiritual perfection is slow and painful. Sanctification is truly a "spiritual exercise." He offered nothing new on prayer, only the reminder to avoid distractions. On meditation he spoke much more personally, but, as others in his tradition, he emphasized emphatically the importance of meditation on the life of Christ, especially his suffering and death. In a treatise *On Consideration* written for Pope Eugenius III (1145–1153), a Cistercian, Bernard underlined the importance of self-examination and reflection on divine truths. For novices in faith, however, he went on to say, there is need for guidance of more mature persons.

Those who have sung the hymns attributed to Bernard will recognize how Christological his piety was. He composed a great number of sermons on Christ, the Virgin Mary, patroness of the Cistercian order, and several saints. He had a special predilection for the birth of Christ. He strained to find words to express his love for mother and child. They remind us eloquently of the love of God. He liked to comment on the circumcision because it served as an extraordinary proof of the humility of the Incarnate Word. He dwelt on the name of Jesus. "When we preach it, it illumines us; when we meditate on it, it nourishes us; when we invoke it, it consoles us and tempers our sorrows" (*Sermon on the Song of Songs* 15.5). Jesus' meeting with his parents in the Temple at age twelve had a powerful witness for Bernard in one thing, his obedience.

Bernard liked also to dwell on Calvary. According to his biographers, he himself prayed often in the monastery church before a crucifix. Jesus' sufferings on the Cross confirmed what all the other privations of his life from birth onwards said: How great is the love of God! God could have repaired the effects of human sin in some other way, no doubt, but "because of his excessive love for us," God did it this way. Bernard could not find words to express his emotion regarding the passion. "Oh, how immense is your goodness, Lord! Oh, how far are your thoughts from ours! Oh, how can your mercy extend even to the impious! Oh, how can I not admire it!"

In an order devoted as his was to the Virgin Mary it is not surprising to find extensive development of Marian piety. Bernard perhaps contributed more than any medieval writer to the advancement of Marian devotion. He was her "knight." He coined and popularized the name of Notre Dame which Catholics have loved to invoke since. His devotion to Mary was proverbial in his own day. He celebrated her virginity and holiness, her divine maternity, the excellence of her virtues, her role as mediatrix between God and human beings, and her glorification in heaven. Bernard approved the idea of Mary as absolutely free of all personal fault, but he rejected the idea of immaculate conception, for, as he viewed it, she would have had to exist before

being conceived. He could scarcely find words to express his joy in the assumption of Mary into heaven. Because of her exalted state, he urged monks to honor her, pray to her, and imitate her virtues. Mary is the dispenser of grace, mediatrix between Jesus and human beings, between Savior and the Church.

Bernard also believed in guardian angels, not only for the Church but for each individual. We each receive an angel to protect, guard, and assist us. He encouraged his monks to call on them often.

In his *Sermon on the Song of Songs* Bernard explicated his mystical theology. His thought is never speculative, but for the most part practical. Bernard was a stranger to Neoplatonic theories such as underlay the thought of Augustine or Pseudo-Dionysius. He spoke out of his own personal experience. His language, like that of the Song of Songs, was romantic, sensuous even. He related numerous times experiences of the "coming" of the Word into his soul. He did not know when or how, but he "felt" the Word present. He also knew ecstatic experiences when, as he described it, "the soul is rapt out of itself" to enjoy the Word.

The Medieval Achievement

Before closing this chapter on life and thought in the Middle Ages from 604 to about 1150, some word of assessment should be added. Moderners, especially Protestant Christians, have taken such a negative stand toward the Middle Ages as a whole that historians today have to emphasize positive elements in the story which get passed over so easily among the many negative elements. Now no one, of course, can dispute the negative aspects, but it is essential to put these in context and not single them out for polemical purposes. Viewed in retrospect from what happened in the fifth through the eighth centuries, Christianity pulled off a rather remarkable feat in the evangelizing and Christianizing of so much of Europe.

What precipitated the collapse of Graeco-Roman civilization, the plunge into what is called the "Dark Ages," was not some inherent fault of Christianity but, quite simply, the barbarian "invasions." The Germanic peoples who gradually triumphed in the West were not cultureless. They had a different culture—one of the fields and the forests. Most of them admired Greek and Roman culture, but in their migrations they could not abandon their own and take over what they admired; they had to integrate the two in some way, just as the Romans had assimilated Greek culture into theirs. In the process of accommodation, Christianity, the religion of the Roman Empire but not yet fully absorbed by the people, played a major role of conserving and revitalizing and integrating or synthesizing. In the East, remember, that culture did not diminish at all. In the West, however, the renaissance took place gradually, first in England and then in Gaul. By the time of Charlemagne it reached full bloom only to suffer a temporary setback from the Viking invasions and then surge again.

For Christianity the main task was not a cultural one, although culture had an integral connection with everything Christians did. The main task was to evangelize and to Christianize. When one assesses Christianity's work during these centuries on those points, it comes out with an astonishing if not unblemished record. Christianity had not had time to complete its work in the Roman Empire before disaster struck. Fortunately, however, churches and people caught up in the spreading of the gospel had never limited their efforts to the Roman Empire. From the first century on, they had let their labors spill over to the people who would one day conquer the Western part of the empire. Ulfilas (ca. 311–383) began his work among the Goths shortly after his consecration as a bishop at Constantinople in 341. Bishops such as Ambrose of Milan (339–397) and Martin of Tours (d. 397) whose sees touched the fringes of the empire as the barbarians pressed southwards had both to win Arians to

Catholic faith and to convert barbarians as well as Romans. Not surprisingly, the impetus for the evangelization of Europe came from areas such as Ireland and England which were largely barbarian.

Debate about the degree to which different people accepted Christianity can go on forever, but the evangelization story is remarkable. First Western, then Central and Northern, and then Eastern Europe as well as lands much farther east heard the Christian message and saw firm foundations laid for continuing evangelization. In the main monks led the way. The *peregrini* of Ireland represented a different type of monasticism than they inherited from Egypt. At the center of their calling was a calling to spread the faith. Linked inseparably with their fearless efforts was the support of tribal chieftains and kings who saw evangelization as an inseparable companion of expansion. First the Merovingians and then the Carolingians, in what must surely be the most questionable part of the whole enterprise, backed the sword of the Spirit with the sword of steel, very much as Constantine had done in the Roman Empire. One cannot doubt the grand vision which inspired someone like Charlemagne. He intended to create a Christian empire like Constantine's, like the Byzantine. Kings elsewhere operated a similar vision, but few had Charlemagne's success.

How Christian did these kingdoms become? How Christian were the people who called themselves Christian? Those are difficult questions in any age and society. A prior question is: How do you judge what is Christian and what is not? Christianity never exists apart from culture. In its origins it existed in Jewish culture, then in hellenistic, then in Roman, then in Persian, then in innumerable other cultures. Which of these provide the perfect standard for evaluation? Some would say the Jewish. If we could restore Christianity or reproduce it in its primitive form, then we would have what Christianity should be. Anyone who reads the New Testament, however,

will have to recognize that primitive Christianity
was far from perfect, and its advance into other
realms would add to its challenge to live up to its
own good news.

If modern observers will turn their attention
away from Rome and the Roman papacy at its
worst during these centuries, they will find
impressive evidence of Christianization as varied
cultures blended into one another. Pastoral care
through the penitential system combined with
regular gathering for worship to effect genuine
transformation of consciousness and behavior.
Christian life in the year 1050, deformities aside,
stood several notches above Christian life in 604,
when the Middle Ages were in infancy. If people
at both of those dates had serious faults and
failures, they shared them with Christians of the
year 70 or the year 2000. Yes, pastoral care
through the penitential system and the worship of
the day had flaws which would cause other
problems in the later Middle Ages, but they were
correctable flaws, and in their own time these
basic institutions did a job of Christianizing.
Once again, moreover, the monks came to the
rescue. They inspired reform and revitalization
that carried over into every aspect of social
experience. Nowhere does that come out more
clearly than in reform of the papacy.

Part 7

The New "Dark Ages" 850–1050 C.E.

□□□

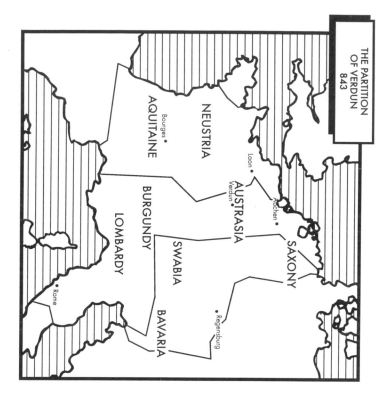

THE PARTITION
OF VERDUN
843

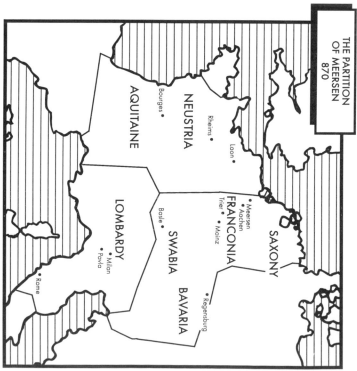

THE PARTITION
OF MEERSEN
870

Chapter 37

Christianizing Northern and Central Europe

The Christianization of Europe continued vigorously during the ninth, tenth, and eleventh centuries. The chief centers of activity were northern and central Europe. The northern mission attracted the interest of West European rulers as well as the Roman Church, the central European mission the interest of both Western and Eastern rulers. All, of course, saw an intimate connection between missions and expansion. Christianized peoples made more obedient subjects.

The Scandinavians

Denmark

By the ninth century Christianity in Western Europe seems to have recovered sufficiently from Viking raids to begin serious efforts to win the Scandinavians. Willibrord made some effort to win converts in Denmark, but its effects did not last long. After him the next serious attempt was by Ansgar. Born in 801 in the northwestern part of France, he entered the monastery of Corbey, one of the most important religious houses in Carolingian territory and of the tradition of Columban. Later he was sent to help found a new monastery in Westphalia, where he served as the first master of scholastics and held the office of preacher. When Charlemagne's successor, Louis the Pious, decided to help Harald gain control of the Danish kingdom, he called for missionaries to confirm converts. The abbot of Corbey suggested Anskar and one other colleague. Conceiving a grand missionary scheme, Louis had Anskar consecrated archbishop of Hamburg with power to appoint bishops and priests, sending him to Rome for papal approval. Pope Gregory IV commissioned Anskar and Ebo, archbishop of Rheims, as papal legates to the Swedes, Danes, Slavs, and others races to the north. Anskar did not have Boniface's spectacular success, but he did win the confidence of Danish kings and made some inroads into Sweden.

Following his death, most gains disappeared. The Vikings raided Frisia and northern Germany. Only Roman tenacity saved the archbishopric of Hamburg and Bremen, which was added to Hamburg during Anskar's lifetime to provide financial support. What turned events around in Scandinavia was the rising power of the Holy Roman Empire under the Saxon dukes, Henry I and Otto I, between 919 and 962. In 934 Henry overcame the Danes and compelled one of their rulers to accept Christianity. Unni, archbishop of Hamburg-Bremen from 919 on, took advantage of this to renew Anskar's work. Although he did not win Gorm, he made a deep impression on his successor, Harald Bluetooth, and obtained his permission to resurrect some of the Christian communities that remained from earlier work. He died in Sweden in 936.

Extension of the Holy Roman Empire aided the mission. Harald Bluetooth and his queen received baptism after Otto defeated him. His son, Sweyn, however, reacted against the faith, but Sweyn's son Canute, evidently reared a Christian by his Polish mother, was a Christian. Since his brother, Harald, succeeded to the throne of Denmark, Canute had to win his own kingdom. He conquered much of England and in 1016 was elected King of all England. In 1018 the death of his brother gave him the throne of Denmark as well. By 1020, firmly established as King of both England and Norway, he energetically espoused the cause of Christianity. He made a pilgrimage to Rome that increased his zeal further. His death did not diminish Christian growth. Denmark pressed for its own metropolitan, but Rome did not agree until about 1100 when Lund obtained that status.

Norway

The Christianization of Norway began during the mid-tenth century, sparked especially by English influence. Haakon, sent as a young child to the English court, was reared a Christian. Accepted as king by most of Norway on his return in 935, he attempted to win the people to the Christian faith. Initially he did so by example. Later, he sent to England for clergy, built churches, and placed priests in them. About 950 he proposed adoption of Christianity. He met strong resistance and pressure from leaders to participate in pagan sacrifices, which he did reluctantly. After his death in 961, his nephews, who succeeded him, violently tried to impose Christianity and aroused popular hatred for it. Following the slaying of the chief, Harald Graafell, about 969 or 970, Harald Bluetooth, King of Denmark, imposed his rule on Norway and ruled it through Haakon the Jarl, whom he persuaded to join him in Christianizing the country. He sent "priests and other learned men" to Norway to instruct and convert the people. This effort seems to have had little lasting effect.

More telling was the work of Olaf Tryggvason. Born about 963 or 964, he was taken captive and sold into slavery by Vikings. Raids into England with the latter brought him into contact with a hermit in the Scilly Islands who awed him with his ability to foresee the future. Olaf and his followers received baptism and returned to England as Christians. In the summer of 996 he returned to Norway determined to win the people to Christian faith. He used as much force as needed to achieve his objective, completing the nominal process within about four years. He also carried Christianity to Iceland and Greenland. Trapped in a naval battle in 1000 by the forces of Sweyn of Sweden, he leaped overboard to his death.

Completion of Tryggvason's work awaited the appearance of Olaf Haraldsson, who claimed the crown of Norway in 1016. Olaf employed English clergy and established ties with the see of Hamburg to effect his goal and, like Olaf Tryggvason, did not hesitate to use force. He too aroused opposition of a personal and political nature and was defeated and slain in battle in 1030 by forces of Canute of Denmark, who wanted to subject Norway to himself. Although these two Olafs did not eliminate paganism, they did establish Christianity as the dominant religion of Norway, and a cult developed around Olaf Haraldsson, St. Olaf. However, a diocesan organization did not develop until the latter half of the eleventh century. Monks, largely from England, helped present the monastic approach to Christianity. Conflict arose over the claim of the archbishops of Hamburg-Bremen to control the churches of the North, for the Norwegian churches developed patterns similar to the original pre-Christian religious and social context. In 1104 Norway was placed under the newly created archepiscopate of Lund. In 1152 the country received its own archbishopric.

Christianity had reached the islands to the west of Scandinavia earlier, but Olaf Tryggvason has received credit for Christianizing them—the Orkneys, the Faroe Islands, the Shetlands, Iceland, and Greenland. He probably did advance his brand of Christianity in the Orkneys and Iceland, but the process continued after his death ca. 1000. Leif Ericson evidently propagated Christianity among the sparse inhabitants of Greenland at the direction of Olaf Tryggvason. From here Ericson probably made contact with the shores of North America, what was called Vinland.

Sweden

Sweden entered the Christian fold last among the three major Scandinavian kingdoms. Anskar won converts there on his several visits, but no evidence of Christian communities existed in 936 when Archbishop Unni of Hamburg visited and died there. The first planting thereafter evidently resulted from merchants or soldiers who went to England and returned. Although King Eric converted momentarily under pressure from Otto III of Germany, he later renounced his faith. The first King of Sweden to spread Christianity was Olaf Skotkonung, a contemporary of Olaf Tryggvason who had helped to defeat him eight years before. Under his son, Anund Jakob, 1021–1051, Christianity continued to spread. Subsequent rulers advanced the Christian cause further. Inge (1066–1111?) is credited with organizing the Church of Sweden. Sverker (1130–1150) invited the Cistercians to Sweden and brought the Church closer to Rome. He began erection of a cathedral at Uppsala. When, after his death in 1156, Sweden was granted an archepiscopate, the seat was fixed at Uppsala and the first holder was a Cistercian.

Central Europe

Bohemia

The conversion of Bohemia and Czechoslovakia did not begin until the late ninth century and was not completed until the tenth, despite their closer proximity to the center of the Carolignian kingdom. Although a group of Bohemian chieftains received baptism in Regensburg in 845, their conversion did not spread among the Czechs. The foothold for conversion of the Slavs in Bohemia came from Moravia. Real advance occurred when Vaclav or Wenceslas took the throne in 923 or 924. Reared as a Christian, he built churches and zealously supported the churches. Strong opposition to him for his pro-German, ascetic style, however, led to opposition and murder by his brother Boleslav. Wenceslas became a national saint. In 950 Otto I imposed his regimen on Boleslav and inaugurated a more favorable era for Christianity. Boleslav II acted energetically on behalf of Christianity during his long reign (967–999). He founded churches and strengthened monasteries. Under direction of Otto I, he helped found the first Bohemian episcopate, at Prague. Under the second bishop, Vojtech or Adalbert, Cluniac reforms were attempted. Opposition, however, forced Adalbert out. After two leaves in Rome he spent the rest of his life as a missionary, perhaps among the Magyars, but chiefly among the Poles and the Prussians, among whom he suffered martyrdom in 997.

The Magyars (Hungarians)

The Magyars started forays into Moravia and Pannonia in the last decade of the ninth century. Masses of them entered modern Hungary about 895–896. During a period of disintegration of the Carolingian kingdom, they invaded Italy and Western Europe. They wreaked havoc on churches and monasteries, killing and taking captive both clergy and laity. As the Saxons gained power, they repulsed the Magyars. In 955 Otto I inflicted a defeat near Augsburg that ended their threat to the West.

From three sides—Saxony, Poland, and the Byzantine Empire—the Hungarians faced aggressive Christian forces which resulted in conversion to Christianity. The Greek Church sent missionaries from the southeast, baptizing two Magyar princes in 949. The successor, Geisa, however, turned Hungary toward the West rather than the East, sending envoys to Otto I in 973. He opened the way for missionaries in his domains. Bishop

Piligrim of Passau dispatched priests to Hungary and reported to Rome the baptism of 5,000 Magyars and the end of opposition to Christianity. He preached throughout the kingdom. In 1000 he requested and received from Pope Sylvester II (997–1003) a royal title and an ecclesiastical organization for Hungary. He founded and endowed monasteries and established two archbishoprics and eight bishoprics. Many missionaries assisted in the evangelization of the country. Although a strong reaction set in after Stephen's death in 1038, Christianity gained renewed support under Ladislas I (1077–1095) and Koloman (1095–1114).

The Poles

Christianity entered Poland through both Slavic and German agents. The first well-authenticated conversion was that of Duke Mieszka, baptized in 966 or 967 under influence of his wife, Dobrawa, sister of Boleslav II of Bohemia. Poland received an episcopate in 968 in Poznan. Mieszka's son Boleslaw Chrobry (992–1025) both extended the state and Christianity . Boleslaw gave vigorous support to missionaries. He assisted Adalbert of Prague in his work. After the latter's martyrdom in 997 he brought his body to the Polish capital of Gniezno, which in 1000 became an archbishopric. He appointed Adalbert's brother archbishop and created three subordinate bishoprics—at Kolberg in Pomerania, Breslau in Silesia, and Cracow. A visit of Otto III to the tomb of Adalbert made the Polish church virtually independent of German imperial control. After Boleslaw's death opposition arose as the Kingdom of Poland split up. Later monarchs, however, restored much of the property and support, but Christianity did not attain the strength it had in the West for a long time.

The Wends

Some Wends, residing in northwestern Germany, were converted under Charlemagne, but the latter made no strong effort to bring them into the Christian fold. His successors also seem to have overlooked them. Therefore, the task of evangelization remained for the Saxons, who effected it with force of arms and establishment of ecclesiastical organization. The conversion process, however, took several centuries. Henry I (919–936) subjected the Wends to German rule, but he got little support from German clergy to convert them to Christianity. Otto I proved more successful. His extension of his realm as far as the Oder opened the way for missionaries. Henry strengthened the church in Wend territory by establishing bishoprics, founding sees at Brandenburg and Havelberg in 948, and arranging financial support. He also set up an archepiscopal see at Magdeburg to supervise the organizing of the church in Wendland. These efforts do not appear to have had great success. Ten years after Otto's death in 973, mob violence broke out against the clergy, evidently from anti-German sentiment. Another occurred in 1018 during the reign of Henry II (1002–1024). The emperors retaliated with great brutality, causing further damage to Christian witness. Not until the end of the eleventh century did Christianity successfully Christianize the territory east of the Elbe.

The Pomeranians

Pomerania entered the Christian fold as a consequence of Danish, Polish, and German efforts. Polish king Boleslaw expanded his kingdom to include Pomerania and established an episcopal see at Kolberg. During the latter half of the eleventh century, however, paganism still thrived. But that began to change in the twelfth century, thanks to Vratislav. Shortly before 1121 Boleslaw III (1102–1139) invaded Pomerania and forcibly baptized a large number of captives. Since Polish bishops refused to accept responsibility for evangelizing the country, Boleslaw sought others. The first, a Spanish monk named Bernhard, failed miserably, so Boleslaw turned to Otto, bishop of Bamberg. Otto, though sixty, undertook the risky mission with the financial and other support of Boleslaw. Vratislav, who had been baptized earlier, received him with honor. Otto used diplomacy rather than force for several months in 1124 and 1125. Although a reaction set in when he withdrew to return to Bamberg, he returned in 1128 with authorization of both the pope, Calixtus II, and the emperor, Lothair. This time he gave permanency to the work, completing the organization of the Pomeranian Church. Although not yet well rooted, Christianity gained among the populace with the influx of large numbers of settlers from Germany and Denmark during the twelfth and thirteenth centuries.

The Obodrites

The Obodrites, living in northwestern Wendland and in Slavic areas between the Elbe and the Oder, had a stormier introduction to Christianity. The most energetic effort to win the Obodrites occurred in the first half of the twelfth century when Vicelin, probably a Saxon, labored there between 1126 and 1154. Commissioned by the archbishop of Hamburg, he became in later years the bishop of Oldenburg. The influx of settlers from Germany and the Netherlands gradually Christianized the area. Henry, Duke of Saxony, completed the German conquest of the area and aided the church with establishment of Cistercian monasteries in their time of vigorous growth. The founding of monasteries hastened the Christianization.

East Prussia, the Baltic Republics, Finland

The evangelization of East Prussia, Lithuania, Latvia, Estonia, and Finland did not really take place until the fifteenth century. Earlier efforts occurred, for example, the ill-fated venture of Adalbert among the Prussians, where he was martyred in 997. In 1009 Bruno of Querfort came to the same tragic end. King Eric of Sweden conquered the Finns in the mid-twelfth century, and many received baptism. An Englishman, Bishop Henry of Uppsala, accompanied Eric and was called founder of the Finnish Church. In 1249 Birger Magnusson again conquered Finland and led the majority of the population to accept Christianity. The most powerful figure in the land was the bishop of Abo. The Lapps became more favorably disposed to Christianity later.

The Danish King Vlademar II (1219–1241) occupied Estonia and began its Christianization, but the Ests rose up and wiped out most traces of this in 1222. In 1238 the northern part of Estonia was restored, allowing continuation of the conversion process.

The Lithuanians were the last of all the Baltic peoples to enter the Christian fold. As late as 1333, Christians fled the kingdom and sought refuge with the Teutonic Knights, whom the Lituanians opposed vigorously.

Christian Missions from the East

Although the Eastern Christian churches lacked the drive found in the West, significant gains did occur on the borders of the Empire. Note was taken in Chapter 31 of the remarkable work of Cyril and Methodius and their disciples among the Slavic peoples during the ninth century and later among the Bulgars. A much larger and more important field for the future of Orthodox Christianity, however, opened during the second half of the tenth century in Kievan Russia. Following the fall of Constantinople to the Ottoman Turks in 1453, Russia assumed a dominant place among the Orthodox churches, Moscow representing itself as the "Third Rome." The Orthodox churches also vied with the Roman Catholic Church in the Balkans, where they had a major victory in the adoption of Orthodoxy by the Serbians during the late twelfth century.

Russia

Christians had long been penetrating into the Ukraine and south Russia. The Patriarch Photius evidently initiated some kind of mission. By the middle of the tenth century there were a number of Christians around Kiev, possibly converted during their employment in Constantinople. Although the ruler Igor (913–945) remained a pagan, his wife, Olga, became a Christian, perhaps about 954, ten years after Igor died. In 957 she made a trip to Constantinople and returned with a priest. She did not win her sons, but her grandson Vladimir was responsible for the conversion of Russia. From several choices he elected Greek Orthodoxy and undertook actively to convert his people. He built churches and founded monasteries. He sent missionaries to other areas besides Kiev. By the end of his reign Russia had three bishoprics, which Vladimir refused to place under control of Constantinople. Vladimir's successor, Yaroslav, furthered the ties with Greek Christianity, but it took decades to evangelize the majority of the people. When the Mongols conquered Russia in the first half of the thirteenth century, they posed a new challenge which led to the deepening of the religious life of the Russian Church and to the geographic extension of it.

The Serbs

Serbia felt pulls both toward Rome and toward Constantinople at times. Roman Catholicism dominated in Hungary and Croatia, Greek Orthodoxy in Bulgaria. In the twelfth century Christianity became thoroughly naturalized in Serbia in Greek Orthodox form. Key to this was Rastko, or Sava, won to the monastic life by a Russian from Mount Athos, in 1192. Three years later his father abdicated the throne and joined him in founding a monastery which he made into a training school for future leaders of the Serbian church. When Rastko or Sava's brother, Stephen, moved the country in the direction of Rome, Sava obtained from the emperor, the patriarch, and the Holy Synod the right of Serbian bishops to consecrate their own archbishops, thus becoming autocephalous (independent). He appointed himself archbishop and drilled Orthodox beliefs and customs into the clergy.

Chapter 38

The Churches and the New "Dark Ages"

The Viking invasions in England and along the western coast of the continent plunged Europe into a new period of cultural confusion and political disarray. They had their greatest impact in England and France, where the Vikings struck harder. In England Alfred the Great (871–899) rallied sufficient forces to limit the Danish hegemony and to effect a revival of Christianity. In France, where the Carolingian Kingdom dissolved completely in 910, political gravity shifted toward the German part over which Louis the German reigned for sixty years (817–876) and which suffered little from the Viking incursions.

The Church in England

Alfred's defeat of the Danes contributed physically to the survival of Christianity in England. Surprised by Danish King Guthrum in January 878, he managed to hide in the marsh island of Athelney and gather around himself a fighting force. In May he fell on the Danes at Edington in Wiltshire and dealt such a decisive defeat that Guthrum had to sue for peace. Not only did he evacuate Wessex, he became a Christian, the first step toward recouping civilized relationships. Alfred dealt another blow to the Danes about 886, regaining London and surrounding areas. By common consent he was becoming King of the English. He dealt further blows between 892 and 896 as the Danes raided Western Mercia, causing them to seek easier pluckings in France.

Alfred also promoted ecclesiastical reform and revival of learning. Well educated himself, he gathered a band of scholars from England, Wales, and the continent. With their assistance he translated a number of works; Gregory the Great's *Dialogues* and *Pastoral Rule*, Boethius's *Consolations*, Orosius' *Seven Books of History*, and Augustine's *Soliloquies*. He founded monasteries at Shaftesbury and Athelney and planned to establish one at Winchester. He also intended to divide dioceses, but this was not effected until ten years after he died in 899. His monastic reforms met with little success, but his literary works impacted the church noticeably.

Alfred's successors from 899 to 975 continued his effective resistance to the Danes, who controlled the midlands of England, the Danelaw. Since the Danes could not be driven out of England, the most effective route lay in Christianization, and all of the kings (Edward the Elder, 899–925; Athelstan, 925–939; Edmund I, 939–946; Eadred, 946–955; and Edgar, 959–975) acted with considerable effectiveness. Like Alfred, Edgar marked out an epoch in reform of both church and state, aided especially by outstanding clergy—Dunstan, archbishop of Canterbury; Oswald, archbishop of York; Ethelwold, bishop of Winchester.

Dunstan (ca. 909–988), attached for some time to the court of King Athelstan, took vows as a monk at Glastonbury and, about 940, became the Abbot. A strict ascetic himself, he insisted on strict observance of the Rule of Benedict. Glastonbury became widely known for learning. Under King Eadred he served as a minister and treasurer. In 957, after his recall by Edgar, then King of Mercia and Northumbria, he was appointed bishop of Worcester and London. When Edgar also claimed the throne of Wessex in 959, Dunstan became archbishop of Canterbury. The king and the archbishop together planned a thorough reform of both church and state. After Edgar's death Dunstan and Oswald secured the election of Edward the Confessor, but following the latter's brief tenure, Dunstan's influence waned. His chief contribution rested in restoration of monastic life in England, which had become almost extinct by the mid-tenth century. He founded monasteries at Peterborough (966), Ely (970), and Thorney (972). He also supported learning and gained fame as a musician, illuminator, and metal worker.

Oswald (d. 992), a Dane by birth, shared Dunstan's zeal for monastic reform. Educated in the household of his uncle, Archbishop Odo of Canterbury, and at the Benedictine monastery of Fleury in France, where he received ordination, he returned to England in 962. Dunstan consecrated him bishop of Worcester and in 972 archbishop of York as well as Worcester in order to assure continuance of monastic reforms, seriously endangered by Elfhere, earl of Mercia, who broke up many communities. Oswald also worked hard to reform clerical morals and to improve their theological knowledge.

Ethelwold (ca. 908–984) was the most zealous of the monastic reformers. Closely associated with Dunstan throughout his life, first as a monk at Glastonbury, he rigidly insisted on following the Rule of Benedict at Abingdon when he became abbot. He took Fleury as a model and told the monks at Abingdon that any who did not want to follow Benedict should leave immediately. In 963 he became bishop of Winchester, where he worked with Oswald to carry on reform.

The quality of the English rulers dropped precipitously after 975 and opened the way for a reemergence of the Sandinavian threat. By this time, however, the Danish invaders came as Christians. In 991 Olaf Tryggvason, an exile from the Norwegian royal house, made his first raid and had to be bought off by the Danegeld. In 994 he linked up with Sweyn, the temporarily exiled King of Denmark, and, though repulsed at London, had again to be bought off. Vikings made repeated raids thereafter. In 1002 King Ethelred committed an atrocious blunder in massacring Danes in his service and inciting Sweyn all the more to conquer England. Only London held out, and Ethelred fled to Normandy. Sweyn was King of England when he died suddenly in 1016. Meanwhile Canute, son of Olaf II of Norway, sailed to England to lay claim to the throne. He ruled from 1016 to 1035. Viking though he was, he was also a genuine believer in Christian faith and a statesman of great ability who admired and sought to achieve the higher civilization of the Christian West.

Canute used his heavy hand to promote peace and justice in alliance with the church. He supported ministers with money. He founded monasteries, turning the secular college of Bury St. Edmunds into one of the wealthiest. He made restitution for the murder of Alphege, archbishop of Canterbury, by giving the see great gifts. One of those on whom he relied heavily was Wulfstan (d. 1023), bishop of London (966–1002) and archbishop of York (1002–1023). A monk probably born in the eastern Danelaw, Wulfstan composed *Institutes of Polity, Civil and Ecclesiastical*, a serious effort to formulate political theory in this troubled era, and wrote much of the legislation during the reigns of Athelred II and Canute from 1008 on. He also drafted various private codes.

Canute might have started a Scandinavian Empire centered on England, but he left no strong successor when he was assassinated in 1035 at age forty. Eventually Edward, son of Ethelred, was elected king and reigned until the end of 1065. Known in history as Edward the Confessor, he was not as monkish as many have thought and he did not possess Canute's outstanding abilities. Brought up in Normandy, he reflected leanings in that direction in the style of Westminster Abbey. When he died, the Norman Duke William made immediate preparations to conquer the country he claimed Edward had promised him.

The Church in Germany

Although in this period the story of the church in Germany is tied integrally to that of the church in France, it is important to distinguish them at certain points. For one thing, the church in Germany did not have foundations in Christianity like the Gallo-Roman Church, for the Roman Empire fixed its boundaries along the Rhine and Danube. Along this frontier, Christianity had only sparse roots but deep enough to withstand the barbarian invasions. When Celtic missionaries came, they found some remains of earlier plantings.

For another thing, the evangelization process took somewhat different form. Whereas in Gaul Christianity spread gradually, in Germany itinerant missionaries planted monasteries which would serve as continuing centers of church life. In some areas, such as Bavaria or Swabia, which were mountainous and covered with forests, bishops planted and nurtured the faith. From Boniface, moreover, they inherited direct ties with Rome and maintained a loyalty to Rome not found in the Frankish domains. In the second and third generations monasteries had immense importance as centers of small administrative towns. Conquest and conversion went hand in hand as nowhere else.

Christianity spread in Germany through the expansion of parishes more than in France. Germany had an estimated 2500 parishes by 850 organized into deaneries. Yet paganism persisted in the forests, so dear to the worship of German peoples before the advent of Christianity.

German Christianity also differentiated classes less than Gallic or Italian. Only the nobles and the higher clergy stood apart from the rest of the people. Because they held large dioceses, German bishops were more significant figures than their French counterparts. Efforts of the emperors to counterbalance the power of the dukes of Lorraine, Franconia, Saxony, Swabia, and Bavaria, moreover, led to assumption of the right of appointment of all bishops except in Bavaria with treatment of them as imperial fiefs. Bishops thus became important political figures who administered their counties. Kings and emperors took care in selection, often appointing their relatives. This led to the problem of "lay investiture," church offices becoming the possession of the state. The German Church was thus on its way to becoming a national church, although the German emperors never legislated for the church as Charlemagne did.

Collapse of the Frankish Kingdom

The Frankish Kingdom grew shaky under Louis the Pious. Just three years after assuming the crown, he divided the reign with his three sons—Lothair, Pippin, and Louis. In 823 he included Charles the Bald. The brothers squabbled and fought constantly. At the death of Louis, Lothair held the kingdom for three years, but in 843, in the Treaty of Verdun, the remaining brothers split it three ways. The Viking raids, begun as early as 750, increased in strength and boldness. Only on rare occasions did the later Carolingians enjoy a victory, and when they did win, as Louis the Stammerer did at Saucourt in 881, it became an occasion for celebration in the famous *Ludwigslied*, a poem of fifty-nine lines. The last Carolingian king of Germany died in

Lorraine in 911, opening the way for the four tribal duchies to establish a framework for a new Germany.

Rise of the Saxon Dukes, Henry I and Otto I

The long tenure of Louis the German (817–876) already assured a shift of political gravity and it is not surprising that Germany was the first of the Frankish kingdoms to recover from the anarchy of the late ninth century. Two factors in Germany favored restoration of the monarchy: (1) the extensive territory still belonging to the crown in Franconia and Swabia, two of the duchies, and (2) the interest of the clergy in supporting the monarchy in order to preserve the church's holdings.

The revival of the German monarchy began with the election of Henry, Duke of Saxony, as King of the Saxons and Franconians. A strong and practical statesman, he brought to the monarchy considerable holdings. Although he had long opposed centralization, he now resolved to gain recognition of the dukes of Swabia and Bavaria. That took six years. He then set out to expand his realm. Henry (919–936) and his son Otto I, the Great (936–973), spread their control gradually through France employing the Carolingian policy of using the church for political ends. Otto, intensely ambitious and devout at the same time, advanced the church's ideals and culture and its civilizing mission at the same time. He halted the Magyars. He extended Germany and Christianity through Wendland. By 962 Italy also succumbed to his influence. And on Candlemas day (February 2) 962 John XII (955–964) placed the crown on his head. The Holy Roman Empire lasted until 1806, but John XII lasted only one more year, for Otto removed him and replaced him with a reformer. Otto clearly intended to reconstruct the empire of Charlemagne.

Winning control of Germany was, of course, not easy. The Saxons had plenty of opponents and open opposition. Otto used the Church to

great effect in establishing control, for the success of his policy depended on control of the German Church. As king, he nominated bishops and abbots and made binding claim on their loyalty. Although "clergy and people" still had some voice in elections, Otto himself made the real decisions. Often he appointed relatives. The bishopric or abbey became his fief. He handed the newly appointed bishop or abbot the crozier with the words, "Receive the Church." He was their master just as much as he was master of state officials.

Otto took keen personal interest in evangelization of the new territories he won. In 950 he forcibly subjected the Duke of Czech Bohemia, Boleslav. He relied on the Church to Christianize the obstinate Wends. In 948 he established missionary bishoprics at Brandenburg and Havelberg. In 968 he founded an archbishopric at Magdeburg to tend to the Christianizing of the Slavs. He set up missionary sees in Serbia, though the area later became Orthodox.

The Ottonians

Otto II (973–983) lacked the remarkable gifts of his father and the Empire suffered accordingly. Ambitious plans for control of Italy failed. The Danes under Sweyn Forkbeard overran the border. The Slavs rebelled. The Obodrites burned Hamburg, the Lyutitzi Brandenburg, and the Bohemians Zeitz. The northern part of Otto the Great's annexations to Germany were lost for more than a century. Otto III (983–1003), far more able, had much greater success. Half-Saxon and Half-Byzantine, by Theophano, wife of Otto II, he dreamed of a remodeled Roman Empire of the West under his leadership with the papacy as his partner, a Christian confederation of Germans, Italians, and Slavs. Deeply influenced by Gerbert, the most distinguished scholar of the age who strove to be appointed to the archbishopric of Rheims, Otto III wanted to transcend the limitations of a German kingship. In 996 he quietly entered Italy to receive the imperial crown. Pope

John XV (985–996), however, had died before he arrived, so the Romans asked him to appoint a successor. He selected the first German to hold the pontifical office, his cousin Bruno, who chose the name Gregory V (996–999). No sooner had the emperor left Rome, however, than the Romans drove Gregory out and set up John XVI, a Calabrian, in his place. In 998 Otto returned, degraded and mutilated John, and in 999 elevated Gerbert, a Frenchman, to the papacy as Sylvester II (999–1003). Otto conceived of himself as a combination of Constantine and Charlemagne, a "Servant of Jesus Christ" in contrast to the *servus servorum Dei* of the popes. He denounced papal claims of the *Donation of Constantine* and treated Rome as his own chief capital.

Otto III had genuine religious enthusiasm. His mentors included the missionary saint Adalbert, to whose shrine in Poland Otto made a pilgrimage just before his death; Romuald; and the Greek Nilus of Calabria. His visit to Poland resulted in the establishment of an archbishopric at Gniezno. Meantime, Pope Sylvester gave a royal charter and a native archbishopric to Stephen I of Hungary.

Since Otto III died childless, the crown shifted to the Bavarian duke Henry, though not without difficulty. Unlike his predecessor, Henry II (1003–1024) did not have such a grand vision for his reign. His seal bore the words *Renovatio Regni Francorum*, "Renewal of the Kingdom of the Franks." His chief concern was Germany, not a restored Roman Empire. Like Otto the Great, however, he ruled the Church, inspiring its reform through synods, and looked to the Church for unwavering support. He controlled nomination of bishops and exacted the enfeoffment of knights on Church lands and full service from them. At the same time he made lavish grants of land and jurisdictions to bishops, more than ever the servants of the crown. It did not occur to him that popes might claim their first allegiance. Within his domain he divided sees and founded them as he saw fit.

Conrad II (1024–1039), more secular than Henry, who had been destined for a religious vocation before his election, followed the same policy as Henry but with much less hesitancy. In Church matters his concern was the interest of the crown. He appointed German bishops to vacant sees who would maintain the union of Germany and the Italian Kingdom. He appointed to all church offices, often after receiving considerable sums of money. He treated bishops as his officials. He allowed no appeals to Rome without his permission, presided over synods, decreed fasts and feasts, moved sees, and called himself the vicar of Christ. In Italy he presided with Pope Benedict IX at synods.

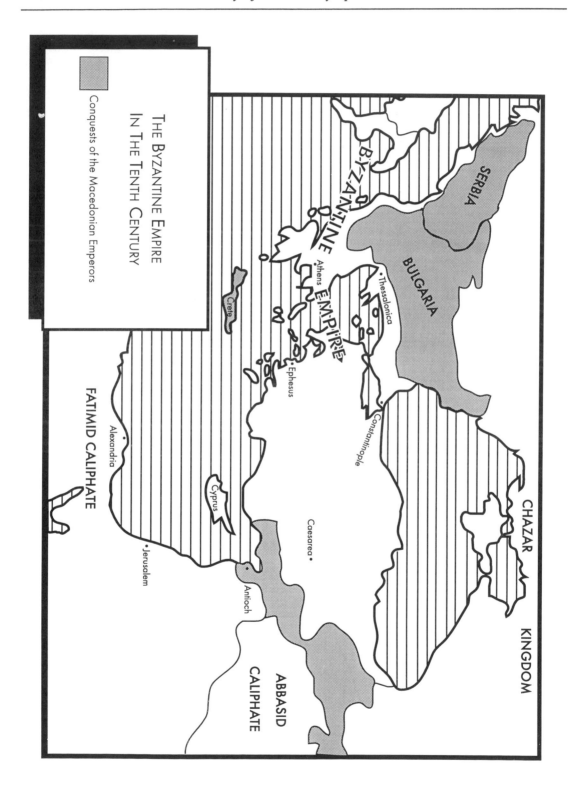

THE BYZANTINE EMPIRE
IN THE TENTH CENTURY

Conquests of the Macedonian Emperors

BYZANTINE

SERBIA

BULGARIA

EMPIRE

Athens

Thessalonica

Crete

Ephesus

Constantinople

Caesarea

Cyprus

CHAZAR

KINGDOM

FATIMID CALIPHATE

Alexandria

Jerusalem

Antioch

ABBASID
CALIPHATE

Chapter 39

Eastern Christendom, 867–1056

The Byzantine Empire enjoyed a resurgence under the Macedonian dynasty (867–1056). Effective military leadership led to significant victories over the Saracens and Bulgars. At the same time the Eastern churches made significant gains in the evangelization of Russia. The one discordant note was struck during another period of anarchy (1025–1056) with yet another schism between East and West, precipitated this time by the ambitious Patriarch Michael Cerularius.

The Macedonian Dynasty

Under the Macedonian Dynasty, 867–1025, the Eastern Empire reached a new level of power, building on the work of the Isaurians. It pursued with considerable success wars against Saracens in both East and West and against the Bulgars. Basil I (867–886) initiated recovery of the eastern Mediterranean, squelching pirates from Africa, Crete, and Cilicia who raided the shores of Greece. In 961 Nicephorus II (963–969) recovered Crete and Cyprus and reasserted Roman control of the sea. The Empire boasted a series of great military leaders in this period, who retook territory in the East lost to the Muslims. Equally significant was the overthrow of Bulgaria during the tenth century. After suffering humiliating defeats in the ninth century at the hands of Krum (806–815) and watching a Bulgarian Empire mushroom on its doorstep under Simeon (893–927), the Byzantines benefited from a rebellion

which precipitated the decline of the Bulgarian Empire under Peter I (927–969). Involved in the revolt were Bogomili, a Neo-Manichaean sect, whose story later intersected that of the Cathari of Southern France. In 967 Emperor Nicephorus II seized the moment to attack the Bulgars with the help of the Grand Duke of Kiev, Sviatoslav (945–973), against whom he shortly turned. His successor, John Tzimisces (969–976), continued the conquest of Bulgaria, after his armies defeated the Russians at Arcadiopolis and Dorostolum and forced them to evacuate the country. The empire reannexed Eastern Bulgaria, but Western or Macedonian Bulgaria continued independent and became a powerful state under Tsar Samuel (976–1014). Not until 1014 did the Byzantines overthrow the Kingdom of Ochrida after thirty years of warfare to regain supremacy over the whole Balkan peninsula.

Byzantium also recovered southern Italy. In 712 the Saracens had seized Corsica, and in the ninth century they took Sicily, Calabria, and Taranto. Basil I recaptured Bari in 876, Taranto in 880, and Calabria in 885. Although the Saracens recovered Sicily and invaded Calabria in 902, the Byzantines overwhelmed them at Garigliano in 915 to retain control of southern Italy for a century. With Greek monasteries and clergy southern Italy became *Magna Graecia*. Although Western emperors tried to displace the Easterners in 968 and 1022, they had little success. By the end of the Macedonian Dynasty in 1025 the Empire controlled southern Italy, the Balkans, and the Eastern frontiers, and its diplomacy reached far beyond.

The Conversion of Russia

For the Church the most significant happening was the conversion of Russia described earlier. Although the Russians first came into contact with the Byzantine Empire during the reign of Michael III (842–867), nothing remained of early efforts except an episcopate dispatched to Kiev by Emperor Basil I (867–886). The reign of Olga opened the way for the conversion of her grandson Vladimir (980–1015), who was to Russia what Clovis was to Gaul. Rejecting both Islam and Roman Catholicism and Judaism, he was deeply impressed with the rites of the Orthodox Church and the power of the Byzantine Empire. Hagia Sophia awed envoys sent by Vladimir to Constantinople. After capturing the trading city of Cherson, Vladimir allied himself with Basil II (976–1025) and received baptism at Cherson in 988, marrying the emperor's sister Anna. As a wedding gift, he gave her the town and returned to Kiev. On his return he began to overturn the pagan cult he had formerly sustained and adopted Christianity as the faith of Russia. Organization of the Orthodox Church in Russia took place, however, chiefly under his son Yaroslav I (1019–1054). The later story belongs to the next phase of medieval history.

The Byzantine Patriarchate

Dominance of the patriarchs of Constantinople by the emperors, the haloed figures in Byzantine church art, created instability. Photius, a winner under Michael III, found himself in a very different situation under Basil I (867–886), when the Synod of Constantinople, which the Latin Church recognizes as the Eighth Ecumenical Council, condemned him and restored Ignatius. Demands made by Pope Hadrian II (867–872) for return of estates belonging to the papacy confiscated by Leo III should be given back and for assignment of Bulgaria to his authority united Basil and Ignatius against the papacy on much the same grounds as Photius and Michael. When Ignatius died in 878, Basil appointed Photius once more. Another Synod of Constantinople, which Eastern Christians count the Eighth Ecumenical Council, confirmed his reinstatement. Photius, however, enjoyed a short period of glory, about seven years. Aspiring to secure his own election or a relative's election as emperor, he acted so aggressively that Leo VI, resenting his domineering style, forced him to retire to a monastery in 886 and then installed his younger brother, Stephen (886–893), as Patriarch. The Eastern clergy wrote Rome to say that Photius's deposition was justified and to affirm the Roman excommunication!

Other Patriarchs fared little better under this system. Leo installed Nicholas (901–907) and removed him a few years later because he refused to sanction the emperor's fourth marriage in violation of canon law. Leo made light of the Patriarch's effort to keep him from entering the Church and deposed him, appointing Euthymius (906–911) in his place. Euthymius recognized the marriage on the grounds that the laws of the Church had to yield to state needs. Leo took pains to cultivate the good will of Pope Sergius III (904–911), but he hardly needed to during the period often characterized as "the great pornocracy" (904–963). In 920 the Synod of Constantinople effected a reunion of Old and New Rome, amazingly under Constantine VII (Porphyrogenitus), whose legitimacy it denied by invalidating the fourth marriage of Leo and the Empress Zoe.

Emperor Nicephorus II (963–969) looked on the Church as an obstacle to the successful pursuit of his military objectives. Jealous of privileges of clergy and monks, in 963 he prohibited the founding of new monasteries and hospitals and voided all wills donating land to the Church. He required imperial approval of all ecclesiastical elections. He left the wealthiest sees vacant so as to collect their revenues and compelled new bishops to pay a large part of their receipts annually to the treasury. The clergy stoutly resisted his demand that all soldiers who fell in battle against the Muslims he counted martyrs and his resettlement of Monophysites in Antioch. Basil II (976–1025) reversed Nicephorus's anticlerical legislation and permitted again the construction of churches and religious houses in his *Novels* (988), issued the same year Vladimir received baptism and began the conversion of Russia.

Successes of the Macedonia Dynasty notwithstanding, the empire was heading toward harsher times already as a series of inept rulers succeeded to the throne. As in the West, so also in the East feudalism was replacing the strong, centralized government of the Macedonians. Like the nobility, the clergy and religious placed control of their properties above the needs of the society. Some patriarchs had sufficient strength to create trouble for the emperors at times.

The Schism of 1054

The strained relations between East and West reached a breaking point again in 1054 at the tail end of the Macedonia Dynasty. Reunion had been restored in 892 by the action of Pope Formosus (891–896), but tension remained over several issues: (1) the Roman claim to universal supremacy, (2) the addition of *filioque* to the Creed, (3) the use of unleavened bread in the eucharist, and several minor matters. More significant were: (1) the politico-ecclesiastical rivalry between the two sees, (2) the overbearing conduct of the papacy, and (3) the rather different character of Eastern and Western Christianity.

The engineer of the split was Michael Cerularius, Patriarch of Constantinople from 1043 to 1058. A bright and energetic man, Cerularius resented the subordinate position Constantinople held after Rome and determined to deliver it from that position. He sensed the opportune mo-

ment had come when Pope Leo IX (1048–1054) took the field against the Normans and was defeated by them June 18, 1053 at Civitate and held captive until March 1054. Cerularius opened his attack by letter to Leo, archbishop of Ochrida, making the following charges against the churches of the West: (1) using unleavened bread in the Eucharist according to Jewish custom, (2) fasting on Saturday in Lent, (3) eating blood and things strangled in violation of Acts 15, and (4) not singing the hallelujah during the fast. Leo replied with a series of countercharges: (1) Cerularius's arrogant use of the title "ecumenical," (2) his attempt to subject the patriarchs of Alexandria and Antioch, (3) rebaptism of Latins by Greeks, (4) clerical marriage, (5) neglect of the baptism of children before the eighth day after birth, and (6) omission of the *filioque* from the Creed. Prospect that the Normans might seize Byzantine possessions in Italy forced Emperor Constantine X (Monomachus) to pressure Cerularius to soften his stand. Both wrote the pope conciliatory letters, the emperor's begging restoration with the See of Peter and remonstrating with his Patriarch. The pope wrote a strong reply critical of Cerularius and sent three legates bearing it to Constantinople. The emperor received them graciously and sought to force a reconciliation, but Cerularius stood firm. Peeved at his intractableness, on July 16, 1054, the legates entered Hagia Sophia and laid a sentence of excommunication on the altar, concluding with a solemn anathema against "Michael, pretended Patriarch, and neophyte" and his friends. July 18, they set out to return to Rome laden with gifts from the emperor to the pope. On July 20, Michael excommunicated the legates in language as abusive as their own. He spent the last years of his patriarchate trying to deliver it from its subordination to the state. It cost him his life when, exasperated by Emperor Isaac Comnenus's impatience on one occasion, he cried out, "It was I who gave you the empire. I, too, can take it from you."

Chapter 40

The Papacy in Need of Reform

The dissolution of the Frankish Kingdom in the late ninth century opened the way for seizure of the coveted papal office by powerful Roman families and for radical degradation of it. Even the great counterreformation historian Baronius lamented the crimes "horrible to be seen" committed by the popes of "the Great Pornocracy." Stepping in to rescue the office from the clutches of the family of Theophylact were the emperors of the rising German kingdom under the Ottonians, beginning with Otto the Great's removal of John XII in 963. German control of the papacy posed a new set of problems, however, for Ottonian policy favored imperial dominance not unlike that practiced by emperors in the Byzantine Empire. Otto and his successors appointed and removed bishops and abbots at will in line with the concerns of the state. To counter this threat, the papacy, aided especially by the reform movement generated by the Abbey of Cluny, strove to liberate itself from lay control through the practice of investiture and to take its future into its own hands.

The Papacy
Dominated by Roman Nobility

This period of papal history, following a series of brief tenures, was one of the most embarrassing in the history of Christianity. Within eight years after the death of Formosus (891–896) nine popes held the office. Formosus' immediate successor, Stephen VI (896–897), had his body exhumed, dressed in pontifical regalia, tried by a Roman synod, condemned, and thrown into the Tiber on the charge that he had left his See of Porto for that of Rome. Two popes later, Formosus got a decent burial.

With the appointment of Sergius III (904–911) the papacy fell under the control of the family of Theophylact, a former leader of the militia appointed to the office of *vestiarius*, an important position in the papal court. The real power, however, rested in the hands of his wife, Theodora, and her daughters, Marozia and Theodora. It was strengthened by the marriage of Marozia to the Margrave Alberic of Spoleto, a relative of Sergius. Marozia managed to continue to exert influence until her death in 931. From 932 until 954 her son Alberic controlled Rome. Another son became Pope John XI (931–935). Before Alberic died, he extracted a promise from Roman nobles to see that his next son, Octavian, would ascend the papal throne when it next became vacant. In 955, as John XII (955–963), he succeeded to the chair of Peter at the age of seventeen. Concerned with restoration of the Papal States, he led an unsuccessful campaign against Capua. Realizing that he could not ward off an attack against them, he sent legates to Otto I in 960, pleading with him to free the Roman Church from the yoke of Berengar and Adalbert. Otto arrived at the gates of Rome toward the end of January, 962. On

February 2, John XII placed crowns on the heads of Otto and his wife. A year later, Otto removed him from his throne and installed a more worthy candidate as one of his first acts of reform.

The Papacy under Reform

Shortly after his coronation, Otto solemnly recognized and confirmed the Carolingian donations and other territorial claims the popes had made since. But he also reiterated imperial privileges concerning papal elections and the emperor's hegemony over the Papal States. Immediately after the emperor's departure, John XII, unhappy with his concessions, entered into an alliance with his former foe Adalbert and also with Greeks and Hungarians. Otto returned immediately to Rome, which admitted him without resistance, and presided over a synod which deposed John, justifying the action by the rule that exceptional circumstances demand exceptional measures. In John XII's place Otto installed a layman, Leo VIII (963–965), against whom Rome revolted as soon as the emperor left. Otto returned and suppressed the rebellion, but when he left again, John XII returned and avenged himself on his enemies. However, he died in May, 964 of a stroke and Otto returned Leo VIII to his throne. After Leo's death in 965 Otto sent two bishops to Rome to watch over the election of John XIII (965–972), whom a rebellious group of aristocrats imprisoned in the Castle San Angelo because he was Otto's choice. Otto returned and remained in Italy until the fall of 972 to consolidate and strengthen his power.

The death of Otto weakened the imperial reform efforts and led to a second period of degradation between 973 and 1046. Powerful Italian families once again sought to wrest control of the papacy from the emperors. Otto II (973–983) made little impact, here as in other areas, but Otto III (983–1002) undertook reform with considerable zeal. Invited by John XV (985–996) to come to Rome to receive his crown, he arrived after the pope had died. In his place he appointed Bruno, son of his nephew, Otto of Carinthia, as the first German pope, who chose the name Gregory V. Gregory (996–999) restored some respect for the papacy when he decided against Gerbert, friend of the emperor, in a dispute over the archbishopric of Rheims. Unfortunately he became a victim of Crescentius, who for years had tried to seize control of the papacy. When Otto left Italy, Crescentius started a revolt and forced Gregory to flee. In his absence Crescentius installed John Philagathos, archbishop of Piacenza, as John XVI. Otto returned soon afterwards with his army and deposed, mutilated, and imprisoned John. He then proceeded to have Crescentius beheaded.

The most significant of Otto's reform popes was Gerbert, the first French pope. Educated by the Benedictines of Aurillac, he enhanced his learning through contact with Arab scholars in Spain. As Sylvester II (999–1003), he attempted genuine reform. Although he reigned briefly, he greatly elevated the power of the papacy.

Otto III's successor, Henry II, Duke of Bavaria (1002–1024), devoted himself chiefly to internal affairs in his kingdom, and it was not long before Roman nobility had again taken control of the papacy. John Crescentius, son of the one Otto had beheaded, seized the papacy and determined holders of the office from 1003 until 1012. His death during the reign of Sergius IV (1009–1012), however, undercut the power of the Crescentii and gave an opening for the counts of Tusculum to secure the Chair of Peter for a member of their family, Theophylact, as Benedict VIII (1012–1024). Henry II favored his election. With the support of the Tuscalans Benedict invited Henry to receive the imperial crown. Benedict turned out to be a genuine reformer who succeeded in breaking the power of the Crescentii. He also conducted military junkets against the Saracens and the Greeks in southern Italy. Benedict supported the Cluniac reform movement underway since the early tenth century. He and Otto both attended the Synod of Pavia in 1022 which condemned marriage of clergy and other abuses.

The Tuscalans did less well with the next two appointments, Romanus, a layman and brother of Benedict VIII, as John XIX (1024–1033) and Theophylact, nephew of John, as Benedict IX (1033–1045). Elected at age ten or twelve, Benedict IX rivaled John XII for the worst pope in history. The Romans drove him from his throne, so that he had to call on the army to restore him in 1044. Meantime, the Crescentii elected an alternate, Sylvester III. Feeling increasingly insecure in his position, Benedict resigned May 1, 1045 in favor of Gregory VI (1045–1046), a zealous reformer. Emperor Henry III (1039–1056), unlike his father Conrad II (1024–1039), had a strong determination to correct abuses and set out for Rome in 1046. At his request a synod met at Sutri on December 20, 1046. It summoned both Gregory VI and Sylvester. Gregory evidently resigned, recognizing the illegitimacy of a pontificate secured by force. The Synod of Sutri deposed Sylvester III and committed him to a monastery. Accompanying Gregory into exile was a young cleric from the Lateran named Hildebrand, into whose hands fell much of Gregory's plan for reform. The emperor nominated Suidger, bishop of Bamberg, to succeed Gregory VI as Pope Clement II (1046–1047). Christmas Day, 1046, he received the imperial crown from the hands of his newly elected pope.

Part 8

The Age of Reform
1050–1200 C.E.

□□□

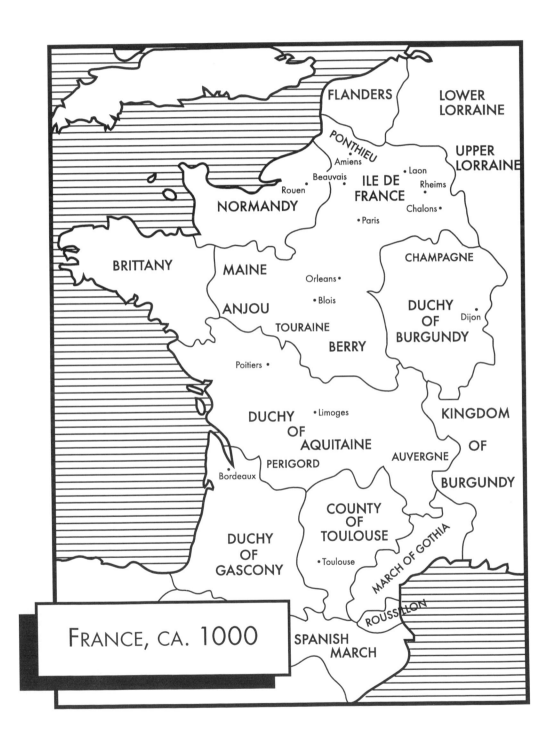

FLANDERS

LOWER LORRAINE

PONTHIEU

• Amiens

UPPER LORRAINE

• Laon

Beauvais •

ILE DE FRANCE

Rheims

Rouen •

• Chalons •

NORMANDY

• Paris

BRITTANY

MAINE

CHAMPAGNE

Orleans •

ANJOU

• Blois

DUCHY OF BURGUNDY

Dijon •

TOURAINE

BERRY

Poitiers •

• Limoges

KINGDOM

DUCHY OF AQUITAINE

OF

PERIGORD

AUVERGNE

BURGUNDY

Bordeaux •

COUNTY OF TOULOUSE

DUCHY OF GASCONY

• Toulouse

MARCH OF GOTHIA

ROUSSILLON

FRANCE, CA. 1000

SPANISH MARCH

Chapter 41

The Hildebrandine Reforms

The moral collapse of the papacy in the tenth and again in the eleventh century put the church on a very dangerous course. Although the impetus for reform came in great part from within, especially in the Cluniac reform movement, another part of it came from without—from secular rulers. Actually threats to the papacy in earlier centuries had already turned the See of Rome in this direction. When Pope Stephen II (752–757) invited the help of Pippin III and Pope Leo III (795–816) the help of Charlemagne, they did not get by without paying a price, that of lay involvement and control. The Merovingians had already laid a heavy hand on the Frankish Church. Under the Carolingians it grew heavier still. Under the German emperors it became intolerable. Not only did the Carolingian and the German rulers exact dues from the princes of the church in their own domain, thinking themselves responsible for the church as well as the state, they did the same for Rome. The demise of decency as powerful Italian families seized control of the papacy gave grounds enough for the emperors to do in Rome as they did in their own domain, select and install persons who best suited the aims of the state. All too often, money entered into the transaction.

Problems

Documents of this period speak of three sets of problems: Nicolaitanism, Simony, and Lay Investiture. Nicolaitanism, taken from the Revela-

tion of John (2:6, 15), referred to clerical license. In the West Popes Siricius (384–399) and Innocent I (402–417) had laid down the "rule" of celibacy for the clergy. Nonetheless, clergy continued to marry, for Leo I (440–461) forbade clergy to put away their wives and required them to live as brother and sister. Gallican councils refused to ordain married men unless both they and their spouses took vows of continence. Subsequently bishops made repeated but not very successful efforts to impose celibacy on those in holy orders. In the tenth century clerical concubinage was rife. The popes did not set a good example either.

Simony, taken from the name of Simon Magus and his desire to buy the power of apostles to perform miracles (Acts 8:14-25), designated the buying and selling of ecclesiastical offices. The Council of Chalcedon (451) prohibited ordination to any order for money, and Gregory the Great (590–604) denounced the practice. Yet the custom of obtaining money for appointments became widespread in the Middle Ages. In the tenth and eleventh centuries kings and emperors, prelates, and lay patrons often granted honors and estates of a see only after they received liberal payments from recipients. John Gratian paid a considerable sum to become Pope Gregory VI (1045–1046) and resigned promptly or was removed at the Synod of Sutri on the charge of simony.

Lay investiture had to do with the granting of symbols of office—ring and crozier—to bishops and abbots. Investiture by a king or nobleman began with the Merovingians and continued under the Carolingians. It grew with the advance of feudalism. Kings and nobles held suzerainty over the clergy. The German emperors brought the practice to its peak during the tenth and eleventh centuries. From their point of view lay control assured that objectives of state and church would mesh and lead to the best possible society. From the point of view of the bishops and abbots it led to constriction of the church's freedom to follow God's leading. In the mid-eleventh century the clash of perspectives on investiture took center stage in the reform of the church.

Recovering Church Control

The first major salvos in the battle to recover Church control of elections were fired by Peter Damian (1007–1072) as a Benedictine hermit at Fonte Avella (1035–1059) and then, after 1057, as cardinal bishop of Ostia. In a eulogy he lauded the Emperor Henry III in 1052 for having "cut off all the heads of the many-headed Hydra of simoniacal heresy with the sword of divine courage." He went on to praise Henry for rejecting the example of predecessors, thus meriting the right to give his approval to popes. In a letter to Cardinal Bishop Boniface of Albano (1060–1071) Peter Damian scored those who "in their pursuit of ecclesiastical honors, give themselves over to the service of rulers with disgusting subservience like captive slaves" and who, to obtain positions they wanted, "have to be lavish with money and also have to fawn on their patrons with soothing flatteries." In a letter to King Henry IV in 1065 he argued separation of spheres—temporal and spiritual. He pleaded with Henry to restore to the Roman Church its proper dignity, to guard it rather than try to rule it.

Cardinal Humbert (d. 1061), a monk of the Lotharingian monastery of Moyenmoutier appointed bishop of Silva Candida by Leo IX in 1050, exercised far less tact than Peter Damian. In three books *Against Simoniacs*, published serially between 1054 and 1058, he refused to admit that ordinations by simoniacs were valid, as Damian did, and thundered against lay investiture. The ring and crozier symbolize the pastoral office; how, then, could someone not a pastor confer them? he demanded to know. As the soul excels the body and commands it, so too does the priestly dignity excel the royal and should be able to advise in all things. Humbert did not go quite as far as Gregory VII to add that the priestly should "command" the royal.

Hildebrand

Working behind the scenes in these years was the ardent reformer Hildebrand, who in 1073 assumed the papal office as Pope Gregory VII (1073–1085). Born in Tuscany around 1020, Hildebrand went to Rome in early years and received his education at a school of the Lateran. He also spent several years at Cluny. Closely associated with Gregory VI, he accompanied him into exile in the Rhine Valley and remained with him until he died in 1048. When Bruno, bishop of Toul, received appointment as Pope Leo IX (1049–1054) he sought to enlist Hildebrand as an adviser. At first the latter refused because the election had taken place at the imperial court at Worms, but he finally consented. From 1049 until his election in 1073 he served as subdeacon under a succession of reforming popes.

Leo IX

Leo IX worked with great zeal to implement reform. Cousin of Emperor Henry III, Bruno, archbishop of Toul, did not relish stepping into the position which had treated its three German popes—Gregory V (996–999), Clement II (1046–1047), and Damasus II (1048)—so badly. Gregory was driven from the see and died at twenty-seven, Clement was poisoned within less than a year, and Damasus lasted only twenty-three days before being poisoned. Further, he recognized the difficulty of reforming an office so heavily fought over and degraded by a succession of popes controlled by rival Roman noble families, the Crescentii and the Tusculans. A German was surely not in a position to negotiate such a delicate situation.

Here is where Hildebrand proved critical. Before leaving the imperial court at Worms, Bruno asked several advisers to accompany him on the way to Rome. At Besancon he met the Abbot of Cluny, Hugo, and Hildebrand. Hildebrand refused. He did not object to Bruno personally but to circumstances in which he was elected. When Bruno asked why Hildebrand would not support him, he replied: "Because you are going to Rome to seize hold of the Roman Church, not in accordance with ecclesiastical statute but by royal and secular force." Bruno responded by laying aside papal dress and donning that of a pilgrim and declared that he would accept the pontificate only if Rome agreed. Reluctantly, Hildebrand then agreed to join him.

Bruno did not proceed in pontifical style. He first visited the See of Toul, then went to Augsburg to dedicate the church of St. Gall, and then to Rome on foot. Before the tomb of Peter, he told the people he had come to learn their will. Although nominated by the emperor, he had to act in accordance with the church's canons and would accept the office only if he had their unanimous vote. This deeply impressed the Romans, and they gave him the vote he insisted on. As his model, he chose Leo I, definer of the concept of papacy and savior of Rome in a critical period.

Because his predecessors had emptied papal coffers, Leo IX had to reorganize papal finances. He arranged for a tithe on all revenues for the preservation and renovation of St. Peter's. On Easter Sunday, 1049, he appointed Hildebrand treasurer and cardinal-subdeacon. He selected mostly foreign prelates to serve as his close collaborators to cut off domination by the Italian noble families. He convened a council whose express purpose was "against the purchase and bartering of ecclesiastical titles and offices, and against concubinage in the clergy." Although the council divided, Leo proceeded to take action against Nicolaitanism and Simony among the clergy. He collected decrees of predecessors against incontinence of priests and supplemented them with some of his own. Like Leo I, he prohibited married clergy from putting away their wives to escape the cost of maintaining them, but he also forbade sexual intercourse with wives. He pressured priests to live in communal houses rather than in private apartments. At the council itself he started investigating which of the bishops present were guilty of simony. One bishop, Kilian of Sutri, could not defend himself against the charge and was stricken with apoplexy. Ten priests suffering from personal scruples asked to be relieved of their rank and office. All agreed that anyone ordained by a simoniac should resign his office. Realizing, however, that too strict judgment might strip Rome of its priests and church services, one group of bishops asked the pope to adopt a more lenient attitude. Leo had to concede that the church could not be reformed overnight. He asked for a milder decree from the assembled bishops, that is, that those ordained by simoniac bishops would have to do penance for forty days but retain their office.

Leo drew up a plan for a "senate of the pope of Rome," what was to become the papal curia. His closest associates included Humbert, whom Leo named bishop of Silva Candida and who accompanied him on his travels as a legate. His advisers also included Peter Damian, who boldly named simoniac bishops, and Hildebrand.

During his five years in office, Leo spent only six months in Rome. The rest of the time he spent traveling throughout the West to see firsthand the maladies afflicting the church. Peter Damian sent the pope a copy of his work *On the Sins of Gomorrah* in which he described the secret sins of secular clergy in central Italy. Leo's investigations bore out the observations of Peter

Damian. He crossed the Alps into Germany, visiting Cologne, Aix-la-Chapelle, and Mainz. In October 1049 he convened a synod at Rheims, where he took part in consecration of a new church of the Virgin dedicated to Remigius, the Apostle of France (d. 532). Although the displeasure of King Henry I of France to Leo's "invasion" of his realm kept many bishops away, Leo proceeded with his plan to reform the church. Hildebrand made the opening speech, enumerating the agenda: simony, illegal use of church and chantry benefices by lay persons, marriage within forbidden degrees, desecration of churches, levying of fees for the arbitrary separation of spouses, withdrawal from monastic vows, military service by the clergy, and treatment of the poor. When Leo called on the bishops to confess any acts of simony, all professed innocence except Guido of Rheims, who kept silent. In a private conference the next day he confessed his guilt and asked pardon. Leo deferred the case until the following April in Rome. By the third day others admitted unwitting guilt of simony and resigned, but Leo proclaimed them innocent and reinstated them. At the same time he excommunicated bishops who stayed away from the council and those who left prematurely.

The Synod of Rheims laid out a plan for general reform of the church: (1) election of bishops or abbots by clergy and people before they can assume office; (2) no buying or selling of holy orders, offices, or altars; (3) no possession of an ecclesiastical office or public altar by a layman; (4) no collecting of taxes or tithes in the forecourt of a church except by the bishop or his deputy; (5) no demanding of fees for burials, baptisms, communion, or visiting the sick; (6) no carrying arms or performing military service by clergy; (7) no usury by cleric or lay person; (8) no resigning of holy orders by monk or cleric; (9) no ill treatment of wandering clergy; (10) no oppressing of the poor by robbery or imprisonment; (11) no contracting of marriage with a

blood relative; and (12) no desertion of a legal wife to marry another.

Leo held another synod at Mainz attended by the Emperor Henry III, secular princes from Germany, Burgundy, and Italy, forty archbishops and bishops, many abbots and clergy, and emissaries of the Byzantine emperor, as well as one bishop from Denmark. Leo asked that the decisions of Rheims be confirmed. He paid frequent visits to Monte Cassino, went on pilgrimages to holy places, and canonized saints. He wove back and forth to Italy, crossing the Alps six times. As a relative of the emperor, he stood in a good position to negotiate control, for instance, the Duchy of Benevento and other Italian towns not in the Papal States for the See of Bamberg and the Abbey of Fulda.

Leo had extraordinary physical stamina, but he erred badly in taking the field against the Normans. The Normans met resistance from neither the German nor the Byzantine emperors. Hildebrand urged Leo to take up the sword himself to defend papal holdings in Benevento. Peter Damian spoke against it and refused to accompany him to the battlefield. Ignoring his own directive forbidding clergy to serve in the army, Leo hired German soldiers. In the spring of 1053 they advanced on the Normans. By this time caught up in the military preparations, Leo would not listen to Norman offers to negotiate, he pressed blindly into battle and suffered a crushing defeat. To save the city of Civitate, the burghers surrendered the pope to them. The Normans treated the pope with deference, but the horrible miscalculation caused a tragic turn of events in his career. For two or three years he had taken big strides in the Cluniac reform. Now he was plunged into despair. For eight months he did not return to Rome. In March 1054 the Normans permitted him to go to Capua, where he engaged in ascetic exercises to cure his illness and regain his strength. He did not recover. Carried to Rome on a litter, he died there on April 19, 1054.

Meanwhile, another misfortune burdened his last days, the schism between the Greek East and the Latin West. For a time he had hoped to enlist both emperors in the defense of Benevento against the Normans, but that did not work out. Michael Cerularius, the Patriarch of Constantinople, thwarted efforts of both the emperor and the pope to effect a reconciliation. July 16, just months after Leo's death, papal legates excommunicated the Patriarch. Four days later, he reciprocated.

Leo to Gregory VII

Leo's successors continued the reform he began with such flourish, but after the death of Henry III their policy began to shift from one of cooperation with the emperor to one of opposition. The chief figure behind the change may have been Hildebrand, for he was the one who had opposed Henry's attitude toward the papacy all along. Although he did not hold a position in the front rank until the death of Cardinal Humbert in 1061, he was gaining in importance. Under Alexander II (1061–1073) he played the part of chief adviser.

Henry's death weakened the imperial position, for his son and heir, Henry IV (1056–1106), was then only six years old. The Tusculan party stood ready to capitalize on diminishment of German power and influence to recapture control of the papacy. The reformers, therefore, recognized how critical it was to assure the complete independence of the papacy either from imperial or any other control and looked toward enemies of the emperor in Germany for help. By the time Henry IV reached the age when he could take over the reins of the empire from Empress Agnes, he faced a head on clash with the reformers as he tried to restore his position to where it was before his father's death.

The first assistance for the reform came from Godfrey, Duke of Lorraine, who had clashed with Henry III from 1044 on. When Henry's last

nominee for the Chair of Peter, Victor II (1054–1057), died, the cardinals elected Godfrey's brother as Pope Stephen IX (1057–1058). Stephen died suddenly after only a year in office, however, and the Crescentii and Tusculans stepped in before the reformers could act and elevated the last Tusculan pope, Benedict X (1058–1059), to the office and took control of Rome. The cardinals had to move to Siena, where they elected the bishop of Florence as Nicholas II (1059–1061). Although he held a brief tenure, Nicholas took major steps to reform the papacy. First, he reversed the anti-Norman policy of Leo IX and Stephen IX, thus gaining the support of the toughest fighters in Europe at the time, whom he used immediately to drive his opponent, Benedict X, out of Rome. He also allied himself with France, thus gaining a second friend in the future conflict with Henry IV. More important than this, he convened the council in Rome in 1059 which decided that henceforth the College of Cardinals would elect the pope, the clergy and people merely giving assent, and that the pope would come only from Roman ranks unless no Roman clergyman was deemed worthy. Under this arrangement, the emperor would still have a veto and no one could take office without his consent, but he would no longer make the actual choice. Although his participation was treated as a concession of the church, Henry IV understandably reacted with hostility. To add insult to injury, the Norman Robert Guiscard swore to lend support to any pope the cardinals selected. The emperor convened a synod in 1060 that condemned Nicholas and annulled his decrees.

The death of Nicholas II, in consequence, was followed by election of competing popes once more. The reformers elected Anselm of Lucca as Alexander II (1061–1073), the combined forces of the emperor, Roman aristocrats, and conservative Lombard bishops Cadalus of Parma as Honorius II (1061–1072). Although German prelates supported the imperial side momentarily, three years later they switched to that of the reformers. Honorius II still held out, however, in Lombardy. During the next ten years, the reform shifted gears again—from moral regeneration of the clerical office to erosion of the rights of the emperor.

Hildebrand as Gregory VII

On his deathbed Alexander II recommended the election of Hildebrand. Committed as he was to the reform, it is ironic that Gregory's own election was irregular. During the funeral solemnities for the deceased pope, the cry went up, "Hildebrand for bishop!" Gregory did not wait for imperial confirmation or seek it; he merely informed Henry IV of his election just as he did other kings and princes, bishops and abbots. At the time Henry had his hands full with a rebellion in Saxony, and Gregory with the Normans, the Roman nobility, and hostile Lombard bishops. Gregory was also contemplating a campaign against the Seljuk Turks, who had crushed the Byzantine army at Manzikert in 1071 and were overrunning the Holy Land. For this he needed Henry's cooperation.

Gregory, however, was intent on reform. Roman synods in 1074 ordered the deposition of all simoniacal priests and forbade married priests to celebrate Mass. Although these provoked resentment in England, France, and Germany, Gregory renewed them a year later. In March of 1075 another Roman synod promulgated a stern decree prohibiting lay investiture. Anyone receiving a bishopric or abbacy from the hands of a lay person not only was not to be considered a bishop but excluded from the grace of St. Peter. Any emperor, king, prince, or other lay person who invested persons as bishops or in other offices would incur the sentence of excommunication. The synod also excommunicated five counselors of Henry for simony.

At the time Henry still had his hands full with rebellious Saxons and concurred in the decision. Soon afterwards, however, he resorted again to appointments. In December 1075 Gregory wrote a strong letter charging him with disrespect and disobedience to the pope, which was the same as disobedience to God's will, and threatened him not only with excommunication but also with deposition. Henry responded immediately by calling a synod to meet at Worms in January 1076. There German and Italian bishops withdrew their obedience. In a letter addressed to "Hildebrand, no longer pope but false monk" damned by the assembled bishops, Henry demanded that Gregory give up the papal throne.

In the violence of his attack, however, Henry miscalculated. He stirred up sympathy for an opponent who had much more support not only among reformers but throughout Germany than he anticipated, especially among rebellious princes. February 22, 1076, Gregory excommunicated Henry, deposed him, and absolved his subjects from their oath of obedience. Henry retaliated by summoning synods at Worms and at Mainz, but only a few bishops attended. At the meeting of the German diet at Tribur, near Mainz, October 16, 1076, the princes demanded that Henry submit to the pope, seek absolution within a year or forfeit his crown, and appear at a diet to be held in Augsburg on February 2, 1077, under the presidency of the pope.

Henry waited two months. Then, in one of the coldest winters know on the Rhine, he crossed the Alps as a penitent, accompanied by his wife and an infant son and one faithful servant, to seek absolution from the pope, who was then residing at the fortress of Countess Matilda, a strong supporter, at Canossa. On January 21, Henry sought absolution in vain. Gregory agreed to give it only if Henry gave up his crown. For three days, January 25 to 28, the emperor stood with bare head and feet in the snow in a coarse woolen shirt. Finally, entreaties of Countess Matilda and the abbot of Cluny, Hugo, forced him to relent on receiving Henry's promise to submit the decision to the forthcoming meeting at Augsburg.

Henry was cast down but not knocked out. A civil war followed in Germany and Italy. Enemies of Henry offered his crown to Rudolph, Duke of Swabia, whom Henry defeated at Melrichstadt in 1078 but who turned to defeat Henry at Muhlheim in 1080. Gregory refused for three years to decide, but he finally cast his lot with Rudolph in March 1080 and pronounced an even severer ban on Henry. Henry replied to this ban by choosing Archbishop Wibert of Ravenna, Gregory's bitter enemy, as Clement III (1080–1100) at Brixen in June, 1080. Although he suffered a defeat in October, his antagonist, Rudolph, died in battle. From that point on, the tide reversed. Rudolph's successor, Hermann of Luxemburg, could not hold his own against Henry. By Easter, 1083, Henry had captured Rome and St. Peter's and installed Wibert. In 1084 he convened a synod which excommunicated Gregory. Wibert crowned Henry emperor on March 31, 1084.

Gregory called on the Norman Duke Robert Guiscard for help. Though the latter secured Rome, he wreaked such havoc on the city that the pope had to ask him to leave. Gregory died an exile in Norman hands at Salerno in 1085, still supported by Countess Matilda but not many others. His exaggerated claims alienated many who had once supported him.

Gregory registered his claims quite forcefully in the famous *Dictatus Papae* in 1075. Just a few of the twenty-seven assertions reveal his attitude quite clearly: (2) That the Roman Pontiff alone is rightly to be called universal. (12) That he may depose emperors. (19) That he himself may be judged by no one. (22) That the Roman Church has never erred, nor ever, by the witness of Scripture, shall err to all eternity. Such assertions as these stood far from the intention of earlier reformers. Although he did not claim authority to select kings and install them, Gregory did claim authority over kings and kingdoms. Reform became, for him, chiefly the crushing of secular power beneath the feet of spiritual.

The End of the Investiture Controversy

The controversy over investiture did not end as Gregory would have wanted but in a compromise in which both king and priest had to yield. Gregory's immediate successors, Victor VI (1085–1087) and Urban II (1088–1099) followed essentially the same policy of papal supremacy Gregory had set forth but with greater moderation. Urban II, remembered especially for calling the First Crusade in 1095, left ample evidence of his policy. He excommunicated Philip I, king of France, for rejecting his legitimate wife, Bertha, for Bertrada of Montfort, the runaway wife of Count Fulco of Anjou. He encouraged Conrad to rebel against his father, Henry IV. He fostered hatred between the Guelphs (papal) and Ghibellines (imperial) in Germany. He convened the Synod of Piacenza in 1095 which condemned Henry for immorality, simony, and Nicolaitanism.

Pascal II (1099–1118) gained a resounding victory over Henry IV, who died at Liège, August 7, 1106, by supporting the rebellion of his son Henry (1106–1125) against him. However, Henry V paid him off in treachery, for he demanded the right of investiture over all the churches of the empire and coronation at Rome. In 1111 he forced the pope to concede by imprisoning him. Synods at Rome and Vienne in 1112, however, repudiated lay investure again.

The compromise settlement was finally effected during the pontificate of Calixtus II (1119–1124), elected at Cluny and consecrated at Vienne. Renewing the policy of Hildebrand, he excommunicated Henry, ratified the prohibition of lay investiture at Rheims in 1120, and secured at Worms in 1122 a *Concordat* between imperial and papal parties. By this compromise agreement, the pope retained the right to deliver the ring and crozier in all churches of the empire, but granted to the emperor the right to hold all elections to all bishoprics and abbeys in his presence without simony or any kind of corruption. Symbols of temporal power (the rod or scepter) were to be delivered by the emperor. The Ninth Ecumenical (First Lateran) Council in 1123 affirmed the *Concordat* of Worms. However, the *Concordat* in no way settled once for all the problem of the church and the state. The struggle in England between Henry II and Thomas Beckett offers clear witness of that.

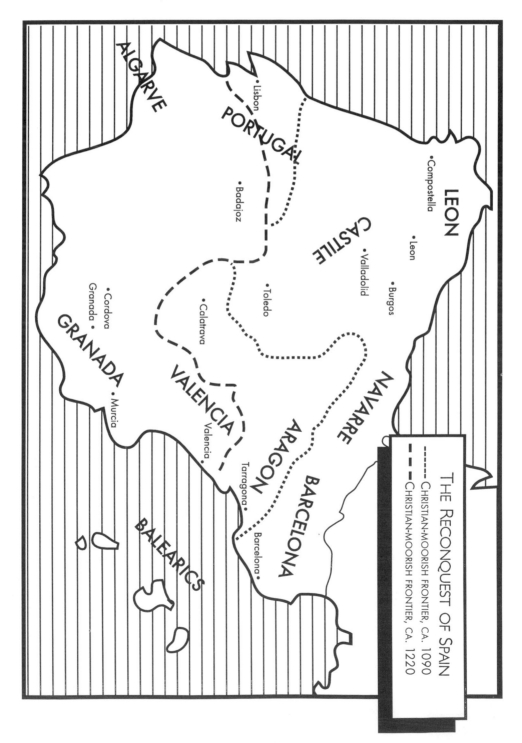

THE RECONQUEST OF SPAIN

------- CHRISTIAN-MOORISH FRONTIER, CA. 1090

┄┄┄┄ CHRISTIAN-MOORISH FRONTIER, CA. 1220

Chapter 42

The Churches of Europe

The late eleventh, twelfth, and thirteenth centuries will probably be remembered more for the crusades which began in 1095 than for anything else. Nonetheless, some other developments were taking place in every part of Europe which had equal or even greater importance for the future of Christianity.

In England the Normans sought to effect hegemony over both state and church, but met effective resistance from the archbishops of Canterbury. The murder of Thomas Beckett in 1170 tilted the balances of power decidedly toward the church.

In France the Normans, a rising power in Europe during the tenth century, helped to revitalize the church, badly depressed with the collapse of the Carolingian kingdom. After a long eclipse the monarchy revived about 1030, and feudal barons, in this climate of Cluniac reform, began to found monasteries and colleges and to turn their proprietary churches over to religious houses. The monastic life so well represented by Cluny and the Cistercians was looked to as the prescription for all ills. Royal reassertion of Carolingian rights to appoint bishops and abbots and to claim revenue from the church, however, brought inevitable conflict with the Gregorian reform.

In Germany the emperors adhered to the spirit of the Concordat of Worms for a time, but Frederick I Barbarossa (1152–1190) returned to earlier policies of imperial dominance, thus setting up an inevitable conflict with the papacy.

In Spain Christianity, which had not fared badly under Islamic rule, enjoyed a resurgence during the eleventh century as the kingdoms of Castile, Aragon, and Navarre came into existence. A crusade organized by Pope Innocent III (1198–1216) initiated the final liberation of the Spanish peninsula from Muslim rule. Ecclesiastical reorganization went hand in hand with the reconquest.

In Scandinavia the Gregorian reforms took effect, partly under Cistercian influence, as evangelization continued. Christianization also continued in the Balkans.

England

Relations between church and crown dominated during this period as the Normans imposed their regime. During the later Saxon period, the church had declined. Edward the Confessor (1042–1066), though saintly, had his heart in Normandy, where he had spent his early years. The problems that plagued the church elsewhere—clerical concubinage, simony, ignorance—also plagued the church in England. The Normans, therefore, faced the challenge of helping a failing church.

William the Conqueror (?1028–1087) brought experience as a reformer. The illegitimate son of Duke Robert I (d. 1035), he struggled to win and keep control of the duchy. Once secure, however, he presided over a continuing revival, organizing the church under strong bishops, all of aristocratic background. Like the Frankish kings, he founded and used monasteries in his reform efforts. Especially notable was the famous Abbey of Bec, founded by Herluin and consecrated by Archbishop Mauger of Rouen, uncle of William, in 1041. Bec supplied the first two archbishops of Canterbury appointed after the conquest, Lanfranc (1070–1089) and Anselm (1093–1109), in addition to numerous other notable bishops, as well as Pope Alexander II (1061–1073), who gave his blessing to the conquest in 1066.

William moved quickly to normanize the church as well as civil affairs. He deposed several bishop and abbots by canonical process. For implementation of his reform he made a very wise selection in appointing Lanfranc as archbishop of Canterbury, for Lanfranc considered loyalty to William a cardinal principle. An Italian, born and educated at Pavia, he entered Bec just a year after its founding and became prior in 1045. In 1063 William appointed him Abbot of St. Stephen's, Caen, one of two monasteries he founded as an act of penance for marrying within prohibited degrees, a punishment Lanfranc negotiated with Rome. Especially adept at organization, he deliberately sought by his replacement of Saxon with Norman bishops and abbots to bring the English church into line with the reforms of Gregory VII. He, however, did not fully implement the Gregorian decrees. Although he took action against simony and clerical immorality, he did not oppose lay investiture, doubtless because of William I's opposition. William learned to trust him implicitly. During the king's many absences, he placed in the hands of Lanfranc and two Norman bishops the management of political affairs. When Norman nobles rebelled against William in 1075, Lanfranc called out the English militia to restore order.

Lanfranc did not succeed everywhere in efforts to reorganize. He ran into trouble with Thomas, the archbishop of York, who refused to recognize the supremacy of Canterbury and tried to impose on other dioceses his own authority. Lanfranc's effort to establish headship over the church throughout England, Wales, Scotland, Ireland, and the northern islands likewise proved abortive. Further, the English clergy did not concede to demands for celibacy. In most of his plans, however, he proved effective. He replaced Anglo-Saxon church law with the new canon law put together on the continent. He reshaped monasteries on the best continental models, compiling his own *Monastic Constitutions*. Although the English church cooperated with the reform on the continent, William the Conqueror rejected Gregory VII's demand for fealty about 1080 and advised Lanfranc to ignore repeated requests to come to Rome to receive instruction.

Normanization under William did not mean exact imitation of the patterns of the Norman church. In England William recruited bishops from the monasteries rather than from the aristocracy. Four other bishops and twenty-two abbots came from Norman monasteries to work in England. William left a few Anglo-Saxons in place. The most notable of these were Ethelwig, Abbot of Evesham, and Wulfstan, a monk and bishop of Worcester (1062–1095). Wulfstan assisted William the Conqueror against the rebellious barons in 1075 and William II against both the barons and the Welsh. Although caught in the middle between Lanfranc and the bishop of York, he assisted the former in suppressing the slave trade between England and Ireland.

The cordial relations between the crown and the see of Canterbury did not last long under the next king and his appointee as archbishop of Canterbury. William Rufus (1087–1100) quickly incurred the condemnation of the church for simony and poor episcopal appointments. When Lanfranc died in 1089, he waited four years before appointing a successor in order to collect the revenues of Canterbury for his treasury. When he did select someone, he made a poor choice in Anselm, who held extreme views about the superiority of spiritual to temporal authority. He believed that no bishop should express obedience by doing homage to a king, specifically one who flaunted his contempt for religion, his greed, and his homosexuality as William Rufus did. In 1097 relations between the two became so strained that Anselm had to flee to Europe. Anselm reached Rome in April 1098, where he refused to receive the pallium from the imperial appointee Clement III (1080–1099), supporting instead Urban II (1088–1097).

Anselm's struggle resumed under Henry I (1100–1135), who defeated and imprisoned his brother Robert and inspired the murder of William Rufus, also his brother, in August of 1100. Although Henry did much to secure order in his dominion, he exacerbated tensions already existing between himself and the church. He recalled Anselm from exile, and the latter gave hasty approval to his coronation by the bishop of London and performed his marriage to the Princess Matilda of Scotland. When Henry renewed the practice of investiture, however, the saintly archbishop challenged him. In 1103 Henry sent Anselm into exile for the second time. After Pope Pascal II (1099–1118) agreed to confirm previous investitures if Henry would give up the right to continue the practice, he recalled Anselm (1106). At a council held at Westminster in 1107 he relinquished the privilege formally.

Theobald also had a stormy relationship with the crown during his tenure as archbishop of Canterbury (1138–1161). Appointed to the position only after Pope Innocent II (1130–1143) had refused to approve a "translation" of Stephen's brother, Henry of Blois, from the see of Winchester, he hesitated initially to decide between the claims of Henry's daughter Matilda and Stephen, whose claim was not ironclad, but finally crowned Stephen in 1141. Like Lanfranc and Anselm, a monk of the Abbey of Bec (prior 1127–1137; abbot, 1137–1138), he operated under a double restriction during much of his

archepiscopal reign. As a consolation for refusing to name him archbishop of Canterbury, Innocent II appointed Henry papal legate, a position above the See of Canterbury, and Theobald did not hold the position until 1150, when, evidently by insistence of Bernard of Clairvaux, Eugenius III (1145–1153) appointed him to it. As a result, Theobald had to battle Henry over the appointment of William as archbishop of York, which he opposed, and over questions of the jurisdictions of the monks of Christ Church, Canterbury. When Theobald disobeyed a command not to attend the Synod of Rheims in 1148, Stephen seized his property and exiled him. Pope Eugenius, however, put England under an interdict and forced Stephen to concede quickly. In 1152 Theobald refused to crown Stephen's son, Eustace, and had to flee to Flanders. After his recall, nonetheless, he reconciled Stephen with Henry of Anjou. On Stephen's death in 1154 he crowned the latter as King Henry II (1154–1189) and recommended Thomas Becket as chancellor. Becket succeeded him as archbishop of Canterbury when he died in 1161.

Becket had served Henry so effectively as Chancellor of the Exchequer that he seemed to the king a natural choice for archbishop. As chancellor, Becket affected a grand style which all the princes of Europe envied and had developed an intimate relationship with Henry, and his policies often favored Henry's interests rather than the church's. But when elected archbishop, he warned the king that he had lost a friend and gained an enemy. Thenceforth, he adopted a very austere lifestyle and took a strong stand against Henry's policies on taxation. In 1163 their relations reached an explosive point when Henry required bishops to sanction beforehand a set of articles, the Constitutions of Clarendon, designed, among other things, to transfer the trial of clergy accused of crimes to secular courts. Becket refused to give his approval. Henry then proceeded to subject him to a series of reprisals, including a demand for a huge sum of money. When

Thomas refused, the king required a council of barons and bishops held at Northampton to pass sentence on him. In 1164 Thomas, however, escaped to France, staying first in a Cistercian monastery at Pontigny and, when Henry threatened to expel all Cistericans from England, in a Benedictine monastery at Sens under special protection of the king of France. Becket appealed to Alexander III (1159–1181), but he evidently got limited help from him, because the pope was too embroiled in his own troubles. From exile Becket excommunicated two bishops who had signed the Constitutions of Clarendon and threatened an interdiction unless the king would give full satisfaction before November 2, 1170. This threat succeeded. Henry and Becket made peace at Freteval, near Tours, July 22. Becket returned to Canterbury December 1, 1170, where the people acclaimed him. Shortly afterwards, however, Henry, in a fit of exasperation, wondered aloud in the presence of four warlike knights—Sir Reginald Fitz-Urse, Sir William de Tracy, Hugh de Moreville, and Richard le Bret—whether no one would rid him of "the insults of this lowborn and turbulent priest." On Tuesday, December 29, 1170, the four rode to Canterbury, seized Becket at the altar as he performed Mass, and slew him. They left crying, "King's men! King's men!"

Henry was to rue his hasty words, for nothing could have shifted the balance of power so rapidly as a martyrdom. Excommunicated by the people, he paid a heavy price for reconciliation at Avranches in Normandy on May 22, 1172: (1) abrogation of the Constitutions of Clarendon, (2) restoration of all rights and possession to the Church of Canterbury, and (3) undertaking of a three years' crusade to Jerusalem or Spain at the request of the pope and supporting of two hundred knights in the Holy Land. On July 12, 1174, depressed by disasters and the rebellion of his wife and son, Henry even made a pilgrimage to the tomb of Becket.

The long conflict between Church and Crown eased during the reign of Richard I (1189–1199), in part because the latter had little interest in anything except the Third Crusade (1189–1192) and in part because he secured the appointment of his principal assistant during the crusade, Hubert Walter, as archbishop of Canterbury (1193–1205). Walter served Richard and John (1199–1216) as Henry II had wished Becket would have served him. As justiciar, he governed England during Richard's absence to fight in wars with France (1194–1198). He made himself unpopular by financial demands he made on behalf of the king. Protests from his own monks at Canterbury forced him to resign the justiciarship in 1198, but he resumed the office when John became king a year later.

Church-Crown tensions heated up again even before a new archbishop assumed the chair at Canterbury. On Hubert Walter's death in 1205 John intended to appoint his secretary the bishop of Norwich, but monks at the cathedral, who held the formal right of election, chose instead one of their own. The resulting stalemate opened the way for the powerful Pope Innocent III (1198–1216) to appoint Cardinal Stephen Langton, with whom he had developed a friendship while they taught together at the University of Paris. John, however, refused to accept the nomination and prevented Langton from receiving any revenues or even landing in England until 1213. In the interim he resided at Pontigny. Pope Innocent placed England under an interdict forbidding services in all parish churches in 1208. John retaliated by seizing church property. The pope then threatened to have the king of France take over the Kingdom of England. Finally, on May 15, 1212, John surrendered the Kingdoms of England and Ireland to the pope and received them back in return for homage and an annual tribute. John had finally had to concede what William the Conqueror had avoided—submission to Rome.

Archbishop Langton (1206–1228) did not take as strong a stand against the king as some predecessors had. Although he seems to have played some part in the framing of Magna Carta which the barons forced on Henry at Runnymede June 15, 1215, his role was probably that of mediator rather than originator. His name heads the list of counselors whom John professed to follow. The action, whatever it was, earned him a suspension from his archbishopric and a period of exile by Pope Innocent III, who bitterly opposed Magna Carta. He could not resume his position until after Innocent's death in 1216. Subsequently he upheld the privileges of his see, but he also protected the interests of Henry III against rebellious barons, at one point, in 1224, ordering the bishops to take over the most important royal castles from the barons.

Magna Carta represented in many ways an epitome of a long struggle. Although the document spoke mainly of baronial rights, its first article guaranteed that the Church of England "may be free and enjoy its liberties and rights unimpaired." Probably, the church was the one body which could prevent the monarchy from tyranny. A powerful king could seize property from, imprison, or execute barons without a lot of quibble, but he could not do the same to bishops.

France

Reform and revitalization of the church in France went on without much assistance or challenge from a monarchy badly weakened by the collapse of the Carolingian Kingdom and the onset of feudalism as a consequence of the Viking invasions. During the tenth century, France had become a melange of provinces in which great vassals fought for territory. Little by little the Capetians shoved aside what remained of the Carolingian dynasty. Although they were deplorably weak themselves for many years, by the last part of the eleventh century Philip (1060–1108) shrewdly took advantage of the weakness of competitors and the support of bishops to advance his cause. He seized revenues of vacant sees and unblushingly took money for appointments. As Gregorian reforms reached into his domain, he fiercely fought for his right to nominate bishops and abbots. He agitated Gregory VII (1073–1085) by overlooking brigandage of petty barons who held his own estates in fief. In 1092 he was excommunicated by Pope Urban II for his abduction of Bertrada, wife of the count of Anjou, and bigamous marriage to her. His bishops, however, supported him because of their interest in a stable monarchy over against feudal anarchy. In 1104 Paschal II absolved him on pretense of separation from Bertrada. Although Philip's successors did not play a prominent role on the European stage, by the end of the twelfth century they had laid down a solid base on which they could build. Basically they pursued two goals: recovery of their authority over the royal domain and then the large autonomous fiefs and opposition to expansion in France by the Norman-Angevin kings of England. They depended heavily on the loyalty of the episcopate and the monasteries.

One of the eminent figures in this regard was Suger (ca. 1081–1151), the Abbot of St.-Denis, near Paris. Born of humble parentage about 1081, he entered St.-Denis at age ten as a fellow student with the future King Louis VI (1108–1137). From 1106 onwards he took an active part in affairs at St.-Denis. Sent frequently by the king on embassies to the papal Curia, he was returning from a visit with Pope Callistus II (1119–1124) when elected Abbot of St.-Denis. Throughout much of his career he served as an adviser to kings, first Louis VI and then Louis VII. During the latter's absence from France on the Second Crusade (1147–1152), he was one of the regents, an office he discharged so well that, on his return, Louis honored him with the title of "Father of the Country." He is best remembered today, of course, for the architecture of the new church of St.-Denis, a forerunner of Gothic.

Louis VII (1137–1180) found it advantageous to throw his weight behind the Gregorian reforms as they gained wider acceptance. Genuinely devout, he offered Becket protection from Henry II, inviting conflict with him as a result.

Philip Augustus (1180–1223), creator of a strong monarchy, however, revived old Carolingian attitudes and asserted his rights vis-à-vis the church, as he moved France toward the commanding position it would hold in Europe from the thirteenth century on. Of great importance was the founding of the University of Paris near the end of the twelfth century.

The story of the church in France at this period cannot be ended without some word about Cluny and the Cistercians. Although their general story was told in an earlier chapter, both had such a profound impact on the period under discussion, 1050–1200, they deserve further comment. Cluny reached the zenith of its influence during the long abbacy of Hugh (1049–1109). Hugh's successor, Pons (1109–1132), created discord and open conflict at Cluny itself which caused irreparable damage to its work. Although it righted itself under Peter the Venerable (1132–1156), it yielded leadership in monastic reform to the Cistercians, who came into their own with Bernard of Clairvaux (abbot, 1115–1153).

Under Hugh Cluny extended its sway throughout Europe—France, Spain and Portugal, Italy, Switzerland, Liège and Flanders, England, and even the Byzantine Empire—but its main impact always was its country of origin. Noreen Hunt has cited several reasons for its success. Among general trends favoring monasticism were: unrest and dissatisfaction with the world, religious benefits monasteries were thought to provide, a general feeling that monasticism benefitted society, political movements such as the Norman conquest or the Spanish reconquest, openness for dissemination of ideas, papal and episcopal encouragement, the drive to reform the church, and, more pragmatically, as a way of getting rid of unwanted property. Cluny, however, had other factors in its favor: location away from areas attacked by the Vikings but yet in the mainstream of north-south European trade routes, long tenures of the first six outstanding abbots, a definite program to offer from the beginning,

features such as the liturgy which appealed to masses of people, appeal to the laity, both lay and clerical patronage, papal patronage, and outstanding Cluniac monks who filled important positions throughout Europe. Confirmation of the dynamic of the movement itself, the Cluniacs themselves did not push their expansion.

The Cistercians doubtless rode the same wave which carried the Cluniacs. While Cluny was toppling under the weight of its success, along came Citeaux and Bernard. Bernard himself had much to do with putting the Cistercians in the forefront of the reform movement. On the negative side, of course, he attacked extravagances in architecture, liturgy, and lifestyle. One of the sad flaws in his own story, as a matter of fact, may be the harshness of his criticisms when mirrored against the gentleness of Peter the Venerable's replies and the humbleness of his reactions. Already having to bring peace to a badly divided monastery, Peter acknowledged the correctness of Bernard's judgments and applied the medicine of Clairvaux. Though not equal to Bernard in gifts of leadership and wisdom, he possessed qualities Bernard did not have, for example, as reflected in sympathy for Abelard and Heloise and in his abilities as a diplomat.

On the positive side, Bernard had no peer in influence and impact. After a few years struggling to build the monastery at Clairvaux, he emerged as the spiritual leader *par excellence*. In 1128 he served as secretary for the Synod of Troyes and obtained recognition of rules for the newly formed Order of Knights Templar, dedicated to the protection of pilgrims in the Holy Land. He helped secure the election of Innocent II (1130–1143) as pope in a struggle with antipope Anacletus II (1130–1138). Not surprisingly, Innocent showered the Cistercians with favors. In 1145 he secured the election of a Cistercian as Pope Eugenius III (1145–1153), further enhancing the order's standing. At this pope's request he preached the Second Crusade, which, sadly, turned out to be a fiasco, to Bernard's bitter disappointment. He led attacks on Abelard (1079–1142) and Henry of Lausanne (d. after 1145), leader of one of many twelfth century sects. At the death of Bernard in 1153 the Cistercians numbered 288 houses. By 1200 their numbers increased to 529. In the thirteenth century they grew to 671. Thereafter, they increased slowly until the Reformation of the sixteenth century to 738, when they lost all of their possessions in England and Scotland, Denmark, Sweden, and Norway. From the mid-twelfth century on, they left a powerful testimony of the growing importance of French Christianity in the world.

Germany

Feudalism filtered into Germany later than in France and was showing its face during the twelfth century in constant struggles between emperors and barons. In the minds of both emperors and common people, however, the vision of a restored Roman or Carolingian Empire remained strong. The two greatest emperors of the twelfth and thirteenth centuries—Frederick Barbarossa (1152–1190) and Frederick II (1212–1250)—intended to restore their control over Italy and with that the papacy. In consequence clashes between papacy and empire constitute the heart of German ecclesiastical history at this time.

Following the death of Henry V (1106–1125), the first two emperors—Lothair II of Saxony (1125–1137) and Conrad III of the House of Hohenstaufen (1138–1152)—stayed within the lines set by the Synod of Worms in 1122. With the death of Henry the crown shifted from the Salian line to Saxons who had supported Rudolph of Swabia and Gregory VII against Henry IV. Throughout his life Lothair held firm to the ecclesiastical party against Henry IV and Henry V. When elected emperor, therefore, he declined to interfere in choice of clergy, and the bishops used their freedom to strengthen their own party. He insisted on Roman approval of all appointments. Papal legates went about Germany freely settling disputes and holding synods and councils.

As imperial power was withdrawn from Rome, however, it left an opening for powerful Italian families, notably the Pierleoni and Frangipani. The Pierleoni dominated in the choice of Callistus II (1119–1124), the Frangipani in that of Honorius II (1124–1130). Conflict between the two resulted in another papal schism in 1130. Because the Pierleoni family claimed a majority in the College of Cardinals, they secured the election of Anacletus, son of Pierleone. Innocent II (1130–1143) was elected first but by a minority of the College. With the help of the Normans Anacletus seized control of Rome and drove Innocent out of the city. He had to flee to France, where he obtained help from Bernard of Clairvaux and Peter the Venerable. Acknowledged as the legitimate pope in both France and England, Innocent enlisted the help of the Emperor Lothair, who turned a deaf ear to Anacletus and conducted Innocent and Bernard to Rome with armed force. On June 4, 1133 the grateful pope placed the imperial crown on Lothair's head. Lothair had to return a second time to liberate Rome from Anacletus, who, with the help of Roger, a Norman duke in southern Italy, and party of the rival emperor, Conrad III, took control of Rome again. Bernard returned to Rome again to strengthen Innocent's position. Anacletus died in 1138 and the Second Lateran Council in 1139 formally announced the end of the schism, but war broke out soon afterwards between Innocent and Roger II. Roger took Innocent prisoner, but released him when he confirmed Roger as king of Sicily.

Conrad pursued the same policies as Lothair as he initiated the Hohenstaufen line, which occupied the German throne until 1254. One of the most worthy popes of the twelfth century, Eugenius III (1145–1153), held the Chair of Peter at this time. A protege of Bernard of Clairvaux, he wore the rough shirt Cistercians wore under his purple. Unfortunately the revolt led by Arnold of Brescia forced him to spend most of his time in exile. Preaching a doctrine of apostolic poverty, Arnold persuaded the Roman people to rise up and expel the pope. His effort at setting up a new republic, however, failed. In 1154 he was banished from Rome and shortly afterwards hanged by order of the Emperor Frederick I.

Although he could lend the church powerful support like this, Frederick (1152–1190) had a very different view of his rights both in civil and religious matters. He envisioned his role as that of Charlemagne, whom he had canonized in 1166, or Otto the Great. Although he did not claim a right to summon councils or to impose forms of worship, he considered himself supreme in all external acts of government within his realm and thus violated both the spirit and the letter of the Concordat of Worms. He appointed and deposed bishops, resolved disputes in elections and other controversies, and prohibited appeals to Rome. The crisis of the papacy under his predecessors also revived opportunities for the emperor to intervene once more in affairs of the papacy.

Frederick met a match in the only Englishman ever elected pope, Nicholas Breakspear. Probably the son of a cleric attached to St. Albans, he studied in France and entered the Augustinian monastery of St. Rufus, near Avignon, where he became abbot in 1137. On a mission to Rome he was retained by Eugenius III, who recognized his gifts, and appointed cardinal bishop of Albano sometime before 1150. Soon thereafter, Eugenius sent him to Scandinavia, where he helped to reform and reorganize the churches of Sweden and Norway. Elected Pope Hadrian IV in 1154, he demanded full homage from Frederick Barbarossa before agreeing to crown him emperor. As the first condition of coronation, Hadrian demanded that Barbarossa surrender Arnold, with which the emperor complied. When the latter failed to follow the expected customs due the pope, Hadrian refused to give the kiss of peace until he did. Later he precipitated a quarrel with Barbarossa when he claimed that the emperor held his crown as a *beneficium*,

fief, from the pope. Following Hadrian's death, this issue flared into a full blown controversy.

A disputed election furnished Frederick I the pretence he needed to intervene again in Italy. Roland Bandinelli, a distinguished canon law expert from Bologna and counselor of Hadrian IV in his contest with the crown, was elected by a large majority as Alexander III. The emperor's party, however, insisted that the electoral decree of Nicholas II required a unanimous vote and elected Cardinal Octavian as Victor IV (1159–1164). Victor immediately took control of the Vatican. When both appealed to the emperor, he immediately convened a Synod at Pavia in 1160 to decide the case. The partisan gathering sided with Octavian and excommunicated Alexander. France, Spain, and England sided with Alexander, who took refuge in France for three years (1162–1165). Germany, Hungary, Bohemia, Norway, and Sweden supported Victor. Italy was divided. When Victor died in April, 1164, Alexander III got the backing of the Lombard league and in September, 1165 returned to Italy and took possession of Rome. In November, 1166 Frederick crossed the Alps, captured Rome, and installed Pascal III (1164–1168), already elected pope after Victor's death. Unfortunately for Frederick, the "Roman fever" struck his army and he suffered a powerful defeat at the hands of the Lombard league at Pavia in September, 1167. After the death of Pascal III in 1168, the schism collapsed, though schismatic cardinals elected two more successors—Callistus III (1168–1178) and Innocent III (1179–1180)—and continued the struggle for ten more years. Forsaken by his strongest ally, Henry the Lion, Frederick lost a bloody battle to the Lombards near Legano, May 29, 1176. Emperor and pope effected a reconciliation at Venice in front of St. Mark's Church on July 24, 1177.

The Peace of Venice recognized Alexander as the legitimate pope and remanded Callistus to an abbey. It acknowledged Beatrice as Frederick's legal wife and his son Henry as king of the

Romans. It restored Rome and the *patrimonium* to the pope but recognized Spoleto, the Romagna, and Ancona as part of the empire.

After an exile of ten years, Alexander reentered Rome March 12, 1178. During Lent, 1179 he convened the Third Lateran (Eleventh Ecumenical) Council to ratify the settlement and deal with certain evils caused by the long schism. Most important among the decisions of the Council was establishing of the policy that popes would be elected by the College of Cardinals by a two-thirds majority. In addition, the council required bishops to be at least thirty years of age, checked extravagances of prelates on visitations, ordered clergy to dismiss concubines, decreed that clergy guilty of unnatural license be expelled from the priesthood and confined to convents, and laid the grounds for a crusade against the heretics of southern France. Soon after this council, Alexander was again driven into exile, dying at Civita Castellana, August 30, 1181.

The four popes between Alexander III and Innocent III held short tenures, but they were not, as often depicted, weak and inept or chosen on account of their compliance toward the emperor. All persisted with the line taken by Alexander. What now occupied the attention of both popes and emperor, however was the Third Crusade. In 1187 Saladin occupied Jerusalem, diverting the attention of Pope Urban III (1185–1187) away from a dispute with Frederick Barbarossa precipitated by Philip, the archbishop of Cologne. His successors, Gregory VIII, who had only two months to serve, and Clement III (1187–1191), healed the rift and put the papacy back in the good graces of the emperor. Frederick, who had always had a fascination with the East, pledged to recover the holy City on March 27, 1188. German princes joined him. Having accompanied his uncle Conrad III (1138–1152) on the disastrous second crusade, he took great precaution. He wrote the king of Hungary, Emperor Isaac II Angelus (1185–1195), and Sultan of Iconium requesting unmolested passage through their

lands. He also wrote Saladin notifying him that if he did not give up the lands seized he could expect war within a year. Saladin replied in a polite but boastful letter accepting the challenge. Frederick left the reins of empire in the hands of his son Henry VI, already designated to succeed him (1190–1197). Frederick left Ratisbon early in May 1189 at the head of 20,000 knights. En route the army ran into all kinds of obstacles— from the Bulgarians, Emperor Isaac Angelus, and Turkish bands. Frederick himself drowned trying to ford the river Salef in Cilicia on horseback. He was buried in the Church of St. Peter at Antioch.

Henry VI (1190–1197) contrasted sharply with his father in virtually every way. Small and gaunt, he had no taste for the military. His chief interest was learning, not sports or arms. Yet he shared Frederick's political outlook. Henry had allied the German Empire with the Normans by marriage to Constance, the aunt and heiress of the king of Sicily, on October 29, 1184. Much of his reign, however, was marked by a struggle with Tancred, count of Lecce, over control of Sicily. The Germans suffered a stinging defeat during the winter of 1191–1192, but the situation reversed in 1194 after Tancred died at Palermo on February 20. By December Henry had conquered Sicily and was crowned king on Christmas day in the cathedral of Palermo. He went out of his way to conciliate the Norman populace. Henry inherited rather cordial relations with pope Clement III (1187–1191), whose desire for a crusade shaped his entire policy. He developed strained relations with Celestine III (1191–1198), however, first of all for his imprisonment of Richard the Lionhearted of England. Richard had fallen into the hands of Prince Leopold of Austria. Henry VI ransomed him and demanded that he give up his alliance with Tancred, lend aid in conciliating the Guelfs (the chief contestants of Hohenstaufen rule in Germany), acknowledge himself as vassal of the emperor, and pay a large sum to ransom himself. For the last Celestine excommunicated him. Henry's interference in appointment of bishops also angered the pope. Henry avoided a complete break with the papacy only by preparations for a crusade in 1195. Shortly after the fleet of crusaders set sail, however, Henry contracted a violent fever and died on September 28, 1197 at age thirty-two. His death marked a significant turn in the affairs of the papacy, for a few months later Innocent III succeeded Celestine and raised the office to the very apogee of power.

Spain

Christians retained a small toehold in Asturias in northwest Spain when the Muslims took over the peninsula. In 718 they fought off a small Muslim army and set up a kingdom under the leadership of Pelayo, a high official from Roderic's court at Toledo. It was from here, over the next several centuries, that they prepared for the reconquest. Help in this came in the purported discovery of the body of the apostle James which led to the establishment of a city, Santiago de Compostela, in 866. Compostela grew into an international shrine drawing pilgrims from all over Europe. By the eleventh century the kingdoms of Leon, Castile, Aragon, and Navarre had emerged. Navarre lay wide open to French political and cultural influence. In consequence, the monks of Cluny entered Navarre and Castile at the invitation of Sancho "the Great" (970–1035). Cluny's reports to Rome led Pope Alexander II to propose the first crusade in 1063 to reconquer the territory taken over by the Muslims. Ferdinand of Castile leaped to the occasion, but it remained for his son Alfonso VI of Leon and Castile (1072–1109) to recapture Toledo in 1085 and to begin the last phase of the conquest. Although he suffered reversals at the hands of a reinforced Muslim army, Ruy Diaz de Bivar, El Cid, Spain's epic hero, inspired continuing efforts, especially after the appearance of "The Poem of El Cid" around 1150. The reconquest reached its conclusion under Alfonso VIII (1158–1214) and

Ferdinand III (1217–1252) of Castile. The latter reconsecrated the great mosque of Cordoba as a cathedral and sent troops across the straits to Morocco to place the Christian emblem over the home of the infidel. Only Granada remained under Moslem control when he died in 1252.

Alexander II (1061–1073) sent Hugh Candidus to Spain as his legate on a mission to reform the church, replacing the Mozarabic rite by the Roman. Concern about Adoptionism may have precipitated this action, but there was also an effort to standardize and to bring Spain under papal suzerainty. Gregory VII (1073–1085) picked up and extended the claim. Although he met opposition from Alfonso VII of Castile, he imposed his will on Aragon, Navarre, and Catalonia. In 1085 Castile also accepted the Roman rite. Spain quickly placed itself fully in the Roman camp.

The reconquest opened the way for the construction of hundreds of churches and monasteries and their endowment with donations of immense tracts of land. The land granted to the Cathedral of Santiago de Compostela, for instance, extended twenty-four miles. To the archbishopric of Toledo Alfonso VI granted farmlands, houses, shops, and mills not only in Toledo but also in nine adjoining towns. The style of churches was mostly Romanesque, as developed in the Carolingian era and invading Spain by way of Provence. Cluny and the Cistercians both had an impact— Cluny with its rich ornamentation and Citeaux with its simplicity and austerity. The Cathedral of Santiago de Campostela, begun early in the twelfth century, is the prime example of the Cluniac pattern. Several monasteries, for example at Poblet and Silos, reflect Cistercian style. As early as the thirteenth century Gothic architecture filtered into Spain, notably in the cathedrals of Leon, Cuenca, Burgos, Toledo, Barcelona, and Mallorca. Later buildings also show mixed styles similar to those found in other countries. Muslim art, called *Mudejar*, also had some impact on Spanish churches, for example, the Church of

San Lorenzo at Shagun, dating from the late twelfth or early thirteenth centuries.

The Spanish kingdoms granted special favors to the clergy and monks. The clergy had personal and royal immunity, which exempted them from trial before ordinary courts and from taxation. Monasteries often possessed great amounts of land, buildings, mills, and other properties on the scale of great landowners. They employed many farm laborers, most of whom were Christian or Muslim serfs. They enjoyed control of their territory much as did the nobles, and they had an obligation to take part in war if circumstances required their help. They often counterbalanced the nobility and aided in the reconquest, contributions remembered often in Spanish churches. The number of monasteries in a district was an index of its prosperity.

The eleventh to the thirteenth centuries were a time of coordination and unification of church life in Spain. In 1085 Alfonso VI conquered Toledo and elevated it to an archbishopric. Under Alfonso VII the northwestern bishoprics submitted to Toledo. Early in the thirteenth century Franciscans and Dominicans entered Spain. Domingo de Guzman, founder of the Dominican Order, was a native of Calahorra. In 1232 Pope Gregory IX (1227–1241) entrusted the Inquisition to the Dominicans. In 1235 the bishop of Tarragona published the first instructions for inquisitors in Spain, drafted by Raymond de Peñafort, a trusted adviser of Gregory.

Under the archbishop of Toledo Don Rodrigo Ximenez de Rada (1170 or 1180–1247) Toledo became an important center of learning. Rodrigo (Roderick) encouraged translations into Castilian and Latin of the writings of Aristotle, Galen, and Euclid with commentary by Arab scholars. He also attracted to Toledo some notable foreign scholars such as Gerard of Cremona, Adelard of Bath, Hermann the Dalmatian and Hermann the German, Michael Scotus, and Albert de Retines. The mass of translation work done at Toledo helped to spread throughout Europe the influence of Eastern learning in such areas as astronomy, medicine, alchemy, mathematics, physics, logic, morals, politics, and other fields. Archbishop Roderick himself wrote the first general history of Spain, using not only Christian but also Arab sources. Originally writing in Latin, he translated the work into Castilian under the title *A History of the Goths*. Roderick also founded the first Spanish university, at Palencia, in 1212 or 1214. Salamanca and Valladolid followed next.

Scandinavia

The earliest efforts at evangelizing Scandinavia left some traces, but lasting effects came later, particularly with the missionaries sent from England. The more the rulers knew of Christianity, the more they insisted on the conversion of their subjects to it. Harald Bluetooth (ca. 950–985) imposed Christianity on Denmark. Sweyn Forkbeard (985–1014) resisted conversion until late in his reign, but Canute (1019–1035) became a strong advocate. Olaf imposed Christianity on Sweden about 1000 C.E. Norway held out the longest. Olaf Tryggveson (997–1000) used the sword to force Christianity on his people. His cousin Olaf (1016–1028), who became the national saint, followed suit. Although conversions were superficial, the next generation took Christianity to heart as the church gained power and its teachings filtered down to the masses.

The church in Scandinavia helped to organize each country, for the first laws regulated the duty of the people to the church and the clergy. Bishops served directly under the king in all three countries. Kings became national saints—Olaf in Norway, Canute in Denmark, and later Eric in Sweden. Harald Hardrada of Norway sternly rebuked Adalbert, archbishop of Hamburg-Bremen (1043–1072), when he pursued forcefully his papal commission as the metropolitan of all Scandinavia. In 1103 Eric secured from Pope Paschal II the right to establish the see of Lund as the Scandinavian metropolis, eclipsing the authority of Hamburg-Bremen once for all. Kings

expanded dioceses as a part of their efforts to organize the society—Sweyn Estrithson (1047–
1074) eight dioceses in Denmark, Olaf the Peace
King (1067–1093) four in Norway, and Eric five
in Sweden. Church and state went hand in hand.

During the twelfth century, Scandinavia
linked itself more closely to the rest of Christendom. Religious movements of Western Europe
entered and drew Scandinavians after them.
Denmark, Norway, and Sweden sent out a stream
of pilgrims, crusaders, and missionaries. Monasteries appeared. The papacy established stronger
ties. In 1152 Nicholas Breakspear, the papal
legate (later Pope Hadrian IV), founded an
archbishopric in Nidaros, Norway. In 1164 Pope
Alexander III made Uppsala the archbishopric of
Sweden, leaving Lund for Denmark.

In all three countries the church assisted the
monarchy in effecting peace and propagating law.
The archbishops of Lund, Nidaros, and Uppsala
took the lead in championing the church's claims.
In Sweden King Eric IX (1155–1160), the national saint, led an anticlerical party, but his grandson
Eric X softened the stand by accepting coronation
from the archbishop of Uppsala in 1210. In
Norway the church obtained a stunning concession from Earl Erling Crooked-Neck when Archbishop Eystein (Augustine) received the kingdom
as a fief, an increase in the immunities of the
church, and the deciding voice in disputed election of a successor. King Sverre (1184–1202),
however, reversed those concession and successfully defied Innocent III, insisting on the supremacy of the king. His son, Haakon III, however,
made peace with the church.

The Balkans

Christianity impressed itself little by little on
the mostly Slavic populace of the Balkans during
this period. Bohemia-Moravia, which held a
certain independence despite its ruler being a
vassal of the emperor of the Holy Roman Empire, received at least a taste of Christianity
during the ninth century, especially through the

work of Cyril and Methodius. Members of the
royal family distinguished themselves by their
commitment to Christian faith. At the beginning
of the tenth century churches sprang up in Bohemia as priests came from neighboring German
provinces. The establishment of the diocese of
Prague in 973–974 raised Bohemia to a new
level. Bohemia and a part of Poland were placed
under the jurisdiction of the archbishop of Mainz.
At about the same time two Benedictine monasteries, one for women at Prague about 967 and
the other for men in Brevnov (near Prague) about
992, initiated a spate of monastic foundations.
Monasteries played a critical role in the economic
development of the country.

As in Germany, so also in Bohemia and
Moravia the church depended entirely on lay authority. Kings appointed bishops and abbots, the
archbishop of Mainz consecrated them, and the
emperor confirmed the appointments. Bishops
had slight impact on affairs of the church, the
papacy even slighter. Priests usually married.
They did not enjoy special privileges or exemptions. Despite efforts of Adalbert, bishop of
Prague, martyred in 997 in Prussia, and of the
papacy to institute the Gregorian ideal, the Bohemian church went its own way until the middle
of the twelfth century. In 1143 it adopted the rule
of celibacy for priests, but it remained unenforced
into the thirteenth century. Henry Zdik, bishop of
Olomouc (d. 1151), attempted to support the reform but had little success. As the church grew,
it came into conflict with the rulers. A conflict between Henry Bretislav, bishop of Prague, and Bohemian Duke Frederick brought Frederick Barbarossa onto the scene, declaring the bishop of
Prague an "immediate" prince of the empire in
1187. In 1197, however, Premsyl Ottokar I
(1197–1130) retrieved the ducal office and ended
the secular authority of the bishop of Prague. In
1198 his status was elevated to the dignity of
king. During the thirteenth century, the church of
Bohemia gradually gained its freedom from lay
authority. With the support of Rome Andrew,

bishop of Prague, forced Ottokar to make considerable concessions for appointment and removal of clergy and for exercise of discipline in ecclesiastical matters.

In Poland Christianity got a firm boost from Boleslav III (1102–1138). He zealously pursued the evangelization of the heathen Slavs. To win over conquered peoples, he called on Otto, bishop of Bamberg, to help in evangelizing the East Pomeranians in 1124 and 1125 and the West Pomeranians in 1128. His enthusiasm for the church resulted in some improvements in ecclesiastical organization and aided it in the areas of education and morality. During the reign of Innocent III (1198–1216), Henry Kietlicz, archbishop of Gniezno, supported the pope in his efforts to introduce into Poland the same ecclesiastical organization and discipline which prevailed in the rest of the West. In 1215 he convened a synod in which the clergy agreed to maintain celibacy. Only gradually, however, did the princes yield their power in appointment of clergy. Little by little, they conceded to clergy the right to elect their bishops and released them from the jurisdiction of civil courts. Lesjek II (1202–1227) formally placed Poland under the authority of Rome.

After the conversion of the Pomeranians the only peoples who remained outside the fold were tribes of Letto-Lithuanian stock. These included the fierce Prussians and the Jadzwings or Yatvags. The brother of Leszek I, Conrad of Mazovia, determined to conquer them for the church and to make them Polish subjects. Despite enlisting support of Innocent III and having the crusade preached in Germany as well as Poland, Conrad's first efforts in 1219 and 1222 proved unavailing. After the Dobryzn Brotherhood he founded was almost annihilated in 1224, Conrad turned to the Teutonic Knights of St. Mary. This seasoned group conquered the main part of Western Prussia between 1234 and 1237. From that time on Polish princes backed the crusade. In 1283 the last Prussian leader, Skurdo, fled to Lithuania. The Prussians were either exterminated or assimilated into Christian societies, either of Germany or Poland. Their conversion, however, placed on the borders of Poland a dangerous German power, which, added to Lithuania, would prove extremely threatening in the future.

Hungary entered the family of Christian nations at the end of the tenth century. Stephen (997–1038) received baptism at the hands of Adalbert in Esztergom. He entered directly into negotiations with Pope Sylvester II (999–1003) to place Hungary directly under the papacy. August 15, 1000 he received the crown sent to him by Sylvester. He divided the kingdom into ten dioceses, each dependent on the diocese of Esztergom (Gran). In the early twelfth century, however, a second province was formed under the archbishopric of Kalocsa.

Under Ladislas I (1077–1095) Christianity obtained a major boost. He managed to make himself independent of both popes and emperors, but he secured the canonization of Stephen and his son Emeric. He fought successfully to incorporate the Cumans and the Patzinaks, blood relations of the Magyars, into the kingdom and the Christian faith. He took severe measures against those who resisted conversion or returned to paganism. In 1092 at Szabolcs he promulgated laws concerning religion that permitted priests to marry, regularized collection of tithes, and enacted penalties against serfs who worked on Sundays. The church, despite his independence, canonized Ladislas.

The Hungarian church was divided into two sections by language and by districts. One section followed the Latin liturgy of the Roman church, the other the Latin liturgy in Slavonic. Transylvania was separated from the rest of Hungary both ethnographically and politically.

Byzantium

A third period of anarchy followed the Macedonian Dynasty in the Byzantine Empire, lasting from 1025 until 1081. The Comneni took control of an empire severely reduced. Already having lost most of southern Italy to the Normans, in 1071 the Byzantines suffered a devastating defeat at Manzikert, which cost them most of Asia, at the hands of the Seljuk Turks. Ten years later, the latter captured Antioch. The Comneni, however, recovered much of the lost territory. In the Balkans the Slavic peoples asserted their independence with the help of Hungary. All of the Comneni were good soldiers and recovered much of the lost territory. What crushed the empire was the crusades.

Following the Turkish victory at Manzikert, Michael VII (Parapinaces) entreated Pope Gregory VII for help, promising the reunion of East and West. Hildebrand welcomed the prospect of reunion and proceeded to take steps to send assistance. However, by December of 1073 he had enlarged his response to the idea of a crusade which would deliver the Eastern Empire and restore access to the Holy Places in Jerusalem. His difficulties with Henry IV prevented him from carrying out his plan. It remained for Urban II (1088–1099) to carry through with the crusade, which began in 1095 and ended with the capture of Jerusalem on July 15, 1097. Urban responded to an appeal from Alexius I (1081–1118), sending legates to Piacenza, March 1–7, 1095 to beg Urban and all Christians to come to the aid of fellow Christians in the East. Although it began under more favorable auspices, the Second Crusade, 1146–1148, proved disastrous to the Eastern Empire and to the crusaders. The Third, 1189–1192, proved more successful in terms of Western recovery of the Holy Places, but it was costly and worsened relations between Greeks and Latins. Within twenty years the Fourth Crusade, 1202–1204, destroyed most of what remained of the Byzantine Empire as Latins set up a kingdom which lasted from 1204 until 1261. What remained of the Byzantine Empire was a small tract of land around Nicaea.

Turbulent as the period was, it led to the last flowering of Byzantine Orthodoxy, in which some significant developments in theology occurred. Seminal in this was Simeon the New Theologian (949–1022), a mystic and spiritual writer. In 977 he entered the Studios as a monk, but a few months later he moved to St. Mamas, also near Constantinople. Ordained a priest in 980, he became abbot a year later. Opposition, however, forced him to resign in 1005 and to go into exile in Asia Minor in 1009. Strongly christocentric and eucharistic in his theology, he assigned a central place to the vision of the Divine Light. He combined the contemplative tradition of Isaac of Nineveh (d. ca. 700) and the coenobitic tradition of Basil of Caesarea and Theodore of the Studios (759–826)

Michael Psellus (ca. 1019–ca. 1078) led a revival of Platonic philosophy. Imperial Secretary to Michael V (1041–1042) and Secretary of state to Constantine IX (1042–1054), he was appointed the first professor of philosophy at the newly founded University of Constantinople in 1045. In 1054 imperial suspicion of his activities caused him to enter a monastery. As soon as Constantine died, however, he returned to the court and took part in intrigues until 1072, when he fell into disfavor and obscurity. His *Chronograph* became an important source for the history of Byzantium from 976 to 1077. Later historians such as Anna Comnena and Zonaras made extensive use of it.

Anna Comnena (1083– after 1148), daughter of Alexius I Comnenus and Irene, was one of the earliest women historians and also one of the most outstanding Byzantine writers. After failing to secure the deposition of her brother John and installation of her husband as emperor, she retired to a convent and composed the *Alexiad*, a history of her father's reign, completed in 1148. Although eulogistic, the work contains critical comments about the crusaders.

Johannes Zonaras (12th century), a canonist and historian, retired from the imperial court during the reign of John II Comnenus (1118–1143) and spent the rest of his life in retirement. He wrote a highly regarded *Epitome of History* covering the period up to 1118. he also commented on Greek canon law.

Out of the "new theology" of Simeon emerged what was known as Hesychasm. Hesychasm reached its full flower in the writings of Gregory of Sinai, Nicephorus of Mount Athos, and Gregory Palamas during the fourteenth century. Hesychasts emphasized the Jesus Prayer as a means of securing "the union of the mind with the heart."

THE BALKANS IN THE THIRTEENTH CENTURY

Chapter 43

The Crusades

Scholars do not agree on the meaning and application of the word crusade. Hans Eberhard Mayer, professor of Medieval and Modern History at the University of Kiel, limits the use of the term to efforts to recover control of Jerusalem. Most other scholars take a broader view. Some would construe anything undertaken against Islam—the Byzantine campaigns of the second half of the tenth century, the reconquest of Spain, as well as the effort to recover the Holy Land—as crusades. Still others interpret the word to designate all Christian military endeavors to eradicate unbelief. Included in this definition would be the crusade against the Albigenses in southern France and several crusades in the northern parts of Europe, especially against the Prussians, the Wends, the Livonians, the Estonians, and the Finns during the twelfth and thirteenth century. According to either of these broader definitions, crusades were essentially evangelistic, concerned with propagation of the true faith.

The question which will always fascinate historians is how Europeans got caught up in such endeavors for nearly two centuries, or, using the broadest definition, three or four centuries. What caused the crusades? Many factors can be cited. (1) To some degree, Christians imitated Muslims, who had taken control of most of the Mediterranean world by Jihad, "Holy War." The concept came from the Old Testament, and Christians simply reversed its application. As Islam weakened, Christians seized the moment. It is perhaps significant that the first crusade to attract papal sponsorship was in Spain. Gregory VII (1073–1085), caught up in his effort to reform the church, seized the reins and sought to take advantage of the enthusiasm of Ferdinand of Castile. (2) The popes themselves deserve much credit for the fervor which ignited the crusaders. Indeed, they often had to cajole and threaten to keep crusades going. Urban II (1088–1099) stood far ahead of others in pushing the first crusade. Eugenius III (1045–1053) was a rather reluctant booster of the second, but Innocent III (1198–1216) had no bounds on his enthusiasm for crusades not only to win the Holy Land but to overcome unbelievers in Spain and the North as well. In the thirteenth century papal enthusiasm had to make up for growing reluctance to undertake these dangerous missions. Wise rulers acted with growing caution.

(3) A more immediate cause for the crusades to the East was the decay of the Byzantine Empire, leaving the West open to an attack from Muslim forces. (4) Correlative to that was the rise of the Seljuk Turks as a major power during the eleventh century. In 1088 Emperor Alexius I Comnenus (1081–1118) appealed to Robert of Flanders for help against them. Although the Eastern army remained disciplined, repeated attacks had worn it down and the Third Anarchy had weakened the government of the empire.

The West, of course, had other motives. (5) One was the sentiment for Holy Places and pilgrimages to them. So long as Westerners had free passage, they did not feel strong pressure for crusades to liberate them. By the late eleventh century the burgeoning power of Muslim forces made pilgrimages increasingly difficult. (6) At the same time Europeans were developing a consciousness of spiritual unity, a manifest destiny extending beyond the bounds of the European continent. They could use pent-up energies they aimed at one another to achieve a more noble mission. Heathen Huns and Northmen no longer distracted. (7) Many crusaders found promises of plenary indulgence for sins a powerful enticement. Laden with guilt, they could earn a clean slate and an eternal reward whether they lived or died. (8) Many others acted out of more mercenary motives. Crusaders, especially in the fourth crusade, laid claim to rich booty when they succeeded in capturing cities. Kings and merchants also benefited handsomely by new trading opportunities. (9) Some got caught up in the militant spirit of the age and love of war or were aroused by the desecrators of the Holy Land. Crusade preachers depicted atrocities committed by Muslims in intimate detail. The "righteous" had to overcome the "demonic."

The First Crusade, 1096–1099

At the Council of Placentia on March 7, 1095 the ambassador of Emperor Alexius put forth a plea to save Constantinople. Pope Urban II, however, deferred action until the Council of Clermont, November 18-27. What he preached on that occasion was not recorded, but some of his correspondence and later accounts give at least the gist of his sermons. The "barbarians" had invaded and ravaged the Eastern churches. Worse still, they had seized the Holy City adorned by Christ's passion and resurrection. In letters Urban urged caution about who should go. Monks and clergy would have to secure permission of their bishops.

The crusade proceeded in two stages. The first was led by Peter the Hermit (1050?–1115) and Walter the Penniless. Peter the Hermit was an electrifying preacher who overshadowed Pope Urban. These poorly armed and poor "crusaders" set out overland through Hungary and Bulgaria to Constantinople. Walter, leading chiefly a French contingent, reached Byzantium without too much trouble. Peter, who delayed at Cologne preaching, arrived later in July with Lorrainers, Rhinelanders, and South Germans as well as other Frenchmen. Some other groups never reached Constantinople. They were slaughtered in Hungary when they ravaged and looted. Some concentrated on attacking Jews in one town after another—Speyer, Worms, Mainz, Trier, and Cologne. When the contingents led by Peter and Walter began to plunder the suburbs around Constantinople, Emperor Alexius advised them to cross the Bosporus. They marched through Nicomedia to Civetot, where the Turks routed them on October 21, 1096. Only a handful survived to return to Constantinople, where Peter the Hermit had remained. The People's Crusade was over, but Peter joined the main group under Godfrey of Bouillon as they came through and went with them to Antioch. During the siege of Antioch in 1098, he attempted to flee but rejoined the crusade and entered Jerusalem with the victorious army. On his return to Europe he became prior of an Augustinian monastery which he had helped found.

The main crusade met with marked success. Led by Godfrey of Bouillon (d. 1100); Hugh of Vermandois, brother of the king of France; Bohemund of Taranto, the oldest son of Robert Guiscard, the Norman king; Raymond of Toulouse, who brought the largest contingent; Count Robert II of Flanders (1093–1111); Tancred, nephew of Bohemund; and a host of nobility, they won major victories at Nicaea on June 19, 1097, Dorylaeum on July 1, Antioch between October 1097 and June 3, 1098, and Jerusalem July 15, 1099. Godfrey, the hero of the campaign, was elected king of Jerusalem on July 22, 1099. The crusaders drenched Jerusalem in blood, hacking people down without respect to race or religion.

The victory produced universal jubilation in the West. Coinciding with the election of Paschall II, it incited many others to step forward and take the Cross, including William IX, the Duke of Aquitaine. Stephen of Blois and Hugh of Vermandois volunteered to go a second time. The bishops of Paris, Laon, and Soissons, and the archbishop of Besancon took the Cross. Unfortunately, the crusaders competed with one another for control of the territories they had conquered.

The Second Crusade, 1145–1149

The Latin conquest ran into a powerful opponent in Zengi, the Atabeg Amir of Mosul and Aleppo. Zengi preached Holy War from the time of his accession. His main objective was the Islamic City State of Damascus, which he had failed to conquer in 1130 and 1135. Unsuccessful there, he turned to attacks on Christian sites. In April 1143 the death of Emperor John II (1118–1143) as a result of a hunting accident opened the way for Zengi to capture Edessa after a siege of four weeks on Christmas eve 1144. Although Zengi was murdered in 1146, one of his sons, Nur ed-Din (1146–1174), gave the crusaders no respite.

News of the fall of Edessa caused a considerable stir in the West, but it did not precipitate an immediate flurry of crusading activity. The push for it may have come from King Louis VII (1137–1180), but he evidently thought in terms of a strictly French armed pilgrimage and not a crusade of the type mounted in 1095. A Frankish embassy and an Armenian delegation put in pleas with Eugenius III (1145–1153) before he issued the first crusading bull on December 1, 1145. It was Bernard of Clairvaux who served as go-between for the king to the pope. Out of this came an amended papal bull, issued March 1, 1146, in which, from the opening phrases, the pope asserted his right to direct the crusade just

as Urban II had done the First Crusade. Bernard himself kindled the flames with his preaching, at first in France but then also in Germany. From March on, he preached incessantly for months. The crusade would be a work of penance, indulgence an end in itself. The East had to be freed from the heathen, the crusader from sin. The day of salvation had arrived. To his credit, Bernard warned against persecution of the Jews. Before Emperor Conrad III (1138–1152) he depicted the final judgment and demanded to know on Christ's behalf what could he have done than he had already done. Conrad took the Cross, and his nephew and numerous nobles followed suit. In February 1147 Otto, bishop of Freising, joined Louis VII and Conrad.

The crusade turned into a fiasco. The German troops behaved so badly when they reached Constantinople that they alienated Emperor Manuel Comnenus (1143–1180). Roger II of Sicily further injured relations by seizing and destroying the centers of the Byzantine silk industry at Thebes and Corinth. Conrad went on ahead of the French forces and suffered a severe defeat at the hands of the Seljuk Turks near Dorylaeum at the end of October. The French suffered from strong anti-Byzantine feelings which already presaged the attack on Constantinople in 1204. Meantime, Louis and Emperor haggled over an agreement to restore Byzantine territory. Although both Conrad and Louis reached the Holy Land, they did not remain long. Conrad returned to Germany in 1148, Louis in 1149. Meantime, Bernard of Clairvaux, Suger of St. Denis, and Peter the Venerable began to speak of a true crusade to make amends for this one. Bernard wrote an apology for the failure of the Second Crusade, attributing it to human sinfulness and God's inscrutable judgment.

The Third Crusade, 1187–1192

The fiasco of the Second Crusade dampened the fervor of Europeans for a time. Frederick Barbarossa (1152–1190) had his hands full in

Italy with the Lombard League and in Germany with the Guelph Henry the Lion, Duke of Saxony and Bavaria. The successes of Saladin, however, were enough to put Europeans on notice again. In 1184–1185 a special embassy from Outremer notified Western rulers of the seriousness of the situation and that Jerusalem would fall if help did not come soon. Meeting with Pope Lucius III (1181–1185) and the emperor at Verona in November 1184, they obtained a promise of a crusade for 1186. Both Henry II of England and Philip Augustus of France assured them only of their good will. What changed hearts was the catastrophic defeat of Christian forces at Hattin in the summer of 1187. Urban III died on hearing the news. His successor Gregory VIII (1187), although pope only two months, played a decisive role in putting the crusade in motion. The first ruler to respond to Gregory's encyclical *Audita tremendi* was William II of Sicily, but he died shortly after dispatching fifty ships to Tripoli. Richard the Lionhearted, count of Poitou and the most chivalrous of Henry II's sons, took the cross first without securing Henry's approval. Frederick Barbarossa delayed until April 1198 before he agreed to go. He immediately laid careful plans to pass through Serbia, Hungary, Byzantium, and the Seljuk stronghold of Rum. He gave Saladin an ultimatum which he rejected. He departed Regensburg in May 1189 with the largest crusading army yet assembled. By April 1190 they moved into Seljuk territory and found the treaty the emperor had arranged with the Sultan Kilij Arslan II worthless. Near Iconium on May 18, 1190 they won a brilliant victory which forced the sultan to come to terms. Sadly, the emperor drowned on June 10, 1190 crossing the River Salef, and the German crusade broke down in confusion. Most of the crusaders headed for Cilician or Syrian ports and sailed for home. The rest marched to Antioch, where they buried the emperor's body after removing the bones which they hoped to carry to Jerusalem but had to bury in the Cathedral at Tyre instead. One important

sidelight was the founding of the Order of Teutonic Knights, a hospital order, in 1190.

The English and French crusade was delayed by a war which broke out between the two kingdoms (1188–1189) and by Richard the Lionhearted's rebellion against his father. Henry, however, died in July 1189 and Richard succeeded him as king (1189–1199). With peace restored on July 4, 1190 the thirty-two year old Richard and the twenty-five year old Philip Augustus departed from Vezelay. They improved their chances of arriving in the Holy Land with less attrition by sailing, Philip from Genoa and Richard from Marseilles. They met and wintered at Messina in Sicily. From here on they bickered constantly, though they united to capture Tyre and lower Saladin's profile. Richard achieved a victory over Saladin at Arsuf on September 7, 1190, but he never reached Jerusalem and was forced to sue for peace. Terms of the treaty, however, secured new freedoms for Christian pilgrims. Altogether, the crusade obtained much better results than the second one. The united forces of Outremer and the West ensured the survival of the crusader states for another century. Although no further help on this scale would come hereafter, Emperor Henry VI (1190–1197) already had grand visions of a new crusade which his premature death would blur. The crusade which occurred turned completely from the original purpose.

The Fourth Crusade, 1198–1204

Henry's death coincided with a major shift in papal competence and authority as Innocent III ascended to the Chair of Peter. In August Innocent announced plans for a new crusade, concentrating on France and on Italian coastal areas which could supply ships. Innocent did not want the kings to go on the crusade but to stay out of the way of preparations. Cardinal legate Peter Capuano and a parish priest, Fulk of Neuilly, preached the crusade with great effectiveness in France. Innocent decreed a crusading tax of one-fortieth on clerical income, exempting the Cistercians because of their refusal to pay. To secure transportation, Innocent turned to Enrico Dandolo, the Doge of Venice (1192–1205). As it turned out, the crusaders did not muster enough money to pay for fifty warships and had to agree to capture the rich trading city of Zara in November 1202.

Early in 1203 envoys from Philip of Swabia (1198–1208) and Alexius IV Angelus, pretender to the throne of Byzantium, approached the crusaders wintering at Zara with a proposal—to restore Isaac II Angelus (1185–1195), blinded and imprisoned by his brother Alexius III (1195–1203). Alexius IV promised the reunion of the Orthodox church with Rome, huge sums of money for the Venetians, and ten thousand Byzantine soldiers to aid the crusade. The French barons quickly agreed and persuaded bishops to do the same. What appealed to the mass of the crusaders was hope of booty, which in Constantinople would be immense. June 24, 1203 the crusading fleet dropped anchor at Chalcedon. July 17 the crusaders attacked from both land and sea. By April 13, 1204 the city had fallen. For three days the crusaders killed and looted. The Byzantine Empire was methodically cut to pieces. Six Venetians and six Frenchmen met to select a new emperor, choosing Baldwin of Flanders (1204–1205). On May 16 Baldwin took the crown of the emperor of Romania, the Latin Empire of Constantinople. It continued until 1261. The Greek capital was moved to Nicaea. The crusade was over. No one mentioned the Holy Land. Among rulers of the Latin Kingdom only Henry, brother of Baldwin, ruled effectively (1206–1216). After him the kingdom went downhill, the vassal states becoming more or less independent. The end of the kingdom came suddenly in 1261 when one of the Nicaean commanders noticed the Latins unprepared to defend themselves. August 15 Emperor Michael VIII Palaeologus (1259–1282) entered the city and began the dynasty which would rule until 1453.

The Children's Crusade, 1212

The tragic outcome of the Fourth Crusade did not cool the ardor for crusading, for a flurry of crusading followed within Europe itself. Innocent III inaugurated crusades against the Albigenses, 1209–1229, and their protector, Raymond VI of Toulouse. In 1212 the kings of Castile, Aragon, and Navarre overwhelmed the Muslim Almohads in the battle of Las Navas de Tolosa. The thirteenth century popes carried on a series of crusades against Hohenstaufen enemies in southern Italy. Similarly the church in northern Germany launched crusades against unconverted peoples there.

The most curious and the most tragic of crusades was the Children's Crusade of 1212. In the spring of 1212 children ages twelve to eighteen gathered behind a boy from Cologne named Nicholas. They intended to do what armed knights had proved unable to do, capture the Church of the Holy Sepulchre. In a year of religious fanaticism they believed the poorest and purest could do what the mighty could not. The only authority who tried to disperse them was the king of France. The main body set out in July under Nicholas's leadership, marched up the Rhine and across the Alps to Italy. August 25 they reached Genoa. What happened thereafter is uncertain. According to one contemporary account, some made their way to Marseilles, where merchants provided seven ships, two of which wrecked off Sardinia, and the others carried them to slave markets in North Africa and Egypt. Some returned home. Others died of deprivation or by violence.

Innocent III, stunned as he may have been that the Fourth Crusade slipped out of his control, still sought to gather up the enthusiasm for a crusade. In 1213 he opened his campaign for a new crusade, using as an excuse the fortifying of Mount Tabor in Galilee by the Ayubids. His bull, *Quia maior* called for all Christians to participate, regardless of rank or ability. Because France and

England were tied up in a murderous war and Emperor Frederick II preoccupied with Otto IV, he did not have to fear their interference. In 1215 he summoned the Fourth Lateran Council largely to establish a new organization. It set June of 1217 for the massing of crusaders at the south Italian ports of Brindisi and Messina. It set up a system for financing and, for the first time, decreed that persons who provided for crusaders would receive the same plenary indulgence as the latter, only a short step from arranging for proxies. Innocent, however, did not live to see the crusade put into effect; he died at Perugia on July 16, 1216. His successor, Honorius III (1216–1227), lacked Innocent's political skills.

The crusaders directed their attack at Damietta in Egypt with a view to weakening the center of Muslim power as a prelude to reconquering Palestine. They succeeded in capturing the Tower of Chains on an island in the midst of the Nile. From September 1218 they received steady reinforcements from Europe, but returnees and then disease wore down their strength. Among those who came to the camp was Francis of Assisi, who hoped to do by love and preaching what the crusaders had not succeeded in doing. By the fall of 1219 Damietta fell to the forces of the crusaders. Unfortunately they did not enjoy peace, for the military commander John of Brienne and the papal cardinal legate Pelagius squabbled over control. John of Brienne sailed back to Acre, but Pelagius proved a very poor leader. Inspired by some Arabic prophecies which he had translated into French, he led the crusaders out of Damietta in conquest of all Egypt. Meantime, the Ayubids recovered and forced Pelagius and the other crusaders to leave Egypt altogether. Pope Honorius III tried to blame Frederick II, but the fault lay much more with the obstinacy of his legate.

The Fifth Crusade, 1228–1229

Crusades followed one another in rapid succession during the thirteenth century without major campaigns of the twelfth. Emperor Frederick II (1220–1250) was the first to try to effect a political rather than a military settlement. In 1215 he took the crusader's vow. Both Innocent III and Honorius III, however, chose to ignore it for a time. After Frederick had overcome his Guelph rival Otto IV in 1220 Honorius called on him to lend active support, crowning him emperor and resigning himself to Frederick ruling his native kingdom of Sicily as well. Frederick reiterated his vow to go on a crusade and requested that Honorius excommunicate any who did not go by the summer of 1219. Following the failure of the crusade in Egypt in 1221, the papal curia pressed for a new crusade. In July 1225 the curia and the emperor made final arrangements in the Treaty of San Germano. Frederick agreed to go on a crusade in August 1227 or forfeit a huge gold deposit and incur the sentence of excommunication. One thing in his favor, however, was sole direction of the crusade. In November 1225 he gained a dynastic claim to Jerusalem by marrying Isabella, daughter of John of Brienne, king of Jerusalem.

The emperor's problems grew more serious under Honorius's successor Gregory IX (1227–1241), who belonged to the same family as Innocent III. When Frederick turned back after setting sail in August 1227 because Ludwig IV, Landgrave of Thuringia, died and he became ill himself, Gregory denounced him and immediately excommunicated him. A little later, after seeking to negotiate a reconciliation, Frederick ignored the pope's command to remain in Italy and went on the crusade anyway on June 28, 1228. After a brief stop at Cyrpus to install imperial garrisons he went on to Acre. Through lengthy negotiations the Sultan al-Kamil came to terms with Frederick in a treaty signed at Jaffa, February 18, 1229. The treaty restored Jerusalem to the Franks along with Bethlehem and Nazareth, but the Muslims were to retain the Dome of the Rock and al-Aqsa mosque. Frederick had obtained what Christians had fought for so long—control over the Sepulchre of Christ. However, the treaty angered the pope, the orthodox Muslims, and the Patriarch of Jerusalem. Because the patriarch would have refused to do so, Frederick crowned himself king.

Frederick did not get to remain long in Jerusalem. John of Brienne, angered by the loss of the Kingdom of Jerusalem, let Pope Gregory persuade him to invade Sicily at the head of the papal army. May 1, 1229 Frederick left Acre and arrived at Brindisi June 10. By the fall of 1229 he had routed the papal army. In May 1230 Gregory made peace at San Germano, lifting the excommunication and recognizing the success of the crusade.

The Sixth Crusade, 1248–1254

By the middle of the thirteenth century Europeans had lost much of their heart for crusading, but the crusader states still existed in Palestine and occasionally evoked enough concern to lead to a new effort. In 1244 the Ayubid rulers entered into a conflict with one another. As preparation for this, as-Salih had contracted for help from Khwarismian troops whom the Mongols had defeated and who were serving as mercenaries in Mesopotamia. The Khwarismians quickly swept through Palestine and, almost unopposed, occupied Jerusalem. They then united with the Egyptian army and dealt a devastating defeat to the Frankish-Damascene army at Gaza on October 17, 1244, the worst setback since Hattin.

In 1245 Pope Innocent IV (1243–1254) issued a call for a new crusade at the Council of Lyons. The only country capable of taking up the challenge at the time was France, where Louis IX (1226–1270) had already anticipated it by taking the cross in December 1244. From 1245 until his death in 1270 he based his policy on the crusade. An able ruler, he had extended Capetian control over most of France and inspired the people to devotion to the church. Louis prepared carefully for the crusade. The church bore most of the cost of the crusade, which amounted to eleven or twelve times the annual royal budget. Accompa-

nying him was Jean de Joinville, who wrote the most vivid account of a crusade still extant. Departing from Marseilles in August 1248, the crusaders wintered at Cyprus. On June 5, 1249 they arrived at Damietta, which they quickly took. Louis spent the summer at Damietta and established a bishopric there in November. November 20 he set out for Cairo, but the crusaders ran into the same problem the crusading army had met in 1221 at Mansourah. Weakened by dysentery, Louis and the troops had to capitulate on April 6, 1250. The crusaders retained Damietta, but they had to pay a huge ransom to obtain the release of the king. Louis, nevertheless, decided to stay in the Holy Land. Although he had only a small contingent of troops left, perhaps 1,700, he profited from a war between the Ayubids and rebellious Mameluks. By making a treaty with the latter, he secured release of the rest of his troops and the cancellation of the unpaid half of his ransom. For four years, 1250 to 1254, he ruled the Holy Land. He rebuilt the fortifications of Jaffa, Acre, Caesarea, and Sidon. By the spring of 1254, however, he realized he could no longer hold the Holy Land against the Ayubids, so on April 24 he left for France. Before departing, he explored the possibility of an alliance with the Mongols against the Muslims. Some Mongols had become Nestorians or been influenced by them. In 1245 to 1247 Pope Innocent IV had sent the Franciscan John of Piano del Carpine to convert the Great Khan, but the latter demanded the submission of the pope. Other embassies also proved unsuccessful. Louis sent as his ambassador to Mongka Khan at Karakorum the Franciscan William of Rubruck, who returned after three years (1253–1256) to report that the Khan would agree to an alliance only if Louis became his vassal. Meantime, the brother of Mongka Khan, Hulagu, conquered one Islamic territory after another. He met defeat, however, in September 1260 at Ain Jalud in Galilee at the hands of the Mameluks, halting the Mongol advance permanently. The eastern part of the Mongol Empire became Buddhist, the rest Muslim, dashing Christian hopes for an alliance with the Mongols.

The Seventh Crusade, 1270–1271

Whether it is appropriate to call Louis' final effort a crusade is difficult to say, but historians have traditionally done so. In 1263 the Sultan of Egypt, Baibars, sacked Nazareth and set out to conquer all of Palestine, using a scorched earth policy. By 1268 he took Antioch and made its French inhabitants pay dearly for their alliance with the Mongols. The rest of North Syria fell without a fight.

In 1267 Louis took the cross again. The French nobility, including Joinville, had little enthusiasm. Nonetheless, Louis sailed to Tunis, where he hoped to convert the sultan, and there he died on August 25, 1270. Edward I of England, after late arrival in Tunis, sailed to Acre, landing in 1271. He departed from the Holy Land in September 1271 after negotiating an eleven year truce with Baibars. Meantime, Charles of Anjou, brother of Louis, manipulated the crusade to his own end. Minor efforts to retain Christian control of the Holy Land continued until 1291, but the days of crusading had passed.

Assessing the Crusades

The crusades succeeded in part, but for the most part they must be assessed as costly failures. If winning the Holy Land was the main goal, they can be thought of as partial successes. The crusaders held Antioch for 170 years, but Jerusalem, their main objective, only for brief periods within the crusading era. If checking the advance of Islam or healing the breach between East and West were the main or subsidiary goals, the crusades must be considered worse than failures. They may have slowed Islamic advance here and there, but in the end they dealt such a terrible blow to the Byzantine Empire that they assured the triumph of the Ottoman Turks in 1453. As Steven Runciman has ably argued,

moreover, they damaged East-West relations almost beyond repair in the Fourth Crusade. From the perspective of the Byzantine Empire it would have been better had the crusades never happened.

Rehashing the reasons for failure may not prove profitable, for the problem lies in the very idea of a military crusade using brute force to achieve religious ends, as critics of crusades began to point out before the crusading fervor subsided. Francis of Assisi (1182–1226) gave eloquent witness of the contradiction when he approached the Sultan of Egypt. Not force, but love must reconcile. Later Ramon Lull (ca. 1233–ca. 1315) tried to translate Francis's ideal into a radically different understanding of mission work. Born in Majorca shortly after its recovery from Islamic rule, he was educated as a knight. However, a powerful experience of conversion redirected him toward a lifelong endeavor to convert Islam to Christianity. From 1287 he traveled constantly, making three trips to North Africa, with that goal in mind. Whether he died as a martyr stoned by Muslim mobs is now questioned, but his life work represented a strong witness against the crusading mentality.

Although the crusades failed to achieve their major goals, they had other important consequences. By design they increased the importance of the papacy. Although they had mixed success in doing so, the popes tried to coordinate the crusades and to keep them under ecclesiastical control. At the same time the crusades gave rise to the military orders, which subsequently played important roles in European politics. The Knights of St. John or Hospitallers, which formed at an early but undetermined date, evidently originated as a hostel for sick and destitute pilgrims. Supported primarily by French backers, they received great privileges from emperors and popes. The Knights of St. John continued strong for two centuries after the crusades, but they began to decay in the late sixteenth century. After 1310 they were known as the Knights of Rhodes, after

1530 as the Knights of Malta. The Knights Templar, founded by Hugo de Payeas and Godfrey St. Omer in 1119 to defend the Holy Sepulchre, grew rapidly and claimed 9,000 members around 1250 with great revenues and extensive privileges. Wearing a white mantle with a red cross, the Templars participated in all crusades except the first and fifth, but they began to degenerate soon after the crusades ended. In 1312 they were dissolved on grounds of immorality. The Order of Teutonic Knights failed to gain the prominence of the other two orders. Dating from around 1190, they served first as a hospital corps on the field of battle. Composed almost exclusively of German constituents, the Order grew rapidly under Hermann von Salza (1210–1239). Several other orders also existed. Military orders supplied a pattern for the Franciscans and Dominicans.

The crusades also had commercial and social impact on Europe. From the beginning they opened up rich trading opportunities in the East which led to the development of towns and sowed the seeds for the decay of feudalism. To a considerable extent they prepared the way for the Renaissance as Westerners again became familiar with classical writings. They stimulated a considerable amount of literature, especially histories of the crusades by Christians, Muslims, and Jews. Theologically, the crusades encouraged a new emphasis on the historical but dying Christ alongside the medieval concept of a sacramental and eternal Christ.

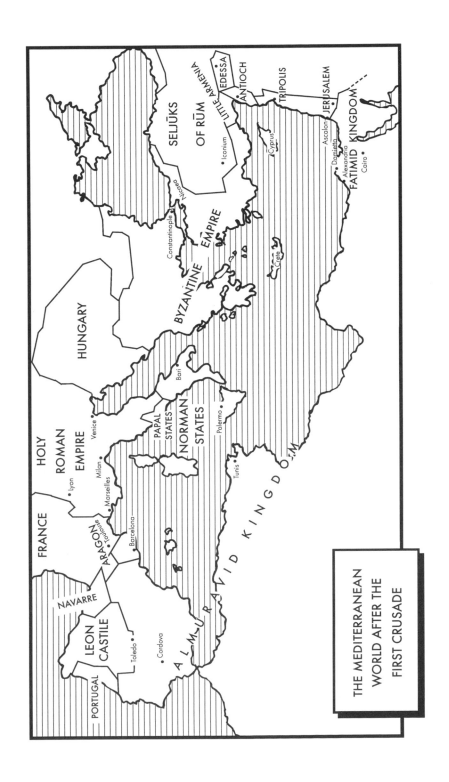

THE MEDITERRANEAN WORLD AFTER THE FIRST CRUSADE

Chapter 44

The Church in Medieval Society

During the eleventh and twelfth centuries the church attained a place in European society it had not enjoyed before. This is not to say that all Europeans became model Christians in the "age of faith." If historians could find records of people at all levels of society—royal, baronial, vassal, and serf—they could substantiate unbelief and impiety of all kinds, not just in dissenting movements but among those who made no overt protest as well. As a matter of fact, the extant records bear witness to a mixture of genuine piety and superstition, faithfulness and unfaithfulness, selflessness and selfishness, among clergy and monks as among the laity. Conceding all of that, nevertheless, medievalists rightly point to a monopoly held by the church in this period well beyond what it could maintain in subsequent centuries. The church baptized all children. It stood ready to punish nonconformity. Its priests judged and punished violations of the church's teachings—usury, witchcraft, violation of marriage laws. Stern laws protected the clergy. The church collected its dues, chiefly the tithe. It stood at the center of medieval villages, towns, or, eventually, cities. Everything of importance revolved around the church. Its bells tolled the hours of the day. Its calendar regulated the week, the month, and the year. It had the answers to all questions of real importance.

The growth of monasteries and increase in their wealth probably offer one of the strongest testimonies to the church's place in medieval society. But the monks did not perform the services which touched the lives of most people. Parish priests rendered that service, often as substitutes (vicars) for the monks. The vicars struggled to survive, but they were the ones who did the most for the masses. They had the education and performed the services people needed—the sacraments, exorcisms, tolling the bells to warn of approaching storms, cursing caterpillars and locusts. Sometimes they identified too readily with their people, for example, in brewing beer in the nave of the church or keeping animals in the church yard. More often, they stood above the laity, a class apart, but not so far above them that they could not enter into their struggle to live.

The development of trade and commerce from about 1100 onwards, partly as a consequence of the crusades, opened up some new problems for the church in society. Heretofore it had stood at the center of an agrarian society in which commerce played a small role. Judging by Gratian's *Decretum*, compiled about 1140, the church took a dim view of trade and it forbade absolutely the lending of money at interest (usury). Yet commerce could hardly go forward without usury. Consequently the church had to distinguish by intention. If merchants loaned money to make money, they committed a mortal sin, but if they loaned money to help a neighbor and sought only to cover the loss they might incur by doing so, they could ask for interest. It was not long, however, before human motivation created a tangled skein. It is easy to see from the crusades that not all Christians acted out of love of neighbor.

The Laity

So much of Christian history has focused on the clergy, the higher ones at that, or the hierarchy that the place of common folk in the church has received far too little notice. No society accentuated the cleavage between clergy and laity more than medieval society in the period under discussion. bishops and abbots stood on the level of nobility, from which most of them came. Other clergy, almost the only educated persons in society, held at least the same stature as knights. The laity had several strata, but even the lay aristocracy, at best modestly educated if not illiterate, learned the arts of war and of government so that they had to employ priests as their "clerks." In England the literate civil servant at court between 1150 and 1250 was still a "cleric." Not until the fourteenth century did laymen and laywomen begin to receive the training needed to fill such positions. The laity heard few sermons which could instruct them in basic Christian teachings. Stained glass windows, which began to appear in the tenth century, did not make up for the loss of education even if they served as "Poor Men's Bibles."

Officially the church emphasized the difference in status and function. In 619 the Second Council of Seville forbade lay persons to hold offices in the church or to act as ecclesiastical judges, quoting Deuteronomy 22:10. Gratian's *Decretum* reiterated the point. Lay persons, Archbishop Stephen Langton declared in 1213, should believe that their prelates would do everything "discreetly and with counsel." Monarchs, of course, did not abide by such dicta, but it was precisely this for which Gregory VII fought with such vigor. What, above everything else, set the clergy apart from the laity was the administration of the sacraments, especially of the eucharist. Although early custom allowed lay persons to administer baptism and to hear confession, by the eleventh century the clergy had virtually precluded both. The more elevated the concept of the sacrament, the greater the gap between clergy and laity.

The laity, of course, did have a role—to protect the church and the clergy. Under the Gregorian reform protection took the form of the crusade. It is perhaps not surprising that the idea for a crusade originated with Gregory VII himself, that is, for the reconquest of Spain, nor that popes after him tried desperately to maintain control over crusades rather than let them fall into the hands of emperors and kings. The powerful Innocent III (1198–1216) was obsessed with that very issue.

It is quite clear, however, that lay persons took a very different view of the relationship between clergy and laity. Kings and princes did not yield their prerogatives to popes and bishops and fought vigorously to retain them. Witness Henry IV against Gregory VII or Henry II of England against Thomas Becket. Or later observe the independence of Emperor Frederick II (1212–1241) for his crusading activities. Yet assertion of the rights of laity occurred also at a more popular level in the formation of sects or heresies, most connected in some way with the social and economic revolution taking place in Europe in the eleventh and twelfth centuries.

The Disaffected

The complexity of dissent in this period should not be underestimated, but these were lay movements from start to finish, even if clergy joined them occasionally. They were widely scattered with their strongest centers at Milan in northern Italy and Toulouse in southern France, both industrializing areas. Numbering 130, according to one medieval source dating around 1200, these diverse groups agreed in their protests of several features of church life in their day. They protested the worldliness and arrogance of the clergy, the formalism of the church's ritual in language they could not understand, and the worldly ambition of papal policy. Some of them, such as the Albigenses, probably merit the classification of heresies because of their radical dualism, but most represented popular protests against abuses in church and society involving no doctrinal deviations on critical points of doctrine. Some groups of those calling themselves Cathari even, such as the Concorezzoni, did not lapse into the worst kind of dualism.

The Cathari

The Cathari, so-called from the Greek word meaning "Pure," were reported as early as 1000 in Italy and southern France, in 1012 in Germany, and in 1022 at Orleans in France and quickly dealt with as heretics. They were labelled with several other names: "New Manichaeans," on account of their dualistic tendencies; "Patarenes," from the quarter in Milan which many inhabited; "Albigenses," from the town of Albi in southern France where they had great strength; "Bulgari, Bugares or Bugies," from Bulgaria; "Tessarants" or "Textores," from the number of weavers in the sect; and "Publicani or Poplicani," as a corruption of the name Paulician. The Paulicians dated from the fifth century in Asia Minor, from which they made their way to Constantinople. They taught a strict dualism and, like the Manichaeans, rejected the Old Testament completely.

The Cathari probably had several antecedents besides the Paulicians. They may have inherited Manichaean tendencies which had never been completely stamped out in northern Italy and southern France. Their teachings had much in common with those of the Bogomiles. In the eighth century the Byzantine emperors settled a number of Paulicians in Thrace. Bogomil, influenced by Paulicianism, introduced the ideas to the Balkans. Around 950 the Patriarch Theophylact (933–956) described Bogomilism as "Manichaeism mixed with Paulicianism." The sect spread rapidly in the Balkans during the eleventh century and, from there, in Italy and France. Despite vigorous efforts at repression, the sect held on. When the Tartars invaded Hungary, they made Bogomilism the national religion, but Catholicism was restored about 1450.

The Cathari taught that there are two churches, one of the wicked and one of the righteous, outside of which there is no salvation. Rome they regarded as the harlot of the Apocalypse, the pope as anti-Christ. They made much use of the scriptures, which they interpreted spiritually and allegorically, but they rejected the Old Testament as a work of the Devil. In accordance with their pronounced dualism, they denied Christ's full humanity. He was created in heaven and not born on earth; rather he passed through Mary as through a pipe. They explained the Fall of angels as a result of Satan's tempting them by bringing a woman, decked in jewels and gold and beautiful to behold, to earth. For nine days and nights angels poured out of heaven until God closed the aperture which Satan had made. The Cathari denied the resurrection of the body. They rejected the eucharist. They renounced marriage as contrary to divine law and held that persons living incontinently could not be saved. They forbade eating of meats, eggs, and cheese as well as the killing of animals, birds, or insects. They rejected oathtaking, priestly vestments, altars, and crosses along with the doctrines of purgatory and indulgences.

In place of the Catholic church's sacraments the Cathari substituted their own. The *Consolamentum* supplanted baptism and, in their understanding, meant much more. It consisted of the laying on of hands and the imposing of the Gospel of John, their favorite, on the candidate's head or breast. The candidate then confessed all sins of thought, word, work, and vision, and placed her or his faith and hope in God and in the *Consolamentum*. After this came the kiss of peace. The *Consolamentum* absolved all previous and future sins and assured salvation. The *Meli-*

oramentum entailed the veneration of the officials who administered the *Consolamentum* by reciting a threefold salutation: "Hail to thee, thrice holy one!" Presumably it replaced the eucharist. The *Endura* involved suicide. The Cathari gave some options on this: voluntary starvation, smothering with a pillow in case of illness, and drinking a concoction composed of ground cucumbers and slivers of glass.

The Cathari divided adherents into two classes. The *Credentes*, "believers," corresponded to the church's catechumens. The *Perfecti* represented those who had received the *Consolamentum* and thus could be called *bons hommes*, "good men," or *Vestiti*, "the girded," for binding themselves with a cord for the *Consolamentum*. Cathari organization is not well known, but it paralleled that of the Catholic church with bishops, their assistants, and deacons.

Persecution of the Cathari became intense in the mid-twelfth century. Given their contempt for the physical, however, shedding of blood only added faggots to the flames, particularly in southern France. About 1200, contemporary accounts estimated their numbers as high as 4,000,000 in over 1000 towns and villages. In 1167 they felt sufficient strength to hold a council at St. Felix de Caraman, near Toulouse. Nicetas of Constantinople, to whom they gave the name pope, attended.

The Cathari broke up into sects around 1200. One document numbered them at seventy-two. The chief centers were Albi in France and Concorrezzi in Italy. The Concorrezzoni were not as radically dualist as the Albigenses.

The Catholic church responded with crusades and the Inquisition. Beginning with Innocent III, the popes authorized four crusades, Innocent excommunicated Raymond of Toulouse, a Cathari sympathizer, and deprived him of his lands for his refusal to persecute them. When Innocent's legate, Peter of Castelnau, was murdered in 1208, the full wrath of the church fell on Raymond and the Cathari in the form of a crusade led by Simon de Montfort. Simon massacred hundreds at Beziers in 1209. At Muret in 1213 he decisively defeated the Cathari led by Peter of Aragon. In 1233 Pope Gregory IX (1227–1241) entrusted the Inquisition to the Dominicans for the final extirpation of the heresy. By the end of the fourteenth century no trace of the Cathari remained.

The Arnoldists

The Arnoldists were named after Arnold of Brescia (d. 1155), their founder and leader. Devoted at an early age to the priesthood, Arnold studied in Paris under Peter Abelard, whom he defended against the attacks of Bernard of Clairvaux. On returning to Italy he became a canon regular and soon began attacks on the worldliness of the church. The church should resign worldly power and possessions. Priests who have worldly possessions forfeit their salvation. The clergy, he argued, should live off of the tithes and voluntary offerings of the people. Sacraments administered by priests not leading an apostolic life are invalid. In 1139 a Roman synod brought charges against him and banished him to France. Bernard of Clairvaux secured the condemnation of his doctrines and those of Abelard at the Council of Sens in 1140. In 1145, nonetheless, he returned to Rome, where Pope Lucius II (1114–1145) received him into communion on the condition that he do penance. Soon thereafter, however, he threw his support behind the party opposing the temporal rule of the pope and earned the excommunication of Eugenius III (1145–1153). For a time this party exerted real influence in Rome, which they wanted to free from papal rule. When Frederick Barbarossa made peace with Eugenius on October 16, 1152, however, the Arnoldists lost power. Frederick captured Arnold. When Nicholas Breakspeare became Pope Hadrian IV, he induced Frederick to turn Arnold over to him. He then had Arnold hanged, his body burned, and the ashes thrown into the Tiber. In 1184 the Council of Verona declared the Arnoldists heretical. Thereafter, they disappeared.

Petrobrusians

Peter de Bruys (d. ca. 1140), known only from the writings of Peter the Venerable and Abelard, was evidently a priest deprived of his office who then began to preach in Dauphine and Provence. He rejected infant baptism, the Mass, church buildings, prayers for the dead, veneration of the Cross, parts of scriptures, and the authority of the church. He gained a considerable following. His teachings were condemned at the Second Lateran Council in 1139. He was burned at St. Gilles, near Nimes, by people infuriated at his burning of crosses.

Henricians

Little is known about Henry of Lausanne (d. after 1145), but he was probably a French monk who became an itinerant preacher. He gave Lenten sermons at Le Mans around 1116 with the permission of the bishop. Attacks on worldliness of the clergy and insistence on the ideal of absolute poverty made him popular with the masses. According to Bernard of Clairvaux, he also denied the objective efficacy of the sacraments and made that dependent on the worthiness of the priest. Expelled from LeMans for heretical teaching at any rate, he continued his preaching throughout southern France. In 1135 the Synod of Pisa arrested him and forced him to recant, but he soon resumed his anticlerical preaching. Arrested again in 1145, he evidently died soon afterwards.

Amalricians

The Amalricians or Amaurians originated from Amalric or Amaury of Bene (d. ca. 1207), a scholastic philosopher who taught at Paris. Like John Scotus Erigena, he maintained the derivation of all things from a single essence and that those who remain steadfast in the love of God cannot sin. His teachings were condemned at the Council of Paris in 1210 and at the Fourth Lateran Council in 1215.

Ortlibarii

Ortlieb of Strassburg (ca. 1200) founded this ascetic sect, about whom little is known except for the condemnation of his teaching by Innocent III. His followers, many of whom were burned at Strassburg in 1212, appealed to the inner authority of the Spirit, held to the eternity of the world, and apparently taught unorthodox views of the Trinity and the Incarnation.

Beguines and Beghards

Both of these were pious associations founded in the lower Rhine area during the late twelfth century for the promotion of warmer piety than existed in the churches. Mostly composed of women, the Beguines took up a semimonastic life in houses which members supported by spinning, weaving, care for the sick, and other activities. They were free, however, to leave the community and marry or to hold private property. The Beghards were the male counterparts to the Beguines. Although usually weavers, dyers, or fullers, they had a common purse and held no private property. Their social doctrines, mysticism, and sympathies with the Spiritual Franciscans caused ecclesiastical authorities to suspect them of heresy. Both groups were condemned at Mainz in 1261, Cologne in 1262, and Vienne in 1312. After some reforms many of the Beghards were permitted by Pope John XXII to continue in 1321 and survived until the French Revolution. The Beguines, on the other hand, directed their energies toward charitable enterprises. During the sixteenth century and again at the French Revolution, they were almost suppressed, but some have continued to this day, especially in Belgium.

Waldenses

The only sect apart from the Beguines to survive to the present day, the Waldenses originated with Peter Valdes, a rich merchant of Lyons.

About 1173 or soon after he felt prompted by Christ's words to the rich youth (Matthew 19:21) and by hearing the story of St. Alexis's decision to leave his wealthy bride for a life of mendicancy and almsgiving to distribute his possessions among the poor and become an itinerant preacher. He provided for his wife and placed his daughters in the Abbey of Fontevrault, a double order of monks and nuns founded about 1100 by Robert Arbrissel. He quickly attracted a following to the New Testament pattern. In 1179 Valdes sought ecclesiastical recognition at the Third Lateran Council. Although Pope Alexander III expressed approval of their vow of poverty, he denied them the right to preach except on invitation of the clergy. Valdes and his followers soon violated this injunction. In 1184 the Council of Verona designated them Humiliati or "Poor Men of Lyons" and anathematized them along with the Cathari. These actions did not halt them.

Unlike the Cathari, the Waldenses did not hold unorthodox views. Indeed, Valdes had made a meticulous confession to Cardinal Henry of Albano between 1179 and 1180. What rankled officials was lay preaching. As the Waldenses articulated their own views, they first of all had to obey God rather than human beings, which Catholics interpreted as a refusal to submit to papal authority. They taught the authority and popular use of the scriptures and the right of lay persons, including women, to preach. Correspondingly, they insisted that spiritual endowment or merit and not the church's ordination gave the right to bind and loose, to consecrate and bless. Some Waldenses, not all, rejected infant baptism. They refused to take oaths and condemned the death penalty. Some also rejected the doctrine of purgatory and prayers for the dead. They regarded themselves as a church within the church. In southern France they elected a superintendent, called *Majoralis omnium*, to whom they ascribed authority as Catholics did to the pope, but elsewhere they had a threefold ministry—priests, teachers, and rectors.

The Waldenses grew rapidly, especially among the lower classes. They spread first in southern France and Spain, then in Germany, Piedmont, and Lombardy. Valdes died sometime between 1205 and 1218. From the time of Innocent III, especially with the establishment of the Inquisition in 1208, the Waldenses suffered severe persecution. Although their numbers dwindled in Lombardy, France, and Spain, they continued strong in the mountain valleys of Savoy and Piedmont in Italy. They also survived in Germany despite the efforts of Conrad of Marburg to suppress them in 1231 to 1233. From Germany they spread to Bohemia, Poland, and Hungary. In Bohemia they associated with the followers of John Huss. During the sixteenth century, they made contact with the Protestant reformers. Pope Innocent VIII had inaugurated a major crusade against them in 1487, but Louis XII of France granted them limited toleration in 1498. Francis I revoked that in 1545, when he launched a severe campaign against Protestants.

Women

Women in this era found themselves featured between extremes. On the one hand, they were portrayed as the instrument of the Devil, inferior to men and evil, the source of the world's sin, the supreme temptress and the most dangerous obstacle to salvation. On the other hand, they could be put on a pedestal, treated with reverence, showered with favors, honored for purity. Both church and society accepted the subjection and the superiority of women at one and the same time. Particularly important for the growth of the latter understanding was the development of the cult of the Virgin Mary. the perfect knight revered the lady. Worship of the lady stood next to the worship of God among the chivalrous aristocracy.

Writings by women began to appear during the twelfth century. Heloise penned flaming love letters to Peter Abelard (1079–1142). Hildegard (1098–1179), Abbess of Rupertsberg near Bingen, earned the title of "the Sibyl of the Rhine." Gifted with supernatural visions from early childhood, she dictated her revelations between 1141 and 1151 in the book entitled *Scivias*. She gained guarded approval for her visions from Pope Eugenius III under influence of Bernard of Clairvaux. Hildegard also wrote a scientific treatise which reflects unusual knowledge for her day, an *Explication of the Symbol of Saint Athanasius*, an *Exposition of the Gospels*, an *Exposition of the Rule of Saint Benedict*, numerous letters, and other writings. During the thirteenth and fourteenth centuries, the number of articulate women mystics increased many times.

Women of the aristocracy played highly significant roles in church and society. The diaconal role of women in early Christianity died out during the eighth century in the West and during the tenth century in the East. However, it continued to have some impact during the high middle ages in the function of abbesses. Women headed convents which included both men and women, a carry over of the diaconal role to the office of abbess as well as the role played by monasticism in the evangelization of Europe. Abbesses held relatively the same position and power as queens and empresses. They did not have sacerdotal powers, to ordain or consecrate the eucharist, but they did have jurisdictional powers. Independently of bishops they levied taxes, regulated monasteries, ruled often enormous territories dependent on the monastery, and presided over the churches and clergy as well as the laity in them. Matilda, daughter of Otto I (962–973) for instance, headed what was known as the Quedlinburg Institute, had the title of *Metropolitana*, and held the jurisdiction of a bishop. Abbesses of the Institute normally held a seat in the Imperial Diet.

Recent research on women religious during the middle ages has demonstrated that many women of wealth and education elected religious vocations as a way of exercising their freedom. Marriage required giving of a dowry much larger than the one which would accompany those entering a religious order. Childbearing entailed great risks. The idea of romantic love in marriage was just beginning to grow in European consciousness, but no one questioned love of God. Women of this period frequently complained of loveless marriages. Not all arranged marriages turned out badly, but many did, so that women chose to exercise other options.

The crusades placed women in positions of responsibility ordinarily filled by men, and women fought to hold onto them. Eleanor of Aquitaine, for example, held the reins of England while her son Richard the Lionhearted was away fighting. Blanche, the mother of Louis IX of France, ruled during his minority and during his absence on the Sixth Crusade. The wives of many nobles served as guardians of the fiefs and managers of the manor while their husbands went away on military expeditions, pilgrimages, or engaged in other business. They superintended the farms, interviewed tenants, and saved up money for the next crusade. When their husbands were taken captive, they secured ransom money. Not very accurate statistics exist, but wars naturally increased the percentage of women compared with men.

The twelfth century in particular was a time for the sensitizing to the feminine. Although the Cistercians did not originate the custom, they made much use of feminine imagery to speak about God or Christ, addressing both God and Jesus as "our Mother." They shared such usages with Anselm and William of St. Thierry (ca. 1085–1148), but they accentuated it far more than others, perhaps, as Carolyn Walker Bynum has emphasized, to add nurturing, affectivity, and accessibility to their concept of authority. Women did not have the same problem because they did not hold the offices of priests and bishops, although those who became abbesses did have some reluctance and sense of unworthiness to govern. Men, however, felt a need to temper the power their offices gave them.

The Clergy

By the eleventh and twelfth centuries parochial organization probably existed in France, Germany, and England and was in process of development in several other countries undergoing evangelization. Synods instructed priests to teach the creed, elementary prayers, and Christian morality. They directed them also to choose promising boys to educate for the clergy.

Under the Gregorian reform pressure was exerted to enforce clerical celibacy, but many priests still had wives or concubines. The Second Lateran Council of 1139 made marriage of priests not only illegal but invalid, but that did not halt the practice in most countries. The schoolmen debated whether celibacy of the clergy was a law of God or of the church and decided that it was the latter. The fact that the Eastern churches permitted marriage of clergy before age thirty-five made it difficult to enforce uniform practice in the West.

The twelfth century witnessed the systematizing of canon law, whose importance had increased in the Gregorian reform. About 1140 Gratian, a Camaldolese monk probably working at the monastery of San Felice at Bologna, published his *Harmony of Discordant Canons*, the most complete collection up to that time. Although a private collection, it became synonymous with canon law itself and continued in use right up to the codification of the *Code of Canon Law* in 1917. From 1130 to 1230 the study of law—canon, civil, and regional—became the chief occupation of scholars.

The chief figure in the clerical hierarchy, of course was the bishop. Bishops selected and trained the parish clergy. They directed their activities. They presided over all diocesan activities. In this period still they had to protect church properties against local barons or monarchs and often to intercede for members of their flock with the same. They themselves stood at the center of the contest between popes and emperors or kings. Many of them, elected from the nobility, naturally leaned toward the secular ruler who was, after all, much closer than the pope geographically and perhaps ideologically. Strong monarchs easily exerted more influence than weak popes beyond the Alps in Italy.

Bishops also took leading roles in the crusades. The most noted example was Otto, bishop of Freising (ca. 1114 or 1115–1158). The son of Leopold III, Margrave of Austria, and Agnes, daughter of Emperor Henry IV, he studied in Paris under Hugo of St. Victor. In 1132 he entered the Cistercian Abbey of Morimond in Champagne; four years later he was elected abbot. In 1138 he was appointed bishop of Freising. In 1147–1148 he took part in the Second Crusade, barely escaping with his life. One of the first to introduce the study of Aristotle to Germany, he is noted chiefly for his historical writings: *A Chronicon or History of Two Cities* (1143–1146) and *Acts of Frederic* (Barbarossa) (1156–1158). Barbarossa was his nephew. Other bishops accompanied the crusaders.

Archbishops or metropolitans exercised jurisdiction over bishops in their provinces. The Gregorian reform created many conflicts at this point because the popes reserved the right of appeal directly to Rome over the head of the archbishop. Strong archbishops sometimes resisted directives from Rome, but, most of the time, the popes won. Sometimes sees made competing claims. In England, for example, Canterbury and York vied with one another for jurisdiction over the British Isles. Lanfranc still struggled to make Canterbury preeminent at the end of the eleventh century, and it was not until the martyrdom of Becket in 1170 that Canterbury finally had a secure position, even in England. Archbishops also had to battle monarchs and emperors to preserve the freedom and integrity of their offices.

Chapter 45

Medieval Thought in the Age of Reform

The age of reform spurred forward by Cluny and Citeaux was accompanied by a revival of learning following the brief "dark ages" brought on by the Viking raids of the ninth and tenth centuries and the lapse into feudalism. The crusades played a significant role in the introduction of Aristotle, for they brought Westerners once again into contact with the riches of the East. Meantime, episcopal or cathedral schools supplanted monastic schools as the key centers of learning. Possessed of greater freedom than the latter, they gathered around them outstanding scholars who eventually formed the first universities in Europe which would play a key role in guiding the church through the Renaissance and Reformation. The Schoolmen, as teachers in the universities came to be called, wedded the best of Aristotle to the most philosophical, if not the best, in Christian thinking.

Education

Credit for the preservation of learning during much of the Middle Ages must go to the monasteries. The monks copied and illuminated manuscripts, collected precious libraries, taught a corpus of students at least for the monasteries themselves if not for the society at large, and inspired a love for learning alongside a desire for God. The Rule of Benedict, so influential throughout the earlier Middle Ages, assumed that knowledge of letters would go hand in hand with the search for God. Monks had to read and write in order to carry out the monastic regimen. Monks were the main architects of the Carolingian renaissance. Although they concentrated always on scriptures and the Fathers of the church, they could not neglect the more general culture which saturated those writings. Interpretation of scriptures necessitated study of grammar and other information supplied by classical sources. Use of the Fathers involved the monks in their comprehensive culture with its classical roots. As Jean Leclercq has pointed out, the monks took from the patristic writers "a terminology and themes and a whole vocabulary whose meaning cannot be grasped if their source is not recognized." (*The Love of Learning and the Desire for God*, 126). What the monks did was to prolong patristic culture to their own age. Bernard of Clairvaux can appropriately be labeled "the last of the Fathers." As to the classics themselves, the monks both lauded and disparaged them, lauded where they found them in harmony with Christian thought and disparaged where they saw conflict with the latter. Some obviously valued them more than others, and from these came a twelfth century renaissance.

During the twelfth century, the European center of learning shifted to northern France to cathedral schools at Bec, Rheims, Orleans, Laon, and Paris. Among the brilliant teachers who attracted scores of students and shaped the future of European education were Anselm of Laon (d. 1117), William of Champeaux (ca. 1070–1121), Bernard of Chartres (d. ca. 1130), William of Conches (ca. 1080–ca. 1154), and, above all, Abelard (1079–1142).

Anselm of Laon's background is obscure until he began teaching at the cathedral school of Laon. Combining the office of chancellor with that of deacon (ca. 1109–1114) and archdeacon (1115–1117), he gained fame as a teacher of liberal arts as well as theology. Although he held traditional views, he employed different methods of study, notably a dialectical approach. His students included William of Champeaux, Gilbert of Poitiers (ca. 1080–1154), and Abelard.

William of Champeaux began to teach in the cathedral schools of Paris, but the ridicule of his brilliant student Peter Abelard drove him away in 1108. He retired them to the Monastery of St. Victor, where he laid the foundations for the Victorine School continued by Hugo and Richard. In 1113 he became the bishop of Chalons and evidently modified his extreme realism.

Bernard of Chartres exerted a strong formative influence on the Platonist tradition of the School of Chartres, already made famous by Fulbert (ca. 960–1028), the bishop of Chartres, who had studied under Gerbert of Aurillac at Rheims and Chartres. William of Conches studied under Bernard of Chartres and furthered his emphasis on the study of profane learning in the interest of promoting Christian humanism. His work on the Trinity came under attack by William of St. Thierry, a Cistercian protege of Bernard of Clairvaux.

The medieval curriculum followed the scheme of the classical trivium—grammar, rhetoric, and dialectic—and quadrivium—arithmetic, geometry, astronomy, and music. The primary textbooks included a mixture of Christian and classical sources: Cassiodorus, the *Isagoge* of Porphyry, Aristotle on the *Categories* and his treatise *On Interpretation*, Boethius on *Music* and *The Consolations of Philosophy*, Martianus Cappella,

and the grammars of Priscian and Donatus. The classics gradually regained popularity among teachers such as Gerbert of Aurillac (ca. 940–1003), Peter Damian (1007–1072), Anselm of Canterbury (ca. 1033–1109), John of Salisbury, Peter Abelard, Robert Grosseteste (ca. 1175–1253), and others. John of Salisbury sought energetically to develop a Christian humanism first at Canterbury under Theobald (1148–1161) and Thomas Becket (1161–1171). His writings included the *Metalogicon*, a defense of the study of grammar, rhetoric, and logic. His letters and other writings reflect extensive knowledge of Latin classical writers, and he was the first medieval writer to acquaint himself with the whole of Aristotle's *Organon*. In 1176 he became bishop of Chartres.

Books were extremely costly and few could afford them. They were handcopied in monastic scriptoria, often with meticulous care, beautifully ornamented, and carefully guarded. Libraries usually contained copies of the scriptures, the Fathers of the church, classical writings, and sometimes contemporary works such as the writings of Anselm, Abelard, Peter the Lombard, and others. A large library would not house more than a few hundred books, but their value would far exceed that of thousands today.

The universities owed their origin to conventual and cathedral schools, to the enthusiasm and skill of individual teachers such as Abelard who drew students from far and near, and to the guilds which provided the pattern for organization. The first universities arose in Italy—Salerno as a center for medical studies and Bologna as a center for the study of both canon and civil law, thanks to the work of Gratian in collecting the canons. The University of Paris dates from the early twelfth century when Peter the Lombard (ca. 1100–1160) taught at the Cathedral School (1134 on), Hugo and Richard at St. Victor, and Peter Abelard at Ste.-Genevieve, but it did not become a community of masters and scholars until the end of the twelfth century. Styled a *Uni-*

versitas Magistrorum in 1207, it received its official approval from Pope Innocent III in 1215. Between 1215 and 1225 Paris formed its "nations"—French, Norman, Picard, and English (later German), and shortly afterwards its four faculties of theology, law, medicine, and arts. Paris established itself quickly as the theological center. Oxford originated during the late twelfth century, but its exact date is uncertain. An edict of 1167 forbade students to go abroad. In 1214 appeared the first reference to a chancellor, who obtained his authority from the bishop of Lincoln. By about 1230 Oxford had established its reputation as a leading university. From boarding houses operated by various religious orders came the colleges, Merton and Balliol vying for the earliest (1263). In Spain Alfonso VIII of Castile established a university at Palencia in 1212, but it was abandoned. Ferdinand III established a second at Salamanca in 1230. Universities appeared all over Europe during the fourteenth and fifteenth centuries.

Universities took on different patterns of organization. Originally the term *universitas* signified an aggregation of students and teachers. The curriculum included at least four faculties—the arts, law, medicine, and theology, listed ascendingly in order of their importance. Each university had its own government, endowments, and privileges. Bologna and Paris served as the two basic models of organization. In Bologna the students controlled, in Paris the teachers. Bologna struggled to develop an arts curriculum, whereas in Paris the liberal arts and theology stood at the center from the beginning.

Precursors

From the time of Augustine and Gregory the Great Platonism dominated in Western thinking in second hand form. The theologian *par excellence* was, of course, Augustine (354–430). Few could have grasped his thought well, for he did not put it in systematic form but in occasional writings addressed to specific situations. From the time of his baptism until about 405 he focused on refutation of the sect he formerly belonged to, the Manichaeans. From 405 until 412 he replied to the Donatists. From 412 until 418 he occupied himself with the Pelagians and simultaneously began the writing of his *magnum opus, The City of God*, a thirteen year effort to defend Christianity against charges of responsibility for the calamities befalling the empire with the invasion of Rome by the Vandals in 410. He also refuted Arianism. Unsystematic though all of this was, the most basic themes gripped Western thinking ever after. Politically Westerners lived with a vision of the City of God, however imperfectly embodied in church or state. Although the Synod of Orange in 529 modified Augustine's concept of grace and the penitential system denied it, people at all levels of life could not forget the Augustinian concept of grace embodied in tangible sacraments. With the later Augustine they also looked to Rome for guidance. Yet the Augustine they knew was the Augustine popularized and communicated in idioms they could understand by Gregory the Great (540–604) and thinkers of their own time.

Another important source of Platonism in the West, as in the East, was the writings which went under the name of Dionysius who met Paul at Mars Hill in Athens (Acts 17:34). Probably composed in Syria around 500, the series—*On the Heavenly Hierarchy, On the Ecclesiastical Hierarchy, On the Names of God, On Mystical Theology*, and ten letters—were mentioned first at the Council of Constantinople in 533 and, in the West, in the writings of Gregory the Great. They acquired great significance in the ninth century in the thought of John Scotus Erigena (ca. 810–ca. 877). They served as a guide to mysticism and mystical theology among the schoolmen—Hugo of St. Victor, Albertus Magnus, Dionysius the Carthusian, and others.

Aristotle's thought was not altogether unknown in the West during the Middle Ages. Boethius (480?–524?) contributed significantly to the revival of interest in Aristotle during the sixth century through his translations and commentaries on the *Organon* of Aristotle and the *Isagoge* of Porphyry and by his own independent writings: *Introduction to Categories of Syllogisms, On Categorical Syllogism, On Hypothetical Syllogism*, and other works on logic as well as his widely read *The Consolations of Philosophy*. John of Damascus's (ca. 675–ca. 749) writings exercised substantial influence on Western thinking. Translated, although inadequately, by Burgundio of Pisa, they were known to Peter the Lombard and Thomas Aquinas.

Aristotelianism gained new importance in the West through Arab and Jewish philosophers, both of whom combined Neoplatonism and Aristotelianism. Avicenna (Ibn Sina) (980–1037), court physician to a number of Persian princes, exerted much influence on the earlier Schoolmen. Averroes (Ibn Rushd, 1126–1198), a native of Cordova in Spain, contributed to scholastic philosophy especially through his commentaries on Aristotle, but his theories first entered the Christian world about 1230 with Roger Bacon (ca. 1214–ca. 1292) and Albertus Magnus (ca. 1200–1280). The chief Jewish Aristotelian was Avicebron or Salomon ben Gabirol (ca. 1020–ca. 1070), whom medieval Christian writers wrongly thought to be an Arab because he wrote in Arabic.

Basic Questions

The encounter of Christians with the Islamic and Jewish worlds and with Aristotle forced upon Christians two basic questions—concerning universal or generic concepts and concerning the relationship between reason and revelation. Different answers to these questions underlay much of the philosophical and theological debate of the twelfth century and after.

Boethius's translation of Porphyry's writings probably precipitated discussion of the question of "universals." Even before the founding of the universities, the question inspired major debate.

Four different positions are discernible. On one extreme, Realists, who were strict Platonists, taught that universals were not mere generalizations of the mind after observing objects, but have real existence. They expressed this in the formula, *universalia ante rem*, "universals exist before particular objects." William of Champeaux (ca. 1070–1121) held this position in its most extreme form and suffered humiliation at the hands of his pupil Peter Abelard on account of it. On the opposite extreme, nominalists taught that universals have no antecedent existence but are mere names, *nomina* in Latin, from which comes Nominalism. They used the formula *universalia post rem*, "universals exist after particular objects." That is, by comparing individual objects and their qualities, one arrives at a "name" or "general concept." The first and most outstanding nominalist was Roscellinus (d. ca. 1125), one of Peter Abelard's teachers. Abelard, however, also attacked Roscellinus' teaching. Between these extremes were two others. Aristotelian or Moderate Realists held that universals have real existence but only in individual objects. They expressed this in the formula *universalia in re*, "universals exist in particular objects," for example, humanity in individual human beings. Most notable scholars in the twelfth century probably adhered to this position. Conceptualists argued that universals exist in the mind but not in reality. Peter Abelard achieved a position between the extreme Realism of William of Champeaux and the extreme Nominalism of Roscellinus. In a subtle way he distinguished apprehension of objects from the objects themselves, particular things remaining outside human perception of them. His views influenced John of Salisbury and others, but his own unfortunate experience diminished their impact later on.

The question of universals had more than philosophical import in the eleventh and twelfth centuries. According to Anselm, Roscellinus' nominalism led him to tritheism, for which the Council of Soissons condemned him in 1092. He argued that to consider the three persons of the Trinity "of one substance," as the Creed of Nicaea-Constantinople stated, would result in confusion of persons, the Father begetting himself in begetting the Son and both the Father and the Spirit becoming incarnate in the Son. Similarly, Berengar of Tours (ca. 1010–1088) disputed the material change in the elements assumed by some as necessary to maintain an idea of Real Presence in the eucharist.

The relationship between faith and reason or revelation and reason has always stimulated considerable debate among Christians, but it reached a new level in the Middle Ages. Anselm, the first of the Schoolmen, makes clear in prefaces to his writings the urgency people felt about the rational tenability of Christian faith. Some had "often and earnestly entreated" him to put in writing his arguments for Christian doctrine not on the basis of scriptures but "with common proofs and with a simple argument . . . enforced by the cogency of reason." The result was the *Monologium* and, soon after it, the *Proslogium* giving a rational explanation and argument for the existence of God. Although very much a heart thinker, Anselm used the most consistent logic even to explain the incarnation in *Cur Deus Homo?*

The leading theologians of this era fell into three categories with minor variations in each. Some argued, with many of the Western Fathers such as Tertullian and Augustine, for the primacy of faith. A few went to the same extremes as Tertullian in rejecting reason altogether. Most notable of these were Bernard of Clairvaux (1090–1153) and, to a lesser degree, Peter Damian (1007–1072) and William of Occam (ca. 1285–1347). More typical were those who favored Augustine's insistence that faith must precede and assist reason. Anselm expressed this in the formula, "I believe in order to understand, not I understand in order to believe." Faith seeks understanding. Reason is employed to assist faith. Others who espoused the same view include: Bonaventure (1221–1274), Duns Scotus (1265–

1308), Roger Bacon (ca. 1214–ca. 1292), and Ramon Lull (ca. 1233–ca. 1315).

A second group emphasized the primacy of reason. It is doubtful whether any Christian thinkers fitted into this subcategory, but some maintained the absoluteness of reason. All propositions of faith must satisfy rational criteria, and faith must not conflict with reason. If so, reason must resolve the conflict. Arab and Jewish scholars would be the best representatives. Some Christian scholars maintained the primacy of reason but submitted to faith on complex matters. Marsilius of Padua (ca. 1275–1342), author of the *Defensor Pacis*, claimed to accept the church's authority on disputed matters, but always with tongue in cheek. Etienne Gilson accused him of having "a slight touch of Voltaire" in his writings. So too the Averroist Siger de Brabant (ca. 1240–ca. 1284), some of whose propositions Stephen Tempier, bishop of Paris, condemned in 1270.

Most of the Schoolmen sought to harmonize reason and revelation in some way. one group of them insisted that revelation must be confirmed by reason. Like John Scotus Erigena, Peter Abelard, certainly in his earlier years, placed strong emphasis on congruence of reason and revelation. "I understand in order to believe." Another group held that reason and revelation travel parallel paths, but that faith goes beyond. So Thomas Aquinas (ca. 1225–1274). From this perspective arose the division between philosophy and theology, philosophy a rational and theology a revelational science. A third group, especially the mystics such as the Victorines and Bonaventure, contended that reason and revelation travel the same path but that faith goes beyond.

The Early Schoolmen

Scholasticism reached its peak with the development of the universities of Europe, but its foundations were well laid by outstanding teachers in the cathedral schools, mostly in France. At the head of the stream stood Anselm, a monk and abbot of Bec who succeeded Lanfranc as archbishop of Canterbury in 1093. Although he is remembered, above all, for his theory of the atonement, he deserves credit also for giving a green light to the development of theology as a rational science, the very thing for which scholasticism became known. In some ways this is surprising because he had highly personal religious experience about which he wrote movingly. His age, however, was one which demanded rational rather than dogmatic demonstration, and he responded with immense dialectical skill. After publishing a series of prayers, in 1078–1079 he wrote his *Monologium*, a rational presentation of Christian belief in the Trinity, and his more famous *Proslogium*, an ontological argument for the existence of God. The ontological argument ran as follows: (1) It is possible to conceive of a Being than which none greater can be conceived. (2) To exist in reality is greater than to exist in thought only. (3) Thus if this Being existed in the understanding only, it would be possible to conceive of a still greater Being, that is, the one that existed in reality, which is a contradiction. (4) Therefore, one must conclude that God exists. Not everyone found this argument compelling. A monk of Marmoutiers, near Tours, named Gaunilo, pointed out that Anselm only proved what he assumed. It would be possible to conceive of an island than which none more paradisal could be conceived, but the fact that one could conceive such would not prove its existence. Anselm's courteous reply reiterated his basic argument, insisting that the island would not make a suitable analogy because God is one of a kind whereas there can be many islands.

During his exile from England in 1098, Anselm completed his greatest theological work, *Cur Deus Homo?* Once again relying on rational argument, he repudiated the *Christus Victor* theory which had dominated early Christian understanding of the atonement and constructed a theory which suited better the medieval outlook. According to his satisfaction theory, human sin has offended God's honor. God's honor must be "satisfied" either by punishment of human beings (according to the principle of justice) or by a substitute (according to the principle of mercy). Human beings could not supply an adequate substitute. Consequently, God provided the substitute in the God–Man, Christ, who more than "satisfied" the sense of justice and honor.

Although his life became a tangled skein early on, Abelard impacted the development of Christian thought in this era at least as heavily as Anselm. Born at Pallet in Brittany of noble parents in 1079, he renounced his rights as the first born of the knight Berengar and chose a life of study. Possessed of a high regard for his own critical powers, he disputed with both of his teachers, Roscellinus the Nominalist and William of Champeaux the Realist. Taking up teaching, he drew such a large following that the latter, in a fit of jealousy, forced him to leave the city. About 1113 he took up the study of theology with Anselm of Laon, the most famous theologian of the day, and then returned to Paris, where his fame spread far and wide. There he met and fell madly in love with Heloise, then only eighteen. According to Bernard of Clairvaux and others, she was a good match for Abelard in terms of sheer mental gifts. Heloise bore Abelard a son, whom they named Astralabius. They married secretly. When she returned to live with her uncle Fulbert after bearing her child, he treated her so badly that Abelard put her in a convent. Fulbert, thinking Abelard wanted to get rid of her, or perhaps just seeking revenge, had Abelard emasculated. The latter then retired to St. Denis for about two years, but his outspoken criticism of the legend of St. Dionysius, patron of the abbey, forced him to flee. He spent some time as a hermit, but in 1125 he became abbot of St. Gildas, a monastery in need of reform and badly located. In 1136 he returned to Paris to teach. Within a short time, unfortunately, he again fell afoul of heresy hunters. William of St. Thierry sent Bernard of Clairvaux a list of thirteen propositions he found objectionable in the teachings of Abelard. Abelard agreed to defend himself at the Council of Sens in 1140. When he arrived, however, he immediately recognized that Bernard had carefully stacked the deck against him and he appealed to Rome. The Council went ahead to condemn his teachings and Bernard secured the confirmation of the condemnation by Pope Innocent II (1130–1143). Befriended by Peter the Venerable, Abelard spent the remainder of his life at Cluny.

Abelard's most telling contribution was his *Sic et non*, a collection of pro and con quotations from the Bible and the church fathers on 158 propositions with no effort to reconcile them. This method supplied the base for Peter the Lombard's *Sentences*, but the latter sought to reconcile conflicting statements. Abelard's handling of the Fathers reflected a critical and rationalistic approach, although he did concede to authority where he had to.

Abelard diverged significantly from Anselm and from traditional Christian thinking in the ethical sphere. In his doctrine of sin he placed the accent on intention rather than on the actual act. Eve sinned, he argued, when she *resolved* to eat the fruit, not in the actual deed. Guilt thus lies in the consciousness of right or wrong. Correspondingly, Abelard attributed a moral influence to the death of Christ. Rejecting both the *Christus Victor* and the Satisfaction theories, he focused on the impact of Christ's death on human beings. In the life and death of Christ God manifested the overwhelming divine love. This love stirs up in human hearts a reciprocal love. Thus by love God draws humankind back to God's self.

Abelard's manner probably had more to do with his downfall than his thought, innovative as some of it might have been. Unrestrained in his public attacks on others, he received little sympathy when he came under personal attack. Already in 1121 his treatise *On Unity and Divine Trinity* came under attack for tritheism, even though he leaned more toward Sabellianism and the charge

did not hold. At Sens in 1140 only a few brave former pupils such as Arnold of Brescia and Gilbert of Poitiers (1080–1154) dared to stand beside him. Gilbert himself, however, came under attack at the Council of Rheims in 1148, though he was not condemned, for his views of the Trinity, and Arnold met a horrible fate in Rome in 1154. Abelard's staunchest friend throughout was, of course, Heloise, who loved him even more passionately than he loved her. She wrote scorching love letters from the monastery she headed as abbess. "God is my witness that if Augustus, the emperor of the whole world, were to honor me with the thought of wedlock, and yield me the empire of the universe, I should deem it more precious and more honorable to be your mistress than to be the queen of a Caesar," she wrote in the first. Abelard replied with far more subdued letters, basically hinting that she cool her ardor some.

Scholasticism began to take on solid form with Peter the Lombard (ca. 1100–1160), the "Master of the Sentences." Born of a poor family near Novara, Italy, thanks to a rich patron Peter received a good education at Bologna, Rheims, and finally, around 1134, Paris. In Paris he taught at the Cathedral School of Notre Dame, where he composed his *Four Books of Sentences*, around 1155 to 1158. He opposed Gilbert of Poitiers at the Council of Rheims in 1148. Except for his appointment as bishop of Paris in 1159, the last decade of his life is obscure.

The Lombard's *magnum opus* owed much to Abelard, Hugo of St. Victor, and the *Decretum* of Gratian. Designed as a textbook for study of doctrine, it employed the following scheme: (1) It propounded a question in theology. (2) It offered a solution from one or more biblical or patristic passages and then (3) adduced authorities which seemed to contradict that solution. (4) It tried to resolve the contradiction either (a) by the hypothesis of dual meanings for the words in question, or (b) by the weighing of authorities, giving preference to the Bible and then to Augustine (as Abelard did). Reason thus assumed a secondary role, less than in Abelard's *Sic et non.* Not at all original, Peter the Lombard arranged the four books on the following pattern: (1) the Trinity, (2) the Creation and Sin, (3) the Incarnation and Virtues, and (4) the Sacraments and the Four Last Things. In Book 2 traditional teaching with Abelardian influence, and in Book 4 Hugo and the *Decretum* of Gratian. Going beyond Hugo, he affirmed seven and only seven sacraments. The *Sentences* came under attack as heretical at the Council of Tours in 1163 and at the Third Lateran Council in 1179, but it soon became the standard textbook on which scholars commented to gain credentials to teach theology.

Hugo of St. Victor (1097–1141) merits mention among the Schoolmen only in part, for he and Richard (d. 1173) headed the revival of mystical theology which occurred at St. Victor's during the twelfth century. Born either in Saxony or in Flanders (near Ypres), he evidently received his early education at the monastery of Hamersleben, near Halberstadt. About 1115 he accompanied his uncle, Archdeacon Hugo of Halberstadt, to France, where he attached himself to the Abbey of St. Victor, the monastery of Augustinian Canons founded by William of Champeaux. Thereafter, he remained at St. Victor until he died except for a brief trip to Rome to visit Pope Innocent II (1130–1143).

Hugo wrote on a variety of subjects. Early in his career, he composed a number of mystical treatises. Later he wrote systematic works, the most mature of which was *On the Sacraments of the Faith* (1140). In addition, he wrote several exegetical works in both periods of his life. He was studiously orthodox, but often interjected fresh insights into old ideas.

A theory of the threefold progression in knowledge of divine things dominated Hugo's mystical theology. Knowledge begins with *cogitatio*, grasping by sensory observation and reflection. It advances through *meditatio*, searching into the hidden sense of what the mind has grasped.

It strives toward *contemplatio*, the final free insight into the inward character of reality.

On the important issue of faith and reason Hugo divided truth into three classes: (1) from reason, (2) according to reason, and (3) above reason. He reacted strongly against the skepticism of Abelard and asserted the primacy of faith. The objects of faith are above reason, but theology can promote understanding of faith. Contra Bernard of Clairvaux, Hugo contended that faith and reason are not inconsistent.

Hugo made a major mark on later theology. Peter the Lombard relied heavily on him in framing the *Sentences*, but he did not produce a work as well organized or articulated. Especially noteworthy was the Lombard's dependence on Hugo's sacramental theology. From Hugo dates the treatment of the doctrine of the sacraments according to the Augustinian definition as a visible sign of an invisible grace.

Mystical Theology

Hugo founded the French mystical school for which St. Victor and Clairvaux became centers. Although Bernard attained far greater prominence, he borrowed much of his theology from Hugo. Richard (d. 1173) and Adam (d. between 1177 and 1192) developed the school further.

Evidently a native of Scotland, Richard came to St. Victor as a young man. In 1159 he was elected subprior, in 1162 prior of the monastery. Although an experiential mystic, he insisted on rational demonstration of theological points and was not content with citing of authorities. In this he pointed toward the view of Thomas Aquinas on the need to establish an empirical basis for the proof of God's existence, but he had even greater confidence than Aquinas that one could arrive at essentials of the doctrine of the Trinity by speculative reasoning. His most important treatise was *On the Trinity*, but most of his mystical theology is found in allegorical commentaries entitled *Benjamin Major* and *Benjamin Minor.*

Alongside the more speculative mysticism of the Victorines stood the more popular affective mysticism of Bernard, William of St. Thierry, Hildegarde of Bingen, and Elizabeth of Schonau. Bernard has received extensive treatment earlier in connection with a discussion of Benedictine piety, and it suffices here to recall his importance in framing the tradition of "Bridal" or "Marriage Mysticism" which received such extensive development in the thirteenth century, especially by women mystics.

William of St. Thierry (ca. 1085–1148), an admirer and associate of Bernard, shared Bernard's concern for orthodoxy and his mystical theology. Born into a noble family at Liège and probably educated at Laon, he entered the Benedictine Abbey of St. Nicasius at Rheims in 1113. In 1119 or 1120 he became Abbot of St. Thierry near Rheims. Having formed a close friendship with Bernard, in 1135 he resigned his abbacy and joined a group of Cistercians in forming a monastery at Signy. A prolific author, he wrote his first two treatises on the relationship between knowledge and love: *On Contemplation of God* and *On the Nature and Worth of Love*. Before leaving St. Thierry he wrote a work *On the Sacrament of the Altar*, which he dedicated to Bernard, and another *On the Nature of the Soul and the Body*, in which he tried to synthesize the teaching of Eastern and Western Fathers. He composed also two commentaries on the Song of Songs. His final work was a life of Bernard. It was William who, in 1138, called Bernard's attention to the errors in Peter Abelard's theology and incited him to obtain a condemnation.

Hildegarde of Bingen (1098–1179) and Elizabeth of Schonau (ca. 1129–1164) blazed the trail for women mystics who wrote revelations during the thirteenth and fourteenth centuries. Hildegarde, a daughter of aristocratic parents born at Bockelheim, was reared by a recluse in a cell on the Diessenberg adjoining the family estate. In 1116 she entered the Benedictine community which had formed around Jutta.

Twenty years later, she succeeded Jutta as abbess. Having had visions since childhood, she began to write them down under direction of her confessor. Between 1141 and 1151 she dictated her *Scivias* ("Know the ways"), recording twenty-six visions on the vices of the world and coming disaster. She reported other visions in her letters, which she addressed to emperors, popes, princes, bishops, and numerous other persons. With encouragement from Bernard of Clairvaux Pope Eugenius III gave cautious approval to her visions in 1147. Subsequently she moved the convent from the Diessenberg to Rupertsburg, near Bingen, from which she journeyed throughout the Rhineland. She exerted wide influence.

Elizabeth of Schonau entered the monastery at Schonau at the age of twelve. In 1152 she began to experience visions described in her three books of *Visions*. Her experiences began with depression and resulted in convulsions and loss of consciousness. In her period of unconsciousness she saw heavenly forms, especially of the Virgin Mary or the saint whose anniversary was observed that day, which she could describe when she regained consciousness. Her visions later became more frequent and lasted longer.

In this context some attention should be given also to Joachim of Fiore (ca. 1132–1202), whose apocalyptic visions exerted a powerful influence in the next centuries over the Spiritual Franciscans and the Fraticelli, who thought of themselves as the new order of spiritual persons forecast in Joachim's scheme. Of obscure background, Joachim experienced conversion as the result of a pilgrimage to the Holy Land as a young man. He entered the Cistercian Order and was elected the Abbot of Corazzo, against his will, in 1177. A few years later, he resigned and devoted himself to writing his apocalyptic works. He lived first at the Abbey of Casamari and then at Fiore, where he founded a monastery which received papal approval in 1196.

Joachim, in three biblical writings, outlined a trinitarian conception of history. The first, *Ordo conjugatorum,* is the age of the Father when humankind lived under the Law which lasted until the end of the Old Testament dispensation. The second, *Ordo clericorum,* is that of the Son wherein humankind lives under grace in the New Testament dispensation. Joachim expected this period to last forty-two generations of about thirty years each, which would come very near the year 1260. The third, *Ordo monachorum,* is the age of the Spirit wherein humankind will live with the freedom of the "Spiritual Understanding" deriving from the Old and the New Testaments. This age would begin about 1260. Joachim lived a life of commendable purity and did not come under censure, but the Fourth Lateran Council in 1215 and the Council of Arles in 1263 condemned some of his views. Both the Spiritual Franciscans and the Fraticelli suffered severe persecution, yet Joachim's ideas continued to captivate the imagination of many throughout the later Middle Ages.

Chapter 46

Art, Architecture, and Music, 604–1300

If art, architecture, and music reveal the deeper concerns and preoccupations of a civilization, it is clear that the Middle Ages in Europe was a period of intense concern for religion. The capabilities in these, to be sure, varied greatly from time to time so that some generations left skimpy contributions behind them. The so-called "Dark Ages" from about 500 to 750, for instance, prevented Westerners from doing much more than maintenance of the churches their forebears had built, much less matching the wonderful artistic achievements of the Byzantines at the time of Justinian I (527–565). These were times of survival, and even in a city such as Rome, the pride of the West even after the fall, works of art were done on a small scale. The "Little Dark Ages" of the late-ninth and early-tenth centuries which followed the Viking invasions caused another lapse in attention to art.

No period, however, was devoid of the creativity which gives rise to expressions of the inner person. Diminishment of capability to perform may dampen creative instincts; it cannot destroy them altogether. Churches and monasteries sprang up everywhere even during the darkest of the "Dark Ages" and wherever these existed art, architecture, and music also existed. Then, when stability returned, art thrived. Accordingly, under the Carolingians art, architecture, and music revived and took strides forward. To a great extent, these imitated the achievements of the past as in-

dicated in the name Romanesque applied to architecture. Yet something new was added as the Germanic peoples manifested their creative gifts. Similarly, under the Ottonians came another resurgence in art, architecture, and music, not advancing basic styles so much as enriching existent ones. From the early Middle Ages, therefore, the modern world has inherited a rich lode of illuminated manuscripts, carved ivories, wood and metal carvings, frescoes, mosaics, sculptures, and tapestries as well as grand churches and monasteries of the Romanesque style. It has also inherited the Gregorian chant.

During the twelfth century, a new style of architecture, Gothic, added to the already rich inheritance of earlier centuries. Gothic perhaps served better than any other style to give expression to medieval aspirations. Its pointed arches and sweeping spires linked heaven and earth in ways the Roman basilica and the rounded arches could not. And what is remarkable is how much building took place during the twelfth and thirteenth centuries as medieval piety peaked. With gifts of emperors, kings, princes, popes, bishops, and just ordinary folk monasteries and churches all over Europe underwent expansion, rebuilding, and building for the first time. Yet, as rich and ready as resources were, the grand works of art took time, often more than a century, so that most of them reflected a mixture of styles linking worshipers over many centuries.

Byzantine Art and Architecture

Distinctively Christian styles of art and architecture gradually emerged in the Later Roman or Byzantine Empire. They represented basically a cross-fertilization of oriental and Graeco-Roman art forms. In art mosaics and icons represented major contributions, but outstanding art was also done in other media and for a variety of purposes. In architecture Hagia Sophia, now a Muslim mosque, is considered to be the crown of Byzantine creativity. Some of the finest specimens of Byzantine art and architecture, however, can be found in the West—at Ravenna, Rome, and in southern Italy, where the Byzantine Empire maintained continuing control for centuries after Justinian reconquered the West.

In Ravenna the Mausoleum of Galla Placidia (425–450); the churches of San Vitale, built by Archbishop Ecclesius (526–532); San Apollinare in Classe, erected by Archbishop Arsicinus (535–539) under patronage of Ostrogothic King Theodoric (493–526); and San Apollinare Nuovo, the palace church of Theodoric; and the baptistry of San Giovanni in Fonte, dedicated to Archbishop Neon (449–452) all feature outstanding mosaics. A dominant theme of Byzantine mosaic art was the triumphant Christ. Even the good shepherd mosaic of the Mausoleum of Galla Placidia has a look of the exalted Judge rather than that of a gentle shepherd. The triumphant Christ typically held the central place in the apse of Byzantine churches, as in San Vitale in Ravenna or in Santa Maria Maggiore in Rome, originally constructed between 420 and 440. Other mosaics regularly combined scenes from salvation history of both Old and New Testaments with some from Christian history. The mosaics of San Vitale featured the triumphant Christ with Emperor Justinian and his court on the left and Empress Theodora and her entourage on the right, the emperor and empress being haloed. Both of them were present for the dedication of San Vitale in 547.

Byzantine churches of the Middle Ages were divided into three zones corresponding to the understanding of the worshipping church. The highest zone, the dome and apse, was reserved for the depiction of the heavenly hierarchy, almost always the Christ Pantocrator and the Madonna as a symbol of the incarnation. The next highest featured scenes from the life of Christ and Mary which had the most important implications for salvation and resurrection. These corresponded to the Christian year. The lowest, terrestrial zone surrounded the community gathered for worship with the church fathers, the martyrs, the saints. The symbolism corresponded to the heavenly hierarchies depicted in the writings of Pseudo-Dionysius. As the present-day saints gather, they gather with the whole host of heaven to participate in the story of salvation. Mosaic art served here in a way painting could not. Complex technical procedures enabled them to become saturated with and reflect light.

Icon art grew out of a strong Eastern predilection for the visual in worship. Although the second commandment inhibited early Christian painting, Eastern theologians found a rationale for icons in the incarnation by way of the Neoplatonic concept of an identity of the image with the idea it manifested. Painted in two dimensions, usually on wood, but also produced in mosaic, ivory, or other forms, icons featured Christ, the Virgin Mary, or other saints as objects of devotion. They became common in the east from the sixth century on. The iconoclastic controversy during the eighth and ninth centuries increased devotion to them among the people. The faithful venerated the icon with kisses, genuflexions, incense, and other forms of reverence and thought they would exercise beneficial powers—preventing illnesses, driving out demons, securing blessings, and channelling divine grace. Not many icons survived the iconoclastic controversy, but St. Catherine's Monastery at the foot of Mount Sinai has conserved several Marianic icons which would have served monks in the sixth century and after.

Illumination of books in the East took an iconographic form. Book illumination came into its own in the tenth century when a revival occurred during the reign of the Macedonians. The Patriarch Photius (878–886) and Emperor Constantine VII Porphyrogenitus (913–959), himself a scholar and artist, boosted art as well as other forms of learning. Artists produced lavishly embellished manuscripts suited to highly cultivated tastes of the day. As models, they used manuscripts of the late classical, early Christian, and sixth and seventh centuries.

A new epoch in Byzantine art dates from the reign of Basil II (876–1025) with the development of a new style which dominated throughout the next three centuries. The whole picture was organized to near mathematical perfection. Similarly space in churches was organized into a formal unity. The eleventh century produced a flood of art of all types—book illustrations, mosaics, decorated book covers; the twelfth century, monumental art and comprehensive decorative programs par excellence. Although the deterioration of the empire deterred production in the East, the Byzantine tradition continued in Norman Sicily, Serbia, Russia, and around the Adriatic Sea.

Byzantine architecture looked to Hagia Sophia as its model. The East developed a different basilical style than the West. Eastern churches had aisles in two stories sometimes extended around the transept. Most were shorter and broader than Western churches. Many churches, especially martyria, used a circular, convergent style or an octagon, to symbolize the day of resurrection. Eastern architects incorporated the dome into both the basilical and the convergent structures.

Hiberno-Saxon Art

Behind the revival of art and architecture which took place in the West during the Carolingian era stood some influential developments in England and Ireland which made their way to the continent by way of Celtic and Anglo-Saxon missionaries. Celtic monks on Iona engaged in manuscript illumination as early as the seventh century. Patterns found in the Book of Kells, traditionally thought to have belonged to Columba but actually dated about 800. The Echternach Gospels may have originated in Ireland about 690. The Lindisfarne Gospels were copied and decorated by Eadfrith, later bishop of Lindisfarne, in honor of St. Cuthbert around 696 to 698. Columban and Gall may have carried some of this artistic tradition to France and Switzerland. Although the monastery bearing his name originated a century afterwards, the great library at St. Gallen collected many illuminated manuscripts, including the St. Gall Gospels, which were made in Ireland, following the pattern of the Book of Kells.

Carolingian Art and Architecture

The Carolingian renaissance erupted suddenly in the reign of Charlemagne (768–814), and Charlemagne himself deserves credit for it. He not only pushed learning, securing the best scholars he could find such as Alcuin; he also advanced art. When he moved his capital to Aachen, he sought to effect there a "New Rome," the center of a renewal of empire. Architecture expressed his claims, but his renaissance, just as the later one, pressed for a revival of stylistic forms of the past, including architecture and art.

In architecture the Carolingians created what is called Romanesque, a revised Roman style. Charlemagne's first building at Aachen was the Palace Chapel, begun in 792 and completed around 800. It followed the pattern of early baptistries and martyria with its octagonal shape and domed roof. The cupola over the octagon symbolized the power of the new ruler. The original mosaics in the cupola, either Christ enthroned or the lamb of the Apocalypse, undergirded the same plot. Other churches built during this period, for instance, St. Michael's at Fulda, also used the circular or octagonal style.

Most Western churches imitated the Roman basilical style employed in early Christian churches. St. Denis near Paris, begun during Pippin III's reign and completed during Charlemagne's, the abbey church of Fulda (791–819), and Saints Petrus and Marcellinus in Seligenstadt (832–840) adopted the pattern of St. Peter's. St. Denis, which supposedly housed the remains of Dionysius of the Areopagus, copied the tomb of Peter. Carolingian churches often had double choirs. The rounded Roman arch is one of the most easily recognizable features of Romanesque.

The court at Aachen was a center of art as well as learning during Charlemagne's late years and after his death. Illumination of manuscripts took place there and in several monasteries around the Frankish kingdom. The illuminations were distinctive not only for their forms, colors, and arrangements of the central motifs but for the details of their borders. The earliest of these, the Godescalc Evangelistary, commissioned by Charlemagne himself and produced between 781 and 783, reflected the influence of the Hiberno-Saxon tradition carried over to the continent. Illuminations adhered closely to the text. Later illuminations reflect more Byzantine influence with richer and more varied colors and more rounded figures. Later artists sought to relate all lines to the central figure in the painting, showing here more direct dependence on classical models. After the death of Charlemagne the court artists passed from view and left hardly a trace of their influence until the tenth century revival under Otto the Great. The one exception was the scriptorium of the Abbey of Fulda, where Hrabanus Maurus became abbot in 822.

One theme strikingly missing from Carolingian illuminations was that of Christ in Majesty. According to the *Caroline Books*, which Charlemagne had issued after the decrees authorizing the use of images in worship at Nicaea in 787 appeared, the likeness of Christ could not be portrayed since he appeared only through his Word. Paintings were not holy objects to be revered but only existed to depict figures, to refresh the memory, and to formulate thoughts. The illuminations of Charlemagne's day depicted only the four evangelists with any regularity. They highlighted the word of the scriptures.

Other important scriptoria where manuscript illumination occurred included Rheims, where Ebbo served as archbishop from 806 to 855 and St. Martin of Tours, where Alcuin became abbot in 776, although he spent little time there. Tours reintroduced the Majestic Christ figure within the framework of cosmology, as in Byzantine art. Metz and St. Gallen were also major centers.

The Carolingians also produced notable sculpture and metalwork. Court artists crafted the bronze doors for the Palace Chapel in the workshop at Aachen. Monumental works in stone also were done, although only fragments have survived. Some of the finest artistic pieces are carvings in ivory—book covers, diptychs, and vessels. St. Gallen served as a center for transmission of traditions, where not only ivory carvings but church vessels and altar pieces made of gold were produced.

Ottonian Art and Architecture

The slump brought on by the Viking and Magyar invasions came to an end under the dynasty begun by Otto I (962–973) as the Cluniac reform impacted all of Europe. Art and architecture took on new life in Germany, Spain, England, and Italy. In Spain the reconquest opened the way for building of churches and monasteries. In England the Norman conquest spurred much building. In Italy the popes found new means to build, refurbish, and embellish in a new way.

The Ottonians followed in the Carolingian path in architecture, giving preference to the three aisled basilica with columns. Otto himself directed the erection of the first at Magdeburg. Otto II paid tribute to his Byzantine wife, Theophana, by erecting the convent church of St. Cyriakus in Gernrode, Saxony, in the Byzantine style.

The Ottonians also imitated the Carolingians in painting. In one area, however, they innovated, that is, in showing miracle stories and other narrative scenes from the Gospels for the first time. Some of the best surviving frescoes are to be found in the church of St. George at Reichenau-Oberzell. In addition, this era produced fine illuminated manuscripts. At first the artists copied Carolingian masterpieces, but they gradually developed a style of their own. The most important center for illumination now appears to have been Trier rather than Reichenau, as was long thought. Echternach branched off from the Trier school, but Regensburg manifested a style of its own, somewhat like that of Tours in the Carolingian era. A network of workshops in art stretched from Salzburg to Bremen. Some were inventive, for example, Cologne, but others were imitative.

The Ottonians also did outstanding sculpture, carving, and metal work. They produced reliquaries, book covers, antependants for altars, and other items. Artists of this period also did much work in gold.

Spanish artists produced colorful illustrations of apocalypses during the latter half of the tenth century. The center of this production was the monastery of San Salvador de Tavara near Zamora. Anglo-Saxon illuminators equalled the Ottonians in skill. The chief school was at Winchester.

Gothic Architecture

Romanesque architecture dominated until the twelfth century, when Gothic endangered its hegemony and then pushed it completely to the side in most countries. Preliminary steps toward Gothic were taken at St. Denis by Abbot Suger (1140–1144). The key lay in constructing the vaulting in such a way that it could support the roof without dependence on walls by buttresses and by the use of pointed arches. Introduction of pointed arches for the vaulting led to its use in all arches. Gothic continued the effort of Romanesque to attain height, but it allowed far more light and created an image of soaring heavenward in a way Romanesque could not.

Gothic received an enthusiastic reception in France. Notre Dame in Paris followed St. Denis in 1163 in rebuilding. Then came Rheims in 1210 and Amiens shortly thereafter. From France the Gothic trend passed almost immediately into Norman England, where Norman elements modified the original. In Germany Gothic caught on more slowly and underwent adaptation, but by the mid-thirteenth century the cathedral of Cologne carried the Gothic principle to its logical conclusion. Where earlier constructions had maintained the side aisles of Romanesque churches, Cologne dispensed with them to create one single large nave. It Italy Gothic did not catch on as it did in other countries. Soon the Renaissance transformed style once again and laid the groundwork for Baroque.

One of the great developments accompanying the move from Romanesque to Gothic was the stained glass window. Though used already in the tenth century, it reached its peak of development in the great Gothic churches like the Cathedral at Chartres. Windows did for Western Christians what mosaics and icon screens did for Eastern: they provided a focus for meditation.

The story of a single cathedral may illustrate the complex process by which the great Gothic churches of the twelfth century and after came into existence. The original York Minster was begun by King Edwin, baptized at York in 627, and completed by his successor, King Oswald (633–642). In 741 this church was badly damaged by fire but rebuilt in a grand style, perhaps on a different site than the original. During the Norman invasions, in 1069, the church was burned and pillaged. Thomas of Bayeux, the Norman archbishop, gathered clergy to patch up what remained, but a Viking raid in 1075 destroyed the Minster for the last time. The archbishop proceeded to abandon the old church and to build a totally new one which was completed before he died in 1100. The cathedral roof suffered severe damage from fire in 1137, and it underwent extensive refurbishing during the archbishopric of Roger of Pont l'Evêque, who left it one of the great Norman masterpieces when he died in 1181. By the thirteenth century its fame spread all over Europe.

The shift to Gothic, however, led to further rebuilding. After the refurbishing of Canterbury in the late twelfth century, York seemed antiquated and cumbersome. The vast remodeling project began under the leadership of Archbishop Walter de Gray (1215–1255) in 1220. The transformation of the Cathedral went on after that for almost two hundred and fifty years. De Gray began revising the south transept. Subsequent work transcended changes in style over that long period of time by almost complete replacement of the Norman original—a new nave, a new choir, and finally a new tower. The chapter house, built between 1260 and 1290, affected a somewhat different style, but that did not detract from the larger design. Construction of the nave took seventy years, 1290–1360. The builders ran into all sorts of difficulties. They originally intended to vault the roof with stone, but they had to change to wood because of the length of the rafters (nearly fifty feet). The black plague in 1347 claimed the lives of a large number of workmen.

Money for this vast project came from a variety of sources. Pilgrims contributed. The archbishops promoted sale of indulgences. They themselves raised much of the money. Large amounts also came from nobles of the north. The Vavasours supplied the stone from their quarries. The Percys gave timber.

Music

The story of music paralleled the story of art during the Middle Ages, experiencing some of the same ups and downs. Early Christianity passed on a vigorous appreciation for hymnody and psalmody, but also a fear of the seductive influence of instrumental music. Reservations even intruded about hymns at times so that the

Council of Laodicea (360–381) forbade singing of all nonbiblical texts, but these were readily overcome in the East. Ephraem Syrus (306–373) popularized a new type of hymn which supplied the model for the Byzantine *kontakion*. In the West also appeared outstanding hymn writers during the fourth and fifth centuries—Ambrose, Hilary of Poitiers, and the Spanish Prudentius. As monasticism rose to a position of great influence, however, psalmody overrode hymnody in the liturgy, though it did not displace it entirely.

Byzantine

Byzantine hymn writing lasted about six centuries, from the second half of the fifth until the end of the eleventh centuries. Prior to the iconoclastic controversy the *kontakion*, a hymn consisting of from eighteen to thirty or more stanzas all structurally alike, prevailed. A single stanza, called *troparion*, varied in length from three to thirteen lines. A soloist sang the *kontakion* and a choir the refrain at the end of each stanza. Stanzas were connected either alphabetically or by an acrostic signaled by the title of the *kontakion*. The title also supplied other information: the day of the feast on which the *kontakion* was to be sung, the feast for which it was composed, and the musical mode of the melody. Hymns were written in an elaborate rhythmical scheme of lines of varying length which required not only real poetic but also musical skills.

Introduction of the *kontakion* into the Byzantine liturgy has been ascribed to Romanus, a native of Emesa on the Orontes, who, after serving as a deacon at Berytus in Phoenicia, came to Constantinople during the patriarchate of Anastasius I (491–518) and joined the clergy of the Theotokos Church. Behind the style, however, stands a long tradition of Syriac hymnody antedating even Ephraem, although Romanus owed much to the latter. As a matter of fact, some of Romanus's *kontakia* are paraphrases of Ephraem's homilies. He differed from Ephraem, however, in conciseness, and his hymns made him

---

the premier Christian poet of the age of Justinian (572–565). Many later hymns were ascribed to Romanus to give them greater weight, but the authorship of the most famous hymn of the period, the *Akathistos*, sung originally for the Feast of the Annunciation, is uncertain.

Towards the end of the seventh century a new kind of hymnography, the *kanon*, supplanted the *kontakion*. A complex form of poetry, it consisted of nine odes which originally had from six to nine *troparia*. Later, because of the introduction of a number of monostrophic stanzas, only three of the troparia of each ode were used in the service. Thence, the ode did not differ from a short *kontakion*. Whereas the *kontakion* was a hymnic homily, the nine odes of the *kanon* had the character of hymns of praise. Originally the kanons were composed for Lent, later for the period between Easter and Pentecost, and eventually for the entire ecclesiastical year.

What probably precipitated the shift from *kontakion* to *canon* was the iconoclastic controversy itself. Hymn writers did not worry about diction as much as they did about the possibility of persecution, exile, and death, and they embodied their mood in their hymns. The mystical element of Byzantine theology thoroughly penetrates the style of the *kanon*. The *kanon* differed significantly from the *kontakion* in its increased use and greater variety of music. The first school of *kanon* writers were monks of St. Sabas monastery in Palestine, near the Dead Sea, who flourished during the eighth century. The most distinguished composers were John of Damascus and his brother Kosmas of Jerusalem.

At the close of the eleventh century ecclesiastical authorities forbade the introduction of new hymns into the liturgy.

Western

In the West hymnody and psalmody played a major role in the celebration of the Vigils, the first of the daily Offices to come into existence. From the celebration of other offices at Jerusa-

lem—Matins, Sext, None, and Vespers—as well as the Sunday Mass and special holy days—Christmas, Epiphany, Holy Week, Easter, Ascension, Pentecost, and the finding of the Cross—came an expansion of the liturgy and of the use of music in the West as well. Throughout the West liturgies and music developed independently in different areas. Although later traditions from the eighth century on pointed to a Roman prototype dating from the time of Leo I (440–461), several other liturgies—Gallican, Celtic, Visigothic, and Milanese—were widely used.

Contemporary studies have raised serious questions about the role of Pope Gregory the Great in the development of what is known as the Gregorian chant. His own writings seldom mention music and when they do, they deemphasize it. In a decree of 595 Gregory explicitly stated that music was only a vehicle of the text, not a concern of the higher clergy, and not a requirement for appointment of deacons. Not until Bede (731) does one find a statement connecting Gregory with development of a musical tradition, evidence which is suspect, for Bede wanted to disavow Celtic influence in favor of Roman.

Some kind of Roman tradition began to prevail during the Carolingian era when Pippin III (741–768) sent Chrodegang, bishop of Metz, to Rome as one of his envoys. Chrodegang, became interested in Roman music. In 754, when Pope Stephen II met the king at Saint Denis, Pippin was exposed to Roman rites and music. Shortly thereafter, Emperor Constantine V (741–775) presented Pippin an organ, an instrument unknown in the West since Roman times. About 760 Pippin brought a singing teacher who had studied at Rome to Metz to establish a *schola cantorum*, school of singers, and another to Rouen, where one of Pippin's brothers was bishop, to do the same. Pope Paul I (757–767) sent Pippin an Antiphonal containing chants of the Mass and a Responsal with those for the Offices. Charlemagne continued the process of

Romanization begun by his father. In 789 he issued his General Admonition insisting that all clergy should learn and use the *cantus Romanus*. In 803 the Synod of Aix-la-Chapelle reiterated this directive and ordered bishops to establish *scholae cantorum*. Carolingian Romanizers took every opportunity to invoke the name of Gregory to promote the Roman over the Gallican or other liturgies.

Throughout these centuries the monastery at Metz served as the major center of musical reform and innovation. In 831–832 Amalarius, bishop of Metz (ca. 780–ca. 850), recognized the problem of diversities in music supposedly stemming from Rome and went to study the sources there. He asked Pope Gregory IV (827–844) for an authentic Antiphonary. When he compared it with the Offices of the Abbey of Corbie, near Amien, however, he found wide variations in order and words, and even in antiphons and responsaries, due to a revision undertaken under Hadrian I (772–795). Consequently, Amalarius set about to compile a new Antiphonary for use at Metz. He drew on the old Metz versions, the Corbie version, and what he had learned from Alcuin as a youth. The Metz revision continued to exert strong influence as late as the twelfth century, for Bernard based his reform of Cistercian chantbooks on the Metz tradition. During the tenth century, when Otto the Great and his successors subjected the papacy, the Metz tradition may have established itself over the older Roman tradition.

Musical notation developed slowly in the West. In the East the Byzantines began to use ecphonetic ("pronouncing aloud") signs as early as the fourth century and had developed a system of fifteen by the eighth. Such signs were not known in the West, however, to Cassiodorus (ca. 485–ca. 580), Isidore of Seville (ca. 560–636), or Alcuin (ca. 735–804). In the middle of the ninth century the West developed neumes, from the Greek *neuma* meaning "nod" or "sign." During the tenth century, neumes appeared throughout France and Germany and even in England. From Byzantium the West also took its tonal system. When Eastern clergy applied the brakes to liturgical and musical developments, however, hardly permitting any change after 1054, the West stepped on the accelerator as new music styles tickled the popular fancy. The most important development in church music was a more ambitious kind of polyphony suited to the vast spaces of the Gothic cathedrals erected in the twelfth and thirteenth century, first in France and then elsewhere.

The first definite mention of polyphony in the West appeared in a treatise *On Harmonic Institution* by Hucbald (ca. 840–930), a monk of the monastery of St. Amand in the diocese of Tournai. Hucbald gave attention to harmony of sounds in the use of instruments and to the need for more precise notations than neumes allowed. Others also worked on the improvement of musical notations during the tenth and eleventh centuries as the organ, previously associated with pagan music, gained acceptance in the church. During the eleventh century, letter notations supplemented the neumes. Subsequently an embryonic staff helped them become more satisfactory means for noting pitch. Between 1025 and 1033 Guido, a Benedictine who taught the choir school of the cathedral at Arezzo, developed precise methods for teaching music. Meantime, the songs of troubadours added some new flavor to the music of the church. By 1300 the Western church had a rich heritage at its disposal.

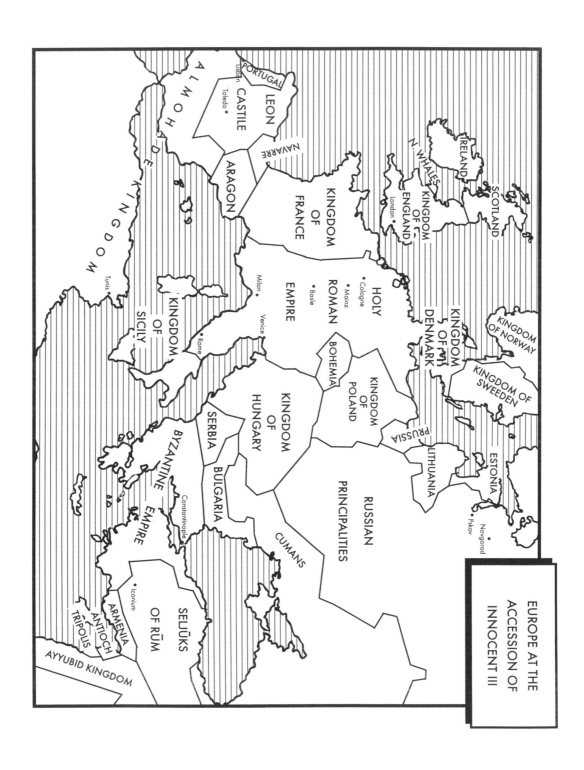

EUROPE AT THE
ACCESSION OF
INNOCENT III

Part 9

The Great Century 1200–1300 C.E.

EASTERN EUROPE
IN THE
THIRTEENTH CENTURY

COURLAND

Riga
KNIGHTS OF THE SWORD

• Memel

• Königsberg

LITHUANIA

• Danzig

PRUSSIA

Stettin •

POMERANIA

KUIAWIA

• Kulm

BRANDENBURG

MAZOVIA

GREAT • Poznan
POLAND

LAUSITZ

• Glogau

POLAND

MEISSEN

Breslau •

Lublin •

Sandomierz

RUSSIA

SILESIA

LESSER
POLAND

• Prague
• Kuttenberg

Cracow •

BOHEMIA MORAVIA

GALICIA

AUSTRIA

• Gran
• Buda-Pest

STYRIA

• Veszprem

HUNGARY

CARINTHIA

TRANSYLVANIA

CROATIA

CUMANS

BOSNIA

SERBIA

BULGARIA

Chapter 47

The Papal Monarchy

The thirteenth was in many ways the church's greatest century, the century of Gothic architecture, powerful popes, great rulers, exciting new religious orders, great mystics, scholasticism, and outstanding writers. Gothic architecture perhaps symbolizes the aspirations of the people—to link heaven and earth, to lift earth heavenward. Some names stand out among all the names of history: Innocent III, Frederick II and Louis IX, Francis of Assisi and Dominic of Calaruega, Gertrude of Helfta and Gertrude of Hackeborn, Albertus Magnus and Thomas Aquinas and Duns Scotus, and Dante. At times the church soared.

Yet the thirteenth was also a time of great troubles, a time when the discerning eye could foresee a radical shift in the church's fortunes. The thirteenth was the age of increasing tensions between church and state, schisms and heresies, the Inquisition and crusades, persecution of Jews, and shift of consciousness that prepared for the Renaissance. It was the age when a crusade supposedly designed to help the Byzantines turned into a crusade that destroyed the Byzantine Empire. It was the age when kings and princes no longer—if they ever did—responded to the church's beck and call. Emperor Frederick II (1212–1250), to the contrary, functioned with few qualms of conscience under repeated papal excommunications, and even the mighty Innocent III (1198–1216) could not prevent the English barons from forcing John Lackland to sign *Mag-*

na carta. At the end of the century, moreover, Boniface VIII (1295–1303) proved utterly impotent to impose his will on Philip the Fair or the French church. The grand phrases of *Unam sanctam* in 1302 fell on deaf ears and inaugurated a series of attacks first on the popes' involvement in temporal affairs, then on their claims in spiritual affairs, and then on the very legitimacy of the office itself.

During the period attention naturally focuses on the papacy, beginning with Innocent III and ending with Boniface VIII. Circumstances aided Innocent in lifting the papacy to its highest level in implementing papal theory laid out by Gregory VII. His crusading fervor, however, took a turn which he surely did not intend when the Fourth Crusade ended up as a crusade against the Byzantine Empire and set in motion forces that would gradually undermine the papacy. His successors could not carry out the lofty objectives Innocent had set. Frederick II frustrated them at every turn, and even the saintly Louis IX (1214–1270), hero of two crusades, resisted papal demands at times. Louis's grandson Philip IV, the Fair, proved still less obliging. Philip asserted vigorously the traditional claims of French monarchs going back to the Merovingians and Carolingians to control everything within his territory, church as well as state. Consequently Boniface VIII's reign ended on a far more discordant note than the one with which Innocent III had begun the century, with the proud pope maligned and charged with heresy.

Innocent III

Descendant of the noble Scotti family, Lotario de' Conti di Segni (1160–1216) received his education at Paris, where he studied theology under Peter of Corbeil, and at Bologna, where he majored in canon law under Uguccio of Ferrara. A person of great political skills, he rose rapidly in papal service. In 1190 his uncle, Pope Clement III, named him a cardinal. In 1198, though not yet ordained, he was elected to succeed Celestine III (1191–1198), who had held him back from further ecclesiastical preferments, at the age of thirty-seven.

No one could contest Innocent's effectiveness in the office, but scholars have debated extensively what claims he made for it. According to an older critical view, Innocent committed the papacy to a vision of unlimited world monarchy that proved disastrous. He wanted to rule the world and would stop at nothing to achieve that end. According to a more recent interpretation, Innocent intervened in the temporal sphere out of the highest spiritual motives and based his theory of church and state on a cautious dualism rather than a theocratic concept giving the pope both spiritual and temporal supremacy. The truth would appear to lie somewhere between the two extremes.

Early in his pontificate Innocent III issued a series of statements that sounded like uninhibited monarchical thinking. Citing both Old and New Testament scriptures in his coronation address, he claimed that the pope, as vicar of Christ, is "set between God and man, lower than God but higher than man, who judges all and is judged by no one." In a letter to the archbishop of Ravenna he asserted that the liberty of the church would fare best "where the Roman church has full power in both temporal and spiritual affairs." He cited Gregory VII's sun/moon analogy in a letter to the prefect Acerbus and the nobles of Tuscany to illustrate that "the royal power derives the splendor of its dignity from the pontifical authority." In a letter to the patriarch of Constantinople George II (1192–1199) he pointed out that James the brother of Jesus left to Peter not only the rule of the universal church "but the whole world." And he explained to Emperor Alexius III (1195–1204) that when Jesus told Peter that "whatsoever you bind upon earth, etc." in Matthew 16:19, he left nothing out when he said "whatsoever." It is difficult to avoid the conclusion that Innocent did hold a theocratic idea of papal world monarchy. Occasional statements qualifying such thinking would be a consequence of special circumstances. Innocent was practical enough to know when the occasion demanded a turn of phrase that would avoid offense.

Although Innocent doubtless deserves most accolades he has received as the greatest of medieval popes, he did not have quite as much success as some have assumed. It is true that he intervened in the disputed imperial election and saw to the installation of Frederick II in 1212, claimed the right to arbitrate the disputes between John Lackland of England and Philip IV of France, helped to crown a king in Bulgaria and tried to remove one in Norway, and extended the boundaries of the papal states in central Italy. He also claimed feudal lordship over Sicily, Aragon, and Hungary, which had placed themselves under papal protection. His weakness, however, showed up in his effort to govern Sicily as the guardian of the infant Frederick II, where what he did actually weakened the strong government set up by the Normans. In the papal states he had to hand over the reins of government as a fief to marquis Azzo VI of Este to ensure respect for this suzerainty because he lacked executive powers to enforce his will.

Innocent's more dramatic success was in Germany, where a contest went on between two uncrowned rivals from the death of Henry VI in 1197 until the death of one of the rivals, Philip of Swabia, the candidate of the Ghibelline majority.

The Guelph minority elected Otto, count of Poitou, the third son of Henry the Lion. At first Innocent maintained neutrality, but he finally sided with Otto, who had previously given assurances that he would not claim certain territories in central Italy. When the supporters of Philip protested, Innocent replied in the bull *Venerabilem* sustaining his right to intervene on the grounds that the emperor was, by right of election, also ruler of Rome. In the case of a divided election, therefore, he could step in. The struggle swayed first in Otto's and then in Philip's favor, but just when it appeared that Innocent might change his allegiance, Philip was assassinated, and Otto took the crown. Otto immediately renewed his promises but then reneged on them, claiming Spolete, Ancona, and the Romagna for the empire and setting out to conquer Sicily. In November 1210 Innocent excommunicated Otto. In September 1211 the German princes gathered at Nuremberg and deposed Otto. In his place they elected Frederick II. Innocent approved the choice, for Frederick had recognized the pope's suzerainty over Sicily and had his son crowned king of Sicily. After his coronation Frederick signed the *Golden Bull* on July 12, 1213, in which he repeated all promises to the pope made by Otto. Otto IV secured the help of John Lackland of England and took up arms against the Hohenstaufen, but he was routed at the Battle of Vouvines on July 27, 1214. The Fourth Lateran Council in 1215, among other things, renewed the ban of excommunication against Otto and acknowledged Frederick as emperor.

Innocent registered mixed success in his interventions in other states. When Philip Augustus of France divorced Ingeborg, his legal wife, and married Agnes of Meran, Innocent, after years of threats, placed France under an interdict until Philip agreed to take back Ingeborg. When John Lackland refused to accept Stephen Langton as archbishop of Canterbury, Innocent again resorted to an interdict in March 1208. John replied with persecution of the church. Innocent

then excommunicated him, released his subjects from their oath of allegiance, and declared him deposed. He then called on Philip Augustus to execute the sentence of deposition in John's continental territories. John resisted for a time until threat of an uprising forced him to capitulate in 1213. John recognized Langton, returned confiscated property to the church, permitted exiled churchmen to return, and received England and Ireland from the pope as a fief, agreeing to pay a yearly tithe. Innocent, however, did not have the same success in opposing *Magna carta*, signed June 15, 1215.

Innocent's political involvements took their worst turn in the Fourth Crusade. He envisioned an attack on Egypt, but, as noted earlier, the crusade resulted in the conquest of Constantinople. Although Innocent at first opposed the expedition for fear it would delay the main objective, he celebrated the victory with the questionable hope that it would reunite the Greek and Latin churches. In the onslaught against Constantinople Egypt was forgotten and relationships between East and West crushed. Within the Latin Kingdom the Greek churches reluctantly submitted to a Latin hierarchy and underwent some latinization, but they did not experience reconciliation.

The most powerful of medieval popes, however, did not let the dream of another crusade die. In 1208 Innocent preached a crusade against the Albigensians in southern France and he sustained the efforts of Albert, bishop of Riga, to effect the conversion of Livonia through a crusade. In 1212 Innocent announced that Livonia had been "subjected for us." In 1215 he convened the Fourth Lateran (Twelfth Ecumenical) Council with a view to launching a new crusade in June 1217.

The crusade Innocent planned did not take place on schedule, but the council did transact other important business. In a decree formulated against the Cathari the council approved the use of the term "transubstantiation" to describe the change of bread and wine in the eucharist. It condemned certain views of Joachim of Fiore and other heretics. It forbade the founding of new religious orders and required existing orders to follow the Cistercian pattern in holding a general chapter every three years. It instructed the faithful to take communion at least once a year, during Easter. It laid down certain plans for reform of the clergy.

Innocent III did not live to see the crusade nor the reforms implemented. To promote the cause of the crusade and to restore peace between Genoa and Pisa, he set out for Lombardy in the early summer of 1216. At Perugia he contracted a fever and died on July 16. He bequeathed to his successors a problem of major proportions. The administrative machinery he set up in no way matched the ambitiousness of his policies. His use of power to achieve political ends only accentuated the problem.

The Popes and the Hohenstaufen

Innocent III's successors strove mightily to effect his dream of a papal monarchy. Unfortunately, they ran into determined opposition in one of the last of the Hohenstaufen, Frederick II (1212–1250). Whereas the reign of Innocent witnessed the culmination of the growth of papal authority which began with Leo IX (1049–1054), that of Innocent IV (1243–1254) signaled the beginning of the decline culminating in the Avignon papacy (1309–1378), the so-called Babylonian Captivity of the church.

Innocent's plans for a crusade went awry in the hands of Honorius III (1216–1227) and Gregory IX (1227–1241) because neither could enlist cooperation of the emperor, although Frederick's independent crusade in 1228 and 1229 turned out rather well. Honorius made the crusade his major endeavor. Capture of Damietta in 1219 raised his hopes still higher, but they crashed when the papal legate Pelagius led the crusaders toward Cairo and into a crushing defeat at Mansurah, forcing evacuation of Damietta. Whether Frederick's procrastination here deserves the criticism

it received then and subsequently or not, the main blame must fall on the shoulders of the legate's disregard of the advice of military leaders.

During these years, Frederick occupied himself almost entirely with reorganizing his Sicilian kingdom, restoring and confirming his own power, and developing an adequate army. He contended that a strong kingdom in Sicily was essential to the prosecution of the crusade he promised to pursue. Perhaps legitimately, he postponed the crusade. Crowned November 22, 1220, he renewed a vow to undertake the crusade in August 1221; then again in 1225 he set August 1227 after his marriage to Princess Isabella of Brienne, heiress of the kingdom of Jerusalem. He and the pope disputed Frederick's interference in the filling of Sicilian bishoprics and in the government of the Papal States. He exacerbated tensions further when he brought Germany and Sicily under a single crown and established a military colony at Lucera, too near papal territory. The gentle Honorius proved no match for the determined monarch. Honorius's most important gift to later generations was his *Census Book of the Roman Church*, an invaluable source of information on papal revenues during the thirteenth century.

Gregory IX (1227–1241), cut from the same cloth as Innocent III, proved much tougher in dealing with the emperor. A nephew of Innocent, Ugolino of Segni, Gregory followed in Innocent's footsteps by studying at Paris and Bologna. In 1198 Innocent appointed him cardinal deacon, in 1206 bishop of Ostia, and later as a papal legate to Germany. In 1217 Gregory was selected to preach the northern crusade, and it was from him that Frederick took the cross in 1220. As soon as he became pope, Gregory insisted that the emperor embark on the crusade and excommunicated him on September 29 when Frederick returned claiming illness. When Frederick did set out, still unreconciled to the church, in 1228, Gregory proclaimed an interdict over Frederick's lands and wherever he should go. While Frederick relied largely on diplomacy to conclude a treaty with the sultan that secured return of the chief cities of the Holy Land to Christians and established the Kingdom of Jerusalem on a firmer basis, Gregory dispatched papal troops to Sicily. Frederick, however, soon returned and regained control. The grand master of the Teutonic Order, Herman of Salza, had to act as intermediary between the pope and the emperor, finally securing a peace settlement on July 23, 1230. The pope lifted his ban. Frederick returned church properties, freed papal territory, conceded the freedom of episcopal elections in Sicily, and recognized the jurisdiction of the church and its right to impose taxes.

The peace lasted several years, but relations between the pope and the emperor became strained again when Gregory IX tried to serve as go-between for Frederick and the Lombard League. After Frederick won a decisive victory over the forces of the League at Cortenuova in 1237, he demanded unconditional surrender of the League, thus provoking desperate resistance of the cities. Frederick incited the Romans against the pope, detained papal ambassadors and imprisoned a legate, ran roughshod over the church in Sicily, and installed his son Enzio over the Kingdom of Sardinia in flagrant disregard of the rights of the papacy. Gregory, in desperation, formed an alliance with the Lombard League and on March 20, 1239, once again excommunicated Frederick. This precipitated the most bitter of their clashes and one that did not end until Gregory died. Gregory unsuccessfully tried to persuade the German princes to elect a new emperor, but they remained committed to Frederick. Frederick retaliated by capturing most of the territory of the Papal States and temporarily threatening Rome. He prevented the assembling of a general council called by Gregory by arresting and imprisoning a hundred clergy attempting to reach Rome by means of a Genoese flotilla. He was well on the way to completing his march on Rome when Gregory died August 22, 1241.

Marking the growth of the monarchical papacy was the issuing of a new law code by Pope Gregory, the *Decretals*, in 1234. Gratian's *Decretum* (ca. 1140), like many other earlier ones, was a private collection of canons; Gregory's was official. It ensured papal supremacy by not only growth of appeals to Rome but of cases of the first instance, making the pope what Geoffrey Barraclough has called "the universal ordinary." It was not until the pontificate of Urban IV (1261–1264), however, that the *Rota Romana* was set up to deal with the many cases that came to Rome. Gregory also took the Inquisition out of the hands of bishops in 1232 and turned it over to the Dominicans and Franciscans, thus tying it more closely to the papacy itself.

The major shift in the fortunes of the papacy took place during the pontificate of Innocent IV (1243–1254). After a seventeen-day stint by Celestine IV (October 25–November 10, 1241), the chair of Peter remained vacant for a year and a half, chiefly because Frederick held two cardinals prisoner and refused to release them. On June 25, 1243, the College of Cardinals unanimously elected a candidate whom Frederick applauded, Sinibaldo Fieschi, count of Baragna, a Genoese noble, as Innocent IV (1243–1254). After lengthy negotiations, pope and emperor concluded a treaty in which the latter accepted virtually all of the pope's demands, including return of the Papal States. It soon became clear, however, that the treaty circled around rather than solved the problem of the Lombard League. When Frederick refused to evacuate the Papal States until his excommunication was lifted, Innocent IV denied absolution and declared him a perjurer. Innocent then fled Rome and went to Lyons. There he convened a general council to pronounce judgment on Frederick and to provide relief for the Holy Land, where Jerusalem had fallen again into Muslim hands. The pope opened the council with an address on the five wounds of Christ, one of which was Frederick's persecution of the church.

In spite of an able defense by Thaddaeus of Suessa, on July 17, 1245, in the third session of the council, Pope Innocent IV declared Frederick guilty of repeated perjuries, sacrileges committed by imprisoning clergy, and heresy and felony for not fulfilling his duties as king of Sicily, and deposed him. Innocent also stripped the emperor of all honors and dignities and released his subjects from the oath of allegiance. Frederick responded by questioning the right of the pope to depose princes or to make pronouncements in temporal affairs. He countered the charge of neglect of duty by accusing the church of the same and calling for the church to return to the poverty and simplicity of the apostolic age. Innocent took up the challenge by ordering a crusade preached against Frederick. With the pope's support the German princes in May 1246 elected Henry Raspe, landgrave of Thuringia, as Frederick's successor, and, when Raspe died in the spring of 1247, William, count of Holland, but these elections did not gain general acceptance in Germany. In Italy Frederick suffered several misfortunes—the defeat of his army in the siege of Parma, the treason of his most able ambassador, and the imprisonment of his son Enzio by the Bolognese—but he was far from finished when he died on December 13, 1250. The archbishop of Palermo restored him to communion before his death.

Frederick's son Conrad IV, appointed heir to the throne in Frederick's will, continued his father's policy which offended the papacy so much, the union of Germany and Sicily, but he died suddenly on May 20, 1254, at age twenty-six, having appointed the pope guardian of his two-year-old son Conradin (Conrad V). Innocent IV happily obliged and immediately recognized Conradin as king of Jerusalem and duke of Swabia and affirmed his right to the crown of Sicily. Although Conradin's half-brother Manfred at first accepted this arrangement and took the office of imperial vicar of Lower Italy, he went to war when Innocent himself assumed control of the kingdom. With the help of the Saracens, Manfred decisively defeated the papal army at Foggia on December 2, 1254. The news hastened the ill pope's death on December 7.

The Turn toward France

As the Hohenstaufen hegemony unraveled, the popes turned toward France, where Louis IX showed a much friendlier and more reliable face. Although the College of Cardinals elected a person far more open to compromise than Gregory IX and Innocent IV as Pope Alexander IV (1254–1261), he too soon found himself at loggerheads with Manfred. Manfred had himself crowned king of Sicily and so threatened the Papal States that Alexander had to leave Rome. In Germany, Alexander IV supported William of Holland, but on his death in 1256 he forbade the election of Conradin and refused to take a stand on the competing candidates, Alfonso X of Castile and Richard of Cornwallis.

On the death of Alexander, the cardinals elected Jacques Pantaleon, patriarch of Jerusalem, who was visiting Rome at the time, to succeed him. The most important acts of Pantaleon's brief pontificate as Urban IV (1261–1264) were to crown Charles, count of Anjou, as king of Sicily and to appoint several Frenchmen to the College of Cardinals, thus inaugurating the intimate connection between the papacy and the French monarchy which would lead to the Babylonian Captivity. Urban was succeeded by another Frenchman, Guy Foulquois le Grow, counselor of Louis IX and archbishop of Narbonne. During his pontificate as Clement IV (1265–1268), Charles of Anjou defeated Manfred at Benevento and took control of Sicily, but he soon alienated the people by his cruelty and greed. The young Conradin, now grown, tried to repulse Charles, but his forces suffered a disastrous defeat at Tagliacozzo. Conradin was handed over to Charles, who had him executed at Naples on October 29, 1268, ending the Hohenstaufen line.

The papal chair remained vacant for almost three years. During the next twenty-three years nine popes occupied it. Gregory X (1271–1276) busied himself with the liberation of the Holy Land, but the Seventh Crusade proved abortive. Gregory also sought to effect a reconciliation with the Byzantines. Emperor Michael Palaeologus (1261–1282) was receptive and sent emissaries to the Council of Lyon in 1274. The Greeks, however, had to make the primary concessions and could not gain acceptance of them when they returned to Constantinople. The Greeks conceded the papal claims to primacy, the *filioque* in the creed, and the right of appeals to Rome in exchange for permission to retain their creed and liturgies. The Council did make an important revision in regard to papal elections, that is, establishing the conclave which would confine the College of Cardinals until they succeeded in choosing a pope.

Meantime, the long interregnum in the empire ended with the deaths of Richard of Cornwall and Alfonso X of Castile. On the advice of Gregory X the German princes elected Rudolph of Hapsburg as emperor. Rudolph renewed promises he had previously made to protect the rights and privileges of the Roman church and to separate Sicily from the empire at Lausanne in October 1275. Rudolph also took the cross, but the crusade never materialized, and Gregory died in January 1276 before he could place the crown on Rudolph's head.

After a succession of three popes lasting less than eighteen months, the cardinals selected Giovanni Gaetano Orsini as Nicholas III (1277–1280). A forceful person in the mold of Innocent III, Nicholas set himself firmly against Charles of Anjou's ambitious plans. Persuading Charles to resign his office as a Roman senator, in 1278 Nicholas issued a constitution forbidding emperors, empresses, or princes to be elected Roman senators and making Roman citizens alone eligible. Nicholas then had himself elected senator for life. Nicholas strengthened the papacy further by

effecting a reconciliation between Rudolph of Hapsburg and Charles of Anjou.

In contrast to Nicholas, noted for his nepotism, his successor Martin IV (1281–1285) catered to Charles of Anjou, restoring him to the dignity of a Roman senator and looking with favor on Charles's attacks on the Byzantine Empire. Martin excommunicated the emperor Michael Palaeologus on a charge of aiding schism and heresy, thus shattering whatever still remained of the reunion of 1274. Martin's support for Charles of Anjou turned sour, however, when the people of Sicily revolted and massacred all French citizens on the island at Easter 1282. although Martin ordered a crusade against Peter III of Aragon, the husband of Manfred's daughter Constance, Charles lost Sicily. Charles's successor Honorius IV (1285–1287) acted more evanhandedly.

As in the eleventh century the papacy once again suffered from rivalry between powerful Italian families, this time the Orsini and the Colonna. Nicholas IV (1288–1292) favored the Colonnas. When he died, the conclave to choose his successor dragged on for two years until Charles II, the son and heir of Charles of Anjou, suggested that Peter de Murrone, a pious hermit, be elected. As Celestine V, Murrone soon recognized his lack of suitability for the office and resigned after only five months. His successor Boniface VIII (1294–1303), fearing lest he change his mind, had Murrone imprisoned until his death on May 9, 1296. Boniface also annulled Murrone's administrative acts.

Boniface VIII

Benedetto Gaetani held the same high concept of the papal office as Gregory VII and Innocent III, but the radical shift in European politics between his pontificate and theirs made his efforts to implement it not only futile but tragic. Born around 1234 at Anagni, he studied at Todi and Spoleto and then served as canon at

Paris, Rome, and elsewhere. In 1276 he entered service of the curia as consistorial advocate and then notary apostolic. Appointed a cardinal deacon in 1281 and a cardinal priest in 1291, he carried out important missions to France and to Italy. Elected pope on December 24, 1294, at Naples, he immediately set out to realize his two chief goals of the pacification of Europe and the liberation of the Holy Land, which had fallen into Muslim hands again in 1291. Boniface achieved neither goal.

Boniface had little success anywhere he turned. He supported Charles II's attempts to recapture Sicily from the house of Aragon, but in the treaty of Caltabellota he had to recognize Frederick of Aragon as the ruler. In Rome he waged a bitter fight against the Cononna family. Two Colonna cardinals established secret contacts with Frederick of Sicily and formed a group hostile to him who contested the abdication of Celestine and Boniface's installation. In May 1297, Stephen Colonna robbed the papal treasury, and Boniface proved unable to back up either his demand for the surrender of Stephen or the occupation of all Colonna fortifications by papal troops. When the Colonnas resisted, Boniface excommunicated the two cardinals and outlawed the house of Colonna, then preached a crusade against his enemies. Papal troops conquered and destroyed their fortifications. The two cardinals fled to Philip IV the Fair of France. In England Edward I (1272–1307) delivered a sharp rebuke when Boniface attempted to deny the English right to the crown of Scotland. Boniface's one political triumph was in Germany, where he bestowed the crown upon Albert I (1298–1308).

More lasting was Boniface's institution in 1300 of the Jubilee Year, promising full remission of sins to all penitents who should visit St. Peter's. It proved so profitable that Clement VI (1342–1352) observed a second jubilee in 1350. Under Urban VI (1378–1389) the jubilee period was shortened to thirty-three years and under Paul II (1470) to twenty-five.

Boniface's most disastrous encounter was with Philip the Fair. Boniface had attempted unsuccessfully to effect a reconciliation between France and England, who battled over the latter's possessions on the continent, chiefly Flanders. On February 25, 1296, Boniface issued the bull *Clericis laicos* forbidding secular rulers to impose and the clergy to pay taxes on church property and revenues without the consent of the papacy, threatening an interdict. Philip responded by prohibiting the exportation of gold and silver from France without a royal permit, thus making it impossible for papal collectors to send money to Rome. Boniface then wrote Philip a conciliatory letter and issued another bull, declaring that *Clericis laicos* did not affect feudal obligations or forbid voluntary contributions from the clergy and leaving in the king's hands the decision as to whether a tribute from the clergy was necessary. A month later, Boniface canonized Louis IX and offered to act as an arbiter between France and England. Tensions eased somewhat, and Boniface recouped some of his financial losses through the first Jubilee Year.

In 1301 the controversy flared up again over a writing, probably by Pierre Dubois, calling on the king to extend his dominion to the walls of Rome and beyond and denying the pope a right to secular power. When Boniface sent the bishop of Parmiers as a legate to France to investigate violations of ecclesiastical privileges and to invite Philip to participate in a crusade, Philip had him arrested on a charge of treasonable activities. Boniface demanded his legate's immediate release and put *Clericis laicos* into effect again. He called representatives of the French church to a council of Rome in the fall of 1302, demanding that Philip himself appear before it to answer serious charges and asserting the superiority of the pope to kings. Philip suppressed his papal bull *Ausculta filii* and circulated in its place a forgery, *Deum time*, that presented papal claims in extreme and abbreviated form to incite French public opinion against the pope. Philip then convened the French parliament and asserted the independence of France of the papacy.

In October 1302, the pope convened a synod in Rome. In connection with the synod he issued the bull *Unam sanctam* that drew on the two-swords theory to dramatize the superiority of ecclesiastical to secular powers. The spiritual sword is to be used *by* the church, the temporal *for* the church. The secular estate may be judged by the spiritual, but the spiritual by no human power. The bull then ended with the assertion that "it is altogether necessary to salvation for every human creature to be subject to the Roman pontiff." Others had made some of the same statements—Innocent III, Bernard of Clairvaux, Hugo of St. Victor, Thomas Aquinas, and the Augustinian Aegydius Colonna—but none so starkly.

Unam sanctam incited Philip to take vigorous action against Boniface. He arrested the papal legate who delivered the bull, forcing Boniface finally to post it on the church doors at Rome as an adequate announcement. Parliament and the French people backed the king and accused the pope of simony, sorcery, immorality, the murder of Celestine, and other crimes. Boniface offered the French crown to Albert I of Hapsburg, but the emperor wisely refused the empty honor. On September 8, 1303, William of Nogaret, assisted by Sciarra Colonna and a band of Ghibellines, arrested Boniface just as he prepared to excommunicate Philip and to release Philip's subjects from their oath of allegiance. Although Boniface obtained release with the help of the citizens of Anagni, he did not long survive his return to Rome. He died on October 11, 1303. With his death the age of papal supremacy ended. Soon to follow was the humiliating submission of the popes to the French monarchy at Avignon.

Politicizing the Papacy

During the thirteenth century, the papacy increasingly took on a political character. Popes laid claim to fullness of power and functioned theoretically without checks. Because the exercise of functions in so many spheres required a huge bureaucracy, centered in the curia, the church became more and more centralized and top-heavy. Thence the religious functions of the papacy receded as legal and political functions moved to the forefront. Political factors became the driving force and with them the need for money. In the early fourteenth century John XXII (1316–1334) spent sixty-three percent of his resources on war. Political activities drove popes to even greater extremes, which brought the papacy into disrepute.

Other factors obviously contributed to papal decline. A. C. Flick has pointed to political, intellectual, economic, and religious factors. Weakening the papacy politically were the decline of the Holy Roman Empire, brought on in part by the popes themselves, the rise of national states with genuine national interests such as France and England, and the preparation of lay lawyers ready to supply arguments against papal pretensions. Intellectually the Renaissance, originally supported by the papacy, supplied an undercurrent of informed criticism of the church and its institutions, including the papacy. Rationalism gradually shoved uncritical acceptance of documents such as the Donation of Constantine or the pseudo-Isidorean decretals ("False Decretals") aside. Economically the rise of mercantile powers with guilds, banks, leagues, and manufacturing processes created institutions almost wholly independent of ecclesiastical authority as, simultaneously, feudal holdings deteriorated and the wealth of kings expanded. Religiously the crusades pointed up the weakness of papal power as they went out of control. Meantime, schisms, and heresies undercut the church's hegemony in European society, representing large numbers of those who found little meaning in the hierarchical, institutional church. Ultimately, however, the popes themselves must shoulder most of the blame in creating a papal monarchy far removed from the spiritual needs of the masses.

Centralization had negative effects not only on the papacy itself but on the whole church. It took away the functions and powers of local clergy and bishops. It weakened the spiritual life of the dioceses, creating absenteeism. The laity felt left out and responded with hostility. Orders such as the Franciscans and Dominicans tried to bridge the growing gulf, but they too got trapped in the highly centralized bureaucracy, ending up as inquisitors rather than, as Francis of Assisi intended, advocates of the poor and marginalized. Bad days lay ahead.

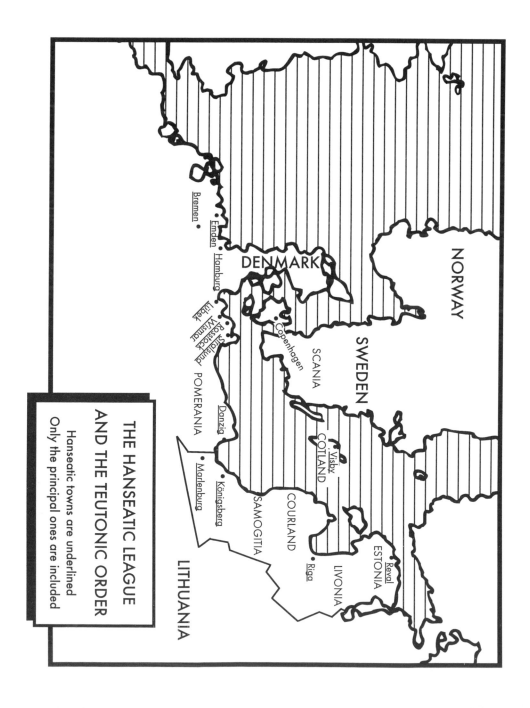

THE HANSEATIC LEAGUE
AND THE TEUTONIC ORDER

Hanseatic towns are underlined
Only the principal ones are included

Chapter 48

Christian Advance and Division

To recount the story of Christianity in Europe during the thirteenth century would require more space than allowable. In this chapter, therefore, the spotlight will fall on areas in which Christianity registered significant advances—the Baltic states and Russia. In the case of the former the story is not an altogether commendable one, for it involved crusades which, like other crusades, entailed a quest for the goods of earth more than a sharing of the gospel. Indeed, in Russia Alexander Nevsky became a hero by saving a Christian settlement from the Christian Swedes and from the Order of Teutonic Knights in 1240 as the Mongols invaded Russia from the East. Crusading, however, had become so woven into Western consciousness as the answer to the Church's problems and needs that it obscured the slower but more lasting efforts of authentic missionaries. It was the means not only to regain control of the Holy Land and to stop the advance of Islam or to reconquer territory lost to Islam, but also to advance the Christian faith into lands not yet evangelized.

The crusades in northern Europe may well have achieved something not possible by other means, but like the other crusades they proved costly. One of the costs was the division of Christendom. Although Christians have usually pointed to the conflict between Michael Cerularius, Patriarch of Constantinople, and Pope Leo IX in 1054 as the breaking point, there are many

reasons why that view requires reexamination. Both East and West continued to act as if no break occurred then. They continued to extend good will to one another. What created a crisis in East/West relations was the crusades, above all, the Fourth Crusade, when Westerners turned on Constantinople itself, the city they had originally set out to help. The war game proved very tricky and costly.

The Wendish Crusade, 1147–1185

During the Second Crusade, nobles in Saxony clamored to attack the pagan Slavs living on their eastern frontier and, with the blessing of Bernard of Clairvaux, who met with them on March 13, 1147, they obtained the authorization of Pope Eugenius III in the Bull *Divina dispensatione* to make war on their own heathen rather than go to Jerusalem. Eugenius bestowed on them the same privileges, merits, and insignia as on the rest of the crusaders. Bernard himself urged them to fight the heathen "until such time as, by God's help, they shall either be converted or wiped out." The alternatives were baptism or death. Danes and Poles joined the Saxons in the effort. All three acted out of less than commendable motives: the Saxons to get tribute or seize more land, the Danes to get revenge against pirates and slavers, and the Poles to intimidate the Prussians. Yet a whole complement of bishops—from Mainz, Halberstadt, Münster, Merseburg, Brandenburg, and Olmutz—as well as the papal legate Anselm of Havelburg marched with them in the late summer of 1147. The first effort proved more successful as a military foray than as a crusade. The few baptisms which occurred had no lasting effect and idols, temples, and sanctuaries remained in place.

After 1147 the wars against the Slavs took place without the benefit of papal authorization for a time, though the campaigns of Henry the Lion and Valdemar, King of Denmark, against the Wends were treated as wars carried on successfully in the wake of the crusade of 1147. Henry and Valdemar often fought one another, but they united in 1160 to defeat the Abotrites and numerous times afterwards against other foes. In 1171 or 1172 Pope Alexander III congratulated and rewarded Valdemar the Great as a "crusader" and issued a Bull which placed the war against the pagans of the North—Estonians and Finns— on the same basis as a crusade to the Holy Land, assuring full penance for all sins of those who died. In 1172 the Danes began bringing Cistercians and in 1177 Premonstratensians with them to occupy Pomeranian abbeys. The fall of Henry the Lion in 1181 left them free to dominate the Abotrites and Pomeranians. In 1185 the Pomeranian Prince Bogislav surrendered the whole of Pomerania to King Canute VI. At the time the Danes were preparing to launch a large scale raid on the Estonians.

The East Baltic Crusades, 1200–1292

Military conquest subjected first the Livonians, Letts, and Estonians and then the Prussians and the Finns. This gave birth to the Latin anchored "dominions" of Livonia and Prussia and the "duchies" of Estonia and Finland. A new archbishopric and eight new bishoprics assumed responsibility for effecting the conversions.

In Livonia the bishop of Riga and the Sword Brothers, armed monks, undertook the subjugation of the Livonians. They used some methods of persuasion such as miracle plays, but for the

most part they used the sword. In 1211 the Sword Brothers and the Christian Letts killed a number of prisoners when the garrison they were besieging refused baptism. Five days later, after both sides suffered heavy casualties, the garrison surrendered and received baptism. Unfortunately the baptisms did not take and the military orders had to fight their battles over again. In this instance, because scandal led to the disbanding of the Sword Brothers, the Teutonic Knights had to carry the campaign after 1237. The main leader of the Riga mission, Hartwig II, archbishop of Bremen (1185–1207), devised a plan to keep the converts baptized, that is, continuous crusade. That turned out to be necessary, for the Livonians won back much of their territory between 1255 and 1260. By 1290 the Teutonic Knights had established a line of forts running from Dunaburg to Memel which kept the Lithuanians out and the missionaries in.

In Prussia the Teutonic Knights had to rescue a mission that had floundered. The "reconquest," mostly by diplomacy, took fifty years. An initial campaign in 1222–1223 turned out rather badly, so the Teutonic Knights established a line of forts which they could use as bases to intimidate various tribes, beginning at the Polish fort of Chelmno in 1230. It took the added assistance of the papal legate and Polish princes to rescue the Knights from Duke Swantopelk of Danzig in 1246. By 1277 the main body of Prussians had been subjugated, but some still made attempts at a revolt in 1286 and 1295.

In Estonia King Canute VI (1182–1202) and Valdemar II (1202–1241) followed up the raid their father, Valdemar I, had undertaken against the Estonians in 1170. Danish fleets attacked Finland in 1191 and 1202 and Estonia in 1194 and 1197, Osel in 1206 and Prussia in 1210. Meantime, Gregory VIII's appeal for crusaders captured the imagination of Danish nobility. In 1218 Pope Honorius III promised Valdemar II that he might annex all the land he could conquer from the heathen. In 1219 the Danes established a fort at Tallinn and proceeded to take control of northern Estonia. Priests and bishops stayed behind with the knights, and the next year Valdemar returned with reinforcements and Dominicans. The Sword Brothers assisted. Although Valdemar had some difficulties with the Teutonic Knights, he joined them in an anti-Russian crusade in 1240–1242.

The Swedes had already made raids on Finland as early as 1142. In 1191 and 1202 Danish fleets raided and established missions there. Thus there existed a community of Christians at Suomi when Innocent III took note of it in a letter to Archbishop Andrew of Lund in 1209. In 1215 a Finnish priest worked among the Estonians. When the Danes captured Estonia, they lost interest in Finland and left it to the Swedes. In 1237 the latter responded to the call of Pope Gregory IX for a crusade against the Tavastians. The expedition in 1240 against Prince Alexander Nevsky of Novgorod, however, met a resounding defeat. An all out effort occurred in 1249 under leadership of Birger Jarl and again in 1292. In 1295 King Birger announced that he had converted the Karelians.

The Lithuanian Crusade, 1283–1410

Papal rhetoric during the thirteenth century laid down a justification for the crusades. Missionaries spread the faith and some barbarians join the household of God. But sometimes the Devil rises up and rages against those of true faith, necessitating the use of armed force. Piety must overcome impiety through the "ministry" of warfare. This is really an act of love, repaying Christ for what he did for us.

From Alexander III on (1159–1181), the popes took increasing interest in the northeast. Innocent III (1198–1216) made it a policy to intervene wherever possible on the grounds that, as the vicar of Christ, the pope has a responsibility to look out for the political and spiritual welfare of humankind and to use whatever powers he could to effect the salvation of all. His successors

pursued the same policy in the face of opposition from emperors and many kings and evidence of their own impotence. The northern crusades were one of their instruments, used, of course, in cooperation with others when they could secure it.

When the Teutonic Knights completed their conquest of the Prussians in 1283, they turned their attention to the Lithuanians in a crusade that lasted until 1410. Actually, the Sword Brothers had taken on the Lithuanians as early as 1203, but they had not succeeded in subduing them. During the thirteenth century, the military prowess of the Lithuanians posed a threat to the Order of Teutonic Knights which had established control in the surrounding area. The fact that the grand princes and warriors of Lithuania remained pagan gave them the excuse they needed to take up arms against them. They adhered steadfastly to their polytheistic faith until 1386, when the Grand Prince Jogailo accepted baptism on the basis of prospect of winning Poland. The conversion process advanced slowly even after that.

Two developments committed the Teutonic Knights irrevocably to the war in Lithuania. One was the fall of Acre in 1291 which precluded any further action in the Holy Land and led to the establishment of their new headquarters in Venice. Meantime, the knight brothers in Prussia strove to shift all resources possible to the northern crusade. The other was the widespread opposition to the Order itself, particularly that of the French King Philip the Fair, who, from 1305 on, argued that it should be abolished. Charges included genocide and murder of pilgrims. Consequently, after 1309, the whole Order focused itself on Prussia and applied the crusade apparatus to Lithuania and the Russian frontier.

Not everyone was convinced that warfare was the way to get converts. The Schoolmen debated the issue and answered no. In 1268 Roger Bacon contended that preaching was the only way to win the heathen and that military monks hindered the process of conversion. He singled out the Teutonic Knights for censure. People would gladly become Christian if they could retain their freedom, but the Teutonic Knights want to enslave them. The reply of supporters of the crusade was that people like the Prussians and the Lithuanians were not harmless. The Knights also invoked their archives, which were filled with papal Bulls authorizing them to fight the heathen. They benefited from a surplus of fighting men who could no longer go east and who had gained experience in many wars around Europe. Crusaders came to Prussia from everywhere—Rhinelanders at the beginning of the fourteenth century, Bohemians in 1323, Alsatians in 1324, Englishmen and Walloons in 1329, Austrians and Frenchmen in 1336, Bavarians and Hollanders in 1337, Hungarians and Burgundians in 1344, and after mid-century Occitanians, Scots, and Italians. King John of Bohemia took the lead in 1328/1329.

The Lithuanian crusade proved exceedingly costly to both sides. The Teutonic Knights acted just as brutally as the Lithuanian warriors. Ironically, when the conquest ended in the baptism of Prince Jogailo, it prepared the way for the united Kingdom of Lithuania and Poland to turn around and recapture territory taken by the Teutonic Knights.

The Novgorod Crusade, 1295–1378

The crusade against Novgorod was obviously the most misdirected of all the northern undertakings. By 1250 the Orthodox had established seventeen monasteries in or near Novgorod, and in succeeding years the number grew. By the end of the fifteenth century they had founded ten monasteries and seven parishes among the Russian Karelians with a total of twenty-six churches. During these centuries of Mongol supremacy in Russia, many believers experienced missionary and monastic vocations. Novgorod itself grew increasingly independent of secular authority and more and more dependent on the power of the archbishop. Conversion and colonial expansion went hand in hand.

The Swedish conquest of Finland and organization of a Latin type Christianity among the Karelians created a potential conflict solved for a time by the making of a Russo-Swedish frontier between 1295 and 1326. In 1326 Novgorod turned from Moscow to Lithuania for protection. Neither Moscow nor Lithuania wanted to provoke the Swedes. Tension did arise in 1337 when Swedish settlers cooperated with the Karelians in an anti-Russian revolt, but a Russian delegation to King Magnus II (1319–1363) patched together a truce, while Magnus was still occupied with recovering territory lost to the Danes. The crusade mentality, however, was growing. In 1340 the Register of Uppsala mentioned "the preaching of the cross against the Karelians" and in the 1340s Bridget, the King's cousin, pressed for a Holy War in the same way Bernard of Clairvaux had, emphasizing the need for the purity of the crusaders. Far better that Magnus stop fighting the Christian Danes and send the troops against the heathen. Moved by political considerations more than Bridget's vision, he undertook a full crusade in 1347 to prove to the Russians whose faith was better. On June 8, 1348 the crusaders set out. When they reached Viborg, Magnus gave them a choice, "Adopt my faith, or I will march against you with my whole force."

Although the Swedish forces succeeded in capturing the fort of Orekhov, they lost it in February, 1349. Shortly after that, the Black Death struck Sweden. When it subsided in August, 1350 Magnus set out again, but he rallied far fewer crusaders. In a Bull dated March 14, 1351, Pope Clement VI (1342–1352) permitted Magnus to collect money to finance the crusade, instructed archbishops and bishops to begin preaching a full crusade against the Russians as soon as the plague subsided, and told the Teutonic Knights to give full assistance. Although the clergy could not prevent Magnus from collecting money, the Hanseatic cities, the Teutonic Knights, the magnates of Norway and Sweden, and others turned against the idea. His main supporter, Clement, died in 1352. Later King Albert (1364–1389) allied himself with the Teutonic Knights of Livonia and, in 1378, Pope Urban VI (1378–1389) authorized the Swedish bishops to grant full indulgence to all who would fight in or pay for a further crusade against the Russians, but nothing came of it. Small Swedish and Finnish campaigns in 1395, 1396, and 1411 also failed. June 22, 1496 Pope Alexander VI issued the last crusading bull for Sweden, but it too fell flat.

Russia

As noted earlier, Russia entered the Christian fold officially with the conversion of Vladimir, grandson of Princess Olga, who had received baptism in Constantinople in 954. Vladimir faced three options: Christianity, Islam, or Judaism. He met with representatives of all three. He decided against Islam because it rejected the use of wine, a beverage he considered indispensable for Russians. He did not want to adopt Judaism because the people were dispersed and homeless. According to the *Povyest*, he sent embassies to cities where both Latin and Byzantine rites were observed who reported that among the Greeks "we knew not whether we were in heaven or on earth." Vladimir decided in favor of the Byzantine Church. Undoubtedly helpful too was his marriage to the sister of the Emperor Basil II (976–1025) around 987, after helping the latter quell a revolt. From this point on Vladimir ardently promoted Orthodox Christianity, erecting many churches and founding many monasteries and using force to make conversions. Immediately after his baptism he gathered the citizens of Kiev at the Dnieper river and had them immersed according to the Byzantine rite. He had pagan idols smashed and thrown in the Dnieper.

Kiev became the seat of the Russian hierarchy. From it missionaries went forth to evangelize, conducting the liturgy and instruction in Slavonic. Vladimir built other churches and established schools to give children a Christian education. Throughout Vladimir's lifetime (956–1015) Christianity met little opposition.

Upon the death of Vladimir his son Svyatopolk seized the throne and murdered two of his brothers, Boris and Gelb, but he did not hold the crown long. One of his surviving brothers, Yaroslav, known as the Wise (1019–1054) defeated him and launched the "Golden Age" of the Russian Church. He initiated the codification of Russian law, limiting the custom of blood vengeance, and promoted the translation of Eastern canon law (*Nomokanon*) to regulate ecclesiastical affairs in the diocese of Kiev. He built a new basilica in the capital, St. Sophia, bringing architects from Constantinople to do the work. He collected a great many religious books, opened other schools, and did other things to promote the faith. Under Yaroslav the Russian Church gained its independence from Byzantium, although the Russian hierarchy was still subject to Constantinople. In 1051 a Russian, Hilarion, was appointed Metropolitan of Kiev. A hermit up to this time, Hilarion encouraged the founding of the first Russian monastery, the Kiev-Pechersk Laura, under Theodosius (1062–1074). Theodosius used the pattern of the Greek Studios which all Russian religious communities followed subsequently. The Pechersk Laura became a center of scholarly endeavor. The monk Nestor began the *Povyest*, a chronicle of the events of early Russian history through the eleventh century.

Following the death of Yaroslav, the Russian monarchy lapsed into bitter feuding among his sons, different ones seeking allies in Hungary, Poland, or even among the Cumans and Petchenegs. Vladimir Monomakh, a grandson of Yaroslav, finally succeeded in gaining recognition as the legitimate heir to the throne of Kiev (1113–1125). A person of exceptional ability, he wrote for his sons a treatise on moral behavior entitled the *Pouchenye* (*Instructions*), in which he urged charity, condemned violence, forbade pillages during travel, and advised sensitivity to others. Unfortunately, after his death, the kingdom once again fell to feuding about the succession. Some cited seniority over primogeniture. The endless disputes caused Kiev to lose its importance as a unifying center. Language and the Church played an increasingly important role in uniting the Russian people. Eventually Moscow, founded in 1156 by Yury Dolgoruky, son of Vladimir Monomakh, would supplant Kiev as the capital. Meantime, in 1175 Andrei Bogulyubsky, Monomakh's grandson, transferred his capital to Vladimir, where he and his successors consolidated power and established a primogeniture. This branch ruled Russia for more than three centuries.

In 1223 the Russian princes encountered the forces of Genghis Khan (d. 1227) for the first time in the Steppes of the Don region. Seventeen years later came the Mongol invasion led by the khan Batu. After overwhelming the White Bulgars in 1236, Batu destroyed Ryazan and Vladimir and halted a march on Novgorod only because of the swamps. In 1240 he burned Kiev and massacred its inhabitants. He proceeded then to Poland and Hungary, where he defeated the full forces of King Bela IV on April 11, 1241. A vacancy in the Great Khanate caused him to withdraw from Europe never to renew the invasion, but he retained control over Russia and the Cumans. The "Tartar Yoke" remained for two centuries. The Great Princes of Vladimir received their authority by charters and had to make frequent trips to the Mongol capital at Saray and to pay liberal bribes in order to keep them. The Orthodox Church fared better in some ways at first, for it was chartered separately by the Tartars and was made tax free in 1270.

Although districts like Novgorod escaped the worst and remained more or less independent, Novgorod itself was threatened from the West, first by Swedish forces and then by Teutonic and Livonian Knights. In 1240 the Swedes seized on the weakening of the Russians by the Mongols to assault Novgorod. Alexander, later Grand Prince of Vladimir, handed them a resounding defeat at the Neva river, from which derived his surname Nevsky. A short time later the Teutonic and Livonian Knights (the Sword Brothers) marched on the land of Russ. Although his forces had inferior equipment, Alexander Nevsky took advantage of winter weather to lure the crusaders onto the ice of Lake Peipus for what came to be known as the "ice slaughter." The battle became a symbol of Russian patriotism and of Russian Orthodox versus Roman Catholic trying to proselytize by force. Western military action deeply scarred the Russian religious consciousness.

Dealing with the khans, Nevsky (1218–1263) relied on skillful diplomacy rather than arms. He gradually gained the confidence of the khans so that he and other princes were entrusted even with collection of taxes, thus relieving their people greatly. The khans even permitted him to establish a bishopric at Saray, the residence of the Khan of the Golden Horde. He died on one of his many journeys to Saray.

In time Moscow supplanted Kiev and Vladimir as the leading civil and ecclesiastical center of Russia. The metropolitan Peter (1308–1326) moved his see, although he still retained the title of metropolitan of Kiev and Vladimir. He too negotiated with the khans and obtained privileges for the church. Under Peter and Alexius (1354–1378) the church strongly supported the Muscovite princes in their effort to establish control and to resist the Mongols. In the mid-fourteenth century the Great Prince Ivan firmly established the primacy of Moscow over other principalities. The khans made the Muscovite prince the collector of taxes throughout Russia, thus confirming his control and enabling him to buy up land. The church also acquired land either from the princes or through donations of the faithful. Since it did not pay taxes, it amassed wealth quickly, soon arousing hostility from the state.

After suffering a severe blow with the Mongol invasions, monasticism revived in Russia during the fourteenth century in a new form. The person responsible for it was Sergius of Radonezh (ca. 1314–1392). Sergius spent many years as a hermit in the forests. After a time he founded a monastery of the coenobitic variety, Holy Trinity. Dimitry, the Grand Prince of Moscow, frequently sought his counsel. In 1380 Sergius advised him to stiffen his resistance to Khan Mamai's imposition of a heavy tribute. On September 8, the united Russian forces defeated Mamai at Kulikovo. Although the Mongols still retained their sway for another century, the situation had changed radically. Dimitry's successors consolidated their control on more centralized lines which some ascribe to Mongol and others to Byzantine influence. Quite clearly, the Russian Church identified with the Byzantine tradition. Nowhere is that more evident than in their attitude toward the Latin Church. Although the Russian Church maintained a reluctance to sever ties with Rome, the Grand Prince Basil II deposed and imprisoned Isidore, the Greek Metropolitan of All Russia, when he returned to Moscow after signing the Decree of Union at the Council of Florence in 1441 and received appointment as a cardinal and papal legate.

Rupturing Relationships, 1054–1453

What happened in 1054 at Constantinople has been viewed traditionally as the final breach between Rome and Constantinople. Today there is nothing "final" about the pronouncements of the Patriarch Michael Cerularius or the papal legates who delivered the Bull of Pope Leo IX, for the two sees have restored relations with one another almost completely. Much scholarly study has demonstrated, moreover, that it was not "final" in 1054 either. Failure to include the popes in the diptychs, official lists, of the Byzantine Church, which is usually taken as proof of the schism, antedated the affair with Cerularius many years. No pope was listed after 1009. What happened in 1054 increased ill will, but it did not cut off relationships between Rome and Constantinople. Nothing demonstrates the point more readily than continuing negotiations between the Byzantine Empire and the papacy.

Following the defeat of the Byzantine army at Manzikert in 1071, which had thrown all of Asia Minor open to invasion by the Seljuk Turks, the Emperor Michael VII (1071–1078) looked to Rome to prevent an invasion by the Norman chieftain, Robert Guiscard. Pope Alexander II (1061–1073), fearful of an alliance between the German emperor and Michael, used the occasion of Michael's accession to broach the issue of Church union. The radically different concepts of union caused the Patriarch John Xiphilinus (1064–1075) to shunt the question aside indefinitely. When word circulated that Robert Guiscard was ready to invade the Balkans in 1073, the Emperor Michael, however, sent an imperial embassy to Rome to offer union if Gregory would restrain Guiscard. Gregory persuaded Guiscard to make peace with Byzantium, but alarmed the Patriarch John when he announced that he would come to Constantinople at the head of a large army to beat back the infidel and hold a synod at Constantinople to settle all religious differences. Soon Gregory had more problems at home than he could handle.

The first formal breach between Rome and Constantinople actually occurred in 1078, when Gregory VII excommunicated Emperor Nicephorus (1078–1081), installed after a palace coup dethroned Michael VII. Here he was victim of a deception pulled by Guiscard, infuriated that Nicephorus prevent the marriage of his daughter to Michael's son. When Alexius Comnenus took the throne in 1081, Gregory excommunicated him also as the Normans began their invasion of Epirus. In retaliation Alexius closed the Latin churches at Constantinople, except for the Venetian, and kept in touch with Gregory's nemesis in Germany, Henry IV. The impasse remained at Gregory's death in 1085. The Normans showed their appreciation to Gregory by sacking Rome. It remained for Urban II (1088–1099) to rectify the error by lifting the excommunication and asking Alexius to allow the Latin churches to reopen. The emperor summoned a synod at Constantinople which decreed that the pope's names had been omitted from the diptychs through carelessness. The Patriarch Nicholas III (1084–1111) assured the pope that the churches were again open, promised to restore his name to the diptychs in eighteen months, and asked him to extend his favor to certain Greek bishops in southern Italy. He also asked for a statement of faith, a request Urban never fulfilled. During the next decade, the churches enjoyed good will.

Latin pilgrims received a welcome at Constantinople, though difficulties sometimes arose. Many Latins resided at the imperial court and discussed religious problems with Greeks in a friendly way. Latin pilgrims did not sense any split between themselves and the Patriarch of Jerusalem. Although Emperor Alexius's reconciliation with Urban II did not please everyone at Constantinople, it was welcomed by the more enlightened. In 1090 the archbishop of Ochrida, Theophylact, one of the best scholars of his day, declared it ridiculous that anyone would want to excommunicate the Latins for their differences of customs. He cited only two points which he thought serious: the *Filioque* added to the Creed and the Petrine claims of the popes. Theophylact urged charity even in these. Urban II held a similar position.

Ironically, Steven Runciman has argued, what caused the worsening of relations between East and West was a desire to help, that is, with the crusades. Urban believed that if Western Christendom would come to the aid of the East, it would put an end to past ill will. When two ambassadors of Emperor Alexius appeared at the Council of Piacenza in March, 1095, he gave them permission to address the council. At Clermont, November 27, 1095, he preached his sermon summoning all of Western Christendom to undertake a Holy War, evidently beginning it with the appeal of the Easterners for help and urging it as a duty of Western Christians to come to their aid.

The crusading armies worsened relations with the Greeks. In the first crusade the band led by Peter the Hermit and Walter the Penniless was uncouth and offensive, hysterical peasants over whom they had no control. They stole and rioted at every turn. The army led by the princes was not much better. The crusaders and the Byzantines mutually disliked one another. When the crusaders captured Antioch, Bohemond of Taranto, son of Robert Guiscard, claimed it rather than giving it to the emperor on the grounds that the latter failed to help the crusaders. The Latins also removed the Patriarch to the vacant chair of Jerusalem. The latter, Arnold of Choques, persecuted Orthodox monks to get them to reveal where they hid the true cross and tried to reserve the Holy Sepulcher for Latin services only. A Greek Patriarch was not restored to Antioch until 1206, by which time the Byzantine Empire had been ruined by the Fourth Crusade. A Greek returned to the Jerusalem patriarchate in 1198. The Latins then set up a patriarch at Acre. The Latin patriarch returned to the city of Jerusalem when it again came into the hands of crusaders, between 1229 and 1244. In 1310 Pope Clement V appointed a Latin Patriarch of Alexandria. In the case of the three patriarchates the schism with Rome was a result of the establishment of crusader colonies in the patriarch's territories.

The Second Crusade engendered further animosities as both the German and the French armies pillaged the suburbs of Constantinople. The crusaders ignored the advice of Emperor Manuel I (1143–1180) and suffered for it. The French bitterly blamed the failure of the crusade on the Byzantines. Bernard and other clergy contemplated preaching a crusade against Constantinople. The whole affair marked a disastrous turning point in East-West relations. After the death of Manuel in 1180 anti-Latin resentment mounted. In 1182 it led to the massacre of Franks and Italians at Constantinople which the West could not forgive. The Third Crusade created less hostility although Frederick Barbarossa had a strong desire to conquer Constantinople and make himself the sole emperor of Christendom. The Fourth Crusade, however, brought relations between the Churches of Rome and Constantinople to the point of crisis. The attempts of subsequent councils failed to overcome the damage the crusades had inflicted.

The Council of Lyons (1274)

The first overt effort at reunion followed the capture of Constantinople by seventy years. Pope Gregory X (1271–1276) longed for a crusade to liberate the Holy Land and saw reunion as an essential step in that direction. When Emperor Michael Palaeologus (1261–1282) wrote to ask his help in compelling Charles of Anjou to give up his plans to recoup the Latin Kingdom lost in 1261, Gregory replied that he could do so only if reunion took place. Already on October 24, 1272 he sent invitations to the emperor and Patriarch Joseph to attend the council. When the huge assembly, estimated at 1,000 prelates, gathered at Lyons, he stated his threefold purpose: reform of the Church, union with the Greeks, and liberation of the Holy Land. On July 6, 1274, the emperor agreed to the Act of Union, acknowledging that the Greek Churches could retain their form of the creed and their ancient rites, and recognizing the right of appeal to Rome.

The Byzantine Church refused to subscribe to the *Filioque* and the doctrine of papal supremacy, the two most offensive points. Violent reactions, aggravated by persecution of monks, took place. Then, in 1281 Pope Martin IV (1281–1285) decided to throw his support behind Charles of Anjou against Michael VIII. In 1282 the emperor died, excommunicated both by the Roman Catholic and the Orthodox churches. Although a small group of Byzantine intellectuals tried later in the century to keep the idea of reunion alive, they had little support either among the clergy or the people. Attempts of emperors to negotiate a union in order to obtain military assistance also ran aground.

The Council of Florence (1439)

The other effort at reunion fared no better despite greater energies poured into it. Originally assembled at Ferrara in January, 1438, the Council transferred to Florence early in 1439. Attended by a large Greek delegation led by Emperor John VIII Palaeologus (1425–1448), the Council proclaimed the union on July 6, 1439. Due to their desperate need for military assistance against the Ottoman Turks, the Greeks readily conceded the unconditional demands made by Pope Eugenius IV (1431–1447) and his advisers: acceptance of the *Filioque*, recognition of papal supremacy, and acknowledgment of the Western doctrine of Purgatory. The one concession made to the Greeks was to continue to use unleavened bread for the Eucharist.

Although some of the Greek party, especially Bessarion, Metropolitan of Nicaea, and Isidore, Metropolitan of Kiev and All Russian, showed real concern for unity, they could not rally support for it in the East. The Patriarchates of Alexandria, Antioch, and Jerusalem and the churches of Russia, Romania, and Serbia all rejected it immediately. In Byzantium only a minority accepted it. Emperors John VIII and Constantine IX (1448–1453) proved unable to force their will on the Church. Most Byzantines felt betrayed. John Bessarion (1403–1472), who showed the most enthusiasm for it, remained in communion with Rome. In 1439 he was named a cardinal by Pope Eugenius IV. He played a prominent role in the revival of Greek studies in the Italian Renaissance. The Union was not proclaimed in the Church of Hagia Sophia until December 12, 1452. Five months later, Constantinople fell to the Turks.

Chapter 49

Church and Synagogue

Christian attitudes toward Jews solidified during the thirteenth century as the Church attained the apogee of power and influence and fostered a crusading mentality. These attitudes had never been good. Before Constantine Christianity's minority status, however, prevented Christians from retaliating for early Jewish intolerance or for Jewish complicity in the death of Christ. The hostility was there. The Council of Elvira in 306, for instance, forbade Catholics to marry Jews or allow Jews to bless their crops and ordered excommunication of Christians who ate with Jews. Catholic men who committed adultery with Jewish women would be permanently excluded from the Church. With Constantine's conversion the situation changed radically. Constantine himself ordered the burning of any Jew who attacked "with stones or some other manifestation of anger" converts to Christianity and threatened penalties for any who converted to Judaism (October 18, 315). Constantius (August 13, 339) prohibited marriage of women in weaving factories to Jews and imposed the death penalty upon Jews who married Christian women. He also forbade Jews to own Christian slaves. Theodosius II (January 31, 439) forbade Jews to hold public offices because it would be inappropriate for "the enemies of the heavenly majesty and of the Roman law" to have power to make judgments against Christians, even bishops, or to build new synagogues. Justinian (July 28, 531) prohibited

Jews from giving testimony against orthodox Christians, though he permitted them to testify in behalf of an orthodox Christian against an unorthodox one.

Ecclesiastical attitudes were, if anything, worse than imperial. The Council of Nicaea in 325 adopted the Roman custom of celebrating Easter on Sunday rather than the Asian custom of observing the Jewish Passover on the grounds that it would be unthinkable to "follow the practice of the Jews, who have impiously defiled their hands with enormous sin" and that Christians should have nothing to do with "the detestable Jewish crowd." In 388 when Emperor Theodosius I (379–395) ordered Christians of Callinicum to rebuild a synagogue they had torn down, Ambrose protested vigorously. Such a mandate could not be justified, for this was only a synagogue, "a home of unbelief, a house of impiety, a receptacle of folly, which God himself has condemned." The Jews had burned many churches in the time of Julian (361–363) without being avenged. Why should the Jews expect that?

Pope Gregory the Great (590–604) set forth what should have become the official policy of the Catholic Church in the Middle Ages. In a letter dated June 1, 591 addressed to Virgilius, bishop of Arles, and Theodorus, bishop of Marseilles, he affirmed efforts to win Jews to the Christian faith but forbade forcible baptisms. Persons baptized, "not by the sweetness of preaching but by compulsion," he observed, would only return to their "former superstition." In October, 598, he ordered his legate in Palermo to see that the bishop, Victor, repay the Jews for synagogues he had seized and hastily consecrated as churches so that they could not be used again as synagogues. The proper price for the synagogues and attached property should be assessed by the Patrician Venantius and the Abbot Urbicus so that the Jews "may in no wise be oppressed or suffer any injustice." Gregory also ordered a search for all books and ornaments carried off and restoration of them. The Jews should neither have freedom to go beyond what the law allows nor suffer damages "contrary to justice and equity."

Visigothic Spain

The first severe persecution of Jews occurred in Visigothic Spain. Recared (586–601), the first Visigothic King to adopt the Catholic faith, pursued an active effort to convert all Jews. His successors went still further and gave Jews the options of conversion or exile. many Jews accepted Christianity publicly but continued to practice Judaism secretly. In 654 these "Judaizing Christians" of Toledo were forced to make a new declaration of faith to King Recceswinth (649–672), promising not to observe Jewish customs or rites or to associate with unbaptized Jews again, marry persons related by blood within the sixth degree, contract marriage with non-Christians, practice circumcision, celebrate the Passover, Sabbath, or other Jewish festivals, or observe food laws. In 681 King Erwig (680–687) decreed that all unbaptized Jews should receive baptism within one year. If they did not, they would have their heads shaved, receive a hundred lashes, and go into exile. Their property would revert to the king.

The situation of the Jewish people improved as a result of the Muslim conquest of Spain. Under the Pact of Omar, originally formulated about 647 after the conquest of Palestine with reference to Christians and other "people of the Book," Jews or Christians were not forced to convert but were placed under severe strictures. They could not erect new monasteries, churches, cells, or hermitages or repair those which needed repair in Muslim quarters. They had to honor and host Muslim travelers. They had to show special respect to them in public. They could not make public display of their religion or make converts. Later they had to pay a head tax in return for protection and exemption from military service and were forbidden to hold public office.

The Frankish Kingdom

The Jews fared better in the Frankish Kingdom than in Spain. Intolerance arose chiefly within the Church. In 615 the Council of Paris, with the Merovingian King's approval, denied Jews any civil or military position which placed them over Christians. If they violated this stricture, they had to receive baptism. Dagobert I (d. 639) ordered all Jews to receive baptism or leave the realm.

Both Charlemagne and his son, Louis the Pious, made toleration the imperial policy, but during the reign of the latter (814–840), Agobard, the archbishop of Lyons, penned strong anti-Jewish documents.

The Crusades

The worst treatment of Jews emerged with the crusades. Although previously they had experienced destruction of property, forcible conversion, and many restrictions, from the first crusade onwards they encountered mob violence. The first wave of crusaders led by Peter the Hermit and Walter the Penniless massacred Jews in German cities such as Speyer, Worms, Mainz, Trier, and Cologne on their way east. At Mainz in May, 1096, the Jews took refuge in the palace of the archbishop, but to no avail. The crusaders, led by a German noble named Emico, smashed the gates and entered anyway. The archbishop's soldiers who had promised to help fled and left the Jews open to the slaughter. Conditioned to accept whatever happened as the will of God, they meekly yielded to their killers. As at Masada in 73 C.E., men and women killed their children and patiently awaited their own deaths. Bernard of Clairvaux, to his credit, spoke out vigorously against persecution of the Jews in connection with the crusade against the Wends, an offshoot of the second crusade to the Holy Land.

The crusading era created a climate of anti-Jewish sentiment which evoked further onslaughts against the Jewish people. In 1173 Thomas of Monmouth wrote a work entitled *The Life and Miracles of St. William of Norwich* which initiated a series of charges of ritual murder of Christian children at Passover time. According to the account of Thomas, a Benedictine monk at Norwich, William had mastered the art of leather making and attracted a Jewish clientele by the time he was twelve. A guileless child of saintly life, he was tricked by a Jewish messenger and brought to their synagogue to serve as their ritual offering at Passover, March 21, 1144. In precise detail Thomas described how the Jewish leaders first tortured and then killed him with merciless cruelty, thus making him a martyr of the type of Christ. In support of this incredible story Thomas cited a Jewish convert named Theobald. Each year, in some part of the world, according to Theobald, Jews had to sacrifice a Christian "in scorn and contempt of Christ" to avenge their sufferings. They cast lots at Narbonne in Spain each year to decide which city would choose the victim. In 1144 the lot fell to Norwich.

In 1171 Jews at Blois in France were accused of having crucified a Christian child during the Passover and throwing the corpse into the Loire river. According to a Jewish *Book of Historical Records* by Ephraim ben Jacob (1132–ca. 1200), the charge arose when a soldier, seeing at dusk a corner of an untanned hide sticking out of the coat of a Jew watering his horse, hurried to report to his master that he saw a Jew throw a little Christian child killed by Jews in the water. The master, wanting to retaliate against a Jewish

woman named Pulcelina, reported the next morning to Theobald V, the Count of Blois (1152–1191). Theobald had all of the Jews of Blois arrested and imprisoned. Since he had no evidence against them, he could not hold them until a priest appeared and suggested the use of the ordeal to prove whether the soldier was lying. When the latter passed the water test by floating, Theobald sought ransoms for their release. The Jews offered small amounts, lest larger ones encourage other arrests. So the count following the advice of the priest, put them in a wooden structure, surrounded it with faggots, and demanded that they convert. Christians beat and tortured them, but they remained steadfast. After trying unsuccessfully to burn three rabbis, the Christians then killed them with swords and set fire to the building, killing the other thirty-one. Another rabbi from the Count of Blois' territory arranged a huge ransom for the remaining Jews in the city.

A mob attack on the Jews of London attended the coronation of Richard the Lion Hearted in September, 1189. Fired with religious zeal by the Third Crusade, the mob spirit spread northwards until it reached the city of York in February and March, 1190. Nobles heavily indebted to the Jewish community used the occasion to stir up hatred of people on lower socioeconomic levels, completely exterminating the Jewish community. According to a *History of English Affairs*, written by William of Newburgh (1136–ca. 1201), a monk and canon of the Augustinian priory at Newburgh, the nobles waited until Richard had departed for France to organize the crusade before they struck. Acting out of diverse motives—recovery of property lost to Jews through usury, payment of expenses for the crusade, money for taxes—they either set fire to part of the city or used the occasion of a huge fire to raid the house of a wealthy Jew who had died of a beating he received from the London mob in 1189. The conspirators killed his widow, children, and all others living in the estate, set fire to the house, and withdrew with their booty. The

Jews sought protection from the Warden of the royal castle at York and brought to the castle huge sums of money. But a few days later the conspirators struck again, this time at the Jewish leader Joce's house. They pillaged it, killed the inhabitants, and set fire to it. Joce and his family and many others, however, had fled to the castle and escaped. The next day a mob rushed to the house and demolished whatever remained. They gave any Jews they found outside the castle the choice of baptism or death. Those who received baptism lived. The mob of Christians butchered those who refused.

Meantime, the Warden of the castle where the Jews had taken refuge began to waver. He went to the sheriff of the county, John Marshal, and complained that the Jews had cheated him out of the castle put in his charge. The sheriff was infuriated. The conspirators fanned the flames. Marshal ordered the summoning of the people to besiege the castle. Masses gathered from everywhere. Although the sheriff tried to countermand his order, he could not turn back the mob of working people, youth, country folk, and soldiers as well as many clergy "among whom a certain hermit seemed more vehement than the rest." Unarmed and with no provisions to withstand a siege, the Jews could not hold the castle. Most of the Jews, on advice of their rabbi, committed suicide. Some offered to convert but were slaughtered by the mob. The mob immediately marched on the Cathedral, secured records of debts owed the Jews, and burned them. Those who had taken the cross set out on the journey before an inquest, the rest remained behind in fear of one. When King Richard ordered an inquiry by the bishop of Ely, William of Longchamp, the main conspirators fled to Scotland. The bishop imposed fines on the citizens of York for not keeping the peace. He could do nothing more to deal with the mob.

The Jewish people had survived much harassment and persecution in France from the time Philip Augustus took the throne in 1179, he looked enviously on the Jews as a source of money to secure his throne and to fight his enemies. Whether he believed Jews guilty of ritual murder is uncertain. In 1180 he imprisoned all Jews in his domain and released them only after they paid huge ransoms. A year later, he annulled all Jewish loans made to Christians and took twenty percent for himself. In 1182 he confiscated all Jewish lands and buildings and drove them out of lands he ruled directly. Some converted and received their possessions back. Others pleaded with counts, barons, archbishops, and bishops to intercede on their behalf but to no avail. In 1198, however, Philip readmitted the Jews, assuring himself of lucrative income through careful regulation of their banking business and imposition of a variety of taxes and duties.

The Thirteenth Century

The Travail of the Jewish people increased markedly in the thirteenth century as Christians smelled total victory in the evangelization of Europe. Like most of his predecessors, Innocent III did not want to destroy the Jewish people, but he did one thing which was to have fateful consequences for the Jews. He required Jews and Muslims to wear special dress in Christian lands which would make them easy to distinguish from Christians. This bit of legislation by the Fourth Lateran Council in 1215 stood behind the expulsions of Jews from Western European countries during the next three centuries.

Beyond that, Innocent sought chiefly scrupulous observance of the anti-Jewish laws enacted by the christianized Roman Empire and the Church. The Fourth Lateran Council threatened the Jews with a social and economic boycott if they charged excessive interest (usury) and threatened to excommunicate Christians who continued to associate with Jews charging high interest rates. It also commanded Christian princes to restrain Jews from such oppressive practices. The Council renewed earlier church regulations prohibiting blaspheming of Christ, election of Jews to public office, reconversion to Judaism. It released all creditors who intended to undertake a crusade, specially naming the Jews, and ordered the Jews to repay interest already collected and count other income they received as payment on the principal of a loan.

Under immense pressure many Jews did convert to Christianity. The struggle which often occurred here is reflected in the story of a conversion which took place at Louvain around 1220. As reported by Caesarius, Prior of the Abbey at Heisterbach, near Bonn (d. ca. 1240), a priest named Rener, Chaplain to the Duke of Louvain, often visited in a Jewish home to argue with the Jew about Christian faith. The man's daughter, Rachel, still a little girl, was won over to the Christian faith and asked for baptism. A woman came to the home and secretly carted her off to a Cistercian convent. When the father discovered this, he offered the Duke of Louvain a huge sum of money to recover his daughter. The Duke was willing, but the priest Rener and the Abbot of Viller, Dom Walter, dissuaded him. The Jewish father then turned to Hugo, bishop of Liège (d. 1229), who sent letters to the convent directing the nuns to return Rachel. When the father came for her, however, accompanied by friends and relatives, she refused, smelling the "Jewish stench" (*Foetor Judaicus*) of her parents. At the end of the year Dom Engilbert, archbishop of Cologne (d. 1225), convened a synod which ordered the bishop of Liège never again to trouble the convent about the girl. Although Hugo remained silent for a time, he eventually sent a letter summoning the girl under penalty of excommunication to come to Liège to answer objections raised by her father. She came "under good protection." When confronted with her father's charge that she was forcibly baptized, she replied, "My father truly has lied in his beard." The Jew's Christian lawyer still pressed her, but the Abbot of Villers intimidated him to relent. When the Abbot of Clairvaux, Wido, visited the convent at the end of the year, he reproached the bishop. The bishop demanded to know what business it was of his. He gave two reasons: "first because I am a Christian, and next, because that convent in which she is living is of the lineage of Clairvaux." The abbot proceeded then to place the girl and her case under papal protection.

Some Jewish converts proved super zealots for their Christian faith. One convert, Nicholas Donin, denounced the "blasphemies" of the Talmud to Pope Gregory IX (1227–1241). The pope in 1239 ordered the prelates and rulers of France, England, Spain, and Portugal to seize all Jewish books and examine them. The only ruler to take the mandate seriously was Louis IX, King of France (1226–1270). Louis ordered the books seized on March 3, 1240. In June he compelled four prominent French rabbis to debate Donin in public. Jewish arguments could not save the Talmud from condemnation and burning in 1242 and 1244. A few years later (1247) Pope Innocent IV (1243–1254) asked the French papal legate, Odo of Chateauroux, to investigate alleged charges of the anti-Christian character of the Talmud. The legate investigated reluctantly, but he issued a final condemnation on May 15, 1248, finding them "full of innumerable errors, abuses, blasphemies, and wickedness such as arouse shame in those who speak of them and horrify the hearer." Gautier, the archbishop of Sens, who tried to salvage the Talmud in 1241, received fierce denunciation from Thomas of Cantimpre, in his treatise on virtues and vices (ca. 1263), who perceived the archbishop's sudden death in 1241 as an act of God. Louis IX, the crusader saint par excellence, delighted in a story about the beating of a knight administered to a Jew when the latter denied belief in the incarnation, virgin birth, and that Mary was Mother of God. To this story, according to John of Joinville, Louis added that only learned clergy should dispute with the Jews. Laymen, when they hear "the Christian law missaid, should not defend the Christian law, unless it be with the sword."

The Jewish people occasionally received better treatment. In the main this occurred in eastern European countries to which they finally migrated—Austria, Hungary, Bohemia, Poland, Silesia, and Lithuania. As a racially and religiously distinct group, they received special charters. With some changes the Charter of the Jews of the Duchy of Austria, issued by Frederick, Duke of Austria and Styria and Lord of Carniola, July 1, 1244, served as a model. This extensive document required a Jewish witness as well as a Christian witness in cases of complaints against a Jew; protected Jewish lenders against capricious accusations; put jurisdiction of important conflicts among Jews in the hands of the duke; mandated a death sentence if a Christian killed a Jew and required appropriate punishment for other crimes; guaranteed Jews freedom of travel in Austria without excessive road fees; mandated the death penalty for Christians desecrating Jewish cemeteries and other punishments for throwing things at a synagogue; gave legal protection in the courts to Jews; ordered the hand cut off in cases where Christians raised it in violence against a Jewish woman; forbade forced quartering in Jewish homes; mandated the death penalty for kidnapping of a Jewish child; threatened punishment of Christians who violated pledges made to Jews; and limited interest to eight percent a week or 173.33 percent annually.

In Western Europe, however, the tide was flowing against the Jewish people and pushing them eastward. In 1265 Alfonso X, the Wise (1252–1284), of Castile, issued *The Seven-Part Code*. Although these regulations did not go into effect until 1348, they prefigured what was happening to compel the exodus from Western countries. All of them—based on Visigothic, later Roman, and ecclesiastical sources—were hostile to the Jews. Castile, however, defended the Jewish people, religion, and property. *The Seven-Part Code* defined what being Jewish meant, described how they should act among Christians, forbade employment in any positions where they could oppress Christians, restricted building of synagogues, protected their Sabbath observances, prohibited reconversion of Christian Jews, ordering the death penalty for that, forbade a Christian man or woman to live with a Jew, mandated the death penalty for a Jewish man having intercourse with a Christian woman, forbade Jews to own Christian slaves, and required Jews to wear special dress.

Christian attitudes grew more and more determined in the fourteenth and fifteenth centuries. Christian tolerance such as existed in Spain still in the thirteenth century gave way to bigotry. In 1328 Christians massacred Jews in Navarre. In 1391 fanatical anti-Jewish riots spread through the Christian portions of Spain as the Reconquest reached its peak. Indeed, this year marked the end of toleration. In 1492 Ferdinand and Isabella ordered all Jews either baptized or to leave Spain. Many converted, but more fled—to Naples, Navarre, Portugal. In these, too, however, they soon met the same kind of intolerance. In Portugal, for instance, the monarch commanded the baptism of all children between ages four and fourteen in 1497. Earlier, he had issued an order requiring all Jews and Muslims to leave the kingdom before the end of October, 1497. The story does not speak too well for Christianity in the West. Too few Christians stood ready to protect the rights of other human beings. The final consequence of the buildup of centuries of hatred became evident in Nazi Germany.

Chapter 50

New Orders for a New Day

By the end of the twelfth century the Benedictine tradition, long so vital to the health and well-being of the church, no longer sufficed to enervate and energize the church and to help it overcome mounting problems. The Cluniacs had brought genuine reform throughout Europe during the tenth and eleventh centuries. The Cistercians continued the movement of renewal as the Cluniac reform mired down in its own success. Yet, although the Cistercians, especially in the person of Bernard of Clairvaux, captured the loyalty of masses, they failed in their cloistered state to reach the masses of people who, alienated from the Catholic Church, had gravitated toward the medieval sects which obviously met needs the church failed to meet. Several other new orders— Camaldolese, Vallombrosians, Carthusians, and Canons Regular—also failed. Why?

A number of factors can be cited. First of all, the Gregorian Reform to which the Cluniacs contributed so significantly widened rather than narrowed the gap between the masses and the church, for Gregory emphasized clerical versus lay authority and involvement. The masses doubtless applauded improvement of clerical morals, which they criticized vigorously, and of monks, but they witnessed growth rather than diminishment of the church's wealth, power, and involvement in secular affairs. By the time of Innocent III (1198–1216), who epitomized more than any other the papal theory envisioned by Gregory VII (1073–1085) and implemented it to a greater degree, the papacy had become monarchical, a worldly power vying with other world powers. Not surprisingly, Arnold of Brescia and Peter Valdes, among others, saw the incongruity of the Church's practice with the gospel it supposedly preached.

Secondly, the European economy shifted dramatically during the twelfth century. Largely agrarian in earlier centuries when the Benedictine concept of stable communities sustained by agriculture worked so well, Europe began to see the growth of towns and trade, a shift to a more urban economy, during the twelfth century. The crusades, as noted earlier, prepared the way for this as they opened up trade routes to the East which necessitated in turn development of industries in the West which could produce goods to sell or exchange. With industries, however primitive, came a shifting of populations as peasants sought out the towns where they could find some relief from the drudgery and poverty of rural life for those who owned no land. Thousands of these persons, having no education and possessing no real skills, begged at the city gates all over Europe around 1200.

Cities put the church in a different position of importance and authority. In a largely agrarian society the Church was the center of everything. In the city it remained important in this time, but it did not have the same importance it had had earlier. And, in the late twelfth century, cities began to show their clout. In 1176 the coalition of Italian cities known as the Lombard League defeated Emperor Frederick Barbarossa at Legnano. They continued to have importance throughout the thirteenth century. During the thirteenth century, German merchants in the Rhineland and Baltic Sea regions formed the Hanseatic League to protect their trading interests. Between 1368 and 1370 they put together enough of an armed force to defeat the Danish King Valdemar IV, who tried to take control of economic activity in the north.

Where the Church lost touch with the masses was in towns where industries were heavily concentrated. One of the alternate names for the Albigenses was *textores* or *tessarants*, "weavers." Many of them undoubtedly worked in the textile industries of Albi or other cities in southern France and northern Italy. The Church identified with the rich and powerful who could contribute to the building of great churches, cathedrals, and monasteries, and it ignored the laborers who worked long hours in tedious and dehumanizing jobs and who found companionship and support in parachurch organizations rather than in the great Church. Preoccupied with a battle for power going on at another level, the hierarchical Church ignored the cries of the powerless long enough for them to earn such popular sympathy that it took crusades, inquisitions, and new religious orders either to stamp them out or to win them back to the Church.

The alienated themselves came up with the idea for a new kind of order such as the Franciscans and Dominicans eventually developed. Peter Valdes founded "the Poor Men of Lyons" before Francis Assisi was born (1182) and when Dominic was only three or four years old, about 1173. Like many others among those who distanced themselves from the Church, he took the one effective route he knew to meet a longing and to solve a problem—back to the Gospels. He responded to the same story so many early hermits

had responded to, Jesus' challenge to the rich youth. Military orders also supplied an example.

The wide gap between Church and people in everyday life was reinforced in what should have united them, that is, in the worship of the Church. The service was in Latin, the language of priests which many of them did not understand. Indeed, according to a contemporary source, Lewis, the bishop of Durham between 1316 and 1333, though of noble birth, did not understand Latin and could hardly pronounce it so that, despite coaching for several days before his consecration, could not say the word "Metropolitan" but finally ended up saying in French, "Let that be taken as read!" If the bishop had such a problem, then imagine where lay persons stood! Priests rarely preached, though many must have offered good pastoral care.

The Old and the New

The new orders which came into existence at this time, the Franciscans and Dominicans, differed from earlier orders, therefore, in several ways. (1) Rather than sustaining themselves by agriculture, they relied on begging as their means of support, at least in the beginning. This helped them to identify with the masses of impoverished people. The Spiritual Franciscans carried poverty to extremes. Conventuals steered midway between the ideal of Francis and the more traditional monastic customs. Dominicans did not make poverty a central concern.

(2) The Franciscans and Dominicans devoted themselves to practical activities in society, whereas the earlier monks had sought to withdraw from society. In actual practice, of course, throughout the Middle Ages in varying degrees, monks played very important roles in society. Scarcely any person in the twelfth century had a more active life than Bernard of Clairvaux. By design, however, they emphasized contemplation over activity and let the cloister be a world apart. The mendicants deliberately tried to carry out a ministry—preaching, teaching, mission work—in

society and thus overcome the Church's problem of estrangement from the people.

(3) Franciscans and Dominicans staffed the newly founded universities of Europe, whereas the earlier monks focused education chiefly on the monastery itself. To some degree, admittedly, the distinction is artificial, for monastic schools conserved the spirit of learning which emerged in the universities. However, other orders did not turn out scholastics as the Franciscans and Dominicans did. Noted Franciscans included John of Giles, Alexander Hales, Adam Marsh, Bonaventure, Duns Scotus, William of Ockham, and Roger Bacon. Dominicans could claim the two most eminent and influential schoolmen: Albertus Magnus and Thomas Aquinas.

(4) The mendicants also differed from earlier monastic orders, except for the Cluniacs, in their immediate subjection to the papacy. Cluny obtained a charter which placed it directly under the apostolic see, but other orders were subject to both religious and secular leaders, and one object of the battle against lay investiture was to free abbots from secular control. Both Franciscans and Dominicans, by contrast, obtained their charters directly from Pope Innocent III. They thus became instruments in the hands of the popes.

(5) Finally, the mendicants developed lay brotherhoods, called Tertiaries or penitential brothers, which provided lay persons opportunities to dedicate themselves in religion very much as members of the orders. Tertiaries followed much the same regimen as other mendicants, but they did not take a vow to live according to the rule of the order.

Francis and the Franciscans

Francis of Assisi founded the first of the mendicant orders, though the Franciscan order subsequently diverged far from what he envisioned. He had in mind something very simple, following Jesus and Jesus' teaching. What resulted was a powerful agency serving the institutional designs of the papacy. Even before Francis

died, the little band of followers had fallen under control of Cardinal Ugolino and modified Francis's simple rule. When Francis returned from the Holy Land in 1221, he became a humble lay brother in an organization he did not intend to found.

Francis of Assisi (1182–1226)

Francis was born while his father, Pietro Bernardone, an affluent cloth merchant, was away on a business trip, and his mother named him Giovanni (John). When his father returned home, he insisted that his new son have the name Francesco, because he loved France so much. Typically of children of affluent parents, Francis lived a carefree and party filled life until about age twenty. When Assisians mounted a campaign against the neighboring city of Perugia in 1201, he did as all other youth his age did. He assembled all the trappings of war and went. However, before he reached the place of battle, he was captured and spent a year in prison waiting for his father to ransom him.

Like many another who has had a similar experience, this event turned Francis's thought in a more serious direction. Over a period of about five years, until 1206, he underwent a kind of "conversion" in which he discovered his vocation and became the husband of "Lady Poverty." The sequence of events is no longer establishable, but a few stories have survived which bore witness to the change. Francis began to repair churches which had fallen into despair. One day, riding his his horse, he heard a leper cry out as required by law. Instinctively he spurred the horse past, but then, as he shot past, he pulled up on the reins, jumped down, and raced back to embrace and kiss the leper. When Assisi mounted a campaign against another city in the region, his father outfitted him again. But this time as he got into the battle line, he noticed a poor knight in tatters, dismounted, and gave horse, armor, and the rest to the knight. He went off into the fields. One day he stole some cloth from his wealthy father's shop, sold it, and took the proceeds to a priest. The priest handed it back, knowing it had not come from Pietro Bernardone. Francis then hurled it down and stalked away. Finally, his father accosted him in front of the cathedral one day and upbraided him. All he had, the very clothes on his back, Pietro Bernardone had given him. To which Francis responded by taking off all his clothes and hurling them at his father's feet. He would have gone away stark naked save for the kindness of the bishop in putting his robe on him.

In 1209 a sermon on Matthew 10:9, "Take neither gold nor silver nor bronze for your purses," so impressed him that had decided to devote himself completely to apostolic poverty. Others followed, and by the end of the year, according to the earliest *Life* by Thomas of Celano, the number had reached eleven, with Francis making twelve.

In 1210 Francis sought the approval of Pope Innocent III. The rule he submitted, evidently contained just three passages of scriptures. "If you wish to be perfect, go, sell what you possess, and give to the poor, and you will have treasure in heaven, and come, follow me" (Matt 19:21). "Take nothing for the journey, neither staff nor purse, nor bread nor silver nor two coats" (Luke 9:3). "If anyone wishes to come behind me, let that person deny self and take up his/her cross and follow me" (Matt 16:24). The canny pope, sensitive in an age heresies to heresy in simple guises, gave qualified approval, according to early Franciscan legend, after a dream in which he saw Francis holding up the walls of the Church which had started to collapse about him. He arranged, however, for Cardinal Uglino, the bishop of Ostia, to keep an eye on what appeared to be a harmless venture with limited impact. Uglino later became Pope Gregory IX (1227–1241).

Francis and the "Minor Brothers," so-named to identify them with the lower classes, scattered to beg on behalf of the sick and poor. They met only once a year in the little church of Portiun-cula in Assisi. In 1212 Clara of Sciffi, touched by a sermon of Francis on voluntary poverty, renounced her family ties and, with Francis's help, instituted the Order of Clarisses. In 1214 and 1215 Francis toured the south of France and Spain on his way to Africa to convert Muslims, but illness prevent him from reaching Africa. In 1219 he went through Eastern Europe to Egypt, where he was present at the siege and capture of Damietta in November.

During Francis's absence, the direction of the Order of Friars Minor passed into the hands of Pietro di Cantona (d. 1221) and then Elias of Cortona (ca. 1180–1253) and the order underwent a complete change. In 1220 it began to erect houses for the friars. At the urging of Cardinal Ugolino, in 1221 a new rule was drawn up which, after further revision, was submitted to Pope Honorius III and received his formal approval on November 29, 1223. The new rule reintroduced the old ideas of monastic submission and added a new element of submission to the pope. Francis, realizing that he did not have the capability of administering so vast an enterprise as the Franciscans had become, stepped aside. Pietro di Catona, a doctor of laws, favored the radical change in the order. Francis submitted to him just as any other member of the order, calling himself "the little brother."

In September 1224 Francis received the stigmata, the nail prints in his hands and feet and the spear wound in his side, on Mount Alvernia, a Franciscan retreat given him and his followers by the Lord of Chiusi. Although some have treated the claims with some skepticism, suggesting that they were self-inflicted, modern understanding of psychosomatic effects would at least leave room for such an experience. Francis so desired to be like Christ in every way that he also experienced the wounds of Christ as he conceived them. He cut through much of the confusion and turmoil of his own day—crusades, power struggles, divisions in church and society—with the simple formula tried over and over again, by literally trying to follow Jesus. Nearly blind and his health broken by his travels, Francis died on October 3, 1226. Less than two years later, July 16, 1228, Pope Gregory IX canonized him.

The Franciscans

A fight between two groups—"spirituals" who wanted to continue Francis's strict adherence to the rule of poverty and subsistence by begging and "conventuals" who wanted to accommodate the order to new realities by establishing houses—fractured the Franciscan Order almost immediately after Francis's death. From 1245 on, the debate grew so violent that it threatened the unity of the order. It subsided temporarily during the generalate of Bonaventure (1257–1274), who wrote a new *Life* of Francis to aid reconciliation. The Franciscans brought their controversy before Pope Clement V between 1310 and 1312. In 1317 and 1318 John XXII (1316–1334) decided against the Spirituals and issued two bulls permitting corporate ownership. Many of the Spirituals left the order and formed the *Fraticelli*. Continuing dispute occurred, nonetheless, and involved the Dominicans as well. It caused a general decline of the order during the fourteenth century. As the order prospered, it became more lax. Reform efforts led to further division—between "Observants" and "Conventuals." The Council of Constance in 1415 accorded the "Observants" special recognition. In 1517 they separated from the Conventuals and declared themselves the true Order of St. Francis. In 1950 the Observants claimed 1500 houses, the Conventuals only 290.

Dominic and the Dominicans

The Dominican Order (Order of Preachers) remained much closer to the design of its founder than the Franciscans did. Although they too got caught up in the Franciscan debate about voluntary poverty, they did not make poverty the central concern from the beginning as Francis and the Franciscans had. Dominic focused on preaching and education from the very first. The issue of poverty intruded because the Dominicans competed with the Franciscans, even borrowing Franciscan stories to paint their portrait of their founder, about whom they had little information.

Dominic (1170–1221)

Dominic does not offer a colorful portrait. Born at Calaruega in Old Castile, Spain, in 1170, probably of the Guzman family, he studied at Palencia in the cathedral school. Although the first university would be founded at Palencia in 1212, it did not offer general studies when Dominic entered at age fourteen. In 1199 he became a canon of the cathedral at Osma, where Martin de Bazan, bishop of Osma (1190–1201) had established the Rule of St. Augustine for his canons. Dominic soon became subprior of this chapter and remained at Osma until 1203. In 1203 he requested Pope Innocent III to release him from this charge so that he might go as a missionary to the Saracens. Innocent refused. As a consequence, he joined Bishop Diego, a Cistercian, on a preaching tour to convert the Albingensians in Languedoc. In 1206 Diego, Dominic, and others founded a convent for women at Prouille, in Albigensian territory, and attached a number of missionaries to it. When Diego died in 1207, Dominic was left to carry on in his place.

In 1208, following the murder of the papal legate Peter of Castelnau, Innocent III initiated a crusade against the Albigenses. During the seven years that the crusade lasted, Dominic strove hard but with little success to win the Albigenses back to the Church. In 1214 Count Simon de Montfort, the chief leader of the crusading army, put the castle of Casseneuil at Dominic's disposal, enabling him to found a specific order for the conversion of the Albigenses. Volunteers joined him. In 1215 the order received the sanction of the bishop of Toulouse and, a few months later, Pope Innocent III, with the proviso that Dominic adopt one of the accepted monastic rules. Dominic chose the Augustinian and defined the purpose of the Order of Preachers as the defense of the faith and the combatting of heresy. In 1216 he went to Rome and gained from Honorius III a formal sanction in two bulls granting special privileges.

During the remaining years of his life, Dominic traveled unceasingly throughout Italy and in Spain (1218) and to Paris (1219) setting up friaries and organizing the order. In 1221 he set out to preach to pagans in Hungary but became ill and had to return to Bologna. He died there on August 6, 1221. Although he lacked the popular appeal of Francis of Assisi, he was canonized in 1234. Dante described the rather severe person of Dominic as "good to his friends but dreadful to his enemies." If the Inquisition entrusted to the Dominicans in 1232 embodied something of his personality, it was an apt characterization.

The Dominicans

Known in England as the Black Friars because of their habits and in France as Jacobins because of the first house they established in Paris, the Dominicans took definite shape at two general meetings in Bologna in 1220 and 1221. At Dominic's insistence the Order of Preachers adopted the Franciscan practice of individual and corporate poverty and subsistence by begging. Corporate poverty meant no ownership except of convents and churches. After Dominic's death the order spread quickly to Greece, Poland, Denmark, and Palestine. It soon extended even to Asia. Official figures recorded 60 convents in 1221, 404 in 1277, and 582 in 1303. They listed 50 houses for women in 1277 and 149 in 1303.

By design the Dominicans focused on education to combat heresy. Privileges extended to them provoked jealousies among other orders. They soon occupied the great theological chairs of Europe—Bologna, Padua, Vienna, Cologne, Prague, Oxford, Salamanca, and Paris. The accommodation of Aristotle to Christian thought was done chiefly by Dominicans, especially Albertus Magnus and Thomas Aquinas. Highly organized, they became the main arm of the papacy. Popes used them to preach crusades,

collect money, and carry out diplomatic missions. From 1232 on, they supplied most of the staff for the Inquisition. During the age of European exploration, they went with Spanish and Portuguese explorers as missionaries in both East and West.

During the fourteenth and fifteenth centuries, the Dominicans engaged in controversies over constitutional and disciplinary issues. After the Black Death some friars evoked a great outcry against the order by gaining individual wealth through preaching and hearing confession and keeping surplus revenues. In 1475 Pope Sixtus IV rescinded the rule of corporate poverty and permitted the order to own property and have permanent sources of income. This did not create the problem it did for the Franciscans because voluntary poverty was not the central concern of the founder.

Like the Franciscans, the Dominicans also established a Second Order for women and a Third Order for lay persons. Dominican nuns, however, were cloistered and contemplative. Notable Dominican women included Catherine of Siena (1347–1380), an activist mystic who had much to do with the return of the papacy to Rome in 1378.

Preachers

Some special word needs to be interjected at this point concerning the Dominicans as preachers. The major reason Dominic and the Dominicans emphasized learning was to equip themselves for effective preaching. "The bow is first bent in study," a Dominican aphorism said, "and then it sends the arrow in preaching." Dominicans soon dominated in education. By the fourteenth century they had drawn up a long and elaborate program lasting as long as fourteen years. Not all of the preachers, by any means, pursued such an extended course, but all were at least trained at a level which could equip them to communicate with village audiences they would likely address. Their education exceeded that of the average parish priest by far.

Franciscan and Dominican preaching would not have differed significantly, but the Dominicans specialized in preaching more than the Franciscans. They were careful to certify those who preached and required maturity and enthusiasm. The young friars had to prove themselves. Skilled preachers could easily abuse the office because of gifts of money or other things. Preaching was the highest calling, however, and the Dominicans harped on matching life and calling. The best preachers took care to let their message fit their congregation.

The friars had to speak to a wide variety of people. Most preferred the uneducated rural folk. Good preachers attracted some who followed them from village to village. The Dominicans seem to have identified with the lower classes, for they took frequent swipes at the wealthy and powerful. They preferred the peasants who lived by honest toil and came really to listen. By contrast the rich seldom show devotion and oppress the poor. The friars discussed such things as the value of time-work over piece-work, commendation of fellow workers, business ethics, taking of interest (usury). They dealt with such moral problems as stealing, cheating, gluttony, drunkenness, and superstition.

The Dominicans played a major role in the missionary thrust of the thirteenth and fourteenth centuries. Dominic himself wanted to preach to the Muslims and the Cumani. His followers created provinces in Hungary in 1221, in Morocco in 1225, and in Scandinavia, Poland, Greece and the Holy Land in 1228. Raymond of Penaforte set up language schools in several places to teach Arabic. Unfortunately the friars underestimated the difficulty of converting Muslims and had little success.

The Inquisition

The Inquisition developed as a response to the massive growth of independent religious groups during the twelfth and thirteenth centuries. Originally the protection of the Church's doctrine and organization rested in the hands of bishops within their dioceses. Bishops worked with secular rulers to assure orthodoxy and order. In the Carolingian era Charlemagne ordered his bishops to make visitations throughout their dioceses and to correct offenses; his successors and the Ottonians followed suit in this to reform the Church and to christianize their domains. As a result of the Gregorian reform in the eleventh century, however, the papacy gathered more and more power into its own hands. Gregory VII (1073–1085) used legates to bring the authority of the pope to bear on affairs in the dioceses. As the problem of dissent in the Church grew greater and greater, the popes took pains to create an inquisition over which they could exercise control. To be effective, they needed experts whose sole business would be to unearth the guilty and to put them out of business. The Dominicans and Franciscans could not have timed their appearance any better. April 20, 1233 Gregory IX issued two Bulls entrusting the Inquisition specially to the Dominicans.

This action should not be seen as an exclusive grant of authority to the Dominicans. Bishops continued to exercise authority in their dioceses and frequently voiced resentment at the invasion of their jurisdiction by the friars. Transfer of the inquisitorial function to the mendicants, as H.C. Lea has pointed out in his classic study of *The Inquisition of the Middle Ages*, made relationships between bishops and friars very delicate, and until the middle of the thirteenth century popes continued to treat suppression of heresy as a matter of episcopal jurisdiction. Increasingly, however, inquisitors saw themselves as independent of and superior to bishops. Because heresy seemed ineradicable, the Inquisition became a permanent institution. Popes took care to enlist secular authorities' support. The Inquisition spread throughout Europe except the British Isles, Denmark, or other Scandinavian countries.

The Inquisition operated rather simply. Its major object was to terrorize any who might contemplate deviating from the Catholic faith. A single inquisitor usually conducted trials, though he often had an assistant. A notary recorded all of the proceedings. Technically the inquisitor did not have power to pronounce sentence. That decision lay in the hands of an assembly. Bishops then had to evaluate the decision of the assembly of experts.

The process of the Inquisition was an arbitrary one. A person would be reported to the inquisitor as a suspected heretic. After a secret inquiry the accused would be cited to appear at a given time and bail taken to secure an appearance. Presumed guilty, the person would either have to admit guilt or deny the accusation. Those who persisted in denial when the evidence seemed to prove otherwise, however, would be labeled obstinate, impenitent heretics and abandoned to the secular arm to be burned at the stake. If they repented, they would be thrust in jail for life. If convicted by an assembly of experts, they would be delivered to the secular arm for execution. Inquisitors had strong reasons for trying to get a confession and could use two means—deception or torture, both mental and physical. For the latter the Inquisition followed the same rules as secular courts. If anyone confessed under torture, the confession had to be confirmed after removal from the torture–chamber. Records always reported free and spontaneous confessions!

The Holy Office of Inquisition did not require much evidence. According to the Council of Narbonne in 1244, saying or signifying that one considered heretics "good" sufficed to condemn a person. An inquisitor usually required two witnesses to condemn a person of good reputation, but he could exercise discretion if testimony seemed weak. Testimony of persons of bad reputation could count as valid evidence. The accused had no rights. The inquisitor could proceed in purely arbitrary fashion.

The accused had little opportunity for defense, despite the fact that the Council of Beziers

in 1246 ruled that they should have. The secrecy of the hearings assured that the judge could act as he thought best and the accused had no right to counsel. The inquisitor even had the right to prosecute those who undertook defense of heretics. So hopeless was defense that many did not even attempt it. In some cases the accused appealed to Rome with some success, if they had sufficient money to satisfy the curia.

The penalties covered a fairly wide spectrum. Technically the inquisitors could not impose the death penalty. They could only withdraw the Church's protection so that the state could act against impenitent sinners. They could not confiscate the property of heretics, except in Italy. At most they could impose fines as penances. Inquisitors, however, could require harsh penances ranging from pious observances to wearing yellow crosses on clothing to imprisonment. Pious observances included recitation of prayers, going to churches, flagellation, pilgrimages, and ecclesiastical fines. Imprisonments involved solitary confinement on a diet of bread and water in frightful facilities. Bernard Gui's Register of Sentences for the years 1308 to 1322 reported the following disposition of 636 cases: 40 delivered to the secular court and burned, 67 bones exhumed and burned, 300 imprisoned, 21 bones exhumed of those who would have been imprisoned, 138 condemned to wear crosses, 16 condemned to perform pilgrimages, 1 banished to the Holy Land, 36 fugitives, 1 condemnation of the Talmud, and 16 houses to be destroyed. Inquisitors reserved the right to mitigate, increase, and reimpose sentences.

Although the Inquisition could not impose the worst penalties, confiscation of property or execution, the state at this time rarely hesitated to exact the penalties asked by the Church. One of Innocent III's first acts was to order confiscation of property of heretics in lands controlled by the papacy and to command temporal princes to do the same in their domains. Usually the Church divided the spoils with secular authorities. Similarly the Church intervened authoritatively when state laws appeared to interfere with effective enforcement. The Church had, by the thirteenth and fourteenth centuries, impressed the duty of safeguarding the Church and kingdom against heresy to assure prompt action. The only penalty thought adequate for impenitent heretics was burning. The percentage of burnings, however, was not too high because it took only an occasional performance to maintain the proper amount of terror in the mind of the public.

The Inquisition surely was one of the saddest chapters in the history of Christianity, and in that of the mendicant orders. No group of Christians ever were more confident that they did God and the Church a service than the inquisitors. Even the great Dominican Thomas Aquinas could justify the extermination of heretics who failed to repent.

Chapter 51

Spirituality

Fourteenth century mysticism has stood so tall in the history of Christian spirituality that it has dwarfed the achievements of the thirteenth. This is unfortunate, for the thirteenth century laid the foundation for fourteenth century spirituality just as the twelfth century has laid one for the thirteenth's. Two traditions—Franciscan and Dominican—stand out, the Franciscan for its affective mystical piety centered on the imitation of Christ and the Dominican for its more speculative mysticism. Yet these did not stand alone. The Beguines and Beghards, pious lay women and men in the Rhineland, exercised a practical piety informed by the bridal mysticism of Bernard of Clairvaux. Cistercians and other Benedictines also continued to produce significant spiritual writers, most notably the nuns at Helfta—Mechtild of Magdeburg (ca. 1210–ca. 1280), Gertrude of Hackeborn (1232–1292), and Gertrude the Great of Helfta (1256–ca. 1302). The thirteenth was also the century of apocalyptic spirituality generated by the writings of Joachim of Fiore and fostered by the Spiritual Franciscans.

The Franciscan Tradition

Francis of Assisi (1182–1226) left behind only about twenty pieces of his writing, but he etched an idea on the minds and hearts of his followers which would incarnate itself in story, song, and art in the thirteenth century. Francis's concern was, above all, to follow Jesus. Ernst Renan called him, "the first perfect Christian since Christ." It would be more accurate to say that he tried harder than anyone to follow Christ as literally as he could, given his understanding of the account in the Gospels. That meant for him a life of poverty, for Jesus had commanded the rich youth to go and sell what he had and give it to the poor and follow him. In Francis's own vivid way of expressing it, he "married Lady Poverty." This step led to his severance of ties with his family, again in literal fulfillment of words of Jesus. Following Jesus in his context caused Francis to lay aside the crusading mentality which dominated his age and to pursue the way of love. The words in his Canticle of Brother Sun, "Blessed are those who endure in peace, for by You, Most High, they shall be crowned," probably addressed conflict in his own native city, but it spoke too to the whole Christian world. "Christ's way is the way of peace." Later generations embodied that in the stories they told about him—his taming the fierce wolf of Gubbio or his preaching to the birds. Imitation of Christ meant harmony even with nature. Ultimately the Little Poor Man of Assisi carried the imitation to such an extreme that he had also to bear the wounds of Christ in his last two years. So intensely had he prayed to be like Christ that he received the stigmata, in his body, as the Apostle Paul expressed it (Col. 1:24), filling up what was lacking of the sufferings of Christ.

Francis has been appropriately characterized as a nature mystic. This would not mean naturalism or pantheism. Francis praised God *for* creation, not creation as God. So intimate and vivid was his sense of the presence of the living God—Father, Son, and Spirit—that nature took on a face and a heart. "Praised be You, my Lord, with all your creatures, . . . Brother Sun, Sister Moon and the stars, Brother Wind, Sister Water, Mother Earth." As he preached to the birds, as his first biographer and one of his first followers, Thomas of Celano, recorded, he took as his text Jesus' own words. "You ought often to praise your Creator and always to love Him who has given you feathers for your clothing and everything you need. God has made you the most noble of his creatures" (Celano, I.58).

Francis's impact registered differently on different people. As noted in an earlier chapter, his own followers divided on the degree to which they needed to adhere to his commitment to poverty. The Spiritual Franciscans insisted on strict adherence to the original vision of Francis, the Conventuals favored accommodation to quite different realities of a prosperous institution. The key figure in effecting a short term reconciliation was John Fidanza or Bonaventure (1221–1274), the fifth Minister General of the Franciscan Order.

Born at Bagnorea, near Viterbo, his devout parents, John of Fidanza and Maria Ritella, dedicated him to Il Poverello as a child when he contracted a dangerous illness in hopes that Francis would cure him. "In childhood," Bonaventure wrote in his preface to his *Life* of Francis, "I was rescued from the jaws of death through his intercession and merits." He studied under the arts faculty at Paris, and, either in 1238 or 1243 entered the Order of Friars Minor. He then studied theology under Alexander of Hales, the most distinguished Franciscan theologian of the day. In 1248 he began to lecture on scriptures. In 1253 he completed a commentary on the *Sentences* of Peter the Lombard and received approv-

al for his doctorate from John of Parma, then minister general of the Order. The opposition of William of Saint Amour and secular teachers at Paris, however, prevented both Bonaventure and Aquinas from obtaining their degrees until an appeal to Rome in 1257. Elected to succeed John of Parma, he set to work reconciling the two factions. In 1263 the Order approved his *Life* of Francis as the official biography and ordered the destruction of all other "legends." He declined Pope Clement IV's invitation to become the archbishop of York in 1265. However, Gregory X (1271–1276), whose election to the papacy he helped to secure, insisted that he become cardinal bishop of Albano in 1273. He played a significant role in the Council of Lyons in 1274, but he died on July 14 during the Council.

Bonaventure propounded an essentially affective type of spirituality. Although it had some roots in Francis's, it was also deeply imprinted with the spirituality of Bernard of Clairvaux and the Victorines. He did not disdain theoretical knowledge as much as either Francis or Bernard, in that regard perhaps more Victorine and influenced by his own age as Aristotelianism gained the ascendancy. He emphasized the will as that by which we love God, desiring above all to put intellect at the service of piety and devotion of the heart. He thus leaned more toward Plato than toward Aristotle. One special feature of his spirituality was devotion to the Trinity.

Bonaventure was the first to speak definitely of the three stages of the spiritual journey: purgative, illuminative, and unitive. These correspond, according to Bonaventure, to the three means: meditation, prayer, and contemplation. In the purgative state the faithful examine their consciences by meditation and lament their faults in prayer. Purified and reconciled, they receive the light of God as a gift of grace and are forced to imitate Jesus, above all, in his suffering and dying. The divine light leads them to fullness of truth, wherein they may experience union with God by love. Like Pseudo-Dionysius, however, Bonaventure considered God in essence beyond knowing to the intellect. Like Bernard, he emphasized love as the means of attaining union.

Bonaventure took his theory of contemplation from Hugo of Saint Victor. The Trinity has imprinted itself on the world, making it a book in which we can read about God. Before the Fall human beings could easily ascend toward God. Now they must have the aid of grace. Three powers help in the ascent: bodily senses, the spirit which bears the imprint of the Trinity, and a supernatural light which resides at the apex of the soul. By love Christians can contemplate the beauty of God residing in the creation. Threes can be found everywhere because of the way the Trinity has imprinted itself on everything, but the Trinity is found especially in the human soul: memory, understanding, and will. As the soul contemplates the Trinity, it becomes like the Trinity. Although this sounds more dogmatic than mystical, Bonaventure thought of theology as an affective science. Yet he was not an experiential mystic himself. When he spoke of ecstasy, he cited the experience of Francis of Assisi.

Bonaventure shared with Anselm and Bernard a special predilection for the passion of Christ. He exhorted his readers to meditate on the suffering Savior in order to become like him. He composed a work entitled *The Tree of Life* to facilitate meditation. Jesus is the mystical tree. This theme inspired a spate of writings on the life of Christ under the name of Bonaventure.

Franciscan preachers disseminated Franciscan piety far and wide. It often came out in far more traditional forms as in the preaching of Anthony of Padua (1195–1231), who stressed repentance, contempt for the world, and use of the Church's means of grace. Contemporary accounts estimated that Anthony sometimes preached to audiences of thirty thousand. He literally wore himself out with itinerant preaching.

A more effective embodiment of the Franciscan ideal was the poet Jacopone da Todi (ca. 1230–1306). Converted after the death of his wife

in 1268, Jacopone became a Franciscan lay brother in 1278. In 1294 he and some other brothers obtained the permission of Pope Celestine V (1294) to form a separate community living the rule of the order in its original strictness. Reversal of the order by Boniface VIII (1294–1303), however, led to his imprisonment from 1298 until 1303. During this period, he wrote many poems in both Latin and the Umbrian dialect. The poems reflected the apocalyptic outlook of Franciscan "Spirituals" and the times and cover a wide range of topics. Some are harsh critiques of the pope, others on traditional themes in spirituality such as the Virgin Mary or penitence. The central theme, however, is love. Jacopone urges the faithful to let their hearts "wing swiftly to love." God will give you His heart if you accept it unconditionally. Love pours into the mind and illumines it, into the heart and inflames it, and into the soul and transforms it. Love besieges the soul and will not give up. No one can measure the love of God.

The Franciscan tradition also inspired some remarkable women mystics such as Angela of Foligno (ca. 1248–1309). Born into a wealthy family, Angela chose a life of contemplation after her husband and children's deaths and became a Franciscan tertiary. She experienced frequent visions related chiefly to the passion of Christ which her confessor, Brother Arnold, transcribed. Later they circulated under the title of *The Book of Visions and Instructions*. True to Francis's original vision, she strove for complete poverty. Not until she reached the point of renouncing all property, she said, did she know the joys of the spiritual life. Where before she had felt only bitterness, now she could "feel the sweetness and consolation of God in her heart." The series of revelations which she experienced reached a peak in 1294, the year of Celestine V's brief pontificate. As she described the greatest of these, "The eyes of my soul were opened, and I beheld the plenitude of God, whereby I did comprehend the whole world, . . ." and a loud voice told her,

"This whole world is full of God!" For her as for Jacopone da Todi the central thing is the love of God which "is never idle, for it constrains us to follow the way of the Cross!"

The Dominican Tradition

The Dominican tradition predictably produced a more rational and speculative piety culminating in the mysticism of German and Dutch Dominicans in the fourteenth century. Dominic himself would account in great part for the difference. His concern was not, like Francis's, the following of Jesus in poverty but preaching, and for preparation of preachers, education. Not surprisingly, therefore, the Dominicans distinguished themselves by occupying the great theological chairs in the universities of Europe and as leaders of the Inquisition. They also gave birth to the new synthesis of thought based on Aristotle.

The Dominicans, nevertheless, spawned also a mystical tradition which emerged full blown in the fourteenth century but had thirteenth century roots. The great period of Dominican mysticism, as a matter of fact, was the period from 1250 to 1350. The Dominican tradition prepared the way for the formation of the group known as "the Friends of God" and later "the Brothers of the Common Life." The earlier manifestation of this mystical stream was strongest among women in cloisters attached to the Order of Preachers, but not exclusive to them. Both men and women recorded profound mystical experiences in *Minnesangen*. Themes sound similar to those of the Franciscans, binding together deep personal piety and profundity of thought, but with inclination toward the *Wesenmystik* tradition of Pseudo-Dionysius. Significant poets included Eberhard of Sax, active in the areas of Basel and Zürich around 1230, Konrad of Wurzburg (d. 1287), and Mechtild, the first to write her songs in German.

Meister Eckhart (ca. 1260–1327) overlaps the thirteenth and the fourteenth centuries. Although his thought would not have been typically Do-minican in an era dominated by Thomism, he exerted a profound influence through John Tauler (1300–1361) and Henry Suso (ca. 1295–1366). Entering the Dominican convent at Erfurt as a youth, he obtained a master's degree at Paris in 1302. In 1304 he became provincial of the province of Saxony. In 1311 he was sent to Paris to teach but returned to Germany around 1313. He lived first at Strassburg and then at Cologne, where he gained fame as a preacher. In 1326 the archbishop of Cologne tried him for heresy. He appealed to Rome but died before a decision was reached. In 1329 Pope John XXII condemned twenty-eight of his propositions. Modern study of Eckhart does not sustain charges of pantheism for which he was condemned.

Deeply influenced by Pseudo-Dionysius, Eckhart emphasized the unknowability of the Godhead in its essence, yet also the importance of striving to know. God is "beyond God." Human beings can know the Trinity by natural reason because the Trinity is close to the natural realities with which they have contact. Just as reality has emanated from the Godhead to the Unspoken Word (the Father) to the Spoken Word (the Son) to Love (the Spirit) to creation, so must they return through each of those stages. The first step is to withdraw from the creaturely to behold the uncreaturely in creatures. Next, they must meditate on the purely spiritual faculties of the soul—memory, understanding, and will. To know God in essence, however, will require "total self-detachment." God dwells in "nakedness." Return to God requires, therefore, being "born again."

The Beguines

During the thirteenth century, crusades and Inquisition notwithstanding, many men and women cultivated their piety in parachurch organizations such as the Beghards and Beguines as well as numerous sects of somewhat questionable orthodoxy. The Beguines attracted cultured and well-educated women to their communities, a few of which still exist. Although persecution decimated their ranks, many remained steadfast in their commitment although often choosing to move to one of the recognized orders.

Marie d'Oignies (1177–1213) was one of the earliest Beguines. She was married for fourteen years. She had much to do with the shape of the Beguine communities and she joined one in caring for patients in the leprosarium at Willenbroek. She practiced strenuous asceticism. She emphasized reverence for the passion of Christ and the eucharist. She had rich charismatic experiences. She withdrew later to Oignies, where she gathered a circle of like-minded women around herself.

Hadewijch is known only through her letters and poetry. She either founded or joined a Beguine group and became its leader. After a time, her leadership was disputed, evidently because of her demands. She fell under suspicion of the Inquisition and may have been exiled from the group. She was highly educated, how is a matter of conjecture. She shows familiarity with Latin, the rules of rhetoric, medieval numerology, Ptolemaic astronomy, and music theory. She knew how to write letters and poetry. She also was proficient in French. Sources of her thought included scriptures, Origen, Hilary of Poitiers, Augustine, Gregory the Great, Isidore of Seville, Hugo, Adam, and Richard of St. Victor, Bernard of Clairvaux, William of Saint Thierry, and Guerric of Igny. She also seems to have known some Eastern writings.

Hadewijch's chief theme, like Bernard's, is love. Like the Dominicans of this period, she frequently used the word *Minne* to describe her experience of intimacy. Hadewijch found the experience of love painful. Love gave but love also withheld consolation. Yet the beloved could not let pain interfere with the desire to serve love. Experience of God was deeply personal, and she confessed that life grieved her sorely. She could neither love nor cease to love. She wondered about the Inquisitors (or possibly her critics): "While they are busy scanning me, Who

shall be loving their love?" Then she added her editorial, "Better had they gone their free way, Where they might have learned to know you." God knows better how to cure what afflicted her.

Benedictines

Despite the ferment of the period, the older orders had not gone out of business entirely. Once again, women supply some of the premier examples. Among Cistercians Lutgard of Aywieres (1182–1246). She entered the Benedictine cloister of St. Catherine at Trond around 1194 as a student. Around 1200 she made a profession and in 1205 became prioress. Soon thereafter she went over to the Cistercian cloister at Aywieres. A vigorous ascetic, she proved a helpful counselor to others, converting sinners and healing the sick. She was one of the first to emphasize reverence for the heart of Jesus.

With the arrival of Mechthild of Magdeburg the convent at Helfta gained recognition as a strong center of spirituality. Born around 1210, she left home around age twenty and joined a Beguinage at Magdeburg. At the order of a Dominican confessor she wrote down her visions between 1250 and 1269 under the title of *The Flowing Light of the Godhead*. Persecution of Beguines forced her in 1270 to join the Cistercian convent at Helfta, which provided a certain amount of protection. There she added another volume to her revelations. This work had a marked impact on subsequent developments in German mysticism. Like Lutgard, Mechthild too emphasized the sacred heart. Her counsel for those who want to grow spiritually is to meditate on the bloodstained body of Christ, his hands and feet and side. She professed numerous experiences of union with the Trinity. Some of her visions aroused criticism and one, in which John the Baptist conducted a Mass, was censured.

Advancing further the reputation of Helfta were Mechthild of Hackeborn (1241–1299) and Gertrude (1232–1292) her sister. In 1258 Mechthild entered the convent at Helfta. After careful preparation she was appointed director of the cloister school and choir. Gertrude evidently edited the *Special Book of Grace*. It is trinitarian and christocentric and emphasizes reverence for the sacred heart of Jesus.

Gertrude the Great (1256–ca. 1302) entered the convent at Helfta at age five and received a good education there. At age twenty-five she experienced a conversion to the contemplative life. During worship services, she had visions which centered on the sacred heart. Her *Legacy of Divine Piety*, based mostly on her notes, and *Spiritual Exercises*, a collection of prayers, have exerted much influence on the development of Catholic devotion to the sacred heart of Jesus.

Chapter 52

Scholasticism

The integration of Aristotle's thought into Christian thinking which is characterized as scholasticism took place slowly during the thirteenth century. Early in the century, official church pronouncements forbade the use of Aristotle in the schools. Augustinianism still prevailed during the first half of the century, and it remained dominant among Franciscans, who never felt comfortable with Aristotle. Bonaventure hardly nodded in Aristotle's direction, and John Duns Scotus deliberately challenged the synthesis of Aristotelian and Christian thought when it finally came into existence.

The synthesis was the achievement of Dominican scholars. Albertus Magnus paved the way for it with his massive learning, but he did not effect the synthesis itself. That was the contribution of Thomas Aquinas. Even here, the effort to integrate Aristotelian into Christian thought did not go unchallenged. Some disciples of Aquinas, notably Siger de Brabant, went a few steps farther than he and earned the condemnation of the archbishop of Paris. Some propositions of Aquinas were included among those censured in 1277 at the Council of Paris. Albertus Magnus had to defend his pupil, who had died three years before. Despite this close call, Thomism gradually gained an ascendant position in the universities, especially among Dominicans.

The Augustinian Era

Aristotle was not the only ingredient entering the stream of Christian thought at this time. The Arab and Jewish scholars—Averroes, Avicenna, and Avicebron—also figured prominently in scholarly debate. In an age of widespread dissent authorities understandably viewed with some caution any efforts to introduce novel ideas. In 1210 the Synod of Sens, after condemning the writings and supporters of David of Dinant, Amaury of Bene, and Maurice of Spain, prohibited the reading of the writings of Aristotle on natural philosophy and of the commentaries on them both in public and in private in Paris under penalty of excommunication. Five years later, the statutes of the University of Paris reiterated this prohibition. Although Pope Gregory IX issued a Bull, *Parens scientiarum*, in 1231, which opened the way to cautious use of Aristotle after the writings "have been examined and purged from all suspicion of error," a university committee never reported on the writings in question. In 1245 Pope Innocent IV extended the decrees of 1210 and 1215 to Toulouse. In practice, however, some teaching of Aristotle must have occurred, for Roger Bacon reported lecturing at Paris on the *Physics* and *Metaphysics* of Aristotle around 1240. By mid-century the papal prohibition had lost its urgency and general sentiment ran in favor of the use of Aristotle. In 1255 all current works of Aristotle were prescribed for the whole Paris Faculty. Belatedly and ineffectively in 1263 Pope Urban IV reiterated the prohibition of books cited at Sens in 1210 when confirming *Parens scientiarum*. By this time Aristotle had become "the philosopher."

The Franciscans

The Franciscans did not join the revolution which took place in the latter half of the thirteenth century. Arriving at the University of Paris just after the Dominicans in 1219, they included several outstanding Englishmen: Haymo of Faversham, Alexander of Hales, Adam Marsh, and Roger Bacon. The most important was Alexander of Hales (ca. 1186–1245), first regent of the Franciscan convent at Paris and teacher of Bonaventure. Born at Halesowen, Worcestershire, he studied at Paris, where he received the doctorate around 1220 or 1221 and began teaching. In his lectures he commented on the *Sentences* of Peter the Lombard. He left Paris briefly in 1231 and 1232 to return to England, where he was made Archdeacon at Coventry, but he soon returned to teach at Paris. In 1236 he joined the Franciscan Order but retained his teaching position. He is considered the founder of the Franciscan school of theology. He died at Paris on August 21, 1245.

Alexander's principal writing was his *Summa universae theologiae*, completed posthumously by his students. It followed the method of the Lombard's *Sentences*, but answers were selected from classical writers as well as the Bible, the Church Fathers, and later theologians. Alexander sampled all of Aristotle and Avicebron, but he borrowed more from the Neoplatonic tradition of Augustine and the Victorines. Two doctrines which he specially developed were the concept of a treasury of merits upon which the practice of distributing and selling of indulgences was based and the indelible character of baptism and ordination. Alexander argued for withdrawal of the cup from the laity.

More influential in shaping the Franciscan tradition than Alexander of Hales was his eminent student Bonaventure. In his *Paradiso* Dante depicted Bonaventure as the equal of Thomas Aquinas. After studying at Paris under Alexander, around 1242–1243, he lectured on the *Sentences* of the Lombard, but he relinquished his post after his appointment as Minister General of the Franciscan Order. As seen in the preceding chapter, Bonaventure contributed far more to spirituality than to scholasticism, even though he wrote a *Commentary on the Sentences* of Peter the Lombard and an exposition of Christian dogma. Quite clearly, he weighted the Franciscan tradition on the Augustinian side. He was the first to declare that he purposely followed Augustine in both philosophy and theology. He built his whole system, as seen in *The Journey of the Mind to God*, on Augustine's epistemology. Although he used Aristotle liberally, he differed quite decidedly from Thomas Aquinas in doing so. He had a very different attitude toward human intellectual activity than Aquinas, and though he used the same terms as Aquinas, he never adopted the Aristotelian outlook. For him the aim of human reflection is to teach how the mind, will, and soul may attain to God. His theology was that of Augustine and his philosophy that of Neoplatonism, both systematized.

Although Paris ranked first in theology at this time, Oxford held a position very close to it, and England sent a large number of its scholars to Paris. Oxford ranked first in logic, mathematics, and science. The most distinguished of Oxford's theologians in the early thirteenth century was Robert Grosseteste (ca. 1175–1253). Born at Stradbroke in Suffolk of poor parents, he studied at Oxford and possibly Paris. Early in the thirteenth century, he began teaching at Oxford. From 1224 until 1235 he taught at the newly founded Franciscan house of studies. In 1235 he became bishop of Lincoln.

As a philosopher, Grosseteste rendered a massive service in putting the Aristotelian corpus into the mainstream. He translated Aristotle's *Nicomachean Ethics* and a treatise *On Virtue*. He commented on part of Aristotle's *Physics* and *Nicomachean Ethics*. Like Bonaventure, however, he followed Augustine and the Arab Neoplatonists rather than Aristotle in his philosophy of nature. He also shared the Franciscan school's emphasis on the primacy of will over intellect. He did not envision a gulf between metaphysics and physics as Aristotelians did.

Other noted Franciscans at Oxford included Roger Bacon (ca. 1214–ca. 1291), the most significant contributor to the development of the physical sciences in the thirteenth century. After studying at Oxford, where he gained his grounding in Aristotelian psychology and metaphysics, he went to Paris about 1240, lecturing on the writings of Aristotle. After some study of theology in Paris, he returned to Oxford around 1247 and continued the study under Adam Marsh and Thomas of Wales. Under influence of Grosseteste, however, he abandoned theology for the natural sciences. Until 1257 he devoted himself entirely to the latter. The poverty of the Franciscans and Bonaventure's lack of sympathy for the sciences, however, hampered his work. In 1277 he was condemned by superiors and put under some restraint. Before his death in 1292 he composed a *Compendium of the Study of Theology*. Although brilliant in assembling data, he never put his thought into a system and carried on a somewhat erratic tirade against theology and philosophy.

The Dominicans

Another Franciscan, Duns Scotus, sowed the seeds for the breakdown of the medieval synthesis, but before examining his thought it will be useful to examine the synthesis itself. Its creators were Albertus Magnus (ca. 1200–1280) and his pupil Thomas Aquinas (1225–1274).

Born of noble parentage at Lauingen, near Ulm, Albertus studied first at Bologna and Padua, where he entered the Dominican Order in 1222.

Returning to Germany to study theology, he lectured in the Dominican houses at Hildesheim, Freiburg-im-Breisgau, Regensburg, and Strassburg. About 1241 the Order sent him to Paris, where he held one of the Dominican chairs of theology from 1245 until 1248. His students included Thomas Aquinas. In 1248 the Order transferred him to Cologne, to which Aquinas followed, where he set up a Dominican *studium generale*. From 1253 to 1256 he served as the Provincial of the province of Germany. He spent the next four years in Rome, summoned there to defend the interests of his order against the attacks of secular teachers at Paris. In 1260 Pope Alexander IV (1254–1261) appointed him archbishop of Regensburg, but he resigned at the end of two years and returned to Cologne. In 1263 and 1264 he preached the crusade in Germany and Bohemia on order of Pope Urban IV (1261–1264). The next few years he spent in Wurzburg, Strassburg, and other Dominican centers. After 1269 he remained in Cologne until his death. In 1277 he defended the teaching of Aristotelians at Paris. His comprehensive learning earned him the title of *doctor universalis*.

Albertus's writings fill thirty-eight volumes and cover nearly every subject—logic, physics, metaphysics, psychology, ethics, and theology. He did not succeed, however, in pulling all of it into a system, as his pupil Thomas Aquinas did. He viewed philosophy, as Arab and Jewish philosophers did, as a natural vision of truth. Aristotle served as his principal guide and source of truth, but he supplemented Aristotle from other sources. His objective was to make all of Aristotle available in the West, and he succeeded in doing so. He reserved the right to criticize his mentor, however, so that he cannot be judged a consistent Aristotelian. Although he drew his doctrine of universals and his epistemology from Aristotle, he took his doctrine of the soul from Plato. Characteristically he tried to harmonize all three major positions on universals—*ante rem, in re*, and *post rem*. He formulated the dictum on revelation and reason which opened the way for the long conflict between theology and science: "Revelation is above but not contrary to reason."

Thomas Aquinas was the youngest son of Count Landulf of Aquino, a relative of both the emperor and the king of France. At age five he entered the Benedictine school at Monte Cassino, where his parents expected him to remain. In 1240 he went to Naples to complete his liberal education. There, he came in contact with the Dominicans and decided to seek admission to that Order. His family, however, seized him and held him captive at Roccasecca for fifteen months in an effort to change his mind. When released in April 1244, he joined the Order. In the fall of 1245 he entered the University of Paris to study under Albertus Magnus, then followed him to Cologne in 1248. In 1252 he returned to Paris to continue his study and to lecture at the Dominican Convent of St.-Jacques. He received his Master of Theology degree in 1256, but, like Bonaventure, had to have intervention of Rome to secure it. For the next ten years he taught in Italy—Anagni and Orvieto (1259–1265), Rome (1265–1267), and Viterbo (1267–1269). The Order returned him to Paris in 1269 but then sent him to Naples to set up a Dominican school in 1272. He died on March 7, 1274 at the Cistercian monastery of Fossanuova on his way to the Council of Lyon. Stephen Tempier, bishop of Paris, condemned several propositions drawn from his writings alongside those of Siger de Brabant in 1277. He also was censured posthumously by Archbishops Kilwardby, a Dominican, (1277) and Peckham (1284) of Canterbury. The Franciscan Order prohibited study of his works for several years. In 1278, however, the Dominicans officially required study of his teaching in the Order of Preachers. He was canonized in 1323 by Pope John XXII. Since the thirteenth century, the Church has added only two dogmas which do not find their base in his teaching—the immaculate conception (1874) and the assumption (1950) of Mary.

Aquinas surpassed his teacher in his ability to weave a mountain of diverse information into an orderly and coherent system. He went farther than Albertus in acceptance of human reason as an adequate instrument for attaining truth within the realm of human experience. He accepted the main lines of Aristotle's system as the basis of his interpretation of the natural order, including ethics and politics. He also took elements from other places as well, and he added a personal dimension not found in Aristotle's arguments for the existence of God.

Thomas Aquinas saw no contradiction between philosophy and theology, but, as he viewed them, they involve different methods. In philosophy knowledge precedes faith, in theology faith precedes knowledge. Higher truths, such as the Trinity, cannot be discovered by reason alone. They require revelation. He accepted Aristotle's rational arguments for the existence of God—first mover, first cause, unconditional being to explain the conditional, perfect being to explain the imperfect, and the rational design of things. Whereas Aristotle's God is impersonal, Thomas's is a dynamic existential reality, the Creator and Source of all being, Being in itself. Creation, therefore, for Aquinas, is the expression of God's love and goodness and not the fulfillment of a deficiency. God did not have to create, but God did anyway.

Aquinas departed quite decisively from Augustine on his anthropology. He rejected the traducian theory as heretical and held that each soul is created at birth. Although Augustine did not take a firm position on the traducian theory, he leaned toward it. Aquinas also emphasized human freedom more than Augustine. Sin is a consequence of inordinate self-love passed on from Adam. Grace is a *donum superadditum*, a gift added to the natural endowment.

Aquinas agreed with Augustine that unbaptized infants perish. Sacraments are visible signs of invisible realities, grace imparted by the Church. They are efficacious, that is, effective for salvation in themselves. There are seven sacraments. As a moderate realist, Aquinas affirmed the doctrine of transubstantiation for the eucharist. penance removes guilt incurred after baptism. Indulgences abound for the dead as well as the living as a part of the treasury of merit established by Christ. Aquinas accepted Anselm's satisfaction theory of the atonement.

Aquinas regarded Rome as the Mother Church to whom all Christians owed absolute obedience. Obedience to the Church is obedience to Christ. The pope must determine doctrine and obliterate heresy. Heretics must be compelled to believe. His thought here gave effective support to the Inquisition.

The Averroists

Some Aristotelians went much farther than Aquinas and Albertus Magnus and brought the effort to appropriate Aristotle's thought for Christian philosophy and theology into a collision with ecclesiastical authorities. At Paris the leaders were members of the Faculty of Arts, notably Siger de Brabant and Boethius of Dacia. Siger (ca. 1240–ca. 1284) joined the arts faculty around 1260. In 1270 Stephen Tempier, bishop of Paris, condemned thirteen errors of "Averroists" and Thomas Aquinas wrote a treatise *On the Unity of the Intellect against the Averroists*. In 1276 Simon de Val, the inquisitor of France, cited Siger and two others for heresy. Siger evidently appealed to the papal curia and fled the country. He was murdered at Orvieto around 1284 by a clergyman in a fit of insanity.

Siger composed his most substantial treatises as "questiones" on the works of Aristotle—*Metaphysics*, *Physics*, and *De Anima*. He envisioned his task as one of exposition of the thought of Aristotle, whether it could be reconciled with revealed truth or not. Views of Siger condemned in 1277 included the idea that the world is eternal and that there is a unity of intellect in the human race. If one follows the latter to its natural end, it

would mean denial of personal immortality and of rewards and punishments in the future life.

The Breakdown of the Synthesis

The Aristotelian triumph did not last long. As early as 1269 to 1271, Aquinas began to run head on into conservatives led by John Peckham (ca. 1223–1292), who occupied the Franciscan chair of theology in Paris at that time. Later elected archbishop of Canterbury (1279), Peckham vigorously opposed the teaching of the unity of intellect in humankind and declared that it be condemned as heretical in 1286. Both Aquinas and Bonaventure died in 1274. Siger had to flee Paris a few years later.

A more serious blow came from another Franciscan, John Duns Scotus (ca. 1265–1308). Little is known about his early life. He joined the Order of Friars Minor around 1280. He may have studied at Cambridge before going to Oxford, where he worked with William of Ware. He received ordination in 1291. He lectured on the *Sentences* of Peter the Lombard first at Cambridge (ca. 1297–1300), then at Oxford (1300–1302 and 1303–1304), and Paris (probably 1302–1303 and after 1304), where he was elected regent in 1305. In 1307, probably for political reasons, he moved to Cologne, where he died in 1308.

Duns Scotus combined elements of the older Augustinianism with the Aristotelianism of his day. Strongly critical of Thomism, he placed his main accent on the primacy of love and will rather than knowledge and reason. He sharply distinguished faith from reason and insisted that natural law depended on the will of God rather than on God's mind, so that it would not be immutable. Although he agreed with Aquinas that faith and reason should not conflict, he argued that reason is unreliable and limited. Consequently, the authority of the Church must ultimately decide what is to be believed. In theology he was the first noted theologian to defend the doctrine of the immaculate conception of Mary on the basis of Christ's mediatorship. He also argued against Thomists that the incarnation would have happened whether the Fall had occurred or not.

The sharp differentiation of faith and reason by Scotus came to fruition in the "razor" of William of Occam (ca. 1285–1347). A native of Ockham in Surrey, he entered the Franciscan Order at an early age. he studied at Oxford around 1310 to 1318. From 1318 until 1324 he lectured on the Bible and the *Sentences* of the Lombard and composed a commentary on the latter. In 1323 John Luttrell, the Chancellor of the University, went to the papal court at Avignon and denounced Occam. John XXII summoned him to answer charges. A commission of six theologians listed fifty-one propositions judged heretical, but the pope made no formal condemnation. On order of the Minister General of the Franciscans in 1327 Occam examined papal constitutions on Franciscan poverty and declared them heretical. He then fled Avignon to Bavaria, where he enjoyed protection of Louis of Bavaria until he died in 1347. Meantime, he wrote numerous treatises attacking the papacy.

A sharp logician in the Augustinian and Franciscan tradition, he emphasized economy ("Occam's razor"). There is no such thing as a "universal" outside the mind of the knower. Individual entities evoke in the mind a sign, to which we give names. From this it follows that none of the so-called "truths" of natural religion can be demonstrated. God cannot be known intuitively but only by revelation. Human beings must be satisfied with what revelation teaches. The soul and its fate cannot be known except by faith. The answer to the human situation lies in the power of God. God's power is absolute. God is free to do whatever God wants. Thus humans have one choice, obedience.

Occam's nominalism dug the grave of scholasticism. It exerted a profound influence on the Protestant reformers, especially Luther, who considered Occam his "dear teacher." The last of the Schoolmen, Gabriel Biel of Tubingen (ca. 1420–1495), did not go far beyond Occam.

Conclusion

Viewed in retrospect from its thirteenth-century pinnacle, the Christian story is a remarkable one. Beginning as a sect of Judaism in a tiny, out-of-the-way corner of the Roman Empire, its founder crucified by Roman authorities as a threat to the *Pax Romana*, Christianity appeared to have bleak prospects not merely for expansion but for survival. Aided by the onetime persecutor Saul of Tarsus, Christianity nonetheless not only survived but grew and endured three centuries of harassment and persecution to become, by the end of the fourth century, the official religion of the Roman Empire, wherein it was illegal *not* to be a Christian.

Migration of the population of Europe placed Christianity again in a precarious position. Although the East Roman or Byzantine Empire remained strong, in the West every semblance of authority dissolved as first one and then another Germanic tribe claimed the hegemony over different parts of the empire. The one institution that offered some promise of uniting these disparate claimants was the Christian church, more specifically the Roman church. To monks go the laurels for the evangelization or reevangelization of Europe. Thanks to them, monasteries and churches gradually covered western, then central, and finally northern Europe. To the papacy, however, we must give credit for rushing into the political and cultural vacuum created by the collapse of the Roman Empire and establishing some kind of order. Not until the Carolingians, Pippin III and Charlemagne, did a secular ruler effectively challenge papal claims as Constantine's successors in the West. Thereafter, first the French monarchs and then the emperors of the Holy Roman Empire and eventually heads of other states placed priestcraft in a precarious position.

All too often, Protestant historians of Christianity in this period have locked onto the story of the papacy and the state and failed to notice the far more remarkable story of the evangelization and Christianization of the peoples of Europe, first the Germanic, then the Slavic, and then the northern Europeans, albeit not by the most commendable methods. Where in the early centuries Christianity adapted an essentially Jewish expression to an essentially Greek and Roman culture, now it accommodated the latter to an essentially German or Slavic or northern European culture. Protestants have often raised critical questions as to how Christian the Christianization was, but, given the shock produced by the Germanic and later Norse invasions, I find the deep impact of Christianity astonishing and remarkable.

Not everything that happened deserves applause, to be sure. Who, for instance, can find much to praise in the papacy during "the Great Pornocracy" (ca. 900–962)? One can only regret, too, the abysmal level of literacy in the West during much of the Middle Ages. By way of defense we must be fair to recognize that this preceded the invention of movable type in 1456 and resulted from cultural lapses brought on by the Germanic invasions rather than church policy and practice. At the same time we should readily acknowledge that the churches in the Middle Ages did a commendable job of forming ordinary saints in Christian culture.

The crown of Western medieval achievements may have been Gothic architecture, which expressed so well the longing to link heaven and earth. If we will avoid the tendency to seize upon the worst examples we can find, we will see that the monasteries really did form men and women of profound personal piety. Parish clergy, likewise, lived lives of authentic commitment, identified with their charges, and served God with gladness rather than for self-serving reasons. Far less than Protestants have suggested or imagined did either monks or clerics plunge to levels of indecency ascribed to them. Protest movements erupted now and then, but they were by no means universal. From the side of the Catholic church the worst occurred in efforts to repress such expressions by way of crusades and inquisitions. The hierarchy would probably have fared better had it left room for dissent and not enlisted state coercion to suppress it.

As we draw this story to a close in 1300, the beginning of the Renaissance, Christianity faced new critical tests to its survival. Prophetic vision should have enabled some to discern the beginnings of a vast revolution in the political and cultural situation of the churches. In the disastrous Fourth Crusade in 1204 the Byzantine Empire had suffered a blow from which it could not recover sufficiently—even though it freed itself from Latin domination in 1261—to stave off the invasion of the Ottoman Turks. In the West, political stability of the Holy Roman Empire was threatened as national loyalties, especially in France, rose and challenged the authority of both emperors and popes. Boniface VIII (1295–1308) seems not to have grasped the reality, but, his exaggerated claims notwithstanding, his exercise of power was a dim candle alongside that of Innocent III a century earlier. Soon the churches all over Europe experienced dislocation from the axial position they had attained during the Middle Ages as traumatic events of the fourteenth century dealt them other devastating blows. Yet Christianity survived and revived, and its day was far from over in 1300.

For Further Reading

Part 1.
The Beginnings to 70 C.E.

Chapter 1. *An Ancient New People.*

Goodenough, Erwin R. *Jewish Symbols in the Greco-Roman Period.* 13 vols. Princeton NJ: Princeton University Press, 1958–1968.

Hengel, Martin. *Judaism and Hellenism: Studies in Their Encounter in Palestine during the Early Hellenistic Period.* 2 vols. Translated by John Bowden. Philadelphia: Fortress Press, 1974.

Moore, George Foote. *Judaism in the First Centuries of the Christian Era. The Age of the Tannaim.* 3 vols. Cambridge MA: Harvard University Press, 1958.

Sanders, E. P., editor. *Jewish and Christian Self-Definition.* Vol. 1. *The Shaping of Christianity in the Second and Third Centuries.* Philadelphia: Fortress Press, 1980.

Sandmel, Samuel. *Judaism and Christian Beginnings.* New York: Oxford University Press, 1978.

Schürer, Emil. *The History of the Jewish People in the Age of Jesus Christ (175 B.C.–A.D. 135).* Rev. ed. by Geza Vermes and Fergus Millar. Edinburgh: T.&T. Clark, 1973.

Chapter 2. *The World of Early Christianity.*

Carcopino, Jérôme. *Daily Life in Ancient Rome.* Trans. E. O. Lorimer. New Haven CT: Yale University Press, 1940.

Dill, Samuel. *Roman Society from Nero to Marcus Aurelius.* Cleveland and New York: World Publishing Co., 1956.

Dodds, E. R. *Pagan and Christian in an Age of Anxiety.* Cambridge: Cambridge University Press, 1965.

Ferguson, Everett. *Backgrounds of Early Christianity.* 2nd ed. Grand Rapids MI: Eerdmans, 1993.

Ferguson, John. *The Religions of the Roman Empire.* Ithaca NY: Cornell University Press, 1970.

Fox, Robin Lane. *Pagans and Christians.* San Francisco: Harper & Row, Publishers, 1986.

Snyder, Graydon F. *Ante Pacem. Archaeological Evidence of Church Life before Constantine.* Macon GA: Mercer University Press, 1985.

Chapter 3. *The Founder of Christianity.*

Bowman, John Wick. *The Intention of Jesus.* Philadelphia: Westminster Press, 1943.

Brandon, S. G. F. *Jesus and the Zealots.* Manchester: University of Manchester Press, 1967.

Crossan, John Dominic. *The Historical Jesus: The Life of a Mediterranean Jewish Peasant.* San Francisco: HarperSanFrancisco (Harper/Collins), 1991.

_____. *Jesus: A Revolutionary Biography.* San Francisco: HarperSanFrancisco (Harper/Collins), 1994.

Dibelius, Martin. *Jesus.* Trans. C. B. Hedrick and F. C. Grant. Philadelphia: Westminster Press, 1949.

Hinson, E. Glenn. *Jesus Christ.* Gaithersburg MD: Consortium Press, 1977.

Jeremias, Joachim. *The Parables of Jesus.* Trans. S. H. Hooke. London: SCM Press, 1950.

Meier, John P. *A Marginal Jew: Rethinking the Historical Jesus.* New York: Doubleday, 1991.

Chapter 4. *Jerusalem and Beyond.*

Becker, Jürgen, ed. *Christian Beginnings.* Trans. Annemarie S. Kidder and Reinhard Krauss. Louisville KY: Westminster/John Knox, 1987.

Conzelmann, Hans. *History of Primitive Christianity.* Trans. John E. Steely. Nashville: Abingdon Press, 1973.

Streeter, B. H. *The Primitive Church*. London: Macmillan & Co., 1929.

Chapter 5. *The Pauline Mission.*

Allen, Roland. *Missionary Methods: St. Paul's or Ours?* 5th ed. London: World Dominion Press, 1960.

Bornkamm, Günther. *Paul*. Trans. D. M. G. Stalker. New York and Evanston: Harper & Row, 1971.

Grassi, Joseph A. *A World to Win: The Missionary Methods of Paul the Apostle*. Maryknoll NY: Maryknoll Publications, 1965.

Part 2.
Into All the World, 70–180.

Chapter 6. *Broadcasting the Seed.*

Green, Michael. *Evangelism in the Early Church*. London: Hodder & Stoughton, 1970.

Frend, W. H. C. *The Rise of Christianity*. Philadelphia: Fortress Press, 1984.

Harnack, Adolf. *The Mission and Expansion of Christianity*. Trans. James Moffatt. London: Williams & Norgate, 1908.

Hinson, E. Glenn. *The Evangelization of the Roman Empire*. Macon GA: Mercer University Press, 1981.

MacMullen, Ramsay. *Christianizing the Roman Empire, A.D. 100–400*. New Haven and London: Yale University Press, 1984.

Chapter 7. *Like Master, So Disciples.*

Benko, Stephen and John J. O'Rourke. *The Catacombs and the Colosseum*. Valley Forge, PA: Judson Press, 1971.

Cadoux, C.J. *The Early Church and the World*. Edinburgh: T.&T. Clark, 1925.

Canfield, Leon Hardy. *The Early Persecutions of the Christians*. New York: Columbia University Press, 1913.

Fiorenza, Elisabeth Schüssler, Editor. *Aspects of Religious Propaganda in Judaism and Early Christianity*. Notre Dame IN: University of Notre Dame Press, 1976.

Frend, W. H. C. *Martyrdom and Persecution in the Early Church*. Garden City NY: Doubleday, 1967.

Grant, Robert M. *Gods and the One God*. Philadelphia: Westminster Press, 1986.

Workman, Herbert B. *Persecution in the Early Church*. 4th ed. London: Epworth Press, 1923.

Chapter 8. *Life Together.*

Baptism.

Aland, Kurt. *Did the Early Church Baptize Infants?* Trans. G. R. Beasley-Murray. Philadelphia: Westminster Press, 1963.

Ferguson, Everett. *Conversion, Catechumenate, and Baptism in the Early Church*. New York: Garland, 1993.

Jeremias, Joachim. *Infant Baptism in the First Four Centuries*. Trans. David Cairns. London: SCM Press, 1960.

_____. *The Origins of Infant Baptism*. London: SCM Press, 1963.

Eucharist and Worship.

Cullmann, Oscar. *Early Christian Worship*. London: SCM Press, 1953.

Delling, Gerhard. *Worship in the New Testament*. Trans. Percy Scott. Philadelphia: Westminster Press, 1962.

Jungmann, Josef A., S.J. *The Early Liturgy*. Trans. Francis A. Brunner. Notre Dame IN: University of Notre Dame Press, 1959.

Burtchaell, James Tunstead. *From Synagogue to Church: Public Services and Offices in the Earliest Christian Communities*. Cambridge: Cambridge University Press, 1992.

Discipline.

Greenslade, S.L. *Shepherding the Flock: Problems of Pastoral Discipline in the Early Church and in the Younger Churches Today*. London: SCM Press, 1967.

Volz, Carl A. *Pastoral Life and Practice in the Early Church*. Minneapolis: Augsburg, 1990.

Structuring for Mission.

Campenhausen, Hans Freiherr von. *Ecclesiastical Authority and Spiritual Power in the Church of the First Three Centuries*. Trans. J. A. Baker. London: Adam & Charles Black, 1969.

Chapter 9. *Struggle for Identity and Unity.*

The Roman Situation.

Bauer, Walter. *Orthodoxy and Heresy in Earliest Christianity.* Trans. Philadelphia Seminar on Christian Origins. Philadelphia: Fortress Press, 1971.

Bowe, Barbara Ellen. *A Church in Crisis: Ecclesiology and Paraenesis in Clement of Rome.* Minneapolis: Fortress Press, 1988.

Frend, W. H. C. *Saints and Sinners in the Early Church: Differing and Conflicting Traditions in the First Six Centuries.* Wilmington DE: Michael Glazier, 1985.

Turner, H. E. W. *The Pattern of Christian Truth.* London: Mobray, 1954.

Jewish Christianity.

Daniélou, Jean. *The Theology of Jewish Christianity.* Trans. by John A. Baker. London: Darton, Longman & Todd, 1964.

Schoeps, Hans-Joachim. *Jewish Christianity.* Trans. Donald R. Hare. Philadelphia: Fortress Press, 1969.

Marcion.

Blackman, E.C. *Marcion and His Influence.* London: S.P.C.K., 1948.

Hoffmann, B. Joseph. *Marcion: On the Restitution of Christianity.* Chico CA: Scholars Press, 1984.

The Gnostics.

Filoramo, Giovanni. *A History of Gnosticism.* Oxford: Basil Blackwell, 1990.

Grant, Robert M. *Gnosticism and Early Christianity.* Rev. ed. New York: Harper & Row, 1959, 1966.

Harnack, Adolf von. *Marcion: The Gospel of an Alien God.* Trans. John E. Steely and Lyle D. Bierma. Durham NC: Labyrinth Press, 1924, 1990.

Jeffers, James S. *Conflict at Rome: Social Order and Hierarchy in Early Christianity.* Minneapolis: Fortress Press, 1991.

Jonas, Hans. *The Gnostic Religion.* Second edition. Boston: Beacon Hill, 1958.

Montanism.

De Soyres, J. *Montanism and the Primitive Church.* Cambridge: Deighton, Bell & Co., 1878.

Huber, Elaine C. *Women and the Authority of inspiration: A Reexamination of Prophetic Movements from a Contemporary Feminist Perspective.* Lanham MD: University Press of America, 1985.

Chapter 10. *Confessing Faith.*

Barnard, L. W. *Athenagoras: A Study in Second Century Christian Apologetic.* Paris: Beauchesne, 1972.

_____. *Justin Martyr: His Life and Thought.* Cambridge: Cambridge University Press, 1967.

Cullmann, Oscar. *The Earliest Christian Confessions.* Trans. J. K. S. Reid. London: Lutterworth Press, 1949.

Goodenough, Erwin R. *The Theology of Justin Martyr.* Amsterdam: Philo Press, 1923, 1968.

Grant, Robert M. *Jesus after the Gospels: The Christ of the Second Century.* Louisville: Westminster/John Knox Press, 1990.

Part 3.
New Status, 175–313 C.E.

Chapter 11. *Victorious Victims.*

See under chapter 6, above.

Chapter 12. *The Seed of the Church.*

Mason, Arthur James. *The Persecution of Diocletian.* Cambridge: Deighton Bell, 1876.

Riddle, Donald. *The Martyrs, a Study in Social Control.* Chicago: University of Chicago Press, 1931.
See also under chapter 7, above.

Chapter 13. *Aliens in Their Own Homeland.*

Christians in Roman Eyes.

Wilken, Robert L. *The Christians as the Romans Saw Them.* New Have and London: Yale University Press, 1984.

Romans in Christian Eyes.

Chadwick, Henry. *Early Christian Thought and the Classical Tradition: Studies in Justin, Clement, and Origen.* New York: Oxford University Press, 1966.

Droge, Arthur J. *Homer or Moses? Early Christian Interpretations of the History of Culture.* Tübingen: J. C. B. Mohr (Paul Siebeck), 1989.

Finney, Paul C. *The Invisible God: The Earliest Christians on Art.* New York: Oxford University Press, 1994.

Hatch, Edwin. *The Influence of Greek Ideas on Christianity.* New York: Harper & Bros., 1967.

Jaeger, Werner. *Early Christianity and Greek Paideia.* Cambridge MA: Harvard University Press, 1961.

Nock, Arthur Darby. *Early Gentile Christianity and Its Hellenistic Background.* New York: Harper & Row, 1964.

Pelikan, Jaroslav. *Christianity and Classical Culture: The Metamorphosis of Natural Theology in the Christian Encounter with Hellenism.* New Haven CT: Yale University Press, 1993.

Weltin, E. G. *Athens and Jerusalem: An Interpretative Essay on Christianity and Classical Culture.* Atlanta: Scholars Press, 1987.

Chapter 14.
The Struggle for Unity in an Age of Persecution.

Frend, W. H. C. *The Donatist Church.* Oxford: Clarendon Press, 1952.

Greenslade, S. L. *Schism in the Early Church.* Second edition. London: SCM Press, 1964.

Willis, Geoffrey. *Saint Augustine and the Donatist Controversy.* London: S.P.C.K., 1950.

Chapter 15. *Christian Spirituality.*

Bouyer, Louis.*The Spirituality of the New Testament and the Fathers.* New York: Desclee Co., 1960.

Crouzel, Henri. *Origen: The Life and Thought of the First Great Theologian.* Trans. A. S. Worrall. San Francisco: Harper & Row, 1989.

McGinn, Bernard, John Meyendorff, and Jean Leclercq, editors. *Christian Spirituality: Origins to the Twelfth Century.* New York: Crossroad, 1985.

Watkins, O. D. *A History of Penance.* Two volumes. London: Longmans, Green & Co., 1920.

Chapter 16. *Life Together.*

Charities and Social Aid.

Garrison, Roman. *Redemptive Almsgiving in Early Christianity.* Sheffield: JSOT Press, 1993.

Hands, A. R. *Charities and Social Aid in Greece and Rome.* Ithaca NY: Cornell University Press, 1968.

Hengel, Martin. *Property and Riches in the Early Church.* Trans. John Bowden. Philadelphia: Fortress Press, 1973.

Fellowship Meals.

Keating, J.F. *The Agape and the Eucharist in the Early Church.* New York: AMS Press, 1901, 1969.

Worship.

Duchesne, Louis. *Christian Worship: Its Origin and Evolution.* Trans. M. L. McClure. Fifth edition. London: S.P.C.K., 1919.

Hahn, Ferdinand. *The Worship of the Early Church.* Trans. David E. Green. Philadelphia: Fortress Press, 1973.

Rordorf, Willy. *Sunday.* Translated by A. A. K. Green. Philadelphia: Westminster Press, 1968.

Art and Architecture.

Davies, J.G. *The Origin and Development of Early Christian Architecture.* London: SCM Press, 1952.

Grabar, André. *The Beginnings of Christian Art, 200–395.* Trans. Stuart Gilbert and James Emmons. London: Thames and Hudson, 1967.

Holy Orders.

Telfer, William. *The Office of a Bishop.* London: Darton, Longman & Todd, 1962.

Chapter 17. *First Principles.*

The Rule of Faith.

Hanson, R. P. C. *Tradition in the Early Church.* Philadelphia: Westminster Press, 1962.

Hultgren, Arland J. *The Rise of normative Christianity.* Minneapolis: Fortress Press, 1994.

Canon of the New Testament.

Baxter, Margaret. *The Formation of the Christian Scriptures.* Philadelphia: Westminster Press, 1988.

Gamble, Harry Y. *The New Testament Canon: Its Making and meaning.* Philadelphia: Fortress Press, 1985.

Knox, John. *Marcion and the New Testament.* Chicago: University of Chicago Press, 1942.

Metzger, Bruce M. *The Canon of the New Testament: Its Origin, Development, and Significance.* Oxford: Clarendon Press, 1987.

Souter, Alexander. *The Text and Canon of the New Testament.* Revised edition by C. S. C. Williams. London: Gerald Duckworth & Co., 1954.

Interpreting the Scriptures.
The Cambridge History of the Bible. Vol. 1. *From the Beginnings to Jerome.* Ed. P. R. Akroyd and C. F. Evans. Cambridge: Cambridge University Press, 1970.
Kugel, James L. and Rowan A. Greer. *Early Biblical Interpretation.* Philadelphia: Westminster Press, 1986.
Shotwell, Willis A. *The Biblical Exegesis of Justin Martyr.* London: S.P.C.K. 1965.

Part 4.
Christianizing an Empire, 313–400 C.E.

Chapter 18. *Constantine.*

Barnes, Timothy D. *Constantine and Eusebius.* Cambridge: Harvard University Press, 1981.
Baynes, Norman H. *Constantine the Great and the Christian Church.* London: Proceedings of the British Academy, 1929.
Coleman, Christopher B. *Constantine the Great and Christianity.* New York: Columbia University Press, 1914.
Eadie, John W. *The Conversion of Constantine.* Huntington NY: R. E. Krieger Publishing Co., 1971, 1977.
Firth, John B. *Constantine the Great: The Reorganization of the Empire and the Triumph of the Church.* London: G. P. Putnam's Sons, 1923.
Jones, A. H. M. *Constantine and the Conversion of Europe.* London: Hodder & Stoughton, 1948.
MacMullen, Ramsay. *Constantine.* New York: Dial Press, 1969.

Chapter 19. *Church and State after Constantine.*

Browning, Robert. *The Emperor Julian.* Berkeley: University of California Press, 1976.
Croke, Brian and Jill Harries. *Religious Conflict in Fourth-Century Rome: A Documentary Study.* Sydney, Australia: Sydney University Press, 1982.
Dudden, F. Homes. *The Life and Times of St. Ambrose.* 2 vols. Oxford: Clarendon Press, 1935.

Greenslade, S. L. *Church and State from Constantine to Theodosius.* London: SCM Press, 1964.
King, N. Q. *The Emperor Theodosius and the Establishment of Christianity.* London: SCM Press, 1961.

Chapter 20. *Christianizing the Roman Empire and Evangelizing the World.*

Alföldi, Andreas. *The Conversion of Constantine and Pagan Rome.* Trans Harold Mattingly. Oxford: Clarendon Press, 1948.
Latourette, Kenneth Scott. *A History of the Expansion of Christianity.* Vol. 1. London: Eyre & Spottiswoode, 1938–1945.
Nock, Arthur Darby. *Conversion: The Old and the New in Religion from Alexander the Great to Augustine of Hippo.* Oxford: Clarendon Press, 1933.
See also under chapter 6, above.

Chapter 21. *A People Rend by Strife.*

Burn, A. E. *The Council of Nicaea.* London: S.P.C.K., 1925.
_____. *The Nicene Creed.* London: Rivingtons, 1909.
Grillmeier, Aloys, S.J. *Christ in Christian Tradition.* Vol. 1. 2nd ed. Trans. John Bowden. Atlanta: John Knox Press, 1975.
Kelly, J. N. D. *Early Christian Creeds.* 3rd ed. London: Longman, 1972.
_____. *Early Christian Doctrines.* Revised edition. New York: Harper & Row, 1978.
Pelikan, Jaroslav. *The Emergence of the Catholic Tradition (100–600).* Chicago: University of Chicago Press, 1971.
Wand, J. W. C. *The Four Councils.* London: Faith Press, 1951.

Chapter 22. *Changing Churches.*

Architecture.
Barnard, J.H. *The Churches of Constantine at Jerusalem.* New York: AMS Press, 1971.
Crowfoot, J. W. *Early Churches in Palestine.* London: British Academy, 1941.
Davies, J. G. *The Origin and Development of Early Christian Architecture.* London: SCM Press, 1952.
Krautheimer, Richard. *Early Christian and Byzantine Architecture.* Baltimore: Penguin Books, 1965.

Art.
Beckwith, John. *Early Christian and Byzantine Art.* Baltimore: Penguin Books, 1970.

The Liturgy
Dix, Gregory. *The Shape of the Liturgy.* Second edition. Westminster: Dacre Press, 1945.

The Calendar.
Davies, J. G. *Holy Week: A Short History.* London: Lutterworth Press, 1963.
McArthur, A. Allan. *The Evolution of the Christian year.* London: SCM Press, 1953.
Rordorf, Willy. *Sunday.* Translated by A. A. K. Graham. Philadelphia: Westminster Press, 1968.

Christian Ministry and Discipline.
Clebsch, William A. and Charles R. Jaekle. *Pastoral Care in Historical Perspectives.* New York: Harper & Row, 1964.
Eastwood, Cyril. *The Royal Priesthood of the Faithful.* Minneapolis: Augsburg Publishing House, 1963.
McNeill, John T. *A History of the Cure of Souls.* New York: Harper & Brothers, 1951.
Niebuhr, H. Richard, and Daniel Day Williams, editors. *The Ministry in Historical Perspectives.* New York: Harper & Brothers, 1956.

Chapter 23. *The Call of the Desert.*

Burns, John. *Ascetics and Ambassadors of Christ: The Monasteries of Palestine, 314–631.* Oxford: Clarendon Press, 1994.
Burton-Christie, Douglas. *The Word in the Desert: Scripture and the Quest for Holiness in Early Christian Monasticism.* New York: Oxford University Press, 1993.
Chitty, Derwas. *The Desert a City.* Oxford: Basil Blackwell, 1966.
Durkett, Eleanor S. *The Gateway to the Middle Ages.* 3 vols. Ann Arbor: University of Michigan Press, 1938.
Wimbusch, Vincent L., editor. *Ascetic Behavior in Greco-Roman Antiquity: A Sourcebook.* Minneapolis: Fortress Press, 1990.

Part 5.
Dividing Worlds, 400–600 C.E.

Chapter 24. *The Barbarian "Invasions."*

Thompson, E.A. *Romans and Barbarians: The Decline of the Western Empire.* Madison: University of Wisconsin Press, 1982.

Chapter 25. *The Ongoing Task.*

Latourette, Kenneth Scott. *A History of the Expansion of Christianity.* Vol. 2. London: Eyre & Spottiswoode, 1938–1945.
Robinson, Charles Henry. *The Conversion of Europe.* London: Longmans, Green & Co., 1917.

Chapter 26. *Solitude the Rage.*

Nigg, Walter. *Warriors of God: The Great Religious Orders and Their Founders.* Trans. Mary Ilford. London: Secker & Warburg, 1959.
Ryan, John, S.J. *Irish Monasticism: Origins and Early Development.* Ithaca NY: Cornell University Press, 1972.
Workman, Herbert B. *The Evolution of the Monastic Ideal.* Boston: Beacon Press, 1913.
Also see under chapter 23, above.

Chapter 27. *East Is East and West Is West.*

French, R.M. *The Eastern Orthodox Church.* London: Hutchinson University Library, 1951.
Zernov, Nicolas. *Eastern Christendom: A Study of the Origin and Development of the Eastern Orthodox Church.* New York: G. P. Putnam's Sons, 1961.

Chapter 28. *Imperial Power and Right Doctrine.*

Attwater, Donald. *St. John Chrysostom.* London: Harvill Press, 1959.
Baur, Chrysostomus. *John Chrysostom and His Time.* 2 vols. Trans. N. Gonzaga. London: Sands and Co., 1960.
Bethune-Baker, James F. *Nestorius and His Teaching: A Fresh Examination of the Evidence.* Cambridge: Cambridge University Press, 1908.

Gray, Patrick T. R. *The Defense of Chalcedon in the East (451–553).* Leiden: E. J. Brill, 1979.

Sellers, R.V. *The Council of Chalcedon: A Historical and Doctrinal Survey.* London: S.P.C.K., 1953.

See also under chapter 21, above.

Chapter 29. *Being Christian in a Collapsing World.*

Bonner, Gerald. *St. Augustine of Hippo: Life and Controversies.* Philadelphia: Westminster Press, 1963.

Brown, Peter. *Augustine of Hippo, a Biography.* London: Faber & Faber, 1967.

Evans, Robert F. *Pelagius: Inquiries and Reappraisals.* New York: Seabury Press, 1968.

Ferguson, John. *Pelagius.* Cambridge, England: W. Heffer, 1956.

Chapter 30. *The Emergence of the Papacy.*

Burn-Murdoch, H. *The Development of the Papacy.* New York: Frederick A. Praeger, 1954.

Dudden, F. Homes. *Gregory the Great: His Place in History and Thought.* 2 vols. London: Longmans, Green, & Co., 1905.

Jalland, T. J. *The Church and the Papacy: A Historical Study.* London: S.P.C.K., 1944.

Kidd, B. J. *The Roman Primacy to A.D. 461.* London: S.P.C.K., 1936.

Part 6.
The Church in Time of Transition, 600–850 C.E.

Chapter 31. *The Continuing Drive.*

Allies, T. W. *The Holy See and the Wandering of the Nations. From St. Leo I to St. Gregory I.* London: Burns & Oates, 1888.

Deanesly, Margaret. *Augustine of Canterbury.* London: Thomas Nelson & Sons, 1964.

See also under chapter 25, above.

Chapter 32. *The Churches of Western Europe.*

France.

Geary, Patrick. *Before France and Germany: The Creation and Transformation of the Merovingian World.* New York: Oxford University Press, 1988.

James, Edward. *The Origins of France: From Clovis to the Capetians, 500–1000.* New York: St. Martin's Press, 1982.

Wallace-Hadrill, J. M. *The Frankish Church.* Oxford: Clarendon Press, 1983.

_____. *The Long-haired Kings.* Toronto: University of Toronto, 1982.

Wemple, Suzanne F. *Women in Frankish Society: Marriage and the Cloister, 500–900.* Philadelphia: University of Pennsylvania Press, 1981.

Winston, Richard. *Charlemagne.* New York: American Heritage Publishing Co., 1968.

England.

Edwards, David L. *Christian England: Its Story to the Reformation.* New York: Oxford University Press, 1980.

Hodgkin, Robert Howard. *A History of the Anglo-Saxons.* 2 vols. Oxford: Clarendon Press, 1935.

Stenton, F. M. *Anglo-Saxon England.* 2nd ed. Oxford: Clarendon Press, 1950.

Wilson, David K. *The Anglo-Saxons.* New York: Praeger, 1960.

Spain.

Coopee, Henry. *History of the Conquest of Spain by the Arab Moors.* Boston: Little, Brown, 1881.

Thompson, E. A. *The Goths in Spain.* Oxford: Clarendon Press, 1969.

Chapter 33. *Eastern Christendom, 610–867.*

Giakalis, Ambrosius. *Images of the Divine: The Theology of Icons at the Seventh Ecumenical Council.* Leiden: E. J. Brill, 1994.

Kidd, B.J. *The Churches of Eastern Christendom from A.D. 451 to the Present Time.* London Faith Press, 1927.

Chapter 34. *The Papacy, 604–867.*

Barraclough, Geoffrey. *the Crucible of Europe: The Ninth and Tenth Centuries in European History.* Berkeley: University of California Press, 1976.

Fichtenau, Heinrich. *The Carolingian Empire.* Trans. Peter Munz. New York: Barnes & Noble, 1963.

See also under chapter 30, above.

Chapter 35.
The Golden Age of Monasticism, 604–1153.

Benedict of Nursia and the Benedictines.
Butler, Edward Cuthbert. *Benedictine Monasticism.* New York: Barnes & Noble, 1962.
Kardong, Terrence. *The Benedictines.* Wilmington, Del.: Michael Glazier, 1988.
Lindsay, T.F. *Saint Benedict, His Life and Work.* London: Burns, Oates, 1949.
McCann, Justin. *Saint Benedict.* London: Sheed & Ward, 1937.

Cluny.
Cowdrey, H. E. J. *The Cluniacs and the Gregorian Reform.* Oxford: Clarendon Press, 1970.
Hunt, Noreen. *Cluniac Monasticism in the Central Middle Ages.* London: Macmillan Co., 1971.
_____. *Cluny under Saint Hugh, 1049–1109.* Notre Dame IN: University of Notre Dame Press, 1968.
Knowles, David. *Cistercians and Cluniacs: The Controversy between St. Bernard and Peter ther Venerable.* London: Oxford University Press, 1955.
Rosenwein, Barbara H. *Rhinoceros Bound: Cluny in the Tenth Century.* Philadelphia: University of Pennsylvania Press, 1982.

Bernard of Clairvaux and the Cistercians.
Gilson, Etienne. *The Mystical Theology of Saint Bernard.* Trans. A. H. C. Downes. Kalamazoo MI: Cistercian Publications, 1990.
Leclercq, Jean. *Bernard of Clairvaux and the Cistercian Spirit.* Trans. Claire Lavoie. Kalamazoo MI: Cistercian Publications, 1976.
Lekai, Louis Julius. *The Cistercians: Ideals and Reality.* Kent: Kent State University Press, 1977.
Merton, Thomas. *The Last of the Fathers.* Westport CT: Greenwood Press, 1970.

Chapter 36. *Early Medieval Theology, Penance, Canon Law, and Spirituality.*

Theologians.
Church, Richard William. *Saint Anselm.* 2nd ed. London: Macmillan Co., 1937.
Kleinz, John Philip. *The Theory of Knowledge of Hugh of Saint Victor.* Washington DC: Catholic University of America Press, 1944.

Southern, R. W. *Saint Anselm: A Portrait in a Landscape.* Cambridge: Cambridge University Press, 1990.

Penance and Canon Law.
McNeill, John T., and Helena M. Gamer. *Medieval Handbooks of Penance.* New York: Columbia University Press, 1938, 1990.

Spirituality.
Leclercq, Jean, Francois Vandenbroucke, and Louis Bouyer. *The Spirituality of the Middle Ages.* New York: Seabury Press, 1982.

Part 7.

The New "Dark Ages," 850–1050.

Chapter 37.
Christianizing Northern and Central Europe.

Drobena, Thomas John. *Heritage of the Slavs: The Christianization of the Slavs and the Great Moravian Empire.* Columbus OH: Kosovo Publishing Co., 1979.
Dvornik, Francis. *Byzantine Missions among the Slavs: SS. Constantine-Cyril and Methodius.* New Brunswick NJ: Rutgers University Press, 1970.
Frances, James. *The Cistercians in Scandinavia.* Kalamazoo MI: Cistercian Publications, 1992.
Hunter, Leslie Stannard. *Scandinavian Churches: A Picture of the Development of the Life of the Churches of Denmark, Finland, Iceland, Norway and Sweden.* London: Faber, 1965.
Spinka, Matthew. *A History of Christianity in the Balkans: A Study of the Spread of Byzantine Culture among the Slavs.* Hamden CT: Archon Books, 1968.

Chapter 38.
The Churches and the New "Dark Ages."

England.
Cheney, William A. *The Cult of Kingship in Anglo-Saxon England: The Transition from Paganism.* Manchester: University of Manchester Press, 1970.
Coulton, G. G. *Medieval Village, Manor, and Monastery.* Cambridge: Cambridge University Press, 1925.

Hunt, William. *The English Church from Its Foundation to the Norman Conquest (597–1066)*. London: Macmillan & Co., 1901.

Southern, R. W. *The Making of the Middle Ages*. New Haven CT: Yale University Press, 1968, 1978.

Germany.

Bernhardt, John William. *Itinerant Kingship and Royal Monasteries in Early Medieval Germany, ca. 936–1075*. Cambridge: Cambridge University Press, 1993.

Gallagher, John Jospeh. *Church and State in Germany under Otto the Great (936–973)*. Washington DC: Catholic University of America Press, 1938.

Kieckhefer, Richard. *Repression of Heresy in Medieval Germany*. Philadelphia: University of Pennsylvania Press, 1979.

Chapter 39. *Eastern Christendom, 867–1056.*

Arnott, Peter. *The Byzantines and Their World*. New York: St. Martin's Press, 1973.

Dvornik, Francis. *The Photian Schism*. Cambridge: Cambridge University Press, 1948.

Every, George. *Misunderstandings between East and West*. Richmond VA: John Knox Press, 1965.

Chapter 40. *The Papacy in Need of Reform.*

Tierney, Brian. *The Crisis of Church and State, 1050–1300*. Englewood Cliffs NJ: Prentice Hall, 1964.

Part 8.
The Age of Reform, 1050–1200.

Chapter 41. *The Hildebrandine Reforms.*

Mathew, Arnold Harris. *The Life and Times of Hildebrand, Pope Gregory VII*. London: Griffiths, 1910.

Pennington, Kenneth. *Pope and Bishops: The Papal Monarchy in the Twelfth and Thirteenth Centuries*. Philadelphia: University of Pennsylvania Press, 1984.

Robinson, I.S. *The Papacy 1073–1198: Continuity and Innovation*. Cambridge: Cambridge University Press, 1990.

Chapter 42. *The Churches in Europe.*

England.

Binns, Alison. *Dedications of Monastic Houses in England and Wales, 1066–1216*. Woodbridge: Boydell Press, 1989.

Cheney, C. R. *The Papacy and England, 12th–14th Centuries*. London: Variorum Reprints, 1942.

Knowles, David. *Medieval Religous Houses, England and Wales*. London: Longman, 1971.

Stephens, W. R. W. *The English Church from the Norman Conquest to the Accession of Edward I (1066–1272)*. London: Macmillan and Co., 1901.

Thompson, Sally. *Women Religious: The Founding of English Nunneries after the Norman Conquest*. Oxford: Clarendon Press, 1991.

Warren, Ann K. *Anchorites and Their Patrons in Medieval England*. Berkeley: University of California Press, 1985.

France.

Marks, Claude. *Pilgrims, Heretics, and Lovers: A Medieval Journey*. New York: Macmillan, 1975.

Masson, Gustave. *The Story of Medieval France*. New York: G. P. Putnam's Sons, 1888.

Germany.

Bryce, James. *The Holy Roman Empire*. New York: Macmillan Co., 1904.

Gallagher, John J. *Church and State in Germany under Otto the Great (936–973)*. Washington DC: Catholic University of America Press, 1938.

Kieckhefer, Richard. *Repression of Heresy in Medieval Germany*. Philadelphia: University of Pennsylvania Press, 1979.

Spain.

Lomax, Derek. *The Church in Medieval Spain*. New York: Oxford University Press.

Scandinavia and the Balkans.
See under chapter 37, above.

Byzantium.

Baynes, Norman H. *The Byzantine Empire*. London: Oxford University Press, 1958.

Hussey, Joan. *The Byzantine Church*. London: Oxford University Press.

Obolensky, Dmitri. *The Byzantine Commonwealth. Eastern Europe, 500–1453*. London: Weidenfeld & Nicolson, 1971.

Chapter 43. *The Crusades.*

Cowdrey, H. E. J. *Popes, Monks, and Crusaders.* London: Hambledon Press, 1984.
Runciman, Steven. *A History of the Crusades.* 3 vols. Cambridge: Cambridge University Press, 1966–1968.
Setton, Kenneth M. *A History of the Crusades.* 6 vols. Madison: University of Wisconsin Press, 1969–1989.

Chapter 44. *The Church in Medieval Society.*

Coulton, G. G. *Life in the Middle Ages.* 4 vols. Cambridge: Cambridge University Press, 1967.
_____. *Medieval Panorama.* Cleveland: World Publishing Co., 1955.
Nigg, Walter. *The Heretics.* Trans. Richard and Clara Winston. New York: Alfred A. Knopf, 1962.
Peters, Edward, editor. *Heresy and Authority in Medieval Europe.* Philadelphia: University of Pennsylvania Press, 1980.
Runciman, Steven. *The Medieval Manichee.* New York: Viking Press, 1962.
Southern, R. W. *Western Society and the Church in the Middle Ages.* Grand Rapids MI: Eerdmans, n.d.

Chapter 45. *Medieval Thought in the Age of Reform.*

Knowles, David. *The Evolution of Medieval Thought.* New York: Vintage Books, 1962.
Leclercq, Jean. *The Love of Learning and the Desire for God.*
Pelikan, Jaroslav. *The Growth of Medieval Theology (600–1300).* Chicago: University of Chicago Press, 1978.
Taylor, Henry Osborne. *The Mediaeval Mind.* 4th ed. Cambridge MA: Harvard University Press, 1925.

Chapter 46. *Art, Architecture, and Music, 604–1300.*

Byzantine Art and Architecture.
Dalton, O.M. *East Christian Art: A Survey of the Monuments.* New York: Hacker Art Books, 1975.

Demus, Otto. *Byzantine Mosaic Decoration: Aspects of Monumental Art in Byzantium.* London: Routledge & Kegan Paul, 1964.
Grabar, Andre. *The Golden Age of Justinian, from the Death of Theodocius to the Rise of Islam.* Trans. Stuart Gilbert and James Emmons. New York: Odyssey Press, 1967.
Rice, David Talbot. *Art of the Byzantine Era.* New York: Praeger, 1963.
Walter, Christopher. *Art and Ritual of the Byzantine Church.* London: Variorum Publications, 1982.

Hiberno-Saxon Art.
Green, Miranda J. *Symbol and Image in Celtic Religious Art.* London: Routledge & Kegan Paul, 1989.
Mahr, Adolf. *Christian Art in Ancient Ireland.* 2 vols. Dublin: Stationery Office of the Saorstat Eiream, 1932–1941.

Carolingian and Ottonian Art and Architecture.
Backes, Magnus. *Art of ther Dark Ages.* Trans. Francisca Garvie. New York: H. N. Abrams, 1969, 1971.

Gothic Architecture.
Bony, Jean. *French Gothic Architecture of the Twelfth and Thirteenth Centuries.* Berkeley: University of California Press, 1983.
Harvey, John Hooper. *The Gothic World, 1100–1600: A Survey of Architecture and Art.* London: Batsford, 1950.
Simpson, Otto Georg von. *The Gothic Cathedral.* 3rd ed. Princeton NJ: Princeton University Press, 1988.

Music.
Catlin, Giulio. *Music of the Middle Ages.* Translated by Steven Botterill. 2 vols. Cambridge: Cambridge University Press, 1984–1985.
Hughes, Andrew. *Medieval Music: The Sixth Liberal Art.* Rev. ed. Toronto: University of Toronto Press, 1980.
Reese, Gustave. *Music in the Middle Ages.* New York: W. W. Norton & Co., 1940.
Seay, Albert. *Music in the Medieval World.* 2nd ed. Englewood Cliffs NJ: Prentice Hall, 1975.

Part 9.
The Great Century, 1200–1300.

Chapter 47. *The Papal Monarchy.*

Pennington, Kenneth. *Pope and Bishops: The Papal Monarchy in the Twelfth and Thirteenth Centuries.* Philadelphia: University of Pennsylvania Press, 1984.

Tout, Thomas Frederick. *The Empire and the Papacy, 918–1273.* London: Rivingtons, 1914.

Ullmann, Walter. *The Growth of Papal Government in the Middle Ages.* New York: Barnes and Noble, 1953.

Chapter 48. *Christian Advance and Division.*

Christiansen, Eric. *The Northern Crusades: The Baltic and the Catholic Frontier, 1100–1525.* Minneapolis: University of Minnesota, 1980.

Iswolsky, Helene. *Christ in Russia.* Milwaukee WI: Bruce Publishing Co., 1960.

Runciman, Steven. *The Eastern Schism: A Study of the Papacy and the Eastern Churches during the XIth and XIIth Centuries.* Oxford: Clarendon Press, 1955.

Chapter 49. *Church and Synagogue.*

Synan, Edward A. *The Popes and the Jews in the Middle Ages.* New York: Macmillan Co., 1965.

Chapter 50. *New Orders for a New Day.*

Francis and the Franciscans.

Armstrong, Edward A. *Saint Francis: Nature Mystic.* Berkeley: University of California Press, 1976.

Bedoyere, Michael de la. *Francis.* New York: Harper & Row, 1962.

Moorman, John R. H. *St. Francis of Assisi.* London: SCM Press, 1950.

Petry, Ray C. *Francis of Assisi: Apostle of Poverty.* Durham NC: Duke University Press, 1941.

Sabatier, Paul. *Life of St. Francis of Assisi.* Translated by Louise Seymour Houghton. London: Hodder & Stoughton, 1894.

Smith, John Holland. *Francis of Assisi.* New York: Charles Scribner's Sons, 1972.

Dominic and the Dominicans.

Bennett, Ralph Francis. *The Early Dominicans: Studies in Thirteenth Century Dominican History.* Cambridge: Cambridge University Press, 1937.

Herkless, John. *Francis and Dominic and the Mendicant Orders.* New York: Scribner's, 1901.

Reaves, John-Baptist. *The Dominicans.* New York: Macmillan Co., 1930.

The Inquisition.

Henningsen, Gustav and John Tedeschi. *The Inquisition in Early Modern Europe: Studies in Sources and Methods.* Dekalb: Northern Illinois University Press, 1986.

Lea, Henry Charles. *The Inquisition of the Middle Ages: Its Organization and Operation.* New York: Citadel Press, 1888, 1961.

Chapter 51. *Spirituality.*

See under chapter 36, above.

Chapter 52. *Scholasticism.*

General.

Copleston, Frederick. *Medieval Philosophy.* London: Methuen & Co., 1952.

Gilson, Etienne H. *History of Christian Philosophy in the Middle Ages.* New York: Random House, 1955.

_____. *Reason and Revelation in the Middle Ages.* New York: Charles Scribner's Sons, 1938.

Thomas, Elliott C. *History of the Schoolmen.* London: Williams & Norgate, 1941.

Vogt, Berard. *The Origin and Development of the Franciscan School. Duns Scotus and St. Thomas.* New York: J. F. Wagner, 1925.

Albertus Magnus.

Albert, S. M. *Albert the Great.* Oxford: Blackfriars Publications, 1948.

Kovach, Francis J., and Robert W. Shahan. *Albert the Great.* Norman: University of Oklahoma Press, 1980.

Bonaventure.

Dobbins, Dunstan John. *Franciscan Mysticism: A Critical Examination of the Mystical Theology of the Seraphic Doctor.* New York: J. F. Wagner, 1927.

Gilson, Etienne H. *The Philosophy of St. Bonaventure.*
    Trans. D. I. Trethowan and F. J. Sheed. New York:
    Sheed & Ward, 1938.

Thomas Aquinas.
Maritain, Jacques. *The Angelic Doctor:The Life and*
    Thought of Saint Thomas Aquinas. Translated by
    J. F. Scanlan. New York: Dial Press, 1931.
    _____. *St. Thomas Aquinas, Angel of the Schools.*
    London: Sheed & Ward, 1933.

Index

The Church Triumphant.
A History of Christianity up to 1300.
  by E. Glenn Hinson.

Mercer University Press, Macon, Georgia 31210-3960.
Isbn 0-86554-436-0.
Catalog and warehouse pick number: MUP/H347.
Text and interior design, composition,
    and layout by Edd Rowell.
Cover design and layout by Edd Rowell.
Illustration from a photograph by Jon Parrish Peede.
Camera-ready pages composed on a Gateway 2000,
    via WordPerfect 5.1 for dos and wpwin 5.1/5.2,
    and printed on a LaserMaster 1000.
Text font: TimesNewRomanPS 10/12.
Display font: TimesNewRomanPS bi and bf.
Titles on cover: Essette Letraset UniversityRoman.
Printed and bound by Braun-Brumfield Inc.,
    Ann Arbor MI 48106.
Printed via offset lithography on 50# Natural Smooth.
Smyth sewn and cased into Kivar 9 lightweight cloth
    printed 4-color process,
        plus polyester film lamination over binder's boards,
        and with headbands and matching endleaves.

[June 1995]